THE WORLD'S HISTORY

VOLUME TWO: SINCE 1300

HOWARD SPODEK

THE WORLD'S HISTORY

VOLUME TWO: SINCE 1300   FOURTH EDITION

Prentice Hall

Boston Columbus Indianapolis New York San Francisco Upper Saddle River
Amsterdam Cape Town Dubai London Madrid Milan Munich Paris Montréal Toronto
Delhi Mexico City São Paulo Sydney Hong Kong Seoul Singapore Taipei Tokyo

Editorial Director: *Leah Jewell*
Executive Editor: *Charles Cavaliere*
Development Editor: *Margaret Manos*
Editorial Assistant: *Lauren Aylward*
Director of Marketing: *Brandy Dawson*
Senior Marketing Manager: *Maureen Prado-Roberts*
Senior Managing Editor: *Ann Marie McCarthy*
Project Manager: *Denise Forlow*
Senior Manufacturing and Operations Manager
for Arts & Sciences: *Nick Sklitsis*
Operations Specialist: *Christina Amato*
Senior Art Director: *Maria Lange*

Credits and acknowledgments borrowed from other sources
and reproduced, with permission, in this textbook appear on
pages 897–98.

This book was designed and produced by
Laurence King Publishing Ltd, London
www.laurenceking.com

Every effort has been made to contact the copyright holders, but
should there be any errors or omissions, Laurence King Publishing
Ltd would be pleased to insert the appropriate acknowledgment in
any subsequent printing of this publication.

Senior Editor: Clare Double
Production: Simon Walsh
Picture Researcher: Claire Gouldstone
Design: Ian Hunt

Front cover: top image Mary Evans Picture Library, bottom image
AKG Images/Stedelijk Museum, Leiden.

Library of Congress Cataloging-in-Publication Data

Spodek, Howard
  The world's history / Howard Spodek. -- 4th ed.
    p. cm.
  Includes bibliographical references and index.
  ISBN 978-0-205-70839-0 (hbk.) -- ISBN 978-0-205-70837-6 (pbk.) -- ISBN 978-0-205-70838-3 (pbk.)
  1. World history. I. Title.
  D20 .S772010
  909--dc22
                        2009031858

10 9 8 7 6 5 4 3 2 1

Prentice Hall
is an imprint of

www.pearsonhighered.com

ISBN 10: 0-205-70837-4
ISBN 13: 978-0-205-70837-6

Brief Contents

Contents

CHAPTER TWENTY-FOUR

Contemporary History: Trade, Social Revolution, Technology, Identity

MAPS

Preface

Why History?

The professional historian and the student of an introductory course often seem to pass each other on different tracks. For the professional, nothing is more fascinating than history. For the student, particularly one in a compulsory course, the whole enterprise often seems a bore. This introductory text is designed to help the student understand and share the fascination of the historian. It will also remind professors of their original attraction to history, before they began the specialization that has almost certainly marked their later careers. Furthermore, it encourages student and professor to explore together the history of the world and the significance of this study.

Professional historians love their field for many reasons. History offers perspective and guidance in forming a personal view of human development. It teaches the necessity of seeing many sides of issues. It explores the complexity and interrelationship of events and makes possible the search for patterns and meaning in human life.

Historians also love to debate. They love the challenge of demonstrating that their interpretations of the pattern and significance of events are the most accurate and the most satisfying in their fit between the available data and theory. Historians also love the detective work of the profession, whether it is searching through old archives, uncovering and using new sources of information, or reinterpreting long-ignored sources. In recent years historians have turned, for example, to oral history, old church records, files of photographs, cave paintings, individual census records, and reinterpretations of mythology.

Historical records are not simply lists of events, however. They are the means by which historians develop their interpretations of those events. Because interpretations differ, there is no single historical record, but various narrations of events each told from a different perspective. Therefore the study of history is intimately linked to the study of values, the values of the historical actors, the historians who have written about them, and of the students engaged in learning about them.

Professional historians consider history to be the king of disciplines. Synthesizing the concepts of fellow social scientists in economics, politics, anthropology, sociology, and geography, historians create a more integrated and comprehensive interpretation of the past. Joining with their colleagues in the humanities, historians delight in hearing and telling exciting stories that recall heroes and villains, the low born and the high, the wisdom and the folly of days gone by. This fusion of all the social sciences and humanities gives the study of history its range, depth, significance, and pleasure. Training in historical thinking provides an excellent introduction to understanding change and continuity in our own day as well as in the past.

Why World History?

Why specifically world history? Why should we teach and study world history, and what should be the content of such a course?

First, world history is a good place to begin for it is a new field for professor and student alike. Neither its content nor its pedagogy is yet fixed. Many of the existing textbooks on the market still have their origins in the study of Western Europe, with segments added to cover the rest of the world. World history as the study of the inter-relationships of all regions of the world, seen from the many perspectives of the different peoples of the earth, is still virgin territory.

Second, for citizens of multicultural, multiethnic nations such as the United States, Canada, South Africa, and India, and for those of the many other countries such as the United Kingdom and Australia which are moving in that direction, a world history course offers the opportunity to gain an appreciation of the national and cultural origins of all their diverse citizens. In this way, the study of world history may help to strengthen the bonds of national citizenship.

Third, as the entire world becomes a single unit for interaction, it becomes an increasingly appropriate subject for historical study. The new reality of global interaction in communication, business, politics, religion, culture, and ecology has helped to generate the new academic subject of world history.

Organization and Approach

The text, like the year-long course, links *chronology*, *themes*, and *geography* in eight units, or Parts, of study. The Parts move progressively along a time line from the emergence of early humans to the present day. Each Part emphasizes a single theme—for example, urbanization or religion or migration—and students learn to use them all to analyze historical events and to develop a grasp of the chronology of human development. The final chapter employs all the themes developed in the first seven Parts as tools for understanding the history of our own times. Geographically, each Part covers the entire globe, although specific topics place greater emphasis on specific regions.

New to the Fourth Edition

Every aspect of the book's program has been exhaustively reviewed and revised for this new edition. The last twelve chapters have been reorganized for clarity and readability and in response to reviewer comments, and the final two chapters dealing with the modern world have been extensively reorganized and rewritten.

Chapters One and Five now open with introductions before the first heading, making all chapters consistent in this edition. Excessive details have been trimmed and many headings reorganized for greater clarity and consistency. Where discussions continued from one chapter to another in the third edition, they have now been consolidated: for example, the Cold War is now discussed in one chapter only, rather than in three; the Soviet Union, too, is addressed in just one chapter.

The pedagogical features were carefully examined, and a completely new and more colorful design makes it easy for students to find Key Topics, Glossary words and special features, such as the "How Do We Know?" boxes. The author has rewritten several Part openers as bridges from one section to the next. Two new How Do We Know? boxes based on the works of art help students learn the skills to make the most of the many illustrations in the book.

Content Changes

Within each Part, materials have been updated, revised, and added. Examples of some of the more notable changes and additions include: A discussion of the fossils of early hominids discovered in Chad; additional materials on early urbanization in India and Africa; new evaluations of the decline of the Roman Empire; consideration of the Gnostic gospels and their significance in understanding early Christianity; the assimilation of Islam into African empires in the tenth through the fifteenth centuries. The third edition Part Five, on world trade, and Part Six, on migration and demography, have been restructured. Part Five is now a single unit on the movement of goods, ideas, and people, while Part Six is devoted to social revolutions. The Scientific Revolution of the sixteenth, seventeenth, and eighteenth centuries gets more coverage. The Industrial Revolution has been placed into a wider context, more clearly setting the stage for the events that began to unfold in the late eighteenth century around the world. As noted, the twentieth century is now given expanded coverage, and divided into two chronological periods, each with its own theme. Throughout the book increased prominence has been given to issues of gender, and every chapter now ends with a What Difference Does It Make? section.

In updating the book to cover the events of contemporary history, new materials have been added to reflect new developments. These include: breakthroughs in applications of genetic information; new interpretations of the significance of gender; rapidly increasing urbanization; China's return to world power status; the increase in religious militancy; globalization in economics and culture; increasing sub-nationalism, guerrilla warfare, and numbers of refugees; and the continuous elaboration of the World Wide Web as a means of communication, and containerization as a means of transportation.

Chapter-by-Chapter Revisions

Chapter One, on human origins, has been arranged to clarify chronology, eliminate repetition, and make the information clearer for students. A new opener introduces the subject of the chapter, and the sections on *Homo erectus*, African palaeontology, and the earliest human culture have been updated.

Chapter Two includes an updated section on Achievements in Literature and Law.

Chapter Five, on early empires, has been thoroughly reorganized and revised for clarity and chronology; new chapter and section introductions have been written; and much internal repetition has been eliminated. A new How Do We Know? box, "Gender Relations in Ancient Greece: Voices from the Vases," adds a feminist perspective on male–female relationships as presented through art. The sections on Egyptian art, the Greek polis, and the Peloponnesian War have been expanded.

Chapter Six, on Rome, has been completely revised and restructured to clarify chronology and generally make the text read more clearly. A new section on Roman engineering has been added.

Chapter Nine contains a new How Do We Know? box on "The Buddha Imagined in Art," which examines the development of Buddhist philosophy through representations of the Buddha and scenes from his life.

Chapter Eleven ends with a rewritten Turning Point on Religion and Trade. This presents a smooth transition from the life with religion at its core to the increasing importance of trade in ordinary people's lives. The text goes into more detail about the various religions' attitudes to trade, making a natural progression from Part Four to Part Five.

Part Five is retitled "Global Trade: The Beginning of the Modern World." The introduction to this section has been expanded and rewritten to give more attention to the traders and navigators who went before Columbus, in enlarging global trade.

Chapter Twelve now begins in 1300, rather than 1100, to accord with many adopters' preferences. This makes a better starting point for the modern world, for those students who are only studying Volume Two. Trade with China now has its own section, rather than being included in the general discussions of Asian trade, and the section on Indian Ocean trade has been reorganized to incorporate a discussion of Arab traders.

Chapter Thirteen has been thoroughly revised, and is now called "The Opening of the Atlantic and the Pacific," better to connect the major regions of the world. There is a new How Do We Know? box, "Eurocentric History?", to introduce and analyze this idea. The sections on European exploration have been combined for clarity. The Renaissance is now treated in a single, unified section with all the relevant material under one heading. There is more material on towns, trading, and economic changes in Europe at that time, to put the Renaissance into context, and there is also a new section on "Economic and Social Changes in Europe."

Chapter Fourteen has been completely revised. There is a new chapter opener, and the text now includes a stronger introduction to the notions of capitalism and mercantilism. At the end of the chapter, the material on trade systems in Asia and elsewhere has been unified under one heading, including a revised section on "Russia's Empire under Peter the Great," with a new map covering all of Russia.

Chapter Fifteen now includes a new section on Russian expansion into Siberia, and the material on African slave trade has been expanded.

Chapter Sixteen has been entirely reorganized to make the material chronological and to create a more fluent structure of sections and headings. There is now a dedicated section on the Scientific Revolution, while the Enlightenment material has been unified. The discussion of Hobbes and Locke now serves as a preliminary to England's civil war and revolution. The sections on South America have been completely reorganized to make clear their role in world revolution.

Chapter Seventeen now contains a unified treatment of Marx and Engels in just one section. The structure of the chapter has been reorganized to consolidate discussions of both labor reform and voting reform into their own sections. In addition, the emphasis has shifted slightly away from the U.S. and Britain to labor movements in the rest of Europe and worldwide.

Chapter Eighteen has a new chapter introduction and clarified, improved definitions of nationalism and imperialism, the chapter's main theme. In particular, the sections on African nationalism have been reorganized, with Islamic revival now given due emphasis in that section, and the sections on European powers in China and Southeast Asia rewritten. The Turning Point after this chapter, on "The Olympics and International Politics," has been updated to include the 2008 Beijing Games.

Chapter Nineteen has been reorganized to eliminate repetition and to make it easier for students to follow. New chapter and section openers offer more analysis and discussion, with fewer details. The section on Technology in the Twentieth Century has been substantially revised.

Chapter Twenty, now subtitled To Hell and Back, has a new introduction. It contains an expanded discussion of fascism and ultra-nationalism, and improved discussion of the governments in Italy, Germany, and Japan, with clearer distinctions between the shifting nation states in this period. The material on World War II has been divided for clarity. There is a new section titled "Remembering the War," discussing the long-term aftermath of World War II and how different countries have recognized, and memorialized, problematic events in their history.

Chapter Twenty-one has a new introduction. The entire examination of the Cold War is now located in this chapter, and it has been rewritten to more clearly demonstrate the relationship between Cold War maneuverings and the politics of newly independent states. The chapter is now in clearer chronological order within each subsection. A new section entitled "1968: Revolt Against Authority," surveys the protest movements of this period around the world. Finally, the discussion of the collapse of the Soviet Union at the end of the Cold War has been moved here from later in the book.

Chapter Twenty-two shows an improved structure and chronology. There is additional material on the position of women in Chinese society and on the Indian struggle for independence.

Part Eight is entirely restructured to explore the applicability of the historical themes we have studied to the understanding of contemporary history, the events through which we ourselves are living. The last two chapters revisit the seven themes. Historians always claim that a knowledge of the past is useful, indispensable, to understanding the present. The rewritten Part Eight tests that belief. It demonstrates ways in which the seven themes developed so far can be used to understand more clearly trends in the contemporary world, from cloning, to the globalization of economics and culture, to the significance of the 2008 Beijing Olympics, to the election of America's first African-American president. The chapters revisit the seven themes of the book: In Chapter Twenty-three, evolution, settlements, politics, and religion; and in Chapter Twenty-four, trade, revolution, and technology, plus an additional theme, identity. The chapters are updated to the present—including the election of Barack Obama—and they encompass new material on globalization; a new section on gender; a discussion of micro-finance; and new material on refugees and global culture.

Special Features

This edition retains all the pedagogical features of the previous edition, highlighted in a new design to make each feature clearly identifiable immediately. The Key Topics at the beginning of each chapter are now placed in a shaded box in the margin, rather than under the main title. The questions at the end of each chapter are now called Asking Questions, to encourage students to consider their own reading as well as the author's. Key Terms are also highlighted in boxes to make them easy to pick out and distinguish from picture or map captions, and there is a summary of each chapter's Key Terms at the end of the chapter. Each of these features is designed to make the text more accessible to students. Collectively, these materials provide a rich, comprehensive, and challenging introduction to the study of world history and the methods and key interpretations of its historians.

● The Introduction to the book describes the key themes of the text and the methods historians use to practice their craft.

● The introduction to each of the eight Parts now includes more specific key references to the chapters that follow.

● Each chapter begins with a list of Key Topics that provide an overview of the chapter.

KEY TOPICS
● Human Origins in Myth and History
● Fossils and Fossil Hunters
● Humans Create Culture
● The Story of Prehistory: What Difference Does It Make?

● Key Terms in each chapter are set in bold face in the text, with a fuller definition given in the margin. The Key Terms are listed at the end of each chapter for easy reference, and collected in the Glossary at the end of the book.

KEY TERM

umma The community of believers in Islam, which transcends ethnic and political boundaries.

- Turning Point essays, some completely new for this edition, illustrate visually the connections between one part and the next. In some cases, the Turning Points tell their own story as well, notably in the bridge into the twenty-first century that uses the modern Olympic Games to illustrate and introduce many of the issues that are to follow. Turning Point Questions ask students to consider the material that has been presented.

TURNING POINT ↗

The Agricultural Village

The evolution of maize from the rather stunted cob of wild corn from the Valley Mexico about 5000 B.C.E. to the more productive and nutritious plant of about 1 B.C.E., reveals the benefits of that came with the creation of agricultural villages. (See Richard MacNeish, "The Origins of New World Civilization," *Scientific American*, November 1964.) Settled agriculture greatly increased the quantity and quality of the food supply. As human populations grew, hunting and gathering alone could not produce enough to feed their numbers. People had to travel ever greater distances, which brought them into direct conflict with their neighbors—who were also hard pushed to hunt and gather adequate food and were also expanding in number. Settled agriculture was the solution. Careful attention to plant and animal patterns on the part of hunter-gatherers had already set the stage.

As they settled down, humans began to domesticate not only food crops but also animals, which served for food, for power and energy in carrying goods and pulling plows, and for products such as milk, wool, fur, and leather. Village dwellers produced tools that were increasingly sophisticated in usefulness and aesthetic beauty. Some of these tools were made of organic materials, such as bone and fiber, but many were made of stone. Villagers became skilled at grinding and polishing the stone tools, and this new era is called the Neolithic or New Stone Age.

Settled agriculture began in the Fertile Crescent—that is, Mesopotamia, the valley between the Tigris and Euphrates Rivers—and in the Nile valley about 12,000 years ago. However, one of the best preserved early villages was discovered in China at Ban Po, near Xian. The residents of Ban Po cultivated millet and domesticated pigs and dogs. They practiced slash-and-burn agriculture, and pollen samples show distinct alternating periods of cultivation and fallow. The most ancient layers of the excavation, which date to about 6000 B.C.E., give a clear idea of the physical form of an early agricultural village.

Immediately adjacent to the excavation, archaeologists have reconstructed a model of the entire prehistoric village. It represents Ban Po's three housing styles:

Model reconstruction of Ban Po.

36

- The How Do We Know? features have been placed in orange boxes. They help the student understand the process of how historians use evidence, both textual and visual, to interpret the past.

- This edition also continues the emphasis on the use of primary sources, for these are the kinds of materials from which the historical record is argued and fashioned. The original source material is presented in black text with the author's commentary in blue. Most chapters have two or more orange Source boxes.

- The Suggested Readings for each chapter have been thoroughly revised and updated to reflect current scholarship. In addition, each item in the bibliography is now annotated to direct students with their reading.

HOW DO WE KNOW?

Some Modern Critiques of Early Urbanization

Sumer's city-states had many accomplishments to their credit, but some historians have pointed out that their civilization came at the cost of increasing warfare, growing social inequality, and the oppression of women. These modern critiques reflect the importance of studying the past in order to understand the present more fully.

Politically, each of the major cities of Sumer was also a state, ruling over the contiguous agricultural areas and often in conflict with neighboring city-states. The artwork of the city-states often depicts royal armies, military expeditions, conquests, and a general appreciation, even an exaltation, of warfare. The fighting seems to have been frequent, and the main combatants were the largest of the city-states. Battles were fought hand-to-hand and also from donkey-drawn chariots.

The warfare was especially destructive because the kings and soldiers believed that they were upholding the honor of their gods. When cities are sacred, conflicts between them mean holy war, fights to the finish. The "Lamentation over the Destruction of Ur," which was addressed to Ningal, goddess of the Ekushnugal Temple, describes that city's utter destruction after the Elamites sacked it, exiled its ruler, and destroyed the temple c. 1950 B.C.E.:

After your city had been destroyed, how now can you exist!
After your house had been destroyed, how has your heart led you on!
Your city has become a strange city; how now can you exist!
Your house has become a house of tears, how has your heart led you on!
Your city which has been made into ruins—you are no longer its mistress!
Your righteous house which has been given over to the pickax—you no longer inhabit it,
Your people have been led to slaughter—you are no longer their queen. (Kramer, *The Sumerians*, p. 142)

Lewis Mumford, one of the most respected modern commentators on the history of cities, regarded this early union of power, religion, and continuous warfare as a permanent curse of urban life. He wrote, "even when it is disguised by seemingly hardheaded economic demands, uniformly turns into a religious performance; nothing less than a wholesale ritual sacrifice."

The first Sumerian cities fostered division of labor into occupational categories. We have noted the roles of kings, priests, landowners, architects, scribes, long-distance traders, local merchants, artisans, cooks, farmers, soldiers, laborers—the whole panoply of occupational categories absent in villages but forming the backbone of a sophisticated urban economy and society. Priests and kings held great wealth and power and largely controlled the means of production, but it is not clear that they formed an exclusive category of "haves" versus "have nots." The spectrum seems to have been more varied, including a

substantial group of middle classes. But there is, nevertheless, much evidence of the enormous power of the aristocracy.

At the bottom of the economic hierarchy were slaves. People entered slavery in four ways: some were captured in battle; some were sentenced to slavery as punishment for crimes; some sold themselves (or their family members) into slavery to cope with poverty and debt; and some were born into slavery. We have no record of the number or proportion of slaves in the general population of Sumer and its cities. The law codes' extensive regulations of slaves and slavery suggest, however, their widespread existence.

The socialist philosopher-historian Karl Marx argued that the rise of cities brought about "the division of the population into two great classes." Marx's formulation was too stark, ignoring the broad range of classes in the city, but he does force us to think about the class structure in our own cities, including the relationship between rich and poor, and its implications for the health of society.

Finally, the transformation of society from a rural, egalitarian, kin base to an urban, hierarchical, territorial, and class base may have provided the entering wedge for the subordination of women. Some women in Sumer had great power. Several seem to have held independent high administrative posts in major temples controlling large land holdings. The high status of Lady Pu-abi (c. 2500 B.C.E.) was revealed in her burial. She was adorned with gold and buried with several other bodies, presumably servants, suggesting a woman of high rank, perhaps a queen. Shagshag, wife of King Uruinimgina (also known as Urukagina), c. 2300 B.C.E., held great powers in the name of her husband.

Women in Sumer generally had certain basic rights, including the rights to hold property, engage in business, and serve as legal witness. Nevertheless, it is clear that women's legal rights were limited by their husbands. Even powerful women were often only pawns in the power struggles of men.

Feminist historian Gerda Lerner argues that before the evolution of city-states, with their warfare and hierarchical class structures, the status of women had been more equal. Kin groups had been the basic economic units of society, and women had had more power in these family groups than they did in the city-states that displaced them. Lerner claims that inequalities between men and women are not products of unchanging biological differences. Rather, the inequalities have been created by humans—and they can be altered by humans.

- What did Lewis Mumford learn about warfare from his study of ancient cities? How did this affect his view of modern warfare?
- What did Karl Marx learn about class relations from his study of ancient cities? How did this affect his view of class relationships in modern (nineteenth-century) cities?
- What did Gerda Lerner learn about gender relationships from studying ancient cities? myhistorylab

---

SOURCE

The Code of Hammurabi

As states grew larger, formal, written law codes replaced the customs and traditions of the farming villages. Around 1750 B.C.E., the Babylonian ruler Hammurabi conquered Mesopotamia, uniting the warring city-states under his rule. To reinforce that unity he set forth a code of laws that covered many aspects of daily life and business.

The code provides a marvelous insight into the problems and nature of urban life at the time. It provides a detailed insight into property rights and urban crime, as well as the social and gender divisions in the society. Finally, it gives students and scholars some idea of how justice was perceived in Hammurabi's world. The code is a list of 282 laws; only some of them are represented here. In the original list, they are not particularly organized so we have reorganized them here.

Property
Property laws incorporated laws of consumer protection for house buyers, boat renters, contractors for services. In one case, a brutal punishment for faulty workmanship indicates that common people, too, were viewed as commodities. The sins of the fathers may be taken out on the children. Some of the specific laws included:

- If [the collapse of a building] has caused the death of a son of the owner of the house, they shall put the son of that builder to death.
- If any one steal the property of a temple or of the court, he shall be put to death, and also the one who receives the stolen thing from him shall be put to death.

Urban Crime
Many laws provided for punishment for robbery and for personal injuries. Many of the latter varied according to the social class of the person inflicting the injury as well as the person suffering the injury:

- If any one is committing a robbery and is caught, then he shall be but to death.
- If a gentleman has destroyed the eye of a member of the aristocracy, they shall destroy his eye.
- If he has broken another gentleman's bone, they shall break his bone.
- If he has destroyed the eye of a commoner or broken the bone of a commoner, he shall pay one mina of silver.
- If he has destroyed the eye of a gentleman's slave or broken the bone of a gentleman's slave, he shall pay one half his value.

Gender in Ancient Babylonia
Numerous laws governed marriage, bride price, dowry, adultery, and incest. Although women did own the dowries given them, their rights of ownership were limited. Marriage is presented in large part as a commercial transaction, in which the groom's family pays a bride-price to the bride's father, while the bride's father gives her a dowry. Childlessness is grounds for divorce but the husband must return his wife's dowry. Behavioral restraints in marriage are unequal: if the husband "has been going out and disparaging her greatly," the wife may leave, taking her dowry; if the wife is "a gadabout, thus neglecting her house (and) humiliating her husband," he may have her drowned.

- If a woman quarrels with her husband, and says: "You are not congenial to me," the reasons for her prejudice must be presented. If she is guiltless, and there is not fault on her part, but he leaves and neglects her, then no guilt attaches to this woman, she shall take her dowry and go back to her father's house.
- If she is not innocent, but leaves her husband, and ruins her house, neglecting her husband, this woman shall be cast into the water.

Stele of Hammurabi, from Susa, Iran, c. 1760 B.C.E. Hammurabi, the great king of Babylon, is the first known ruler to have created a detailed legal code; other societies with unknown rulers developed much earlier codes. On this commemorative stone slab, Hammurabi, standing, is receiving the Babylonian laws from the sun-god Shamash. The laws themselves are inscribed below on the stele. (Louvre, Paris)

● Each chapter text ends with a discussion of legacies to the future, namely, What Difference Does It Make?

● Each chapter concludes with Asking Questions to help students to re-examine the material. The questions are also useful for classroom debates and could serve as essay topics.

New Layout and Design

Readers will notice a brighter, clearer design. There's added color to engage the interest, and a clearer distinction between the various types of box and charts, plus a slightly squarer, more compact page size that is easier to handle. In the Source boxes, colored type has been used to mark the difference between the text of the historical source and the author's discussion of it.

Maps and Illustrations

To aid the student, extensive, clear, and informative charts and maps represent information graphically and geographically. There are more than 20 new and amended maps in this edition, some quite innovative, such as a map of greenhouse gas emissions. A wide range of illustrations, most in color, supplement the written word. For the fourth edition we have added more than 80 new illustrations.

Support Materials for Instructors and Students

The World's History comes with an extensive package of supplementary print and multimedia materials for both instructors and students, many of which are available free to qualified adopters.

MyHistoryLab (www.myhistorylab.com) MyHistory-Lab provides students with an online package complete with the electronic textbook and numerous study aids. With several hundred primary sources, many of which are assignable and link to a gradebook, pre- and post-tests that link to a gradebook and result in individual-

ized study plans, videos, and images, as well as map activities with gradable quizzes, the site offers students a unique, interactive experience that brings history to life. The comprehensive site also includes a History Bookshelf with 100 of the most commonly assigned books in history classes, and a History Toolkit with tutorials and helpful links. Other features include gradable assignments and chapter review materials, as well as a Test Item File.

Instructor's Manual/Test Item File The Instructor's Manual contains chapter summaries, key points and vital concepts, and information on audiovisual resources that can be used in developing and preparing lecture presentations. The Test Item File includes over 1,500 multiple-choice, matching, true/false, and essay test questions. Available for download from the Instructor's Resource Center.

MyTest MyTest is a browser-based test management program. The program allows instructors to select items from the Test Item File in order to create tests. It also allows for online testing.

The Instructor's Resource Center (www.pearson highered.com) Text-specific materials, such as the instructor's manual/test item file, are available for download by adopters.

Digital Transparency Masters provide instructors with full color PDFs of all the maps, charts, and graphs in the text for use in the classroom. These PDFs can be printed to acetate for use with overhead projectors. Available for download from the Instructor's Resource Center.

PowerPoint Presentations include key points and terms for a lecture on the chapter, as well as full-color slides of selected important maps, graphs, and charts within a particular chapter. The presentations are available for download from the Instructor's Resource Center.

Popular Valuepacks for *The World's History*

Titles from the renowned Penguin Classics series can be bundled with *The World's History* for a nominal charge. Please contact your Pearson Arts and Sciences sales representative for details.

Connections: Key Themes in World History. Series Editor Alfred J. Andrea. Concise and tightly focused, the titles in the popular Connections Series are designed to place the latest research on selected topics of global significance, such as disease, trade, slavery, exploration, and modernization, into an accessible format for students. Available at a 50% discount when bundled with *The World's History.*

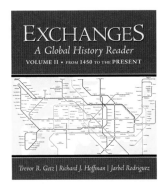

Getz/Hoffman/Rodriguez, *Exchanges: A Global History Reader* introduces students to the discipline of world history. Unlike other source collections, *Exchanges* helps students look beyond strictly delineated regionalism and chronological structures to understand history as a series of ongoing debates. Available at a 50% discount when bundled with *The World's History.*

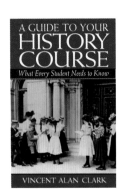

Clark, *A Guide to Your History Course: What Every Student Needs to Know.* This concise, spiral-bound guidebook orients to the issues and problems they will face in the history classroom. Available at a 50% discount when bundled with *The World's History.*

The Prentice Hall Atlas of World History, Second Edition includes over 100 full-color maps in world history, drawn by Dorling Kindersley, one of the world's most respected cartographic publishers. Copies of the *Atlas* can be bundled with *The World's History* for a nominal charge. Contact your Pearson Arts and Sciences sales representative for details.

Acknowledgments for the Fourth Edition

Each edition, each evolution of the text, brings new, indispensble colleagues who make the enterprise what it continues to become. This revision began once again at Laurence King Publishing in London, under the guidance of Lee Ripley, moved then to Kara Hattersley-Smith, and then to Clare Double and, under her supervision, to the illustrators, designers, proofreaders, and other personnel who have added their suggestions, based on a wealth of experience, and kept the project on task. Freelance editor Margaret Manos of New York and New Hampshire read the text—old and new—with great sensitivity and worked wonders in reorganizing, clarifying, streamlining, and improving readability. She sifted through the many external reviews and focused their key comments and criticisms into improving the revision process. She frequently sharpened perspectives, especially on issues of feminism and European and American history. In some important cases she helped select artwork that added insight and aesthetics to the arguments of the book. At Pearson, Charles Cavaliere continued to exercise the quiet, overarching supervision of the entire project, with his enduring concern for accuracy and elegance of presentation, integrity of perspective, and marketability of the final product.

Kara Hattersley-Smith, Editorial Manager, assures me that this transoceanic venture has proceeded smoothly, aided by Clare Double, Senior Editor, Ian Hunt, Designer, and Claire Gouldstone, Picture Researcher. Without them, there would be no fourth edition, and I am grateful for their patient and firm guidance and wise diplomacy.

I have also benefited immensely from the kindness of the many students (especially my own students at Temple University), colleagues, and teachers who have used this book and took time to share with me their advice and suggestions. I thank them all and hope that they will see the benefits of their good counsel in this edition.

One element that has not changed in this new edition is the mental image I keep before me of my own children—albeit at a younger age, since by now their knowledge in so many fields surpasses my own—and of my students. I write for them.

Grateful acknowledgments are also extended to the following reviewers of the fourth edition: Jeff Burson, Macon State College; Nupur Chaudhuri, Texas Southern University; Peter Dykema, Arkansas Tech University; Nancy Fitch, California State University; David L.

Longfellow, Baylor University; Maxim Matusevich, Seton Hall University; Louis M. McDermott, California Maritime Academy.

The author and publisher would like to thank Philip J. Ethington for supplying the map on p. 815.

About the Author

Howard Spodek received his B.A. degree from Columbia University (1963), majoring in history and specializing in Columbia's newly designed program in Asian Studies. He received his M.A. (1966) and Ph.D. (1972) from the University of Chicago, majoring in history and specializing in India. His first trip to India was on a Fulbright Fellowship, 1964–66, and he has spent a total of some seven years studying and teaching in India. He has also traveled widely throughout the United States, Latin America, Asia, Africa, and Europe. He has been a faculty member at Temple University since 1972, appointed Full Professor in 1984. He was awarded Temple's Great Teacher award in 1993.

Spodek's work in world history began in 1988 when he became Academic Director of a comprehensive, innovative program working with teachers in the School District of Philadelphia to improve their knowledge base in world history and facilitate a rewriting of the world history program in the schools. Immediately following this program, he became principal investigator of a program that brought college professors and high school teachers together to reconsider, revise, and, in many cases, initiate the teaching of world history in several of the colleges and universities in the Philadelphia metropolitan area. Those projects led directly to the writing of the first edition of the current text (1997).

Howard Spodek has published extensively on urbanization in India, including *Urban-Rural Integration in Regional Development* (1976); *Urban Form and Meaning in South-East Asia* (editor, with Doris Srinivasan, 1993); and a wide array of articles, including analyses of working women's organizations. In addition he wrote and produced the documentary film, *Ahmedabad* (1983). He has written on his experiences with world history faculty at the college and high school levels in articles in *The History Teacher* (1992, 1995). He has received funding for his research, writing, teaching, and film from Fulbright, the National Endowment for the Humanities, the National Science Foundation, the American Institute of Indian Studies, and the Smithsonian Institution.

Howard Spodek

Introduction:
The World Through Historians' Eyes

Themes and Turning Points

Most readers of this textbook have probably not taken many courses in history. Few are (thus far) planning to major in history, much less become professional historians. A lot therefore rides on this single text. It must present a general introduction to world history that interests, engages, and even fascinates the reader through its subject matter, its narrative, and its analysis. It must open the eyes, minds, and hearts of students who come to this course believing that history is only about the past, and mostly a matter of learning names, dates, and places. It must introduce them to the methods and "habits of mind" of the historian. It must demonstrate how knowledge of the contents and methods of world history—and of this book in particular—will broaden their horizons and also have practical usefulness.

"Usefulness" is not always associated with the study of history. Indeed, in everyday conversation, the phrase "that's history" means that an event is no longer significant. It may once have been important, but it is not now. From this point of view, "history" is a record of people and events that are dead and gone. For the historian, however, the opposite is true. The past has made us who we are, and continues to influence who we are becoming. In this sense, the past is not dead, just as people whom we have known personally and who have influenced our lives are not "dead," even though they may no longer be with us. This text will highlight ways in which the past continues to have profound effects on the present and future. It will help us understand who we have become.

History does not provide specific answers to today's problems, but it does provide examples and case studies

that help us improve our thinking. Generals study past wars to understand how modern battles may be fought; economists study past periods of growth and recession to understand how we can encourage the former and avoid the latter. Understanding the ways in which families and relationships have functioned in the past helps us find ways to make our own families and relationships more satisfying today.

World history gives us the largest possible canvas on which to carry out these studies. We cannot, however, study everything that ever happened. We must choose what to include and what to exclude. We must choose strategies that maximize our ability to understand our lives today in the context of the whole range of human experience.

In this text we choose two fundamental organizing principles as our framework for the study and teaching of world history. First, we choose a series of eight chronological turning points, each of which changed the patterns of human life. Second, we explain the importance of each of these changes in terms of the new themes they introduced into human experience. These two elements—chronological turning points and interpretive themes—go together.

This text is organized around seven turning points and themes. Others might also have been chosen, but these turning points represent some of the most important transformations in human life. The thematic analysis of these turning points encourages students to grapple with the origins and continuing presence of eight of the most significant themes in life: the biological and cultural qualities that make humans the special creatures that we are; the settlements we create and live in; the political power that we assemble and sometimes oppose; the religious systems through which many people find meaning in their individual lives and communities; the movement of trade and people that has linked the peoples of the world ever more closely, sometimes in cooperation, sometimes in competition, and sometimes in conflict; the political, industrial, and social revolutions, especially of the seventeenth through the twentieth centuries; the continuing technological developments that

Learning about silkworms, from a book on the silk industry (gouache on paper). Chinese school, nineteenth century. This painting suggests some of the concerns of modern world history that have previously received less attention: Non-Western regions presented in their own right, and not only in their relationship to the West; daily activities and ordinary people; the human conditions of production and trade; the activities of women. Also, the use of art and illustration is a powerful tool in our becoming acquainted with the peoples of the world throughout time.

continue to reshape our world; and the quest for personal and group identity, so prevalent in our own times.

Because real life does not fit neatly into exact chronological periods, there will be significant overlap among the turning points. Readers may argue that the themes are also not limited to single chronological periods. For example, political regimes, religious systems, and economic organizations appear at all times in history. This argument is, of course, correct: "Everything is related to everything else," and in reality each chronological period will include several themes. We have chosen, however, to highlight particular themes in particular historical periods so that students will understand these themes more thoroughly and learn to employ them as tools of analysis in forming their own understanding of our world.

Chronological Turning Points and Part Themes

PART ONE. The emergence of the first humans. Biological and early cultural evolution, to 10,000 B.C.E.
THEME: Historians and anthropologists search for and interpret artifacts and records to determine what is human about humans.

Turning Point: The Agricultural Village.
PART TWO. Creating settlements, first agricultural villages and, later, cities. 10,000 B.C.E. to 1000 C.E.
THEME: Settlements—villages, towns, and cities—are created to meet community needs.

Turning Point: From City-state to Empire.
PART THREE. The creation of early empires, 2000 B.C.E. to 1100 C.E., from Sargon of Assyria through Alexander the Great, Qin and Han China, Republican and Imperial Rome, and India of the Mauryas and Guptas.
THEME: Imperial political power is generated, increased, consolidated, and resisted.

Turning Point: Politics and Religion.
PART FOUR. The creation and diffusion of global religions: Judaism, Christianity, Islam, Hinduism, and Buddhism. 2500 B.C.E. to 1500 C.E.
THEME: Spiritual feelings are mobilized into powerful religious systems, some of which attain global scope.

Turning Point: Religion and Trade.
PART FIVE. Global movement of goods and people, and the linking of continents; 1300–1700.
THEME: The flows of goods and people are channeled

into global networks, while trade broadened knowledge and outlooks, changing political structures, too.

Turning Point: Comparisons Across Time.
PART SIX. Revolutions, both political and industrial, 1640–1914.
THEME: Vast, abrupt changes in political and economic systems create new social values and systems affecting individuals, families, and communities.

Turning Point: The Olympics and International Politics.
PART SEVEN. Technological change and its human control; 1914–1991.
THEME: New technological systems—both simple and complex—are instituted to improve or threaten human life.

Turning Point: From Past to Present to Future.
PART EIGHT. The application of historical themes to an understanding of contemporary history.
THEME: A brief review of the seven themes developed until now, and an exploration of their applicability to understanding our own times, the last 20–30 years. Includes a final consideration of ways in which individuals and groups form their own identities in the space between past and present.

Global Scope

The scope of this text, and of each turning point and theme within it, is global. For example, the study of the Industrial Revolution in Europe includes its funding—in part—from the wealth that poured into Europe from its New World conquests of people, land, gold, and silver, and from African slave labor; its global extensions in the form of imperialism in Asia, Africa, Australia, and Latin America; and the interactions of colonizers and colonized in response to the new opportunities and challenges.

Social Science Methods, Comparative History, and the Study of Values

Comparative History and the Methods of the Social Sciences

The global, interactive, and comparative format of this text provides also an introduction to social science methodology. The methods of the social sciences are embedded in the structure of the book. Because each part is built on comparisons among different regions of the world, the reader will become accustomed to posing hypotheses based on general principles and to testing them against comparative data from around the world.

This method of moving back and forth between general theory and specific case study, testing the degree to which the general theory and the specific data fit each other, is at the heart of the social sciences. For example, in Part Two we will explore the general characteristics of cities, and then examine how well the generalizations hold up through case studies of various cities around the world. In Part Three we will seek general theories of the rise and fall of early empires based on comparisons of China, Rome, and India. In Part Four we will search for commonalities among religious systems through a survey of five world religions. In Part Eight we begin with an analysis of new issues of political and cultural identity and then examine their significance in a series of brief case studies in different regions of the world. These comparisons enable us more clearly to think about and to understand the workings of cities, empires, and religions not only of the past, but also of our own time and place.

Multiple Perspectives

The text highlights the importance of multiple perspectives in studying and interpreting history. The answers we get—the narrative histories we write—are based on the questions we ask. Each part suggests a variety of questions that can be asked about the historical event that is being studied and a variety of interpretations that can emerge in the process of answering them. Often there is more than one "correct" way of understanding change over time and its significance. Different questions will trigger very different research and very different answers. For example, in Part Five we ask about the stages and processes by which Western commercial power began to surpass that of Asia. This question presupposes the fact that at earlier times Asian power had been superior and raises the additional questions why it declined and why European power advanced. In Part Six we ask how the Industrial Revolution affected and changed relationships between men and women; this question will yield different research and a different narrative from questions about, for example, women's contributions to industrialization, which is a useful question, but a different one.

Through the systematic study of the past in this thematic, comparative framework, students will gain tools for understanding and making their own place in the world. They will not only learn how the peoples of the world have gotten to where we are, but also consider the possibility of setting out in new directions for new goals.

Evaluating Values

This form of analysis will also introduce a study of values. In order to understand the choices made by people in the past, we must attempt to understand the values that informed their thinking and actions. These values may be similar to, or quite different from, our own. In order to understand the interpretations introduced by later historians, we must understand the historians' values as well. These, too, may be similar to, or different from, our own. Historians usually had personal perspectives from which they viewed the past, and these perspectives influenced their interpretations. Finally, in order for student-readers to form their own understanding of the past, and to make it more useful in their own lives, they must also see how their own values influence their evaluation of past events.

For most of the past century, social scientists spoke of creating "value free" disciplines. Today, most scholars believe that this is impossible. We cannot be "value free." On the contrary, we must attempt to understand the values that have inspired historical actors, previous historians, and ourselves. Coming to an understanding of the values of others—historical actors and historians who have studied them—will help readers to recognize and formulate their own values, a central part of a liberal arts education.

History and Identity

History is among the most passionate and bitterly contentious of disciplines because most people and groups locate a large part of their identity in their history. Americans may take pride in their nationality, for example, for having created a representative, constitutional democracy that has endured for over 200 years (see Part Six). Yet they may be saddened, shamed, or perhaps incensed by the existence of 250 years of slavery followed by inequalities in race relations continuing to the present (see Part Five). Christians may take pride in 2,000 years of missions of compassion toward the poor and downtrodden, yet they may be saddened, shamed, or even incensed by an almost equally long record of religious warfare and of persecution of those whose beliefs differed from their own (see Part Four).

As various ethnic, religious, class, and gender groups represent themselves in public political life, they seek not only to understand the history that has made them what they are, but also to persuade others to understand that history in the same way, to create a new consciousness. Feminist historians, for example, find in their reading of history that patriarchy, a system of male-created and male-dominated institutions, has subordinated women. From available data and their interpretation of them, they attempt to weave a persuasive argument that will win over others to their position.

Some will not be persuaded. They may not even agree that women have been subordinated to men, but argue that both genders have shared in a great deal of suffering (and joy) throughout history (see Parts One and Seven). The historical debates over the origins and evolution of gender relationships evoke strong emotions because people's self-image, the image of their group, and the perceptions others hold of them are all at stake. And the stakes can be high.

Control of Historical Records

From earliest times, control over the historical records and their interpretation has been fundamental to control over people's thoughts. The first emperor of China, Qin Shihuang (r. 221–207 B.C.E.), the man who built the concept of a united China that has lasted until today attempted to destroy all knowledge of the past:

> He then abolished the ways of ancient sage kings and put to the torch the writings of the Hundred Schools in an attempt to keep the people in ignorance. He demolished the walls of major cities and put to death men of fame and talent. (deBary, I: 229).

So wrote Jia Yi (201–168? B.C.E.), poet and statesman of the succeeding Han dynasty. Shihuang wished that only his interpretation of China's past, and his place in it, be preserved. Later intellectuals condemned his actions— but the lost records were irretrievable (see Part Three).

In similar fashion, the first great historian of the Christian Church, Eusebius of Caesarea (c. 260–339) in his accounts of the early Christians in the Roman Empire, chose carefully to include elements that he considered of "profit" to his mission, and to exclude those that were not.

> It is not for us to describe their miserable vicissitudes [in persecution] … just as it is not a part of our task to leave on record their faction-fights and their unnatural conduct towards each other, prior to the persecution. That is why we have decided to say no more about them than suffices for us to justify God's Judgment … We shall rather set forth in our whole narrative only what may be of profit, first, to our own times, and then to later times. (MacMullen, p. 6).

Historical Revision

Interpretations of events may become highly contested and revised even after several centuries have passed. Colonial governments seeking to control subject peoples sometimes argued that the conquered people were so backward that they benefited from the conquest. Later historians, with more distance and more detachment, were often less kind to the colonizers. Some 1,900 years ago the historian Tacitus was writing bitterly of the ancient Romans in their conquest of England: "Robbery, butchery, rapine, the liars call Empire; they create a desolation and call it peace." (Agricola, 30)

In our own era, the many nations that have won their freedom from colonialism echo similar resentments against their foreign rulers and set out to revise the historical record in keeping with their newly won political freedom. Jawaharlal Nehru, the first prime minister of independent India (1947–64), wrote in 1944 from the prison cell in which he had been imprisoned for his leadership of his country's independence movement:

> British accounts of India's history, more especially of what is called the British period, are bitterly resented. History is almost always written by the victors and conquerors and gives their viewpoint; or, at any rate, the victors' version is given prominence and holds the field. (Nehru, p. 289)

Philip Curtin, historian of Africa and of slavery, elaborates an equally critical view of European colonial accounts of Africa's history:

> African history was seriously neglected until the 1950s … The colonial period in Africa left an intellectual legacy to be overcome, just as it had in other parts of the world. … The colonial imprint on historical knowledge emerged in the nineteenth and early twentieth centuries as a false perspective, a Eurocentric view of world history created at a time of European domination … Even where Europeans never ruled, European knowledge was often accepted as modern knowledge, including aspects of the Eurocentric historiography. (Curtin, p. 54)

Instead, Curtin continues, a proper historiography must:

> show the African past from an African point of view … For Africans, to know about the past of their own societies is a form of self-knowledge crucial to a sense of identity in a diverse and rapidly changing world. A recovery of African history has been an important part of African development over recent decades. (p. 54)

Religious and ethnic groups, too, may seek to control historical records. In 1542, the Roman Catholic Church established an Index of Prohibited Books to ban writings it considered heretical. (The Spanish Inquisition, ironically, stored away many records that later scholars used to recreate its history and the history of those it persecuted.) More recently, despite all the evidence of the Holocaust, the murder of six million Jews by the Nazi government of Germany during World War II, a few people have claimed that the murders never took place. They deny the existence of such racial and religious hatred and of its consequences, and ignore deep-seated

Lenin addressing troops in Sverdlov Square, Moscow, May 5, 1920. The leaders of the Russian Communist revolution crudely refashioned the historical record to suit the wishes of the winners. After Lenin's death in 1924, his second-in-command Leon Trotsky (pictured sitting on the podium in the left-hand picture) lost to Josef Stalin the bitter power struggle that ensued. Not only was Trotsky banished from the Soviet Union, but so was his appearance in the official archives (see doctored picture below).

Indians giving Hernán Cortés a headband, from Diego Duran's *Historia de las Indias,* **1547.** Bent on conquest and plunder, the bearded Spaniard Cortés arrived on the Atlantic coast of Mexico in 1519. His forces sacked the ancient city of Tenochtitlán, decimated the Aztec people and imprisoned their chief, Montezuma, before proclaiming the Aztec Empire "New Spain." By stark contrast, this bland Spanish watercolor shows local tribesmen respectfully paying homage to the invader as if he were a god; in ignoring the brutality exercised in the colonization of South America, the artist is, in effect, "rewriting" history. (Biblioteca National, Madrid)

problems in the relationships between majority and minority populations.

The significance of the voyages of Columbus was once celebrated uncritically in the United States in tribute both to "the Admiral of the Ocean Sea" himself and to the courage and enterprise of the European explorers and early settlers who brought their civilizations to the Americas. In South America, however, where Native American Indians are more numerous and people of European ancestry often form a smaller proportion of the population, the celebrations have been far more ambivalent, muted, and meditative.

In 1992, on the five hundredth anniversary of Columbus' first voyage to the Americas, altogether new and more sobering elements entered the commemoration ceremonies, even in the United States. The negative consequences of Columbus' voyages, previously ignored, were now recalled and emphasized: the death of up to 90 percent of the Native American Indian population in the century after the arrival of Europeans; the Atlantic slave trade, initiated by trade in Indian slaves; and the exploitation of the natural resources of a continent until then little touched by humans. The ecological consequences, which are only now beginning to receive more attention, were not all negative, however. They included the fruitful exchange of natural products between the hemispheres. Horses, wheat, and sheep were introduced to the Americas; potatoes, tomatoes, and corn to Afro-Eurasia. Unfortunately, the spread of syphilis was one of the consequences of the exchange; scholars disagree on who transmitted this disease to whom (see Part Five).

Thugs sometimes gain control of national histories. George Orwell's satirical novel *Animal Farm* (published in 1945) presented an allegory in which pigs come to rule a farm. Among their many acts of domination, the pigs seize control of the historical records of the farm animals' failed experiment in equality and impose their own official interpretation, which justifies their own rule. The rewriting of history and suppression of alternative records by the Communist Party of the former Soviet Union between 1917 and 1989 reveals the bitter truth underlying Orwell's satire (see Part Seven).

Although the American experience is much different, in the United States, too, records have been suppressed. Scholars are still trying to use the Freedom of Information Act to pry open sealed diplomatic archives. (Most official archives everywhere have 20-, 30-, or 40-year rules governing the waiting period before certain sensitive records are opened to the public. These rules, which are designed to protect living people and contemporary policies from excessive scrutiny, are the general rule everywhere.)

What Do We Know?
How Do We Know It?
What Difference Does It Make?

So, historical records are not simply lists of events. They are the means by which individuals and groups develop their interpretations of these events. All people develop their own interpretations of past events; historians do it professionally. Because interpretations differ, there is no single historical record, but various narrations of events, each told from a different perspective. Therefore the study of history is intimately linked to the study of values.

To construct their interpretations, historians examine the values—the motives, wishes, desires, visions—of people of the past. In interpreting those values, historians must confront and engage their own values, comparing and contrasting these values with those of people in the past. For example, they ask how various people viewed slavery, or child labor, or education, or art and music in societies of the past. In the back of their minds they compare and contrast those older values with values held by various people today and especially with their own personal values. They ask: How and why have values changed or remained the same through the passage of time? Why, and in what ways, do my values compare and contrast with values of the past? By learning to pose such questions, students will be better equipped to discover and create their own place in the continuing movement of human history. This text, therefore consistently addresses three fundamental questions:

What Do We Know?
How Do We Know It?
What Difference Does It Make?

Even when historians agree on which events are most significant, they may differ in evaluating why the events are significant. One historian's interpretation of events may be diametrically opposed to another's. For example, virtually all historians agree that part of the significance of World War II lay in its new policies and technologies of destruction: nuclear weapons in battle and genocide behind the lines. In terms of interpretation, pessimists might stress the continuing menace of these legacies of

terror, while optimists might argue that the very violence of the war and the Holocaust triggered a search for limits on nuclear arms and greater tolerance for minorities. With each success in nuclear arms limitation and in toleration, the optimists seem more persuasive; with each spread of nuclear weapons and each outbreak of genocide, the pessimists seem to win.

The study of history is thus an interpretation of significance as well as an investigation of facts. The significance of events is determined by their consequences. Sometimes we do not know what the consequences are; or the consequences may not have run their course; or we may differ in our assessments of the consequences. This play between past events and their current consequences is what historian E.H. Carr had in mind in his famous description of history as "an unending dialogue between the present and the past." (Carr, p. 30)

Tools

The study of history requires many tools, and this text includes most of the principal ones:

- Primary sources are accounts that were produced at the time an event occurred. Those who produced them were eyewitnesses with direct knowledge of what happened. The core of historical study is an encounter with primary materials, usually documents, but including other artifacts—for example, letters, diaries, newspaper accounts, photographs, and artwork. Every chapter in this text includes representative primary materials.
- Visual images, a strong feature of this book, complement the written text, offering non-verbal "texts" of the time. These are often central pieces of evidence. For example, in Chapter Nine we illustrate the influence of Hinduism and Buddhism in Southeast Asia through the temple architecture of the region.
- Maps place events in space and in geographical relationship to one another.
- Chronological timelines situate events in time and sequence.
- Brief charts supply summaries as well as contextual information on topics such as religion, science, and trade.

Asking Questions

- Please review the seven themes and turning points selected here. From what you already know of world history, do these seem well chosen? Would you select different or additional themes and turning points for your account? If so, which ones and why?
- Examine how one of the values in which you believe has come from historical experience, either your own experience or that of relatives and friends, or the experience of groups to which you belong.
- When you tell other people about yourself, what "records" from your past do you highlight? Which ones do you leave out of the story, or even conceal? Are there any that you would like to destroy? Can you destroy them? How does the audience you are speaking to affect your choice of "records"?

Suggested Readings

Basic, Comprehensive, Introductory Materials

Carr, E.H. *What Is History?* (Harmondsworth, Middlesex: Penguin Books, 1964). A classic introduction to the study of history and historiography from the point of view of a master.

Tosh, John. *The Pursuit of History: Aims, Methods, and New Directions in the Study of Modern History* (London: Longman, 4th ed., 2006). Excellent, comprehensive introduction to the study of history, with discussions of many different kinds of historical study, their methods and purposes.

Tosh, John, ed. *Historians on History: Readings* (Harlow, England: Pearson, 2nd ed. 2009). Excellent selection of brief extracts from major historians who have given new direction to the field, mostly practicing in the last half-century.

More Specialized Materials

Bennett, Judith M. "Medieval Women, Modern Women: Across the Great Divide," in David Aers, ed., *Culture and History, 1350–1600: Essays on English Communities, Identities, and Writing* (New York: Harvester Wheat-

sheaf, 1992), pp. 147–75. Discusses continuity, in contrast to change, in women's history.

Curtin, Philip D. "Recent Trends in African Historiography and Their Contribution to History in General," in Joseph Ki-Zerbo, ed., *General History of Africa, Vol. I: Methodology and African Pre-History* (Berkeley: University of California Press, 1981), pp. 54–71. An excellent introduction to this fine series commissioned by the United Nations.

Dunn, Ross. *The New World History: A Teacher's Companion* (Boston: Bedford/St. Martin's, 2000). Excellent selections both on what the new world history ought to be, and what it is as major historians write it.

deBary, William Theodore, *et al.*, comps. *Sources of Chinese Tradition*, 2 vols. (New York: Columbia University Press, 2nd ed., 1999, 2000). *The* anthology of materials on the subject.

Lerner, Gerda. *The Creation of Patriarchy* (New York: Oxford University Press, 1986). A controversial study of patriarchy in ancient Mesopotamia by a distinguished historian of the United States. Lerner retooled to study this fundamental feminist question.

MacMullen, Ramsay. *Christianizing the Roman Empire (A.D. 100–400)* (New Haven: Yale University Press, 1984). Excellent analysis of the factors leading to Christianity's success in the Roman Empire. Gives major role to government support.

Manning, Patrick. *Navigating World History: Historians Create a Global Past* (New York: Palgrave Macmillan, 2003). A major historian presents a magisterial, somewhat dense, survey of the field.

Nehru, Jawaharlal. *The Discovery of India* (Delhi: Oxford University Press, 1989). A history of his country, written in jail during the freedom struggle by the man who became India's first prime minister.

Orwell, George. *Animal Farm* (New York: Harcourt, Brace, 1946). A classic satire on government by thugs; aimed at the USSR.

Tacitus, Cornelius. *Tacitus' Agricola, Germany, and Dialogue on Orators*, trans. Herbert W. Benario (Norman: University of Oklahoma Press, 1991). One of ancient Rome's great historians who understood the cruelty underlying the power of empire.

TURNING POINT ↗

Religion and Trade

Organized religions have very diverse attitudes towards trade. They differ from time to time, from place to place, and even internally, from one branch to another.

For Christianity, the relationship between religion and trade was complex. Jesus' teachings condemned the pursuit of wealth. Both the Gospel of Matthew (6:24) and of Luke (16:13) quote him: "No servant can be the slave of two masters … You cannot serve God and Money." Christian clergy were sworn to lives of poverty, as well as chastity and obedience.

Large and popular religions must, however, have some flexibility in their belief systems, and we find in Christianity many examples of the accommodation of spiritual and financial interests. The Church became wealthy because many Christians gave 10 percent of their earnings to the Church, in a process called tithing. In exchange, the Church might bless their economic interests. In the first illustration on p. 386, a bishop blesses the annual market at St. Denis, near Paris.

As the Roman Catholic Church became increasingly wealthy, however, reformers lamented its departure from the ascetic standards of its early years. Martin Luther broke from the Church in the early sixteenth century, in part as a protest against the Church's sale of "indulgences," documents granting the forgiveness of sin in exchange for donations to the Church. Money, Luther argued, could not take the place of honest penance.

For Islam, with which we concluded Part Four, a concern with trade and commerce came naturally. The Prophet Muhammad was himself a caravan driver by profession, and he married his employer, Khadija, the owner of the caravan company. To promote a fruitful relationship between religious authority and economic power, the Umayyad dynasty moved its headquarters out of the relatively remote Arabian Peninsula to Damascus (661), an important node on the West Asian trade routes. A century later (750), the Abbasid dynasty moved to an even more central location for trade—

The Pope's Selling of Indulgences, Lucas Cranach the Elder, 1521. Woodcut. When the Pope began selling indulgences, pardons for sin issued on God's behalf, the German monk Martin Luther, outraged, declared that only God could grant pardons, and condemned the Church for greed. The artist Lucas Cranach, supporting Luther, depicted the Pope as the Antichrist.

TURNING POINT ↗

Baghdad—and throughout the Islamic world mosques were built with commercial enterprises surrounding them, the profits of these businesses helping to support the mosque. (See accompanying illustration of the Mosque of Bajazet, below.)

Judaism, too, accommodated both religion and trade. The Bible represents favorably the Jewish patriarchs' concerns for the welfare of their families. Islam and Judaism both recognized the importance of harnessing business to the needs of the community.

A bishop blessing the annual market, St. Denis, near Paris, fourteenth century. Miniature. (Bibliothèque Nationale, Paris) Because St. Denis, the first bishop of Paris, was martyred, about 250, and buried nearby, this site became a pilgrim center. Almost 1,000 years later, King Dagobert I conferred on the townspeople the right to hold a market. St. Denis then attracted merchants from all over Europe, and even from the Byzantine Empire. The bishop's blessing suggests the combined significance of religion and trade in this town.

Mosque of Bajazet with the Seraskier's Gate, Istanbul, **Griffiths, c. 1850.** Engraving from Julia Pardoe, *Beauties of the Bosphoros,* p. 106, published London: George Virtue, 1838. "The mosque of Bajazet is built in the immediate neighborhood of the great Tcharchi, or Bazar, and hence the square is constantly thronged with merchants, traders, and strangers passing to and from this great commercial mart …" (Stapleton Collection, England)

His Holiness Pramukh Swami Maharaj sanctifying books of account during the *Chopada Puja* ceremony at the Shri Swaminarayan Mandir, Neasden, London. More typically, in India, each merchant hosts an individual ceremony for his own business firm. Here, in London, the priest is blessing the account books of many different businessmen in a single collective ceremony.

Both created legal codes commanding concern for the poor, condemning greed, and providing regulations for trade in the interests of the public good.

Hinduism, too, designates the pursuit of wealth and power as an important goal in life and sets aside the longest stage of the life cycle to the practicalities of administering a household. One whole caste category, the *vaishyas*, is composed of business people. In parts of India, at the new year, businessmen invite *brahmin* priests to bless their account books in an elaborate ceremony called *chopada puja*, or the worship of the account books. The illustration above indicates that as Hindu businessmen have traveled overseas in modern times, they have continued this custom of integrating business practice with religious ritual.

Resentment of the power of the brahmins, however, was a concern of early Buddhism. Many of its adherents and supporters were political rulers, most notably the Emperor Asoka, and people of the business castes. They employed *brahmin* priests to perform religious rituals, but created no such hereditary group within their own religion.

As we trace the expansion of trade from regional exchange to global enterprise, we shall see that religious belief and affiliation were often critically important to the businessmen we study.

Turning Point Questions

1. To what degree have religious and business leaders accommodated one another—or failed to find such accommodation?
2. What have been the terms of the accommodation?
3. How have the members of each group benefited or lost out from the accommodation or the failure of accommodation?

PART FIVE

GLOBAL TRADE: THE BEGINNING OF THE MODERN WORLD

1300–1700

Trade, Traders, Disease, and Migration

Many westerners, and especially Americans, begin the study of modern history with the voyages of Christopher Columbus. Historians often refer to this story, beginning with Columbus, as the "master narrative" because it has dominated the study of world history for many years and because it has been perpetuated by the "masters," the heirs of Columbus' voyages and conquests, the people who have benefited from them.

There are good reasons for identifying Columbus' four expeditions between 1492 and 1504 as the turning point that ushers in the modern age in world history. They transformed the Atlantic from a moat that separated the eastern and western hemispheres into a bridge that joined them. They inspired Ferdinand Magellan (c. 1480–1521) to explore the Atlantic and the Pacific, bringing the entire globe into touch. The consequences were immense, and immensely different for different peoples. No sooner did Europeans "discover" the New World than they conquered the land and its peoples. European kings, merchants, and priests grew rich, powerful, and proud on the basis of the gold and silver they brought from the New World, the land they seized and cultivated there, the laborers they forced into servitude, and the souls they claimed for Christianity. Columbus opened the door.

More recent narratives give greater importance to the preexisting trade networks that drew Columbus into his search for Atlantic routes to India and China. They point to the lucrative Indian Ocean trade, from which Spain felt excluded, as the inspiration for his voyages. They begin their story with an account of the trade networks of this earlier period, usually from about 1300. By that date the sea routes were fully operational, and even the land routes, the silk routes across Asia, were functional once again, protected by their Mongol conquerors. Newer narratives also underline the continuing independence of the great Asian nations, in particular India and China.

Like Latin America, Asia too succumbed to significant European control: India after 1757 and China still later, after 1839. From this Asian perspective, 1492 appears less compelling as a turning point. The newer narratives do not question the significance of Columbus' voyages in creating a new world geography, boosting the power of the Spanish throne, and making South America Latin through the introduction of Christianity and the Iberian cultures and languages of Spain and Portugal. They do, however, consider these transformations in the context of the history of the entire world. Our account of trade in world history follows these more recent interpretations. We begin in the period around 1300, when Indian Ocean trade was flourishing but Spain and Portugal were blocked from participating. We evaluate the blockages: the policies of the pope; the Ottoman Empire; the traders of Venice. Sailing for Spain, Columbus attempted to enter that lucrative trade network through the back door.

In Chapter Twelve we explore the role of traders and their relationship with political rulers from 1300 to 1500. We study the geography of the principal trade routes. They were not yet unified, or global, but they were linked. Long-distance merchants coordinated delivery of goods from one end of Afro-Eurasia to the other. Through the thirteenth and fourteenth centuries Mongol descendants of Chinggis Khan provided security along central Asia's silk routes, opening them after hundreds of years of abandonment. Traders and travelers like Marco Polo and Ibn Battuta explored these routes; we read a few of their adventures. Epidemics sometimes accompanied trade missions. The devastating "Black Death" wiped out more than one-third of the population in many places from China to Western Europe, with relationships of wealth and power dramatically restructured in its wake.

Chapter Thirteen turns to the Atlantic and Mediterranean coasts of Europe. As Viking sailors and marauders began to settle in their northern lands, commercial shipping began to ply the waters between the Ocean and the Sea in greater safety. Shipping increased as Europe grew wealthier from improvements in agriculture and renewed urban growth. The businessmen and artisans of newly prospering European cities developed new institutions, such as guilds; supported new inventions, such as the printing press; and accepted new philosophies of business, such as early capitalism, based on free markets, risk-taking, and the principles of supply-and-demand economics. Religious philosophy, too, was evolving to accommodate more earthly desires for personal profit.

Europe was changing, in part, because it was learning from its Arab neighbors in Spain and on the southern shore of the Mediterranean. Europeans incorporated into their fleets the caravel ships and triangular lateen sails used by Arab sailors. Christian scholars and artists began to reclaim the cultural heritages of the ancient Greeks and Romans, which they had forgotten, relearning them from the Muslims and Jews who had kept them alive. They called the culture that emerged a *renaissance*, a rebirth of humanistic creativity that had been lost for over 1,000 years. Both the Church and prosperous businessmen supported the new forms of cultural expression.

Western Europe's economic growth was blocked, however, by Arab and Venetian control over trade routes in the eastern Mediterranean and beyond. Portugal, situated on the Atlantic, circumvented these blockages by circumnavigating Africa. When Columbus promised the new rulers of Spain that he could find yet another new route to the riches of the East by crossing the Atlantic, and win new converts to Christianity in the bargain, they agreed to support his risky venture.

Columbus' voyages did initiate new chapters in world history, as we see in Chapter Fourteen. They opened vast new resources of wealth—in land, in gold and silver, and in captive labor—for Europe to exploit (or develop, depending on your point of view). They heralded the destruction of powerful Native American empires and the deaths of millions of Native Americans, through warfare and disease. They made South America into Latin America, by imposing the languages, cultures, and religion of Spain and Portugal. The Columbian Exchange of crops enriched diets and nutrition throughout the world, while the exchange of microbes, especially smallpox, killed millions, especially Native Americans.

The Portuguese also sailed eastward, around the coast of Africa, attempting to control Indian Ocean shipping—local peoples viewed this as piracy—and to convert souls to Christianity, sometimes threatening death as the alternative. In the longer run, northern Europeans in the Netherlands, England, and France, more devoted to commerce than the Iberians, reaped still greater profit from the new, global opportunities. Many northern Europeans left Catholicism for Protestant denominations, provoking a lasting historical debate over the relationship between commercial success and religious affiliation.

Other world empires responded to these new developments in varied ways. Alarmed by the new power of the Western Europeans, Russia tried to catch up militarily and commercially, although the Russian monarchy held on to its political powers. The Ottoman Empire was strong enough militarily to lay siege to Vienna in 1529 and to battle again to take the city in 1683—both times unsuccessfully—but its commerce slipped into the hands of foreigners, especially the French, and the empire began its long descent. The Mughals ruled India effectively from 1556 until the early 1700s, but then, as their power faltered internally, Europeans began to expand into the interior from their small trading fortresses along the coasts. The Chinese excluded most European commerce throughout this period, although Jesuit priests won hundreds of thousands of converts. India and China would ultimately succumb to European control, but only after centuries of internal decay that opened the gates.

The unification of world trade and transportation also brought vast migrations. Chapter Fifteen introduces demography as a means of following the lives of these migrants, mostly common people who left no written records. Millions left Europe in search of economic, and sometimes religious, opportunity. They founded "New Europes" in the Americas, South Africa, Australia, and New Zealand, as well as colonial outposts around the world. Millions of Asians migrated from one region of that immense continent to another in the armies of the Ottomans conquering Turkey, the Mughals conquering India, and the Safavids conquering Persia. Millions of Chinese migrated northward as they drove the Mongols out of China's walls and as hardy crops of the Columbian Exchange opened new territories to fruitful cultivation. Urban concentrations increased as new dynasties and rulers constructed new capitals. Two of the most devastating demographic changes in history also marked this period: the dying off of tens of millions of Native Americans, the victims of warfare and disease, and the forced transportation of some ten million people taken as slaves from Africa, mostly to work the sugar plantations of the New World. Almost all of the individual stories of the migrants are lost, but demography helps us to recover their collective experience.

CHAPTER TWELVE

Establishing World Trade Routes

The Geography and Philosophies of Early Economic Systems
1300–1500

Today, long-distance, international trade forms a substantial part of the world's commerce and includes even the most basic products of everyday food and clothing. In earlier times, however, long-distance trade represented only a small fraction of overall trade, mostly supplying such luxuries as silks, gold, and spices for the wealthy classes. Because these goods were extremely valuable relative to their weight, merchants could carry them over thousands of miles and still sell them for handsome profits. Some commercial goods, such as raw wool and cotton, were traded over distances of a few hundred miles. The transportation costs of such raw materials were justified by the **value added** during further processing into finished goods after importation.

Before 1500, by far the largest share of trade was local—food crops traded for local hand manufactures or raw materials. These goods were necessities, but they had little value in relationship to their weight. Often, they were bartered in exchange for other local goods rather than sold for money in more distant markets. This local exchange of goods is a fundamental part of local and regional history, but the study of world history focuses on long-distance trade and its importance in knitting together distant regions of the world.

Trade provides an index of economic vitality. It stimulates economic growth: people produce goods and provide services only if markets exist for them. Anyone who has ever looked for a job has experienced this economic truth. If jobs exist, people can find work; if jobs do not exist, people remain unemployed and economically unproductive. Similarly, both production and consumption are limited by the availability of markets. If markets are accessible, products can be bought and sold; if not, then trade, production, and consumption all stagnate.

World Trade: A Historical Analysis

Historians studying world trade seek to understand its social as well as its economic outcomes. What social benefits have been achieved by different systems of trade? Which systems have favored which members of society? Which systems have harmed which members of society? What have been the trade-offs between benefit and harm under each system? These questions, of course, are not merely historical. The present-day debates over the "globalization" of trade—the transformation of the world into a single marketplace—demonstrate their enduring relevance. Recurrent protests around the globe against the World Trade Organization's intentions to

KEY TOPICS
- World Trade: A Historical Analysis
- Trade in the Americas Before 1500
- Trade in Sub-Saharan Africa
- Asia's Complex Trade Patterns
- China: A Magnet for Traders
- Central Asia: The Mongols and the Silk Routes
- World Trade Routes Before Columbus: What Difference Do They Make?

Trade in the Gulf of Cambay, Boucicault Master, India, 1410. **Vellum.** As the main port of northwestern India, Cambay excited the wonder of painters and artists in far-off Europe. This illustration from the *Livre des Merveilles* (*The Book of Wonders*) (1410) represents Cambay's ships and traders in European guise, not surprisingly, because the artist had never been to the city. (Bibliothèque Nationale, Paris)

value added An economist's term for the increase in value from the cost of raw materials to the cost of finished products. It is the value added to the raw material by processing, manufacture, and marketing.

free market economy An economic system in which the means of production are largely privately owned and there is little or no government control over the markets.

supply and **demand** In economics, the relationship between the amount of a commodity that producers are able and willing to sell (supply) and the quantity that consumers can afford and wish to buy (demand).

moral economy An economy whose goal is providing basic necessities for all members of a society before allowing any particular members to take profits; in contrast to a free market economy.

trade diaspora A dispersion over far-flung territories of a group of people who have a common bond. Usually this is an ancestral bond, such as in the Jewish diaspora and the African diaspora. A trade diaspora refers to the network of international traders who relate to one another through the bonds of their trade.

silk route The set of rough roads, transportation links, across central Asia carrying trade and cultural exchange as far as China, India, and the eastern Mediterranean. The routes flourished only when governments were strong enough to protect them and keep them safe.

expand and regulate international trade (see Chapter Twenty-four) indicate that intense passions continue to surround these questions today.

To what degree should governments regulate or control economic markets? In a completely **free market economy**, conditions of trade would not be regulated; prices would vary only in terms of the relationship between the **supply** of goods and the **demand** for them, and people would be free to conduct business as they chose. Societies, however, do regulate trade. For example, governments that wish to ensure that everyone has food may declare that agricultural production should be expanded and industrial production limited. In wartime, governments may ration food and essential commodities to ensure that everyone has access to at least minimum quantities. By taxing some items at high rates and others at low rates, governments can selectively promote or limit production and trade. Business may be more regulated or less regulated, but government never leaves it completely unregulated.

Even in the earliest societies, such as Egypt, Mesopotamia, and China, government officials, often in alliance with priests, had the power to regulate trade. Nevertheless, market economies based on private profit existed here as well. This trade for private profit was embedded in deeper political, social, religious, and moral structures of society. For example, governments intervened in civilian economies to ensure adequate supplies of war materials for their armies. Concern for the general welfare, or fear of civic unrest, encouraged other interventions to ensure adequate food and basic necessities for the poor; scholars sometimes contrast this **moral economy** with the free market economy.

Long-distance private trade flourished most profitably in major port cities around the world. The merchants who carried on this port-city trade were often foreigners, with some independence from local political and social structures. Although they might occupy marginal positions in their host societies, they held central positions in the international trade networks. These long-distance merchants encouraged and brokered trade between the society in which they were living and the far-flung networks of international merchants. They formed **trade diasporas,** networks of interconnected commercial communities living and working in major trade cities dispersed throughout Africa, Europe, and Asia. Trade diasporas appear in the archaeological record as early as 3500 B.C.E. Some endured for millennia.

During the height of the Roman Empire, for example, traders from Rome sailed the waters of the Mediterranean Sea and the Indian Ocean, on rare occasions all the way to China. Most of these traders were not ethnically Roman. Usually they were descendants of the major trading communities of the eastern Mediterranean: Jews, Greek-speaking Egyptians, and Arabs. Long after the sack of Rome, small religious communities of Jews, Christians, and Muslim Arabs persisted along the southwest coast of India, a heritage of these ancient diaspora traders. Typically, the merchants who conducted trade were marginal to their host societies rather than citizens within them. They were not unregulated by the hosts, nor were they totally subordinated, but they were allowed to make profits in return for the benefits they brought to the port city.

In a world that had no international courts or legal systems, shared religion and ethnicity often formed the basis for conducting long-distance trade. For example, while small in number, Jews were able to carry on international trade across the entire eastern hemisphere. Their religious diaspora in numerous far-distant points of settlement supported their trade diaspora. Dispersed in small communities from China to Western Europe and Africa, their common faith formed a bond of trust, and this trust enabled them to establish highly efficient trade networks. During the period of Tang-Abbasid control over the **silk route**—the eighth and early ninth centuries C.E.—Jews were a preeminent trading community along the trade routes

AT A GLANCE: WORLD TRADE, GLOBAL (compare p. 428)

DATE	POLITICAL/SOCIAL EVENTS	TRADE DEVELOPMENTS	EXPLORATION
1050	• Almoravids destroy Kingdom of Ghana (1067)		
1100		• Age of Great Zimbabwe in southern Africa	
1150		• Papermaking spreads from Muslim world to Europe	
1200	• Foundation of first Muslim empire in India • Chinggis Khan establishes Mongol Empire (1206–1405) • Collapse of Mayan civilization in Central America; rise of Incas in Peru • Rise of Mali, West Africa		
1250	• Osman I founds Ottoman dynasty in Turkey (1290–1326) • Emergence of Empire of Benin • Mongols fail to conquer Japan (1281)		• Marco Polo arrives in China (1275)
1300	• Height of Mali (Mandingo) Empire under Sultan Mansa Musa		• Ibn Battuta's travels in East Asia and Africa (c. 1330–60)
1350	• Ming dynasty in China (1368)		
1400	• Ottoman Turks establish foothold in Europe at Gallipoli	• China reconstructs and extends Grand Canal	
1450		• Decline of Kilwa and Great Zimbabwe in southeast Africa (c. 1450)	
1500	• Zenith of Songay Empire of the middle Niger region (1492–1529) • Hernán Cortés and Spanish conquistadores defeat Aztecs and seize Mexico (1519–21) • Francisco Pizarro and Spanish conquistadores defeat Incas and seize Peru		

linking Europe and China. Charlemagne's ninth-century European empire employed them to carry trade in southern Europe. Baghdad, astride many of the key trade routes in western Asia, held the most prominent Jewish community in the world at the time, and there were also notable Jewish communities in Calicut and Cochin in southern India and in Kaifeng, China. When the Portuguese explorer Vasco da Gama reached Calicut in 1498, a local Jewish merchant was able to serve as interpreter. Cairo, Egypt, one of the world's great trade centers, also sheltered a significant Jewish community.

Other groups of global traders also formed commercial networks on the basis of shared religion and ethnicity, although they were generally less extensive geographically, for example Christian Armenians, Jain and Hindu Gujaratis from western India, and Fukienese from the southeast coast of China. Like the Jews, these trading communities operated within their own social and religious networks, enjoying trade relations with local people, but not encouraging their religious conversion. On the other hand, overseas Muslim trade communities often sought to attract converts to Islam, as happened especially in Indonesia and Southeast Asia.

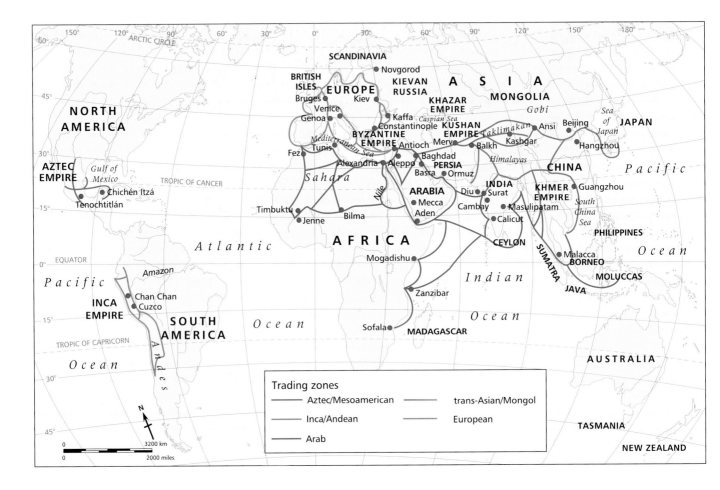

World trade routes. Between 1100 and 1500 a relay system of trade by land and sea connected almost all populous regions of Eurasia, as well as North and East Africa. Long-distance traders carried goods along their own segments of these routes, and then turned them over to traders in the next sector. The western hemisphere was still separate, and had two major trade networks of its own.

Trade in the Americas Before 1500

The western hemisphere spawned two major trade networks. The northern network served primarily the area that is Mexico today, although in those years this region was dominated by several different groups. The southern network, in today's Ecuador, Peru, and northern Chile, ran north–south in two parallel routes, one along the Pacific Coast, the other inland along the spine of the Andes Mountains. East–west routes, linking the coastal settlements with those of the mountains, rose to altitudes of 15,000 feet. In both North and South America goods were carried by pack animals and by humans; the American Indians had not invented the wheel. Boats were used on streams and rivers. Along the South American coast, near the equator, the Incas sailed boats constructed of balsa wood, while the Mayans of the Yucatan paddled canoes through their river systems. There was little traffic between North and South America and virtually none between the eastern and western hemispheres, except for rare voyages, such as that by Leif Eriksson, the Viking explorer who reached Newfoundland about the year 1000.

The Inca Empire

In the Andes Mountains of South America, a significant and long-lasting hub of civilization grew up after 600 C.E. A series of different peoples dominated the regions and by the time the Incas consolidated their empire in the early fifteenth century,

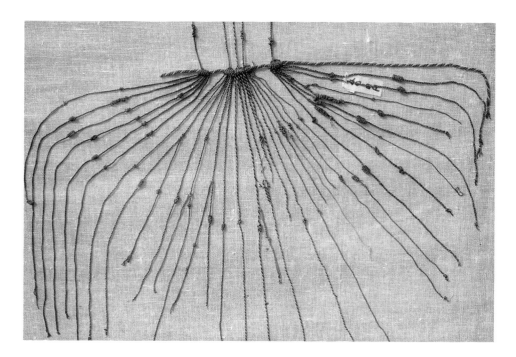

Photograph of a *quipu*. In the Inca empire, which extended from Ecuador to central Chile, trading was facilitated by an extensive road network. This *quipu*, a device of knotted string used to record dates and accounts, would have been a handy aid to the traveling South American businessman in the early 1400s.

these mountain peoples had built an extensive network of trade roads, connecting settlements over hundreds of miles north to south and linking together some 32 million people (see map p. 99).

Inca trade was conducted up and down the mountainsides. With peaks rising up to 20,000 feet, the Andes hosted several different ecological zones, encouraging product differentiation and trade. The valleys below produced sweet potatoes, maize, manioc, squash, beans, chile peppers, peanuts, and cotton. The hills above provided white potatoes, a cereal grain called quinoa, coca, medicines, feathers, and animal skins. The highland people specialized in manufacture and crafts, including gold working.

The state controlled this trade between the ecological zones. Under Inca rulers, from the early 1400s until the Spanish conquest in 1535, many of the best of the 15,000 miles of roads through the Andes were open only to government officials.

Central America and Mexico

In the Yucatán peninsula of Mesoamerica the Mayan peoples had flourished from 200 B.C.E. to 900 C.E. Initially Mayan traders operated without interference, amassing a disproportionate share of wealth. Archaeologists suggest that the increasing wealth of the traders created social tensions and that ultimately the traders were brought under the control of the state, creating a new set of unequal relations dominated by kings rather than merchants.

By the time the Spanish arrived in the 1520s, the Maya were in decline, and the Aztecs dominated the valley of Mexico. The Spanish soldiers wrote vivid accounts of the great marketplace of the Aztec capital, Tenochtitlán. As the Spanish leader Hernán Cortés summarizes in one of his letters:

This city has many squares where trading is done and markets are held continuously. There is also one square twice as big as that of Salamanca, with arcades all around … There are streets of herbalists where all the medicinal herbs and roots found in the land

La Gran Tenochtitlán, **Diego Rivera. 1945.** The great Mexican muralist, Diego Rivera, told the story of the history of his people on the walls of several of Mexico City's most prominent civic buildings with a boldness that attracted casual passersby as well as art connoisseurs. His depiction of the Aztec capital, Tenochtitlán, before the arrival of Europeans, suggests the majesty of the city, but does not overlook the harshness of the life of many of its inhabitants. (Palacio Nacional, Mexico City)

are sold. There are shops like apothecaries', where they sell ready-made medicines as well as liquid ointments and plasters. There are shops like barbers', where they have their hair washed and shaved, and shops where they sell food and drink. (*The Second Letter*, pp. 103–04)

The market met every fifth day, with perhaps 40,000 to 50,000 merchants swarming in, rowing their canoes across the lake to the island on which Tenochtitlán was built. In many ways, the market was like the great fairs of medieval Europe, drawing merchants from distant corners of the kingdom and beyond.

But how independent were these Tenochtitlán merchants? The Spanish described the city's market as being under tight government control. In addition to officers who kept the peace, collected taxes, and checked the accuracy of weights and measures, a court of 12 judges sat to decide cases immediately.

A guild of traders, called *pochteca*, carried on long-distance trade, which expanded steadily through the fifteenth century. They led trade expeditions for hundreds of miles, exchanging city-crafted obsidian knives, fur blankets, clothes, herbs, and dyes for such raw materials as jade, seashells, jaguar skins, feathers from forest birds, and, in the greatest volume, cotton from the Gulf coast. The traders gathered both goods and military intelligence for the ruling Aztec families. Royal troops protected them and sometimes used attacks on traveling *pochteca* as a justification for punitive reprisals and the confiscation of land. The *pochteca* lived in their own wards in the towns, had their own magistrates, and supervised the markets on their own. They were to marry only within the guild and, though they remained commoners, they could send their sons to temple schools. Their main god, Yiacatecutli, resembles the Toltec god Quetzalcoatl, and this, too, suggests that they were to some degree foreigners living in a trade diaspora, with a high degree of independence from the state and temple.

The civilizational hubs in Mexico and in the Andes functioned independently of one another and both flourished, of course, prior to Columbus, and almost entirely isolated from the rest of the world. When Europeans arrived in the sixteenth century brandishing new weapons, commanding new military organizations, and transmitting new diseases, the Americans were unprepared for the challenges.

Trade in Sub-Saharan Africa

Africa south of the Sahara was well integrated into extensive webs of trade relationships. In West Africa, traders dispatched caravans of goods on camelback across the Sahara, linking the forest cultivators and miners in the south with the merchants and rulers of the Mediterranean coast. In East Africa traders along the coast procured gold and ivory from the interior of the continent and sold them to the seafaring merchants of the Indian Ocean.

West Africa

The domestication of the camel in the second to fifth century C.E. opened the possibility of regular trans-Saharan trade. Oases provided the necessary watering points for caravans, as well as producing dates, a major commodity of trade. The first written records since Roman times of this trans-Saharan trade begin with the arrival of Muslim traders in the eighth century.

For the most part, African political units were local, but three large empires arose in succession around the northern bend in the Niger, near Timbuktu, where the sahel, the arid fringe of the desert, meets the vast Sahara itself. These three empires—

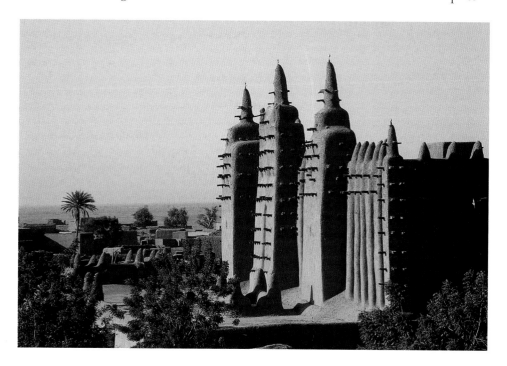

Mosque at Jenne, Mali, first built fourteenth century C.E. The spectacular mud-brick mosques found in the major towns of the African savanna states, such as Jenne and Timbuktu, point to the acceptance of Islam by the merchant and ruling classes in the thirteenth and fourteenth centuries. The mud, which washes away in the rain, needs continual renewal —hence the built-in "scaffolding" of the structure.

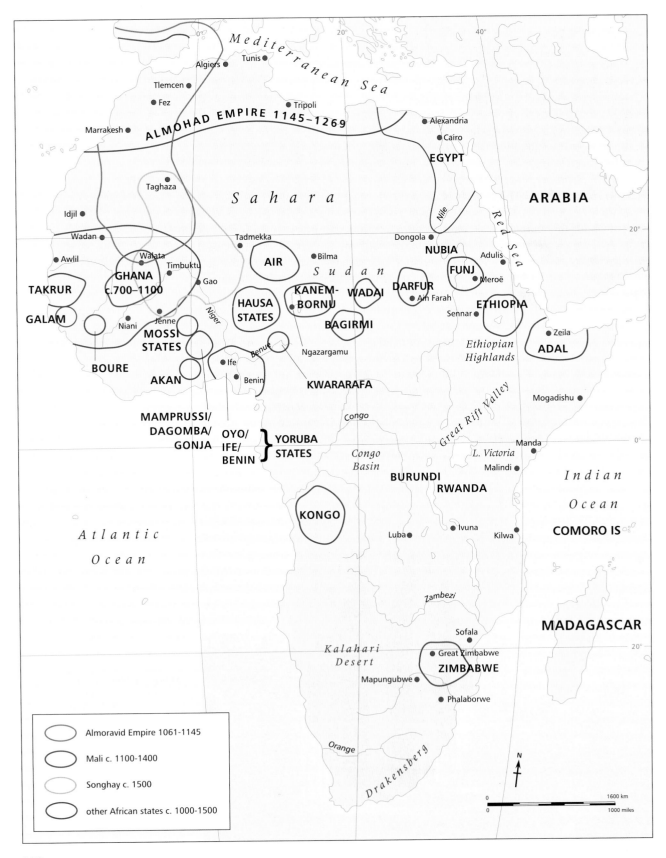

Mediterranean Sea

Algiers • Tunis •

Tlemcen •

• Fez

Tripoli •

Marrakesh •

ALMOHAD EMPIRE 1145–1269

Alexandria •

Cairo •

EGYPT

S a h a r a

Taghaza •

ARABIA

Idjil •

Wadan •

Nile

Dongola •

NUBIA

Red Sea

Adulis •

• Awlil

Walata •

Tadmekka •

AIR

• Bilma

S u d a n

FUNJ

Meroë •

Timbuktu •

GHANA
c.700–1100

Gao •

KANEM-
BORNU

WADAI

DARFUR

• Ain Farah

ETHIOPIA

TAKRUR

HAUSA
STATES

BAGIRMI

Sennar •

Zeila •

GALAM

Niani •

• Jenne

Niger

MOSSI
STATES

Ngazargamu •

ADAL

BOURE

AKAN

Benue

• Ife

Benin •

KWARARAFA

Ethiopian
Highlands

Mogadishu •

MAMPRUSSI/
DAGOMBA/
GONJA

OYO/
IFE/
BENIN

} YORUBA
STATES

Congo

Great Rift Valley

Manda •

KONGO

Congo
Basin

L. Victoria

Malindi •

BURUNDI

RWANDA

I n d i a n

O c e a n

A t l a n t i c

O c e a n

Luba •

Ivuna •

Kilwa •

COMORO IS

Zambezi

MADAGASCAR

Sofala •

Kalahari
Desert

• Great Zimbabwe

ZIMBABWE

Mapungubwe •

• Phalaborwe

Orange

N

Drakensberg

0	1600 km
0	1000 miles

⬭	Almoravid Empire 1061-1145
⬭	Mali c. 1100-1400
⬭	Songhay c. 1500
⬭	other African states c. 1000-1500

Ghana (*c.* 700–*c.* 1100), Mali (*c.* 1100–*c.* 1400), and Songhay (*c.* 1300–*c.* 1600)—kept the trade routes open and secure. In contrast with most governments in other parts of the world, which amassed wealth and power by controlling land and agriculture, these empires drew their power from control over trade, traders, and trade routes.

Gold, slaves, cloth, ivory, ebony, pepper, and kola nuts (stimulants) moved north across the Sahara; salt, dates, horses, brass, copper, glassware, beads, leather, textiles, clothing, and foodstuffs moved south. Gold was the central attraction. In the fourteenth century, the gold mines of West Africa provided about two-thirds of the gold used in trade in the eastern hemisphere. In 1324, when the Muslim emperor of Mali, Mansa Musa (r. 1307–32), passed through Cairo on his way to Mecca, he dispensed so much gold in gifts to court officials and in purchases in the bazaar that prices in Cairo were inflated for years to come. A European map of 1375 showing a seated Mansa Musa as ruler of Mali is noted as follows: "So abundant is the gold found in his country that he is the richest and most noble king in all the land."

There were many natural break-points for the north–south trade. From the Mediterranean coast to the northern fringe of the desert, trade was borne by pack horse; across the desert, via oases, by camel; across the arid sahel and the grassy savannah lands south of the Sahara again by pack animal; and, finally, through the tropical forest, impenetrable to larger animals and afflicted with the lethal tsetse fly, it was borne by human porters. For the most part, locally dominant trade groups carried the trade from one market center to the next in short relays. A few trading communities, however, notably the Soninke and, especially, their Mande-speaking Dyula branch, established trade diasporas that negotiated with the rulers.

East Africa

In the fourth century, the kingdom of Axum in Christian Ethiopia dominated the trade of the Red Sea and to some extent the Arabian Sea. With the rise of Islam, however, Arab traders gained control of the flow of merchandise and Arab armies began restricting Ethiopian power. After the ninth century, and south of the Horn of Africa, Arab merchants provided the main trading link between East Africa and the Indian Ocean. The first major port to spring up had been Manda, followed in the thirteenth century by Kilwa. The ruling Arab dynasty along the coast also seized control of the port of Sofala further to the south. Through local African merchants they exchanged goods with the peoples of the interior, especially at the trading post of Great Zimbabwe. Here they found abundant supplies of valuable metals such as gold and copper (often cast into ingots) and animal products: ivory, horns, skins, and tortoise shells. Slaves were also an important commodity. Great Zimbabwe was the largest and most remarkable of all the developing towns. Architecturally, it featured a 100-acre stone enclosure and another 100 smaller enclosures in the surrounding region.

From these inland sources, goods were transported to the coastal ports and shipped onward to Arabia and India in exchange for spices, pottery, glass beads, and cloth. In the port cities of Africa's east coast, the Swahili language of the nearby

African kingdoms. Many states appeared in 1000–1500 in northern and western Africa, their power based on control over long-distance trade—gold, ivory, and slaves moving north; metalware, textiles, and salt carried south. Ghana, Mali, and Songhay are discussed in the text. These states, protected from marauders by the Sahara, could usually maintain their independence.

Great Zimbabwe. The biggest and most celebrated of several stone enclosures in East Africa dating from the tenth to fifteenth centuries, Great Zimbabwe provided raw materials for trade at the coastal settlements, especially gold, copper, tin, and iron, and was also a trading post for luxury goods—Islamic pottery and cowrie shells were dug up at the site.

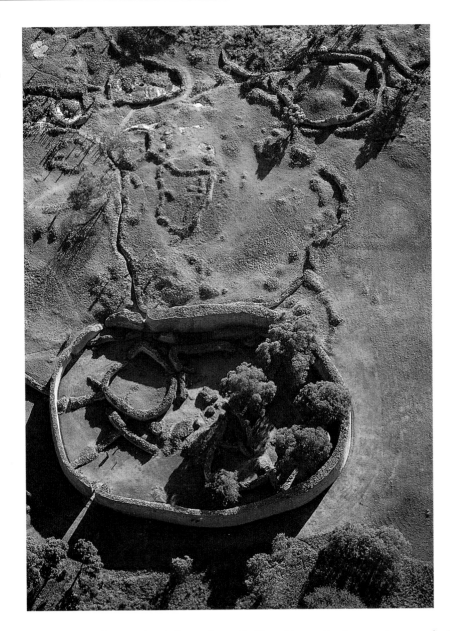

African peoples received from these Indian Ocean traders a strong admixture of Arabic vocabulary, enriching Swahili and ensuring its place as the dominant language of the coastal trade.

Asia's Complex Trade Patterns

As the largest continent, with the largest population and the oldest civilizations, Asia's trade networks date back thousands of years. By 1250, a set of interlinked trade networks connected the main population and production centers of Asia, Africa, and Europe. The map on p. 404 illustrates the comprehensive geographic coverage of these networks. From east to west, Japan and China were linked by land routes to central Asia and by sea lanes to the Indian Ocean. Both land and sea routes continued westward to Arabia, western Asia, and on to the Mediterranean and

Europe. Well-developed sea traffic linked also to the East African coast, where land routes extended into the African continent. North–south routes ran through China, central and western Asia, and Europe, and from the Mediterranean across the Sahara by camel. Centralized transportation companies that could carry goods all the way from East Asia to Western Europe did not yet exist, but arrangements could be made for even this long voyage to be completed stage by stage.

The South Pacific

Austronesian-speaking peoples migrated from south China and Southeast Asia perhaps 6,000 years ago to Taiwan, the Philippines, and eastern Indonesia. Those who settled in the islands adjacent to these areas are known as Melanesians. Those who continued on eastward are called Polynesians. These Polynesians continued to sail eastward in single and double canoes, 100 to 150 feet long, made of wooden components lashed together by cords of fiber. These ships, with their single, square, woven-mat sails, carried not only men and women but also food supplies and even livestock. These simple, elegant craft transported the Polynesians on vast ocean voyages as far northeastward as Hawaii (400 C.E.), as far southeastward as Easter Island (400 C.E.), and as far southwestward as New Zealand (750 C.E.). They were the greatest seafaring peoples of premodern times. Students of Polynesian history marvel both at the enormous stone statues they erected on some of the Polynesian islands, most spectacularly on Easter Island, and at the accomplishments of their sea voyages. Polynesians apparently visited every island within the huge triangle of Hawaii, Easter Island, and New Zealand. Nevertheless, despite traveling through thousands of years and thousands of miles, they preserved several remarkably similar elements of culture throughout their domains. Anthropologists note these

HOW DO WE KNOW?

The Records in the Cairo Genizah

Information on Mediterranean cultures and their trade connections into the Indian Ocean, from the tenth through the thirteenth centuries, has come to historians from the Cairo Genizah (Hebrew for a repository of old papers), studied by Solomon Goitein from the 1950s through the 1980s. Jewish law requires that the written name of "God" not be destroyed but stored for later burial; the Genizah was the storage point in Cairo for such documents for several centuries. Because paper was scarce and often reused, the manuscripts in the Genizah include massive bundles of notes and manuscripts on secular as well as sacred aspects of life: on trade and commerce, on social organization in general, and on the Jewish community in particular. Marriage contracts "state in detail and with great variety the conditions regulating the future relations of the newly married, and thus constitute a precious source for our knowledge of family life" (I:10). Wills and inventories of estates are "veritable mines of information" (I:10). Letters of correspondence, both personal and business, "form the largest and most important group [of manuscripts]. They are our main source not only for our knowledge of commerce and industry, but also for various other subjects, such as travel and seafaring" (I:11). "There are

hundreds of letters addressed to various authorities containing reports, petitions, requests for help, demands for redress of injustice, applications for appointments, and a great variety of other matters" (I:12). Religious responses are frequent, questions and answers between commoners and sages concerning religious philosophy, doctrine, and practice. Most women were illiterate, but they dictated many letters to scribes: "We hear the female voice guiding the male pen" (I:12). For the most part the writing is in Arabic, but transcribed in Hebrew letters.

Because the Jewish community was interwoven with all the others, these centuries-old manuscripts have proven to be a gold mine for historians studying the life of Cairo, its citizens, and their external connections throughout the Mediterranean Sea and the Indian Ocean.

- Given the nature of the Genizah repository, what kinds of records do you think would be most fully represented? Least well represented?
- How might records of family life and records dictated by women help to fill out the records of business transactions?
- How important was Cairo as a trade center at this time?

similarities in tools, names of plants, terms of kinship, and artistic styles across the islands of Polynesia even today.

Did Polynesians sail across the Pacific and establish contact with the Americas? The distances are not impossible. The Hawaiian Islands are closer to the Americas than to Asia, and Easter Island is only 2,200 miles off the coast of South America. Many scholars do argue that contact was accomplished; they cite the sweet potatoes and manioc of South America that somehow reached Polynesia as their evidence. But whatever the capabilities of the Polynesians and their canoes, and whatever the origins of these food supplies, the Polynesians did not establish permanent connections to the Americas.

The South China Sea

Extraordinary as the Polynesian sailors were, apparently they adopted their sails from the Malay sailors of the South China Sea, probably late in the first millennium B.C.E. These sailors left four major legacies to world seafaring, one primarily in their own neighborhood, the other three of much wider significance. The first was the most important: cargo ships—*jongs,* or junks as they are usually called in English. These ships, with multilayered hulls, two to four masts, two rudders, and a normal capacity of 400 to 500 tons, seem to have inspired the junks used by Chinese merchant sailors to the north. Second, their balance-lug square sails seem to have inspired a series of adaptations and inventions, from the square sails used by the

King Edward I Returns from Gascony, **Anon., 1470. Miniature.** This is an example of a ship with triangular lateen sails. Europeans adapted these sails from Arab models because they enabled ships to tack against the wind as well as run with it. (British Library, London)

Polynesians, to the triangular sails used by Arab sailors, called **lateen sails**. The square balance-lug sail could be turned to face into the wind or to tack against it, allowing the sailors much greater maneuverability. As the sail was turned, from an angle it appeared to be triangular, and sailors learned that a triangular sail would fill with wind just as efficiently, while being easier to manage. Thus the lateen sail was born and ultimately carried to the sailing paths of the world. Arab sailors introduced them into the Mediterranean where they were copied by Europeans and used for their voyages in the Atlantic. (Other authorities believe that the balance-lug sail developed on the Nile River, also in the first millennium B.C.E., and they argue that this Egyptian invention was the background source for the Arab lateen sails.)

Third, the Malay sailors studied the patterns of the seasonal monsoon winds of the Indian Ocean and learned to sail with them. Rain-laden monsoon winds are attracted from the Indian Ocean inward toward central Asia during the summer months, when the continental interior is much hotter than the oceans around it; in the cooler months, dry winds blow outward from the continent toward the ocean, when the ocean is warmer than the interior.

Finally, using their ship technology and knowledge of the winds, Malay sailors made regular voyages of 3,000 miles across the Indian Ocean—probably via the Maldives, the Seychelles, and the Comoro Islands—to the large island of Madagascar, 250 miles off the coast of East Africa, where they established themselves as the majority population, as they remain to this day. The Malay brought to Madagascar bananas, coconuts, taro, and their language, which also continues as the dominant language of the island.

Along with their settlements, the Malay sailors established sea routes from East Africa to China. They carried frankincense and myrrh from East Africa, Arabia, southwest Iran, and the Makran coast of India to present-day Vietnam and China. From Timor, 1,800 miles to the southeast of Vietnam, they brought aromatic woods, especially sandalwood. From the "Spice Islands," the Moluccas, 1,000 miles east of Java, they brought cloves, nutmeg, and mace. For more than a thousand years they were the master sailors of the South China Sea.

The Indian Ocean

The great crossroads of the world's shipping lanes in the period 1300–1500 was the Indian Ocean. Its waters encompass three distinct geographical sectors, each with its own cultural orientation. The western sector—the Arabian Sea—sweeps from the East African coast across Arabia and continues on to the west coast of India. From the time of Alexander the Great and the Roman Empire, Greek sailors plied these lanes. By the first century B.C.E. Greek sailors (like the Malays far to the east) had learned to use the monsoon winds to navigate these waters swiftly and efficiently. From the fourth to the eighth centuries, following the decline and fall of the Roman Empire, two new groups dominated this western region of the Indian Ocean: sailors from Axum (modern Ethiopia and Eritrea) and its Red Sea port of Adulis, and sailors from Sassanian Persia, a west Asian empire on the ascendant at the time.

Arab Traders. From the eighth to the sixteenth century, Arab Muslim traders and sailors became masters of the Arabian Sea, named for them, and the Indian Ocean sea lanes. This was the area made famous by the legendary exploits of Sinbad the Sailor.

Islam encouraged trade. The *hajj* (pilgrimage), required of every Muslim at least once during his or her lifetime, necessitated travel, and international trade connections flourished as a result. A Muslim trade colony had operated in Sri Lanka as

KEY TERM

lateen sail A triangular sail affixed to a long yard or crossbar at an angle of about 45 degrees to the mast, with the other free corner secured near the stern. The sail was capable of tacking against the wind on either side. So named when they appeared in the Mediterranean, where they were associated with Latin culture, although their origin was actually far away.

403

Trading ports and cities, Indian Ocean, 1200–1500 C.E. The Indian Ocean was the pivot of long-distance seaborne trade from the Mediterranean to the South China Sea. Each of its port cities housed a rich diversity of merchants of many ethnicities and cultures. Trade goods did not travel on a single ship the whole length of this region. Rather, they would be loaded at a port in one of the three regions, offloaded and reloaded in the next for shipment to the third region.

early as about 700 C.E. Arab traders sailed with the monsoon winds first to India, then on to Southeast Asia, and some even on to the southeast coast of China. Catching the proper seasonal winds in each direction and using their lateen sails to maximum effect, sailors could complete a round trip from Mesopotamia to China in less than two years. Muslim Arab traders played critical roles, as well, in the development of African trade networks, by land from north to south across the Sahara and by sea from the East African coast to various ports along the shores of the Indian Ocean.

Lacking wood in Arabia, Arab sailors depended on others to build their ships, or they obtained teak from southern India to build their own. For reasons that remain unclear, they did not use metal nails in ship construction, but "stitched" the wooden planks together with coir—the fiber of coconut husks—or other fibers. Like the Malay and the Greek sailors before them, they learned to sail with the monsoon winds. The Arab Muslim Ahmad Ibn Majid included extensive recommendations on travel dates appropriate to the monsoon winds in his comprehensive fifteenth-century guide to navigation throughout the Indian Ocean.

The rise of Arab Muslim sea traders was a remarkable transformation for this ethnic and religious group. The Arabs had been quite accustomed to trade—Muhammad himself was a camel driver and leader of caravans—but trade by sea was different. They took to this new way of life eagerly and came to dominate the sea lanes from the Mediterranean coast in the west all the way east to Guangzhou (Canton) and Hangzhou in China, frequently displacing previous communities of sailors. (For the commercial and cultural importance of Hindu and Buddhist sailors and traders in these areas from the seventh to the tenth century, see Chapter Eight.)

Islam Spreads. Along with their trade goods, Muslims also conveyed their religious ideas. Distant merchants, who encountered Muslims in order to trade, slowly absorbed elements of Islam. In the thirteenth century, as the Muslim sultanate of Delhi came to rule northern India, many of the Hindu ocean-going traders, especially those along the west coast in Gujarat, converted to Islam. In regions as distant as Malaysia and Indonesia locals began to assimilate to the religion. Carried not by military power but by traders, Islam came to be the dominant religion in Indonesia (the most populous Muslim country in the world today), and to attract tens of millions of Chinese adherents. When the ruler of Malacca converted to Islam, about

Arab trader, illustration from the *Maqamat* of al-Hariri, twelfth century. Regional shipping routes linked into the oceanic, intercontinental routes. This ship, with Arab passengers and Indian, and perhaps African, crew, sailed the Persian Gulf connecting Mesopotamia and the Indian Ocean.

405

SOURCE

The Arabian Nights

Arab Muslim traders of the Indian Ocean fill the pages of some of the best-loved tales of world literature. *The Thousand Nights and One Night*, also called the *Arabian Nights*, fables originally written in Persian during the years of the Abbasid Empire (750–1258), include the tales of the seven voyages of Sinbad (Sindbad) the Sailor, who won a fortune through a series of hazardous (if unbelievable) adventures at sea. The adventures, supposedly told night after night by Scheherazade to the emperor, Haroun al-Rashid (r. 786–809), as a ploy to postpone her scheduled execution, are fanciful, but Sinbad's descriptions of his departures on each of his voyages are based on the reality of Indian Ocean shipping. This translation from the beginning of the third voyage is by Richard F. Burton, who brought the complete tales to the English-speaking world in the late nineteenth century.

> I returned from my second voyage overjoyed at my safety and with great increase of wealth, Allah having requited me all that I had wasted and lost, and I abode awhile in Baghdad-city savouring the utmost ease and prosperity

and comfort and happiness, till the carnal man was once more seized with longing for travel and diversion and adventure, and yearned after traffic and lucre and emolument, for that the human heart is naturally prone to evil. So making up my mind I laid in great plenty of goods suitable for a sea voyage and repairing to Bassorah [Basra], went down to the shore and found there a fine ship ready to sail, with a full crew and a numerous company of merchants, men of worth and substance; Faith, piety and consideration. I embarked with them and we set sail on the blessing of Allah Almighty and on His aidance and His favour to bring our voyage to a safe and prosperous issue and already we congratulated one another on our good fortune and bon voyage. We fared on from sea to sea and from island to island and city to city, in all delight and contentment, buying and selling wherever we touched, and taking our solace and our pleasure, till one day … [and here begin the fabulous adventures of the third voyage]. (*The Thousand Nights and One Night*, Vol. 4, pp. 2031–32)

1400, the trading circuit of Muslim merchants was complete. The entire length of the Indian Ocean littoral, from East Africa through India and on to Indonesia, housed a Muslim, largely Arab, trading diaspora.

Arabs did not sail into the Atlantic or Pacific Oceans; they had no need. They sailed at will throughout the most lucrative seas of the world they knew. They had no problem of access. While Europeans explored new routes to reach the wealth of India and China in the fifteenth century, the Arabs were already there.

China: A Magnet for Traders

By 1500 China was the most economically advanced region in the world, a magnet for world trade. China is so huge, however, that its internal trade far outweighed its external trade. It is so rich and varied in its productivity that others came to China to obtain its products far more regularly than the Chinese traveled abroad in search of the products of others. China's policies towards trade varied during the centuries we are considering here, partly as a result of changes in imperial policies, partly in response to external pressures. Even though it possessed a highly integrated system of internal markets and reached extraordinary levels of agricultural and industrial productivity, the Song dynasty (960–1279) was overrun by Mongol invaders and had to abandon territories, relocate to the south, and reconstruct its economy. The Ming dynasty (1368–1644) overthrew the Mongols and undertook a series of spectacular ocean voyages. Then, in a reversal of policy, later Ming emperors forbade the Chinese to trade overseas. Nevertheless, merchants from abroad continued to pour in, eager to do business with the Middle Kingdom.

International Trade

As early as the fourth century C.E. the Chinese traded in the South China Sea and the Indian Ocean, although probably only as far west as Sri Lanka. With the decline of the Tang dynasty in the ninth century, the Chinese largely withdrew from this oceanic trade and concentrated instead on inland issues, reflecting their geographical location in the Yellow River valley and the north. After 1127, however, they returned to oceanic enterprise, when the Song dynasty was driven from northern China by the invasions of the Tatars and other northern peoples. With various outside groups in control of the old overland silk routes, seaborne trade was an obvious transportation and communication alternative. Thanks to their industrial innovations the Song could supplement the traditional exports of silk and porcelain with products also of iron and steel. To carry their expanding trade, the Chinese mastered the craft of building large ships, and Chinese merchants established new patterns of commercial exchange, including sophisticated credit systems. In addition to a merchant marine, China constructed a powerful navy.

The great luxury products of China—silk, porcelain, and tea—continued to attract thousands of foreign merchants. Many were Muslim Arabs. A few Lombards, Germans, and French also came to trade. They were treated as welcome guests, and special quarters in the port cities were set aside for them. In issues that involved no Chinese but only these foreigners, they could apply their own laws. Shops with foreign goods and foreign schools catered to their interests. Nevertheless, these merchants followed Chinese commercial rules, and many became quite Sinicized in their manners. When they ended their sojourn in China, they were often feted with large farewell feasts.

The Voyages of Zheng He. In the early years of the Ming dynasty, China's emperors adopted policies of expansionism by land and self-assertion at sea. The Ming Emperor Yung-lo (r. 1402–24) dispatched a series of seven ocean-going expeditions under the Muslim eunuch Zheng He. The first voyage set out in 1405 with 62 large

A Chinese Junk, from *Jan Huyghen van Linschoten: His Discourse of Voyages into the East and West Indies*, **Johannes Baptista van Doetechum, 1579–92. Engraving.** Apparently first an invention of the Malay sailors of the South China Sea, and adapted by the Chinese, these ships could carry more than 1,000 tons of cargo and hundreds of sailors. (Private collection)

SOURCE

Chinese Ships in South Indian Harbors: An Account by Ibn Battuta

The fourteenth-century traveler Ibn Battuta (1304–68) did not usually comment on ships and sailors. He was far more interested in his encounters with people on land. In the south Indian port of Calicut, however, he was so impressed with the capacity and design of the Chinese ships in the harbor that he gave a remarkable description. He notes that, while the Chinese allowed only Chinese ships to dock in their ports, the pilots and crew were not necessarily Chinese:

> We traveled to the city of Calicut, which is one of the chief ports in Malabar [the southwest coast of India], and one of the largest harbors in the world. It is visited by men from China, Sumatra, Ceylon, the Maldives, Yemen, and Fars [Persia], and in it gather merchants from all quarters … there were at the time thirteen Chinese vessels, and we disembarked. Every one of us was lodged in a house and we stayed there three months as the guests of the infidel [Zamorin ruler of Calicut], awaiting the season of the voyage to China. On the Sea of China traveling is done in Chinese ships only, so we shall describe their arrangements.
>
> The Chinese vessels are of three kinds; large ships called *chunks* [junks], middle-sized ones called *zaws* [dhows], and small ones called *kakams*. The large ships have anything from twelve down to three sails, which are made of bamboo rods plaited like mats. They are never lowered, but turned according to the direction of the wind; at anchor they are left floating in the wind. A ship carries a complement of a thousand men, six hundred of whom are sailors and four hundred men-at-arms, including archers, men with shields and arbalests, who throw naphtha. Each large vessel is accompanied by three smaller ones, the "half," the "third," and the "quarter." These vessels are built only in the towns of Zaytun and Canton. The vessel has four decks and contains rooms, cabins, and saloons for merchants; a cabin has chambers and a lavatory, and can be locked by its occupant, who takes along with him slave girls and wives. Often a man will live in his cabin unknown to any of the others on board until they meet on reaching some town. The sailors have their children living on board ship, and they cultivate green stuffs, vegetables and ginger in wooden tanks. The owner's factor [representative] on board ship is like a great *amir* [nobleman]. When he goes on shore he is preceded by archers and Abyssinians with javelins, swords, drums, trumpets, and bugles. On reaching the house where he stays they stand their lances on both sides of the door, and continue thus during his stay. Some of the Chinese own large numbers of ships on which their factors are sent to foreign countries. There is no people in the world wealthier than the Chinese. (Ibn Battuta, pp. 234–36)

junks, 100 smaller ships, and 30,000 crew. The largest ships were 450 feet long, displaced 1,600 tons, and held a crew of about 500; they were the largest ships built anywhere up to that time. They carried silks, porcelains, and pepper. The first expedition sailed as far as Calicut, near the southwest tip of India. In six further missions between 1407 and 1433, Zheng He sailed to ports all along the Indian Ocean shores, at least twice reaching the East African ports of Mogadishu, Brava, Malindi, and Kilwa. Interested in exotic treasures that could not be found in China, Emperor Yung-lo seemed most pleased with a giraffe sent to him by the sultan of Malindi on the fourth voyage, in 1416–19. These colossal expeditions demonstrated both the skill of Admiral Zheng He and the vision of Emperor Yung-lo. On the basis of these voyages, many historians believe that the Chinese would have been able to cross either the Atlantic or the Pacific Ocean—had they wished. But they did not push their expeditions any further and, in 1433, the Ming emperor terminated his sponsorship of the Indian Ocean voyages.

Why did the emperor end these voyages? Why did China not dispatch missions to Europe, and even to the western hemisphere? Why did the Chinese choose instead only to receive European shipping, beginning with the Portuguese in 1514?

Many answers seem plausible. The Ming turned their energies inward, toward consolidation and internal development. At first they pushed the Mongols further north from the Great Wall fortification along the northern border, but an invasion of Mongolia failed in 1449. Thereafter, the Ming limited their military goals, rebuilt the Great Wall, and restricted their forces to more defensible borders.

In 1411 the Ming reconstructed and extended the Grand Canal from Hangzhou in the south to Beijing in the north. The canal was a cheap, efficient means of shipping the grain and produce required by the northern capital. The man-made inland waterway also reduced the importance of coastal shipping, further enabling the Ming emperors to turn their backs on the sea. The faction of eunuchs, dedicated court servants like Zheng He, who urged the government to continue its sponsorship of foreign trade, lost out to factions that promoted internal development. International private shipping was also curtailed.

The Ming government limited contacts with foreigners and prohibited private overseas trade by Chinese merchants. In 1371, coastal residents were forbidden to travel overseas. In response to the smuggling that resulted, the government issued further prohibitions in 1390, 1394, 1397, 1433, 1449, and 1452. The repetition of this legislation reveals that smuggling did continue, but, for the most part, private Chinese sailors were cut off from foreign trade. The government envisioned the expeditions of Zheng He as political missions to exact tribute from outlying countries. Although products were exchanged on these voyages, trade was not their official purpose. So, while both private and government trade flourished in the interior of China, and while thousands of Chinese emigrated to carry on private businesses throughout Southeast Asia, China's official overseas trade came to a

Ink and watercolor print showing silk manufacture, Chinese, early seventeenth century. During the Song dynasty (960–1279), long-distance trade across central Asia dwindled. Maritime trade, with its very much safer and cheaper routes, now offered a viable alternative, and silk, along with porcelain and tea, continued to attract the merchants of the world. Unwinding filaments from silkworm cocoons in order to make yarn was considered women's work, as this Ming dynasty print suggests. (Victoria & Victoria & Albert Museum, London)

409

SOURCE

River Trade in China

Just as the vast and profitable trade in silk depended ultimately on the hard work of millions of spinners and weavers and their families, so river trade in China depended, at least partially, on the investments of common people. The four sources below support that assertion. The first is from Marco Polo attesting to the abundance of river trade in China. The second is from Pao Hui, writing in the thirteenth century about the financing of overseas river trade. The third is a Song dynasty scroll illustrating the multitude of Chinese junks sailing on the Yellow River at Kaifeng. The fourth, a prose poem, desribes the contribution of the women who produced and marketed the silk for which China was famous.

First, Marco Polo writing of the Yangzi River:

I assure that this river runs for such a distance and through so many regions and there are so many cities on its banks that truth to tell, in the amount of shipping it carries and the total volume and value of its traffic, it exceeds all the rivers of the Christians put together and their seas into the bargain. I give you my word that I have seen in this city [I-ching] fully five thousand ships at once, all afloat on this river. Then you may reflect, since this city, which is not very big has so many ships, how many there must be in the others. (cited in Elvin, pp. 144–45)

Then compare Pao Hui on the financing of river trade in Southern Song China:

All the people along the coast are on intimate terms with the merchants who engage in overseas trade, either because they are fellow countrymen or personal acquaintances. Leakage [of copper currency] through entrusting occurs when the former give the latter money to take with them on their ships for the purchase and return conveyance of foreign goods. They invest from ten to a hundred strings of cash, and regularly make profits of several hundred per cent. (Shiba Yoshinobu, p. 33)

Third, examine Zhang Zeduan's twelfth-century scroll painting, *Going on the River at the Qingming Festival* (opposite). At this time, the city of Kaifeng, situated on the Yellow River and at the crossroads of some of China's most important canals, was the hub of water-borne traffic for all of northern China. Inland Kaifeng and Hangzhou, on the coast, were China's most important regional capitals. They formed the apex of a regional system of urbanization that unified the whole country.

Market towns sprang up throughout China, enabling almost every rural family to sell its products for cash and to buy city goods. In turn, the small market towns were linked to larger cities, which provided more specialized products and access to government administrators. Here, families could buy and sell, arrange a marriage, determine the latest government rulings, hear about new farming possibilities, learn the dates and the results of academic examinations. These towns were so widespread that nearly every farm family lived within reach of one.

At the base were the rural families, struggling to survive by producing commodities demanded by the traders. Hand manufacture, especially of cotton and silk cloth, often supplemented farm production in rural areas. Invention made the process more productive. In particular a reeling machine, invented around the eleventh century, drew several silk filaments at once from silkworm cocoons immersed in boiling water. It then drew the filaments through eyelets and hooks and finally banded them into silk thread.

The rural producers were integrated into the market system either through direct, personal access or through brokers who supplied raw materials and bought the finished product. Women were the chief producers in this supplemental rural industry. They also carried the finished product to market. Conditions of production and of marketing could be savage. Xu Xianzhong's "Prose Poem on Cotton Cloth," our fourth source, presents the harshness of both aspects. It is not clear whether the women in the marketplace are selling their cloth, or themselves, or both:

Why do you ignore their toil? Why are you touched
Only by the loveliness that is born from toil?
…
Shall I tell you how their work exhausts them?
By hand and treadle they turn the rollers of wood and iron,
Feeling their fibre in between their fingers;
The cotton comes out fluffy and the seeds fall away.
The string of the cotton bow is stretched so taut
It twangs with a sob from its pillar.
They draw out slivers, spin them on their wheels
To the accompaniment of a medley of creakings.
Working through the darkness by candlelight,
Forgetful of bed. When energy ebbs, they sing.
The quilts are cold. Unheard, the waterclock flows over.
…
When a woman leaves for market
She does not look at her hungry husband.
Afraid her cloth's not good enough,
She adorns her face with cream and powder,
Touches men's shoulders to arouse their lust,
And sells herself with pleasant words.
Money she thinks of as a beast its prey;
Merchants she coaxes as she would her father.
Nor is her burden lifted till one buys.

(Elvin, pp. 273–74)

standstill. Zheng He's expeditions stand out as spectacular exceptions to the generally complacent and inward-looking character of the Chinese Empire.

These decisions to limit China's international trade proved costly. Chinese society became introverted and, although economic growth continued, Chinese culture stagnated. Under the Song dynasty, Chinese technology had been the most innovative in the world. Creativity continued even under the Mongols, but by the beginning of the Ming dynasty, China was less imaginative. Military technology improved but then it, too, stagnated. China had invented gunpowder before 1000 C.E., but used it only sporadically. In the early fifteenth century Ming cannon were at least equal to those anywhere in the world, but metal was in short supply, and further development was limited. The Ming laid siege to few fortress cities, so they felt little need for heavy artillery. In fighting against invasions from the north, the crossbow seemed more effective. At first, when China was much more advanced than its adversaries, decisions to limit further military innovation seemed inconsequential. Later, however, they would render the country vulnerable to distant, newly rising powers.

Internal Trade

When Marco Polo arrived in China in 1275, the splendor and wealth of the country overwhelmed him. He described its Mongol ruler, Kublai Khan, as "the mightiest man, whether in respect of subjects or of territory or of treasure, who is in the world today or who ever has been, from Adam our first parent down to the present moment." Polo correctly reported that China in the late 1200s was the richest, most technologically progressive, and largest country in the world.

The foundations of China's wealth had been in place for centuries. We have already read in Chapter Seven of China's generally growing population, territory, power, and wealth through its successive dynasties from Qin to Tang. Under the Song, China underwent an economic revolution. A revolution in agriculture underpinned the advance: better soil preparation and conservation; improved seeds that often allowed more than one crop per season; better water control and irrigation; and more local specialization of crops. The new techniques were implemented most intensively in the lower Yangzi valley, as the Song moved south from China's historic northern base

Going on the River at the Qingming Festival, Kaifeng, **Zhang Zeduan, Song dynasty scroll.** The multitude of Chinese junks on the Yellow River suggest the well-developed channels of trade in northern China. (National Palace Museum, Taiwan)

Statuette of silk route trader, Chinese, tenth century. Statuettes, found in tombs in China from the time of the Tang dynasty, record the presence of traders from Mediterranean regions who traversed the thousands of miles of the silk routes. From their features, scholars believe that they were Semitic peoples: Jews from the Fertile Crescent, Egyptians, and other Levantines. Some of them eventually settled along the trans-Asian routes. (Seattle Art Museum)

around the Yellow River. Indeed, they maintained regional capitals, two of which also served as national capitals: Kaifeng in the north and Hangzhou in the south, near the mouth of the Yangzi. Thanks to the invention of woodblock printing in the ninth century under the Tang dynasty, ideas could spread rapidly. One of the first uses of print had been to conserve and spread religious concepts; the oldest printed book extant in the world is a copy of the Buddhist *Diamond Sutra* from 868. Now the new method of printing was put into the service of disseminating the new farming methods.

Agricultural improvements—plus China's traditional excellence in textile production and remarkable innovations in the most advanced coal and iron industry in the world—inspired a trade revolution. Common people became involved in the mass production of goods for sale. Domestically this included the production of military goods for an army of over a million men. Trade became monetized, with copper as the principal currency. Chinese currency was so popular in Japan at this time that it became the most important medium of trade. In 1024, in Sichuan province, paper money was printed for the first time in the world. (Sometimes the government printed an excess of paper money, giving rise to inflation.) Merchants invented new credit mechanisms to facilitate trade. Government control of trade—quite marked under the Tang—was sharply reduced in favor of greater market freedom, and trade made up an increasing share of government revenue. Customs offices in the nine official ports, especially the largest, Canton and Zaitun (Quanzhou), collected import taxes of 10 to 15 percent of the value of goods. In 1128, maritime trade brought in 20 percent of China's total cash revenues. Merchants were valued for the taxes the state could collect from them. Those who paid the most were rewarded with official rank.

The international merchants were at the peak of a highly integrated national system of trade and commerce, a system that was built on domestic as well as international water transport. To integrate the system of waterways, portage of goods was arranged at points of dangerous rapids and cataracts. To ensure smooth passage, double locks were installed on the man-made Grand Canal; this system helped to link the agricultural wealth of the south with the administrative cities of the north. Tugboats with human-powered paddle-wheels serviced the main ports. Chinese ocean-going ships, equipped with axial rudders, watertight bulkheads, and magnetic compasses, gained a reputation as the best in the world.

Central Asia: The Mongols and the Silk Routes

The Song dynasty (960–1279) developed the waterways of China, but the great central Asian overland silk routes had declined after the ninth century along with the Tang dynasty that had protected and encouraged them. Under the Mongol Empire (1206–1405), the largest land empire ever known, traffic on the silk routes revived.

The two million Mongols who inhabited the plateau region of central Asia were divided into several warring tribes, each led by a *khan*, or ruler. The land was poor and the climate harsh. The Mongols shepherded their cattle, sheep, and goats in a circular pattern of migration called **transhumance**: in the brief summers they moved their herds northward to pasture; in winter they turned back south. They spent most of their waking hours on horseback and mastered the art of warfare from the stirrups, with bow and arrow as well as sword by their side.

Intercontinental Trade Flourishes

Cultural historians credit the Mongols with little permanent contribution because they were absorbed into other, more settled and sophisticated cultures. But they did

The Mongol Empire

Because it was the largest contiguous land empire in history, understanding the entire Mongol Empire requires language competence in Mongolian, Chinese, Persian, Arabic, Turkish, Japanese, Russian, Armenian, Georgian, and Latin. No scholar can be expected to master all of these languages, but serious scholars are expected to know at least one or two of them and to use others in translation. Surprisingly, Mongolian may not be the most important. Before Chinggis Khan, the language was not written and there are no archives of the Mongol Empire, at least none that have survived. The only major historical text in Mongolian is *The Secret History of the Mongols*, and, although some scholars think it inauthentic, it is our principal source for the biography of Chinggis Khan. Another text from the days of Chinggis Khan, the *Altan Debter*, or *Golden Book*, is lost, but Persian and Chinese historians mention it, and their references show the book to be consistent with, although not the same as, *The Secret History*.

Chinese and Persian texts are the next most important, discussing Mongol rule over the two empires flanking, and captured by, the Mongol Empire. In China, the major text is the official dynastic history of the Yuan, or Mongol, dynasty. In Persia, several authors are important, most notably Rashid al-Din. Until his time, the Mongol conquest posed a problem for Muslim historians: The conquest of the Abbasid Empire was not supposed to happen. Muslims were to conquer others, as they had done with great consistency; they were not supposed to be conquered themselves. During Rashid al-Din's time, however, the Mongols converted to Islam. Rashid al-Din must have understood this well, since he himself had converted from Judaism. Rashid al-Din wrote the history of the Mongol Empire which, he said, marked a new era in world history. Later, he wrote *Jami' al-tawarikh*, a *Collection of Histories*, recording the history of all the peoples touched by the Mongols from the Chinese in the east to the Franks in the west. It was the first example of the form of a world history. For the last 20 years of his life, until he was assassinated as the result of a court intrigue in 1318, Rashid al-Din served as principal adviser to the Il-Khan ruler of Persia.

Distant Europe held relatively little importance for the Mongols, but a number of European sources discuss their conquests. These included men such as Giovanni de Piano Carpini, who was sent by Pope Innocent IV to visit the Khans, and William of Rubruck, who visited the Mongols at the behest of the king of France, Louis IX. The most comprehensive account is by Matthew Paris, who chronicled European reactions to the Mongol advances from his post at St. Albans, England, but the most popular came from travelers, of whom the most famous was Marco Polo.

- Mongolian may not be the most important language in the study of the Mongolian empire, yet the most important biography of Chinggis Khan is in Mongolian. How do you explain this paradox?
- Why are Chinese and Persian important languages for studying the Mongol Empire?
- Would you consider Rashid al-Din's *Collection of Histories* a history of the world? Why or why not?

myhistorylab

establish, for about a century, the *Pax Mongolica*, the Mongolian Peace, over a vast region, in which intercontinental trade could flourish across the reopened silk routes. Reports from two world travelers, Ibn Battuta (1304–68) of Morocco and Marco Polo (1254–1324) of Venice, give vivid insights into that exotic trade route.

During his 30 years and 73,000 miles of travel, Ibn Battuta commented extensively on conditions of travel and trade. For example, in central Asia he encountered a military expedition of Oz Beg Khan (d. 1341), the ruler of the khanate, or sub-empire, of the Golden Horde:

> We saw a vast city on the move with its inhabitants, with mosques and bazaars in it, the smoke of the kitchens rising in the air (for they cook while on the march), and horse-drawn wagons transporting the people. (Dunn, p. 167)

The tents of this camp/city were Mongol **yurts**. Made of wooden poles covered with leather pelts, and with rugs on the floor, they could be readily disassembled for travel.

Later, Ibn Battuta was granted his request to travel with one of Oz Beg Khan's wives along the trade route as she returned to her father's home in Constantinople to give birth to her child. Ibn Battuta reported that the princess traveled with 5,000 horsemen under military command, 500 of her own troops and servants, 200 female slave girls, 20 Greek and Indian pages, 400 wagons, 2,000 horses, and 500 oxen and camels. They crossed from Islamic Mongol territory to Christian Byzantium.

KEY TERMS

transhumance A pattern of seasonal migration.

yurt A portable dwelling used by the nomadic people of central Asia, consisting of a tentlike structure of skin, felt, or handwoven textiles arranged over wooden poles, simply furnished with rugs.

Marco Polo was a merchant in a family of merchants, and his account of his travels to and in China was particularly attuned to patterns of trade. His numerous descriptions of urban markets support the idea of an urban-centered trade diaspora. For example, consider his description of Tabriz in northwest Persia:

Marco Polo, from *Li Livres du Graunt Caam, c.* 1400. The great world traveler is shown setting sail for China from Venice in 1271. Europe was eager for news of the Mongol Empire—potential allies against the Muslim enemy—and a steady stream of intrepid merchants and missionaries brought back amazing reports of the Khan's court. The exotic reminiscences of Marco Polo are by far the most famous. (Bodleian Library, Oxford)

The people of Tabriz live by trade and industry; for cloth of gold and silk is woven here in great quantity and of great value. The city is so favourably situated that it is a market for merchandise from India and Baghdad, from Mosul and Hormuz, and from many other places; and many Latin merchants come here to buy the merchandise imported from foreign lands. It is also a market for precious stones, which are found here in great abundance. It is a city where good profits are made by travelling merchants. The inhabitants are a mixed lot and good for very little. There are Armenians and Nestorians, Jacobites and Georgians and Persians; and there are also worshippers of Mahomet, who are the natives of the city and are called Tabrizis. (Marco Polo, p. 57)

Central Asian routes challenged travelers and their animals. Despite the *Pax Mongolica*, merchants still had to be prepared to defend themselves from attack. As Marco Polo recounts:

> Among the people of these kingdoms there are many who are brutal and bloodthirsty. They are forever slaughtering one another; and, were it not for fear of the government … they would do great mischief to travelling merchants. The government imposes severe penalties upon them and has ordered that along all dangerous routes the inhabitants at the request of the merchants shall supply good and efficient escorts from district to district for their safe conduct on payment of two or three groats for each loaded beast according to the length of the journey. Yet, for all that the government can do, these brigands are not to be deterred from frequent depredations. Unless the merchants are well armed and equipped with bows, they slay and harry them unsparingly. (Polo, p. 61)

For those merchants and statesmen who did reach Beijing, the *khan* maintained a massive service industry to provide hospitality. Polo noted, in particular, an army of prostitutes:

> I assure you that there are fully 20,000 of them, all serving the needs of men for money. They have a captain general, and there are chiefs of hundreds and of thousands responsible to the captain. This is because, whenever ambassadors come to the Great Khan on his business and are maintained at his expense, which is done on a lavish scale, the captain is called upon to provide one of these women every night for the ambassador and one for each of his attendants. They are changed each night and receive no payment; for this is the tax they pay to the Great Khan. (Polo, p. 129)

Almost everything we know about Marco Polo's life is based on the colorful account he left us of his travels through Asia. Little is known of his childhood years in Venice or his education. Marco's father and uncle, both Venetian merchants, traveled from their home in 1260 on a trade mission as far as the northern end of the Caspian Sea. Then war broke out, and their route back home was blocked. But the route eastward was open, so the brothers traveled on to Beijing, where Chinggis Khan's grandson, Kublai Khan (1215–94), ruled.

The Great Khan invited the men to return with more information on Christianity and a delegation from the pope. The information and delegation never materialized, but in 1271 the two brothers, bringing along the 17-year-old Marco, set out for China again. They arrived in 1275 and remained there for 17 years. How exactly they occupied themselves during this time is unclear from Marco's account, but it was not uncommon for foreigners to find employment in the Mongol state. Kublai Khan, it appears, was so enchanted by Marco's tales of foreign lands that he sent him on repeated reconnaissance trips throughout the empire. The Polos eventually set off for home in about 1292, reaching Venice in 1295 and reuniting with relatives and friends who had believed them long-since dead.

Soon after his homecoming, Marco was captured in battle by Genoese sailors and imprisoned. He dictated the tales of his travels to his fellow prisoner Rustichello, a writer of romances. Europe now had its most complete and consistent account up to that date of the silk route and of the fabulous Chinese empire of Kublai Khan. Marco's *Travels* was soon translated into several European languages, introducing to Christian Europe a new understanding of the world.

For seven centuries scholars have hotly debated the authenticity of Marco Polo's account. No original copy of *The Travels* exists, and scholars have been faced with some 140 manuscript versions that were copied in various languages and dialects from scribe to scribe before the invention of printing. In a book titled *Did Marco Polo Go to China?* Frances Wood emphasizes the arguments against. Polo did not mention any of the phenomena that should have caught his attention during his reported time in China: Chinese writing, tea, chopsticks, foot binding, the Great Wall. Despite his claims to frequent meetings with Kublai Khan, Marco Polo is not mentioned in any Chinese records of the time. Wood concludes that Polo's work is actually based on materials gathered from others and that he himself never traveled beyond the Black Sea. As a travel narrative, Wood asserts, the book must be a fabrication, but as an account of what was known of China at the time, it is a rich and influential source of information. However, many commentators are equally adamant that Polo did complete all the travels that he claimed; the debate over the extent of his journeys continues.

Chinggis Khan

The reopening and protection of the silk routes in the time of Marco Polo was the work of the Mongols, who emerged out of Mongolia on a career of world conquest, led by Chinggis Khan. Temujin, later called Chinggis (Genghis) Khan, was born about 1162 into one of the more powerful and more militant Mongol tribes. His father, chief of his tribe, was poisoned by a rival tribe. About three generations before Temujin's birth, one of his ancestors, Kabul Khan, had briefly united the Mongols, and Temujin made it his own mission to unify them once again. He conquered the surrounding tribes, one by one, and united them at Karakorum, his capital. Although skilled at negotiation, Temujin was also infamous for his brutality. Historian Rashid

Chinggis Khan, from Rashid al-Din's *World History*, thirteenth century. Chinggis Khan's conquests had as much impact on western Asia as they did on China. This Persian illustration of Chinggis pursuing his enemies comes from a history, which some consider to be the first world history, written by Rashid al-Din (1247–1318), a Persian administrator employed by Mongol Il-Khans in Iran. (Bibliothèque Nationale, Paris)

416

al-Din (1247–1318), writing almost a century after Temujin's conquests, reports his declaration of purpose, emphasizing women as the spoils of warfare:

> Man's greatest good fortune is to chase and defeat his enemy, seize all his possessions, leave his married women weeping and wailing, ride his gelding, and use the bodies of his women as a nightshirt and support, gazing upon and kissing their rosy breasts, sucking their lips which are as sweet as the berries of their breasts. (cited in Ratchnevsky, p. 153)

Temujin defeated the Tartars and killed all surviving males taller than a cart axle. He defeated the rival Mongol clans and boiled alive all their chiefs. In 1206, an assembly of all the chiefs of the steppe regions proclaimed him Chinggis Khan—"Universal Ruler." He organized them for further battle under a pyramid of officers leading units of 100, 1,000, and 10,000 mounted warriors, commanded, as they grew older, by his four sons. Promotion within the fighting machine was by merit. Internal feuding among the Mongols ended and a new legal code, based on written and recorded case law, called for high moral standards from all Mongols.

Chinggis turned east toward China. On the way he captured the Tangut kingdom of Xixia, and from Chinese engineers he mastered the weapons of siege warfare: the mangonel and trebuchet, which could catapult great rocks; giant crossbows mounted on stands; and gunpowder, which could be launched from longbows in bamboo-tube rockets. In 1211 Chinggis pierced the Great Wall of China, and in 1215 he conquered the capital, Zhongdu (modern Beijing), killing thousands.

Chinggis departed from China to conquer other kingdoms. His officials and successors continued moving south, however, until they captured all of China, establishing the Yuan dynasty (1276–1368). They conquered Korea, large parts of Southeast Asia as far as Java, and attempted, but failed, to take Japan as well. The planned assault on Japan in 1281 was stopped by *kamikaze*, divine winds, which prevented the Mongol fleet from sailing.

Chinggis himself turned west, conquering the Kara-Khitai Empire, which included the major cities of Tashkent and Samarkand. He turned southward toward India, reaching the Indus River and stationing troops in the Punjab, but he was unable to penetrate further. Turning northwest, he proceeded to conquer Khwarizm. In the great cities of Bukhara, Nishapur, Merv, Herat, Balkh, and Gurgan, millions were reported killed, surely an exaggeration, but still an indication of great slaughter. Chinggis went on to capture Tabriz and Tbilisi.

After Chinggis' death in 1227, his four sons continued the expansion relentlessly. In the northwest they defeated the Bulgars along the Volga and the Cumans of the southern steppes and then entered Russia. They took Moscow, destroyed Kiev, overran Moravia and Silesia, and set their sights on the conquest of Hungary. To the terrified peoples in their path, it looked as if nothing could stop the Mongols' relentless expansion. But in 1241, internal quarrels did what opposing armies could not: they brought the Mongol advance in Europe to a halt. During the dispute over succession that followed the death of Chinggis' son Ogedei (1185–1241), the Mongols withdrew east of Kiev. They never resumed their westward movement, and central and Western Europe remained untouched.

In the southwest, under Chinggis' grandson Hulegu (*c.* 1217–65), the Mongols captured and destroyed Baghdad in 1258, ending the five-century-old Abbasid dynasty by killing the caliph. But in the next year, Mongke, Chinggis' grandson and the fourth and last successor to his title as "Great Khan," died while campaigning in China, and many of the Mongol forces withdrew to attend a general conclave in Karakorum to choose his successor. In 1260, Mongol forces were defeated by a

Mamluk army at the battle of Ain Jalut, in modern Jordan, ending forever their drive to the southwest (see map p. 361).

The End of the Mongol Empire

Mongol rule was extensive but brief. At their apogee, 1279–1350, the Mongols had ruled all of China, almost all of Russia, Iran, Iraq, and central Asia. The huge empire was administered through four separate geographical khanates, each under the authority of a branch of Chinggis Khan's family. Over time central authority declined and the four khanates separated, each becoming an independent empire.

The Mongols could not govern their empire from horseback, and they were soon absorbed by the peoples they had conquered. They intermarried freely with the Turks, who had joined them as allies in conquest. In Russia, Mongols and Turks merged with Slavs and Finns in a new Turkish-speaking ethnic group, the Tartars. In Persia and China they assimilated into local culture, converting to various beliefs, including Christianity, Buddhism, and Confucianism. In most of the areas inhabited by Muslims, the Mongols and their Turkish allies typically converted to Islam.

As the four segments of Chinggis Khan's empire went their own separate ways, slowly they were driven from their conquests. By 1335 the male line of Chinggis and his grandson Hulegu died out in the Il-Khan Empire in Persia. The Ming dynasty defeated and evicted the Mongol rulers in 1368, ending the Yuan dynasty. The Chagatai khanate was destroyed by Timur after 1369. In 1480, Russia's Ivan III defeated the Golden Horde (named not, as one might think, for their numbers, but for their tents, *ordu* in Turkish) and pushed them out of his territories, although the last Mongol state in the Crimea was conquered only in the eighteenth century.

From Mongol to Ming: Dynastic Transition

During the 90 years of Mongol rule, 1279–1368, China's population plummeted from a high of 100 million to just over 50 million. Despite the splendor of Kublai Khan in his capital at Beijing, the Chinese economy did not serve everyone equally well. Marco Polo told of especially bitter poverty and class division in south China where the Han Chinese of the Southern Song dynasty experienced Mongol rule as cruel and exploitative:

> In the province of Manzi almost all the poor and needy sell some of their sons and daughters to the rich and noble, so that they may support themselves on the price paid for them and the children may be better fed in their new homes. (Polo, p. 227)

Revolution simmered until 1368, when the Ming dynasty overthrew the Mongols and ruled for almost three centuries, until 1644.

Under the Ming dynasty, the population increased sharply. By 1450 it had reached 100 million again, and by 1580 the population was at least 130 million. Plagues and rebellions caused the population to fall back to 100 million by 1650, but from that trough it rose consistently into present times.

The population settled new territories as it grew. The origins of the Chinese Empire had been in the Yellow River valley in the north. At the time of the Han dynasty, more than 80 percent of the population of China lived north of the Yangzi valley. Under the late Tang dynasty, the population was divided about equally between north and south. Warfare with the Mongols in the north drove more migrants south, and at the height of the Mongol Yuan dynasty up to 90 percent of the population lived in the south. Economically, the south produced rice, cotton, and tea, three of China's most valuable products, not available in the northern climate. Closer to the sea lanes of Southeast Asia and the Indian Ocean, the south also developed China's principal ports for international commerce. The Song built a powerful navy and Chinese merchants carried on regular trade with Southeast Asia, India, and the Persian Gulf. After the Mongols were defeated, however, migration began to reverse. By about 1500, 25 percent lived in the north and movement back in that direction was increasing.

World Trade Routes Before Columbus: What Difference Do They Make?

The years around 1500 marked a turning point in world trade patterns. Before 1500, trading routes crisscrossed Africa, Europe, and Asia. These routes connected with one another, although they were not unified into a single system of trade. Long-distance trade goods would travel in stages, carried first by one set of traders and then transferred to another, as goods were transported to their final destination. The most important long-distance traders were the Muslim Arab sailors and merchants of the Indian Ocean routes and beyond to the ports of China. Chinese traders dominated the East Asian waterways and only occasionally sailed into the Indian Ocean. In the thirteenth and fourteenth centuries, Mongol rulers provided protection along the old silk routes, reopening these land passages through central Asia. At this time, however, few European traders ventured into eastern Asia.

The western hemisphere had two sets of regional routes—mostly unconnected with each other—one centering on Mesoamerica, the other on the Andes Mountains of South America. The Americas remained separated from the rest of the world by the vast expanses of the Atlantic and Pacific Oceans.

As European traders grew more active after 1500, they attempted to subordinate preexisting regional systems to their own centralized control from European head-quarters. Within a single generation they seized control of the Americas. Asian powers, however, were much more powerful and they tended to pay little attention to the newly arriving Europeans. Following early, problematic encounters, China and Japan mostly kept them out. European control increased as northwestern Europe industrialized after 1750. Then the European traders, and their governments, supported by new productivity at home as well as by new ships and new guns, began to assert their control over global trade. They challenged the legacies of Arab and Chinese supremacy in the east, and Native American isolation in the west, and began to introduce new regimes of trade and domination into world history.

Asking Questions

- What is a "trade diaspora"? What was the importance of trade diasporas to the spread of world trade before 1500? What advantages did Jews and Muslims have for engaging in world trade in the period 1300–1500?
- What were the principal interregional trading networks in 1300?
- What is a lateen sail? Where did it originate? What is its significance?
- How would you compare the relative importance of inland and overseas trade for China in the fifteenth century?
- How did the Mongol Empire facilitate world trade?
- Trace the rise of Arab seafaring to show how it came to be predominant in the Indian Ocean and South China Sea.

Suggested Readings

KEY TERMS

value added see p. 392

free market economy see p. 392

supply and **demand** see p. 392

moral economy see p. 392

trade diaspora see p. 392

silk route see p. 392

lateen sail see p. 403

transhumance see p. 413

yurt see p. 413

PRINCIPAL SOURCES

Abu-Lughod, Janet L. *Before European Hegemony: The World System* A.D. *1250–1350* (New York: Oxford University Press, 1989). A resume of the principal trade routes around 1250. Unfortunately omits African routes.

Adas, Michael, ed. *Islamic and European Expansion* (Philadelphia, PA: Temple University Press, 1993). Key collection of historiographical essays on major topics in world history, 1200–1900. Articles by Eaton and Tucker on Islam, and McNeill on "gunpowder empires" are especially helpful for this unit.

Chaudhuri, K.N. *Trade and Civilization in the Indian Ocean: An Economic History from the Rise of Islam to 1750* (Cambridge: Cambridge University Press, 1985). A survey of goods, traders, ships, regulations, and competition among those who sailed and claimed to control the Indian Ocean.

Cortés, Hernán. *Letters from Mexico*, trans. from the Spanish and ed. Anthony Pagden (New Haven, CT: Yale University Press, 1986). Newest edition of Cortés' letters.

Curtin, Philip. *Cross-Cultural Trade in World History* (Cambridge: Cambridge University Press, 1984). Classical statement of the significance and ubiquity of trade diasporas.

Dunn, Ross. *The Adventures of Ibn Battuta* (Berkeley, CA: University of California Press, 1986). Dunn uses Ibn Battuta and his travels as the center-point of an analysis of Islamic life throughout the Islamic ecumene in the fourteenth century.

Elvin, Mark. *The Pattern of the Chinese Past* (Stanford, CA: Stanford University Press, 1973). Primarily economic history, focused heavily on the central questions of why China did so well economically until about 1700, and then why it did so badly after that time.

Mann, Charles O. *1491: New Revelations of the Americas before Columbus* (New York: Vintage Books, 2006). A popularly written survey, comprehensive, up-to-date. Also seeks comparisons between the past and the present.

ADDITIONAL SOURCES

The Thousand Nights and One Night: A Plain and Literal Translation of the Arabian Nights Entertainment, 6 vols. in 3, trans. Richard F. Burton (New York: Heritage Press, 1946). These charming tales are set in a world of Arab sea trade.

Bentley, Jerry H. *Old World Encounters* (New York: Oxford University Press, 1993). Survey of the range of crosscultural, long-distance encounters—especially through trade, religion, and culture—throughout Afro-Eurasia from earliest times to about 1500. Engaging.

Chaudhuri, K. N. *Asia Before Europe* (Cambridge: Cambridge University Press, 1990). Survey of the economic and political systems of Asia before the impact of colonialism and the Industrial Revolution. Comprehensive, comparative, and thoughtful.

Columbia College, Columbia University. *Introduction to Contemporary Civilization in the West*, Vol. I (New York: Columbia University Press, 2nd ed., 1954). Very well-chosen, long source readings from leading thinkers of the time and place. Vol. I covers about 1000 to 1800.

Crosby, Alfred W. *Ecological Imperialism: The Biological Expansion of Europe, 900–1900* (Cambridge: Cambridge University Press, 1986). The biological—mostly destructive—impact of European settlement around the world, a tragedy for native peoples from the Americas to Oceania.

Frank, Andre Gunder and Barry K. Gills, eds. *The World System: Five Hundred Years or Five Thousand?* (London: Routledge, 1993). In this somewhat tendentious, but well argued, account, globalization is nothing new.

Ghosh, Amitav. *In An Antique Land* (New York: Knopf, 1993). A novel, travelogue, historical fiction of Indian Ocean exchanges in the twelfth century and today. Captivating. Much of the tale is based on the research in Goitein's study, below.

Goitein, Shelomo Dov. *A Mediterranean Society: The Jewish Communities of the Arab World as Portrayed in the Documents of the Cairo Genizah*, 6 vols. (Berkeley, CA: University of California Press, 1967–83). Extraordinary research resulting from the examination of a discovered treasury of about 10,000 documents from about 1000 to 1300. Despite the title, gives insight into a variety of communities of the time.

Hanbury-Tenison, Robin. *The Oxford Book of Exploration* (New York: Oxford University Press, 1994). An excellent collection of primary sources on exploration.

Hourani, George Fadlo. *Arab Seafaring in the Indian Ocean in Ancient and Early Medieval Times* (Princeton, NJ: Princeton University Press, 1951, reprinted 1995). The standard introduction. Examines the trade routes and the ships prior to and after the coming of Islam.

Ibn Battuta. *Travels in Asia and Africa 1325–1354*, trans. and selected from the Arabic by H.A.R. Gibb (New Delhi: Saeed International, edition 1990). Selections from the writings of one of the greatest travelers in history.

Ibn Majid, Ahmad. *Arab Navigation in the Indian Ocean Before the Coming of the Portuguese*, trans., introduced, and annotated by G.R. Tibbetts (London: Royal Asiatic Society of Great Britain and Ireland, 1971). Translation of Ibn Majid's classic fifteenth-century guide for navigators, along with very extensive discussion by Tibbetts placing the author and work in context and discussing contemporary theories of navigation.

Komaroff, Linda and Stefano Carboni, eds. *The Legacy of Genghis Khan: Courtly Art and Culture in Western Asia, 1256–1353* (New York: Metropolitan Museum of Art and New Haven, CT: Yale University Press, 2002). Lavishly illustrated catalogue of blockbuster art exhibit, with numerous interpretive essays as well.

Levathes, Louise. *When China Ruled the Seas: The Treasure Fleet of the Dragon Throne, 1405–33* (New York: Oxford University Press, 1996). Scholarly study of the expeditions of Zheng He.

Ma, Laurence J.C. *Commercial Development and Urban Change in Sung China (960–1279)* (Ann Arbor, MI: Department of Geography, University of Michigan, 1971). Careful, scholarly, detailed research monograph.

Menzies, Gavin. *1421: The Year China Discovered America* (New York: William Morrow, 2003). Menzies brings together many scraps of evidence in concocting the argument that Zheng He actually did sail to America. The evidence does not hold.

Polanyi, Karl, Conrad M. Arensberg, and Harry W. Pearson, eds. *Trade and Market in the Early Empires* (Chicago, IL: The Free Press, 1957). Fundamental argument by historical anthropologists that early trade was mostly regulated by rulers and priests.

Polo, Marco. *The Travels*, trans. from the French by Ronald Latham (London: Penguin Books, 1958). One of the most fascinating and influential travelogues ever written.

Ratchnevsky, Paul. *Genghis Khan: His Life and Legacy*, trans. and ed. Thomas Nivison Haining (Oxford: Blackwell, 1991). The current standard biography of the personally elusive Chinggis Khan.

Raychaudhuri, Tapan and Irfan Habib, eds. *The Cambridge Economic History of India. Volume 1: c. 122–c. 1750* (Cambridge: Cambridge University Press, 1982). Collection of articles of fundamental significance.

Risso, Patricia. *Merchants and Faith. Muslim Commerce and Culture in the Indian Ocean.* (Boulder, CO: Westview Press, 1995). Among the questions explored: "What difference did it make to be a Muslim?"

Schele, Linda and David Freidel. *A Forest of Kings: The Untold Story of the Ancient Maya* (New York: William Morrow and Co., 1990). The story of the deciphering of the Mayan ideographs and the histories of warfare that they reveal, by two of the leading researchers.

Shaffer, Lynda Norene. *Maritime Southeast Asia to 1500* (Armonk, NY: M.E. Sharpe, 1996). Useful survey on the voyages, trade goods, markets, towns, and government of the region—from earliest times.

Shiba Yoshinobu. *Commerce and Society in Sung China*, trans. Mark Elvin (Ann Arbor, MI: Michigan Abstracts of Chinese and Japanese Works on Chinese History, 1970). Scholarly source materials with annotations from the economic transformation of the Song dynasty.

Skinner, G. William. "Marketing and Social Structure in Rural China," *Journal of Asian Studies* XXIV, No. 1 (November 1964), pp. 3–43. Classic account of the interlocking structure of urban development in China from local market towns through national capitals of trade.

Toussaint, Auguste. *History of the Indian Ocean*, trans. June Guicharnaud (Chicago, IL: University of Chicago Press, 1966). Broad historical sweep of exploration, trade, cultural exchange, fighting, and rule in and of the Indian Ocean from earliest times to the 1960s. Very useful survey.

Wood, Frances. *Did Marco Polo Go to China?* (Boulder, CO: Westview Press, 1996). One of the more recent, and lucid, statements of the controversy, by the head of the China Department at the British Library.

ILLE DE MAGELLAM

MER DV SV

CHAPTER THIRTEEN

The Opening of the Atlantic and the Pacific

Economic Growth, Religion and Renaissance, Global Connections
1300–1500

Until 1492, no continuous links connected the eastern and western hemispheres, although there had certainly been some voyages between them. The expeditions of Leif Eriksson and other Vikings from Scandinavia around the year 1000 are well documented and authenticated by the artifacts they left behind in their temporary settlements on the northeast coast of North America. Some of the foods of Polynesia—sweet potatoes and manioc—that apparently came from South America present evidence of contacts, even more fleeting, across the Pacific. However, permanent contact between the two major continental landmasses of the world was established only with Christopher Columbus' conquest of the Atlantic Ocean in 1492. The consequences for the people of both hemispheres were enormous.

We have seen, in Chapter Twelve, that three other groups—the Polynesians, Arab traders, and the Chinese—had the capacity to cross the oceans prior to Columbus' expedition, but chose not to. The Europeans, with the exception of the Vikings, also did not venture out into the oceans, so long as the ports of the Middle East provided access to the great markets of Asia. Only when that access was reduced, profits were curtailed, and their own economics and technologies grew stronger, in the fifteenth century, did they launch their voyages across the Atlantic. Even then, they were not exploring for new lands, but only for new routes to well-known markets. In a surprise that altered the history of the world forever, the attractions of Asian trade led, by accident, to the European discovery and conquest of entire continents, with their own civilizations, of which the Europeans had known nothing.

In order to comprehend the enormity of this turn of events, we briefly look backward in time to the previous economic and cultural transformations in Europe that made the Atlantic voyages possible, and forward to the European economic and cultural **Renaissance**, or "rebirth," that accompanied, and resulted from, them. Developments in trade and commerce never take place in a vacuum, as these cultural changes make abundantly clear.

KEY TOPICS
- Economic and Social Changes in Europe
- The Renaissance
- A New World
- Legacies to the Future: What Difference Do They Make?

KEY TERM

Renaissance From the French word meaning "rebirth," a period of cultural and intellectual creativity in Western Europe between 1300 and 1570. The artists and intellectuals who created the movement saw themselves reconnecting with the traditions of ancient Greece and Rome, thus giving a "rebirth" to European culture. The cultural rebirth was accompanied by an expanding urban economy, another rebirth.

French caravel, 1555. Watercolor on paper. The sturdy caravel, with its three masts and its array of both square and lateen, triangular, sails, was adapted by Europeans from the Arab ships of the Indian Ocean and became the ship of choice for oceanic exploration. Columbus and Vasco da Gama both sailed in caravels. By arming his caravel with cannons, Gama transformed it into a weapon of war.

Oseberg Viking ship. The Vikings built magnificent ships that enabled them to sail the coasts of Western Europe, penetrate the Mediterranean Sea, trade on the rivers of northern Russia, and even cross the Atlantic, reaching North America. The Oseberg ship, named for the place in which it was excavated in 1904–05, was buried about 834, and remains one of the finest Viking ships still in existence. (Vikingskiphuset Museum, Bygdøy, Oslo, Norway)

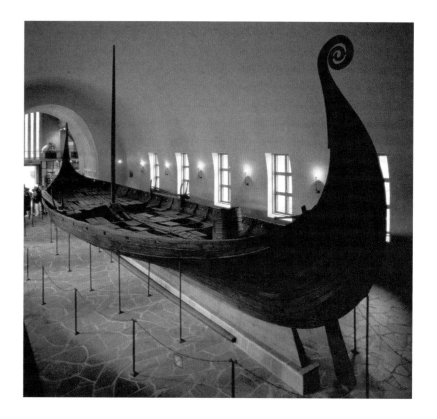

Economic and Social Changes in Europe

By the mid-1200s, Western Europeans were beginning to emerge from agrarian, manorial economies and from the localized political systems of administration and order that had marked the Middle Ages. As forests were cut down and additional lands were brought under metal-tipped plows pulled by horses with more efficient harnesses, agricultural productivity increased. Crop surpluses became available for sale to feed the craftsmen and merchants who began to migrate off the countryside into towns. Cities, which for centuries centered primarily on their churches, now increased the size of their marketplaces. Giovanni Villani describes the consumption patterns in Florence, Italy, in 1338. Its population of about 100,000 made it the fifth largest city in Europe, and every day its residents consumed "over 2,300 bushels of grain and drank in excess of 70,000 quarts of wine. Some 4,000 cattle and 100,000 sheep, goats, and swine were slaughtered each year to provide the city with meat" (cited in Brucker, pp. 51–52). The basis of Florence's wealth, like that of many cities in northern Italy and Flanders, in particular, was cloth manufacture. Villani reports that its textile industry employed 30,000 workers. As their manufacture and trade increased, Western Europeans felt increasingly aggrieved by the difficulties of doing business in the Middle East and the eastern Mediterranean.

Workers and the Landed Gentry

As business increased, local traders and manufacturers formed trade organizations called **guilds**. These guilds regulated prices, wages, the quality and quantity of production and trade, and the recruitment, training, and certification of apprentices, journeymen, and masters. The guilds also represented their members in town

KEY TERM

guild A sworn association of people who gather for some common purpose. In the towns of medieval Europe, guilds of craftsmen or merchants were formed to protect and further their business interests and for mutual aid. Compare guilds in India, p. 248.

governments and thus helped to keep industrial and commercial interests at the forefront of the civic agenda. Guilds were the principal means through which the commercial classes—merchants, artisans, and learned professionals—could counter the entrenched prerogatives of the landed aristocrats and win legal privileges for themselves, their businesses, and their cities. Guild members were mostly males, but widowed female heads of households and workshops were also included among the voting members.

Most guilds were organized within a single locality, but international traders organized international guilds corresponding to their commercial interests. The most famous and powerful of them was the Hanseatic League. More geographically dispersed and ethnically diverse, and therefore less closely knit, than a true guild, it was founded in the mid-thirteenth century to represent the interests of leading shippers of the cities of Germany and the Baltic and North Seas. From its headquarters in the city of Lübeck, the League established its own commercial trading posts as far west as London and Bruges (in modern Belgium), as far east as Novgorod in Russia. Throughout the region, it lobbied for legal systems that favored its members. Sturdy cargo ships belonging to the League carried grain, timber, furs, tar, honey, and flax westward from Russia and Poland, and woolen goods eastward

Scandinavian, Arab Muslim, and East Slav invasions, ninth to tenth centuries. Europe was subjected to repeated invasions that temporarily disturbed the continent but then increased its power. The Vikings settled and developed Scandinavia, and their interaction with the Slavs gave shape to Russia. The Muslims brought with them an understanding of the culture of ancient Greece and Rome that Europeans had forgotten. (Adapted from *The Times Atlas of World History*, 5th ed. London. Times Books.)

"Eurocentric" History?

As the study of world history moves toward modern times, a central question arises: How much attention, and what kind of attention, should we allot to the role of Europe? To what degree should world history be "Eurocentric"? The question has two dimensions: How significant were Europe's innovations, spread throughout the world by industrialization and imperialism? On balance, was Europe's influence beneficial or detrimental?

Europe usually gets more space than other regions in the modern world, because many innovations that have made the modern world what it is—capitalism, the nation-state, the Industrial Revolution, global imperialism—found first and deepest expression in the West. Some historians, like David Landes, renowned for his studies in the history of economics and technology, therefore embraced a Eurocentric approach enthusiastically. "As the historical record shows, for the last thousand years, Europe (the West) has been the prime mover of development and modernity" (p. xxi). And, Landes argues, development and modernity have been for the best: "Some would say that Eurocentrism is bad for us, indeed bad for the world, hence to be avoided. Those people should avoid it. As for me, I prefer truth to goodthink. I feel surer of my ground" (p. xxi).

William McNeill, author of the influential world history *The Rise of the West* (1963), responded more cautiously. When his classic book was republished in 1991, he wrote a retrospective introduction, in which he regretted some elements of his earlier excessive "Eurocentrism": "I gave undue attention to Latin Christendom," he wrote (p. xviii); "My failure to understand China's primacy between A.D. 1000 and 1500 is particularly regrettable" (p. xix).

How had he made these two interrelated errors? First, McNeill explains, "*The Rise of the West* tends to march with big battalions, looking at history from the point of view of the winners—that is, of the skilled and privileged managers of society—and shows scant concern for the sufferings of the victims of historical change." Second, "in the years 1954 to 1963, when the book was being written, the United States was, of course, passing through the apex of its postwar capacity to influence others thanks to its superior skills and wealth." Looking for "winners," McNeill read the emerging American power—based on earlier European power—of his own day backward into the past. Nevertheless, McNeill presents not an abject apology for his earlier writing, but an explanation: Winners do have disproportionate influence compared to victims; America's rise to power was a part of world history. Eurocentricity (including its American offspring) seemed a natural approach.

From his revised perspective, McNeill suggests an alternative to Eurocentrism: "I should have made room for the ecumenical process. How this might be done remains to be seen. Somehow an appreciation of the autonomy of separate civilizations (and of all the other less massive and less skilled cultures of the earth) across the past two thousand years needs to be combined with the portrait of an emerging world system, connecting greater and greater numbers of persons across civilized boundaries" (p. xxii).

Many scholars have come to a similar conclusion and have chosen to emphasize the interconnections among peoples. In *Europe and the People without History*, Eric Wolf, a historical anthropologist, writes: "Following the global effects of European

from England. From Sweden they carried copper and iron ore. In the fourteenth century about 100 towns were affiliated with the League. Nevertheless, as states such as the Netherlands (United Provinces), England, and Sweden grew powerful and asserted their control of the Baltic, the League began to die a natural death, after dominating the commerce of its region for almost two centuries.

Textiles and Social Conflict

In two regions of Western Europe, northern Italy and Flanders, the manufacture of textiles came to dominate the urban economies. In these regions early modern European capitalism was born. Capitalist entrepreneurs organized production, employed large numbers of laborers, and created markets for buying and selling, taking economic risks in hope of making profits. In Florence, between 200 and 300 workshops provided a livelihood for almost a third of the city's population, producing a total of 100,000 pieces of woolen cloth each year. Other cities of northern Italy, though smaller, had similar workshops.

The new organization of textile production created a complex class structure. Among the manual workers in the chain of production, guild masters and the aspiring journeymen and apprentices within the guilds held the best positions:

HOW DO WE KNOW?

expansion leads to a consideration of the search for American silver, the fur trade, the slave trade, and the quest for new sources of wealth in Asia … I then trace the transition to capitalism in the course of the industrial revolution, examine its impact on areas of the world supplying resources to the industrial centers, and sketch out the formation of working classes and their migrations within and between the continents" (p. 23). Europeans may have initiated many of these changes, but each of the world's peoples responded in its own way.

Indian-born, Western-educated historian and anthropologist Dipesh Chakrabarty takes Wolf's position a step further. He acknowledges the enormous contribution of the West to the modern world:

> Concepts such as citizenship, the state, civil society, public sphere, human rights, equality before the law, the individual, distinctions between public and private, the idea of the subject, democracy, popular sovereignty, social justice, scientific rationality, and so on all bear the burden of European thought and history. One simply cannot think of political modernity without these and other related concepts that found a climactic form in the course of the European Enlightenment and the nineteenth century. (p. 4)

But Chakrabarty cautions against the Eurocentric argument that European innovations would be adopted wholesale by the rest of the world, "first in Europe, then elsewhere." Instead, like Wolf, he argues that people of other regions have adapted these innovations, each in its own way. One of his first examples is universal suffrage. Introduced first in the West, where literacy rates were relatively high, it was subsequently introduced more widely, including in countries, such as India, with very low levels of literacy. But India is not simply in the preliminary stages of developing European democracy. It is generating a new form of democracy, with different kinds of interest groups, different methods of communication, and different kinds of relationships with the spirit world and ancestors, than Europe evolved. This is all right. Europe had its way of doing things; India and other countries have theirs. Europe is not the decisive guide and mentor to others; its way is not the only way. Chakrabarty titles his book *Provincializing Europe*.

The debate over the place of Europe in world history continues. It is difficult to envision a history of the modern world that does not give Europe an important place, because of its own cultural innovations and because of its globe-spanning industries and empires. But Europe is not itself unified; and, despite Landes' claims, not all its effects were positive. Each people created its own response to the Europeans, expressing its own unique character, which deserves its own separate study.

- Landes specializes in the history of technology; McNeill is a generalist; and both Wolf and Chakrabarty are trained in anthropology as well as history. To what extent do you think their specializations influence their attitudes toward Eurocentrism?
- With which of the four scholars do you most agree? Disagree? Why?
- Compare and contrast the accounts of Columbus' arrival in the New World as they might be written by a Eurocentric scholar and by one of the Taino people of the Caribbean who met him.

PEARSON myhistorylab

Sheep in pen being milked, Luttrell Psalter, fourteenth century. Woolen-cloth merchants had congregated in Flanders from an early stage, and by the twelfth century the industry there needed English wool to function to capacity. Prior to medieval times overland traders could transport profitably only small and valuable objects over long distances; by the fourteenth century the emergence of sea routes meant that bulk goods, such as wool and grain, could be traded internationally. (British Museum, London)

427

AT A GLANCE: WORLD TRADE, MOSTLY EUROPEAN (compare p. 393)

DATE	POLITICAL/SOCIAL EVENTS	TRADE DEVELOPMENTS	EXPLORATION
1150	• Salah al-Din, sultan of Turkish Syria and Egypt, retakes Jerusalem (1187) • St. Francis of Assisi (1181–1226) • St. Dominic (1170–1221) • St. Clare of Assisi (1194–1253)	• Market fairs in the Champagne region, France	
1200		• Rise of craft guilds in towns of Western Europe • Foundation of Hanseatic League (1241)	
1250		• Increasing Venetian links with central Asia and China (1255–95) • Revolt of craftworkers in Flanders	
1300	• Hundred Years War between England and France (1337–1453) • Black Death in Europe (1346–50)	• West Africa provides two-thirds of the gold of the eastern hemisphere	
1350	• Ghettoization of Jews in Western Europe • Ashigawa Shoguns dominate Japan (1338–1573)	• Revolts of urban workers in Italy and Flanders	
1400	• Ottoman Turks establish foothold in Europe at Gallipoli	• Great Chinese naval expeditions reach east coast of Africa and India under Zheng He	• Portugal's Prince Henry the Navigator sponsors expeditions to West Africa
1450	• Printing of Gutenberg Bible (1455) • Wars of the Roses in England (1453–85) • Turks capture Constantinople (1453) • Jews driven from Spain (1492) • Treaty of Tordesillas (1494)	• Medici family in Florence: Giovanni, Cosimo, Lorenzo	• Bartholomeu Dias sails round Cape of Good Hope (1488) • Columbus reaches the Americas (1492) • Vasco da Gama reaches the Malabar coast, India (1498)
1500	• Machiavelli, *The Prince* (1513) • Muslims in Spain forced to convert or leave	• Portugal sets up trading port of Goa, in India (1502); Portuguese ships armed with cannons	• Ferdinand Magellan's voyage around globe (1519–22)

shearing the sheep; fulling the cloth (that is, shrinking and thickening it by moistening, heating, and pressing it); and dyeing the wool. Weavers, carders, and combers were lower on the pay and social scales. The weavers, more skilled than the others, were better positioned to organize themselves into a guild.

Capitalist traders, in search of private profit, organized the manufacture in a **putting-out system**. They estimated the market demand for production and supplied workers with the raw materials and equipment necessary to meet it. Laborers then produced the finished products, sometimes in workshops but more typically in their own homes. Usually they were paid by the piece. An army of poor people washed, warped, and spun the wool. The additional income of female and child laborers, employed at even lower pay and in worse conditions than the men, enabled working families to survive.

Occasionally class antagonisms between employer and employee grew into open conflict. Revolts broke out in the Flemish cities of Douai, Tournai, Ypres, and Bruges at the end of the thirteenth century. The leaders were mostly craftsmen, and they

KEY TERM

putting-out system In the putting-out system, employers provide employees with raw materials and the orders for turning them into finished products, which they then buy on completion. The employees carry out the work at home.

usually demanded that guild members be allowed to participate in city government and thus have a voice in the regulation of the conditions of trade and manufacture. Workers outside the guild organizations could only hope that increased wages, shorter hours, and better conditions of work might trickle down to their level as well.

In the fourteenth century, such class antagonisms multiplied. Increasingly impoverished workers, suffering also from plagues, wars, and bad harvests, confronted increasingly wealthy traders and industrialists. Workers were forbidden to strike and, in some towns, even to assemble. Nevertheless, class unrest continued to grow, especially in Florence, the greatest industrial center of Western Europe. In 1345, ten wool-carders were hanged for organizing workers.

Aerial view of present-day Delft, west Netherlands. Here, gabled medieval townhouses are seen surrounding the bustling market square in Delft. Since the late 1500s the town has been famous for its pottery and porcelain known as delftware. Dutch products began to compete in European markets with porcelain imports from China.

Painting of Hertogenbosch, Netherlands, 1530. Compare today's photograph of a medieval square on market day (left) with this view of a cloth market in another Dutch town painted in 1530. The layout and construction of the stalls are virtually identical.

Business and the Church

In its efforts to establish its independent power, the urban business community confronted not only landed aristocrats and organizations of urban workers, but an often hostile clergy as well. From earliest times, the Roman Catholic Church had taken a dim view of the quest for private profit and wealth. St. Augustine (354–430) perpetuated the disdain. In the High Middle Ages theologians seriously debated whether it was possible for a merchant to attain salvation.

Because the Church forbade Christians to take and give interest on loans, Jews carried out much of the business of money-lending. In fact, Jews were so much a part of the merchant classes in early medieval northern Europe that a traditional administrative phrase referred to "Jews and other merchants." Church laws forbidding Jews to own land also pushed them into urban life and commerce. By the end of the thirteenth century, Christian rulers forced Jews to live in **ghettos**, specific areas of the cities to which they were confined each night. In European society, Jews were stigmatized four times over: alien by religion, foreign by ancestry, money-lenders by occupation, and segregated by residence. Nevertheless, Jews were tolerated as an economically vital trade diaspora until local people mastered the intricacies of business. After that, Jews were often persecuted, sometimes murdered, and repeatedly exiled—from England in 1290, from France in 1394, from Spain in 1492, and from many German cities.

As commerce increased, however, the Roman Catholic Church began to revise its opposition to business and businessmen. St. Thomas Aquinas (1225–74) addressed the issue directly in his *Summa Theologiae*. Justifying commerce, he wrote: "Buying and selling seem to be established for the common advantage of both parties." Aquinas wrote of a "just" price, determined by negotiation between buyer and seller. Profit was allowed if its uses were deemed appropriate: "Nothing prevents gain from being directed to some necessary or even virtuous end, and thus trading becomes lawful." Traders were allowed compensation for their labor, and businessmen were allowed to charge interest on commercial loans.

Plague and Social Unrest

Europe's growing economy was undermined in the fourteenth century by extraordinary disasters: famine, civil upheavals, and, worst of all, a plague that killed

---

SOURCE

Giovanni Boccaccio Describes the Black Death

Giovanni Boccaccio (1313–75) captured the horror of the Black Death in the introduction to his otherwise droll and humanistic classic of the era, *The Decameron*:

> In the year of Our Lord 1348 the deadly plague broke out in the great city of Florence ... At the onset of the disease both men and women were afflicted by a sort of swelling in the groin or under the armpits which sometimes attained the size of a common apple or egg. Some of these swellings were larger and some smaller, and all were commonly called boils. From these two starting points the boils began in a little while to spread and appear generally all over the body. Afterwards,

the manifestation of the disease changed into black or livid spots on the arms, thighs, and the whole person ... Neither the advice of physicians nor the virtue of any medicine seemed to help ... almost everyone died within three days of the appearance of the signs—some sooner, some later ...

> The calamity had instilled such horror into the hearts of men and women that brother abandoned brother, uncles, sisters, and wives left their dear ones to perish and, what is more serious and almost incredible, parents avoided visiting or nursing their very children, as though these were not their own flesh. (xxiii–xxiv)

one-third of the population. Until recently, the plague, called the Black Death, was believed to be the bubonic plague, but research within the last decade suggests that it may have been a different, undetermined, form of plague. Whatever it was, the disease apparently followed the Mongols from central Asia into China in 1331 and decimated its population. China's population, estimated at 123 million in 1200, dropped to 65 million in the census of 1393. (Part of the decrease was caused by warfare between the Chinese and the Mongols, but a large part must also have been caused by the plague.) The plague reached Crimea in 1346. There, plague-infested rats boarded ships, disembarking with the disease at all the ports of Europe and the Near East. Within the next five years it killed one in three people, reducing Europe's population from 70 million in 1300 to only 45 million in 1400. (The ravages of the Black Death foreshadowed even worse epidemics that would sweep across the continents of the new world, as Native Americans were exposed to diseases from the eastern hemisphere for the first time.)

The catastrophe reshuffled the social classes. Peasants who survived benefited from the labor shortages that followed, gaining higher wages and access to more land, freedom from labor services, and geographical mobility. They began to form a new class of property-owning farmers. Together with urban industrial workers and guild members, they rioted more frequently and boldly against kings and nobles who attempted to raise taxes to fund their wars.

In urban areas, too, workers became scarce, and those who survived demanded higher wages, better working conditions, and more civic rights. In Florence, for example, the Ciompi (the lowest class of workers, named for the neighborhood of Florence in which they lived) revolted, supported by lower-level artisans. In 1378 they presented their demands to city officials: open access to the guilds, the right to unionize, a reduction of worker fines and punishments, and the right "to participate

The routes of the plague. The central and eastern Asian stability imposed by Mongol rule—the "Mongol Peace"—brought mixed benefits. Trade flourished, and travelers such as Ibn Battuta and Marco Polo were able to write remarkable accounts of the lands they visited. At the same time, however, vectors for other travelers, such as the rats that carried plague, also opened up. The Black Death, originating in central Asia, was one of a succession of plagues that followed the trade routes by land and sea, decimating parts of Europe and China.

The Triumph of Death, **French, 1503.** This sixteenth-century work recalls the enormous loss of life caused by the plague of 1348. Brought back from east Asia by Genoese merchants, it is estimated to have killed between 20 and 50 percent of Europe's inhabitants. Contemporary medicine was impotent in the face of the disease, whose onset meant almost certain death. (Bibliothèque Nationale, Paris)

in the government of the City." They gained some of their goals, but Florence's powerful business leaders ultimately triumphed. By 1382 the major guilds were back in control, and soon a more dictatorial government was in power. Similar revolts occurred in Flanders, but on a smaller scale, and with no more success.

In the aftermath of the Black Death the dissolution of the norms of everyday life, and of the certainties of the class structure, inspired Europeans to reassess their fundamental values and institutions. People's beliefs in God and their own future were shaken to their foundations. Some kind of new culture, some kind of renaissance, was waiting to be born.

The Renaissance

The new economy underpinned the European Renaissance—a rebirth of Classical ideals in European thought, literature, art, manners, and sensibilities. Many of the wealthier merchants became patrons of the arts, encouraging an outpouring of painting, sculpture, architecture, poetry, and prose. They identified with their cities, sponsoring creative town planning to increase their efficiency as markets and their beauty as artistic designs, and hiring superb architects to enhance their visual splendor. Both patrons and artists were usually devout members of the Church, and an increasingly wealthy Church became one of the greatest of the patrons of the arts. Nevertheless, the creativity of the Renaissance gave a new orientation to religious expression, more earthy, more fleshy, more this-worldly than it had been throughout **medieval**—"middle period"—European times. Scholars of the fifteenth century already drew this three-part division of time into the ancient, medieval, and Renaissance worlds. They saw the Renaissance as a reconnection with the culture of the ancient world of Greece and Rome, across a thousand years of medieval time, and they praised themselves and their colleagues for making the great leap backward in time.

The Roots of the Renaissance

When so great a transformation as the Renaissance takes place, however, affecting economics, technology, religion, culture, aesthetics, and social and political structures, it is not usually possible to determine exactly what is cause and what is effect, nor to specify an exact date of its initiation. Some historians do attempt to show that a single cause predominates—some, for example, stressing economics, others political or social influences—but most usually see the various transformations as intertwined. For the Renaissance, for example, even when historians emphasize one aspect or another, as we have done with trade, they identify its roots in other aspects of life as well. They detect glimmerings of the Renaissance in a shift in religious as well as

The Renaissance in Italy, 1300–1570. From 1300 to 1570 in Italy, artists and intellectuals worked to fuse the Christian tradition (originating in antiquity but developed during the Middle Ages) with the Greco-Roman tradition in a movement fundamental for the later evolution of the modern civilization of the West: the Renaissance. This map shows the principal places that are associated with the names of important figures.

Leonardo da Vinci (1452–1519)

Isotta Nogarola (1418–66)

DUCHY OF MILAN

DUCHY OF SAVOY

Giovanni Bellini (c.1430–1516)

Milan

Verona

Venice

Francis Petrarch (1304–74)

Padua

Turin

MONFERRATO

Po

Piacenza

Mantua

MARQUISATE OF MANTUA

ISTRIA

SALUZZO

Genoa

Ferrara

DUCHY OF FERRARA

REPUBLIC OF VENICE

DUCHY OF MODENA

Lucca

REPUBLIC OF FLORENCE

Piero della Francesca (c.1420–92)

REPUBLIC OF GENOA

Pisa

Arno

Florence

Urbino

DALMATIA

Siena

Tiber

Perugia

REPUBLIC OF SIENA

Apennines

Adriatic Sea

CORSICA

PAPAL STATES

Dante Alighieri (1265–1321)
Giotto di Bondone (1267–1337)
Giovanni Boccaccio (1313–75)
Filippo Brunelleschi (1377–1446)
Lorenzo Ghiberti (1378–1455)
Poggio Bracciolini (1381–1459)
Donatello (1386–1466)
Cosimo de'Medici (1389–1464)
Paolo Uccello (1397–1475)
Masaccio (1401–28)
Leon Battista Alberti (1404–72)
Marsilio Ficino (1433–99)
Sandro Botticelli (1445–1510)
Lorenzo de'Medici (1449–92)
Pico della Mirandola (1463–94)
Niccolò Machiavelli (1469–1527)
Michelangelo Buonarroti (1475–1564)

Rome

NAPLES (to Aragon)

Bari

Brindisi

SARDINIA (to Aragon)

Naples

Lorenzo Valla (1407–57)
Raphael (1483–1520)

Tyrrhenian Sea

Mediterranean Sea

SICILY (to Aragon)

N
W   E
S

0   300 km

0   150 miles

KEY TERM

medieval The "middle period." Europeans of the Renaissance period, who felt that they were, at last, reconnecting with the glories of ancient Greece and Rome, called the ten centuries in between the end of the Roman empire and the beginning of the Renaissance "the medieval period." They used the term pejoratively. More recent scholars see that very long period as far more complicated and diverse and carve it up by specific geographical regions and into much smaller periods of time.

secular values toward a more worldly and rational, less ascetic, less spiritual emphasis. They date the beginnings of this shift, as we have seen in Chapter Eleven, at least as early as the mid-eleventh century. At that time, contacts with Arab Muslim civilization reacquainted European scholars with ancient Greek philosophies, which Arab scholars had kept alive. These changes in philosophic values supported the opening to trade, just as trade later gave support to new directions in philosophy.

Christian Scholars. Christian scholars, especially in Spain, where Christians, Muslims, and Jews lived side by side, began the systematic translation of Arabic texts into Latin. They sought to reestablish the link with the ancient Roman and Greek texts that the Arabs had preserved and developed, and that the Christian world had lost. The works of Muslim philosophers Avicenna (Ibn Sina) (980–1037) and Averroes (Ibn Rushd) (1126–98), and the Jewish philosopher Maimonides (1135–1204) helped

LEFT *Avicenna*, **French School, eighteenth century. Oil on canvas.** Ibn Sina, called Avicenna by Christian Europeans, was one of the foremost Islamic students of Aristotle's work. He influenced Church scholars, who relearned Greek scholarship through him. (Bibliothèque de la Faculté de Médecine, Paris)

RIGHT *St. Francis*, **Simone Martini, c. 1320. Fresco.** St. Francis of Assisi gave away all his possessions to the poor. When his father disowned him, he stripped naked and, cloaked in a robe given by the bishop of Assisi, went from place to place begging for food, offering service, and preaching. The religious order that he founded became the largest in Europe. (S. Francesco, Assisi)

restore the emphasis upon logic and philosophy that Aristotle had taught. In the eleventh century, Church leaders began to suggest that pure faith was not enough to attain salvation. With St. Anselm (1033–1109) they stressed the need for an intellectual basis for faith; with Peter Abelard (1079–1142), they emphasized the need for a rational approach to the interpretation of texts. Meanwhile, the new wealth and power of their Church offended some Roman Catholics, and they challenged the Church to live up to its early ideals of compassion for the poor and simplicity in everyday living. New orders of priests and nuns began to form as a way of returning to these early ideals: Franciscans followed the teachings of St. Francis of Assisi (1182–1226), Dominicans followed St. Dominic (1170–1221), and the "Poor Clares," an order of nuns, followed St. Clare of Assisi (1194–1253).

Universities. Universities were founded to preserve, enhance, and transmit knowledge. Most emphasized practical disciplines: medical studies at Salerno, legal studies at Bologna, theological studies at Paris—all founded before 1200. Later, students and professors from Paris crossed the English Channel and founded the University of Oxford about 1200, with Cambridge following shortly afterward. By 1300 there were about a dozen universities in Western Europe; by 1500, nearly a hundred.

Curricula centered on theology, but also included grammar, dialectic, rhetoric, arithmetic, music, geometry, and astronomy. The theology curriculum, in particular, required the approval of the Church. This could be problematic, as illustrated in the career of St. Thomas Aquinas. St. Thomas, the greatest Christian theologian of his age, paved the way for the new ideas of the Renaissance. Contentiously, he also welcomed the systematic rationality of Aristotle. While many Church leaders rejected Aristotelian logic as contradicting the teachings of the Church, Aquinas declared that logic and reason, as taught by Aristotle, and faith, as taught by the Church, were complementary. In places where they did appear to conflict, he conceded that divine truths must take precedence: "Some divine truths are attainable by human reason, while others altogether surpass the power of human reason."

Aquinas was ahead of his time. For more than 50 years, the Franciscan order of priests banned the reading of his works. Universities at Paris and Oxford condemned many of his doctrines. But within a century, Aquinas' synthesis of logic and faith, of Aristotle and the Church, became the new standard orthodoxy of Roman Catholicism. Although Aquinas gave divine revelation precedence over human reason, on the eve of the Renaissance he opened the door of the Church to the importance of reason in all human endeavors.

In addition to modifications in official theology, the coming together of dozens of exuberant young male students in the universities, no matter how rigorous the rules and regulations, led to quests for individual expression and challenges to authority. The "Golliard Poets" took their name from the biblical Goliath, a kind of early antichrist. These poets reveled in the pleasures of youth and ridiculed the conventions of sobriety, solemnity, and sanctity. They wrote parodies that were usually irreverent and sometimes obscene, for example, a *Drunkard's Mass*, a *Glutton's Mass*, and an *Office of Ribalds*. They mocked the most sacred beliefs of their time, declaring "I believe in dice … and love the tavern more than Jesus." They declared their blessings for one another: "Fraud be with you."

Such turmoil in religious and philosophical attitudes, both official and unofficial, helped pave the way for the transformations of the Renaissance.

Theological lecture at the Sorbonne, Paris, fifteenth century. Manuscript illumination. Sponsored by the Church, universities were founded primarily for the study of theology, but some included specializations in medicine and law. All the students were male and most were quite serious-minded. (Bibliothèque de Troyes)

HOW DO WE KNOW?

Islamic Influences on the European Renaissance

Arab thinkers, their translations of classical Greek works, and their comments on them, helped inspire the European Renaissance. Averroes' Arabic translations of and commentaries on Aristotle revealed that philosopher's works to Western Europeans who had lost contact with the originals. In addition to his philosophy, Avicenna's *Qanun* (Canon) of medicine remained central to European medical thought for centuries. Al-Khuwarizmi's work in mathematics remained influential or centuries, and lives on in our lexicon today in the word *algorithm*, based on his name. From the tenth to the twelfth century Arabs, Christians, and Jews lived in such proximity, and even harmony, in parts of Spain—the home of these three scholars—that linguistic borrowing back and forth became common. Poetic and prose forms were also borrowed, especially from Arabic literature to Latin and the Romance languages. European scholars, such as Gerard of Cremona, sought out the best in Arabic thought in order to translate it. We have also seen that Europeans adapted Arab technology, such as the caravel, which gave them access to the oceans of the world.

Despite this rich harvest of culture and technology from the Arab world, we have the harsh, even hysterical judgment of Petrarch (1304–74), one of the greatest Italian poets of the Renaissance, often called "the father of humanism":

> I implore you to keep these Arabs from giving me advice about my personal condition. Let them stay in exile. I hate the whole lot … You know what kind of physicians the Arabs are. I know what kind of poets they are. Nobody has such winning ways; nobody, also, is more tender and more lacking in vigor, and, to use the right words, meaner and more perverted. The minds of men are inclined to act differently; but, as you used to say, every man radiates his own peculiar mental disposition. To sum up: I will not be persuaded that any good can come from Arabia. (Cassirer *et al.*, p. 142)

What has happened between the early welcome given to Arabic learning and its bitter, summary rejection by Petrarch? Several interpretations are possible. First, Arabic influence was always greatest in Spain, where Muslims ruled much of the country for centuries, in some regions for almost eight centuries. Other European countries were less influenced. Even in Spain, as Christians began to reconquer the country, they began to focus on Muslims as political and religious enemies rather than as cultural colleagues. A similar change occurred over time throughout the Christian world as the launching of the crusades, after 1095, crystallized a new political antagonism between the two religious communities. The passing of time also brought new cultural currents to Europe, as the development of new vernaculars, especially in the Romance languages, such as Spanish, Italian, and French, broadened and deepened the base of culture, making it more nationalistic. The Western Europeans also developed their own intellectual competences and institutions, reducing their reliance on others. The European Renaissance took Western Europeans in new directions.

Scholars sometimes designate three different periods as "renaissances" in Western Europe. The first was the Carolingian Renaissance, initiated by Charlemagne, about 800; the second was the Renaissance of the High Middle Ages, about the middle of the eleventh to the middle of the thirteenth centuries, significantly influenced by Muslim scholarship and learning; the third was the best known, and most influential, the Renaissance of the mid-fourteenth to the mid-sixteenth centuries. Each of the later renaissances built on the earlier ones, but also discarded some of their qualities. In Petrarch's dismissal of Arabic poetry and of Arabs generally we see a dramatic transformation in the attitudes of Christian thinkers, as their own religious and philosophical traditions become less open, and more hostile, to the influences of other cultures.

- The fourteenth-century Renaissance took place primarily in Italy and in northwestern Europe. Why do you think it did not take place in Spain, where so much earlier cultural development took place?
- Petrarch turned against Arabic learning, but not against the early Greek philosophers. Would such a division have been possible in twelfth-century Spain? Why or why not?
- Arabic learning could be seen as more successful because it continued to hew to traditional paths, whereas Western Christian scholarship could be seen as a failure for turning in new directions. Would you accept such a characterization?

PEARSON
myhistorylab

Humanism

The Renaissance began in the cities of Italy, where thriving economies provided an economic foundation, the Church provided an intellectual foundation, and both the Church and commercial elites provided patronage to artists and intellectuals. Italy was also the heartland of the Roman Empire, a natural place in which to forge a reconnection to that ancient world. The central motivating philosophy of the Renaissance was **humanism**, the belief that the proper study of man is man. Asserting the importance of the individual, humanism challenged the monopoly of the Church over the interpretation of cultural life. Renaissance humanism held strongly to a belief in God, but assigned him a less overwhelming, less intimidating role in human life and action. In his *Oration on the Dignity of Man*, Giovanni Pico della Mirandola (1463–94) places in the mouth of God himself the most succinct statement of this humanistic perspective of the Renaissance:

> I have given you, Adam, neither a predetermined place nor a particular aspect nor any special prerogatives in order that you may take and possess these through your own decision and choice. The limitations on the nature of other creatures are contained within my prescribed laws. You shall determine your own nature without constraint from any barrier, by means of the freedom to whose power I have entrusted you … I have made you neither heavenly nor earthly, neither mortal nor immortal so that, like a free and sovereign artificer, you might mold and fashion yourself into that form you yourself shall have chosen.

According to this typical Renaissance perspective, God gives humankind the power to shape its own destiny.

New Artistic Styles

Renaissance art continued to emphasize religious themes, but it also began to reflect the influence of humanistic and commercial values. Masaccio's painting of *Trinity with the*

LEFT *Vitruvian Man*, Leonardo da Vinci, c. 1492. Pen and ink on paper. Renaissance artists studied the proportions of the human body carefully and represented it accurately. Leonardo's drawing suggests the geometric perfection of the body, relating it both to the circle and the square, and thus to a perfect and harmonious cosmos. (Galleria dell'Accademia, Venice)

ABOVE *Trinity with the Virgin, St. John, and Donors*, Masaccio, 1427. During the Renaissance, people began to rethink their relationship to God and the world around them; at the same time, artists were developing a new means of depicting reality. According to some art history scholars, Masaccio's monumental fresco is the first painting created in correct geometric perspective (the single vanishing point lies at the foot of the cross). (S. Maria Novella, Florence)

Virgin (1427) demonstrates the evolution of geometric perspective in painting, revealing not only a new artistic technique but also a new, objective interrelationship of individuals with the world.

By the fifteenth century, religious, commercial, and artistic sensibilities appear joined together. Portraiture flourished as major artists depicted their patrons, frequently elites of the Church and of commerce. *The Arnolfini Wedding Portrait*, painted in 1434 in Flanders by Jan van Eyck, presents the marriage of an international businessman, probably an Italian stationed in Flanders. Simultaneously van Eyck signalled the economic success of his subject through the elegance of the physical setting of the marriage and his religious concerns through the symbolism of the dog (Fido?), representing fidelity; the removed clogs indicating that the ground is sacred; and the mirror suggesting the all-seeing eye of God.

The richest fruits of Renaissance creativity matured in Florence, where the illustrious Medici family provided lavish patronage. The family's fortune had been built by the merchant banker Giovanni de' Medici (1360–1429), and was enhanced by his son Cosimo (1389–1464) and great-grandson Lorenzo (1449–92). In this supportive environment creative artists developed and expressed their genius. They included Michelangelo Buonarotti (1475–1564), the sculptor of such masterpieces as the *David*, which is in Florence, and the painter of the Sistine Chapel ceiling in Rome; Leonardo da Vinci (1452–1519), scientific inventor and painter of the *Mona Lisa* (also known as *La Gioconda*); and Niccolò Machiavelli (1469–1527), author of *The Prince*, a harsh and hard-nosed philosophy of government. At the same time, the general population of the city of Florence enjoyed high standards of literacy and expressiveness. Michelangelo's subsequent move to Rome, where he sculpted the statues of *Moses* and the *Pietà*, and painted the Sistine Chapel, reminds us that the Church, too, remained a great patron of the arts.

The Arnolfini Wedding Portrait, Jan van Eyck, 1434. Giovanni Arnolfini, an Italian merchant living in Flanders, commissioned this pictorial record of his marriage. On the far wall, van Eyck has written in Latin "Jan van Eyck was here," much as a notary would sign a document. Art historians assure us that although the wife may look pregnant on her marriage day, in fact this is simply what women looked like in the large-hooped skirts of the day. (National Gallery, London)

Developments in Technology

Creativity flourished in the practical arts as well as the fine arts and contributed substantially to the rise of merchant power. Local techniques were enhanced by innovations encountered in the course of trade, especially with the Arab world. Improvements in sailing technology included a new design in the ships themselves. In the thirteenth century the caravel of the Mediterranean, with its lateen sails, used mostly by Arab sailors, was blended with the straight sternpost and stern rudder of northern Europe. The caravel could also be rerigged with a square sail for greater speed in a tail wind. The astrolabe, again an Arab invention, helped sailors determine their longitude at sea. The rediscovery in the early fifteenth century of Ptolemy's *Geography*, written in the second

Sistine Chapel ceiling (post restoration), Michelangelo Buonarroti, 1508–12. Fresco. Renaissance humanism praised the ability of human beings to be creative and original, yet it continued to be anchored in religious imagery. Pope Sixtus IV commissioned Michelangelo to use his imagination in painting the Sistine Chapel ceiling in the Vatican, Rome, with Biblical scenes. (Vatican Museums and Galleries, Vatican City)

century C.E. and preserved in the Arab world, helped to spark interest in proper mapping. (An error in longitude in Ptolemy's map led Columbus to underestimate the circumference of the globe by about one-third. This error emboldened him to set out across the Atlantic and, later, to believe mistakenly that he had reached East Asia.)

Cannons, especially when mounted on ships, gave European merchants firepower not available to others. Although the Chinese had invented gunpowder centuries before, the Europeans put it to use in warfare in the fourteenth century and became the masters of gunmaking. By the early 1400s they were firing cannonballs. The Ottoman Turks employed Western European Christians to build and operate the cannons they used in 1453 to besiege and conquer Constantinople. The Turkish rulers of Persia also employed European gunners and gun manufacturers, and copied their works. By the late 1400s European warring powers were energetically competing in an "arms race" to develop the most powerful and effective cannons and guns. Leonardo and others worked on the mathematics of the projectiles. When Portuguese ships began to sail into the waters of the Indian Ocean after 1498,

The cannon. From the 1450s, innovations in weapons changed the nature of warfare. The most dramatic changes affected the cannon, as shown here in *Four Books of Knighthood*, 1528.

claiming the right to regulate commerce, their guns and cannons sank all opposition. Some historians have called this era the Age of Gunpowder Empires.

The Chinese had also invented the principle of movable type and the printing press, but, again, the Europeans surpassed them in implementation. Movable type was better suited to Europe's alphabetic languages than to Chinese ideographs. By 1455, in Mainz, Germany, Johannes Gutenberg (*c.* 1390–1486) had printed the first major book set in movable type, the Bible. By the end of the century at least 10 million individual books in some 30,000 different editions had been produced and distributed.

The Chinese also created clocks centuries before the Europeans, as early as the eleventh century, although they were apparently turned by water-wheels and regulated by an elaborate escapement mechanism. European cities recognized the need to announce the passage of time, but at first did it simply by ringing bells in public, imprecisely. Around 1300, Europeans invented their first mechanical clocks, about the same time as they invented cannons and spectacles. No one knows exactly who did it or where. A church in Milan installed a clock made of iron in 1309. The Milanese were also the first to erect a public clock to strike the hours, in 1335. It had no hands, only a bell that rang once for one o'clock, twice for two o'clock, and so on. Perhaps the inspiration for the new invention came from China, but in any case, as historian Alfred Crosby points out in his study of the importance of quantification for the economic development of urban Europe, "Hours were of central significance to city dwellers, whom buying and selling had already initiated into the vogue of quantification."

In fourteenth-century Italy, two centuries after the decimal system had been absorbed from India via the Arab world, businesspeople began to develop double-entry bookkeeping. This facilitated the accurate accounting of transactions and the efficient tracking of business profits and losses. In 1494 Luca Pacioli (*c.* 1445–*c.* 1514), a Franciscan friar and mathematician, published the method in systematic form.

By the end of the fifteenth century, some people in Western Europe were ready for new adventures. The Renaissance brought new energy not only through its humanistic philosophy and art, but also through its technological inventions. Newly emerging political rulers and urban businessmen in Western Europe were also inspired. One of their more practical goals was very specific: to gain direct access to the wealth of the Indies and China. They did that. In the process they also discovered a new world.

A New World

In the centuries after the demise of the Roman Empire, the Mediterranean Sea and its coastline had gradually devolved into three cultural and political spheres: Muslim, Byzantine, and Roman Catholic. By about 950, Muslims had established their dominion by land along the eastern and southern coasts of the Mediterranean and held parts of southern Italy as well as major islands in the Mediterranean: Cyprus, Crete, and Sicily. The southern and southeastern Mediterranean had become a "Muslim lake." Even so, the Byzantine Empire continued to control the northeastern shores of the Mediterranean, while various Frankish and Germanic Christian powers held the north-central coast. (See map p. 360.)

These divisions had three results. First, the Mediterranean became a war zone. Warfare between the Christians of southern Europe and the Muslims of the Middle East and North Africa persisted from the eighth century until 1571, when the naval Battle of Lepanto, in Greek waters, fixed generally accepted zones of control between

The Conquest of Granada on January 2, 1492, Rodrigo Aleman, Toledo Cathedral, late fifteenth century. The conquest of Granada by the Catholic King Ferdinand II and Queen Isabella I of Spain marked the final victory of the *reconquista*, the Christian recovery of all of Spain from Muslim rule. Here the Moorish king Boabdil is handing over the keys to the town.

them. Second, trade stability oscillated in response to Europe's internal economy and warfare in the Mediterranean. Third, and most important to our story here, the European merchants felt hemmed in. The valuable merchandise and profitable trade coming from the Indian Ocean basin—the spices of India and Indonesia; the silk and porcelain of China; and the gold and ivory and slaves of East Africa—were controlled by Middle Eastern Muslim traders.

This last, the eastern Mediterranean trade blockage, is often seen as a religious confrontation, but in fact trade opportunities often trumped religious rivalries. The crusades, beginning in 1096, which brought Christians and Muslims into armed conflict, simultaneously brought new opportunities for commerce across the Mediterranean to Middle Eastern ports and increased demand for the merchandise that arrived there from Asia. Although on several occasions popes forbade Catholics to trade with Muslims, these prohibitions were generally disregarded. Religious and ethnic differences may have compounded tensions, but the main contest was the competition for profits among the very diverse groups of traders.

European merchants and princes began to seek alternative routes to the lucrative products of the Indian Ocean. This search took on special intensity in Western Europe, which was geographically farther from the Middle East and closer to the Atlantic. Beginning in 1277, a maritime route between Italy and Spain in the Mediterranean and England and Flanders in northwestern Europe brought regular trade to Europe's north Atlantic coast. By the early fifteenth century, European trade generally was picking up, as the continent recovered from the devastation of the Black Death. Increasingly prosperous, and bold, Western Europeans were prepared to attempt two new routes to Asia: one south around the coast of Africa and then east to India; the other, west across the Atlantic.

Most of the dynamism of Western European trade through the fifteenth century emanated from the relatively secular city-states of Flanders and Italy, but in the Iberian peninsula Portugal and Spain created a powerful new merger of the missionary desire to spread Catholicism with the economic desire for wealth. The

Portuguese crown dispatched sailing expeditions along the African coast that ultimately reached the Cape of Good Hope, turned north into the Indian Ocean and onward to India, and were poised to continue on to China. The newly unified government of Spain commissioned Christopher Columbus to sail westward in search of a new route to the Indies. Instead he discovered a "New World."

The Early Explorers, 800–1000

There had been some excursions onto the waters of the Atlantic Ocean before Christopher Columbus made his famous voyage in 1492. From the eighth until the twelfth century, the European North Atlantic was primarily the province of marauding raiders from the north. These Vikings, the ancestors of today's Norwegians, Swedes, and Danes, were colonizers, fishermen, and traders. One group from Norway began to settle Iceland around 870 and Greenland about 982. Under Leif Eriksson they reached Newfoundland in North America about 1000 and established a settlement there as well, but it did not endure. Danes and Norwegians plundered along the entire Atlantic coast of Europe. In 859 they sailed through the Strait of Gibraltar and attacked ports along the Mediterranean. Arabs from North Africa and Spain were launching similar attacks in the Mediterranean at about the same time.

These Vikings were also traders and colonizers who often fostered urban development in the places they conquered. (See map p. 425.) They founded the town of Dublin, in Ireland, in 841, and they conquered much of northern England, establishing the kingdom of York in the 870s. Vikings also conquered the French territory of Normandy in the late eighth century, from where in 1066 their leader, William of Normandy (William the Conqueror), conquered England. The Normans, as these "Northmen" came to be known, also founded a kingdom in southern Italy and Sicily and established a principality in Antioch.

The Swedes turned eastward across the Baltic Sea and founded trading cities along the river systems of Russia, establishing their capital first at Novgorod in the early ninth century and in Kiev in 882. They proceeded all the way south to the Black Sea, where they traded with the Byzantine Empire. Swedish settlements became catalysts for the formation of the political and economic organization of the Slavic people in whose midst they were established. Kiev became the capital of the first Russian state; its people were called the "Rus." By about 1000 the Vikings became more peaceful, and their raids ceased as their home regions in Scandinavia developed into organized states and accepted Christianity. They lost interest, as well, in further exploration westward across the ocean.

Earlier voyages across the North Atlantic other than those of the Vikings are not recorded historically, and are unlikely to have occurred. There is no known crossing of the South Atlantic. Africans carried on only limited coastal shipping, and Europeans were leery of the hazards of the West African coast, especially south of Cape Bojador. In addition, they recognized that the prevailing winds on the African coast blew from north to south, and they feared that, while they might be able to proceed to the south, they might not be able to return north.

Down Africa's Atlantic Coast

Portugal was particularly well situated geographically to explore the Atlantic coast of Africa as the opening step in finding an alternative route to India, despite the fears of the unknown. In 1415 Portugal captured Ceuta on the Moroccan coast of North Africa, one of the major points of the trans-Saharan trade in gold and slaves and under the control of Muslims. Then, to get closer to the sources of supply, Portuguese

Spanish explorers:
→ Columbus 1493–94
--→ Columbus 1498
·····→ Columbus 1502–04
·····→ Ponce de León 1512–13
→ Magellan & Elcano 1519–22

Portuguese explorers:
→ Dias 1487–88
→ da Gama 1497–98
→ Coelho & Vespucci 1501

Chinese explorers:
→ Zheng He 1405–33

English explorers:
→ Cabot 1497
→ Hudson 1610

French explorers:
→ Cartier 1534–35

Dutch explorers:
→ Barents 1596–97

— major empires c.1500
● Portuguese possessions c.1600
▨ areas of Portuguese sugar cane plantations
● Spanish possessions c.1600

ships, under the direction of Prince Henry (1394–1460), later called the Navigator, sailed down the coast of West Africa.

Henry had several motivations, only one of which was to defeat Muslim power over African trade routes. (He was inspired by legends of a Christian king, Prester John, sometimes said to rule in Mesopotamia, sometimes in Africa, who he thought would be an ally in his crusade.) Henry was also simply curious about the possibilities of oceanic exploration, and he believed it might be possible to reach India by sailing around Africa, although no one in Europe had any idea of the size and shape of that continent. Henry established a center for the study of navigation and shipbuilding at the southwestern tip of Portugal. His staff of experts tested existing navigational tools, such as the astrolabe and the compass, and created new geographical and mathematical tables.

World exploration, 1450–1600.
Spanish and Portuguese explorers and traders had established settlements in South America and the Caribbean by 1600, and commercial depots on the coasts of Africa, India, the Pacific islands, China, and Japan—at a time when English, Dutch, and French explorations of North America had just begun.

Slowly, Prince Henry's men attempted a series of explorations, each reaching just a little further down the African coast. Fearing the shoals, they sailed out to the west, into the ocean, and allowed the northern winds to blow them south. On an expedition in 1444 they captured some 200 Africans and brought them back to Portugal for sale as slaves. Prince Henry died in 1460, but the project continued. As the Portuguese expeditions rounded the hump of West Africa, they proved their profitability. They reached what the Portuguese called the grain coast, the ivory coast, the gold coast, and the slave coast—each named for its principal exports to Portugal. In 1488, Portuguese explorer Bartolomeu Dias (c. 1450–1500) reached the southern tip of Africa and turned northward for 300 miles. He would have continued onward—toward India—with his two caravels, but his crew refused to go further. The route, however, now lay open.

Dias' career intersected with that of Christopher Columbus (1451–1506). Columbus was in Lisbon seeking support for his intended exploration westward across the Atlantic just as Dias returned. Dias' report made clear that an alternative route to India had been found; there was no need to risk the transatlantic attempt. The Portuguese crown rejected Columbus' appeal, and so he went to the Spanish court, where he was received more favorably.

Crossing the Atlantic

By 1488, Columbus had already been trying for three years to gain backing for his venture. He was known in Portugal, for he had sailed on various Portuguese ships as far north as the Arctic Circle, south almost to the equator, east to the Aegean, and west to the Azores. Finally, in Spain he received the backing he needed from the newly merged thrones of Ferdinand of Aragon and Isabella of Castile. In his 1492 voyage, Columbus depended on two geographical estimates and he got both wrong. He underestimated the total circumference of the earth and he overestimated the total east–west span of the Eurasian continent. The globe was bigger than he thought, and so was the oceanic distance that he had to traverse. And nowhere in his figures was there the space for two continents of which he and the people of Europe knew nothing, despite Leif Eriksson's earlier voyages. When Columbus arrived in the Bahamas, he thought he had reached islands off the eastern coast of Asia. Although he found only a little gold, he believed—and promised his patrons—that an abundance of it yet awaited him. He promised also a virtually limitless supply of cotton, spices and aromatics, timber, and slaves. He characterized the people of the lands he had come upon as ready for conversion to Christianity. He reported all these observations in a letter addressed to Ferdinand and Isabella (see box p. 446).

Six months later Columbus embarked on a much larger expedition with 17 ships, 1,200 men (including six priests to carry on the work of conversion), and enough supplies to establish a permanent settlement. The expedition, however, yielded no serious commercial gains and it took Columbus two years to gain support for a third expedition, in 1498, with only six ships. For the first time, he landed on the continental landmass, in what is today Venezuela. Even at the end of his life, after yet another, fourth, voyage that brought him to Central America, Columbus recognized neither the enormity of his mistake nor the enormity of his discovery. He never realized that he had not found China, Japan, India, or islands off the coast of Asia. Nor did he realize that he had discovered a "New World."

Amerigo Vespucci (1454–1512) of Florence was the first person to recognize Columbus' error and his success. In 1499, sailing with a Spanish fleet after Columbus' third expedition, Vespucci traveled some 1,200 miles along the coast of South America. He recognized clearly that this was a continental landmass, but he did not yet realize which one. In a second voyage, 1501–02, this one under the flag of Portugal, he traveled some 2,400 miles down the coast of South America. He reported carefully on all that he saw: humans and their customs and tools, animals, plants, and hints of great treasures. Unlike Columbus, however, Vespucci was cautious: "The natives told us of gold and other metals and many miracle-working drugs, but I am one of those followers of Saint Thomas, who are slow to believe. Time will reveal everything" (Boorstin, p. 250). On his return to Spain, Vespucci was asked by Queen Isabella to establish a school for pilots and a clearing house for information brought back from the New World. In 1507 the clergyman and mapmaker Martin Waldseemüller published a new map of the world as known at the time, and on it he named the new western areas "America." In 1538, Gerardus Mercator published his large and influential map of the world designating two new continents as North America and South America. Vespucci himself died in 1512 of malaria, contracted on his voyages.

Crossing the Pacific

Only the eastern coast of the Americas was known to Europeans when Spaniard Vasco Nuñez de Balboa (1474–1517) followed the guidance of one of his Native American allies, crossed the Isthmus of Panama, climbed a peak, and, in 1513, became the first European to see the Pacific Ocean. Four years later, Balboa was falsely accused of treason against the king of Spain and was beheaded. With the recognition that the Americas were continental in size, and that another ocean lay

Vasco da Gama, **Portuguese School, c. 1524.** Gama's 1497–99 expedition on behalf of the Portuguese crown completed the sea link from Europe around Africa to India. On his next voyage, 1502–03, he established the policy of using military force to create Portuguese power in the Indian Ocean.

The Journal of Columbus' First Voyage to the Americas

Columbus kept a day-by-day journal of his first voyage. The original has been lost, but fortunately the priest Bartolomé de Las Casas (1474–1566) prepared an abstract, which he used in writing his own *Historia de las Indias*. Columbus' leading biographer in English, Samuel Eliot Morison, calls the abstract "The most important document in the entire history of American discovery." This account of what Columbus saw and how he related to it is written sometimes in the first person of Columbus, sometimes in the third person, as the voice of Las Casas. Note especially the overwhelming importance given to religion:

Prologue: Your Highnesses, as Catholic Christians and Princes devoted to the Holy Christian Faith and the propagators thereof, and enemies of the sect of Mahomet and of all idolatries and heresies, resolved to send me, Christopher Columbus, to the said regions of India, to see the said princes and peoples and lands and the disposition of them and of all, and the manner which may be undertaken their conversion to our Holy Faith, and ordained that I should not go by (the usual way) to the Orient, but by the route of the Occident, by which no one to this day knows for sure that anyone has gone …

12 October 1492: At two hours after midnight appeared the land, at a distance of two leagues … Presently they saw naked people, and the Admiral went ashore in his barge, and [others] followed. The Admiral broke out the royal standard, and the captains [displayed] two banners of the Green Cross, which the Admiral flew on all the vessels as a signal, with an F and a Y, one at one arm of the cross and the other on the other, and over each letter his or her crown … and said that they should bear faith and witness how he before them all was taking, as in fact he took, possession of the said island for the King and Queen …

15 October: It was my wish to bypass no island without taking possession, although having taken one you can claim all …

22 October: All this night and today I was here, waiting to see if the king here or other people would bring gold or anything substantial, and many of this people came, like the others of the other islands, as naked and as painted, some of them white, others red, others black, and [painted] in many ways … any little thing I gave them, and also our coming, they considered a great wonder, and believed that we had come from the sky …

1 November: It is certain that this is the mainland and that I am before Zayto [Zaytun] and Quisay [Hangzhou] [two great port cities of China], 100 leagues more or less distant the one from the other …

6 November: If they had access to devout religious persons knowing the language, they would all turn Christian, and so I hope in Our Lord that Your Highnesses will do something about it with much care … And after your days (for we are all mortal) … you will be well received before the eternal Creator …

12 November: Yesterday came aboard the ship a dugout with six young men, and five came on board; these I ordered to be detained and I am bringing them. Afterwards I sent to a house which is on the western bank of the river, and they brought seven women, small and large, and three boys. I did this because the [Indian] men would behave better in Spain with women of their country than without them …

27 November: Your Highnesses ought not to consent that any foreigner does business or sets foot here, except Christian Catholics, since this was the end and the beginning of the enterprise …

22 December: The Indians were so free, and the Spaniards so covetous and overreaching, that it was not enough that for a lace-tip or a little piece of glass and crockery or other things of no value, the Indians should give them what they asked; even without giving anything they [the Spaniards] wanted to get and take all, which the Admiral had always forbidden …

23 December: In that hour … more than 1000 persons had come to the ship, and that all brought something that they owned, and that before they come within half a crossbow shot of the ship, they stand up in their canoes with what they brought in their hands, saying "Take! Take!" (Morrison, pp. 41–179)

between them and Asia, Charles V of Spain commissioned Ferdinand Magellan (c. 1480–1521) to sail west, find a passage around the southern tip of South America, and proceed across the Pacific—no matter how long the voyage—and reach the Spice Islands of East Asia. Magellan set out in 1519 with five ships and about 250 sailors from several different European countries. The voyage became the first circumnavigation of the globe, yielding the first accurate picture of the full magnitude of the planet and completing the picture of most of its main contours. It took just 12 days less than three years. Only 18 men completed the trip. Magellan himself was killed in a skirmish with Mactan tribal warriors on the Philippine island of Cebu. Europeans became aware of Australia and its peoples in the 1500s, but did not map it carefully until the late 1700s.

Legacies to the Future: What Difference Do They Make?

Voyages of exploration, trade, conquest, and settlement evoke a sense of wonder at the skill and daring of the captains and sailors who embarked for the unknown with so few and such small ships and such limited equipment, and the foresight of the governments and businesspeople who organized and financed them. Each participant was called by a different set of values: the desire to chart the unknown; the pressure to find a new home; the quest for profit; the urge to proselytize; the lust for conquest; the competition for national superiority. Often, many of these motives were mixed together. The legacy of these people is the achievement of a geographically known and integrated globe. It is not, however, a single, simple legacy, but a variegated set of mixed legacies that includes competition, greed, self-righteousness, and violence. Few participants prepared for oceanic voyages with the greater good of the entire world at heart. Most, instead, sought benefits for themselves, their region or nation, or their religious group. They looked out on a huge and diverse world from relatively narrow and often self-interested perspectives.

By 1500 European traders had established a permanent connection between the eastern and western hemispheres for the first time, following Columbus' voyages across the Atlantic and Magellan's circumnavigation of the world. Inspired by the early explorations of Henry the Navigator around the west coast of Africa, Portuguese sailors rounded the Cape of Good Hope and opened new routes into the Indian Ocean. These explorations followed upon centuries of Western European economic expansion, national consolidation, and intellectual renaissance. Explorers were motivated by their mixed desire for knowledge, profit, national aggrandizement, and Christian proselytizing.

Asking Questions

- Of the groups—Polynesians, Malays, Indians, Chinese, Arabs, and Europeans— discussed in this chapter and in Chapter Twelve, why do you think that the Europeans were the first to circumnavigate the globe?
- How did the Portuguese displace the Arabs as the predominant maritime power in the Indian Ocean?
- Why do you think that Columbus could not, or did not, recognize that he had not reached East Asia? (There is no single correct answer to this question.)
- What were the demographic, economic, and social effects of the Black Death in the fourteenth century?
- What was the European Renaissance? To what did degree did it develop from contacts with non-European peoples?

Suggested Readings

KEY TERMS

Renaissance see p. 423

guild see p. 424

putting-out system see p. 428

ghetto see p. 430

medieval see p. 433

humanism see p. 436

PRINCIPAL SOURCES

Adas, Michael, ed. *Islamic and European Expansion* (Philadelphia, PA: Temple University Press, 1993). Key collection of historiographical essays on major topics in world history, 1200–1900. Articles by Eaton and Tucker on Islam, and McNeill on "gunpowder empires" are especially helpful for this section.

Boorstin, Daniel J. *The Discoverers* (New York: Random House, 1983). Extremely well written, engaging history of four kinds of invention and discovery. One is maritime, mostly European explorers and cartographers 1400–1800.

Chakrabarty, Dipesh. *Provincializing Europe: Postcolonial Thought and Historical Difference* (Princeton, NJ: Princeton University Press, 2000).

Chaudhuri, K.N. *Trade and Civilization in the Indian Ocean: An Economic History from the Rise of Islam to 1750* (Cambridge: Cambridge University Press, 1985). A survey of goods, traders, ships, regulations, and competition among those who sailed and claimed to control the Indian Ocean.

Crosby, Alfred W. *Ecological Imperialism: The Biological Expansion of Europe, 900–1900* (Cambridge: Cambridge University Press, 1986). The biological—mostly destructive—impact of European settlement around the world: a tragedy for native peoples from the Americas to Oceania.

Curtin, Philip. *Cross-Cultural Trade in World History* (Cambridge: Cambridge University Press, 1984). Classical statement of the significance and ubiquity of trade diasporas.

Landes, David S. *The Wealth and Poverty of Nations: Why Some are So Rich and Some So Poor* (New York: W.W. Norton, 1999). Credits the Western European world with creating the institutions that made its economic growth flourish.

McNeill, William H. *The Rise of the West: A History of the Human Community, with a Retrospective Essay* (Chicago, IL: University of Chicago Press, 1991). Reopened the professional field of modern history. Analyzed the basis of power, and those who created it, in global perspective, in each time period.

Wolf, Eric R. *Europe and the People without History* (Berkeley, CA: University of California Press, 1982). Laments history's emphasis on the powerful, and attempts to correct the imbalance by bringing into the historical record peoples who have been left out.

SECONDARY SOURCES

Aquinas, St. Thomas. *Summa contra Gentiles* and *Governance of Rulers* (excerpts) in *Introduction to Contemporary Civilization in the West*, cited below. Aquinas defined the field of thirteenth-century Roman Catholic theology—and beyond.

Bloch, Marc. *Feudal Society*, 2 vols. (Chicago, IL: University of Chicago Press, 1961). Classic, if dated, comprehensive view of the workings of feudalism in Western Europe.

Boccaccio, Giovanni. *The Decameron*, trans. Frances Winwar (New York: Modern Library, 1955). Delightful tales, set against the background of the Black Death, which raged through Western Europe in the 1340s.

Braudel, Fernand. *Capitalism and Material Life, 1400–1800*, trans. Miriam Kochan (New York: Harper and Row, 1973). Comprehensive survey of the beginnings of the modern capitalist system in Europe.

——. *The Mediterranean and the Mediterranean World in the Age of Philip II*, trans. Sian Reynolds (New York: Harper and Row, 2 vols, 1973). Magisterial work that introduces Braudel's concept of three complementary time frames in the study of history, short range, middle range, and *longue durée*.

Brucker, Gene. *Renaissance Florence* (Berkeley, CA: University of California Press, 1969).

Chaudhuri, K.N. *Asia Before Europe* (Cambridge: Cambridge University Press, 1990). Survey of the economic and political systems of Asia before the impact of colonialism and the Industrial Revolution. Comprehensive, comparative, and thoughtful.

Cipolla, Carlo. *Clocks and Culture, 1300–1700* (New York: W.W. Norton, 2003). Presents the technology of early clocks, and then credits them with increasing people's sensitivity to the importance of time, especially in the world of work.

Cohn, Samuel K., Jr. *The Black Death Transformed: Disease and Culture in Early Renaissance Europe* (London: Arnold, 2002). Studies and summarizes the research on the nature of the Black Death and its longer-term effects.

Columbia College, Columbia University. *Introduction to Contemporary Civilization in the West*, Vol. 1 (New York: Columbia University Press, 2nd ed., 1954). Very well-chosen, long source readings from leading thinkers of the time and place. Vol. I covers about 1000–1800.

Crosby, Alfred. *The Measure of Reality: Quantification in Western Europe, 1250–1600* (Cambridge: Cambridge University Press, 1997). By quantifying the processes of work and productivity, people gained greater understanding and control of them, and increased their efficiency.

Fernandez-Armesto, Felipe. *Columbus* (New York: Oxford University Press, 1991). Careful, sensitive biography of the man and his times.

Frank, Andre Gunder and Barry K. Gills, eds. *The World System: Five Hundred Years or Five Thousand?* (London: Routledge, 1993). In this somewhat tendentious, but well-argued, account, globalization is nothing new.

Gabrieli, F. "The Transmission of Learning and Literary Influences to Western Europe,' in Holt, P.M., Ann K.S. Lambton, and Bernard Lewis, eds. *The Cambridge History of Islam*, Vol. 2B: *Islamic Society and Civilization* (Cambridge: Cambridge University Press, 1970), pp. 851–89. Comprehensive summary of the influence of Islamic learning on Europe, especially good on contrasting different time periods.

The Hammond Atlas of World History ed. Richard Overy (Maplewood, NJ: Hammond, 1999). Excellent, standard historical atlas.

Havighurst, Alfred F., ed. *The Pirenne Thesis: Analysis, Criticism, and Revision* (Lexington, MA: D.C. Heath, rev. ed. 1969). Well-selected pieces from Pirenne, his critics, and supporters. Well introduced, supported, and summarized, although mostly European in orientation.

Hohenberg, Paul M. and Lynn Hollen Lees. *The Making of Urban Europe*, 1000–1950 (Cambridge, MA: Harvard University Press, 1985). Brief, but comprehensive text on the significance of cities to the history of Europe. Special attention to the social development of cities and their residents.

Kee, Howard Clark, *et al. Christianity: A Social and Cultural History* (New York: Macmillan, 1991). An accessible and insightful introduction to a huge subject.

Levenson, Jay A. *Circa 1492: Art in the Age of Exploration* (Washington, DC: National Gallery of Art, 1991). Catalogue of an astounding art exhibit, covering the arts in all the major regions of the world at the time of Columbus' voyages.

Lindberg, Carter. "The Late Middle Ages and the Reformations of the Sixteenth Century," in Kee *et al. Christianity*, pp. 257–423. Excellent survey.

Morison, Samuel Eliot, trans. and ed. *Journals and Other Documents on the Life and Voyages of Christopher Columbus* (New York: The Heritage Press, 1963). The crucial documents.

Nicholas, David. *The Evolution of the Medieval World* (New York: Longman, 1992). Useful survey.

Pirenne, Henri. *Medieval Cities: Their Origins and the Revival of Trade*, trans. Frank D. Halsey (Princeton, NJ: Princeton University Press, 1925). Classic statement of the importance of free merchants to the rise of commercial cities and the development of the modern world. Dated, and more limited than claimed, but pathbreaking and enormously influential.

Pirenne, Henri. *Mohammed and Charlemagne*, trans. Bernard Miall (New York: W.W. Norton, 1939). Key revisionist text citing the Islamic victories in the Mediterranean as the end of Roman Europe and the beginning of rebirth in the north under Charlemagne.

Polanyi, Karl, Conrad M. Arensberg, and Harry W. Pearson, eds. *Trade and Market in the Early Empires* (Chicago, IL: The Free Press, 1957). Fundamental argument by historical anthropologists that early trade was mostly regulated by rulers and priests.

Reynolds, Susan. *Fiefs and Vassals* (Oxford: Clarendon Press, 1994). Scholarly, influential examination of "feudalism," arguing that the word is misused to cover too wide a variety of regional and temporal patterns.

Subrahmanyam, Sanjay. *The Career and Legend of Vasco da Gama* (Cambridge: Cambridge University Press, 1997). The most thorough available account of the man, his contributions, and the historical puzzles surrounding them, presented in overwhelming scholarly detail.

Tuchman, Barbara. *A Distant Mirror: The Calamitous Fourteenth Century* (New York: Knopf, 1978). Engaging history of a century filled with war and plague.

Wills, John E., Jr. "Maritime Asia, 1500–1800: The Interactive Emergence of European Domination," *American Historical Review* XCVIII, No. 1 (February 1993), pp. 83–105. Survey of European entrance into and domination of Indian Ocean and Chinese sea lanes.

CHAPTER FOURTEEN

The Unification of World Trade

New Philosophies for New Trade Patterns
1500–1776

By 1500, ocean voyages of exploration and trade had bridged the eastern and western hemispheres, initiating a new phase of world history. Most regions of the world began to enter into a single system of trade and exchange.

In Western Europe, these overseas trade opportunities were restructuring public life, increasing the power of private businessmen. In other parts of the world, however, government continued to be a more formidable force, more important than private business. The largest city in Europe, for example, was not an Atlantic Ocean port but Constantinople (modern-day Istanbul), the capital of the Ottoman Empire. It, too, was an important commercial city, serving the eastern Mediterranean and the Middle East, but it owed its size—700,000 residents—and importance more to its political role than to its trade (which was, in any case, falling into the hands of foreigners). In India, China, and Japan government authorities generally dominated business interests. There were exceptions, but government control was the usual pattern.

Each major region of the world also had a very different experience in confronting the new international world system of trade being fashioned by the Europeans. The Americas, for example, succumbed almost immediately. The Chinese, on the other hand, remained somewhat independent of the system until the mid-nineteenth century, and in some ways China at first actually dominated the system. Even though the Chinese and Indians were not the shippers carrying the goods overseas, it was their products and their economies that evoked a very large proportion of international trade. Chinese products—especially tea, silk, and porcelain—were the objects of a great deal of the trade. The Europeans sailed in order to get them, as well as the spices and textiles of India and Indonesia; and to get gold and, later, some ten million slaves from Africa. Almost half the silver of the New World mines went to China to pay for exports to Europe. Asians and Africans may not have sailed as widely and aggressively as Europeans did after 1500, but it was the goods of Asia and Africa that motivated the European voyages.

The Birth of Capitalism

In Western Europe, a system of trade and exchange emerged, dedicated to the pursuit of private economic profit through the private ownership of wealth and the means of its production. The system took root in the textile workshops of Italy in the south and Flanders in the north, and soon extended to banking and international

KEY TOPICS
- The Birth of Capitalism
- The Empires of Spain and Portugal
- Trade and Religion in Western Europe
- The Nation-state
- Diverse Cultures, Diverse Trade Systems
- The Influence of World Trade: What Difference Does It Make?

Persian forces under Imam Quli Khan fighting to capture the port of Hormuz from the Portuguese. Miniature, seventeenth century. Since 1507, the Portuguese had controlled the port of Hormuz and, with it, the Persian Gulf, effectively blocking other countries from trading with Persia and the Mesopotamian region by sea. In 1622, British and Persian forces combined to remove the Portuguese garrison from Hormuz, opening trade and shifting the balance of power.

SOURCE

Adam Smith on Capitalism

By the late eighteenth century, as European economies were expanding, they became the subject of discussion and debate among businesspeople, political leaders, and philosophers. Adam Smith (1723–90) had already established his reputation as a moral philosopher before he turned to writing what became his most famous work. In 1776 Smith published *The Wealth of Nations*, a book of 1,000 pages, the first systematic explanation of a newly emerging philosophy of economics, later called capitalism.

In contrast to the mercantilist views of his day, Smith argued that national wealth was not to be measured by treasuries of precious metals, but rather by quantities of productivity and of trade. He opened his great work with an illustration from a pin factory where a division of labor into specialized tasks of production increased output dramatically. Smith further argued that when workers specialize in what they do best, and then exchange their products in the market, productivity increases. The competitive free market guides production: Goods that consumers want to buy attract higher prices, and producers supply them in order to earn good profits; unwanted goods earn no profits, and producers stop producing them. This law of supply and demand in the market, argues Smith, leads to the production of the amounts and kinds of goods that suit the wishes of consumers and the capacity of producers. According to Smith's Law of Accumulation, profits are reinvested in further production.

Smith reached a new and surprising conclusion: Wealth comes not from the command of a ruler, nor the regulations of the clergy, nor the altruism of members of the community, but as a result of people pursuing their own economic self-interest and exchanging the fruits of their labor in the market.

> It is not from the benevolence of the butcher, the brewer, or the baker that we expect our dinner, but from their regard to their self-interest. We address ourselves, not to their humanity, but to their self-love, and never talk to them of our necessities, but of their advantages. (Smith, p. 14)

Although Smith did not use the term, today we call the system he analyzed capitalism—that is, most wealth, or capital, rests in private, nongovernmental hands, and economic decisions on price, supply, and demand are made through the free market rather than by government decision. Critics of this capitalist market system, in which buyer and seller negotiate freely over prices, equated capitalism's self-interest with greed, but Smith explained how competition transformed self-interest into community benefit: If a greedy producer charges too much for his goods, someone else will undercut him and lower prices will result; if he pays his employees too little, they will abandon him and seek work elsewhere. Out of the conflicting self-interests of individual members of the society, paradoxically, social harmony will emerge. Smith, who was a professor of moral philosophy at the University of Edinburgh, disagreed with those who said that rulers or priests must regulate the economy to achieve equity. Like an "invisible hand," the impersonal market would do the job.

Believing that the free, unregulated market would correct most economic imbalances, Smith opposed government intervention. He argued for a hands-off government policy of laissez-faire toward the market—that is, let people do as they choose. But he did recognize that some necessities for economic growth were beyond the powers of any single, small producer. "The erection and maintenance of the public works which facilitate the commerce of any country, such as good roads, bridges, navigable canals, harbors, et cetera, must require very different degrees of expense" (Vol. 5, p. 1), and therefore Smith urged government to promote these public works. He believed that education was fundamental to economic productivity. Private education was more effective than public education, but government-supported public education was better than none.

Smith recognized, of course, that the market did not always succeed in balancing supply and demand. Huge businesses that formed virtual monopolies could control whole industries and manipulate market forces. Their size gave them unfair leverage and Smith wanted them broken up. *The Wealth of Nations* attacked the British East India Company, the joint stock company that monopolized virtually all of Britain's trade in Asia and had even become the acting government of Bengal in India. Smith argued that its monopoly should be broken. His plea, however, did not bring about a change.

Capitalism was the prevailing economic philosophy in Britain in the years of its economic supremacy in the nineteenth century, and the new system spread to many other countries as well. As we shall see in the following chapters, many critics blamed capitalism for the inhumanity and cruelty of the slave trade, the seizure of colonies overseas, and the vulnerability of workers at home. Smith understood these problems, but argued that they were corruptions of the market system rather than natural products of it. He condemned slavery as a form of kidnapping and theft of human beings, rather than a free-market exchange. Similarly he deplored the European destruction of the native American states and populations as a violation of human ethics:

> The savage injustice of the Europeans rendered an event which ought to have been beneficial to all ruinous and destructive to several of those unfortunate countries. (Smith, p. 416)

trade. Through the power of their wealth, that is, their capital, and of their collective organization, the owners of these workshops, the bankers, and the traders began to develop the economic system that we now call **capitalism**.

Capitalism claimed to allow individuals to exchange their products and labor in free, unregulated markets. It fought off the restrictive rules of church and government. It argued instead that in a free-market exchange the prices of goods and of labor would result from the balance between supply and demand. These market prices would serve as a message to producers and consumers, alerting them as to what the market did and did not want at the moment. The lure of the market would encourage people to risk investing their accumulated wealth in economic activities that might earn profits (although they might also suffer losses).

Despite these free-market claims, and their desire to be free of regulation, capitalists frequently persuaded governments to support and assist them in their money-making projects. In exchange, capitalists lent their financial support to government. In cities such as Venice, in the thirteenth century, capitalists gained control of the economy, as the city grew to a population of nearly 200,000. By the 1300s, through banking and trade, they gained control of the government of the city of Florence, with its 100,000 residents. Capitalist philosophies began to overcome more restrictive economic philosophies.

Major Western European governments had been following principles of **mercantilism**, the belief that government should regulate trade—especially by restricting the outflow of gold and silver—for the greater strength of the state. Slowly these governments were persuaded that allowing businessmen more freedom of trade would in fact benefit the state even more by generating more taxable wealth. Capitalists and governments worked together to achieve the goals of both: protection and encouragement for the businessmen, taxes for the state.

Western European businessmen led in sponsoring new international trade initiatives that emphasized private profit and national aggrandizement. As a result, the trading centers of northwestern Europe grew ever larger. By 1700, London had a population of 550,000; Paris, 530,000; Lisbon, 188,000; and Amsterdam, 172,000. Each of these cities was both a national capital and a major trading center. Economic and political interests reinforced one another.

The Empires of Spain and Portugal

The first European nations to dominate the new overseas trade and colonization, however, were Spain and Portugal, countries in which business communities were relatively weak. Here political rulers made the principal economic decisions. Both countries faced directly on the Atlantic Ocean. Portugal's rulers saw the Atlantic as their front door. Spain's rulers, just consolidating their country in 1492, saw it as a route to riches, power, and proselytizing.

Spain's New World Conquests

The four voyages of Christopher Columbus between 1492 and 1504 revealed to the Spanish crown some of the opportunities for agricultural development, religious conversion, and exploitation of resources in gold and silver to be found in the Americas. Spanish settlers began to colonize the islands of the Caribbean and the north coast of South America. In response to tales of great riches, Spanish *conquistadores* marched inland to conquer what they could. In 1519, Hernán Cortés began his expedition from Veracruz with 600 Spaniards, a few guns, and 16 horses.

KEY TERMS

capitalism An economic system characterized by private or corporate ownership of the means of production and by private control over decisions on prices, production, and distribution of goods in a free, competitive market of supply and demand.

mercantilism An economic policy pursued by many European nations between the sixteenth and eighteenth centuries. It aimed to strengthen an individual nation's economic power at the expense of its rivals by stockpiling reserves of bullion, which involved government regulations of trade.

conquistadores The Spanish soldiers who invaded and conquered the kingdoms of the New World, especially in Mexico and Peru.

AT A GLANCE: THE INTERCONNECTING WORLD

DATE	EUROPE	THE AMERICAS	ASIA AND AFRICA
1500	• Communero revolt in Spain (1520–21) • Luther excommunicated (1521)	• Four voyages of Christopher Columbus (1492–1504) • Cortés conquers Tenochtitlán (1521)	• Portuguese establish trading posts in East Africa (1505) • Portugal captures Goa, India (1510) • Portuguese missionaries arrive in China (1514)
1525	• Henry VIII becomes head of new Anglican church (1534) • First stock exchange in Antwerp (1538) • Calvin establishes Presbyterian theocracy in Geneva (1541)	• Pizarro captures Inca emperor Atahualpa (1532) • Potosí silver mine discovered (1545)	• Mughals invade India (1526) • St. Francis Xavier arrives in Japan (1549)
1550	• Council of Trent (1545–63) • End of Hundred Years War (1558) • Tobacco first introduced into Europe (1559); potato (c. 1565)	• Portuguese begin sugar cultivation in Brazil (c. 1560)	• Akbar consolidates Mughal Empire (1556–1605) • Spanish capture Manila, Philippines (1571) • Portuguese establish colony in Angola (1571)
1575	• Spanish Armada defeated by England (1588) • Henry IV of France issues Edict of Nantes (1598)		• Matteo Ricci arrives in China (1582) • Japan invades Korea (1592)
1600	• Dutch, English, and French East India Companies founded • The Netherlands win independence from Spain; Bank of Amsterdam established (1609)		• Tokugawa shoguns begin consolidation of Japan (1603) • Christianity outlawed in Japan (1606) • Dutch found Batavia (Jakarta), Indonesia (1619)
1625	• Portugal declares independence from Spain (1640) • Russia captures Siberia (1649)		• Manchus conquer China and form Qing dynasty (1644)
1650	• English Navigation Act (1651) • Louis XIV of France, the "Sun King" (1643–1715)		• Dutch capture Cape of Good Hope (1652)
1675	• War of the League of Augsburg (1688–97) • Bank of England created (1694)		• Qing dynasty establishes "Canton system" (1683)
1700	• Peter the Great founds St. Petersburg (1704) • War of the Spanish Succession (1702–13) • Act of Union creates Great Britain (1707)		• Edo, Japan, has one million people
1725	• War of Austrian Succession (1740–8)		
1750	• Seven Years War (1756–63) • Adam Smith, *The Wealth of Nations* (1776)	• War of American Independence (1775–81)	• After English victory at Plassey, English gain Bengal (1757)

Because the Aztecs under Moctezuma II dominated and plundered the various tribes living in the surrounding region, Cortés was joined by thousands of Native Americans who wished to overthrow the powerful Aztec empire at Tenochtitlán, modern-day Mexico City. Cortés' small force entered the city without a struggle, possibly helped by a woman, Malinche or Marina, who became his mistress and translator. The peace didn't last, however, and after the Spaniards massacred several Aztec leaders during a festival, the population revolted. They killed Moctezuma, believing that he had collaborated with Cortés, and they forced the *conquistadores* out of the city. Cortés suffered heavy losses, perhaps as many as two-thirds of his men and several horses, but the Spaniards reached Tlaxcala, where their new Native American allies nursed them back to health and helped them retake Tenochtitlán. The Spaniards conquered the capital city again in 1521 after a bitter four-month siege, and the empire fell to them. In the next 20 years they captured the Yucatán and most of Central America, although revolts continued in the region. Cortés became ruler of the Kingdom of New Spain, reorganized in 1535 as the Vice-Royalty of New Spain.

In South America, Vasco Nuñez de Balboa found a portage across the Isthmus of Panama in 1513. Now the Spanish could transport their ships from the Atlantic coast overland across the Isthmus and sail south along the Pacific Coast to Peru. Rumors of great stores of gold encouraged these voyages to the Inca Empire. Like the Aztecs, the Inca were divided. In 1525, after the death of Huayna Capec, possibly from smallpox, a civil war broke out between two of his sons—Huáscar and Atahualpa—over who should rule the empire. Fighting was fierce and ended only in 1532, when Atahualpa captured Huáscar and executed him. In the same year, Francisco Pizarro, leading a force of some 200 men, captured Atahualpa. Although given a room full of gold as ransom for the emperor's life, Pizarro feared a revolt and killed him. In 1533 he captured the Inca capital, Cuzco. The Spanish *conquistadores* fought among themselves for years until Spain established the Vice-Royalty of Peru in the mid-sixteenth century as the South American counterpart to the Vice-Royalty of New Spain in the north. Revolts against the Spaniards continued until they captured and beheaded the last Inca emperor, Tupac Amarú, in 1572.

Emperor Atahualpa arrested by Francisco Pizarro in 1532. When Pizarro landed on the northern coast of Peru on May 13, 1532 he brought with him a force of 200 men with horses, guns, and swords. The Inca emperor Atahualpa, backed up by thousands of troops, felt he had little to fear from the Spanish and, as this contemporary Peruvian drawing shows, he accepted Pizarro's seemingly friendly invitation to meet accompanied only by his bodyguards. It was a trap, and Pizarro arrested and later executed him. (Compare this picture to the picture on p. I-15 of Cortés and the Aztecs in Mexico.)

Why the Inca and Aztec Empires Fell. How had a few hundred Spanish soldiers and their Native American allies succeeded in overthrowing the two largest empires in the Americas? The answer has four parts. First, as we have seen, the conquered Native Americans were not a single united people, but many different, competitive, and even warring peoples. In conquering the dominant groups—Moctezuma's Aztecs in Mexico and Atahualpa's Inca in Peru—the Spanish found many allies among the enemies of these groups. In addition, the Inca were weakened by their own civil war. Second, unlike the Native Americans, the Spanish possessed firearms, steel armor and weapons, and horses—animals never before seen in the Americas. The Spaniards also fought differently from the indigenous populations, shooting their guns from a distance rather than engaging in the hand-to-hand warfare practiced by the Aztecs. Third, the Aztecs and Inca were demoralized when their commanders-in-chief were captured. The two Indian empires were highly centralized, and the removal of their leaders left them disorganized. (Less centralized and more remote groups, like the Araucanians of central Chile, held out far longer, *encomienda* A concession from the Spanish crown to a colonist, giving the colonist permission to exact tribute from a specified number of Native Americans living in a specific area. Conditions were cruel and the Spanish attempted to convert the Indians to Christianity.

repartimiento A system by which the Spanish crown allowed colonists to employ Indians for forced labor. Conditions were virtual slavery.

mit'a A system of forced labor in Peru, begun under Inca rule, by which indigenous communities were required to contribute a set number of laborers for public works for a given period. Conditions were virtual slavery.

hacienda A large rural estate in Spanish America, originating with Spanish colonization in the sixteenth century.

winning a revered place in Latin American history and poetry.) And, finally, Native Americans had no immunity to European diseases, such as smallpox, that were new to the Americas. The diseases proved far more deadly than the warfare.

Legend once had it that the Indians viewed the invading Spanish as gods. In this telling, the Spanish gods were returning to their homelands and were therefore deserving of obedience, rather than resistance. Recent scholarship has dispelled this as a fiction created by the Spanish.

Making the Conquests Pay. After the conquests, the Spanish began to reorganize the economies of the Americas. They established the *encomienda* system, assigning the taxes and the labor of local Indian populations to Spanish colonists who were also to convert them to Christianity, if possible. The Native Americans were enslaved under conditions of great cruelty. The *encomienda* system was first established on the island of Hispaniola, where in 20 years the native population fell from several million to 29,000. Humane voices, especially of priests such as Bartolomé de Las Casas, opposed the *encomienda* system, but it continued until so many Indians had died that it could no longer function. In most of Mexico and Peru the system had ended by the late 1500s, but it operated for another century in Venezuela; for another two centuries, until 1791, in Chile; and until the early 1800s in Paraguay.

The systems that replaced it were not much more humane. The *repartimiento* system in central Mexico and the similar *mit'a* system in Peru forced the local population into low-paid or unpaid labor for a portion of each year on Spanish-owned farms, in mines and workshops, and on public works projects. These systems, too, were forms of unofficial slavery. Not all labor was coerced, however. Spanish-owned plantations or *haciendas*, agricultural estates producing commercial crops and livestock, employed both free and indentured labor. The *haciendas* often produced commercially the newly imported products of the eastern hemisphere— wheat, cattle, pigs, sheep, chickens, horses, and mules—in addition to the indigenous local crops of maize, potatoes, and manioc (cassava).

Inca–Spanish wooden drinking vessel, Peru, c. 1650. This painted Inca ritual drinking vessel made of wood, known as a *kero*, represents people of three different cultures: to the left, an Inca dignitary; in the center, a Spaniard playing a trumpet; and on the right, one of the earliest depictions of a black African in South America, a man playing a drum.

Perhaps the worst conditions existed in silver mines, which also used paid labor at very low wages. The immense Potosí mine in Upper Peru (today's Bolivia) employed 40,000 Native American miners in the seventeenth century. Tunnels destroyed the landscape, and working conditions were inhuman. Children were put to work, forced to crawl through cracks into the mines and to labor without breaks.

From the Spanish perspective, the most valuable products of the Americas throughout the sixteenth century were gold and silver. The mine at Potosí, discovered in 1545, was the largest silver mine in the world. Smaller mines were opened in Mexico in 1545 and 1558. In 1556 a new method of separating silver from ore by using mercury, available from Almadén in Spain, was discovered. (The toxic qualities of mercury were not known at the time.) Between 1550 and 1800 Mexico and South America produced more than 80 percent of the world's silver and more than 70 percent of its gold.

The precious metals were exported each year from Latin America eastward to Europe and westward to the Philippines, where the Spanish had captured Manila in 1571 and established it as their chief trade center for East Asia. They were ultimately used to pay for purchases of silks, tea, textiles, and spices from India and China. Between one-third and one-half of all American silver produced between 1527 and 1821 found its way to China. The Mexican peso became a legal currency in China. Asian traders demanded payment in gold and especially silver because Europe itself produced very little of interest to them.

Plan of Potosí and the Cerro Rico (Rich Hill), Upper Peru. This seventeenth-century painting shows Potosí and the hills in which the lucrative silver mines were located. The mines at Potosí employed some 40,000 poorly paid Indian laborers and tens of thousands of horses—shown in this painting ascending and descending the hills—to transport the material and drive the machinery.

Merchant Profits. The gold and silver mines of the Americas, which brought enslavement and poverty to the Native Americans, benefited the Spaniards themselves less than they did the merchants of Antwerp, Genoa, Amsterdam, London, and Paris. The Spanish did not have the commercial infrastructure to employ their newly captured resources in profitable investments, and they lacked the ships to carry the trade generated by the new finds of gold and silver. The experienced merchants of the trade cities of Europe organized the necessary commercial services. They exchanged the raw metals for cash and bills of exchange, provided loans to tide over the period from the arrival of one shipment of silver to the next, arranged the purchase of goods needed by the Spanish, and supplied the necessary shipping. In the sixteenth century, the most important of these commercial centers was Antwerp (Belgium), with its skilled and wealthy merchants from Antwerp and from England, France, Portugal, Italy, Spain, and Germany.

Warfare and Bankruptcy. Many regions of Europe at this time were "owned" by particular families, who had the responsibility to protect them and the rights to tax them and bequeath them to others. These families often intermarried, in which case sometimes whole countries changed rulers. Spain's Charles V (r. 1515–56) inherited Spain and the Spanish colonies in Africa, the Americas, Naples, and Sicily from his mother's parents, Ferdinand and Isabella. From his father's family, the House of Burgundy, he inherited the Netherlands and the German lands owned by the Habsburg family. Charles became the most powerful ruler in Europe.

Raised in Flanders, Charles V spoke no Spanish, and his pride and foreignness alienated the Spanish. He appointed foreign courtiers from Flanders to offices in Spain, and he used Spanish wealth to fund his political programs in central European territories. Spaniards revolted. The nobles wanted to stop the drain of money to central Europe and the assignment of offices to foreigners. They wanted Charles to return to Spain. As civil order broke down, artisans and business classes in Castile revolted against the great landholders in the Communero revolt of 1520–21. The revolutionaries held conflicting goals, however, and as they fought one another to exhaustion Charles easily retained his hold on government.

But when Charles entered into wars against the Ottoman Turkish Empire in eastern Europe and on the Mediterranean, and into Christian religious wars in northern and central Europe (see next section), he bankrupted even the silver-rich treasury of Spain. After Charles' abdication in 1556, his son Philip II (r. 1556–98) continued the politics of warfare and suffered much the same fate. Even Philip's military victories were financial defeats.

Portugal's Empire

Isabella and Ferdinand united their thrones, creating modern Spain, in 1492, but the western third of the Iberian peninsula, Portugal, remained a separate state. (For 60 years, from 1580 to 1640, it was incorporated into Spain, but otherwise it has remained separate until today.) In terms of worldwide exploration and trade, Portugal, under the leadership of Prince Henry the Navigator, who sponsored many voyages along the coast of Africa, had entered the field earlier and more vigorously than Spain (see Chapter Thirteen).

The Portuguese in Africa. Portugal sought souls for Christianity, gold for its national treasury, grain and fish for its domestic food supply, and slaves for its new sugar plantations. Portuguese entrepreneurs, having seen sugar plantations in the eastern Mediterranean, planted their own on Madeira and other islands in the Atlantic Ocean off the coast of Africa. (Spanish landlords and businessmen did the same in the Canary Islands.) These new plantations needed laborers. Portugal went to Africa to obtain them.

As the Portuguese explored Africa they also built fortresses—such as El Mina in modern Ghana—as assembly and shipping points for their purchases of slaves and gold. For the most part, the Portuguese remained in their coastal enclaves of fortresses, trading posts, and Christian missionary outposts. At some points, however, the Portuguese did venture inland to explore, trade, evangelize, and attempt to conquer. From El Mina, on the Gold Coast, for example, they went inland to trade directly with Mane and Soninke merchants. In the Kingdom of Kongo, they converted King Nzinga Mbembe (1507–43) and many of his people to Christianity, although the Portuguese slave trade in the Kongo ultimately alienated the people from their king. King Mbembe wrote to the king of Portugal that the slave trade was destroying the Kingdom of Kongo as its people turned predatory toward one another. He wanted

The fortress of São Jorge da Mina (later called El Mina), African Gold Coast, 1482. Built at the order of King John II of Portugal in 1482, this fortress—like many others—provided a fortified trading post designed both to protect Portuguese trade from rival Europeans and to serve as a supply base. At the beginning of the sixteenth century trade was in gold and kola nuts with imports of American crops such as maize and cassava, and trans-shipment of slaves. It was not until the late seventeenth century that the export of slaves became the main trade on the Gold Coast. The European traders remained mostly in such fortresses along the coast, and relied on African traders to bring goods from the interior to them.

the trade stopped, on humanitarian grounds. His plea was ignored. The Portuguese, and the Kongolese themselves, desired the profits of the trade.

In Angola, on the west coast, the Portuguese went directly inland to bring slaves to the coast, and claimed the region as their colony in 1484. By 1500, Lisbon was receiving some 1,500 pounds of gold and 10,000 slaves each year from West Africa. On the east coast of Africa, the Portuguese sacked the Swahili trading city of Kilwa to gain control of the Indian Ocean trade, and claimed Mozambique for its rich gold supplies. Although the Portuguese mostly stayed in coastal enclaves like Sofala, and established an outpost on Mozambique Island, they also traveled inland along the Zambezi River.

The Portuguese in Brazil. In 1500, a Portuguese expedition headed for India was blown off course in the Atlantic and landed in Brazil. The Portuguese claimed the land but did little to develop it until pressed by competition from other European powers. By the mid-sixteenth century they had established some coastal towns, including a colonial capital at Salvador, introduced Jesuit missionaries, and planted the first of the plantations that would make Brazil the first of the huge plantation colonies in the Americas. By 1700 Brazil had 150,000 slaves—half its total population—working its sugar plantations.

By this time, other nations, such as Spain, had developed sugar plantations in the Caribbean, contesting Brazil's leadership and undercutting prices and profits. In 1695, however, gold and diamonds were discovered in the interior mountains of Brazil (in the state later named Minas Gerais, General Mines), and by the mid-eighteenth century Brazil was mining some 3,000 tons of gold each year, mostly through slave labor. Unfortunately, as often happens with windfall profits from the discovery of raw materials, Portugal and Brazil spent the profits on goods from other countries, especially Britain, without developing new economic enterprises of their own. When the gold began to run out in the mid-eighteenth century, Brazil and Portugal found themselves in debt to Britain, and hooked on British imports, but without further means of paying.

The Portuguese in the Indian Ocean. Throughout the sixteenth century, even taking into account the emerging sugar profits from Brazil, Portugal's main overseas interests lay in Asia. In 1498 Vasco da Gama had extended Portugal's voyages of exploration eastward. Departing from the east coast of Africa, with the assistance of a local pilot who knew the route, he sailed into one of the world's liveliest arenas of trade, the Indian Ocean and the west coast of India. Almost immediately the Portuguese introduced armed violence into trade relations that had been peaceful. In 1500 an armed Portuguese expedition sailed under Pedro Alvarez Cabral (c. 1468–1520) under instructions from the government to establish a fort and trading post at Cochin, India, to promote relations with other "Christian kingdoms" in India, and to impede Muslim shipping to the Red Sea. Cabral had numerous armed engagements with ships in the Indian Ocean and in ports on India's southwest coast. In fighting at Calicut, 54 of Cabral's men were killed and substantial goods were lost. In response, Cabral bombarded Cochin, killing between 400 and 500 people and destroying considerable goods and property.

When da Gama returned on his second voyage in 1502 he came with 21 armed ships to assert Portuguese power. At the height of their Indian Ocean power, Portugal held some 50 ports, with Goa serving as their Indian Ocean capital. To the extent that they could enforce it, the Portuguese forced ocean traders to pay them a tax of passage—previously unheard of—and demanded that they put into port at Portuguese centers, especially Goa. The Portuguese were making money as much from their own kind of piracy as from trade. Their reputation for violence spread.

By 1600, however, it became clear that the Portuguese could not maintain their coercive system. Many of their own merchants operated as private traders despite the official state monopoly; Portuguese officers were often corrupt; their military was not well disciplined; and they lacked the manpower to actually enforce the controls that they asserted over Indian Ocean traders. Most of all, the much larger ocean-going nations of England and France, and the Netherlands as well, entered the Indian Ocean waters in substantial force, and tiny Portugal was no match for them. Portugal remained in the east, but only as a minor power.

The Spanish and the Portuguese Empires: An Evaluation

Those who claim that Europe's wealth was built on the exploitation of people overseas certainly have some justification, but the experiences of Spain and Portugal demonstrate that exploitation alone was not enough. To build and sustain wealth, countries must be able to use wealth effectively. They must conceive and implement policies of economic growth. They require banks and instruments of exchange to store and transmit money. They need commercial intelligence to create and evaluate strategies for investing capital sensibly and profitably. They must develop efficient means of transporting goods and people. They must not allow their commercial aims to be excessively deflected by warfare. Both Spain and Portugal lacked these facilities. Furthermore, both were hierarchical societies where prestige belonged to those in the aristocracy. It was common in both Spain and Portugal to use mercantile wealth to buy into the nobility and purchase land, and then cease to engage in trade and commerce. Thus, both countries built enormous global empires based on their ocean explorations, but by the end of the sixteenth century both these empires were on the wane, first challenged and then surpassed by countries that established successful commercial communities.

Culturally, Spain and Portugal were far more successful. The influence of their languages and cultures remains dominant in Latin America today, and they continue to have an effect on areas as far-flung as the Philippines (for Spain) and Angola, Mozambique, Goa, and tiny Macao (for Portugal). But as economic and political powers, Spain and Portugal, despite their early, extraordinary successes, were soon eclipsed by the commercially astute nations of northwestern Europe.

Trade and Religion in Western Europe

Spain's King Charles V and his son Philip II fought wars explicitly devoted to matters of religion. These wars siphoned off the vast treasures that Spain brought from the Americas and diverted her from economic and commercial growth. To understand the choice that Spain made for religious warfare, we must analyze the competing claims between Catholics and Protestants that divided Western Europe in the sixteenth and seventeenth centuries. We will also consider scholarly arguments over the extent to which religious philosophies have a direct impact on national economic development. (See box on Weber and Tawney on Religion and Capitalism, p. 465.)

The first European trading empires, about 1750. European sea-borne intercontinental trade was dominated by Spain and Portugal in the sixteenth century. The Spanish rapidly colonized Central America, the Andes Mountain regions, and the Philippines. The Portuguese concentrated on the coasts of Brazil, East and West Africa, and the Arabian Sea ports of India. A century later the Dutch, English, and French followed, establishing settler colonies in North America and South Africa and fortified trading posts along the coasts elsewhere. Compare with the maps on pp. 608 and 609, noting the expansion of European empires.

461

indulgences In the Roman Catholic Church, the remission from the punishments of sin, obtainable through good works or special prayers and granted by the Church through the merits of Christ and the saints. In the sixteenth century, the Church began to sell indulgences, precipitating the reforms of Martin Luther.

The Protestant Reformation

Catholicism had won the hearts, spirits, and tithes of the overwhelming majority of the population of Western and central Europe. By 1500 the Roman Catholic Church had become so wealthy and powerful that several reformers charged the Church with straying from Jesus' early simplicity and his message of compassion for the poor.

Martin Luther (1483–1546), a pious German monk who lived in a monastery in Wittenberg and taught in the university there, shared these criticisms of the Church's wealth and further asserted that the Church claimed too much power over individual conscience. Luther doubted the importance of most of the sacraments and the authority of the Church. He kept his doubts private, however, until in 1517 a friar came to Wittenberg selling **indulgences**. These were pardons, marketed by the Church, offering individuals exemption from punishment for their sins in exchange for donations to the Church. Outraged, Luther posted on the door of the castle church his Ninety-Five Theses, statements of his belief, asserting that faith alone justifies the believer in the eyes of God. Priests, he wrote, were not needed to mediate between humans and God. Only God had the power to absolve people of their sins. Pressed by Church authorities to recant, Luther refused, declaring, "it is neither right nor safe to act against conscience."

When Pope Leo X excommunicated Luther, several local rulers in Germany protected him. They used the occasion to assert their independence of Charles V, who was not only king of Spain but also Holy Roman Emperor, with powers over Germany. (From this time, Luther often aligned himself with local rulers. When a revolt of peasants against their landlords swept Germany in 1524, Luther urged the local princes to suppress the revolt by force, and thousands were killed.) The kings of Denmark and Sweden and many of Germany's princes adopted Luther's doctrine (called Lutheranism in America), and this region of northern Europe became the heartland of the new denomination. Printing presses using movable type, introduced into Europe by Johannes Gutenberg about 1450, helped to spread the new message

John Calvin weighing the Bible against popish pomp. Woodcut. Calvin had studied the writings of the first generation of reformers such as Martin Luther and accepted without question the idea of justification by faith alone and the Biblical foundation of religious authority. This contemporary woodcut shows him weighing what he saw as the extraneous ceremonial trappings and overweening bishops of the Catholic Church against the simple truth of the Bible.

while Luther's new German translation of the Bible made the sacred text available to ordinary readers who could not read Latin, the language of earlier Christianity, and freed them from dependence on priestly readings and interpretations.

In Geneva, Switzerland, John Calvin (1509–64) preached another doctrine of reform. Like Luther, Calvin spoke of justification by faith alone and of the supremacy of individual conscience, and he denied the authority of the Church. Calvin went beyond Luther, though, in arguing that God grants his grace to whomever he chooses, regardless of individual behavior. Unlike Luther, Calvin rejected alliances with government, although he did create a religious community that dominated the government of the city of Geneva. Calvinism spread widely in Western and central Europe, and in New England, without the patronage of any political authority. (In the United States Calvinism is the dominant faith of Presbyterianism, named for its elected leaders, or presbyters.)

A third major strand of reform arose in England, where King Henry VIII (r. 1509–47) broke from the Church, not for reasons of doctrine, but to claim authority over the entire Catholic establishment within England—churches, monasteries, and clergy—and to gain for himself a divorce, which the Church had

The Reformation in Europe.
The tide of religious reform was felt throughout Europe and changed its political map. The early commitment of most of northern Europe to Calvinism, Lutheranism, or Anglicanism was counterbalanced by the recovery to Catholicism of France and Poland. Counter-Reformation zeal, combined with political confrontation and dynastic rivalry, culminated in the Thirty Years War (1618–48), fought across Europe's heartland at enormous cost.

463

forbidden, from the first of his six wives. Henry had no doctrinal quarrel with Rome. He simply wanted to head the English Church himself, and in 1534 Parliament named him "Protector and Only Supreme Head of the Church and Clergy of England," a title that was passed on in slightly modified form to later English sovereigns. In England, Henry's new church was called Anglican. (Its members in the United States are called Episcopalians.)

Each of the three reform movements rejected the authority of the pope, stressed the freedom of individual conscience in matters of faith, and permitted their clergy to marry. Collectively, these various protests against the power and doctrine of the Catholic Church were called Protestantism, or the **Protestant Reformation**.

The Counter-Reformation. Its religious monopoly challenged, the Catholic Church countered with the Council of Trent, a gathering of Church authorities who met irregularly for 18 years, from 1545 to 1563, to address questions of Church doctrine and internal reform. The Council reaffirmed the basic doctrines of Catholicism. It reasserted the necessity of the celibacy of the clergy and encouraged greater religious devotion among them. And it created new religious orders to purify the Church and transmit its teachings. The Society of Jesus, founded in 1534 by Ignatius Loyola (1491–1556), was especially dedicated to education, secular as well as religious, and to carrying the message of the Church around the world. From 1540 Francis Xavier (1506–52) introduced the Jesuit vision to India, Indonesia, and Japan, baptizing thousands of new Christians. In Paris in 1625, Vincent de Paul (1581–1660) began his work among the wretched of the slums, a humanitarian mission that continues around the world today.

The Catholic Church was fighting for an international, universal vision of the world under its own leadership. Meanwhile, the various Protestant movements encouraged separate national states. In response, several of the new national states encouraged the Protestant movement.

Spanish Defeats

Inspired by Protestant doctrines and chafing under Spanish rule, the Netherlands, including today's Holland and Belgium, rose in revolt against control by the Habsburg family. Although geographically small, they were among the wealthiest of Philip's possessions. They were offended by the excessive quantity and deficient quality of the Spanish administrators sent to govern them. They also feared that Philip would extend to the Netherlands and all non-Catholics the **Spanish Inquisition**, a royal court originally established to combat Judaism in Spain.

Many of the peoples of the Netherlands had abandoned Catholicism for new Protestant movements, and many Protestants from other countries had come seeking asylum. In the Netherlands, Protestants and Catholics had reached an accommodation and neither community wished to see that harmony destroyed by the Inquisition. Philip's government refused to pay attention, and the Netherlands erupted in fury. A civil war ensued in which thousands were killed, property was destroyed, and churches were desecrated. By 1576, however, the Netherlands had suffered enough, and representatives of all the Netherlands united across religious lines to expel the Spanish.

In the same year, Queen Elizabeth I of England (r. 1558–1603), the daughter of Henry VIII, publicly aligned her country with the rebels in the Netherlands and began to pursue a policy of alliance with Protestant forces throughout Europe. In reply, Philip II prepared to invade England. In 1588 the Spanish Armada set sail for England with 130 ships, 30,000 men, and 2,400 pieces of artillery. In an astonishing

KEY TERMS

Protestant Reformation The movement, in sixteenth-century Europe, in which Luther, Calvin, Henry VIII, and others broke away from the Catholic Church.

Spanish Inquisition A court established with the consent of the Vatican to search out and punish Jews who claimed to have converted to Christianity but were still secretly practicing the Jewish religion, which had been outlawed in Spain in 1492. Subsequently the Inquisition, which was not bound by civil law and which employed torture, also turned against Christians who were not properly observant.

Weber and Tawney on Religion and Capitalism

The social scientist Max Weber (1864–1920), writing *The Protestant Ethic and the Spirit of Capitalism* in the early twentieth century, argued that Protestantism's emphasis on individual achievement and divine grace tended to promote economic enterprise and capitalism. Weber claimed that Protestant ministers urged their followers to demonstrate their virtue through devotion to thrift, discipline, industriousness, and business.

> Striving for wealth is objectionable only when it has the aim of a carefree and merry existence. But as exercise of duty in a calling it is not only morally permitted but actually commanded … Worldly Protestant asceticism acted effectively against the spontaneous enjoyment of wealth; it limited consumption, especially that of luxuries. On the other hand, it eliminated traditional inhibitions against the acquisition of property; it burst the bonds of the profit motive by not only legalizing it, but even viewing it as directly willed by God … He desired rational and utilitarian use of wealth for the purposes of the individual and the community. (Columbia University, pp. 84, 89)

According to Weber, Protestantism encouraged entrepreneurs to dedicate themselves to making money and laborers to finding satisfaction in hard work.

> The bourgeois entrepreneur could, and felt that he ought to, follow his economic self-interest in the certainty of being in God's good grace, and of being visibly blessed by Him. This remained true as long as he observed the formal rules of the game, kept his morals spotless, and did not make objectionable use of his wealth. In addition, the power of religious asceticism made available to him sober, conscientious, eminently capable workers who regarded their labor as their divinely ordained purpose in life. Even more, it gave him the comforting assurance that the unequal distribution of the goods of this world was the direct consequence of God's Providence which followed out His unknown aims by these distinctions as well as by this selective show of grace. (Columbia University, p. 93)

Weber extended these arguments to assert that, ultimately, Protestant religious leaders had made the pursuit of profit through hard work into the essence of religion.

Subsequent authors, however, notably the British social historian R.H. Tawney, rejected Weber's arguments. Capitalist thought and practice had preceded Protestantism, and some Catholic areas, such as northern Italy and parts of France, were strongly capitalistic, while some Protestant areas, notably in north Germany, were not. "There was plenty of the 'capitalist spirit' in fifteenth-century Venice and Florence, or in south Germany and Flanders, for the simple reason that these areas were the greatest commercial and financial centers of the age, though all were, at least nominally, Catholic" (Tawney, p. 262, n. 32). It was difficult to show any historically consistent correlation between religious doctrines and economic policy.

Tawney's most significant quarrel with Weber, however, was over Weber's argument that religion had ceded the central place in life to the pursuit of economic gain, at least temporarily. Weber was not pleased with this transformation, but he claimed to observe it. Tawney, on the contrary, argued that moral issues concerning the welfare of the entire society always underpin economic ones. They never become secondary.

> A reasonable estimate of economic organization must allow for the fact that, unless industry is to be paralyzed by recurrent revolts on the part of outraged human nature, it must satisfy criteria which are not purely economic … natural appetites may be purified or restrained, as, in fact, in some considerable measure they already have been, by being submitted to the control of some larger body of interests. (Tawney, p. 233)

Debates over the relationship between religious doctrine and business practice continue unabated and unresolved today in relation to religion in general and to all major religions in particular. These debates continue also outside the Western world. Today when East Asian economies are flourishing, Confucian traditions are praised for encouraging development. A century ago, the same traditions, interpreted differently, had been blamed for a lack of development.

- Can you cite examples of religious sentiments influencing economic actions?
- Can you cite examples of economic actions having no relation to religious, moral, or social concerns?
- Do you side with Weber's argument that to a large degree the pursuit of economic growth has taken precedence over religious, moral, and social concerns? Or would you agree with Tawney that, in the long run, economic issues must always be subordinated to larger issues?

reversal, the Armada was destroyed by the English and by a fierce storm, which was quickly named "the Protestant wind."

Spain entered a century-long decline. The northern Netherlands won its independence in 1609, although Spain did not acknowledge it until 1648, after years of intermittent warfare. In 1640 Portugal, which had been united with Spain since 1580, declared its independence once again, and constituent units of Spain, especially Catalonia in the northeast, fought costly, if unsuccessful, wars for independence. Philip III (r. 1598–1621) and Philip IV (r. 1621–65) were incompetent rulers; Charles II (r. 1665–1700) was mentally incapable of ruling. Finally, about mid-century, the stream of silver from the Americas dried up, dwindling from 135 million pesos in the decade 1591–1600 to 19 million in 1651–60. Spain had squandered a fabulous windfall of silver and gold. England, France, and the Netherlands emerged as the rising powers of Europe; their self-confidence and their economies flourished; and their merchant classes organized to travel the world.

The Dutch Republic: Seaborne Merchant Enterprise

In the early seventeenth century, the Dutch had the most efficient economic system in Europe. The Dutch Republic bordered the North Sea and lived from its largesse. Fishing was its great national industry. One out of every four Dutch persons was reliant on the herring industry—catching, salting, smoking, pickling, and selling. Others depended on cod fishing and whaling. Using windmills to pump water from low lands enclosed in dikes, the Dutch reclaimed land from the sea—364,565 acres between 1540 and 1715—and from inland lakes—another 84,638 acres. With such an investment of capital and effort the Dutch worked their land carefully and efficiently. They developed new methods of crop rotation, planting turnips in the fall to provide winter food for humans and sheep. At other times of year they raised peas, beans, and clover to restore nitrogen to the soil. With these cropping patterns, the Dutch no longer had to leave one-third of their land fallow each year. They farmed it all, increasing productivity by 50 percent. In addition, the Dutch established one of the largest textile industries in Europe, based on wool from their own sheep and on huge quantities imported from England.

On the seas and in the rivers, the Dutch were sailing 10,000 ships as early as 1600, and for the next century they dominated the shipping of northern Europe. From the Baltic they brought timber and grain to Amsterdam and Western Europe. In exchange, from the ports of Portugal, Spain, and France they carried salt, oil, wool, wine, and, most of all, the silver and gold of the New World. Often they warehoused in Amsterdam the trade goods en route to other ports, earning additional profits on the storage. They used substantial amounts of the timber themselves to build the most seaworthy, yet economical, ships of the day.

The Dutch also developed commercial institutions to underpin their dominance in trade. The **bourse**, or stock exchange, was opened in Amsterdam in the mid-sixteenth century as the Dutch were gaining control of the Baltic trade, and it was reopened in 1592 as they captured a dominant role in supplying grain to Mediterranean countries. In 1598 they initiated a Chamber of Insurance; in 1609 the Bank of Amsterdam was established. This bank accepted coins from all over the world, assessed their gold and silver content, and exchanged them for gold florin coins that were fixed in weight and value and became the standard everywhere. The Dutch government guaranteed the safety of deposits in the national bank, thereby attracting capital from throughout Europe. Depositors were able to draw checks on their accounts. For two centuries, until the French Revolution in 1789, Amsterdam was the financial center of Europe.

KEY TERM

bourse Another name for stock exchange, especially in Europe.

In 1602 Dutch businessmen founded the Dutch East India Company, a joint stock company dedicated to trade in Asia. The Company captured several Portuguese ports, but concentrated on the most lucrative of all the East Asian centers, Java and the Moluccas, the Spice Islands of today's Indonesia. In 1619 the Dutch East India Company founded Jakarta, which served as its regional headquarters until 1950 when Indonesia won its independence. In 1623 they seized Amboina in the Moluccas, killing a group of Englishmen they found there, and forcing the English back to India. The profits from these possessions reinforced Dutch economic precedence in Europe.

In 1600 a group of Dutch traders reached Japan. In 1641, all other foreigners were expelled, but, because they did not engage in missionary activity, the Dutch were permitted a small settlement on Deshima Island, off Nagasaki, and for two centuries they were the only European traders allowed in Japan. In 1652, the Dutch captured from the Portuguese the Cape of Good Hope, at the southernmost tip of Africa and established there the first settlement of Afrikaners, South Africans of Dutch descent.

In the Americas, the Dutch West India Company raided the shipping of the Spanish and the Portuguese, and then founded their own rich sugar plantations in Caracas, Curaçao, and Guiana. For a few decades they held Bahia in Brazil, but the Portuguese drove them out in 1654. In North America they established New Amsterdam on Manhattan Island.

Despite their commercial skill and success, the Dutch could not ultimately retain their supremacy. The English Navigation Act of 1651 permitted imports to England and its dependencies only in English ships or in those of the exporting country, and this effectively restricted Dutch shipping. Three indecisive, draining

The Return to Amsterdam of the Dutch East India Fleet, **Andries van Eertvelt, 1599.** In 1602 the Dutch East India Company was granted a monopoly over Dutch trade and authorized to seize control of the Portuguese trade routes in the Indian Ocean. The company owned a fleet of ships armed with cannon which carried pepper, indigo, raw silk, saltpeter, and textiles from India to Western Europe. In the later 1600s, large-scale exports of textiles were also carried from India to Africa in payment for slaves going to the Caribbean. (Johnny Van Haeften Gallery, London)

SOURCE

National Joint Stock Companies: Instruments of Trade and Colonization

National joint stock companies were one of the key commercial innovations of Dutch, French, and British financiers in the seventeenth century, giving them an enormous advantage in overseas trade. Forerunners of the modern business corporation, the companies sold stock publicly, sometimes for a single expedition, more commonly for all the expeditions and activities of the company. Financiers invested in expectation of the great profits that might come from successful shipping ventures. Their potential losses and liabilities were limited to the value of their investment; the rest of their personal property was protected. Individual states gave legal charters to these companies in expectation of the benefits of trade for the country. These national companies were chartered for expeditions throughout the world. Those headed toward the Americas were designated "West India Companies," those toward Asia were "East India Companies." The companies of each state usually saw themselves in competition with each other, sometimes leading to armed struggle. And their missions included colonization, and sometimes proselytizing, as well as trade.

The government "Edict Providing for the Establishment of a Company of the West Indies," establishing the French West India Company in 1664, is representative of the aspirations of the state and of the merchants looking to the Americas for both settlement and trade:

> We have recognized that colonial trade and navigation are the only and true means of raising commerce to the brilliant position it holds in foreign lands; to achieve this and to stimulate our subjects to form powerful companies we have promised them such great advantages that there is reason to hope that all those who take interests in the glory of the State, and who wish to profit by honorable and legitimate means will willingly participate … but as it is not sufficient for these companies to take possession of the lands which we grant them, and have them cleared and cultivated by the people they send there at great expense, if they do not equip themselves to carry on … commerce … it is also absolutely necessary, in order to carry on this trade, to provide numerous ships to carry each day the goods which are to be sold in the said countries, and bring back to France those which they export. (Columbia College, *Contemporary Civilization*, I:815–20)

Investment in the Company was open to foreigners as well as to native-born French. The Company was "obliged to introduce into the lands granted above, the number of clergy necessary for preaching the Holy Gospel, and instructing these peoples in the faith of the Catholic, Apostolic and Roman religion; and also to build churches." It also had many of the attributes of a sovereign state:

> The said Company may build forts in all places it shall judge necessary for the defense of the said country … may arm and equip for war such number of vessels as it shall deem fitting for the defense of the said countries and the security of the said commerce … may negotiate peace and alliances in our name, with the Kings and Princes of the countries where it wishes to establish its settlements and trade … and, in case of insult, declare war on them, attack them, and defend itself by force of arms (ibid).

In the Indian Ocean, trade in spices was a large part of the Companies' business. Between them the British and Dutch East India Companies carried 13.5 million pounds of pepper to Europe in the peak year of 1670, the British share mostly from India, the Dutch share from Indonesia. Other goods included indigo, raw silk, saltpeter, and, increasingly, Indian textiles. There were also large-scale exports of textiles carried by Europeans from India to Africa in payment for slaves going to the Caribbean.

The Companies' ships were armed. Their representatives established fortresses and trading centers on the coasts of Asia and of the Americas, and the Companies became, in effect, miniature governments. Malachy Postlethwayt's *Universal Dictionary* of 1751 wrote that the Dutch East India Company

> makes peace and war at pleasure, and by its own authority; administers justice to all … settles colonies, builds fortifications, levies troops, maintains numerous armies and garrisons, fits out fleets, and coins money. (cited in Tracy, *The Political Economy of Merchant Empires*, p. 196)

In India, in the seventeenth century, the British, French, and Dutch East India Companies set up trading posts within towns. Until the end of the century, the Mughal emperors and local governments generally welcomed the foreign traders as means of stimulating the Indian economy through trade and enriching the government through taxes. Following its victories at Plassey in 1757 and Buxar in 1765, however, the British East India Company became the *de facto* government of the province of Bengal in India—with the rights of collecting taxes and the responsibility for providing order and administration. The Company's holdings continued to expand until it was effectively the ruler of almost all of India. The British government regulated the East India Company from its founding in 1600, and finally disbanded it and took over direct rule of India after the Indian revolt of 1857.

wars followed, from 1652 to 1674. Additional years of warfare on land against France further exhausted Dutch resources. In 1700 the Dutch Republic had a population of 2 million people; at this time the population of the British Isles was 9 million, and that of France 19 million. An aggressive, skilled, small country simply could not continue to compete with two aggressive, skilled, large countries.

France: A Nation Consolidated

In the second half of the sixteenth century, France endured four decades of civil warfare because the crown was unable to control the various factions, religious groups, and regions of the country. Struggles between Catholics and Protestants, called Huguenots in France, helped to fuel the warfare. So, too, did the desire of the nobles to have more independence from the king. In 1589 Henry of Navarre, a Huguenot, came to the throne as Henry IV (r. 1589–1610). Recognizing the importance of Catholicism to the majority of the French people, he joined the Catholic Church with the apocryphal comment, "Paris is worth a Mass." In 1598, however, hoping to heal the schism between the religious communities, he issued the Edict of Nantes, which gave Protestants the same civil rights as

Indian cotton cloth, late seventeenth century. This detailed portrayal of Dutch traders suggests that they have come from far across the seas to trade in a rich array of goods. The Indian gentleman on the far right may find the Dutch doffing of caps and handshakes a strange form of greeting, quite different from the form used in India of joining one's hands in the "namaste" salutation.

Catholics. He was not entirely successful, however, and, indeed, was assassinated by a Catholic militant. His successor, Louis XIII (r. 1610–43), following the advice of his chief minister, Cardinal Richelieu, built up France's armies, cultivated allies among France's neighbors, and encouraged his nobles to invest in trade by land and sea. Internally he captured several Huguenot strongholds in France and concluded a truce with these French Protestants. Externally he joined with Protestant rulers in Sweden, the Netherlands, and parts of Germany to defeat the Catholic Habsburg Empire and increase the stature of France.

Louis XIV, in an extraordinarily long and forceful reign (r. 1643–1715), made France the most powerful country in Europe. Under the Sun King, as Louis was known, France set the standard throughout Europe for administration, war, diplomacy, language, thought, literature, music, architecture, fashion, cooking, and etiquette. Although they had been slower than other European countries to enter transoceanic trade, the French now began to assert a global presence, trading in India, Madagascar, the American Great Lakes, and the Mississippi River; establishing colonies in the West Indies; and staking a claim to Canada. By 1690 Louis XIV had raised an army of 400,000 men, equal to the combined armies of England, the Habsburg Empire, Prussia, Russia, and the Dutch Republic. At this time, the French navy was also larger than the English, with 120 ships of the line (warships) compared to the English navy's 100. Also, as we have seen, in 1700, France had a population of 19 million, more than double that of the British Isles.

Louis XIV boasted "L'état, c'est moi" ("I am the state"), by which he meant that the powers of the state rested in him alone. His leading religious adviser, Bishop Jacques-

Bénigne Bossuet (1627–1704), linked the king's power to divine right, asserting that "Royalty has its origin in the divinity itself." Louis XIV continued to assert the right of the king to appoint the Catholic clergy in France, and in 1685 he revoked the Edict of Nantes in the belief that a single, dominant religion was more important than the toleration of minorities within his kingdom. This act cost France the services of many of its Huguenot artisans, who fled to the Netherlands and Britain.

Economically, Louis XIV's chief economic adviser, Jean-Baptiste Colbert (1625–96), pursued a policy of mercantilism—fostering the economic welfare of his own state against all others—by strengthening state control over the national economy even more aggressively than had Richelieu. To facilitate trade, he abolished local taxes on trade throughout central France (a region as large as England), although his government was not powerful enough to do away with these internal tariffs throughout the entire country. Colbert established a Commercial Code to unify business practice throughout the country. To improve communication and transportation, he built roads and canals, including a link between the Bay of Biscay and the Mediterranean. He set quality standards for hand manufacturers and gave financial incentives to the French manufacturers of such luxury goods as silks, tapestries, glass, and woolens. Meanwhile, the needs of the army created huge national markets for uniforms, equipment, and provisions. All these policies benefited private business as well as the state. Nevertheless, many businesspeople, who sought greater freedom of trade, rejected the mercantilist assertion that the export of gold and silver weakened the national economy and that state monopolies should dominate certain economic fields, including much of foreign trade.

The growth of French military and economic strength disturbed the **balance of power** among the leading states of Europe and precipitated a series of wars. The War of the League of Augsburg, 1688–97, and the War of the Spanish Succession, 1702–13, reduced France's power when she was forced to cede to Britain the North American colonies of Newfoundland and Nova Scotia and all French claims to the Hudson Bay territory. Britain began to pull ahead in overseas possessions.

Britain: Establishing Commercial Supremacy

In the same wars, Britain won from Spain the *asiento*, the right to carry all the slave cargoes from Africa to Spanish America, plus one shipload of more conventional goods each year to Panama. These officially recognized trading rights also provided cover for British ships to engage in the business of piracy and smuggling, which flourished in the Caribbean, where buccaneers preyed on Spanish commerce.

In the eighteenth century the most valued properties in the Americas were the sugar-producing islands of the Caribbean. In the Atlantic the most valuable trade was in human cargo—the slaves who worked the sugar plantations. In Asia, control of sea lanes and of the outposts established by the various East India companies was the prize.

Competition for dominance in all three regions continued between the French and the British through three more wars in the eighteenth century: the War of Austrian Succession, 1740–48; the Seven Years War, 1756–63; and the War of American Independence (the American Revolution), 1775–81. These wars demonstrated the importance of sea power, and here Britain triumphed. Around 1790, the French population outnumbered the British 28 million to 16 million, and French armies outnumbered the British by an even greater ratio, 180,000 to 40,000. But the British navy had 195 ships of the line, compared with France's 81.

Suffering defeats at sea, the French retreated from their colonial positions. In the Peace Settlement at Paris in 1763, at the end of the Seven Years War, they turned over their immense, but thinly populated, holdings in North America east of the Mississippi to the British, and those west of the Mississippi to Spain. They kept their rich, sugar-producing islands in the Caribbean: Saint-Domingue (Haiti), Guadeloupe, and Martinique. In India, although they lost out in other locations, they kept Pondicherry on the southeast coast and a few additional commercial locations. The French navy was deployed against the British in America during the American Revolution, but it was completely crushed during the Napoleonic Wars. The British, though they lost the 13 colonies of the United States in 1783, triumphed everywhere else because of the great strength of their navy. They held Canada. They held their islands in the Caribbean. They increased their holdings in India, and they dominated the sea lanes both across the Atlantic Ocean and through the Indian Ocean.

Institutionally, Britain surpassed all other European countries, even the Netherlands, in supporting sophisticated economic enterprise. Recognizing the importance of a stable currency, England had fixed the value of the pound sterling in 1560–61 at 4 ounces of silver, and maintained that valuation for two and a half centuries. Britain surpassed Amsterdam as the center of Europe's international trade. The Bank of England, created in 1694, could transact its business with a currency of fixed value. Moreover, Britain never defaulted on her debts and so earned the trust of the international financial community. In times of war as well as peace, Britain could borrow whatever sums she needed. Politically, Britain developed a new system of constitutional monarchy after 1688 that gave strong support to private commercial interests, as we shall see in more detail in Chapter Fifteen. The French later ridiculed Britain as "a nation of shopkeepers," but geographically, militarily, institutionally, politically, and agriculturally, the British were building the capacity to become the most effective businessmen in the world. They were building a nation-state and a capitalist economy.

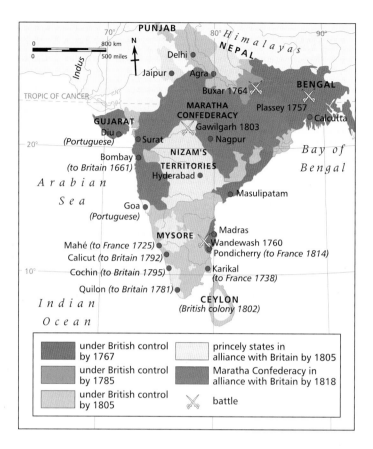

British power in India to 1818.
The weakening of the Mughal Empire created a situation that was exploited by the British and French East India Companies. They created strategic alliances with local independent princes and competed for power on land and sea. With Clive's victory at Plassey (1757) the English gained Bengal, a power base that allowed them to expand steadily, but their control over India was not secure until their final defeat of the Maratha confederation in 1818.

The Nation-state

The term "**nation-state**" is generally used to describe a politically sovereign state with a socially cohesive population. The *state* occupies a geographic territory, is administered by its own independent government, and controls adequate size and force not to be swallowed up by another. The *nation* is based on some combination of shared language, religion, history, ethnicity, future aspiration. Usually the nation also defines itself, in part, in terms of its relationships with other nation-states. Nation-states may emerge from the break-up of larger empires—which may contain several nations within themselves—or from the coalescence of small units into larger ones through conquest or merger. Both these processes had been continuing in Western Europe for centuries. Small units, like the region around Paris under Hugh Capet, were expanding into states, while large units, like Charlemagne's empire, were dissolving.

KEY TERM

the other Using the term "the other" establishes a relationship between two individuals or groups that define themselves in terms of contrast with one another. Normally the definition implies that one has most of the virtues, and "the other" has most of the vices. Occasionally the word is used in verb form, "othering," meaning the process of defining "the other" in negative terms, and oneself in terms of positive virtues.

The nation-states of Europe developed relatively efficient central governments that were capable of collecting taxes, keeping the peace, and raising and deploying armies and navies effectively in waging war. Their authority was generally recognized and accepted—even welcomed—by most of the people within their borders. That authority was different in different nation-states: England, France, and Portugal were monarchies; the Netherlands was ruled by a coalition of businessmen; Spain was a part of the larger Habsburg Empire.

Nation-states took an interest in the economic welfare of their people, although here, too, different states adopted different policies at different times, some capitalist, some mercantilist but with independent merchants, some state-controlled. They engaged in external, overseas trade and commerce and, in this period of time, colonization. The development of overseas trade and colonization was a large part of their transformation from small, locally governed units into nation-states. They also defined themselves by their relationship to one another—generally competitive, often hostile, sometimes belligerent.

By the mid-1700s the nation-states of Western Europe had become the object of both fear and emulation. They were feared because of their economic and military powers. They could, and did, fight wars, conquer territories, create colonies, and dominate trade networks. Some societies feared these new nation-states and kept them at arm's length as long as they could. China and Japan, for example, remained essentially closed for centuries. Other governments emulated them, to develop the strength to resist them even while becoming more like them. This was the response of Russia under Peter the Great (see p. 474).

In their competition over trade routes and colonies around the world, the nation-states of Europe came to define themselves in relation to one another and in relation to the other civilizations with which they were engaging. This self-definition in terms of "**the other**" is certainly not the only element in the definition of the nation-state, but it is important. Moreover, as the European nation-states encountered other peoples around the world, these peoples too began to redefine themselves politically and culturally. This encounter evoked many different responses. In the rest of this chapter we shall consider some of the most important in this early era of European trade and colonial expansion.

Diverse Cultures, Diverse Trade Systems

In Western Europe the business classes were thriving, gaining a measure of legal independence from government, and winning the sanction of those governments to carve out global trading networks. Individual nations were often at war with one another, and, in the process, they redrew specific national borders, and then consolidated them into nation-states. This pattern was by no means universal.

In most other parts of Eurasia, huge polyglot empires, composed of diverse peoples speaking diverse languages, were more typical than small nation-states. Their emperors usually allowed trade and traders to flourish, but only under imperial supervision or outright control. The empires of Russia, the Ottomans, the Mughals, the Chinese (under the Ming and Qing dynasties), Japan, and Southeast Asia provide case studies of various styles of political rule and relationships between rulers and merchants. As Europeans arrived, these empires had to design policies to deal with them. Some of the empires were losing control of their own administrations as European traders gained increasing power in Asia. Others saw the threat of overwhelming European economic invasion and took precautions to avoid that fate.

Russia prepared new ports to take advantage of new possibilities, but also built up its armaments to assure that it would not lose control. China and Japan chose instead to shut the European traders out.

Russia's Empire under Peter the Great

At the end of the seventeenth century Russia had little direct contact with the market economies of northwestern Europe. The country was geographically remote by land, and by sea its principal ocean port was Archangel (Arkhangelsk) at the extreme north, on the White Sea, ice-bound for most of the year. The foreign trade that did exist was carried by foreign ships traveling Russia's great rivers, especially the Volga. Russia belonged to the Greek Orthodox branch of Christianity, so communication with the Church of Rome and its Western European networks was also limited. Mongol rule had oriented Russia's ties more toward central Asia than toward Western Europe. Finally, to the west, Russia was surrounded by generally hostile neighbors: Swedes, Poles, Germans, and Lithuanians.

Russia began to take its modern form only after Ivan III (r. 1462–1505) overthrew Mongol domination in 1480. Muscovy, the territory around Moscow, became the core of an expanding independent state. At first, Russia expanded southeastward, defeating the khanate of Astrakhan in 1556 and capturing the Volga River basin south to the Caspian Sea with its access to the silk trade of Persia. It also expanded eastward all the way to the Pacific (1649), capturing Siberia and its rich population of fur-bearing animals; their pelts became one of Russia's principal exports.

The expansion of Russia, 1462–1881. By the end of the fourteenth century, Mongol forces in Russia were destroyed, mostly by Timur, and Russia began expansion which took it all the way from its center in Moscow, westward to the Baltic Sea, and eastward across Siberia to the Pacific Ocean. The territories gained by Peter the Great were especially important, not because of their size but because they included the strategic warm-water port that became St. Petersburg. Catherine's conquests took Russia further into Europe in the west, and to the Black Sea in the south.

The Principality of Moscow c.1300	Vasily III (1505–33)	Alexis (1645–76)	Elizabeth (1741–62)	Nicholas I (1825–1855)
The Grand Principality of Moscow 1462	Ivan IV the Terrible (1533–84)	Peter I the Great (1682–1725)	Catherine II the Great (1762–96)	Alexander II (1855–1881)
Ivan III the Great (1462–1505)	Michael Romanov (1613–45)	Anna (1730–40)	Alexander I (1801–1825)	acquired (1533–1689)

serf An agricultural worker or peasant bound to the land and legally dependent on the lord. Serfs had their own homes, plots, and livestock, but they owed the lord labor, dues, and services. These services could be commuted to rent, but serfs remained chattels of the lord unless they were emancipated, or escaped. Serfdom declined in Western Europe in the late medieval period, but persisted in parts of eastern Europe until the nineteenth century.

Peter the Great. Alarmed by the growing power of his Western European neighbors and by Russia's relative weakness, Peter the Great undertook to modernize his country, especially its military, economic, and cultural life. He built his program, however, on the backs of Russia's serfs.

Because of its isolation and foreign rule, Russia had only a tiny urban trading class and very few big city markets. As late as 1811, only 4 percent of its population was urban. The overwhelming majority of its people lived as **serfs**, bound not directly to specific owners, but to specific land and its landlords, with little possibility for economic, social, or geographic mobility. After 1675 landlords gained the right to sell serfs off the land, even to urban owners. Occasional serf uprisings, such as that led by Stepan Razin (Stenka Razin; d. 1671) in 1667, were brutally suppressed, and the gulf between free persons and serfs increased.

When Peter I, the Great (r. 1682–96 as co-emperor, or tsar, with his half-brother; 1696–1725 as sole emperor), became sole emperor, he saw Sweden as his principal external enemy. Sweden already held Finland and the entire eastern shore of the Baltic, bottling up Russia without any Baltic port. Worse, in a crushing blow, 8,000 Swedish troops defeated 40,000 Russians at the Battle of Narva in 1700. Humiliated, Peter set out to construct in Russia a powerful state based on a powerful army and navy. In 1697, traveling under an assumed name in order to evade royal protocol, Peter embarked on a "Grand Embassy of Western Europe," especially England and the Netherlands, but also Baltic ports and the Holy Roman Empire. He searched for allies for the wars he expected against the Turks as Russia pushed toward the Black Sea; he gathered information on the economic, cultural, and military-industrial practices of the Western European powers; and for several months he even worked as a ship's carpenter in Amsterdam.

Impressed by the strength of the Western European countries, Peter invited military experts from the West to Russia to train and lead his troops. He bought Western European artillery and copied it. He established naval forces and reorganized the army along Western lines, in uniformed regiments, armed with muskets. He promoted metallurgy, mining, and textile manufacture, largely as means of supplying his troops. By 1703–04 Peter had started to build a new capital, an all-weather port and "window on the West," in St. Petersburg, on land that he conquered from Sweden. Commercially, geographically, and architecturally, he designed St. Petersburg as a Western city. In the construction of the city 30,000 people died from disease, drowning, or lack of food.

In 1709, when Sweden again invaded Russia, Peter was prepared. He retreated until the Swedes fell from the exhaustion of pursuing him through the severe Russian winter. Then, holding his ground at Poltava in south Russia, he defeated the remaining Swedish troops. The Swedish army was finished as an imperial force, and Russia began to seize additional Baltic possessions.

Peter's goals for Westernization were not exclusively military. He wanted Russia to be counted among the powers of Europe, and this would require cultural and economic ties as well. Peter required Western-style education for all male nobles. He established schools for their children, and sent many to study in Western Europe. He demanded that aristocrats acquire the morals and tastes of Europe's elites. He made them abandon their Russian dress in favor of the clothing of Western Europe, and he forced the men to shave or trim their beards in the Western style. He introduced "cipher schools" for teaching basic reading and arithmetic, established a printing press, established and edited Russia's first newspaper, and funded the Academy of Sciences, which opened in 1724, a year before his death. Collectively, all these revolutionary reforms drove a wedge between the nobility and the mass of Russians.

Economically, Peter pushed for the creation of new enterprises. He built a fleet on the Baltic and encouraged exports. He organized new companies headed by groups of Russians and foreigners, and supplied them with working capital and serf laborers. He accepted the mercantilist concept of an economically strong state and saw no role for a free market in achieving it. To finance these state-organized initiatives, Peter introduced heavy taxes, which fell especially severely on the peasantry.

No democrat, Peter demanded loyalty and obedience to himself. He created a new system of administration with himself as head. He brought the Eastern Orthodox Church under state control and subordinated its clergy to his authority. He streamlined local and central government. He created a new "state service," including both civil and military officials, and made appointments to it completely without regard to family status, birth, or seniority. Foreigners could serve within this service, serfs could be elevated, and nobles could be demoted. All depended on performance. In 1722 he introduced a new Table of Ranks, which automatically gave noble status to officials who reached the eighth position out of 14. The newly elevated nobility were the chief administrators of his new policies of Westernization. These revolutionary moves did not survive long after Peter's death.

Peter strengthened the economic and political position of the ruling classes, the landowners, and the rising urban professional and business classes, while exploiting the peasantry ruthlessly. He allotted to the nobility some 175,000 serfs and 100,000 acres of land in the first half of his reign alone. Conscription, programs of forced labor, a poll tax, and indirect taxes on everything from beekeeping to salt provoked two major uprisings in the Russian interior between 1705 and 1708. Peter suppressed them brutally. An iron-willed autocrat, Peter brought his nation into Europe and made it an important military and economic power, but millions of Russians paid a terrible price.

Peter achieved many of his goals, establishing a strong central administration, a powerful military, some commercial enterprise, international trade connections, and diplomatic contact with the nations of Western Europe. He did not, however, free Russia's merchants to carry on the kinds of independent economic activity characteristic of Western European commerce. He kept the largest enterprises, like weapons manufacture and shipping, in the hands of the state. Considered an **enlightened despot**—a ruler who advanced new concepts of intellectual inquiry and legal rights, at least for the nobility, but held on to power for himself—Peter died in 1725. Since he had killed his own son rather than permit him to sidetrack reforms, Peter was succeeded for two years by his wife and then by other family members.

In 1762 Catherine II, the Great, assumed the throne by overthrowing Tsar Peter III, her husband. She ruled for 34 years. Catherine won especially important victories over Poles and Turks, expanding the borders of Russia to the Black and Caspian Seas. Despite her pronouncements calling for greater freedoms for her people, she proved

The Founding of St. Petersburg, Bartolomeo Carlo Rastrelli, Russia, 1723. This bronze relief commemorates the founding of St. Petersburg in 1704. Peter the Great intended his capital to be an all-weather port and a "window on the West." As part of his drive for Westernization he decreed that the aristocracy must abandon their Russian dress in favor of European clothes. The garb of the men depicted here indicates clearly that the edict was already in place. (Hermitage, St. Petersburg)

KEY TERM

enlightened despotism A benevolent form of absolutism, a system of government in which the ruler has absolute rights over his or her subjects. The term implies that the ruler acts for the good of the people, not in self interest.

Idris Giving Instruction to Mankind on the Art of Weaving, **Mughal period, c. 1590.** In the Islamic tradition, the mythical Idris gives instruction and protection to pious and skilled weavers. Here weavers wash, dry, spin, skein, and weave their wool, while courtiers present rolls of cloth for inspection. Most production was localized, as suggested here, although a few examples of large, well-organized workshops, with wage labor and centralized management, mostly under the control of Mughal courts, also existed. When pressured, weavers organized in boycotts and strikes to resist the exactions of rulers and merchants, and to defend the honor of their religion.

at least as despotic as Peter the Great. After brutally suppressing a revolt by hundreds of thousands of serfs led by Yemelyan Pugachev (1726–75), she reduced the already low status of Russia's own serfs and expanded the burden of serfdom onto the peoples of the newly conquered lands as well.

Ottomans and Mughals

Two powerful empires, the Ottoman and the Mughal, were rising in Asia at about the same time as Spain and Portugal were advancing in Europe and overseas. Indeed, there was some connection. In 1600 all four empires were approaching the height of their powers. By 1700 all were in severe decline because of overextension, draining warfare, weak state systems, and lack of attention to technological improvements, especially in the military. All four also allowed control of their economic affairs to fall into the hands of foreigners. By the end of our period, all were subordinated to greater or lesser degree under the power of the newly risen French and British.

The Ottomans did not control their own trade and its profits. At first, because of political alliances with France, only French ships were allowed to trade with the Ottomans. After 1580, trade opened more widely and the English and Dutch entered the trade, along with Jews, Armenians, Venetians, and Genoese. The situation came to resemble Spain's, in which the empire's new riches went into the hands of foreign merchants. A shift in the balance of trade also weakened the central government. To pay for increasing amounts of imported manufactured goods the Ottomans exported more agricultural raw materials, increasing the wealth of landed estate holders and enabling them to break free of central control.

In India, between 1556 and 1605, the Mughal emperor Akbar established one of the great empires of the world. Akbar's administrative reforms brought change in trade and economies as well. City markets encouraged the production of luxury goods for the court and everyday goods for the common people. Even parts of village India—90 percent of India's population—were drawn into the city-based cash economy.

The markets contained a wide array of craftsmen, shop-keepers, and sophisticated specialists. Money-lenders and money-changers were active throughout the urban system, enabling the smooth transfer of funds across the empire. Their *hundis* (bills of exchange) were accepted throughout the empire, and these financial instruments facilitated the work of government officials in collecting and transmitting in cash the taxes and rents on land. Indian cities boasted very wealthy financiers and important guild organizations. The guilds, much like those in Europe, regulated and supervised the major trades. Business flourished and prospered. After all, among the multitude of India's castes, some were charged specifically with carrying on business.

Indian traders were highly mobile and therefore had some independence from the political fortunes of the rulers of the time. If particular rulers could not defend their territory against foreign invasion or maintain internal law and order, or if they tried to extort excessive taxes, the merchant communities could leave for other cities more amenable to their pursuits. Conversely, rulers who wanted to improve their commercial prospects lured these footloose merchants with offers of free land and low taxes. Thus, even in the event of political decline or catastrophe, India's business might shift location and continue to flourish.

Indian businessmen continued to carry on coastal and oceangoing trade, but the imperial government could not support these ventures very effectively. India had no navy. In 1686, for example, the British blocked Indian trade between Bengal and Southeast Asia and even seized ships belonging to the officers and family members of the Mughal rulers. Emperor Aurangzeb replied by land, forcing the British out of their settlement at Hoogly. But the British relocated, built a new town, Calcutta, and continued their maritime commerce and armed competition. Furthermore, although Indian businessmen created sophisticated economic institutions within family-held firms, they did not usually develop impersonal business firms like the European joint stock companies. When the European joint stock companies arrived on the subcontinent, they opened a new scale of overseas operations. Finally, Indian merchants did not normally arm themselves or contract for armed forces, as did many European merchants, especially the joint stock companies. Although they might flee particular rulers, business elites did not directly challenge the power of the ruler or seek to supplant it by recruiting their own forces.

Ming and Qing Dynasties in China

The Ming dynasty in China, as we saw in Chapter Twelve, had largely closed China to foreign trade in favor of developing the internal economy and defending the northern borders against Mongol and Manchu attack. The Ming repaired the Great Wall and extended it by an additional 600 miles. Having limited the size and power of their navy, the Ming were harassed by Japanese and Chinese pirates on their coasts. The Ming responded meekly by avoiding the sea and reviving the system of inland transportation by canals. The pirate attacks increased and became minor invasions of the mainland, even into the Yangzi River basin. Following national unification at the end of the sixteenth century, the new Japanese government brought their pirates under control, but in 1592 Japan invaded Korea, intending ultimately to invade China. Warfare continued for years, mostly within the Korean peninsula, but also within northern China, until Japan finally withdrew in 1598.

The Western presence was limited at this stage. The few Portuguese who arrived in China after 1514 were mostly Jesuit missionaries whose influence was felt far more in the culture of the court than in the commerce of the marketplace. Matteo Ricci (1552–1610), one of the most prominent of the Jesuit missionaries to China, shared with government officials in Beijing his knowledge of mathematics, cartography, astronomy, mechanics, and clocks, while he mastered the Chinese language and many of the Confucian classics. The Jesuits concentrated their efforts on winning the elites of China, and by 1700 some 300,000 Chinese had converted to Christianity.

Despite the shutdown of most international trade, China's economy expanded, at least until about 1600. China, after all, contained one-fifth of the world's population and generated an immense internal economy. The canal system encouraged north–south trade. Using kaolin clay, Chinese artisans created porcelain more beautiful and stronger than ever. Weaving and dyeing of silk expanded near Suzhou; cotton textiles flourished at Nanjing; Hebei specialized in iron manufacture.

In the late Ming period, private seagoing trade with Southeast Asia began to flourish again, often carried by families who had sent emigrants to the region and thus had local contacts. Within China, however, local authorities on the south China coast regulated and limited this trade. Fascinating research by a modern scholar on the success of overseas Chinese merchants suggests that had the Chinese government supported its own traders at home, instead of restricting them, they too might have been effective in building overseas merchant empires. The Chinese merchants:

> could, in terms of entrepreneurship and daring, do everything that the various Europeans could do. But they were helpless to produce the necessary institutional change in China to match European or even Japanese power. They were never the instruments of any effort by Ming or Qing authorities to build merchant empires; nor could they hope to get mandarin or ideological support for any innovative efforts of their own. (Gungwu, cited in Tracy, *The Rise of Merchant Empires*, p. 401)

When Europeans came to trade, the Chinese government restricted them to coastal enclaves. First, the Ming dynasty limited the Portuguese to Macao in 1557 (where they remained until 1999 under agreement with the current Chinese government). Nevertheless, as noted above, between one-third and one-half of all the silver of the New World ultimately went to China to pay for purchases of silk, porcelain, tea, and other products. Despite this new wealth, by the time the Dutch and British arrived in the 1600s the quality of the Ming administration had weakened.

Portuguese ships and sailors, lacquer screen, Chinese, seventeenth century. The faces of the sailors and the ship itself are not depicted as hostile, although at the beginning of the previous century the Portuguese had been expelled for aggressive actions and by mid-century were restricted to coastal enclaves.

The Qing dynasty, ruled by Manchus from north of the Great Wall, captured the government of China in 1644 and secured the southeast coast in 1683. They established the "Canton system," restricting European traders to the area around Canton (Guangzhou), and entrusting their supervision and control to a monopoly of Chinese firms called the Cohong. Because of these restrictions, and because of the vast size of China, European merchants had little effect on China. Also, like the Mughals in India, the Manchu rulers of China were an inland people, far more concerned with control of land than trade by sea. While they limited overseas trade, they expanded their political control into central Asia, doubling the size of the empire.

Although most historians emphasize the role of Europe in enlarging the world economy through overseas voyages, some note that it was the vast internal markets of China and the wealth of its luxury goods—along with the spices of India and the Spice Islands—that attracted the Europeans. According to this perspective, the dominant economic force in the world economy between 1500 and 1776 was not the vigor of European exploration and trade but the richness of Asian markets that attracted them in the first place. The "pull" of the Chinese market attracted the "push" of the European merchants.

Tokugawa Japan

As in China, the early European influences on Japan were both economic and religious. Roman Catholicism appeared with the arrival of the Jesuit priest Francis Xavier (1506–52) in 1549. Like Matteo Ricci in China, Xavier adapted to local cultural practices in dress, food, residence, and, of course, language. For their religious ideas, their culture, and trade, Europeans were at first warmly welcomed. Japan's **shogun**, or chief military administrator, Oda Nobunaga (1534–82), encouraged the Jesuits in their missionary work, and even after Nobunaga's assassination, Christianity found a foothold in Japan. As in China, converts numbered in the hundreds of thousands, and they were mostly from among the Japanese elites. (Among the European contributions to Japanese everyday life were tobacco, bread, playing cards, and deep-fat frying, which inspired the Japanese specialty of tempura.)

The Japanese government became apprehensive about so large a group of elite converts. There had been early signs of the change in policy. In 1597, after a Spanish ship captain boasted of the power of his king, and after Spain had colonized Manila, making that power more blatant, the shogun Toyotomi Hideyoshi crucified six Franciscan missionaries and 18 Japanese converts. In 1606 Christianity was outlawed, and in 1614 Shogun Tokugawa Ieyasu began to expel all Christian missionaries. Three thousand Japanese Christians were murdered. In 1623 the British left Japan; in 1624 the Spanish were expelled; in 1630 Japanese were forbidden to travel overseas. In 1637–38, in reaction to a revolt, which was more a rural economic protest than a religious uprising, 37,000 Christians were killed. The Portuguese were expelled. Only a small contingent of Dutch traders was permitted to remain, confined to Deshima Island off Nagasaki. A limited number of Chinese ships continued to visit Japan each year and some diplomatic contact with Korea continued, but Japan chose to live largely in isolation.

As in China, the suppression of contact with outsiders did not cripple Japan. Its process of political consolidation continued, from the 1600 Battle of Sekigahara until 1651. The country was unified and peaceful. Privately held guns were virtually banned. Agriculture prospered as the area of land under cultivation doubled, and the production of cash crops, such as indigo, tobacco (from the New World), sugar cane, and mulberry leaves as food for silkworms, increased. The population almost doubled, from 18 million in 1600 to 30 million by the mid-1700s, at which point it stabilized temporarily.

The new government was in the hands of the *samurai* warrior classes, who made up about 7 percent of the population. They benefited most from the improved conditions, and there were some violent protests against increasing disparities in income, but standards of living and of education generally improved. City merchants, *chonin*, emerged as a newly wealthy and powerful class, dealing in the new cash commodities of farm and hand manufacture. They supplied banking, shipping, loans, and other commercial services, and founded family businesses, some of which endure even today. The Tokugawa capital Edo (Tokyo) grew to a million people by 1700, among the largest cities in the world at the time. In a reversal of the European pattern of the time, Japan was doing well despite cutting off almost all international trade.

Southeast Asia

Southeast Asia was one of the great prizes of international commercial competition throughout our period, and foreign merchants from China, Japan, India, Arabia, and Europe were active in its markets. Yet the indigenous merchants of the region did not themselves become major factors in the international side of the trade. Foreign

KEY TERMS

shogun The military dictator of Japan, a hereditary title held by three families between 1192 and 1867. Although they were legally subservient to the emperor, their military power gave them effective control of the country.

samurai The hereditary warrior-aristocrats of Japanese society, known for their codes of honor and loyalty. Only *samurai* were permitted to wear swords in their everyday dress.

How Europe Surpassed China Economically and Militarily

During the period covered in this chapter, the relative balance of power between Europe and Asia was shifting. The most remarkable shift was the slow, steady economic progress of Western European nations compared to China, still the most powerful and wealthy nation of the time. We have examined advances in European shipping and armaments, and the consolidation of their commercial classes and their nation-states. Why did China not keep pace?

Mark Elvin, an economic historian, tackled this question in a classic study, *The Pattern of the Chinese Past* (1973), a sketch of Chinese economic and social history from earliest times. In a series of chapters Elvin praises the creativity of the Tang and Song dynasties, crediting the period from the eighth to the twelfth centuries with "revolutions" in farming, water transport, money and credit, market structure and urbanization, science and technology. But "the dynamic quality of the medieval Chinese economy disappeared ... some time around the middle of the fourteenth century" (p. 203). Elvin gives three reasons for this disappearance: The Chinese frontier began to fill up with people and resources; commerce with the outside world decreased sharply; and philosophy became introspective, less concerned with engaging practical problems. The result was "quantitative growth, qualitative standstill," or what Elvin calls a "high-equilibrium trap." That is, economic growth continued and new natural resources were tapped, but most of the gains were eaten up by the population growth. For example, Elvin writes, in the sixteenth through the nineteenth centuries, New World crops were introduced, agricultural techniques were improved, market networks were extended, the legal status of the peasantry was improved, and entrepreneurship and invention flourished. But the population doubled from about 200 million people in 1580 to about 400 million in 1850. "Agricultural productivity per acre had nearly reached the limits of what was possible without industrial-scientific inputs" (p. 312), and these inputs were simply unavailable. Technological innovation occurred, but resources for implementing them were scarce. Wood, clothing fibers, land, draft animals, and metals were in short supply. In this "high-level equilibrium trap," the Chinese economy worked well enough in its traditional forms that there were few incentives for making changes. More important, the changes that would have been necessary to increase production substantially would have required more capital and human resources than were available. China was stuck.

Had the West faced such a trap, and, if so, how had it avoided it? Kenneth Pomeranz, another economic historian, gives his answers in *The Great Divergence: China, Europe, and the Making of the Modern World Economy* (2000). Yes, he says, "Europe, too, could have wound up on an 'east Asian,' labor-intensive path" (p. 13) in which there were few incentives and even fewer resources available to create innovations to improve productivity. Its escape was "the result of important and sharp discontinuities, based on both fossil fuels [coal] and access to New World resources" (p. 13). The fossil fuels became important only later, during the Industrial Revolution, but the New World resources became important almost immediately after their discovery by Europeans. The New World "relieved the strain on Europe's supply of what was truly scarce: land and energy ... crucial factors leading out of a world of Malthusian constraints" (p. 23). The New World provided a place for some of Europe's "excess" population. It also provided richly productive land, an abundance of gold and silver, the lucrative slave trade, and millions of slaves who created a new market for European products. (Here Pomeranz is not considering the fate of the slaves.)

Was the lucky discovery of the New World the major differentiation between the European economic experience and the Chinese? Pomeranz also credits "war, armed long distance trade and colonization" (p. 166). The joint stock company organized for overseas trade and colonization was a significant breakthrough for the "unified management of trading voyages and cargoes too big for a single investor" (p. 171). The backing of the state for these ventures—without excessive, crippling interference—was probably another (p. 173). The use of "force to create monopolies or near-monopolies (mostly in spices)" was a third (p. 182). The competition among the European powers for trading and colonizing supremacy was a fourth element in driving their economic success (p. 194).

Between Elvin and Pomeranz we get a comprehensive, comparative survey of the factors at work in China and in Europe—ecological, demographic, and institutional—that led to China's stagnation and Western Europe's dynamism in economic creativity in the era of the Ming and early Qing dynasties in China, the era of overseas exploration, trade, and early colonization in Western Europe.

- When did the economic productivity and wealth of Western Europe surpass that of China?
- To what degree did the stagnation in China's economy result from a lack of planning and hard work?
- To what degree did the success of Western Europe's economy result from planning and hard work?

myhistorylab

traders began their activities on the coast and then moved inland, taking control of local markets. They also fought among themselves. By 1640, for example, the Dutch East India Company expelled from the Indonesian archipelago not only the local merchants but also European competitors. By this time, the spice trade was beginning to level off and the Dutch were in the process of restructuring the economies of

Southeast Asia, especially Indonesia, to produce such commercial crops as sugar, coffee, and tobacco. In the Philippines, the Spanish asserted similar power.

Local rulers entered into commercial agreements with the foreign traders that enriched themselves, but not their merchant communities. Commercial profits were repatriated from Southeast Asia back to Europe, creating ever more serious imbalances of power and wealth. Capitalist enterprise in the hands of merchants, backed by the state and by military power, was radiating outward from Europe; Southeast Asia had become a participant in this new system, and a victim of it.

The Influence of World Trade: What Difference Does It Make?

We close this exploration of world trade in the year 1776. We have witnessed enormous changes from 1300, when we began, in Chapter Twelve, and even from 1500, when European explorers began their oceanic voyages. During these centuries, an entirely new set of trade networks opened, crisscrossing the Atlantic Ocean. Major elements in these new trade relationships included the export from the western hemisphere of enormous quantities of gold and silver to Europe and to Asia, and the export of millions of people in slavery from Africa to the plantations of the Americas.

The earlier center of ocean trade, the Indian Ocean, continued to be important, but now European traders—Portuguese, followed by Dutch, British, and French— gained control of the intercontinental segments of that trade. The variety of traders in coastal port cities around the world increased, with some exceptions, as in Japan, and the trade outposts of the Europeans were fortified militarily. Within Europe, the power of nation-states and of private traders increased, in large part because of the profits of international trade and because of the perceived need to support it with oceangoing fleets and navies. The new philosophy of capitalism explained and justified the rising power of private business at home and abroad. New religious denominations also arose, with philosophies that rationalized the new economic acquisitiveness. Competition increased in the technology of shipping, the sophistication of commercial strategies, the manufacture of armaments, and the training and disciplining of armed forces at home and overseas. Leadership passed from the Spanish and Portuguese to the Dutch, French, and British.

Throughout this era, the most powerful and wealthy of the world's empires were in Asia, but by the end of it, Europeans, hungry for profit, and often eager to spread the gospel of Christianity, were fashioning the frameworks for their own overseas empires of unprecedented size.

Asking Questions

- Define capitalism and discuss its strengths and weaknesses as an economic system as described by Adam Smith.
- What were the chief causes of the decline of the Portuguese empire and of the Spanish empire?
- What were the chief causes of the rise of the British, French, and Dutch empires?
- What is a nation-state? Why did European rulers seek to consolidate their countries as nation-states in the period 1500–1750?
- What were the goals of Russia's Peter the Great? In what ways did contact with the outside world encourage him to pursue these goals? To what extent did he accomplish them?

Suggested Readings

PRINCIPAL SOURCES

Braudel, Fernand. *Capitalism and Material Life 1400–1800,* trans. Miriam Kochan (New York: Harper and Row, 1973). Highly influential overview of the beginning of capitalism as the guiding economic force in modern Europe.

Brockey, Liam Matthew. *Journey to the East: The Jesuit Mission to China, 1579–1724.* (Cambridge, MA: Harvard University Press, 2007). Discusses the life and work of Jesuit missionaries more typical than Matteo Ricci, who was larger than life.

Chaudhuri, K.N. *Trade and Civilization in the Indian Ocean* (Cambridge: Cambridge University Press, 1985). Comprehensive survey of the ecology, politics, traders, and trade of the Indian Ocean.

Elvin, Mark. *The Pattern of the Chinese Past* (Stanford, CA: Stanford University Press, 1973). An interpretive economic history from pre-Han to Qing China. Thoughtful analyses of successes and failures.

Kennedy, Paul. *The Rise and Fall of the Great Powers* (New York: Vintage Books, 1987). Examines histories of great power rivalries, including the Western European rivalries in the age of exploration and trade. Seeks balance between military power and economic health.

McNeill, William H. "The Age of Gunpowder Empires, 1450–1800," in Michael Adas, ed. *Islamic and European Expansion* (Philadelphia, PA: Temple University Press, 1993), pp. 103–09. Brief survey of the effects of gunpowder on warfare and on the nations that used it in warfare.

Mintz, Sidney W. *Sweetness and Power: The Place of Sugar in Modern History* (New York: Penguin Books, 1985). Anthropological focus on the Caribbean sugar plantation, but places it also in the context of world trade patterns, advertising, and changing food choices.

Perdue, Peter. *China Marches West: The Qing Conquest of Central Eurasia* (Cambridge, MA: Harvard University Press, 2005). Brilliant study of the statecraft, military actions, and ethnic and ecological significance of Qing China's enormous territorial conquests.

Thornton, John. *Africa and Africans in the Making of the Atlantic World, 1400–1680* (Cambridge: Cambridge University Press, 1992). Sees Africans as active participants in the slave trade and other trading activities, not simply as passive recipients in the affairs of others.

Tracy, James D., ed. *The Political Economy of Merchant Empires* (Cambridge: Cambridge University Press, 1991). An excellent account of the merchant empires that emerged in the Early Modern period.

Tracy, James D., ed. *The Rise of Merchant Empires* (Cambridge: Cambridge University Press, 1990). Tracy brings together the papers of an exciting academic conference on the merchant empires of the age of exploration and early colonization. Specialized, but very important coverage. "The Rise" discusses primarily the merchant activity; "Political Economy," primarily the imperial effects.

ADDITIONAL SOURCES

Bayly, C.A. *Indian Society and the Making of the British Empire* (Cambridge: Cambridge University Press, 1988). Sees the effects of British colonization in the early years through the eyes and activities of Indians.

Braudel, Fernand. *Civilization and Capitalism 15th–18th Century.* Volume 2: *The Wheels of Commerce,* trans. Sian Reynolds (New York: Harper and Row, 1986). Remarkable synthesis of the transformation of early modern Europe through its economy, social life, and culture. Volume 1 is published as *Capitalism and Material Life, 1400–1800,* see above.

——. *Civilization and Capitalism 15th–18th Century.* Vol. 3: *The Perspective of the World,* trans. Sian Reynolds (New York: Harper and Row, 1986). Third volume in the series, looks more at the importance of international relations.

——. *The Mediterranean and the Mediterranean World in the Age of Philip II,* 2 vols, trans. Sian Reynolds (New York: Harper Torchbooks, Vol. 1: 1972; Vol. 2: 1973). This study of the Mediterranean demonstrated Braudel's style of history, including geological influences, long-time institutional influences, and short-run political and personal influences. Highly influential for its style of history as well as its subject matter.

Columbia University. *Introduction to Contemporary Civilization in the West,* 2 vols. (New York: Columbia University Press, 2nd ed., 1954). A superb reader of some of the most influential thinkers, presented in long, rich excerpts.

Curtin, Philip, Steven Feierman, Leonard Thompson, and Jan Vansina. *African History from Earliest Times to Independence* (New York: Longman, 2nd ed., 1995). Excellent textbook survey emphasizing anthropology as well as history.

Das Gupta, Ashin and M.N. Pearson, eds. *India and the Indian Ocean 1500–1800* (Calcutta: Oxford University Press, 1987). Articles on the vital trade and politics of the major actors in the Indian Ocean.

Duara, Prasenjit. *Rescuing History from the Nation* (Chicago, IL: University of Chicago Press, 1995). A critical challenge to the idea that the nation-state is a creation of the modern West and that it has a fixed meaning.

Ebrey, Patricia Buckley. *Cambridge Illustrated History of China* (Cambridge: Cambridge University Press, 1996). Excellent basic survey. Pictures help tell the story. Some emphasis on women in Chinese history.

Gungwu, Wang, "Merchants without Empire: The Hokkien Sojourning Communities," in Tracy, ed., *The Rise of Merchant Empires*, pp. 400–21. Traces the overseas activities of merchants of the south China coast, whose opportunities in China were blocked by government.

Kamen, Henry. *Empire: How Spain Became a World Power, 1492–1763* (New York: HarperCollins, 2003). Analyzes the empire globally, accounting for the many non-Spanish groups that participated in constructing and administering it.

Lapidus, Ira. *A History of Islamic Societies* (Cambridge: Cambridge University Press, 2nd ed., 2002). A 1,000-plus-page, comprehensive, well-written history.

Palmer, R.R. and Joel Colton. *A History of the Modern World* (New York: Knopf, 9th ed., 2002). Once *the* major text; now considered too Eurocentric, and very Francophile, but still excellent.

Pearson, M.N., "Merchants and States," in Tracy, ed., *The Political Economy of Merchant Empires*, 41–116. Discusses the role of the state in encouraging business, mostly in Europe, but considers Asia as well.

Pomeranz, Kenneth. *The Great Divergence: China, Europe, and the Making of the Modern World Economy* (Princeton, NJ: Princeton University Press, 2000). How did Europe surpass China? An economic historian explores various explanations. He suggests: The exploitation of New World resources; coal in Britain; armed merchant exploration and trade.

Reid, Anthony. *Southeast Asia in the Age of Commerce 1450–1680.* Vol 1: *The Land Below the Winds*; Vol 2: *Expansion and Crisis* (New Haven, CT: Yale University Press, Vol. 1: 1988; Vol. 2:

1993). Excellent collection of conference papers on foreign merchant impacts on Southeast Asia.

Rothermund, Dietmar. *Asian Trade and European Expansion in the Age of Mercantilism* (Delhi: Manohar, 1981). Survey of economic history.

Schama, Simon. *The Embarrassment of Riches* (New York: Knopf, 1987). Study of the early modern Netherlands, especially its artistic wealth.

Smith, Adam. *An Inquiry into the Nature and Causes of the Wealth of Nations* (New York: Modern Library, 1937). The classic philosophical rationale for capitalism.

Spence, Jonathan D. *The Memory Palace of Matteo Ricci* (New York: Penguin Books, 1985). An account of the work and the significance of Matteo Ricci in China, filled with cultural information, as on the function of memory.

Steensgaard, Niels. *The Asian Trade Revolution of the Seventeenth Century* (Chicago, IL: University of Chicago Press, 1973). Argues that most Asian traders were small-scale and not well organized.

Tawney, R.H. *Religion and the Rise of Capitalism* (New York: Harcourt, Brace, & Co., 1926). Argues, against Max Weber, that Catholicism also showed substantial economic entrepreneurship and that religious and moral principles will always be included in economic considerations.

Thomas, Hugh. *Rivers of Gold: The Rise of the Spanish Empire, from Columbus to Magellan* (New York: Random House, 2004). The first 30 years of conquest seen largely through the eyes of the men who carried it out.

Weber, Max. *The Protestant Ethic and the Spirit of Capitalism*, trans. Talcott Parsons (London, 1930). Argues that religious beliefs do have considerable impact on economic performance. Also, in the modern world, religious enthusiasm had been supplanted by economic aspirations.

Wolf, Eric. *Europe and the People without History* (Berkeley, CA: University of California Press, 1982). Historical anthropologist demonstrates that non-European societies are not unchanging. Their recent history has been heavily influenced by the capitalist West.

For quizzes, flashcards, primary sources, interactive maps, videos, and other activities related to this chapter please go to
www.myhistorylab.com

1508

CHAPTER FIFTEEN

Migration

Demographic Changes in a New Global World
1300–1750

Conventionally, historians write about particular individuals and particular events. In the twentieth century, however, and especially in its second half, historians began to examine **demographics**—that is, human populations viewed collectively, in quantitative terms. Demographers utilize "vital statistics" such as life expectancy, birth rates, death rates, and marriage rates in order to address such questions as: When and why do populations grow and decline? What are the impacts of disease, war, and famine? What are the effects of improvements in agriculture and living standards? What is the distribution of population by age, gender, class, and household size? Through large-scale analyses, demographers seek to identify and interpret patterns of change. Although the statistics may at first seem dry, they can tell fascinating stories.

Today, governments gather statistical information as a matter of course. However, to find information on earlier periods that lack such systematic official data collection, historians must search other sources. Church registers of births and deaths, travelers' accounts, ships' records of passengers and cargo, for example, can all provide demographic data. In this chapter we shall examine demographic data specifically concerned with migration, the movement of populations across geographical space, from one region to another, and between countryside and city.

New topics in the study of the past are often inspired by new experiences in the present. In our own time, demographic shifts are dramatically altering our world, both in the population explosion that has doubled the earth's population in the last 30 years and in the migrations of hundreds of millions of people from one region to another and from rural areas to cities. The United States, in particular, stresses its identity as a nation of immigrants. Its population also shifts internally, especially from north to south and from east to west, and also from countryside to city and from city to suburb. European countries, which have not usually considered themselves as homes for new immigrants, are experiencing the inflow of millions of immigrants from poorer countries seeking economic opportunities. China, having relaxed its restrictions on internal immigration, is experiencing the migration of millions of citizens from villages in its interior to cities along its coast. Such demographic transformations evoke comparisons with earlier historical eras, especially the period 1500–1750, when the populations of whole continents were restructured, and when cities, some of them newly founded, experienced enormous population growth.

There is another reason for choosing to study aggregate populations. Such studies are often the closest we can come to understanding the lives of average people.

KEY TOPICS
- The "New Europes"
- Russian Expansion
- Slavery: Enforced Migration, 1500–1750
- Asian Migrations, 1300–1750
- Global Population Growth and Movement
- Cities and Demographics
- Migration and Demography: What Difference Do They Make?

Portrait of a Black Man, **Albrecht Dürer, 1508. Charcoal on paper.** In the late 1400s, several delegations of Africans from the Atlantic Coast came to Europe, especially Portugal, in Portuguese ships, mostly for commercial exchange, Christian religious pursuits, and new weapons technology. The largest number of Africans in Europe at this time, however, were brought as slaves. This *Portrait of a Black Man* by the great German painter Albrecht Dürer is exceptional, portraying the subject as intelligent, clear-eyed, thoughtful, and independent of spirit. (Graphische Sammlung Albertina, Vienna)

Most people could neither read nor write; they have left us no written record. Although we are not able to know their individual biographies, through demographic studies of aggregate groups we may be able to gain a better understanding of the societies in which they lived and died.

Finally, sometimes research is motivated by the availability of new tools. Population history requires quantitative information and the statistical tools to work with it. Within the last generation demographers have made great strides in developing new methodology, some of it as a result of new data-processing capabilities. Demographic computer modeling provides additional, new replies to the question: "How do we know?"

Here we will explore four major subjects: First, the formation of "New Europes" around the globe as settlers from Europe set out in all directions, often with catastrophic consequences for native populations. Second, the trade in slaves that brought some ten million people from Africa to the Americas—against a background of the long-standing historic trade in slaves in many parts of the globe. Third, the overland migrations of Mongols and Turks, who emerged from central Asia to invade China in the east, Russia and the Balkans in the west, and India in the south. Finally, we will analyze migrations from rural areas to cities in several different parts of the world and compare and contrast peoples' reasons for moving.

The "New Europes"

From 1500 to 1750 developments within Europe increased Europe's influence in the world and expedited the emigration of millions of Europeans to establish "**New Europes**" around the globe. These developments included:

- the increasing powers of traders in the diaspora cities of trade around the globe;
- the increasing power of European nation-states and their support for overseas trade;
- the shifting of trade to the Atlantic (rather than the Indian) Ocean;
- the increasing pace of technological invention in Europe, especially in guns and ships;
- the increasing discipline and order within European armies;
- the importation of immense quantities of gold and silver from the New World, much of which was sent to China and India to pay for imports to Europe;
- the exploitation of the labor of millions of slaves taken from Africa to work the plantations of the New World; and
- the spreading of the message of aggressive Christianity.

As we have seen in Chapter Fourteen, in the sixteenth century both Spain and Portugal built enormous global empires. The voyages of Columbus revealed gold and silver reserves in the Americas, and many Europeans who came after him were prepared to kill Native Americans and to take over their lands. Cortés conquered the Aztec nation of Mexico in 1519 and Pizarro conquered the Incas in 1533. The death and destruction that followed were monumental, but warfare was not the greatest killer.

The Columbian Exchange

The peoples of the eastern and western hemispheres had had no sustained contact for thousands of years. Columbus' voyages therefore ushered in a new era of interaction. This "Columbian Exchange" brought not only new opportunities, but catastrophe as well. The new opportunities came with the intercontinental exchange of plants and animals. The catastrophe befell the Amerindians, who had no resistance to the diseases carried by the Europeans.

The Devastation of the Amerindian Population.

Historian Alfred Crosby, a pioneer in the study of the exchange of microbes, cites the lowest currently accepted estimate of the Amerindian population in 1492 as 33 million, the highest as perhaps 50 million. By comparison, Europe at the time had a population of 80 million. The death of millions of Amerindians followed almost immediately after Europeans began to arrive. At their lowest point after the coming of Europeans, the populations of the western hemisphere dropped to 4.5 million. The biggest killers in this demographic catastrophe were not guns, but diseases: smallpox, measles, whooping cough, chickenpox, bubonic plague, malaria, diphtheria, amoebic dysentery, and influenza. The populations of the New World, separated by thousands of years and thousands of miles from those of the Old, had little resistance to its diseases. Up to 90 percent of the population died.

Aztec smallpox victims, sixteenth century. The Spanish conquest of the Americas owed more to the diseases they brought with them than to their armed forces. The Native Americans had never encountered these diseases, especially smallpox, and had no immunity. They died in horrific numbers—up to 90 percent in many regions. (Peabody Museum of Archaeology and Ethnology, Harvard University)

Benefits of the Columbian Exchanges. More happily, links between the hemispheres also brought an exchange of food sources. From South America, the cassava spread to Africa and Asia and the white potato to northern Europe. Sweet potatoes traveled to China, as did maize (corn); China is today the second largest producer of corn, after the United States. Today, Russia produces ten times more potatoes by weight than does South America, while Africa produces almost twice as much cassava as does South America.

Flora and fauna migrated from east to west as well. Wheat was the leading Old World crop to come to the New World, but perhaps an even greater contribution came in domesticated animals: cattle, sheep, pigs, and goats. Domesticated horses, too, were imported from the Old World to the New. In the long run, these exchanges of food sources did much to increase the population of the world more than ten times, from about 500 million in 1492 to more than 6.7 billion today. But not everyone participated in this growth. There were demographic winners and losers. Peoples of the European continent in 1492 were the biggest winners; Asians generally did well; Amerindians and other indigenous populations in all of the "New Europes" were among the biggest losers. Millions of Africans were forcibly transported overseas into chattel slavery, initiating new diaspora communities, but under abysmal conditions.

North America

By the early 1600s, Spanish supremacy in the New World was being challenged by the Dutch Republic, England, and France. All three had developed expertise in the construction of high-quality ships, and all three fostered business groups skilled in trade and motivated by profit, with strong ties to political leadership. At first, all three concentrated on the Caribbean and its potential for profits from plantations. They seized and settled outposts: England most notably in the Bahamas and Jamaica,

European settlement in eastern North America. Along the Atlantic coast of North America and Canada, Britain established an array of colonies. Thirteen of them revolted in 1776 to form the United States, but the northern areas remained loyal. The British restricted settlement across the Appalachian Mountains so that land was held by indigenous nations and, still further west, claimed by the French. Florida was held by the British from 1763 to 1783, but otherwise was a Spanish possession until invaded and conquered by the United States in 1818.

France in Saint-Domingue (modern Haiti), and the Dutch along the Brazilian coast and in Curaçao. Later they turned to the North American mainland.

North America had its own attractions for farmers, artisans, laborers, and agricultural workers who came to settle. Some of the earliest settlers were pushed out of Europe by the "**price revolution**" created by the availability of New World silver. The influx of the precious metal into Europe, and into the European trade networks in Asia, inflated prices; wages did not keep pace. Pressured by this decline in their economic condition, people living at the margins of European society sought the opportunity of new frontiers in North America.

Later, through the seventeenth and early eighteenth centuries, the European invaders into the New World came in different waves and appropriated different regions for their purposes. In Virginia they came at first looking for gold, beaver furs, deer skin, and a northwest passage to Asia. They failed in all these goals, and at first they failed even to survive. Of the first 900 colonists arriving in 1607–09, only 60 were alive at the end of the two years, most dying from famine and disease. Some 9,000 came between 1610 and 1622; at the later date, only 2,000 were alive.

After 1618 the crown-appointed administrators of the colony offered 50 acres to any settler who would come, and by this date Virginia's tobacco crop became the staple product of its economy. Settlers continued to come, but the life was difficult, attractive mostly to people of the lower social classes. Many signed on as

indentured laborers, contracting to work for a fixed period of years, usually about seven, in exchange for ocean passage and fixed labor with a specific employer in the New World. About 75 percent of these laborers were male, most between 15 and 24 years of age. Since their masters cared little for them, they were bought and sold, sometimes worked to death, and treated not much differently from slaves. With life so cheap, at the whim of both man and nature, the further massacre of Native Americans, who were seen as alien, savage, non-Christian, and an obstacle to European invasion and expansion, became a way of life for the land-hungry settlers.

Maryland also grew tobacco, but its goals included more than mere economic profit. In 1632 the English Crown had given the land to George Calvert, Lord Baltimore, and he established here a religious refuge for Catholics, who were at that time an oppressed minority in England. Catholics formed a minority of the population of the colony, but they were legally protected. Their relationships with the Native Americans, however, were also murderous.

In New England, the first collective settlement of Europeans was the Pilgrim colony founded in 1620. Dissenters from the official doctrines of the Church of England, the Pilgrims also sought a religious haven in the New World. Their community was bound together by the Mayflower Compact, an agreement they drafted on board ship to the New World, establishing a governing body "for the general good of the colony; unto which, we promise all due submission and obedience." Of the 102 Pilgrims who landed at Plymouth, fewer than half survived the first year, but, with the help of Native Americans who befriended the settlers, the colony took root.

In 1630 another group of settlers, the Puritans, arrived in New England. The Pilgrims wished to separate from the Church of England; the Puritans wished only to purify it. They were richer and better educated than the Pilgrims. Many had some college education. English King Charles I (whom many suspected of secret Catholicism and who clashed with Protestant hardliners at home), eager to get them out of England, gave them a charter to establish the Company of the Massachusetts Bay. By the end of the year, 1,000 had settled; within a decade, 20,000. Many more chose to settle in the sugar plantations of the Caribbean islands.

The Puritans had left England for their own religious freedom, but in New England, they denied it to others. People like Roger Williams, a minister who endorsed the separation of Church and state, were forced to flee. The Puritans were narrow in their outlook, but fiercely devoted to community, discipline, work, education, and spreading their view of religion. They scorned Native Americans, fought them, and confiscated their land with little compunction.

The Dutch began to explore and develop the land at the mouth of the Hudson River in 1609, and claimed it in the name of the Dutch Republic in 1624. The next year they purchased an island from the Manhatta Indians and established on it the town of New Amsterdam. The British captured this settlement from the Dutch in 1664 and, the next year, renamed it New York. The area developed its own polyglot, pragmatic, tolerant business ethic under the successive administrations of these two European colonizing countries.

Perhaps the most inspiring settlement was the Quaker colony of Pennsylvania, founded by William Penn, a British aristocrat

KEY TERM

indentured labor Labor performed under signed indenture, or contract, which binds the laborer to work for a specific employer, for a specified time, usually years, often in a distant place, in exchange for transportation and maintenance.

Puritans arrive in New England. Religious freedom and economic opportunity were the two great attractions for European immigrants to the New World. Many of the immigrants from England were dissenters from the established official Church. Their independence was a background factor that later helped to inspire the American Revolution in 1776. Some of the dissenters, however, like the Puritans, were themselves intolerant toward others who settled in their communities, forcing them to conform or to leave.

who had joined the Society of Friends, as Quakers are called formally, inspired by a lecture on the Society's basic principles of freedom of conscience, nonviolence, and pacifism. Pennsylvania and its first capital, Philadelphia (whose name means "brotherly love"), became known throughout Western Europe for religious toleration, and people of many countries and faiths immigrated there: "English, Highland Scots, French, Germans, Irish, Welsh, Swedes, Finns, and Swiss … Mennonites, Lutherans, Dutch Reformed, Baptists, Anglicans, Presbyterians, Catholics, Jews," and a few hermits and mystics. Indeed, even Native Americans immigrated to flee the violence against them that was endemic elsewhere. Unfortunately, the non-Quaker immigrant-invaders did not share Penn's early commitment to tolerant, peaceful interracial relationships with the Native Americans, regulated by legal contracts and personal contacts. After Penn's death, they too pushed them off the land, although with less violence than elsewhere.

While the English were establishing numerous, diverse, thriving colonies along the Atlantic Coast, from Newfoundland to South Carolina, and inland on Hudson's Bay, the French were settling, lightly, the inland waterways of the St. Lawrence River, the Great Lakes, and the Mississippi River, as well as Gulf Coast Louisiana. During the global warfare between Britain and France, the Seven Years War of 1756–63, British military forces conquered the North American mainland from the Atlantic to the Mississippi. Their victory ensured that North America would be English-speaking. French cultural influences and migration, however, continued to be felt in the region of Quebec, and it continues as a French-speaking province today. By 1750, about four million people of European origin inhabited North America.

The Antipodes: Australia and New Zealand, 1600–1900

Crossing the Atlantic became relatively quick and easy, but reaching Australia and New Zealand, on the opposite side of the globe, was quite a different matter. Even their neighbors had established only minimal contacts with them. There had been some landings by Asians in the sixteenth century. They came to the north coast of Australia in search of a species of sea slug that looked like a withered penis when smoked and dried. The slugs became Indonesia's largest export to the Chinese, who valued them as aphrodisiacs.

Spanish copies of Portuguese charts suggest that Portuguese sailors had landed on and mapped the northern and eastern coasts of Australia, and that the Spanish may also have known about them, but no continuing contact resulted. In the early 1600s, a few Dutch sailors reached parts of the coast, several wrecking their ships in the process. Between 1642 and 1644, under commission from the Dutch East India Company, the Dutch commander Abel Tasman (c. 1605–59) began the systematic exploration of New Zealand; the sea—later named for him—that separates Australia from New Zealand; the island that was later named Tasmania; and the north coast of Australia. He reported "naked beach-roving wretches, destitute even of rice … miserably poor, and in many places of a very bad disposition" (cited in Hughes, p. 48). With such unpromising descriptions reaching England, and the general decline of Spanish, Dutch, and Portuguese power, Australia remained almost untouched by Europeans for a century and a half, and the pattern of immigration from Europe lags behind the pattern going to the western hemisphere by a similar amount of time. Then the English conquered and sent migrants to the Pacific Islands.

In 1768, the English Captain James Cook (1728–79) set out on a three-year voyage, which took him to Tahiti to record astronomical observations; to Australia to determine the nature of the "Southern Continent" reported by Tasman; to map New Zealand; and, thanks to the zeal of a young amateur botanist, Joseph Banks

SOURCE

Captain Cook Encounters the Aboriginals of Australia

Abel Tasman's description of the fierce Maori of New Zealand discouraged Europeans from further explorations of those islands. A similarly dismal, and racist, report on Australia was written by the only European to have visited it, William Dampier, who had come to the north coast from New Holland (Indonesia) in 1688:

> The inhabitants of this country are the miserablest people in the World … They have great Heads, round Foreheads, and great Brows. Their Eye-lids are always half closed, to keep the Flies out of their Eyes … therefore they cannot see far.
>
> They are long-visaged, and of a very unpleasing aspect; having no one graceful feature in their faces.
>
> They have no houses, but lye in the open Air, without any covering; the Earth being their Bed, and the Heaven their Canopy …
>
> I did not perceive that they did worship anything. (cited in Hughes, p. 48)

Captain Cook's view was the absolute contrary:

> They may appear to some to be the most wretched people upon Earth, but in reality they are far happier than we Europeans; being wholy unacquainted not only with the superfluous, but the necessary Conveniencies so much sought after in Europe, they are happy in not knowing the use of them. They live in Tranquility which is not disturb'd by the Inequality of Condition: The Earth and sea of their own accord furnishes them with all things necessary for life, they covet not Magnificent Houses, Houshold-stuff, etc., they live in a warm and fine Climate and enjoy a very wholesome Air, so that they have very little need of Clothing and this they seem to be fully sencible of, for many to whome we gave Cloth etc. to, left it carlessly upon the Sea beach and in the woods as a thing they had no manner of use for. In short they seem'd to set no Value upon any thing we gave them, nor would they ever part with any thing of their own for any one article we could offer them; this in my opinion argues that they think themselves provided with all the necessarys of Life and that they have no superfluities. (Cook, Vol. I, p. 399)

Cook took with him on the voyage a young botanist, Joseph Banks. Banks' descriptions of the Aboriginals presented them as timid, without property, and few in number. Although Banks was not proposing colonization, those who wished it could find encouragement in his comments. Banks and his associate Daniel Solander brought back from the three-year trip some 30,000 specimens representing 3,000 species, of which 1,600 had never before been seen by European scientists. Not all of these were from Australia, but in honor of the work of Banks and Solander, Cook named his principal harbor in Australia "Botany Bay."

Australia was distant from Europe, but based on Cook's discoveries, it seemed to hold rich promise for future encounters.

(1743–1820), to report on the natural resources of all these distant lands. The success of Cook's three-year voyage was made possible by discoveries of proper food supplements to prevent scurvy among the sailors and of new instrumentation to chart longitude and thus establish location at sea. Cook's descriptions of the people he encountered in Australia differed sharply from those of Tasman. He found them peaceful—unlike the Maori of New Zealand. This sealed the fate of Australia.

On the basis of Cook's report, the British government decided that Australia could serve as the "dumping ground" it had been seeking for the prisoners who were overcrowding the jails at home. (Until the Revolutionary War, the American colonies had served this purpose.) British settlement in Australia thus began in the form of penal colonies. From 1788, when the first shipload of convicts arrived, until the 1850s, "transportation" to Australia was the only alternative to hanging for British prisoners. Under the "assignment system," convicts were assigned for the duration of their sentences to particular masters, about 90 percent of them private individuals, about 10 percent government officials superintending public works projects. Conditions among the prisoners were extremely harsh, and sexual relationships in particular reflected both the demography and the harshness. Men outnumbered women among the prisoners by a ratio of 6 to 1; in the cities, 4 to 1; in the countryside, 20 to 1. Both prostitution and rape were common among the

A government jail gang, Sydney, New South Wales, eighteenth century. After they lost their colonies in the American Revolution and their prison colonies among them, the British were searching for a new pen for their convicts. Australia met their needs. The first shipload of convicts arrived in 1788, the last in 1868. (Private collection)

women; homosexuality flourished among the men. Beginning in 1835, new prison acts in Britain began to provide for prisons at home, and the use of Australia as a prison colony quickly declined. By 1868, the last convict ship unloaded its cargo—Irish prisoners deposited in Western Australia.

The early British colonization of Australia began at Botany Bay, adjacent to Sydney, and then at other points along the southeast coast, the best watered and most fertile part of Australia. Because mountains flanked close against the coast and fresh water was scarce, progress inland was problematic, and settlement by Europeans was slow, based on commercial agriculture in wool, dairy cattle, and sugar cultivation.

The coming of Europeans, even in small numbers, destroyed the fragile ecology of the indigenous civilization, which survived only in the center and far north of the continent. As in other "New Europes," European diseases killed off the overwhelming majority of the Aborigines, the indigenous Australians. In addition, their hunting grounds were displaced by the sheep and cattle, fences and pasturage of the British settlers. Finally, the savagery and the explicit policies of the British, both official and unofficial, overwhelmed them. A large proprietor of sheep and cattle

> narrated as a good thing, that he had been one of party who had pursued the blacks, in consequence of cattle having been rushed by them, and he was sure they shot upwards of a hundred … [H]e maintained that there was nothing wrong in it, that it was preposterous to suppose they had souls. (Hughes, p. 277)

At first, the Australian Aborigines, who lived nomadically by hunting and gathering, retreated in the face of white advances, but later they began to resist, defending their ancestral territories as best they could with bows and arrows and spears against British weaponry. They resisted in some places for up to ten years, stealing British guns and learning to use them, attacking sheep, cattle, horses, and homes. British response to the resistance was intensified by the belief that the Aborigines could neither be attracted nor compelled into productive work for the British. In 1788,

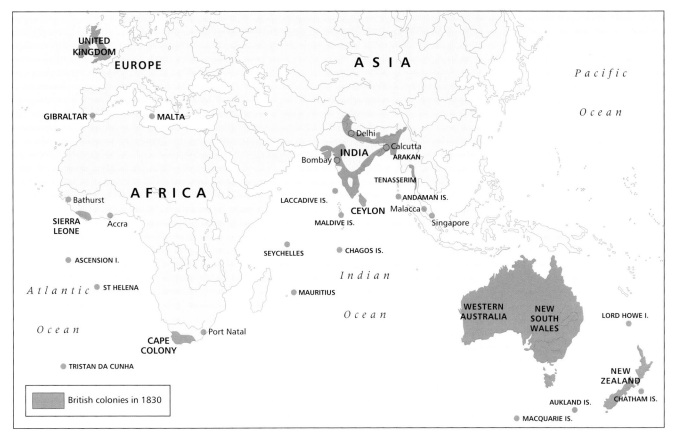

United Kingdom
EUROPE
ASIA
Pacific Ocean
GIBRALTAR • MALTA
Delhi
Calcutta
Bombay INDIA ARAKAN
AFRICA
TENASSERIM
LACCADIVE IS. ANDAMAN IS.
CEYLON Malacca
Bathurst MALDIVE IS. Singapore
SIERRA LEONE Accra
CHAGOS IS.
SEYCHELLES
ASCENSION I.
Indian Ocean
Atlantic ST HELENA
Ocean MAURITIUS
WESTERN AUSTRALIA NEW SOUTH WALES
LORD HOWE I.
CAPE COLONY Port Natal
NEW ZEALAND
TRISTAN DA CUNHA
AUKLAND IS. CHATHAM IS.
MACQUARIE IS.

British colonies in 1830

British territory 1806
British expansion by 1830
British expansion by 1854
Great Trek from 1835
Transvaal (South African Republic 1852)
Orange Free State 1854

Limpopo
Johannesburg
Kalahari Pretoria
Witwatersrand Delagoa Bay
BECHUANA Vaal SWAZI
Orange Kimberley
Bloemfontein BASUTO ZULU
GRIQUA PONDO NATAL Durban
Atlantic Ocean Graff-Reinet
Cape Town CAPE COLONY XOSA
Cape of Good Hope Port Elizabeth
Indian Ocean

QUEENSLAND 1859
Great Dividing Range
Moreton Bay
SOUTH AUSTRALIA 1836 Brisbane
NEW SOUTH WALES 1855
Darling Port Macquarie
Port Augusta Murray Bathurst Botany Bay
Murrumbidgee Newcastle
Adelaide Sydney
VICTORIA 1855 Tasman Sea
Melbourne
Bass Strait
Port Dalrymple Launceston
Macquarie Harbour Hobart TASMANIA Port Arthur
Southern Ocean

area settled by 1830
area settled by 1850
1855 date of creation of state
▲ penal colonies

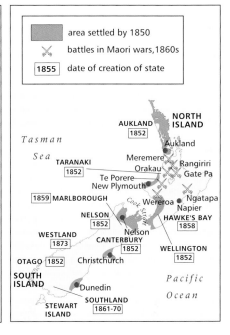

area settled by 1850
battles in Maori wars, 1860s
1855 date of creation of state

NORTH ISLAND
AUKLAND 1852
Tasman Sea Aukland
TARANAKI 1852 Meremere Orakau Rangiriri Gate Pa
Te Porere
New Plymouth Wereroa Ngatapa
1859 MARLBOROUGH Napier
NELSON 1852 HAWKE'S BAY 1858
WESTLAND 1873 CANTERBURY 1852
Nelson WELLINGTON 1852
OTAGO 1852 Christchurch
SOUTH ISLAND
Dunedin SOUTHLAND 1861-70
STEWART ISLAND
Pacific Ocean

British settlement in India, Australia, New Zealand, and South Africa. From India, the British sought the profits of trade and, later, the glory of conquest and the extortion of taxes and cheap labor. Elsewhere they sought to establish settler colonies. British colonists ousted the Dutch from Cape Colony, grasped the habitable littoral of southeast Australia (initially colonizing it with prisoners and other social outcasts), and claimed the world's most southerly inhabitable territory, New Zealand, as a promised land for its swelling early nineteenth-century population.

493

A model war canoe, Gisborne, New Zealand, eighteenth century. Until the end of the eighteenth century, a Maori war canoe was the most prized and decorated clan possession.

when Europeans first arrived to settle Australia, there had been perhaps 300,000 Aborigines. By 2000, the 19 million inhabitants of Australia were 92 percent European, 7 percent Asian, and 1 percent Aboriginal. Today, most of Australia's 50,000 full-blooded Aborigines, and many of its 150,000 part-Aborigines, live on reservations in arid inland regions.

The devastation caused by the arrival of British settlers was repeated in New Zealand. The Maori, an east Polynesian people, had arrived and settled in New Zealand about 750 C.E. They had lived there for almost a thousand years, probably in isolation, until Tasman reached New Zealand's west coast in 1642. The Maori killed four members of his party and prevented his landing. More than a century later, James Cook explored New Zealand for four months and found the Maori brave, warlike, and cannibalistic. Joseph Banks, who was on the voyage, wrote: "I suppose they live intirely [sic] on fish, dogs, and enemies."

The people may have been fierce, but the seals and whales in the coastal waters, and the flax and timber on the land, attracted hunters and traders from Australia, America, and Britain. The first missionaries came in 1814 to convert the Maori. Warfare against and among the Maori was made more deadly by weapons introduced by Europeans. Diseases accompanying the European arrival, especially

Captain Hobson signing the Treaty of Waitanga with Maori chiefs, 1840. The treaty was intended to secure the annexation of New Zealand to the British government, while guaranteeing the constitutional rights of the Maoris. But language difficulties and cultural differences caused misinterpretation of the fine print and the settlers' sense of racial superiority over the "natives" eventually precipitated wars and the conquest of Maori lands.

494

tuberculosis, venereal diseases, and measles, cut the Maori population from about 200,000 when Cook arrived to perhaps 100,000 in 1840 and to 42,000 by the end of the century. In 1840, British settlers signed a treaty with a group of Maori chiefs that gave sovereignty to the British Crown. Although they declared equal rights under law for Maoris and Europeans, in practice they enforced racial inequality. The British confiscated Maori lands on North Island and precipitated wars that drove the Maori from some of New Zealand's richest lands.

South Africa, 1652–1820

The Dutch East India Company sent the first European settlers to South Africa in 1652. They established Cape Town to facilitate shipping between Europe and Asia. The Company soon invited Dutch, French, and German settlers to move inland and to create ranches in Cape Colony. By 1700, the Europeans held most of the good farmland in the region; by 1795, they had spread 300 miles north and 500 miles east of Cape Town. The colony then had a total population of 60,000, of which one-third were whites. Most of the African peoples were of two main ethnic groups—the Khoikhoi herdsmen and the San hunters—with some from other African groups and some peoples of mixed ancestry.

In 1795, Britain took control of the Cape Colony from its Dutch settlers to prevent it from falling to France, which had conquered the Netherlands during the Wars of the French Revolution. In 1814, the Dutch formally ceded the Cape to the British, and the first British colonists arrived in 1820. The continuing struggle for land and power among the British, Dutch, and Africans is discussed in Chapter Sixteen.

Russian Expansion

Russian penetration of Siberia began in the late sixteenth and early seventeenth centuries. Trappers, traders, and explorers moved in as Russian troops and Cossacks continued to reclaim land from the Mongol conquerors. They built trading forts and declared Russian sovereignty all the way to the Bering Sea, and, in the late eighteenth century, even on to Alaska. Later they were joined by Russian farmers seeking to establish farms to provide food for the settlers in this bleak region. Many of the local inhabitants—living nomadic lives with their reindeer, or persisting as hunter-gatherers—succumbed to new diseases carried by the invaders, the universal consequence. Many survivors, however, saw new opportunities offered by the traders and began to alter their way of life, settling into villages. Most adopted Christianity.

In the eighteenth century the fur trade declined; mining, especially of silver, remained as the most important local industry. Meanwhile, the Russian government used Siberia as a prison for its political prisoners and for common criminals as well. Larger-scale settlement in this remote region came only much later, aboard the trans-Siberian railway, which began to reach this region in 1891.

Slavery: Enforced Migration, 1500–1750

Most European emigrants were free people who moved by choice. But throughout the seventeenth and eighteenth centuries, Africa contributed more immigrants to the New World than did Europe. These Africans came as slaves, taken as captives and transported against their will. Trading in African slaves was not new. The Romans had included Africans among their slaves and, as we have seen in

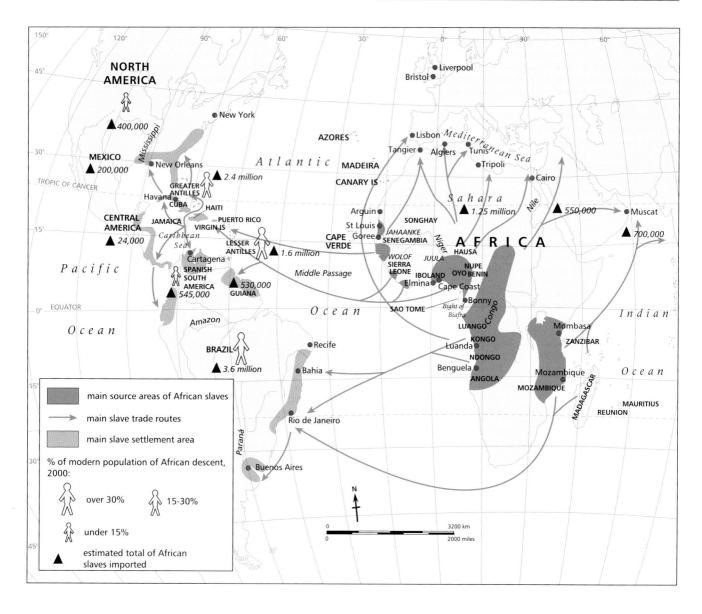

The African slave trade,
c. 1550–1800. A trade in sub-Saharan African slaves dated from the Roman Empire, and had been lucratively developed by Arab merchants from the eighth century. But the impact of Western European entrepreneurs, seeking cheap labor for the Americas, was unparalleled. The millions of Africans who survived the Middle Passage by boat from Africa to the Americas between about 1550 and the late nineteenth century formed a new African diaspora in the New World.

Chapter Twelve, since about the seventh century C.E. Arab camel caravans had carried gold and slaves northward across the Sahara to the Mediterranean in exchange for European cotton and woolen textiles, copper, and brass. On its east coast, Africa had long been integrated into the Indian Ocean trade by Muslim and Arab traders. They exported from Africa gold, slaves, ivory, and amber, and imported cotton and silk cloth.

Portuguese and, later, other European ships reoriented the trade routes of Africa to the Atlantic coast. Caravans continued to cross the desert, but far more trade now came to the new coastal town fortresses constructed at such places as St. Louis, Cape Coast, Elmina, Bonny, Luanda, Benguela, and on São Tomé Island. Here, Africans brought gold and slaves to trade to the European shippers. The number of slaves sold rose from under 1,000 a year in 1451–75, when Portugal began to trade in slaves from the West African coast, to about 7,500 a year, in the first half of the seventeenth century, to about 50,000 a year throughout the eighteenth and first half of the nineteenth centuries. In all, the transatlantic slave trade carried some ten million people from Africa to the western hemisphere to work as slaves, generally on sugar, tobacco, and cotton plantations.

The Plantation Economy

The slaves took on economic importance in direct proportion to the expansion of the sugar plantation economy of the Caribbean after 1650. In the 1700s, the plantations reached their maximum productivity and profitability. Between 1713 and 1792 Britain alone imported £162 million of goods from the Caribbean, almost all of it sugar. This was half again as much as all British imports from Asia during the same period. France held the richest single sugar colony in the Caribbean, Saint-Domingue.

Historian Philip Curtin analyzed the structure of the plantation economy that produced the sugar, and stressed six key points:

- It relied on slave labor.
- It was organized as an early, large-scale capitalist enterprise with gangs of laborers.
- Its owners held legal rights over the lives of the workers.
- It supplied a crop for export to distant European markets but often did not grow its own food; it was completely reliant on international trade for profits and for necessities.
- Its "political control over the system lay on another continent and in another kind of society."
- In its organization, the sugar plantation was a forerunner of factory labor.

Slaves died young on the sugar plantations of the Caribbean and Brazil, where owners often believed it was cheaper to work them to death and buy replacements from among those coming from Africa rather than to feed, clothe, and house them adequately to sustain life. In North America, which concentrated on producing other crops and where planters encouraged their slaves to reproduce, they fared somewhat better.

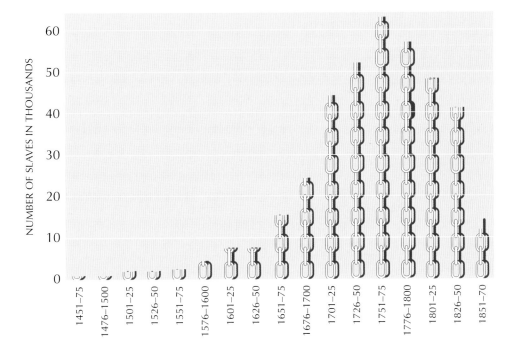

Major trends of the Atlantic slave trade in annual average number of slaves imported. Sixty percent of all slaves delivered to the New World arrived between 1721 and 1820; 80 percent between 1701 and 1850. The British abolition of the slave trade in 1807 had some effect, but it did not stop the trade. (Source: Curtin, *The Atlantic Slave Trade*)

HOW DO WE KNOW?

How Many Slaves?

Philip Curtin's *The Atlantic Slave Trade: A Census*, published in 1969, remains the landmark study on the demographics of the slave trade. Concluding that the existing estimate of 15 million slaves carried from Africa to the New World had been accepted with little basis in research, Curtin investigated the numbers. He limited his research to data already published rather than undertaking original archival searches of his own. From the import records of specific African and American ports, shipping records, and projections based on historical slave populations in the Americas, Curtin produced the first systematic analysis of the quantity of slaves delivered to the Americas.

Curtin begins his analysis with the importation of slaves into Europe, including Sicily, Portugal, Spain, and Italy, as well as to the sugar-producing islands off the coasts of these countries. Evaluating and revising the statistics of previous demographers for the period 1450–1500, Curtin estimates that 50,000 Africans were imported as slaves into Europe and 25,000 into the Atlantic islands of Madeira, Cape Verde, and the Canaries. Another 100,000 were transported off the African coast to São Tomé.

Based primarily on the records of *asientos*, shipping licenses issued by Spanish authorities to foreign firms between 1521 and 1773, and on government records, especially from Britain, Curtin estimates that until 1865 the entire import of Africans to Spanish America was 1,552,000, with 702,000 of these going to Cuba. For the entire period from 1640 to 1807 (when Britain outlawed the slave trade), Curtin estimates that 1,665,000 people were imported as slaves to the British West Indies. He estimates that 1,600,200 were imported to the French West Indies between 1664

and 1838, and more than double these numbers to Portuguese America. To Brazil alone, with its massive sugar plantations, Curtin accepts the estimates of two earlier demographers, who suggested a figure of about 3,646,800. To the Dutch West Indies, 500,000 people were imported as slaves; to the Danish West Indies, now the American Virgin Islands, 28,000. Imports to the United States and pre-1776 North America totaled about 399,000.

Thus, Curtin's estimate for the total importation of slaves to the Americas is 9,566,000. Overall, he notes, "more Africans than Europeans arrived in the Americas between, say, 1492 and 1770" (p. 87). Curtin notes that, although his estimates could well be off by as much as 50 percent, they are, nevertheless, "correct enough to point out contradictions in present hypotheses and to raise new questions for comparative demography and social history" (p. 93).

The United States and Canada imported only 4.2 percent of all the slaves imported into the Americas, about 400,000 out of 9,566,000. Curtin writes:

> Contrary to the parochial view of history that most North Americans pick up in school, the United States was only a marginal recipient of slaves from Africa. The real center of the trade was tropical America, with almost 90 percent going to the Atlantic fringe from Brazil through the Guianas to the Caribbean coast and islands. (p. 74)

Curtin also explored the effects on reproduction of the slave trade. Only about one-third of the slaves sold overseas were

The Slave Trade Reinterpreted

From the fifteenth to the nineteenth centuries, individual states were taking form on the African continent. The largest, like the Songhay Empire of West Africa, was about the size of France or Spain. Medium-size states, the size of Portugal or of England, were more numerous, including the Oyo Empire in Nigeria, Nupe, Igala, and Benin in the lower Niger valley, the Hausa states of northern Nigeria, and Kongo, in Central Africa. Slavery and the slave trade were important to the rise and decline of these states. In a region where land was not privately owned, slaves represented the main form of wealth. A rich state held many slaves. Slaves were a source of labor, a means for their owners to increase wealth. The trade in slaves was a means of further increasing wealth. Long before Europeans arrived on the Atlantic coast, slavery was big business in these African states.

This prevalence of slavery in Africa helps to explain a turnabout in the interpretation of the slave trade. In this interpretation, Africans are active participants who helped build up this important trade. When European traders offered new opportunities, African businessmen, who were already active in the internal slave trade, joined in, continuing to control the trade up to the water's edge. European demand drove the vast increase in the slave trade, but Europeans lacked the military strength, the immunity to disease, and the knowledge of the terrain to enter the interior of the

HOW DO WE KNOW?

women, so that in Africa population losses to the next generation were proportionately limited, but in the Americas, with fewer females, the slaves did not reproduce their own numbers. These rates of reproduction were, however, different in different areas. North America imported relatively few slaves because those who were imported reproduced more abundantly than slaves elsewhere, for reasons yet unknown:

> Rather than sustaining the regular excess of deaths over births typical of tropical America, the North American colonies developed a pattern of natural growth among the slaves … By the end of the eighteenth century, North American slave populations were growing at nearly the same rate as that of the settler populations from Europe … Historians have neglected [this] almost completely, even though it has an obvious and important bearing on such recent historical problems as the comparative history of slavery in the New World. Nor have demographic historians yet produced a complete or satisfactory explanation of this phenomenon. (p. 73)

Various hypotheses have attempted to explain the higher rates of reproduction in North America. The first, and perhaps most obvious, holds that slaves in North America were better treated than elsewhere. The second argues that slaves in North America apparently breast-fed their children for only one year, in contrast to the two years more typical in the Caribbean. Breast-feeding has a contraceptive effect that would have reduced birth rates more in the Caribbean than in the U.S.

Additional demographic inquiries have followed Curtin's *Census.* For example, Curtin pointed out that the location of the most active slave trading varied over time, according to the law of supply and demand. Where slaves were plentiful, often because of warfare and the seizing of captives who could be sold into slavery, prices fell; then more European slavers arrived to take advantage of the low prices, increasing demand, raising prices, and encouraging European slavers to look elsewhere. The marketplace shifted as prices oscillated. The result seems to be that no area was constantly a supplier, but that each area had time to recover some of its population losses. On the other hand, no area remained immune to the economic attractions of the market. The sale and purchase of slaves infected the entire coastline.

Later historians have sought to locate more precisely the geographical source of slaves exported from Africa. Paul Lovejoy, for example, found that of the 5.5 million exported in the 100 years between 1701 and 1800, the three largest sources were west-central Africa, with 2 million, the Bight of Biafra, with 814,000, and the Senegambia, with 201,000. (Lovejoy)

Curtin's work inspired additional statistical research, and we now have a clear, empirical basis for understanding the general dimensions of three centuries of Atlantic trade in human beings.

- Philip Curtin's studies of the slave trade say very little about moral issues. What is the importance of information about the systems and statistics of plantation slavery, separate from the consideration of moral issues?
- Please give examples of ways in which the slave trade was subject to the economic laws of supply and demand.
- What regions of the Americas imported the most slaves?

A slave market, from *Al Magamat (The Meetings),* fourteenth century. Muslims owned and traded slaves from the earliest days of the Islamic religion. Their trade in slaves included Africa, southeastern Europe, Arabia, and the lands surrounding the Indian Ocean. Islamic law governing the treatment of slaves made the practice relatively humane; slaves were used more frequently for domestic service than for gang labor. In principle, Muslims were not permitted to enslave other Muslims. Practice often differed, but granting freedom to Muslim slaves was considered virtuous. (Bibliothèque Nationale, Paris)

continent. They stayed in coastal enclaves, while Africans captured the slaves and brought them to be purchased. Occasionally, African rulers attempted to limit the trade, but both African and European traders seemed beyond their control.

Some of the trading communities of Africa—ethnic groups that traditionally facilitated and controlled trade—probably profited, including the Jahaanke of the Gambia–Niger River region; the Juula of northern Ghana, Ivory Coast, and the Upper Niger River; the Wolof of Senegal; and the Awka and Aro of Iboland in Nigeria. A new community of African–Portuguese traders was also born as Portuguese and Africans along the coast bonded and had children.

The effects of the slave trade on the total economy of Africa remain disputed. Some scholars, following the pioneering work of Walter Rodney in his *How Europe Underdeveloped Africa* (1972), cite dire economic consequences. Some more recent writers, however, suggest that the slave trade, despite its enormous absolute size, was small relative to the total size of Africa's population and internal economy and therefore had little effect. This debate over size and significance continues. No one, however, can estimate the lost opportunities for African development represented by the export of so many millions of its strongest and most resilient men and women.

Crosby points out that Africa received new crops such as maize and manioc (cassava) as part of the Atlantic exchange. These became staple foods and, ironically, may actually have increased the population more than the export of slaves depleted it. And, of course, slavery established a new population of African origin throughout the western hemisphere.

Asian Migrations, 1300–1750

Just as Europeans were transforming the Americas and other parts of the world through their migrations, Asians were moving into other parts of the world they conquered. In Chapters Twelve and Thirteen, we analyzed the geographical patterns and economic institutions of trade and traders, and found that they developed differently in Europe and in Asia. The differences became especially sharp as the Europeans set out on their voyages of transoceanic exploration and trade across the Atlantic. Patterns of migration also differed sharply between Europe and Asia—and yet there were striking similarities.

Vast, successive waves of immigrant conquerors swept out of central Asia between 1300 and 1750, creating three new empires and several new ruling dynasties within the already existing empire of China. Turkic-speaking invaders founded the Ottoman Empire that sprawled across western Asia, southeastern Europe, and North Africa; the Safavid Empire in Persia; and the Mughal Empire in South Asia. In China, the Mongol descendants of Chinggis Khan and, later, the Manchus introduced new dynasties to the existing empire.

The conquests of the Western Europeans and the central Asians show remarkable similarities. The time frame for these invasions and conquests is roughly parallel. (The Ottoman conquests, blocking access to the eastern Mediterranean and the Middle East, provided the inspiration for the Europeans to launch their overseas explorations.) The distances they traveled, across thousands of miles, were equally vast. Both were ultimately motivated by a desire to conquer and subdue that frequently led to ruthless cruelty. Both imposed new cultures on the peoples they conquered—but the degree of this imposition was starkly different.

The contrasts are altogether quite remarkable. The Asians traveled over land. Although they could be very violent, they did not so utterly destroy the peoples they conquered, perhaps because the peoples the Asians conquered had immunity to each

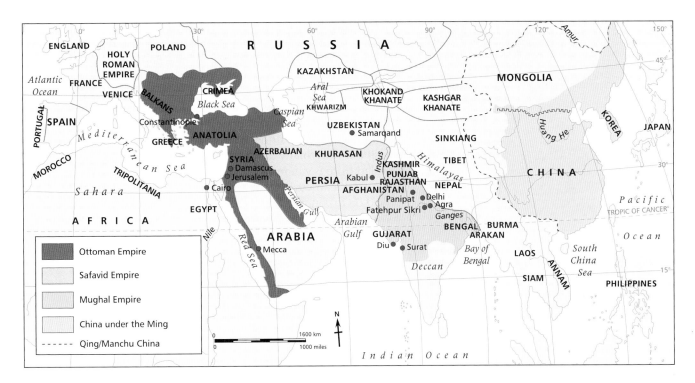

other's diseases thanks to their long contact with each other. Since the Asian conquerors were mostly nomadic horsemen with little experience of sedentary society, they were limited in the degree to which they could influence their subjects. Instead, over time they tended to adopt the ideas and institutions of the peoples they conquered. They did not displace existing societies with new ones of their own design. In large measure they were assimilated by the peoples they defeated. By the early eighteenth century, as Western Europe was increasing in power and wealth, most of the Asian empires were in decline.

The Ottoman Empire, 1300–1700

The Ottoman Empire was named for Osman, a Turkish leader whose military victory in 1301 established its foundation in northwest Anatolia. As the Ottomans expanded from this local base they confronted the Byzantine Empire to the west and the Seljuq Turks—another Turkic-speaking group—to the east. Through the thirteenth and fourteenth centuries they expanded their holdings, capturing much of Anatolia and crossing into Europe to take Gallipoli in 1354. The Ottoman Empire rose to prominence at the same time as Spain and Portugal did in Western Europe and was at its height in 1600. By 1700, however, it had begun to decline.

Three groups led and sustained the Turkish invasions. The *gazis* were Turkish warriors inspired by Islam to conquer territories and bring them under the *dar al-Islam*, a government hospitable to Islam. **Sufis** were members of religious orders, often practicing mystical and ecstatic rituals, who accompanied the troops and introduced Islam within the conquered regions. Finally, the janissaries were slaves captured or bought from among the conquered populations, usually from among the Christians of the Balkans, to be converted to Islam and serve in the elite Turkish armies and, occasionally, in the administration. In 1527 the slave infantry numbered about 28,000. In conquering Anatolia, Turks displaced the local agricultural communities and became the majority population.

Eurasian empires, 1650. Eurasia on the eve of European expansion was dominated by a complex of huge, interlocking, land-based empires, linked by overland trade routes, and by the Arab trading ecumene of the Indian Ocean. The four empires highlighted here were land-based, inward-looking, and ill-prepared for the challenge of European imperialism that would arrive by sea and, over the next 400 years, effectively undermine them.

KEY TERM

Sufi In Islam, a member of one of the orders practicing mystical forms of worship that first arose in the eighth and ninth centuries C.E.

501

Siege of Beograd (Belgrade) by Mehmed II, sixteenth-century Persian manuscript. After the setback of defeat by the central Asian conqueror Tamerlane in 1402, the Ottoman Empire rebuilt, consolidated, and extended its power. A major watershed was passed when Sultan Mehmed II conquered Constantinople (Istanbul) in 1453, making it the third and last Ottoman capital city. This Turkish empire endured for 600 years (1300–1922) and at its height spanned three continents. (Topkapi Palace, Istanbul)

After establishing a foothold in Europe, the Ottomans invited Turkish warriors into the Balkans and occupied northern Greece, Macedonia, and Bulgaria. At the Battle of Kosovo in 1389 they secured Serbia and took control of the western Balkans. Demographically, however, the invaders were not so numerous in this region, nor did they force widespread conversion. A census of 1520–30 showed that about one-fifth of the Balkan population was Muslim, about four-fifths was Christian, and there was a small Jewish minority, many of whom moved to the empire after they were expelled from Spain in 1492.

Under Mehmed II, "The Conqueror" (r. 1451–81), the Ottomans moved on to conquer Constantinople in 1453 and then the remainder of Anatolia, the Crimea on the north of the Black Sea, and substantial areas of Venice's empire in Greece and the Aegean. They began the process of rebuilding Constantinople into a great capital city, and by 1600 it had become the largest city in Europe with 700,000 inhabitants. The capital attracted a great influx of immigrant scholars to its *madrasas*, religious schools, and to its bureaucratic jobs, which required Islamic learning and knowledge of the law.

Selim I (r. 1512–20) decisively defeated the Shi'a Safavid Empire in Persia at the Battle of Chaldiran in 1514. He turned next against the Mamluk Empire of Egypt, conquering its key cities of Aleppo and Damascus, and its capital, Cairo. These victories also gave the Ottomans control of the holy cities of Jerusalem, Mecca, and Medina, and of both coasts of the Red Sea.

Suleiman (Süleyman) I, "the Magnificent" (r. 1520–66), returned to battle in Europe, adding Hungary to his empire and pushing to the gates of Vienna. As they entered central Europe, the Ottomans confronted the Habsburg Empire. Alliances here crossed religious lines, with Catholic France sometimes joining with the Muslim Ottomans in alliance against the Catholic Habsburgs. In a series of battles, which collectively formed a kind of world war, the Ottomans were defeated at sea in 1571 at Lepanto, off the coast of Greece, by a coalition of the papacy, Venice, and the Habsburgs. Finally, in 1580, a peace treaty confirmed the informal boundaries that still endure in the Mediterranean today between predominantly Christian Europe to the north and west, and predominantly Muslim North Africa and western Asia to the south and east.

Battles on land continued until 1606, when the peace treaty of Zsitva Torok confirmed Ottoman rule over Romania, Hungary, and Transylvania, but recognized the Habsburgs as their equals. Financially and militarily drained by two centuries of warfare with the Habsburgs in the Balkans and southeastern Europe, the Ottomans halted their expansion into these areas in 1606. In 1683, a last attempt to seize Vienna failed. North of the Black Sea, where Russia, Poland, and the Ottomans fought, the empire had greater success, taking control of substantial parts of the Ukraine in 1676. These victories, however, marked the maximum extent of Ottoman dominance in the region. Russia had built up its military power under Peter I, the Great (r. 1682–1725), and consolidated it under Catherine II, the Great (r. 1762–96), and now, in the mid-1700s, pushed the Ottomans back. Attempting to regain lost territory, throughout the late 1700s the Ottomans once again brought in Western European experts to retrain their military, as they had in capturing Constantinople, but this effort was too little, too late. The Ottoman Empire had fallen too far behind the Western Europeans and the Russians both economically and militarily. They could no longer catch up.

Through both immigration and natural increase, the population of the Ottoman Empire seems to have more than doubled, from 12–13 million in 1520–30 in the early years of the rule of Suleiman I (at a time when Spain may have had 5 million inhabitants; England 2.5 million; Portugal 1 million), to 17–18 million in 1580, to possibly 30–35 million by 1600. This doubling, or even tripling, of the Empire's population was consistent with the general population increase of the Mediterranean basin, which rose from 30–35 million in 1500 to 60–70 million in 1600.

India: The Mughal Empire, 1526–1707

The Mughals, a mixture of Mongol and Turkish peoples from central Asia, rose to power a little later than the Ottomans. In 1526 Babur (Zahir-ud-Din Mohammad, 1483–1530), a descendant of Timur the Lame on his father's side and of Chinggis Khan on his mother's side, invaded India and conquered Delhi and Agra, establishing himself as sultan. His son, Humayun, was defeated in battles with Afghans and driven out of India, but he fought his way back through Afghanistan and into north India before his death. The task of continuing the conquest and consolidating its administration fell to Humayun's son, Akbar (1542–1605), perhaps India's greatest ruler.

Akbar, Emperor of India. Born in 1542, Akbar was reared in exile with his father, the Mughal ruler Humayun, in the rugged terrain of Afghanistan. His childhood was dominated by physical pursuits, and he grew up without learning to read and write, although he loved to have others read to him. Akbar's father Humayun succeeded in returning to India and re-establishing his authority in Delhi, but when he died (after falling down a staircase), Akbar acceded to the throne aged 14 years.

Ottoman empires, 1300–1700. As the Mongols ceased their advance, some of the peoples who had traveled with them began to assert their power. The Ottoman Turks began to establish their new empire, which conquered Constantinople in 1453 and thrust far into southeastern Europe as well as the Mediterranean coast. Babur, a Mughal, began the conquest of India in 1526 and his grandson Akbar proceeded to construct one of the largest, most powerful, and most cultured empires of his day.

503

Abul-Fazl presenting his book of the Akbarnama to Akbar, c. 1600. Surrounded by his courtiers, the emperor Akbar receives from his principal administrator, Abul-Fazl, the Akbarnama, an array of Mughal miniature paintings that illustrate the military, diplomatic, economic, and administrative life of Akbar's empire and government. Note the diversity in appearance and dress of the courtiers. Abul-Fazl himself was an Indian Muslim educated in Persian fashion, while Akbar was a soldier of Turkish and Mongol descent. At its best, such diversity was a mark of strength in the Mughal court. (Chester Beatty Library, Dublin)

Four years later, he began to govern as absolute monarch. Raised on stories of his ancestors, Timur the Lame and Chinggis Khan, and of his grandfather, Babur, Akbar now set about creating an empire of his own. He showed no mercy to those who would not submit to his rule. In 1568 protracted fighting in the Mewar district culminated in a siege of the historic fortress of Chitor and ultimately the massacre of its entire population of 30,000 inhabitants. In 1572–73 Akbar conquered Gujarat, gaining control of its extensive commercial networks and its rich resources of cotton and indigo. Then came Bengal to the east, with its rice, silk, and saltpeter, Kashmir to the north, Orissa to the south, and Sind to the west. Each new conquest brought greater riches.

A great conqueror, Akbar spent years on the move with his troops, but he also built new capitals for himself, first at Agra (where his grandson would build the Taj Mahal), later at nearby Fatehpur Sikri. With his chief revenue officer, Todar Mal, he established an administrative bureaucracy modeled on a military hierarchy. He surveyed each region of India down to the village level, evaluated its fertility, and established the land revenue each was to pay. His administrators collected the payment in cash. These reforms brought village India into a cash economy, while city markets encouraged the production of luxury goods for the court and everyday goods for the common people. Mughal officials, aware that their wealth would revert to the emperor at their death, lived a life of lavish consumption.

Akbar understood immediately that as a foreigner and a Muslim in an overwhelmingly Hindu country, he would have to temper conquest with conciliation. He allowed the fiercely independent Hindu Rajputs, who controlled the hilly territory of Rajasthan, to keep their ancestral lands, and he offered them roles in his government and armies. In return they paid tribute to him, supplied him with troops, and gave him their daughters in marriage alliances, since Muslims could practice polygamy. He appointed Hindus to a third of the posts in his centralized administration. Two-thirds went to Muslims who immigrated in large numbers from Iran, Afghanistan, and central Asia to the expanding Mughal court. In 1562 Akbar discontinued the practice of enslaving prisoners-of-war and forcing them to convert to Islam. In 1563 he abolished a tax on Hindu pilgrims traveling to sacred shrines. The next year, most importantly, he revoked the *jizya*, the head tax levied on non-Muslims. Between 20 and 25 percent of India's population became Muslim, most through conversion, the rest the result of immigration from outside.

Akbar encouraged and participated personally in religious discussions among Muslims, Hindus, Parsis (Indians who followed Zoroaster; their name means "Persians," from the area in which Zoroaster had his greatest influence), and Christians. (Jesuits visiting the court mistook Akbar's inquiries into Catholic doctrine as a willingness to convert.) Muslim Sufis spread their message in Hindi, a modern derivative of Sanskrit, the sacred language of Hindus. At the same time they inspired the creation of the Urdu (camp) language, the language of common exchange between the invaders and the resident population. Urdu used the syntactical structure of Hindi, the alphabet of Arabic and Persian, and a vocabulary of words drawn from Sanskrit, Persian, and Arabic. Akbar, in particular, encouraged these kinds of cultural **syncretism** and the mixing of groups. His tolerant practices and mixing of groups encouraged still more individuals to migrate to India.

In 1582 Akbar declared a new personal religion, the *Din-i-Ilahi*, or Divine Faith, an amalgam of Islamic, Hindu, and Parsi perspectives. He also incorporated some concepts of divine rights, declaring himself the vice-regent of God and appointing himself ultimate arbiter on disputes concerning Islamic law. Elaborate ceremonials at court emphasized the emperor's supremacy, and he was careful to encourage reverence among the common people as well. Orthodox Muslims, however, saw Akbar's pronouncements as heresies and went into opposition. Several were jailed.

In 1600, at the height of Akbar's rule, the population of India reached 140–150 million, with about 110 million contained within the Mughal Empire, about the same population as China and twice that of the Ottoman Empire at its largest. The population increase that occurred all over Afro-Eurasia at this time affected India as well, and the population of the subcontinent in 1800 probably reached about 200 million.

During a reign that spanned half a century, Akbar presided over a glittering court, in which the fine arts, literature, and architecture flourished. He transformed himself from conquering despot of a foreign religious minority to respected emperor of all Hindustan. In a half-century of rule, 1556–1605, Akbar had established one of the great empires of the world.

Akbar's great-grandson, and third successor, Aurangzeb (Alamgir, 1658–1707), continued the Mughal conquest almost to the southern tip of the country. But Aurangzeb forsook Akbar's tolerance. He imposed a poll tax on Hindus and desecrated their shrines and statues, antagonizing them and fomenting resentment. Aurangzeb's military adventures in the south overextended his armies and overtaxed the peasantry to the point of revolt. Hindu Marathas in western India and **Sikhs** in the north, as well as the Afghan Nadir Shah, who invaded from Iran in 1739, rose against the Mughal Empire. By the middle of the eighteenth century, the empire lay weak and open to new invaders from Western Europe—the British and the French.

Safavid Persia, 1400–1700

In the thirteenth century the Mongols and Turks first devastated and then repopulated Persia. The invaders systematically exterminated the populations of the first cities they confronted; others, hearing of the massacres, fled. The invading Mongols and Turks then settled on the land, reducing to serfdom those who remained behind, and taxing them into poverty. By the end of the century, however, the invaders began to assimilate Persian ways, rebuilding the cities; redeveloping the irrigation works; supporting agriculture and trade, including the silk routes to China; and adopting both the religion of Islam and the culture of Persia, with its monarchical traditions.

In 1370 the successor to the Chagatai branch of the Mongols, Timur the Lame (*c.* 1336–1405), came to power, ruling Iran and much of northern India, Anatolia, and northern Syria from his capital in Samarqand until his death in 1405. With this further set of invasions, Turkish peoples came to constitute about 25 percent of Iran's population, which is the ratio today. The Mongol/Turkish invaders were pastoral peoples, and under their rule substantial agricultural land once again reverted to pasturage and villagers turned to nomadic existences, farming in valley bottoms and herding sheep in nearby mountain highlands.

Culturally, some of the Turks, as well as other ethnic groups in Iran, later came to accept the militantly religious teachings of Shaykh Safi al-Din (1252–1334). His followers, called Safavids, claimed political as well as religious authority. In 1501, a disciple of the

The defeat of Pir Padishah by Shah Rukh in 1403, Persian, 1420–30. Shah Rukh, son of Timur the Lame, was a direct ancestor of the Safavid Persians. During his reign, he had to deal with several rebellions, including one by the Sarbadars, a brigand community in Khurasan. Leading the decisive charge, Shah Rukh's army commander beheads one of the rebel cavalrymen. (Victoria & Albert Museum, London)

teachings of Safi, Shah Isma'il (1487–1524), declared himself the hidden imam, the long-awaited political/religious messiah of Shi'ite Muslims. He occupied Tabriz and proclaimed himself the Shah of Iran.

The Safavids found it difficult to bring together the diverse peoples and interests of Iran. The greatest achievement was by Shah Abbas (1588–1629), who built up the military capacity of the country. He did this, in part, by importing European weapons, equipment, technicians, and advisers. He acquired and built muskets and artillery that were capable of matching the Ottomans. Like other Safavid rulers, he brought slaves from Georgia, Armenia, and Turkish lands to form the core of his armies. Abbas also built a great, new capital city at Isfahan. He encouraged trade and commerce there by inviting Armenian merchants as well as many artisans, including ceramicists who could produce "Chinese" porcelains. He invited some Chinese potters to teach Iranians their trade, and some of them remained and settled in Isfahan. Abbas, however, murdered competing religious leaders and groups, including other Shi'a groups as well as Sunnis and Sufis. His successors in the middle of the century gave official sanction to efforts to convert both Jews and Zoroastrians to Islam by force. But they did not succeed in bringing all the powers of his decentralized realm into a centralized monarchy.

By the end of the seventeenth century, the Safavid army was unraveling, its central administration was failing, regional powers were reasserting themselves, and Iran was in anarchy. Despite the occasional brilliant military conqueror, such as Nadir Shah (1688–1747), another Turkish/Mongol immigrant who took the throne in 1736, Iran was already moving toward partition, first internally, and later at the hands of Europeans and Russians.

China: The Ming and Manchu Dynasties, 1368–1750

In 1211 Chinggis Khan invaded and conquered China, destroying the Song dynasty in the process. His descendants established the Yuan dynasty, which ruled for a century (1271–1368) until the Ming dynasty drove them out and established its own long and successful rule (1368–1644).

By 1600 China's economy was flourishing and the country contained 20 percent of the world's population, about 150 million people. Ming border policy was to pacify and to accommodate the Mongol peoples of the north. The emperors stationed large numbers of troops there and rebuilt the Great Wall. Ming anxieties were well founded. In 1644 China was once again conquered by invaders from the north, the Jurchen, or Manchus, of Manchuria. The Manchu invasions undercut China's power and sophistication, and contributed—along with natural disasters, virulent epidemics,

Attacks on the borders by land and sea. Chinese picture scroll, early seventeenth century. Through the fifteenth and sixteenth centuries, the Ming dynasty was bedeviled by raids and attacks from the barbarian peoples on China's northern frontiers. The Great Wall underwent major reconstruction in this period. Meanwhile coastal residents were forced to take to their boats to battle the pirates who attacked their settlements. (Historiographical Institute, University of Tokyo)

and the failure of irrigation systems—to a catastrophic, but temporary, fall in China's population. The Mandate of Heaven passed from the Ming as the Manchus established a new dynasty, the Qing (1644–1911).

The Qing expanded the borders of China, more than doubling the geographical size of the country. They conquered and controlled Tibet, Xinjiang, Outer Mongolia, and the Tarim Basin, the heartland of the old silk routes. One of their most important European contacts was with Russia, and disputes between the two empires were negotiated in the Treaty of Nerchinsk (1689), the first Chinese–European treaty negotiated on terms of equality. The treaty facilitated trade between China and Russia and delimited their border along the Amur River, although the border between Mongolia and Siberia was not fixed.

The country's population began to grow again in the eighteenth century, fed by new crops introduced into China from the New World. Sweet potatoes, for example, were widespread in coastal China by the mid-eighteenth century, while maize and the Irish potato became common in the north and in the southwest at the same time. Peanuts had spread rapidly in south and southwestern China in the late Ming, and were also becoming an important crop in north China by the end of Qianlong's reign (r. 1736–95). All these crops helped to improve the health of China's rural workers and, because the crops grew well, even in poor and hilly land, they enabled the population to increase rapidly.

Global Population Growth and Movement

Population size is both the result and the cause of larger changes in society. The numbers are important markers.

Demographers estimate that Europe's population more than tripled between 1000 and 1700, with the greatest growth coming after the Black Death of 1348–51. The plague killed off perhaps a third of Europe's population, but it soon increased again to its former levels and then continued to multiply. The New World across the Atlantic provided a new home to some of the increased millions.

In the tropical and subtropical regions of the New World, European settlers introduced plantations, which created an immense demand for labor. Beginning in the early 1500s, as we have seen, Africans were seized as slaves to fill that demand. By the time the Atlantic slave trade was successfully abolished, three and a half centuries later, Africa had lost some ten million people (see "How do we know?" box, p. 498). Meanwhile, the native populations of the Americas were even more devastated, with up to 90 percent of their people lost, in some areas, although the total population in the Americas was slowly augmented by immigration from Europe. The population of Asia more than held its own with about two-thirds of the world's population. Between 1000 and 1800 the proportion actually grew from 63 percent to 69 percent of the total. Although there were massive population movements of Mongols and Turks, these migrations do not affect these counts since almost all of the movement was from one location to another within Asia.

Europeans increased fastest of all. They multiplied not only within Europe but, in the words of Alfred Crosby, a leading scholar on the demographic effects of European expansion, they also "leapfrogged around the globe [to found] Neo-Europes, lands thousands of kilometers from Europe and from each other" (Crosby, p. 2). In 1800 North America held almost five million whites, South America about 500,000, Australia 10,000, and New Zealand a few thousand.

Then came the deluge. "Between 1820 and 1930, well over fifty million Europeans migrated to the Neo-European lands overseas … approximately one-fifth of the entire population of Europe at the beginning of that period" (Crosby, p. 5). The number of peoples of European ancestry who were settled outside Europe grew from 5.7 million in 1810 to 200 million in 1910. These nineteenth-century figures take us into the times of the Industrial Revolution and its massive transformations, which are covered in the next part of this book; but the demographic diffusion across the world had already begun by 1800.

The expansion of Europe was not unique in world history, yet it was probably the most numerically sizable and geographically widespread mass migration ever seen: a migration across vast expanses of water, creating permanent links among continents of the world that had been almost entirely separate, and bringing European dominion over three continents besides its own.

Cities and Demographics

Studies of population movement analyze not only migration across global regions, but also the movement from rural to urban areas, and from one urban area to another. Because cities serve as centers for rule, administration, economic production, trade, art, and culture, migrations into (and out of) cities also tell us something of the transformation of society. The movement from nomadic to urban society is one of the most striking examples.

As we know from Part Two, "Settling Down," we expect urban occupations, diversity of population, and rates of innovation to be very different from those of the countryside. What then was happening in terms of rural–urban movement in the various regions of the world—and in the capital cities of the empires—that we have been studying? Although an examination of capital cities is not decisive, it is suggestive. We expect that capitals of strong states will attract large and vibrant populations. Here we will look at four capital cities that were especially important in attracting migrants in the various empires we have examined.

World population totals and distribution. In the last 1,000 years, the world's population has multiplied 20 times from less than 300 million to 6,000 million (the United Nations estimate as of October 1999). Moreover, the distribution of that population by geographical origins has shifted. For most of the millennium, the proportion of people in Europe grew fastest, but in the last century, that trend reversed. Since 1900, the percentage of people in Africa, the Americas, and Oceania has grown fastest. The decline in population in the Americas, 1000–1700, represents the death of Native Americans; the rise after 1700 represents, in large part, immigration from Europe and Africa. In all time periods Asia has held by far the largest proportion of the world's population.

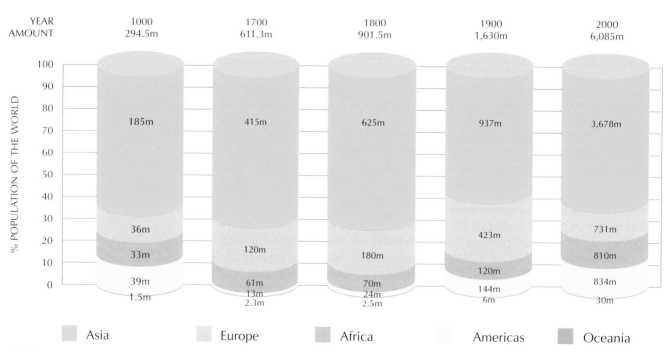

Delhi/Shahjahanabad

Each Mughal emperor built his own capital. Akbar ruled primarily from Agra, about 100 miles south of Delhi, but in 1569 he built a new capital at Fatehpur Sikri, about 20 miles from Agra, to honor a Sufi saint who had prayed there for a male heir for the emperor. By the end of the century, however, a shortage of water forced Akbar to abandon his beautiful, architecturally eclectic capital city and return to Agra. His son, Jahangir, preferred to rule from Lahore and he built up that Punjabi city as his capital. Akbar's grandson, Shah Jahan (r. 1628–58), rebuilt Delhi as his own capital and gave it his own name.

Built in a semicircular shape, with a radius of 10–12 miles, Shahjahanabad (City of Shah Jahan) had a population apparently reaching two million by the mid-seventeenth century. As a newly rebuilt city, almost all its residents were immigrants. The merchant and artisan population, in particular, was composed of foreign merchants such as Armenians, Persians, central Asians, and Kashmiris.

Shah Jahan leaving the Great Mosque at Delhi by elephant, seventeenth century. Akbar's grandson Shah Jahan restored and rebuilt Delhi in the 1600s to serve as the capital of the Mughal Empire. In 1739 the Persian emperor Nadir Shah conquered the city and looted its treasures, including the famous Peacock Throne. Today, with neighboring New Delhi, it is India's capital and third largest city.

Stephen Blake, in his study *Shahjahanabad*, describes the Delhi of Shah Jahan as recapturing the spirit of imperial authority vested in it over centuries, most recently by the Delhi sultanate. It served also as a religious center, a place of pilgrimage revered throughout India for its tombs and graves of saints and holy men. The inner city was encircled by a massive stone wall, 3.8 miles long, 27 feet high, and 12 feet thick. At the convergence of the main streets stood the palace-fort, the home of the emperor, the administrative center of the Mughal Empire. The city had its splendors. The poet Amir Khusrau inscribed on the walls of the private audience hall of the emperor: "If there is a paradise on earth, it is here, it is here, it is here." Opposite it, 1,000 yards west, set on a small hill, rose the *masjid-i-jami*, the Friday mosque, or chief public mosque of the city. In keeping with Islamic architectural principles, gardens with streams of water running through them to delight the eye and the ear were included in the landscaping.

The larger city housed an assembly of military camps, each under the leadership of one of the emperor's leading generals. M. Gentile, a visiting Frenchman in the mid-eighteenth century, wrote: "There are many mansions of the nobles, which one can compare to small towns and in which reside the women, equipment, and bazaars (or public markets) of the nobles" (Blake, p. 179). The twentieth-century historian Percival Spear referred to Shahjahanabad's "nomadic court and its tents of stone" (Toynbee, p. 237), the architecture reminding him that the Mughals "had started as nomads in the central Asian steppes, and until their last days they never forgot their origin" (p. 238). Each nobleman also built his own mosque. But the main function of the city was as the center of administrative and military power. Visitors to India observed that in reality the largest city in India was the military camp commanded by the emperor in the field. When he went to war, as Aurangzeb did for years at a time, hundreds of thousands of soldiers and camp followers accompanied him; Shahjahanabad itself was deserted.

Isfahan

In Iran, Shah Abbas (1537–1628) made Isfahan his capital in 1598. One of the largest and most beautiful cities of its time, it contained perhaps a half-million people in its 25-mile circumference. Its two most monumental features were a 2½-mile-long elegant promenade, the Chahar Bagh, lined by gardens and court residences encouraged by Shah Abbas and, in the center of the city, the *maidan*, a large public square a third of a mile long by a tenth of a mile wide. The *maidan* was lined on one side by two tiers of shops, and on the other sides by the royal palace, the royal mosque, and the smaller Lutfullah mosque. The *maidan* served as marketplace, meeting place, and even as a sportsfield where polo was played.

Shah Abbas fostered artisanal production and trade, and Isfahan welcomed merchants and craftsmen from around the world. In the extended bazaar, which stretched for 1½ miles from the *maidan* to the main mosque, were located shops, factories, and warehouses, as well as smaller mosques, *madrasas*, baths, and *caravanserais* (travelers' hostels). Up to 25,000 people worked in the textile industry alone. Chinese ceramicists were imported to train workers in porcelain manufacture, and carpets and metalwork were also anchors of Isfahan's craft production.

Despite their differences in religion, Shah Abbas and the European powers shared a common political and military opposition to the Ottoman Empire, which lay between them. In the early 1600s Shah Abbas allowed both the English and the Dutch to open trade offices in Isfahan. He also practiced religious tolerance towards foreigners, perhaps for reasons of practical statecraft. Various Roman Catholic missions were established. Christian Armenians, forced by Shah Abbas to immigrate from their earlier home in Julfa to expand Isfahan's commerce, built their own suburb, New Julfa, appropriate to their status as prosperous merchants. A Jewish quarter also grew up in the northwestern part of the city, but later in Shah Abbas' reign Jews were persecuted and forced to convert to Islam or to leave.

Shah Abbas maintained absolute command and imported soldiers who were totally loyal to him. He also kept his forces supplied with up-to-date weapons, for he understood that Iran's status and survival depended upon them, surrounded as it was by the hostile Ottoman Empire to the west, continuing threats from nomads to the north, and a powerful, if friendly, Mughal Empire to the east. In a report of 1605 to Pope Paul V, the friar Paul Simon described the Shah as ruthless, dictatorial, and militarily prepared with forces recruited from far and near:

> His militia is divided into three kinds of troops: one of Georgians, who will be about 25,000 and are mounted; the second force … is made up of slaves of various races, many of them Christian renegades: their number will be as many again … The third body consists of soldiers whom the great governors of Persia are obliged to maintain and pay the whole year; they will be about 50,000. (Andrea and Overfield, pp. 91–92)

Constantinople (Istanbul)

Constantinople had been the capital of the much-reduced Byzantine Empire when Sultan Mehmed II captured it and made it his own capital in 1453. In 1478 Constantinople had about 80,000 inhabitants; between 1520 and 1535, there were 400,000; and some Western observers estimated a population of 700,000 by 1600. Istanbul had become a city of Turks—58 percent of the population in the sixteenth and seventeenth centuries—but there were also Greeks, Jews, Armenians, and Tziganes, or gypsies.

The vast **conurbation** was composed of three major segments plus numerous suburbs. Central Constantinople housed the government center, with trees, gardens, fountains, promenades, and 400 mosques; sprawling, uneven bazaars where luxuries as well as day-to-day necessities could be purchased; and the Serai, near the tip of the peninsula, where the government officials lived in their palaces and gardens. Across the small waterway, called the Golden Horn, were the ports and major commercial establishments of Galata. Here the Western ships came; here were the

KEY TERM

conurbation An enormous, complex city, made up of many parts, each of which may be a small town or city by itself —a megalopolis.

Constantinople, late fifteenth century. Constantinople, spanning the Straits that separate Europe and Asia, has been a pivotal location from the time Constantine established it as the eastern capital of the Roman Empire. The segments of the city reflect the rule and civilization of Rome, the Byzantine Empire, and, after 1453, the Ottoman Empire. In addition, as a great trading city, it houses communities of businessmen from around the world.

Jewish businessmen; the shops and warehouses; cabarets; the French ambassador; Latin and Greek merchants dressing in the Turkish style and living in grand houses. On Galata, too, were the two major arsenals—that of Kasim Pasha and the Topkhana—marking the Ottoman commitment to military power. On the Asian side of the Straits of the Bosphorus was the third part of Istanbul, Üsküdar, a more Turkish city, and the terminus of the great land routes through Asia.

Historian Fernand Braudel sees in Constantinople the prototype of the great modern European capitals that would arise a century later. Economically these cities produced little, but they processed goods passing through, and were the "hothouses of civilization," where new ideas and innovations arose and created a new order. Braudel remarks that cities that were only political capitals would not fare well in the next century; those that were economically productive would. Beginning in the late sixteenth century, the economy of Istanbul was undercut by changes in the world economy. As trade shifted to the Atlantic and to European powers that sailed around the African continent instead of through the Middle East, the Ottoman Empire and its capital were left as a backwater.

London

By comparison with the Asian and east European capitals, London had a very different pattern of immigration and employment. While Delhi, Isfahan, and Constantinople declined during the late seventeenth and early eighteenth centuries in response to negative political and economic factors, London grew, primarily because of economic factors.

SOURCE

Ibn Khaldun on Urban Life in the Fourteenth Century

The great social philosopher Ibn Khaldun of Tunis (1332–1406) described the transition from nomadic to sedentary and urban forms, and the "softening" of the invaders that occurred in the process of urbanization. Ibn Khaldun's analysis presents a very early philosophy of the flowering and decline of civilization, an analysis that other historians would later repeat. This analysis also presents Arab peoples as nomadic and rough, at first, but urbane and sophisticated after two or three generations of urban life.

It is rare that the age of the state should exceed three generations, a generation being the average age of an individual, that is forty years or the time necessary for full growth and development.

We said that the age of the state rarely exceeds three generations because the first generation still retains its nomadic roughness and savagery, and such nomadic characteristics as a hard life, courage, predatoriness, and the desire to share glory. All this means that the strength of the solidarity uniting the people is still firm, which makes that people feared and powerful and able to dominate others.

The second generation, however, have already passed from the nomadic to the sedentary way of life, owing to the power they wield and the luxury they enjoy. They have abandoned their rough life for an easy and luxurious one …

As for the third generation, they have completely forgotten the nomadic and rough stage, as though it had never existed. They have also lost their love of power and their social solidarity through having been accustomed to being ruled. Luxury corrupts them, because of the pleasant and easy way of living in which they have been brought up. As a result, they become a liability on the state, like women and children who need to be protected …

… the rulers of a state, once they have become sedentary, always imitate in their ways of living those of the state to which they have succeeded and whose condition they have seen and generally adopted.

This is what happened to the Arabs, when they conquered and ruled over the Persian and Byzantine empires … Up until then they had known nothing of civilization. (Ibn Khaldun, pp. 117–19)

Ibn Khaldun's depiction of nomadic conquerors being ultimately absorbed and assimilated into the civilizations they conquer presents a process that is frequently repeated in world history. We have seen it in the barbarian conquests of Rome and China in Chapters Six and Seven. His portrait of the decadence and decay of civilizations does not, however, fit all cases. In India, for example, Aurangzeb provoked fatal rebellions when he tried to rule too strictly over too many people, from too remote a location. Aurangzeb's fatal flaw was not decadence but excessive zeal.

E.A. Wrigley, one of the founding members of the Cambridge Group for the History of Population and Social Structure, has examined the changing demography of London between 1650 and 1750 to analyze the city's relationship with British society and economy. Wrigley begins with London's extraordinary population growth, from 200,000 in 1600, to 400,000 in 1650, to 575,000 by 1700, when it became the largest city in Western Europe, to 675,000 in 1750, and 900,000 in 1800. London dominated the development of all of England. In 1650 London held 7 percent of England's total population; in 1750, 11 percent.

Before the twentieth century, as a rule, large cities everywhere in the world were so unsanitary that death rates exceeded birth rates, so London's population growth reflects not only births within the city, but also large-scale immigration to compensate for high death rates. Wrigley estimates that by the end of the 1600s, 8,000 people a year were migrating into London. Since the entire population of England at this time was only five million, and growing at the rate of about 16,000 each year, London was siphoning half of England's population growth into itself.

With so high a proportion of England's population living in London, or at least visiting the city for a substantial part of their lives, the capital must have had significant influence on the country as a whole. Wrigley suggests that the high levels of population growth in London in the seventeenth century may have been a significant factor in giving birth to the industrialization of the eighteenth.

Wrigley suggests several relevant causal relationships. The first group concerns economics: London's growth promoted the creation of a national market, including transportation and communication facilities; it evoked increasing agricultural productivity to feed the urban population; it developed new sources of raw materials, especially coal, to provide for them; it led to the development of new commercial instruments; and it had the effect of increasing productivity and purchasing power. Demographically, London's high death and immigration rates kept England's rate of population growth relatively low. Sociologically, London's growth disseminated new ways of thinking about economics and its importance. Londoners placed increasing value on production and consumption for the common person, encouraging higher levels of entrepreneurship throughout the country.

London's growth could have led simply to the urban ruling elites commandeering the production of the countryside for their own benefit. Such parasitism was common in imperial capitals elsewhere, as we have just seen in the Asian capital cities. In London, however, a government increasingly dominated by commercial classes reinforced the values of production and increased consumption for the common person.

Migration and Demography: What Difference Do They Make?

Numbers count. Demography helps us to discover patterns in history and to formulate questions about issues that need further study. In this chapter, we have employed the methods and insights of demography to examine four great migrations in world history between 1500 and 1750. We have explored the formation of "New Europes" around the globe, the numbers and motivations of the new immigrants, and the (often catastrophic) fate of the original inhabitants. Second, we have analyzed the size, geography, and economic consequences of the slave trade both in Africa, where people were seized, sold, and exported, and in the plantation economies that absorbed most of them. Third, we have compared the migrations and conquests of Turkic-speaking and Mongol peoples from central Asia—establishing new empires in India, Persia, and the Middle East, and a new dynasty in China—with the transatlantic migrations. Finally we have discussed the move from rural areas to cities—the spread of urbanization—and contrasted the motives for this move in more traditional political capitals of empire with those in younger, more trade-oriented capitals.

These migrations have attracted the continuing interest of demographic historians. Their research has helped us to assess the connections between these great migrations of the past and events in our own world. They have also helped alert us to related demographic processes continuing in our own world today: rapid population growth and its consequences for global ecology; global migrations for economic opportunity—both of highly skilled technical workers seeking high-paying jobs and of unskilled day laborers seeking subsistence work; the migration of jobs from richer, higher-wage areas of the world to poorer, lower-wage areas of the world (labor remaining stationary but jobs moving from one location to another); migration from rural areas to cities and from cities to suburbs; migration of refugees fleeing warfare and oppressive governments; the global diffusion of diseases, such as AIDS, that seem to originate in one location and spread rapidly around the world.

These migration issues also alert us to related policy issues that persist in our own times. For example, language policies in areas of the United States with large Hispanic populations, and cultural policies in areas of Europe with large-scale Muslim immigration. Another issue is the encouraging of migration as a policy to change the ethnic composition of a region. The Chinese government today, for example, encourages people of Han Chinese ancestry to immigrate into Tibet and Xinjiang in order to make these two provinces more Chinese and less Tibetan and

Uighur. Even worse, some governments have undertaken programs of mass murder—genocide—to rid their territories of unwanted peoples. The government of Serbia, for example, implemented "ethnic cleansing" in 1999 against Albanian Muslims as part of the battle for control of Kosovo province (with constant, conscious references on both sides to the conquest of Kosovo by the Ottoman Turks in 1389); the Ottoman Turkish government murdered more than 1.5 million Armenians in 1915. In the most extreme case, German national policy in the 1930s and 1940s sought to exterminate the Jews. These and other issues of demography continue to arise around the globe and alter human history. We will return to them repeatedly in our study.

Asking Questions

- What were the "New Europes"? What characteristics did they share?
- What were the main reasons for the rise of slavery in the Atlantic Ocean basin between 1400 and 1750?
- What were the similarities and the differences between the great migrations from the eastern hemisphere across the Atlantic to the western hemisphere, 1500–1750, and the migrations from central Asia to Turkey, Iran, and India at about the same time and slightly earlier?
- The populations of which continents were growing fastest and which slowest in the period 1000–1800? How do you explain the differences between their comparative growth (or decline) in these years?
- What were the principal reasons for the growth of most very large cities before the Industrial Revolution of about 1800?

Suggested Readings

PRINCIPAL SOURCES

Braudel, Fernand. *Capitalism and Material Life 1400–1800*, trans. Miriam Kochan (New York: Harper & Row, 1973). Introduction to a whole new way of thinking about the rise of capitalism in Europe, emphasizing both institutions and natural ecology.

———. *The Mediterranean and the Mediterranean World in the Age of Philip II*, 2 vols., trans. Sian Reynolds (New York: Harper and Row, 1973). Braudel looks at long-run ecological issues, medium-run institutional configurations, and short-run political decisions in this landmark study.

Crosby, Alfred W. *Ecological Imperialism: The Biological Expansion of Europe, 900–1900* (Cambridge: Cambridge University Press, 1986). Extremely well-written and well-argued discussion of the biological consequences of the encounters of distant civilizations with one another.

Curtin, Philip D. *The Atlantic Slave Trade: A Census* (Madison, WI: University of Wisconsin Press, 1969). The pioneering work in quantifying the Atlantic slave trade.

———. *The Rise and Fall of the Plantation Complex:*

Essays in Atlantic History (Cambridge: Cambridge University Press, 1990). Comprehensive account of the plantation organization, economy, and significance.

Hughes, Robert. *The Fatal Shore. The Epic of Australia's Founding* (New York: Knopf, 1986). Engagingly written, exciting, thoughtful presentation of Australian history from the first arrival of Europeans to about 1870, when the system of penal transportation ended.

Mintz, Sidney W. *Sweetness and Power: The Place of Sugar in Modern History* (New York: Penguin Books, 1985). Fascinating anthropological study that begins with the Caribbean sugar plantation, extends to the uses of sugar by the wealthy, the sugared cup of tea of the British industrial worker, the Chinese tea crop, and the advertising industry that brought much of this together.

Northrup, David, ed. *The Atlantic Slave Trade* (Lexington, MA: D.C. Heath, 1994; 2nd ed., 2001). Excellent selection of articles on causes, effects, demography, and economics of the slave trade and of abolition.

———. *Indentured Labor in the Age of Imperialism, 1834–1922* (Cambridge: Cambridge University

Press, 1995). Comprehensive survey of the system of indentured labor that followed the abolition of the slave trade and slavery, and its demographics.

ADDITIONAL SOURCES

Andrea, Alfred J. and James H. Overfield, eds. *The Human Record: Sources of Global History*, Vol. 2 (Florence, KY: Wadsworth Publishing Co., 6th ed., 2008). The excerpts are extremely well chosen for global and topical coverage.

Blake, Stephen P. *Shahjahanabad* (Cambridge: Cambridge University Press, 1990). Scholarly study of the capital city of Shah Jahan, demonstrating the influence of military camp architecture and design.

Cook, James. *The Journals of Captain James Cook on His Voyages of Discovery*, ed. J.C. Beaglehole, 2 vols. (Cambridge: Cambridge University Press [for the Hakluyt Society], 1955 and 1961). Read Cook's own accounts in his own words.

Frykenberg, R.E., ed. *Delhi through the Ages: Essays in Urban History, Culture and Society* (Delhi: Oxford University Press, 1986). Wide-ranging collection of scholarly articles from an important conference, covering Delhi from earliest times to almost the present.

Gates, Henry Louis, Jr. *Wonders of The African World* (New York: Knopf, 1999). Introduction to Africa for a general audience by a leading Harvard scholar.

Henige, David, "Measuring the Immeasurable: The Atlantic Slave Trade, West African Population and the Pyrrhonian Critic," *Journal of African History* XXVII.2 (1986), pp. 303–13. Surveys the attempts to evaluate the effects of the slave trade and emigration on African life.

Ibn Khaldun. *An Arab Philosophy of History*, trans. Charles Issawi (London: John Murray, 1950). In the fourteenth century, Ibn Khaldun of Tunis, an early social scientist, proposed a reading of history consistent with the experiences of both the nomadic and the sedentary people of North Africa and the Middle East.

Inalcik, Halil. *The Ottoman Empire: The Classical Age, 1300–1600*, trans. Norman Itzkowitz and Colin Imber (New York: Praeger Publishers, 1973). A standard, accessible history by an eminent scholar.

Keegan, John. *A History of Warfare* (New York: Knopf, 1993). An eminent British scholar analyzes why, how, and with what weapons people have fought throughout history and across geography.

Klein, Herbert S. "Economic Aspects of the Eighteenth-century Atlantic Slave Trade," in James D. Tracy, ed., *The Rise of Merchant Empires* (Cambridge: Cambridge University Press, 1990), pp. 287–310. Important analyses of the slave trade, including slaves' birth and survival rates.

Lapidus, Ira M. *A History of Islamic Societies* (Berkeley, CA: University of California Press, 1988). Comprehensive, global presentation.

Lovejoy, Paul E. "The Volume of the Atlantic Slave Trade: A Synthesis," *Journal of African History* XXIII (1982), pp. 473–501. Another contribution to the demographic study.

Northrup, David. *Africa's Discovery of Europe, 1450–1850* (New York: Oxford University Press, 2nd ed., 2009). First contacts both in Africa and Europe, seen through African eyes. Innovative scholarly contribution.

Robinson, Francis. *Atlas of the Islamic World since 1500* (New York: Facts on File, Inc., 1982). Excellent reference by an outstanding British scholar. Well written, beautifully illustrated.

Rodney, Walter. *How Europe Underdeveloped Africa* (Washington, DC: Howard University Press, 1972). Classic statement of the exploitation of Africa by the European slave trade and imperialism.

Segal, Ronald. *Islam's Black Slaves: The Other Black Diaspora* (New York: Farrar, Straus, and Giroux, 2001). A survey of the history of the Arab slave trade in Africa and the Indian Ocean region.

Spence, Jonathan D. *The Search for Modern China* (New York: W.W. Norton and Co., 1990). A standard history, engagingly written, thorough, good on narrative and analysis.

Thornton, John. *Africa and Africans in the Making of the Atlantic World, 1400–1640* (Cambridge: Cambridge University Press, 1992). Sees Africans as active in creating their own world, including as businessmen conducting the slave trade.

The [London] Times Atlas of World History, ed. Geoffrey Parker (London: Times Books, 5th ed., 1999). Invaluable reference. Well-balanced treatment of all world areas.

Toynbee, Arnold. *Cities of Destiny* (New York: Weathervane Books, 1967). Colorful introduction to some of the most famous and influential cities. Illustrations and maps are lavish in this coffee-table book.

Willigan, J. Dennis and Katherine A. Lynch. *Sources and Methods of Historical Demography* (New York: Academic Press, 1982). Useful introduction to significance and methods.

Wolf, Eric. *Europe and the People without History* (Berkeley, CA: University of California Press, 1982). A historical anthropologist writes revisionist history bringing third world people into history as important agents in creating the world as it is, in a generally Marxist framework

Wrigley, E.A. *Population and History* (New York: McGraw-Hill Book Company, 1969). Explains the uses of demographic study in history.

——. "A Simple Model of London's Importance in Changing English Society and Economy 1650–1750," *Past and Present* XXXVII (1967), pp. 44–70. Demographic analysis suggests the importance of London in preparing the way for the industrialization of England.

For quizzes, flashcards, primary sources, interactive maps, videos, and other activities related to this chapter please go to

www.myhistorylab.com

Comparisons Across Time

In this picture album we revisit three important places across about a century of time. This before-and-after perspective yields some startling comparisons—and a deeper understanding of the last century and a half.

The first two pictures are from Philadelphia, their perspectives separated by three city blocks and 125 years. The first is a painting of Independence Hall, where the Second Continental Congress met to adopt the Declaration of Independence on July 4, 1776. The second is a photograph of Strawbridge and Clothier, a department store. Although no industry appears in the photograph, the electric trolley cars, the new "downtown," and the store itself speak volumes about the city's transformation. The photograph, too, represents a new medium invented only in the 1830s. From 1780 to 1907 the city had grown from about 25,000 to 1,250,000 people.

The illustrations from India suggest the continuous build-up of British imperial power and wealth. In 1775 the British annexed Benares to their holdings in eastern India, providing the background for this imagined, fawning reception of Warren Hastings, the British Governor General, by the Rajah of Benares. But it hardly compares

Independence Hall, Philadelphia, c. 1780. Painting.

with the triumphal splendor and majesty staged for George V and Queen Mary when they visited India. Their 1911 state visit marked a high point of imperial splendor.

The final pairing of pictures creates a great irony. François Biard has painted a disturbing image of the traffic in people, as they are inspected, purchased, branded, and whipped at a slave market on the African coast. A white man brands one female slave, while a black man whips another. To the rear right of the market, rows of shackled slaves await their turn on the block. Despite its touches of voyeurism and pornography, Biard's painting unequivocally condemns slavery. Slavery was abolished throughout the European-controlled world in the nineteenth century. But in Africa, European colonialism sanctioned new kinds of plantations—for example, for the production of rubber in the Congo. The equivalent of slavery, and worse, was simply moved back to the African continent itself. The photograph from *The Illustrated London News*, 1905, represents the processing of the raw natural rubber as an energetic activity for a lively group, but the presence of the overseer suggests that the truth was much harsher, as we shall read in this part of the book.

Strawbridge and Clothier Department Store, Philadelphia, c. 1907.

Cheyle Singh, Rajah of Benares, flatters Warren Hastings, Anon., 1784. Engraving.

King George V and Queen Mary of England in Delhi during a state visit (*durbar*) to India, 1911.

Beating Rubber and Beating Time–To the Tune of an Old Love Song, Norman H. Hardy. Illustration from *The Illustrated London News*, October 2, 1905.

Slave Market on the Kambia River, Africa, François Biard, 1840. Painting.

Turning Point Questions

1. These six pictures are either illustrations or photographs. Which medium seems more powerful to you?

2. Within each pairing, do you think the sequence of representations suggests "progress," a process much heralded in the nineteenth century, or only difference? Why? From whose perspective?

PART SIX
SOCIAL CHANGE
1640–1914

Western Revolutions and their Influence

[handwritten margin note: GLOBAL SIGNIFICANCE OF THESIS?]

Explosive events, "revolutions," punctuated the years 1640–1914. One cluster of revolutions—in England, North America, France, Haiti, and Latin America—advocated for new political philosophies and introduced new political structures. Many historians refer to them collectively as constituting the "Age of Democratic Revolution." Beginning about the same time, a series of innovations in economic organization and the uses of machinery dramatically increased the quantity and quality of economic productivity. Most historians name this transformation the "Industrial Revolution." These revolutions in politics and economics inspired equally dramatic social revolutions, which affected the individual, the family, the neighborhood, and the community. All three of these revolutions originated in Western Europe, but ultimately people all over the world were affected. They formulated their own varied responses, adaptations, and, sometimes, rejections. For purposes of analysis, this Part will consider these three revolutions sequentially: political in Chapter Sixteen, industrial in Chapter Seventeen, and social in Chapter Eighteen.

[handwritten margin note: GEOGRAPHY STUDIES TIE-IN]

The triple revolution unfolded rather quickly, but the groundwork had been laid over centuries, and we begin by examining the background. We have seen in Parts Four and Five unprecedented expansion in global

[handwritten note: EXPANDING GLOBALIZATION: WHAT CAUSED REVOLUTIONS, RELIGION? TRADE?]

exploration, commerce, and migration from the thirteenth century. By the seventeenth century traditional political, economic, and social philosophies and organizations seemed to be increasingly obsolete. Europeans were establishing political colonialism, economic imperialism, and Christian missions, first in the Americas and then, more slowly, around the globe. The new forms percolated into everyday life and consciousness everywhere. Each society adapted in its own way, however, so the results were diverse and quite often unexpected.

In the midst of all of the institutional changes, new ideas also flourished, many of them in the realm of science, and these ideas inspired further revolutions. Attempts to understand the universe through an application of mathematics to the study of the natural sciences culminated in Sir Isaac Newton's theory of universal gravitation. Social philosophers subsequently began to apply Newtonian, systematic, rational, scientific thinking to understanding the social, political, and economic worlds. (Some of Newton's thinking, on the other hand, was mystical and far-fetched.) Some applied it in ways that encouraged revolts against existing political systems. We begin our study of political, industrial, and social revolution with an analysis of some of the new ideas that provided their philosophical rationale.

[handwritten notes:
SCIENTIFIC REVOLUTION
AGE OF ENLIGHTENMENT
LOGICAL & SCIENTIFIC STUDY
LEADS TO NEW PHILOSOPHICAL PURSUITS]

[handwritten notes:
REVOLUTION TRIFECTA
POLITICAL: DEMOCRATIC
INDUSTRIAL
SOCIAL]

***Execution of the Defenders of Madrid, 3rd May, 1808,* Francisco de Goya, 1814.** Goya, a Spaniard,
saw the French Revolution and the Napoleonic Wars that followed through the prism of their violence.
The bitter warfare at the French invasion of Spain, and the Spanish resistance, inspired this agonized
painting. (Prado, Madrid)

El sueño de la razon produce monstruos.

CHAPTER SIXTEEN

Political Revolutions in Europe and the Americas

The Birth of Political Rights in the Age of Enlightenment

1649–1830

A revolution is a fundamental and often rapid change in the way a system operates—whether political, economic, intellectual, or social. A political revolution, for example, not only removes some people from office and replaces them with others; it also changes the fundamental basis on which the new leaders come to power, the authority they claim, and their mission in office. Leaders of revolutions usually state their goals in terms of high, non-negotiable principles. As revolutionary struggles unfold and as different groups rise and fall, however, they may lurch from one political position to another relatively swiftly and often violently.

In a major revolution several groups may participate and cooperate in the struggle to replace an existing government. Nevertheless, each group may have its own goals, and these goals may be in conflict. Once it becomes likely that a new government will replace the old, the conflicts among the revolutionary partners begin to surface. Each group seeks to privilege its own programs and personnel and to have them incorporated into the new government. This struggle to control the new government may be even more brutal, violent, chaotic, and unpredictable than the battle to overthrow the old. The stakes are high. Major revolutions have long-term effects, not only for participants in that place and time but also for people of later generations and far-flung locations.

The three political revolutions we consider here all share these characteristics of major revolutions. The "Glorious Revolution" of 1688 in England, the revolt of the American colonies against British rule in 1776, and the French Revolution of 1789 all removed one set of rulers and replaced them with another, changed the basis of authority of the state and its relationship to its citizens, and proposed new missions for the state. (By "state" we mean the entire mechanism of government, its officers, its institutions, and its organization.) All of these revolutions were fought in the name of principle. The revolution in England was considered "bloodless," although it was the culmination of a lengthy period of national violence and civil warfare. The American and French Revolutions precipitated lengthy wars.

KEY TOPICS
- The Scientific Revolution
- Human Rights: Philosophical Rationales
- Civil War and Revolution in England, 1642–51
- The Enlightenment
- Revolution in North America, 1776
- The French Revolution and Napoleon, 1789–1812
- Haiti: Slave Revolution and the Overthrow of Colonialism, 1791–1804
- Independence and Disillusionment in Latin America, 1810–30
- Political Revolutions: What Difference Do They Make?

The Sleep of Reason Produces Monsters, **Francisco de Goya, 1797. Engraving.** Goya (1746–1828) creates a terrifying scene challenging a key tenet of the Enlightenment: that human reason will produce progress. The title, *The Sleep of Reason Produces Monsters,* is seen within the etching itself (in Spanish) and suggests that when the mind's defenses are down, as in sleep, we are prey to internal monsters. Reason has its limits. Around 1900, the first psychoanalyst, Sigmund Freud, explored the limits of reason more thoroughly.

AT A GLANCE: THE AGE OF REVOLUTIONS

DATE	EUROPE	NORTH AMERICA	LATIN AMERICA
1640	• Galileo dies; Newton is born (1642) • Civil wars in England (1642–46; 1647–49; 1649–51) • Execution of King Charles I of England (1649) • Restoration of English monarchy (1660) • Royal Society of London founded (1662)		• Portugal takes Brazil from the Dutch (1654)
1670	• The "Glorious Revolution" in England (1688) • The English Bill of Rights (1689) • John Locke's *Second Treatise on Government* (1689) • *Philosophes*: Diderot (1713–84); Voltaire (1694–1778); Rousseau (1712–78); Montesquieu (1689–1755)		
1760	• Tennis Court Oath (June 20, 1789) • French Revolution (1789–99) • "March of the Women" (1789) • "Great Fear" (1789) • "Second French Revolution" (1791–99)	• British levy taxes on Americans in the Stamp Act (1765) • American Declaration of Independence (1776); War of Independence (1775–81) • Constitution (1789)	• Revolts against European rule in Peru, Colombia, and Brazil (1780–98) • Tupac Amaru revolt, Peru (1780)
1790	• "Reign of Terror" (1793–95) • Napoleon seizes power (1799); Emperor (1804) • Napoleon issues Civil Code (1804) • Napoleon invades Russia; finally defeated (1812)	• Bill of Rights ratified (1791) • Louisiana Purchase from France (1803)	• Toussaint L'Ouverture leads slave revolt against French in Saint-Domingue (Haiti) (1791) • Haiti proclaims independence (1804) • Joseph Bonaparte, King of Spain (1808) • Bolívar and San Martin lead revolts against Spain (1808–28) • Paraguay declares independence (1810–11)
1820	• Congress of Vienna (1814–15) • Reform Act extends voting franchise in Britain (1832) • Britain abolishes slavery in its empire (1833)	• President Andrew Jackson evicts Cherokee Indian Nation: "Trail of Tears" (1838) • Warfare with Mexico ends in victory for America (1848) • United States abolishes slavery (1863, 1865)	• Mexico wins independence (1821) • Prince Pedro declares Brazil independent (1822)

All three of these revolutions have been characterized as "democratic" because they increased the participation of more (but not all) of the people in government. All of them at some time tried to balance two additional, competing goals: they sought to protect the rights of propertied people while increasing the power of the government (although not of the king). These goals were not, and to this day are not, fully compatible. Individual rights to private property and the rights of the state often conflict. So we must be careful in our understanding of the "democracy" that emerged from these revolutions.

[handwritten margin notes:]
DEMOCRATIC
REVOLUTION
- HIGHER PARTICIPATION OF SOME PEOPLES
- PROTECTION OF RIGHTS
- INCREASE GOVERNMENT POWER, NOT MONARCHAL POWER

[handwritten bottom notes:]
"PERFECT DEMOCRACY"
GOVERNMENTAL POWER & PERSONAL RIGHTS
CONFLICT EVEN TODAY

Collectively, for Europeans and Americans, the revolutions that occurred in the years between 1688 and 1789:

- situated the authority of government on earth rather than in heaven and thus increased the influence of the secular over the otherworldly;
- rejected the theory that governments were based on a **divine right of kings** in favor of the theory that governments derive their just powers from the consent of the governed;
- encouraged the creation of an effective bureaucracy to administer the affairs of government;
- emphasized the principle of individual merit, of "a career open to talent," rather than promoting people on the basis of personal and hereditary connections;
- helped to solidify the nation-state as the principal unit of government;
- extended effective power over the state to classes of people hitherto excluded, especially to men of the professions and business;
- encouraged the growth of business and industry for private profit;
- inspired the revolutionary leaders to export their new ideologies and methods to new geographical areas, sometimes by force; and
- precipitated wars of heretofore unknown degrees of military mobilization, geographical extent, and human destructiveness.

[handwritten margin notes: SEPERATION OF CHURCH AND STATE; → SOCIAL CHANGE STILL PRESENT TODAY HILTON'S; CAPITALISM; GLOBALIZATION; CONFLICT]

"Liberty," "equality," "fraternity," "natural rights," "the pursuit of happiness," "property," and "no taxation without representation" were the battle cries of these various revolutions. As frequently happens, the results were often unintended, unanticipated, and ironic. The political forms that actually resulted did increase human freedom for many people in many countries, but they often coexisted with slavery, patriarchy, colonialism, and warfare.

These ironies reveal themselves more starkly in two further revolutions that were inspired in part by these first three. In 1791, the slaves of Haiti, a French colony, revolted and abolished slavery. The French ultimately refused to sanction the revolution against slavery—despite their own revolution for human rights. Then, in the first three decades of the nineteenth century, many of the colonies of Spain and Portugal in Latin America fought for and won their independence. But the triumphant generals of the revolution fought among themselves and their dreams of vast, unified, powerful nations dissolved into the reality of smaller, weaker states. The triumphant elite—the descendants of the European settlers in these colonies—suppressed indigenous peoples, people of mixed Spanish–Amerindian ancestry, and of African descent, thereby spreading disillusionment throughout the continent.

[handwritten margin notes: ROAD PAVED WITH GOOD INTENTIONS; UNINTENDED CONSEQUENCES —WHAT WERE THEY? —WHAT IS STILL PRESENT TODAY?; TRADED ONE COLLAR FOR ANOTHER; PRESENT DAY: MIDDLE EAST]

The Scientific Revolution

Revolutions in thought preceded the major political revolutions. People changed their ideas about government before they actually changed the government. And even before they changed their ideas about the political universe, they changed their ideas about the natural universe.

[handwritten margin note: HOW DID THE SCI. REV. LEAD TO THE POLI. REV AND SOCIO. REV.]

Advancements in Science

In his 1985 book *Revolution in Science*, I. Bernard Cohen writes that the study of the history of science is a surprisingly new field. Although some of the scientists we shall consider here spoke of their findings as revolutionary, the first academic historian to write of a scientific revolution seems to have been a Ph.D. candidate at Columbia University, Martha (Bronfenbrenner) Ornstein. In her 1913 dissertation she summarized the importance of the array of scientific discoveries and inventions that included the telescope, which "utterly revolutionized the science of astronomy," "revolutionary changes in optics," "Linnaeus's revolutionary work" in plant and animal classification, "the revolution in the universities" toward systematic, empirical research, and the role of scientific societies as carriers of culture. There had been, she wrote, "a revolution in the established habits of thought and inquiry, compared to which most revolutions registered in history seem insignificant".

In 1948, in a series of lectures, one of the most distinguished of professional historians, Herbert Butterfield, wrote that the scientific revolution of the seventeenth century "overturned the authority in science not only of the Middle Ages but of the ancient world ... [It] outshines everything since the rise of Christianity and reduces the Renaissance and Reformation to the rank of mere episodes, mere internal displacements, within the system of medieval Christendom." This was not a one-time revolution. Butterfield saw it as a kind of "continuing historical, or history making force acting right up to the present time." Beginning in the 1950s, especially in *The Copernican Revolution* (1957) and *The Structure of Scientific Revolutions* (1962, 3rd ed., 1996), Thomas Kuhn turned his attention to the process of scientific investigation as a method of thought and research that constantly challenges conventional thinking and stands ready to overthrow it. Kuhn argued that most scientific research is based on small, incremental advances in human knowledge. He called this "normal science." "Revolutionary science" occurs when scientists break completely with existing explanations of their field, finding them inadequate, and create new theories that are better able to account for all the data available. Galileo and Newton created revolutionary science.

A Community of Scientists

What made seventeenth-century science revolutionary? First, the seventeenth century marked the move from the individual scientist working alone to the creation of a community of scientists, in touch with one another, sharing knowledge and ideas, and building a collective structure of thought and method. It would still be possible for a scientific genius like Leonardo da Vinci (1452–1519) to die with his work unrecognized, and even unknown, but this was becoming less likely. Leonardo, most famous for his paintings *The Last Supper* and the *Mona Lisa*, also carried out research in human anatomy through the dissection of cadavers; he wrote of the circulation of the blood through the body and of the path of the earth around the sun; he drew sketches for inventions such as submarines and airplanes. But he did not circulate these scientific and technological ideas. At the time of his death they remained confined to his own notebooks and were not discovered and publicized until the twentieth century. The creation of scientific academies in the seventeenth century made it much less likely that such genius would remain hidden.

Second, science added four new qualities to its methods: mathematical formulations, quantifying and expressing relationships in nature in mathematical forms; **empiricism**, accepting the evidence of direct observation over theoretical and philosophical explanations; technological innovations in equipment, such as the telescope and microscope; and a belief in the freedom of inquiry, encouraging scientists to follow their findings and their imagination regardless of received opinion and official doctrines. All of these qualities are found in the great revolution in astronomy and physics from Copernicus through Kepler and Galileo, and on to Newton.

KEY TERM

empiricism The theory that all knowledge originates in experience; the practice of relying on direct observation of events and experience for determining reality.

524

Nicholas Copernicus. Nicholas Copernicus (1473–1543), an outstanding Polish astronomer, was commissioned by Pope Paul III to devise a new calendar that would correct the errors of the Julian calendar. The Julian calendar was based on a 365¼-day year, while the actual time it takes the earth to circle the sun is 11 minutes and 14 seconds less. So the calendar year was continuously losing time, just a few minutes each year, but by the sixteenth century this amounted to about ten days, and holidays, such as Christmas and Easter, began to slip backward into different seasons. The pope commissioned Copernicus to analyze the astronomy underlying the calendar.

In the sixteenth century, people accepted the model of the second-century C.E. Greek astronomer Ptolemy, which shows the earth at the center of the universe. The sun, the moon, the planets, and the stars went around it. As a mathematician, Copernicus began tracking the movements of all these bodies.

He was able to fashion a mathematical system that showed the earth at the center of the universe, as accepted belief had it, but he also found a much simpler, though still complicated, formula that showed the sun, not the earth, at the center of the solar system. His new formulation also showed the earth turning on its axis every 24 hours, rather than having the entire cosmos revolve around the earth. As a rule, scientists faced with more than one workable explanation choose the simpler one, and with his new, simpler model of a solar system Copernicus could explain the calendrical difficulties that had been his principal assignment. But this new explanation would land him in serious trouble with the Church, and he knew it.

The concept of the earth at the center of the universe as taught by Ptolemy had been adopted as the official doctrine of the Catholic Church because it was consistent with biblical passages (Joshua 10:13; Ecclesiastes 1:4–5) that spoke of the sun's circle around the earth. The consequences of challenging that belief frightened Copernicus, as he wrote to the pope in his letter of transmission introducing his findings:

> I may well presume, most Holy Father, that certain people, as soon as they hear that in this book about the Revolutions of the Spheres of the Universe I ascribe movement to the earthly globe, will cry out that … I should at once be hissed off the stage … Thinking therefore within myself that to ascribe movement to the Earth must indeed seem an absurd performance on my part to those who know that many centuries have consented to the establishment of the contrary judgment, namely that the Earth is placed immovably as the central point in the middle of the Universe, I hesitated long whether, on the one hand, I should give to the light these my Commentaries written to prove the Earth's motion … These misgivings and actual protests have been overcome by my friends … [one of whom] often urged and even importuned me to publish this work which I had kept in store not for nine years only, but to a fourth period of nine years … They urged that I should not, on account of my fears, refuse any longer to contribute the fruits of my labors to the common advantage of those interested in mathematics … Yielding then to their persuasion I at last permitted my friends to publish that work which they have so long demanded. (Kuhn, 1957, pp. 137–38)

Map of the heavens according to Nicholas Copernicus, c. 1543. Copernicus placed the sun in the middle of his solar system with the earth circling around it. He also demonstrated the tilt and rotation of the earth's axis as it traveled in its yearly orbit. In these findings he differed from Ptolemy, the second-century C.E. Greek astronomer, but he did continue to see the solar system as bounded, with an array of fixed stars and constellations marking its outer limits.

[handwritten margin notes: "ACCEPTANCE OF IMPLIED THEORIES"]

[handwritten note: "THINKING IN OPPOSITION OF ESTABLISHED 'SCIENTIFIC' FINDINGS AND IN OPPOSITION WITH GOD"]

In the end, Copernicus stuck to the principles of his mathematical commitments and his conscience. He presented the truth as he understood it, but he published his complete findings only on his deathbed. They created much less stir than might have been expected, since they were published as a mathematical study, *De Revolutionibus*, comprehensible only to the most learned astronomers and mathematicians of his day. They became more the object of technical study than of theological debate.

Johannes Kepler. Copernicus' model, although a huge step forward, still was not entirely satisfactory because it still represented the planets' orbits as circular. They are not. The breakthrough that enshrined the sun-centered universe was made by Johannes Kepler (1571–1630). For ten years Kepler worked through the rich data he inherited from Copernicus and from the greatest astronomer of the next generation, Tycho Brahe (1546–1601), and finally reached a new understanding. The sun was at the center of the solar system and the planets, including the earth, moved around it. Their orbits, however, were not circles but ellipses, and they moved not at a fixed speed, but at varying speeds depending on their position on the ellipse. With these new insights, Kepler designed a model of the solar system that was simple, comprehensive, and mathematically consistent with the data available. He published his results in 1609 in *On the Motion of Mars*.

The theological argument was now clearly drawn. The earth was no longer the center of God's creation. Kuhn writes, "Copernicanism required a transformation in man's view of his relation to God and of the bases of his morality." There was no longer a fixed, heavenly location for God's throne. The perfection of the universe—with the earth at the center of a series of fixed, concentric, crystalline circles in which the planets traveled—was contaminated. Protestant leaders, believing in the literal word of the Bible, and led by Martin Luther himself, attacked the heliocentric universe of Copernicus as early as 1539. The Catholic Church, at first allowing much more latitude to individual belief in this matter, was slower to condemn, but in 1610 the Church officially designated the Copernican model a heresy, and in 1616, *De Revolutionibus* and all other writings that affirmed the earth's motion were put on the Index, an official list of writings that were forbidden to be taught or even read.

Galileo Galilei. For many years the split between the mathematical astronomers and the Church continued rather quietly, with the mathematicians generally winning out among educated audiences. Then, in 1609, the Italian astronomer Galileo Galilei (1564–1642), turned the newly invented telescope skyward and changed forever what we know about the heavens, how we know it, and its significance in the eyes of the nonspecialist, general public. Galileo added new empirical evidence and new technology to the toolkit of astronomy, opening new avenues of knowledge and popularizing them. The telescope had been created in the Netherlands; Galileo was the first to turn it toward the skies, and he made one discovery after another: The Milky Way is not just a dull glow in the sky but a gigantic collection of stars; the moon's surface is irregular, covered with craters and hills; the moon's radiant light is a reflection from the sun; the sun has "imperfections," dark spots that appear and disappear across its surface; the earth is not the only planet with moons—Galileo observed at least four satellites circling Jupiter.

Galileo demonstrating his telescopic discovery of Jupiter's satellites to the councilors of Venice in 1610. Wood engraving, French, nineteenth century. Galileo opened entire new vistas in astronomy by improving the telescope and turning it towards the heavens. He trusted his direct observations even when they brought him into confrontations with Church authorities who preferred to believe Biblical and ancient Greek perspectives.

Handwritten margin notes:
THE OPPRESSION OF SCIENTIFIC EXPANSION DUE TO ESTABLISHED DOCTRINE

BUILDING OFF OTHER RESEARCH

"FIRST" COLLABORATIVE EFFORT?

DISMISSING OF FINDINGS IN CONTRAST WITH LONG HELD BELIEFS AND THE ESTABLISHED ORDER

Galileo wrote, "We shall prove the earth to be a wandering body [in orbit around the sun] … This we shall support by an infinitude of arguments drawn from nature" (Galilei, p. 45). Over and over Galileo stressed the validity of his own empirical observations. "With the aid of the telescope this has been scrutinized so directly and with such ocular certainty that all the disputes which have vexed the philosophers through so many ages have been resolved, and we are at last freed from wordy debates about it." "One may learn with all the certainty of sense evidence"; "All these facts were discovered and observed by me not many days ago with the aid of a spyglass which I devised, after first being illuminated by divine grace"; "our own eyes show us." Galileo appealed to sense evidence, to direct observation, to empirically based information, and demonstrated its complete accessibility to anyone who looks through a telescope. He wrote for a general audience, not for university scholars; he wrote in Italian, not in Latin. The publication of Galileo's discoveries increased public interest in astronomy, and that public interest gradually turned into public acceptance.

[margin note: OBSERVABLE, EMPIRICAL, DATA BUILT OF COPERNICUS' THEORIES AND MATHEMATICAL STUDIES]

The Catholic Church, deeply enmeshed in its cold war with Protestantism, finally turned against him. In 1633 Galileo was tried by the Inquisition and found guilty of having taught his doctrines against the orders of the Church. Under threat of torture, the 69-year-old scientist publicly recanted his beliefs and was sentenced to house arrest for the rest of his life. (In 1992, on the 350th anniversary of Galileo's death, Pope John Paul II called the Church's error the result of "a tragic mutual incomprehension." There is no "incompatibility between the spirit of science and its rules of research on the one hand and the Christian faith on the other." On the contrary, he asserted, "It is a duty for theologians to keep themselves regularly informed of scientific advances." *L'Osservatore Romano*, November 4, 1992.)

[margin note: 350 YEARS BEFORE A PUBLIC "MERGING" OF FAITH AND SCIENCE]

Isaac Newton. In the same year as Galileo's death, 1642, Isaac Newton was born in England, on Christmas Day. He studied at Cambridge University and became a professor of mathematics there at age 26. In the course of his research, he discovered the calculus, a discovery he shared, separately, with the German mathematician Gottfried Wilhelm Leibnitz (1646–1716). A mathematical system especially useful in calculating motion along curved lines, the calculus was immediately valuable in predicting the celestial course of planets and the earthly trajectory of artillery shells. Another area of Newton's early research was in optics, focusing on the spectrum of light as it passed through a prism. Then he turned his attention to the new issues raised by Copernicus, Kepler, and Galileo: Why do heavy bodies always fall toward earth even as the earth is moving through space? What moves the earth? What moves the planets and what keeps them in their orbits? Before Copernicus, Ptolemy's view of the fixed spheres of the universe answered those questions. But without those fixed spheres, how should we understand the movements of the heavens?

[margin note: NEW FINDINGS RAISE MORE QUESTIONS, AND SCIENCE BUILDS ON SCIENCE]

In finding the universal law of gravity, Newton showed that the laws of planetary motion formulated by Kepler, the laws of earthly movement discovered by Galileo, and the principles of inertia of motion identified by the French mathematician and philosopher René Descartes (1596–1650), were all consistent. The universal principle of gravitation, coupled with the principle of inertia—that a body once set in motion tends to continue moving at the same speed in the same direction—gives a form for understanding the means by which the universe holds together. Moreover, these forces of inertia and gravity are universal, operating in the same way on earth as in the wider universe. Discovering the universal law of gravity required a leap of the imagination; working out its mathematics was the toil of genius. Newton worked out the formula for the pull of gravity: All matter moves as if every particle attracts every

[margin note: THE FINDINGS OF 5 SEPERATE PEOPLE OVER THE COURSE OF A CENTURY OR MORE, VALIDATED]

Newton experiments with light.
Newton's first published papers
were in optics. Here he worked
as an experimental scientist rather
than as a theoretical mathematician.
By passing the rays of the sun
through a prism he demonstrated
that white light was an amalgam of
colored rays. Using this information
he built a reflecting telescope, using
a mirror to focus light, thus avoiding
the chromatic aberration that
appeared in a refracting telescope.

ASTRONOMY
MATHEMATICS
PHYSICS
BIOLOGY

CLASSIFICATION OF
SPECIES

other particle with a force proportional to the product of the two masses, and inversely proportional to the square of the distance between them. This force is universal gravitation. In 1687 Newton published the results in his *Mathematical Principles of Natural Philosophy.*

Like all later scientists, Newton did not try to explain why this force worked, only how it worked. This new law had enormous philosophical implications, for it explained the "glue" in the Copernican system of the universe. It also had very practical consequences in the understanding and prediction of the tides. The great advances in mathematics underpinned not only theoretical research, but also practical invention in the form of time-keeping, mapping, and processes that required accuracy, such as the aiming of artillery and the construction of steam engines.

In recognition of his revolutionary contributions, in 1703 Newton was named President of the Royal Society, England's national academy of science. The Royal Society stressed its commitment to resisting arbitrary authority, including the authority of ancient, received wisdom. It chose as its motto *"Nullius in verba,"* meaning "Nothing in words": scientific facts should be found and verified through experimentation. The king of England had given a royal charter to the Royal Society of London in 1662, creating what continues today as the world's oldest surviving national academy of science. The Society marked the transformation of science from the work of individual, somewhat isolated scholars to an institutionalized, recognized set of disciplines of national importance.

NO BLIND ACCEPTANCE, EXPERIMENTAL PROOF

William Harvey, Anthony van Leeuwenhoek, Carolus Linnaeus. The discoveries in astronomy, physics, and mathematics were the leading sectors in the scientific revolution of the seventeenth century, but they were not alone. In England, William Harvey published *On the Movement of the Heart and Blood* (1628), based on years of laboratory research and vivisection of animals, demonstrating the circulation of blood through the body. In the Netherlands, Anthony van Leeuwenhoek (1632–1723) improved the newly invented microscope, the other great advance in optics along with the telescope, to see and then create drawings of blood corpuscles, spermatozoa, and bacteria. His observations enabled him to argue that reproduction even among tiny creatures occurred through sexual mating, not spontaneous generation. Leeuwenhoek was a businessman in the cloth trade, not specially educated in the sciences, and his election as a Fellow of the Royal Society of London in 1680 demonstrated that amateurs were welcome in this new research.

Leeuwenhoek's researches expanded the knowledge of the number and variety of tiny, microscopic creatures. Carolus Linnaeus (1707–78) developed a system of classification for these and all other known creatures in nature, *Systema Naturae* (1735), including an analysis of sexual reproduction in plants. The further evolution of eighteenth-century science was well underway.

The new science expanded human powers and self-understanding. Some scholars, frightened by the new discoveries, agreed with Blaise Pascal, a devout Christian French mathematician: "I am terrified by the eternal silence of these infinite spaces."

But more took heart, along with Alexander Pope, that a brave, new world was dawning:

> Nature and nature's law lay hid in night;
> God said, "Let Newton be," and all was light.

The new world of science swept away much superstition, at least for the time, and suggested that rationality and science could create a new world in which people could trust their senses to gather empirical information and to act upon it, a world in which the laws of nature could be discovered and calculated, a world in which science would inspire technological invention in the practical arts of making human life more productive and more comfortable. Throughout the eighteenth century, this vision of natural law and the power of human reason to improve the world spilled over from science and technology to philosophy and political theory. Not everyone agreed, however, on what constituted an improvement.

FIRST INSTANCES OF RELIGION & SCIENCE COEXISTING?

SCIENTIFIC REVOLUTION SPARKS POLITICAL & SOCIAL CHANGE

Human Rights: Philosophical Rationales

The political and social "sciences" are not as precise as the natural sciences. The processes of human life in society do not lend themselves to laboratory experiments and mathematical formulas. Nevertheless, the study of society and the creation of institutions for governing it do rest on philosophies that can be examined and revised in light of practical experience. In the seventeenth and eighteenth centuries theoretical speculation about society and politics translated into revolutionary practice. The role of the monarch, of hereditary power, of property, of citizenship, of the power of the state—all were undergoing intense review, in theory and in practice. For example, the political theories of two Englishmen, Thomas Hobbes (1588–1679) and John Locke (1632–1704), laid the foundations for their country's Glorious Revolution of 1688.

Hobbes and Limits on Power

The philosophy justifying England's Glorious Revolution of 1688 had developed over many years. Thomas Hobbes at first seemed to justify the enormous, existing power of the king over the citizens. In his most influential work, *Leviathan* (1651), he declared: "Nothing the sovereign representative can do to a subject, on what pretence soever, can properly be called injustice, or injury." This appears to be a justification for the absolute power of the king, but Hobbes was actually providing a rationale for limiting that power. He declared that the king could claim his authority not by virtue of special, personal rights, nor by virtue of representing God on earth, but because "Every subject is author of every act the sovereign doth." In other words, the king has authority to the extent that he represents the will of the people.

The "State of Nature." Hobbes, like others of his time, was trying to understand the English monarchy in terms of its origins. He postulated the myth of a prehistoric, individualistic, unruly, **state of nature**, which people had rejected in order to create a society that would protect them individually and collectively. Uncontrolled by law and a king, Hobbes famously wrote, "the life of man [is] solitary, poor, nasty, brutish, and short … During the time men live without a common power to keep them all in awe, they are in that condition which is called war; and such a war, as is of every man against every man." To escape such lawlessness, men had exchanged their individual liberties for social and political order. Their (mythical) **social contract**, not divine appointment, had created monarchy in order to serve the people.

KEY TERMS

state of nature The mythical situation in which people lived without any legal codes or contracts, each free to do exactly as he or she pleased, without the restrictions of law and society, but also without the protections of law and society.

social contract A mythical, unwritten agreement among early people in a "state of nature" to establish some form of government. This "contract" generally defines the rights and obligations of the individuals and of the government.

529

Locke and the Right of Revolution

The political accomplishments of the Glorious Revolution are even more closely associated with the writings of John Locke (1632–1704), who had fled England for the Netherlands in 1683, returning only after the revolution was complete. While he was in the Netherlands, Locke wrote his most important essay on political philosophy, *The Second Treatise on Government*, although it was not published until 1689, after the Glorious Revolution had been implemented and Locke felt safe to return to England. Since Locke's philosophy parallels not only the English revolution but also many subsequent ones, his arguments deserve careful attention.

Like Hobbes, Locke argued that government is a secular compact entered into voluntarily and freely by individuals. If there are to be kings, they too must live under the constitution. Locke, like Hobbes, based his argument on a mythical, prehistoric, "state of nature," which people forsook in order to provide for their common defense and needs. He, however, stressed the importance of common consent in the earlier mythical contract. The contract continues to be legitimate only so long as the consent continues. If they no longer consent to the contract, the people have the right to terminate it. Going beyond Hobbes, Locke explicitly proclaimed the right of revolution in his *Second Treatise on Government*:

> There remains still in the people a supreme power to remove or alter the legislative, when they find the legislative act contrary to the trust reposed in them. For all power given with trust for the attaining of an end, being limited by that end, whenever that end is manifestly neglected, or opposed, the trust must necessarily be forfeited, and the power devolves into the hands of those that gave it, who may place it anew where they shall think best for their safety and security. (p. 92)

Locke postulated the "equal right that every man hath to his natural freedom, without being subjected to the will or authority of any other man" ... "Absolute monarchy, which by some men is counted the only government in the world, is indeed inconsistent with civil society." Majority rule is Locke's basis of government: "The act of the majority passes for the act of the whole, and of course determines as having by the law of nature and reason, the power of the whole."

Locke, Hobbes, and Property

Locke was not proposing radical democracy; he was not advocating one person, one vote. For Locke, government existed to serve the interests of property owners: "Government has no other end but the preservation of property." "The great and chief end therefore, of men's uniting into commonwealths, and putting themselves under government, is the preservation of their property." Indeed, after the initial, mythical social contract had established the government's authority, succeeding generations had signalled their continuing acceptance of that contract by allowing their property to be protected by the government. "The supreme power cannot take from any man any part of his property without his own consent. For the preservation of property being the end of government, and that for which men enter into society, it necessarily supposes and requires, that the people should have property." Taxes, therefore, cannot be levied unilaterally or arbitrarily. "If anyone shall claim a power to lay and levy taxes on the people, by his own authority, and without such consent of the people, he thereby invades the fundamental law of property, and subverts the end of government."

Hobbes had already indicated the growing importance of property and industry to seventeenth-century England. Without peace and stability, he wrote:

SOURCE

Universal Suffrage vs. Property Rights

E.P. Thompson, the twentieth-century British historian, emphasized the contributions of common people to history. In his groundbreaking *The Making of the English Working Class* (pp. 22–3), Thompson cites statements made in 1647 at an army council meeting. Participants were attempting to determine the role of the common people in electing Parliament.

Oliver Cromwell's son-in-law, General Ireton, proposed extending the franchise, but only to men of property, fearing that private property might otherwise be abolished: "No person hath a right to an interest or share in the disposing of the affairs of the kingdom … that hath not a permanent fixed interest in this kingdom … If you admit any man that hath a breath and being, Why may not those men vote against all property?"

The common soldiers replied more democratically and more bitterly. One asserted: "There are many thousands of us soldiers that have ventured our lives; we have had little property in the kingdom as to our estates, yet we have had a birthright. But it seems now, except a man hath a fixed estate in this kingdom, he hath no right … I wonder we were so much deceived." In short, if we are asked to fight on behalf of the government, we should have a voice in electing it.

there is no place for industry; because the fruit thereof is uncertain; and consequently no culture of the earth; no navigation, nor use of the commodities that may be imported by sea; no commodious building; no instruments of moving, and removing, such things as require much force; no knowledge of the face of the earth; no account of time; no arts; no letters; no society. (p. 895)

Hobbes wanted an economically productive society that promoted agriculture, industry, commerce, and invention. Locke saw private ownership of property and private profit as the means to achieving that end. He considered the property-owning classes of England the nation's proper leaders and administrators. He asserted the importance of the **enclosure acts** by which England was dividing up the common lands of each village, turning them into private property, and selling them. These enclosure acts were creating a new, wealthier landlord class, which turned its energies to increasing agricultural productivity. At the same time the acts forced those rural people who had owned no land of their own, but who had been grazing their animals on common land, to give up their independence. Most found work with more prosperous landlords and some moved to the cities in search of new jobs.

DISPLACEMENT OF THE POOR

Neither Hobbes nor Locke showed concern for the nonpropertied classes. In their mythical state of nature land had been abundant—available for the taking—and anyone could become a property owner. But in the time in which they actually lived and wrote, as in our own time, access to unclaimed, unowned property was not so easy. Indeed, when Locke notes that "the turfs my servant has cut … become my property," he assigns the labor of the landless servant to his landed master. In practice, Locke's theory justified the government of England by Parliament under constitutional law, which limited the power of the king and transferred it to the hands of the propertied classes—the system that was evolving in his time. Locke's is the voice of the improving landlords and the rising commercial classes who made the Glorious Revolution.

Civil War and Revolution in England, 1642–51

At about the time Hobbes was writing, England was in continuing revolt against its sovereigns. Religion was the burning issue, and it seemed that no sovereign could satisfy the conflicting wishes of dissenters—Roman Catholics, Presbyterians, Puritans, and Quakers—and the official Anglican Church. Frustrations simmered but

KEY TERM

enclosure acts Laws passed in England from 1450–1640, and culminating 1750–1860, which converted public lands held in common into parcels of land to be sold to private owners.

had no focus until both James I (r. 1603–25) and his son Charles I (r. 1625–49) ran out of money to administer their governments and convened Parliament to request additional funds. They did not expect that Parliament would question their right to levy taxes as they chose; Parliament did not expect that the kings would reject its restrictions on royal power. They were both wrong. The struggle between kings and Parliament ultimately resulted in civil war and the beheading of the king. The question still remained, however, of the future religion of country. That issue was resolved—in favor of Protestantism—in the Glorious Revolution of 1688.

Civil War, 1642–51

Many members of Parliament—landowners, increasingly wealthy city merchants, lawyers, Puritans and other religious dissenters, as well as Anglican clergy—refused to give the kings the money they requested. They challenged royal authority, proposed increased power for an elected legislature, promotion by merit in government jobs, and, most of all, religious tolerance in private and public life. Rejecting these proposals, Charles I attempted to levy taxes without the sanction of Parliament. Civil war ensued, from 1642 to 1651, and the Parliament that Charles had convened in 1640 ultimately executed him. Oliver Cromwell, an ardent Calvinist and military genius, ruled as Lord Protector of England from 1653 until his death in 1658. He defeated those who rebelled against his new government in both Ireland and Scotland and joined these two kingdoms to England to form the British Commonwealth. In spite of his victories, neither Cromwell nor Parliament was able to achieve a new form of effective government and the monarchy was restored in 1660. (The new government dug up Cromwell's body from Westminster Abbey, hung it in chains, beheaded it, and left the head impaled on a pole outside the Abbey for several years.) Nevertheless, the Civil War established the principle that the monarchy could be abolished. It provided the theoretical framework that led to the subsequent revolution of 1688.

An Eyewitness Representation of the Execution of Charles I, by Weesop, 1649. Charles' belief in the divine right of kings and the authority of the Church of England led eventually to a civil war with Parliament—which he and his supporters lost. At his subsequent trial, the king was sentenced to death as a tyrant, murderer, and enemy of the nation and beheaded at Whitehall, London, on January 30, 1649. (Private collection)

PARLIAMENT
.VS
MONARCH
+
RELIGION

= CIVIL WAR

The Glorious Revolution, 1688

Charles II (r. 1660–85) and his brother James II (r. 1685–90) continued to claim more powers than Parliament wished to sanction. James II, a Catholic, favored Catholics in many of his official appointments. When a son was born to James, leading nobles feared that James and his successors might reinstitute Catholicism as England's official religion a century and a half after Henry VIII had disestablished it in favor of the Church of England. They invited James II's daughter, Mary, and her husband William of Orange, ruler of the United Provinces of the Netherlands, both resolute Protestants, to come to England to rule as king and queen. Responding to Parliament's invitation, William and Mary arrived in England in 1688, marking the Glorious Revolution. They confirmed their new rule by defeating the troops still loyal to James II at the Battle of the Boyne in Ireland in 1690.

The Bill of Rights. Although the new monarchs had been invited primarily to resolve religious conflicts, their ascension to the throne also resolved the power conflict between monarch and Parliament. The Bill of Rights that was enacted by Parliament in 1689 stated principles that had been evolving for decades in the relationship between the monarchy and the people of England. It stipulated, among other clauses, that no taxes could be raised, nor armies recruited without prior parliamentary approval; no subject could be arrested and detained without legal process; and no law could be suspended by the king unilaterally. The Glorious Revolution thus not only displaced one monarch in favor of another but also limited the powers of the monarchy under constitutional law. Parliament had asserted its power over the king. After all, the new king and queen had been selected by noblemen and confirmed by Parliament. In addition, as William continued his wars against France, he had to defer to Parliament for funds.

[handwritten margin note: FIRST SET OF "CONSTITUTIONAL RIGHTS"]

The Glorious Revolution also brought some resolution to the issues of religion in politics that had beset England for so long, although rebellion against the religious provisions continued in Scotland and especially Ireland. The Anglican Church remained the established Church of England, but the Toleration Act of 1689 granted Puritan Dissenters—but not Roman Catholics—the right of free public worship. Parliament did not yet revoke the Test Act, which reserved military and civil offices for Anglicans only. Cromwell had already permitted Jews to return to England, almost 400 years after their expulsion in 1290.

The Enlightenment

In the century between the Glorious Revolution in England and the American and French Revolutions, a movement in philosophic thought emerged called the Enlightenment. Its intellectual center was in France, although key participants lived in America, Scotland, England, Prussia, Russia, and elsewhere. (Locke, for example, is usually considered an early Enlightenment thinker.) The French leaders of the Enlightenment were called *philosophes* ("philosophers") and they built on the scientific revolution of the sixteenth and seventeenth centuries. In contrast to such Roman Catholic doctrines as original sin and the authority of the Church over human reason, the *philosophes* argued that human progress was possible through the steady and unrestricted expansion of knowledge, or "enlightenment." Their challenge to authority that was not based on rationality and their belief that human institutions should be administered by the most competent people and serve the welfare of the general population, rather than an elite, hereditary minority, helped inspire the American and the French Revolutions.

KEY TERM

philosophes A group of eighteenth-century writers and philosophers, mostly French, who emphasized the supremacy of human reason as the key to progress. They advocated freedom of expression and social, economic, and political reform.

The *Philosophes* — FRENCH

The *philosophes* believed in a world of rationality, in which collected human knowledge and systematic thought could serve as powerful tools for finding order in the universe and for solving key problems in political and economic life. "The perfectibility of humanity is indefinite," proclaimed the Marquis de Condorcet (1743–94). Their concerns for clarity of thought, combined with the desire to solve practical problems in public life, gave them considerable influence over the restructuring of new political institutions in their age of revolution. The authors of the American Declaration of Independence and of the French Declaration of the Rights of Man and the Citizen drew much of their inspiration from the *philosophes*. The *philosophes* believed in order, but also in freedom of thought and expression. For them, public discussion and debate were the means toward finding better ideas and solutions. Indeed, the *philosophes* were in constant dialogue and debate with one another. They often met in salons, comfortable settings for dinner and conversation, often hosted by talented, educated, aristocratic women.

WATCHMAKER

In terms of spiritual and religious beliefs, most *philosophes* were deists: They allowed that the world may have required an original creator, like Aristotle's prime mover, but once the processes of life had begun, he had withdrawn. Their metaphor was that of a watchmaker who built the mechanism, started it moving, and then departed. Humanity's fate thereafter was in its own hands.

Charles de Secondat, baron de Montesquieu. Travel influenced the *philosophes'* thought, opening their minds to a wider range of ideas. Charles de Secondat, the baron de Montesquieu (1689–1755), traveled widely and wrote the *Persian Letters*, satiric criticism of French institutions, including the monarchy and the Catholic Church, in the form of dispatches supposedly sent by two visitors to France to readers at home. Twenty-seven years later, in 1748, Montesquieu wrote his most influential work, *The Spirit of Laws*, in which he recognized that different countries need different kinds of governments, and advocated a separation of powers based on his (mis)understanding of the British system of government. The authors of the United States Constitution later acknowledged their debt to Montesquieu's thought.

Denis Diderot's *Encyclopedia*. The most famous academic product of the *philosophes* and the Enlightenment was the *Encyclopedia, or Rational Dictionary of the Arts, Sciences, and Crafts*, compiled by Denis Diderot (1713–84) and containing articles by leading scholars and *philosophes*. The *Encyclopedia* reaffirmed the faith in human progress based on education:

> The aim of an *Encyclopedia* is to collect all the knowledge that now lies scattered over the face of the earth, to make known its general structure to the men among whom we live, and to transmit it to those who will come after us, in order that the labors of past ages may be useful to the ages that will follow, that our grandsons, as they become better educated, may become at the same time more virtuous and more happy, and that we may not die without having deserved well of the human race. (Columbia University, *Contemporary Civilization*, pp. 988–89)

Diderot called for further social and political revolution. "We are beginning to shake off the yoke of authority and tradition in order to hold fast to the laws of reason." Challenging authority meant being open to multiple perspectives rather than holding a single truth, and Diderot built this concept into the structure of his volumes.

By giving cross-references to articles where solid principles serve as foundation for the diametrically opposed truths we shall be able to throw down the whole edifice of mud and scatter the idle heap of dust. … If these cross-references, which now confirm and now refute, are carried out artistically according to a plan carefully conceived in advance, they will give to the *Encyclopedia* the … ability to change men's common way of thinking. (p. 996)

The *Encyclopedia* ultimately filled 17 volumes of text and 11 of illustrations.

Voltaire. Another *philosophe*, François-Marie Arouet, better known as Voltaire (1694–1778), declared *"Ecrasez l'infame!"*—"Crush the infamy!" of superstition, intolerance, organized religion, and the power of the clergy. Voltaire wrote extensively: *Elements of the Philosophy of Newton* (1738) explicated new scientific evidence of the rational order and the human ability to comprehend the universe; *Philosophical Letters on the English* (1734) argued for freedom of religion, inquiry, and the press; *Essai sur les moeurs* (1756), translated as *Universal History*, gave a humanistic context to historical development and placed the responsibility for human fate in human hands.

"Enlightened Despotism"

The *philosophes* were not, however, committed to popular democracy. Voltaire, for example, preferred benevolent and enlightened despotism to badly administered self-rule. In the best of all possible worlds, there would be an enlightened ruler like Frederick II, the Great, of Prussia (r. 1740–86), at whose court Voltaire lived for several years, or Catherine II, the Great, empress of Russia (r. 1762–96), of whom he was a close friend, or their contemporary, Joseph II, emperor of Austria (r. 1765–90). All three ruled countries in which the administration was efficient, taxes were reasonable, agricultural and handicraft production was encouraged, freedom of expression and religion was allowed, the military was strengthened, and powerful empires resulted. The enlightened despot acted in disciplined ways, subject in his or her mind to the law of nature. But the population at large had no say or vote in the administration. In other words, for these rulers, and for Voltaire, good government did not necessarily require self-government.

Proclaiming the concept of enlightened despotism, colonial governments often claimed the mantle of the Enlightenment to justify their rule, arguing that they were utilizing knowledge and reason, to soften the use of brute force, as the foundation of their administration. In 1784 Warren Hastings, Governor General of the British holdings in India, explained:

Every accumulation of knowledge and especially such as is obtained by social communication with people over whom we exercise dominion founded on the right of conquest, is useful to the state … it attracts and conciliates distant affections; it lessens the weight of the chain by which the natives are held in subjection; and it imprints on the hearts of our countrymen the sense of obligation and benevolence. (Metcalf and Metcalf, p. 61)

The Philosophers at Supper, Jean Huber, 1750. Voltaire (1), Condorcet (5), and Diderot (6) are among the figures depicted in this engraving, a visual checklist of important Enlightenment thinkers. Seeing the Western world as emerging from centuries of darkness and ignorance, these Frenchmen promoted reason, science, and a respect for humanity—ideas that would underpin the intellectual case for the French Revolution of 1789. (Bibliothèque Nationale, Paris)

[handwritten marginal note: PROBABLY BIASED CONSIDERING HE IS UPPER CLASS]

KEY TERM

enlightened despotism Rule by a government that is not subject to democratic control, but nevertheless is efficient and humane. The ruler/despot was usually a king or emperor.

Implementing this Enlightenment philosophy, Hastings founded, for example, the Asiatic Society of Bengal, dedicated primarily to the translation and analysis of ancient Indian texts.

Jean-Jacques Rousseau. Skepticism regarding democratic government was carried further in the works of Jean-Jacques Rousseau (1712–78), perhaps the most enigmatic and ambiguous of all of the eighteenth-century French thinkers. Rousseau questioned the primacy of intellect and human ingenuity. Like Hobbes and Locke, he wrote of the "state of nature," but, unlike them, he seemed, in some ways, to wish to return to it. His *Social Contract* (1762) opened with the lament "Man is born free; and everywhere he is in chains." In his *Discourse on the Origin of Inequality* (1755) Rousseau wrote:

> There is hardly any inequality in the state of nature; all the inequality which now prevails owes its strength and growth to the development of our faculties and the advance of the human mind, and becomes at last permanent and legitimate by the establishment of property and laws. (Columbia University, *Contemporary Civilization*, p. 1147)

Rousseau proposed a democracy far more radical than that of the other *philosophes*, yet he also seemed to justify a repressive tyranny of the majority. Like Locke and Hobbes, Rousseau mythologized an original social contract, which transformed the state of nature into a community, and he attributed great power to that community: "Each of us puts his person and all his power in common under the supreme direction of the general will." "Whoever refuses to obey the general will shall be compelled to do so by the whole body. This means nothing less than that he will be forced to be free" (p. 1153).

Political philosophers have argued for more than two centuries over the paradox of Rousseau's "general will." How is the citizen "forced to be free"? Is this a proclamation of freedom, justification for suppressing minorities, or a proposal for creating a totalitarian state?

Adam Smith. Adam Smith, whose advocacy of the free market we have already examined (see Chapter Fourteen), is sometimes grouped with the *philosophes*, with whom he carried on extensive discussions and correspondence. Like Locke, Smith believed it was normal for people to want to "better their condition" materially. He saw that this attempt was not always successful, but suggested:

> it is well that nature imposes upon us in this manner. It is this deception which rouses and keeps in continual motion the industry of mankind. It is this which first prompted them to cultivate the ground, to build houses, to found cities and commonwealths, and to invent and improve all the sciences and arts, which ennoble and embellish human life. (*Moral Sentiments*, IV.1.10)

Much less optimistically, Smith recognized that private enrichment would engender jealousy and envy. Private property, therefore, needed to be protected and this, he agreed with Locke, was the task of government:

> Civil government, so far as it is instituted for the security of property, is in reality instituted for the defense of the rich against the poor, or of those who have some property against those who have none at all. (*The Wealth of Nations*, p. 674)

At the time of the American and French Revolutions these arguments for enlightenment, rationality, experimental science, secularism, private profit and ownership, "fellow feeling," and limitations on the power of government all clamored for changes in politics, economics, and social life. But what would be the substance and direction of those changes? How would they be implemented and by whom?

Revolution in North America, 1776

As British settlers began to colonize North America, Australia, and South Africa in the seventeenth and eighteenth centuries, they assumed that they shared in the political and legal rights of all Britons. By the 1760s, however, North American settlers were beginning to resent British control over their political and economic life. Control over American trade, restrictions on the development of American shipping, and the resulting limitations on the development of certain kinds of manufacture, were as galling as the issue of taxation. The 1763 British victory over the French in the Seven Years War in North America, concluding a global cluster of wars between the two powers, ended the threat of attacks by French or Native Americans, and freed the American colonists from further need of British troops. However, the British continued to maintain a large army in North America and to tax the colonies directly to pay for it. The 1765 Stamp Act levied taxes on a long list of commercial and legal documents. The colonists protested with riots, destruction of government property, and a boycott of British goods until Parliament repealed the Act.

Further imperious decrees of King George III stoked increasing anger until, finally, the Americans revolted, declaring themselves an independent country in 1776 and fighting a war to end British rule over them. The American Declaration of Independence set out their list of "injuries and usurpations." It reflected the American resolve to secure the same legal rights as Britons had won at home almost a century earlier. It charged the king with "taking away our Charters, abolishing our most valuable Laws, and altering fundamentally the Forms of our Governments." It blamed the king for abrogating the social contract that bound the colonies to Britain. It declared, ultimately, the right of revolution.

The American Revolution went further in establishing political democracy than had the Glorious Revolution in Britain. It abolished the monarchy entirely, replacing it with an elected government. Having declared that "all men are created equal," with unalienable rights not only to life and liberty, but also to the vague but seductive "pursuit of happiness," the revolutionaries now set out to consolidate their commitments in a new legal structure. Their leaders, men like George Washington, Benjamin Franklin, Thomas Jefferson, and James Madison, were soldiers, entrepreneurs, and statesmen of considerable erudition, common sense, restraint, and balance.

The Boston Tea Party, 1773. Protesting against the British tax on tea. American colonists cheer as some radicals dressed up as Native Americans throw tea overboard from British ships into the Boston harbor. (Yale University Art Gallery, New Haven, Connecticut)

The Constitution and the Bill of Rights, 1789

After the Americans won their war for independence, 1775–81, and achieved a peace treaty with Britain in 1783, political leaders of the 13 colonies met in Philadelphia to establish a framework for their new nation. They drafted a new Constitution, which took effect in 1789, and a Bill of Rights, which was ratified in 1791. The American Bill of Rights, the first ten amendments to the Constitution, guaranteed to Americans not only the basic rights enjoyed by the British at the time, but more: freedom of religion (and the separation of Church and state), press, assembly, and petition; the right to bear arms; protection against unreasonable searches and against cruel and unusual punishment; and the right to a speedy and proper trial by a jury of peers. The Americans established a federal system of government. The states individually set the rules for voting and many, but not all, removed the property requirements. By 1800 Vermont had instituted universal manhood suffrage, and South Carolina, Pennsylvania, New Hampshire, and Delaware extended the vote to almost every adult white male taxpayer.

Historians of the early United States situate the more radical American approach to political liberty in at least four factors: religious, geographic, social, and philosophical. First, a disproportionate share of the settlers coming to America from Britain and Europe were religious dissenters, seeking spiritual independence outside the established churches of their countries. Their widespread, popular beliefs in the importance of individual liberties carried over from religion into politics.

Second, the availability of apparently open land presented abundant individual opportunity to the new Americans (as they dispossessed Native Americans). Later, the historian Frederick Jackson Turner would formulate his "frontier thesis," arguing that the relative freedom and openness of American life was based, psychologically as well as materially, on the presence of seemingly endless open frontier land. Third, the absence of landed and aristocratic privilege, and the strength of artisan classes in the urban population. Finally, eighteenth-century political thought had generally grown more radical, especially among the *philosophes* in France. By the time the Americans wrote their Bill of Rights, the French Revolution was well underway.

The First Anti-imperial Revolution

The American Revolution, in addition to securing British rights for Americans, was also, and perhaps more importantly, the first modern anticolonial revolution. The trade and taxation policies imposed by Britain had pushed businessmen and artisans into opposition to British rule. Other nations, notably France, eager to embarrass Britain and to detach its most promising colonies, provided financial and

Signing of the Declaration of Independence, July 4, 1776, **John Trumbull, 1786–97.** What began as a protest against colonial trade restrictions and the limiting of political liberty grew into a revolutionary struggle and the birth of a nation. The Declaration of Independence enshrined the principles underlying the new United States and later influenced freedom-fighters all over the world. (Capitol Collection, Washington)

military support, which helped the Americans to win their independence. One of the goals of the revolution was to open the North American continent west of the Appalachian Mountains to settlement. The British prohibition on this westward movement stood in their way, quite different from Spanish and Portuguese settlement policy in Latin America.

As the newly independent Americans migrated westward, annexing land as they went, they began to develop imperial interests of their own, expressed in the mystique of "manifest destiny." This popular belief in America's natural growth across the continent inspired the European Americans in their constant warfare against Native American Indians. It led Thomas Jefferson to acquire the huge Louisiana Purchase from France in 1803. Texans were encouraged to assert their independence from Mexico in 1836 and were then absorbed into the American Union in 1845. Warfare with Mexico in 1846–48 ended in victory for the United States and the annexation of the southwest. Other annexations of land in North America took place more peacefully, with negotiations with Britain for the Oregon country in 1844–46 and with Russia for the purchase of Alaska in 1867.

Nevertheless, over the centuries America served as an inspiration to anticolonial forces. Jawaharlal Nehru, leading India's twentieth-century struggle for independence from Britain, cited the American Revolution as a model for his own country: "This political change in America was important and destined to bear great results. The American colonies which became free then have grown today [1932] into the most powerful, the richest, and industrially the most advanced country in the world."

The "Other"

The American Revolution, however, did not bring democracy to everyone. The greatest shortcoming was slavery. The system was finally ended only by the American Civil War (1861–65), the bloodiest in the history of the nation. Even afterward, racial discrimination characterized American law until the 1960s and continues to mark American practice up to the present. The status of the Native American population actually worsened after the revolution, as settlers of European extraction headed west, first by wagon train and later by railroad. They slaughtered American Indians, pushed them out of the way, confined them to remote, semibarren reservations, destroyed the buffalo herds on which their nomadic existence depended, and discouraged the preservation of their separate cultures and languages. For the indigenous peoples the effects of the revolution were exactly opposite to those of the settler-invaders: expansion became contraction, democracy became tyranny, prosperity became poverty, and liberty became confinement.

The hypocrisy of democratic statements, on the one hand, and atrocities against American Indians, on the other, peaked in the presidency of Andrew Jackson (1829–37). Jackson fought against economic and political privilege and to extend opportunity to the common man, yet he ordered the United States Army to evict the Cherokee Nation from their lands in Georgia and to drive them to the "Great American Desert" in the west, in direct defiance of the Supreme Court of the United States. About 25 percent of the 15,000 Indians forced onto this "Trail of Tears" died *en route*.

How did America reconcile its ideals of equality and liberty with the enslavement of blacks and the confinement of American Indians? It did so by considering nonwhites and non-Europeans as "other"—that is, as biologically inferior. The concept of race was often used as a definition, usually made by a quick, if approximate and sometimes inaccurate, visual measure, and often as a legal standard. The fixing of legal identity by race, based on identification primarily by color, became especially

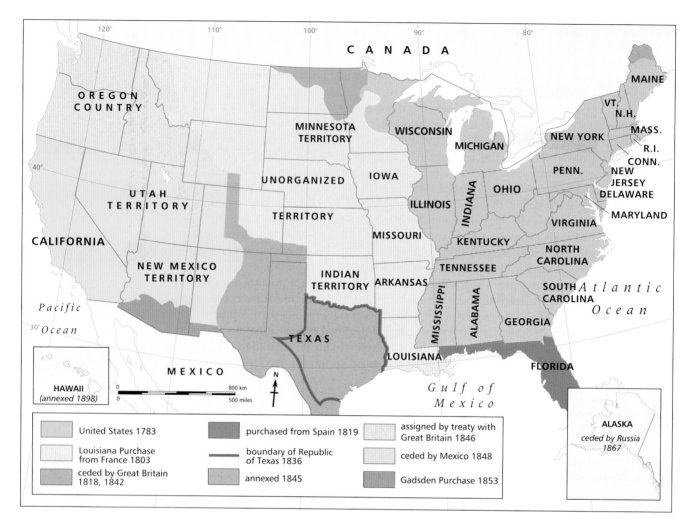

The growth of the United States. The westward expansion of the United States was effected by territorial cession, acquisition, and conquest. Following independence in 1783, the Louisiana Purchase from France (1803), and the annexations of west and east Florida from Spain, doubled the nation's size. Another doubling occurred with the annexation of Texas (1845); the acquisition of Oregon Territory (1846); military victory over Mexico (1848), which brought the southwest; the purchase of Alaska from Russia (1867); and the annexation of Hawaii in 1898. In less than a century the United States had become one of the world's largest nations. In all cases, European immigrants and their descendants displaced Native Americans.

common in the southern United States in dealing with slaves, ex-slaves, and free blacks. For many years, racial definition was also used as a legal standard in excluding Asians from immigrating. If nonwhites were considered not quite equal biologically, the unalienable right to liberty could be abridged. Once the revolutionary principle of equality was accepted in America and elsewhere, the battle was drawn between those who wished to narrow its application to an "in-group" while excluding "others" and those who wished to apply it to all peoples. That battle continues today, in law and in practice, in the United States and around the globe.

The French Revolution and Napoleon, 1789–1812

The American Revolution, with its combined messages of colonial revolt, constitutional government, individual freedom, and equality under law, inspired many peoples at the time and over the centuries. But in comparison with European countries and their experiences, America and its revolution were unique. At the end of the eighteenth century, America was a country of four million people on the fringes of a continental wilderness, without traditions of class and clerical privilege, and founded in large measure by dissidents. Building on already existing British freedoms and fighting a war (with the support of several international allies) against a distant colonial government, the leaders of the revolution were an educated, comfortable elite. The French Revolution, on the other hand, was an internal revolt against entrenched feudal, clerical, and monarchical privilege within the most populous (24 million people) and most powerful European state of its time. It unleashed powerful, combative internal factions, none of which could control the direction or the velocity of revolutionary events inside or outside of France. The French Revolution immediately affected all of Europe, most of the western hemisphere, and indeed the whole world. Some would argue that the battles over its central principles continue even today. The twentieth-century Chinese leader Zhou Enlai, when asked to assess the effects of the French Revolution, famously replied: "It's too soon to tell."

From Protests to Revolution, 1789–91

The French Revolution, like the English civil wars of the 1640s, was triggered by the king's need for funds. Much like Charles I, King Louis XVI (r. 1774–92) decided to solicit these funds by convening leaders of the French people through the Estates-General in 1789.

From this point on, political, social, and ideological change proceeded very rapidly as political institutions, social classes, and philosophical beliefs challenged one another in a continuous unfolding of critical events. France was divided, hierarchically, into three Estates: the clergy, numbering about 100,000 and controlling perhaps 10 percent of the land of France; the nobility, perhaps 300,000 men, who owned approximately 25 percent of the land; and everyone else. The Third Estate included a rising and prosperous group of urban merchants and professionals (estimated at 8 percent of the total population), as well as working-class artisans, and the 80 percent of the French population who were farmers. The wealth that the king wished to tap was concentrated in the first two estates and in the **bourgeoisie**, the leading urban professional and commercial classes, of the Third Estate.

The Estates-General had not been convened since 1614, and the procedures for its meeting were disputed, revealing grievances not only against the king but also among the representatives. The nobles wished to seize the moment to make the Estates-General into the constitutional government of France, with the king subordinate to it. They wanted guarantees of personal liberty, freedom of the press and speech, and freedom from arbitrary arrest. They also wanted minimal taxation, but they might have conceded this point in exchange for greater political power. Under their proposed constitution, the Estates-General would meet in three separate chambers: one for the nobility; one for the clergy, in which the nobility also had a powerful voice; and a third for everyone else.

The Third Estate, which had long regarded the nobility as parasitic and resented their multitude of special privileges, viewed the new proposals with suspicion. The members of the Third Estate drew their inspiration for a more democratic, representative, inclusive, and accountable government from the writings of the *philosophes*, and the experience of the revolutions in England and, especially, in America. Their local spokesman and leading pamphleteer was actually a clergyman, the Abbé Emmanuel-Joseph Sieyès (1748–1836), who wrote *What Is the Third Estate?* (1789). The tract opened with a catechism of three political questions and answers: "(1) What is the Third Estate? Everything. (2) What has it been in the political order up to the present? Nothing. (3) What does it demand? To Become Something." The leaders of the Third Estate asked for an end to the privileges that had enriched and empowered the clergy and the nobility while reducing the opportunities available to everyone else and impoverishing the French crown. Many saw the king as an ally in the struggle against the nobility. They proposed that the entire Estates-General meet

KEY TERM

bourgeoisie From the French word for town, *bourg*. Originally applied to the inhabitants of walled towns, who occupied a socio-economic position between the rural peasantry and the feudal aristocracy. With the development of industry, it became identified more with employers, as well as with other members of the "middle class," professionals, artisans, and shopkeepers.

The Oath of the Tennis Court, Jacques-Louis David, 1790. In this dramatic composition, David captures the moment when the Third Estate asserted their sovereignty as the elected representatives of France. The merchants, professionals, and artisans who attended the hastily convened meeting swore to remain in session until they had drawn up a new constitution—one that would end the vested interests of the nobility and clergy. (Musée Carnavalet, Paris)

in a single body, since the king had granted them as many representatives as both of the other two estates combined.

When the Parlement of Paris ruled that the three estates should meet separately, as the nobility had wished, the Third Estate was enraged. For six weeks its members boycotted the Estates-General when it was convened in May 1789. On June 13 a few priests joined them, and four days later the Third Estate, with its allies, declared itself the "National Assembly." The king locked them out of their meeting hall. On June 20 they met on a nearby indoor tennis court and swore the "Oath of the Tennis Court," claiming legal power, and declaring that they would not disband until a new constitution was drafted. Louis XVI, frightened by these events, and unwilling or unable to assert his own leadership, called up some 18,000 troops to defend himself from possible attack at his palace in Versailles where all these events were taking place.

The Revolt of the Poor. Meanwhile, in Paris, 12 miles away, and throughout France, mobs of people were rising against organized authority. The harvest had been poor, and the price of bread in 1789 was near record heights. Some farmers refused to pay their taxes and their manorial dues, and many city people were hungry. Beggars and brigands began to roam the countryside and move toward Paris.

In the capital, mobs stormed the Bastille, which was a combination of jail and armory. Meeting violent resistance, they murdered the governor of the Bastille, the mayor of Paris, and a number of soldiers. Encouraged by the events in Paris, peasants in the countryside organized against France's remaining feudal institutions. They seized and destroyed documents that demanded feudal dues and taxes. The peasants felt an (unfounded) "Great Fear," as it was

SOURCE

Olympe de Gouges, "The Rights of Women"

Writing under the pen name Olympe de Gouges, Marie Gouze (1748–93) directly appropriated the language of the Revolution's *Declaration of the Rights of Man and the Citizen* (1789). Her *Declaration of the Rights of Woman and the Citizen* exposed the former's lack of concern for the rights of women:

Article I. Woman is born free and remains equal in rights to man. Social distinctions can be founded only on general utility …

Article XVII. The right of property is inviolable and sacred to both sexes, jointly or separately. (Bell and Offen, pp. 105–06)

Gouges addressed this document to the French queen, Marie-Antoinette, urging her to adopt this feminist program as her own and thus win over France to the royalist cause. In 1793 the radical Jacobins in the Assembly, condemning Gouges for both royalism and feminism, had her guillotined.

called, that landlords were attempting to block reform by hiring thugs to burn the harvest. In response, peasants attacked the estates of the nobility and the clergy, and their managers, although they launched few violent attacks on individual persons.

In an attempt to contain these revolutionary disorders, the king, in Versailles, now recognized the National Assembly, the new group formed by the Third Estate and its allies, as representatives of the people. He authorized it to draft a new constitution.

The National Assembly abolished what was left of feudalism and serfdom, the tithe for the Church, and the special privileges of the nobility. It issued the "Declaration of the Rights of Man and the Citizen" with 17 articles, including:

- Men are born and remain free and equal in rights; social distinctions may be based only upon general usefulness.
- The aim of every political association is the preservation of the natural and unalienable rights of man; these rights are liberty, property, security, and resistance to oppression.
- The source of all sovereignty resides essentially in the nation …
- Law is the expression of the general will … All citizens, being equal before it, are equally admissible to all public offices, positions, and employments, according to their capacity, and without other distinction than that of virtues and talents …
- For the maintenance of the public force and for the expenses of administration a common tax is indispensable; it must be assessed equally on all citizens in proportion to their means …
- Society has the right to require of every public agent an accounting of his administration.

The Declaration further affirmed freedom of thought, religion, petition, and due process under law. It represented a triumph for the doctrines of the *philosophes*.

Meanwhile, hungry mobs in Paris continued edging toward insurrection. In October, led by a demonstration of housewives, market women, and revolutionary militants protesting the high price of bread, 20,000 Parisians marched to the royal palace in Versailles. This "March of the Women" broke into the palace, overwhelmed the National Guard, and forced the royal family to return to Paris where they could be kept under surveillance.

Over the next two years, the National Assembly drew up a constitution, which called for a constitutional monarchy; did away with the titles and perquisites of nobility and clergy; introduced uniform government across the country; disestablished the Roman Catholic clergy and confiscated the property of the Church; and convened a new Legislative Assembly, for which about one-half of adult, male Frenchmen were entitled to vote, essentially by a property qualification. Protestants, Jews, and agnostics were admitted to full citizenship and could vote and run for office if they met the property qualifications. Citizenship would be based not on religious affiliation but on residence in the country and allegiance to its government. Except for the radical—and polarizing—anticlerical

Women marching to Versailles on October 5, 1789. Engraving. Angered by reports of a luxurious banquet staged by the king, while they themselves lacked adequate food, a large crowd of Parisians, mostly women, stormed Versailles and laid siege to the royal palace. Louis XVI and his family were saved by the intervention of the French general, the Marquis de Lafayette. (They were eventually executed.)

543

Le ROI ESCLAVE ou les SUJETS ROIS   FEMALE PATRIOTISM

The women of Les Halles taking Louis XVI from Versailles, 1789. Engraving. The illustration on p. 543 shows the women setting out for Versailles, angry, determined, and struggling. Here they return in triumph with their quarry. Contemporary cartoons and engravings told the story of the revolution as it unfolded. (Bibliothèque Nationale, Paris)

KEY TERMS

Jacobins A French revolutionary party founded in 1789. It later became the most radical party of the revolution, responsible for implementing the Reign of Terror and the execution of the king (1793).

Girondins French revolutionary group formed largely from the middle classes, many of them originally from the Gironde region. Relatively moderate.

Montagnards Members of a radical French revolutionary party, closely associated with the Jacobins and supported by the artisans, shopkeepers, and sansculottes. They opposed the more moderate Girondins.

sansculottes From the French, "without knee-breeches." Members of the militant, generally poorer classes of Paris, so-called because they wore trousers rather than the knee-breeches of affluent society.

position, the actions of the French Revolution thus far seemed quite similar to those of England and America. They were consistent with the optimistic and activist worldview of the *philosophes*. The new constitution was finally promulgated in September 1791, following a wave of strikes and an official ban on labor organizations.

International War, the "Second" Revolution, and the Terror, 1791–99

In June 1791, Louis XVI and his queen Marie-Antoinette attempted to flee France but were apprehended and held as virtual prisoners in the royal palace. Shocked and frightened, thousands of aristocrats emigrated to neighboring countries that were more respectful of monarchy and aristocracy. News of the abolition of feudal privilege and of the Civil Constitution of the Clergy filled the nobility and clergy across Europe with dread. Leopold II, the Habsburg emperor (r. 1790–92) and brother of Marie-Antoinette, entered into discussions with other rulers to consider war against the new French government. The French National Assembly, meeting under the new constitution, began to mobilize both in response to this threat and in anticipation of extending the revolution. In April 1792, it declared war on the Austrian monarchy and, for the next 23 years, France would be at war with several of the major countries of Europe.

Events careened onward at a revolutionary pace. The war went poorly and mobs stormed the royal palace attempting to kill the king and beginning the Second French Revolution. Louis sought protection in the National Assembly and was imprisoned; all his official powers were terminated. The Assembly disbanded and called for a new National Convention—to be elected by universal male suffrage—to draw up a new constitution. Amid mob violence, the new Convention met in September 1792. Its leaders were **Jacobins**, members of a nationwide network of political clubs named (ironically) for a former convent in Paris where they had first met. They divided into the more moderate **Girondins**, named for a region of France and in general representing the provinces, and the **Montagnards**, representatives mostly from Paris, who drew their name from the benches they occupied on the uppermost left side of the assembly hall. By 361 to 359 votes, the Convention voted to execute the king in January 1793. The "Second Revolution" was well underway.

Outside the Assembly, the Paris Commune, the government of Paris, represented the workers, merchants, and artisans of the city, who were generally more radical than the Convention. They were called the **sansculottes**, "without breeches," because the men wore long trousers rather than the knee breeches of the middle and aristocratic classes. In June 1793, the Commune invaded the National Convention and forced the arrest of 31 Girondins on charges of treason, leaving the more radical Montagnards in control.

To govern in the midst of the combined international and civil warfare, the Convention created a Committee of Public Safety, which launched a Reign of Terror against "counterrevolutionaries." It executed about 40,000 people between mid-1793 and mid-1794. At Nantes, in the Vendée region of western France, the center of the royalist counterrevolution, the Committee intentionally drowned 2,000 people. To wage war abroad it instituted a *levée en masse*, or national military draft, which raised an unprecedented army of 800,000 men, and mobilized the economic resources of France to support it.

The Committee intensified the campaign against feudal privilege, rejecting the payment of compensation to the manor lords, who lost their special rights over their tenants. It promoted instruction in practical farming and craft production, spoke of introducing universal elementary education, and abolished slavery throughout France's colonies. It introduced a new calendar, counting Year 1 from the founding of the French Republic in 1792, giving new names to the 12 months, and dividing each month into three weeks of ten days each. In 1794 the most important leader of the Committee, Maximilien Robespierre (1758–94), introduced the Worship of the Supreme Being, a kind of generalized civic religious ritual that alienated the Catholic majority in France.

By July 1794, however, French armies were winning wars against the other European powers, and the domestic economy seemed to be recovering. The members of the Convention, partly out of fear for their own lives, managed to end both the mob-inspired violence and the official Terror. The Convention outlawed and guillotined Robespierre. It relaxed price controls and, when working-class mobs threatened the Convention, called in the troops and suppressed the revolt. In 1795 it instituted yet another constitution, this time calling for a three-stage election of a representative government. Almost all adult males could vote for electors who, in turn, chose a national legislative assembly composed of men who did have to meet property qualifications and who, in turn, chose an executive of five Directors. When the 1795 elections were threatened by insurrection, the Convention called upon General Napoleon Bonaparte (1769–1821) to protect the process.

The Directory, as the executive body was called, governed from 1795 to 1799. With the execution of the monarch, the manorial system and the privileges of the nobility and clergy had come to an end, and the Directory ratified the new peasant and commercial landowners in the possession of their new property. However, the Directory itself was unpopular and unstable, and the greater freedom benefited its opponents while at the same time enabling the Catholic Church to make a strong comeback. The elections of Directors in 1797, 1798, and 1799 were disputed, and on each occasion army officers were called in to dismiss the Directors, until, in 1799, Bonaparte, acting with the Abbé Sieyès, staged a *coup d'état* and had himself appointed First Consul. In 1802 his position was upgraded to consul for life and, in 1804, to emperor. Losing the right of free elections, France itself became a (benevolent) despotism. The process that historians usually call the French Revolution was over.

Napoleon Crossing the Alps, Jacques-Louis David, *c.* 1800. Having chronicled the revolution with his brush, David became Napoleon's official painter. The heroic style of the portrait projects the emperor's enormous confidence as he heads for military glory in the Italian campaigns of 1796–97. The truth of the journey was rather different: Napoleon crossed the Alps on a docile but footsure mule, not a fiery stallion. (Palace of Versailles, near Paris)

HOW DO WE KNOW?

The Historiography of the French Revolution

The study of the French Revolution remains the preeminent subject of French historiography, producing a seemingly endless variety of interpretations. Three approaches, however, have predominated. The first emphasizes the importance of ideas, stressing the *philosophes* as the precursors of revolution. This interpretation tends to focus on the first three months of the revolution and the significance of the *Declaration of the Rights of Man and the Citizen*. R.R. Palmer's *The Age of the Democratic Revolution* (1959), for example, favors this reading. A second interpretation stresses the significance of class interests in the revolution, and tends to highlight the next chronological stage, as urban workers and rural peasantry escalated their protests and demonstrations. Georges Lefebvre's *The Coming of the French Revolution* (1939) represents this position. A more recent interpretation (influenced by literary theory) speaks of the revolution as "discourse," an interplay of ideas and interest groups that constantly shifts, or "skids," as events unfold. As the direction of the revolution changed irrevocably with each new event—for example, the execution of Louis XVI—ideas were reassessed and classes reshuffled themselves into new alignments. François Furet's *Interpreting the French Revolution* (1978) is the leading statement of this point of view. Our narrative incorporates elements of all three interpretive perspectives.

There is a broader issue, too. Historians sometimes envision events as part of a long sweep of related trends. Sometimes they see them as contingencies, occurring because of circumstances that are unique and unpredictable. The French Revolution presents both aspects. On the one hand, it was an outgrowth of larger trends, the ideals of the *philosophes* and the legacies of the revolutions in England and America. On the other hand, specific events unfolded day by day in quite unpredictable ways; had they turned out differently—for example, had the one vote majority to guillotine the king been reversed—the outcome of the revolution might have been quite different. To understand the French Revolution, both these perspectives—the grand sweep and the contingency—are necessary.

- In your own understanding of historical change, which do you think counts for more, the ideas or interests? Why?
- In the French Revolution, what is the evidence for the importance of ideas? For the importance of interests?
- In your own understanding of historical change, which do you think counts for more, the grand sweep or contingency? Give an example from one of the revolutions, other than the French Revolution, that illustrates your point of view.

Napoleon in Power, 1799–1812

As head of government, Napoleon Bonaparte consolidated and even expanded many of the innovations of the revolution. To maintain the equality of classes and to systematize the administration of justice, he codified the laws of France. The Code Napoléon or Civil Code, which was issued in 1804, pressed for equality before the law and the principle of a career open to talents, that is, the idea that all people should have access to professional advancement according to their ability, rather than according to birth or social status. Uniform codes of criminal, commercial, and penal law were also introduced. The administration was organized into a smoothly functioning service throughout France.

Fearing a counterrevolution led by the Church, Napoleon reached a concordat or agreement with the pope. The French government continued to hold the former Church lands, but agreed in exchange to pay the salaries of the clergy (including Protestants and others) and to allow the pope to regain authority over the appointment and discipline of Roman Catholic clergy. Protestants, dissenters, Jews, and others were reaffirmed in full citizenship, with all the rights and obligations that such status entailed, as long as they swore their allegiance to the state. In many conquered cities, including Rome and Frankfurt, French armies pulled down the ghetto walls that for centuries had segregated Jews. The government hired a large bureaucracy to administer the state. It selected personnel mostly on the revolutionary principle of a "career open to talent."

This openness of opportunity suited Napoleon very well. He had come from the island of Corsica, of a modest family, and made his mark as a military officer. He had no respect for unearned authority. Nor was he formally religious. He earned his power through his military, administrative, and leadership skills. In a striking exception to the principle of advancement by merit, however, Napoleon appointed his brothers as kings of Spain, Holland, and Westphalia, his brother-in-law as king of Naples, and his stepson as viceroy of the kingdom of Italy. He himself continued to lead the forces of France in military victories over the powers of Europe.

The Napoleonic Wars and the Spread of Revolution, 1799–1812

As a son of the revolution, Napoleon sought to spread its principles by force of arms. By 1810 he had conquered or entered into alliances with all the major powers and regions of Europe except Portugal, the Ottoman-held Balkans, and Britain. In each conquered state, Napoleon introduced the principal legal and administrative reforms of the revolution: an end to feudal privilege, equality of rights, religious toleration, codified law, free trade, and efficient and systematic administration, including statistical accounting, registration of documents, and the use of the metric system. In many areas of Europe, Napoleon was welcomed for the reforms he brought.

There were, however, flaws in Napoleon's policies, and they finally destroyed him. First, Napoleon attempted to conquer Britain, and ultimately the naval power of that island nation and the land forces of its allies, especially those of Russia,

The empire of Napoleon.
Napoleon, fired by revolutionary zeal, fought brilliantly to bring much of Europe under his dominion, often installing relatives as rulers. Napoleonic institutions were introduced to Italy, the Low Countries, Germany, and Poland by force of arms. By 1812 Napoleon seemed invincible, but Britain's strength at sea and Napoleon's disastrous losses on land in his invasion of Russia (1812) led to his downfall.

KEY TERMS

Congress of Vienna The Congress brought together diplomats from the leading countries of Europe to resolve issues raised by the Napoleonic Wars and their aftermath. It redrew national borders, established a balance of power, and enshrined conservative government in Europe for about 30 years.

vodoun (**voodoo**) A religion of the Caribbean region which blended religious practices brought from Africa with those of Catholicism brought from Europe.

maroon An escaped slave who fled to remote, often hilly areas, and joined with others to create small, free colonies. The process of flight followed by community building is called **maroonage**.

mulatto In the Americas, a person of mixed race, usually with parents of European and African origin.

proved too strong. Napoleon could not break the British hold on continental shipping and he was defeated at sea by Lord Nelson at the Battle of Trafalgar in 1805. When the Russian emperor supported Britain, Napoleon invaded Russia in 1812 and mired his army irretrievably in the vastness of that country during the bitterness of its winter. During that campaign, 400,000 of Napoleon's troops died from battle, starvation, and exposure; another 100,000 were captured.

Finally, the nations Napoleon conquered began to experience the stirrings of nationalism and the desire for self-rule. Haiti, which had achieved virtual independence in the 1790s, resisted Napoleon's attempt to reimpose French rule and reinstitute slavery in the island. Some 50,000 French troops perished in Haiti, most by diseases such as yellow fever, but many at the hands of revolutionary slaves. European peoples, too, did not want their countries to be colonies of France. By 1813 Napoleon had been defeated by his disastrous losses in Russia and by a coalition of European armies; the French were driven back to their borders. In 1814 Napoleon abdicated and Louis XVIII (r. 1814–15; 1815–24) assumed the throne of France. Napoleon escaped from exile on the Mediterranean island of Elba only to be defeated and exiled again in 1815, this time to St. Helena in the South Atlantic. The Napoleonic era was over. The **Congress of Vienna,** an assembly of representatives of all the powers of Europe, led by the most influential states, concluded diplomatic agreements that established a balance of power (see Key Term p. 470) between them and redrew the postwar map of Europe. Political conservatism enveloped France and Europe for a generation.

Haiti: Slave Revolution and the Overthrow of Colonialism, 1791–1804

The formal philosophy and rhetoric of enlightenment and revolution proclaimed the natural desire of all humans to be free, and in the slave plantations of the Caribbean local slave revolts were common, feared, and ruthlessly suppressed. In the western sector of the island of Hispaniola in the colony of Saint-Domingue (modern Haiti), French planters had established one of the most brutal of the slave plantation systems. By 1791, 500,000 black slaves formed the overwhelming majority of the population, with 40,000 whites, many of them owners of plantations and slaves, and 30,000 free people of color, both mulatto and black. For decades, the slaves had escaped psychologically and culturally through the practice of *vodoun* (**voodoo**), a religion that blended the Catholicism of their masters with religious practices brought from Africa. Physically, they had escaped through **maroonage**, flight from the plantations to the surrounding hills. Sometimes the escaped slaves, **maroons**, established their own colonies. In the 1750s one of the maroons, François Makandal, built among the maroon colonies a network of resistance to slavery. Inspired to independence by *vodoun* beliefs, and using poison to attack individual plantation owners, Makandal apparently planned to poison the water supply of Le Cap, the main town of northern Saint-Domingue. He was captured and burned at the stake in 1758.

The Slave Revolt

In 1791, slave revolts broke out across Saint-Domingue. The inspiration seems to have been the natural desire for freedom, perhaps abetted by news of the American and French Revolutions. One of the earliest rallying cries, delivered by the poet Boukman Dutty in Haitian-French patois, *"Coute la liberté li pale nan coeur nous tous"* ("Listen to the voice of liberty which speaks in the hearts of all of us") implied no knowledge of those revolutions.

The revolt spread. From guerrilla warfare by maroon bands, it grew to general armed struggle and civil warfare. In the western part of Saint-Domingue, white planters welcomed the support of British troops who came as allies to suppress the slave revolt and also to drive out the French. The **mulattoes**—those of mixed race parentage—were free people, and some of them owned slaves. They now sought their own rights of representation and were divided over the issue of slavery. In the eastern part of Saint-Domingue, a new leader, Toussaint L'Ouverture (*c.* 1743–1803), a freed black, established an alliance with the Spanish rulers against both the slave system in Saint-Domingue (but not in the Spanish part of the island) and the French. Toussaint incorporated the rhetoric of the French Revolution into his own. In 1794, under Robespierre, the French National Assembly abolished slavery in all French colonies. In response, Toussaint linked himself to France as he continued his war against slaveowners, who were now aligned with the British and who resisted the new French decree. By May 1800 Toussaint had become the effective ruler of Saint-Domingue.

The Anti-imperial Revolt, 1804

When Napoleon came to power in 1799 he reversed French policy on slavery. He dispatched 20,000 French troops to recapture the island and to reinstitute slavery, as he did in Guadeloupe in 1802. Napoleon's representative deceived Toussaint into suspending his revolution. Toussaint was imprisoned in 1802 and exiled to France, where he died the next year. Nevertheless, unified black and mulatto armies, now under many different cooperating leaders, continued the struggle against France, drove out its forces, and, once again, abolished slavery. As many as 50,000 French troops died of yellow fever, and thousands more became military casualties. On January 1, 1804, Saint-Domingue at last proclaimed its independence and its new name of Haiti, the Carib name for "mountain." This completed the only known successful slave revolution in history.

Pierre Dominique Toussaint L'Ouverture, **early nineteenth-century French lithograph.** The colony of Saint-Domingue (present-day Haiti) in the West Indies had made a fortune for the French through sugar plantations worked by African slaves. In the 1790s, under the leadership of Toussaint L'Ouverture, it became the site of a slave revolution that eventually led to independence. The former slave acquired his surname because of the ferocity with which he made an opening ("ouverture") in the enemy ranks.

The revolution in Haiti. One of the most dramatic revolutions occurred on the Caribbean island of Hispaniola. A slave revolt in 1791 in the French region, Saint-Domingue, spread rapidly, briefly penetrating and uniting with the Spanish sector, Santo Domingo. Despite interventions by French and British forces, and the incarceration and exile of its leader, Toussaint L'Ouverture, in 1802, Haiti gained its independence from France in 1804, the first successful slave revolt in history.

Abolition: Historians Debate the Causes

Why were the slave trade, and then slavery itself, abolished in the Atlantic countries? To what extent was the spread of democratic revolution responsible? Analyses differ. Historians who emphasize the significance of the Haitian Revolution, as C.L.R. James and David Nicholls do, stress the fear that the uprising of the slaves engendered among slave owners. In the lands of the Caribbean, including northeastern Brazil, black slaves working the high-mortality plantations formed up to 90 percent of the population. Local rebellions already occurred frequently, and large-scale revolution now appeared as a real possibility. The abolition of the slave trade provided some limit on the size of the slave population, although total abolition—a much more expensive act for the slave owners—would come only later.

A second school of thought, shared by historians such as David Brion Davis and Orlando Patterson, stresses the importance of compassion as a motive. Davis emphasizes the increasing influence of humanitarian sentiment in European Christian thought from the seventeenth century:

> The philosophy of benevolence was a product of the seventeenth century, when certain British Protestants, shaken by theological controversy and the implications of modern science, looked increasingly to human nature and conduct as a basis for faith. In their impatience with theological dogma, their distaste for the doctrine of original sin, their appreciation for human feeling and sentiment, and their confidence in man's capacity for moral improvement, these Latitudinarians, as they were called, anticipated the main concerns of the Enlightenment, and laid an indispensable foundation for social reform. (Davis, 1975, pp. 348–49)

The emphasis on compassion increased in reaction against the growing scale and unprecedented cruelty of slavery in the New World. Among Christian groups opposing slavery, Quakers and Methodists stood out. The birth and growth of both these denominations—Quakerism under the leadership of George Fox (1624–91) and Methodism under John Wesley (1703–91)—were contemporary with the development of mass slavery in the Americas. Other branches of Christianity had long since made peace with the institution of slavery, contenting themselves with promising a gentler existence in life after death. Quakers and Methodists, however, had to confront the reality of slavery for the first time in one of its cruelest, New World, forms. In Britain, William Wilberforce (1759–1833), a philanthropist and member of the Clapham Sect—a group of well-to-do Evangelicals—played a major part in the antislavery movement. As a member of Parliament, he led the campaign to abolish the slave trade and to emancipate existing slaves.

The *philosophes* argued a third, similar but more intellectual, position against slavery. They argued that slavery violated the law of nature; it was inconsistent with the nature of humankind. Montesquieu (1689–1755), in his assessments of the nature of

laws and government, argued that "the call for slavery was the call of the wealthy and the decadent, not for the general welfare of mankind."

Finally, an economic critique began to develop in the eighteenth century. Slavery was not profitable to the society, certainly not to the slave, and not to the development of a more productive economy in the long run. In *The Wealth of Nations* Adam Smith argued that slavery, like all examples of monopoly and special privilege, inhibited economic growth. Lacking the opportunity to acquire wealth and property for himself, the slave would find it in his interest to work as little as possible. Slave owners advocated their system not so much for its economic benefits but for the power it gave them over others, despite economic losses. The leading exponents of this rationale for abolition in recent times have been Marxists, led by Eric Williams in his classic *Capitalism and Slavery* (1944). Many economic historians disagreed with this analysis, most notably Robert Fogel and Stanley Engerman, who published *Time on the Cross* in 1974, an elaborate two-volume statistical study linking economics with statistics (econometrics) to show the profitability of slavery. Historian Seymour Drescher argued bluntly (1977) that abolition was "econocide," economic disaster, for Britain. Drescher sided with the humanitarian assessment: abolition was implemented despite its economic costs.

What to do without slaves? The successor system to slavery was not free labor. Indentured labor, supplied in large part by vast contract immigration from India and China, filled the labor needs of the postslavery Caribbean as well as those of new plantation economies in the Indian Ocean in Fiji, Mauritius, and Réunion, and in South and East Africa. Although not quite slaves, indentured servants traded many of their basic economic and political rights for a number of years in exchange for their livelihood.

Finally, with the export of slave labor from Africa banned, European entrepreneurs began in the later 1800s to explore the possibilities of shifting the production of primary products to Africa itself and to employ on-site personnel to perform the necessary work. Although this system sounded like free labor, in fact the wages were so low and conditions so abysmal, that many observers saw these economic initiatives as a newer form of slavery transplanted back to Africa.

- What evidence have we seen in this chapter that the Haitian revolution played an important part in the abolition of slavery?
- What evidence do you have from this chapter, and from other studies, that would support the importance of humanitarianism in the abolition of slavery? What evidence do you have for the importance of economics?
- What is the difference between slavery and indentured labor?

Britain Abolishes the Slave Trade, 1807

Initially, the British tried to assist in putting down the slave rebellion in Haiti. When they failed, their subsequent decision to limit the spread of slavery by abolishing the slave trade in 1807 reflected, in part, their fear of further revolts. In 1833 Britain abolished slavery throughout its Empire, although "freed" slaves were required to work for their former masters for a period of time to compensate them for their loss of "property." The United States, a slave-holding country, feared that the Haitian slave revolt might spread northward and prohibited all trade with Haiti in 1806. In 1808, following Britain's lead, America outlawed participation in the international slave trade, although it abolished internal slavery only with the Civil War (1861–65). Elsewhere, however, the Atlantic slave trade continued at about three-quarters of its highest volume. That trade did not end effectively until slavery was abolished in 1876 in Puerto Rico, in 1886 in Cuba, and in 1888 in Brazil.

Independence and Disillusionment in Latin America, 1810–30

In the period 1810 to 1826 virtually all the countries of Latin America expelled their European colonial rulers and established their independence. Latin Americans drew inspiration from the intellectual and political legacies of the American, French, and Haitian revolutions, although few wanted to move so far toward democratic rights as the Europeans had done, and many were frightened by the events in Haiti.

All of Latin America—except for Portuguese Brazil—was wrested from Spain by the sword. The greatest of the revolutionary leaders—Simón Bolívar of Venezuela in the north, José de San Martín of Argentina in the south, Antonio José de Sucré of Ecuador, and Bernardo O'Higgins of Chile—combined military skills with intellectual, administrative, and diplomatic accomplishments.

Independence Movements

Amerindians and **mestizos** led the first series of revolts, in the late 1700s. In 1780, in Cuzco, Peru, Tupac Amaru, a mestizo with Inca ancestors, led 70,000 rebels against Spanish rule. **Creoles** did not join in the fighting, and Tupac Amaru was captured and executed in 1783. The entire revolt was brutally crushed. The Comunero Revolt in Colombia in 1781 drove the viceroy from Bogotá but ended with few concessions by the Spanish and internal fighting among the rebels. Mulattoes led a revolt in Bahia, Brazil, in 1798. At the time of all these revolts, Spain and Portugal were still independent, powerful countries and, with the aid of Creoles and *mazombos*, they suppressed the revolts. In general, the Creoles and mazombos saw their fate linked more to the Spanish and Portuguese rulers than to the Amerindians or to those of mixed parentage.

The Napoleonic wars in Spain, however, gave the colonies the opportunity to declare their independence, with the Creoles now leading the way. The revolts were bloody and successful. In virtually every Latin American revolt, leadership was provided by a Creole elite, most of whom feared the potential power of the Amerindian, mestizo, mulatto, and African majority. Such men as Father Miguel Hidalgo (1753–1811) in Mexico, Simón Bolívar (1783–1830) in northern South America, and José de San Martín (1778–1850) in southern South America, were all Creoles, as were their leading generals, administrators, and supporters. They were familiar with European traditions and events, and many of them had studied in

KEY TERMS

mestizo A person of mixed race. In Central and South America it usually denotes a person of combined Indian and European descent.

Creole In the sixteenth to eighteenth centuries, a white person born in Spanish America of Spanish parents.

mazombo An American-born direct descendant of Portuguese settlers.

Liberation movements in Latin America. The collapse of Iberian rule in Latin America was virtually complete by 1826. Sustained campaigns by Simón Bolívar and Antonio José de Sucre demolished Spanish control of Venezuela, Colombia, and Peru while, from the south, José de San Martín led the Argentine and Chilean Army of the Andes north to Lima. In 1822, the Portuguese crown prince Pedro declared Brazil's independence from Portugal, without the need of an armed struggle. Liberation brought many internal power struggles and divisions, leaving the present-day South American map with an array of some 20 republics.

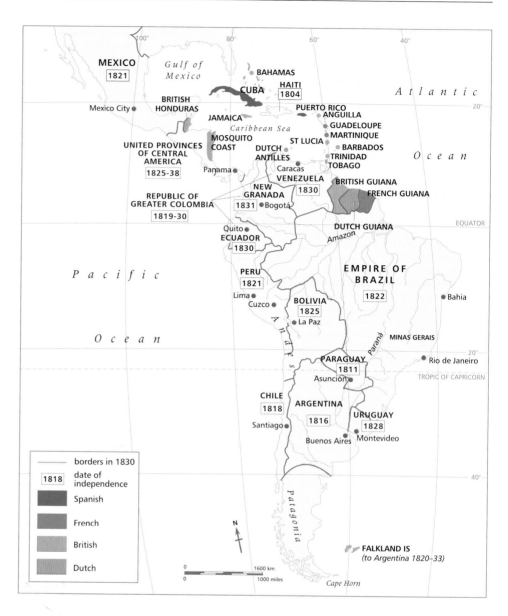

Europe. Indeed, the revolutions benefited the Creoles most, although they formed less than 5 percent of the total population. These elites were determined to preserve the old system, with its low-paid and slave labor. The new Creole elites simply drove out the Spanish and Portuguese rulers and took their places. Other Latin Americans, mestizos and Amerindians, gained little. On the Caribbean islands of Cuba and Puerto Rico there were no rebellions. Here the elites, frightened lest the slave revolt of Haiti be repeated on their own islands, remained loyal to Spain.

Simón Bolívar. As soldier, diplomat, general, administrator, visionary, newspaper publisher, law giver, national president, dictator, lover, and disillusioned revolutionary, Simón Bolívar dominated public life in Latin America for most of two decades, from 1810 until his death in 1830. Son of a Venezuelan Creole aristocrat, Bolívar studied in Europe from age 16 to 19, primarily in Spain. He married in 1802 and returned to Caracas with his bride. Within a year she died of yellow fever. Devastated, Bolívar vowed to devote his life to politics. He returned to Europe for travel and continued study of the *philosophes*. Returning to Venezuela in 1807, he joined in the movements for independence that swept the region, especially after Napoleon's troops invaded Spain, undercutting Spanish authority and power in the Americas.

He failed in many of his early efforts. Assigned to diplomatic duty in England, he was unable to gain recognition and material support for the Venezuelan revolution. In 1811 he was serving as an army officer when Venezuela lost its independence within a year of declaring it. In 1813 he captured Caracas and reasserted Venezuelan independence, but he was defeated and exiled in 1814. Despite the military defeats, he wrote visionary documents. His *Manifesto of Cartagena*, 1812, was a rallying cry for revolutionary forces to continue the struggle against Spain. His *Letter from Jamaica*, written in exile in September 1815, vowed to end not only Latin America's political suppression, but also its economic servitude.

Bolívar renewed his military expeditions and began to earn fabulous success, especially after he received monetary and military support from Haiti and Britain in return for freeing South American slaves. In 1819 his forces defeated the Spanish and established the Republic of Colombia with himself as president and military dictator. Within two more years they liberated Venezuela and Ecuador, filling out the borders of the federation. In Quito, Ecuador, he met Manuela Saenz, who left her husband to join him. She remained with Bolívar for the rest of his life, despite his numerous affairs and the public scandal of their own relationship.

As Bolívar made conquests from the north, various movements began their struggles for independence from the region of Rio Plate, now Argentina. José San Martín emerged as one of the great military strategists of history. He put together an Army of the Andes and promised freedom to slaves who joined his forces. He later claimed they were his best soldiers. Bringing together former slaves and soldiers, he crossed the high Andes Mountains with mules and llamas, successfully defeating the Spaniards in Chile and mounting attacks on Peru. He refused to rule over Chile in favor of Bernardo O'Higgins, the Creole leader there, but he couldn't effectively take Peru. Ultimately, he met with Bolívar in Guayaquil, Ecuador, in 1822. No one really knows what they discussed, but after the meeting, San Martín retired to France, leaving the conquest of South America to Bolívar.

By 1825, through brilliant military action Bolívar captured Peru and Upper Peru, later named Bolivia in his honor, and became president of both. Just as his dreams of a single united region seemed to reach fruition, however, they dissolved in warfare among his generals, who now fought for the independence of each of the constituent units. Bolívar tried to hold the federation together through dictatorial rulings, but his highhandedness further alienated his former supporters and he narrowly escaped an assassination attempt in 1828 as Manuela Saenz covered his exit. Bolívar withdrew from political leadership in 1830. A few months later he died in the agony of tuberculosis, indebted and disillusioned.

Bolívar's dream of "Gran Colombia" dissolved into Colombia, Venezuela, and Ecuador. Further south, the Spanish viceroyalty of La Plata dissolved into Argentina, Paraguay, Uruguay, and Bolivia. For a decade, 1829–39, under General Andrés Santa Cruz, a mestizo, Peru and Bolivia were united, but then broke apart, to the relief of some of their neighbors. Chile, isolated by the Andes to its east, and open to the outside world via the Pacific Ocean to its west, also became a separate, independent nation. In total, 18 nations emerged from Spanish America.

Simón Bolívar, Antonio Salas (attrib.), 1825. Bolívar was the most important military leader of the Latin American revolution. Despite a life of extraordinary adventure and accomplishment, he failed to bring about the unification of South America that he so passionately desired.

Simon Bolívar el Libertador

Warfare among many of the new states and the violent repression of the Indian and African-American populations (25 percent of Brazil's population in 1850 were slaves) gave prominence and power both to national armies and to private military forces throughout Latin America. The military strongmen, or **caudillos,** came to control local areas and even national governments. Personal rule, restrained only minimally by official codes of law and formal election procedures, prevailed in many countries up to the late twentieth century. (See box on Pablo Neruda's epic history of Latin America in verse, *Canto General*, p. 556.)

Mexico. The early Mexican independence movement differed from that in South America because of its attack on Creole elites. The priests Father Miguel Hidalgo and Father José Maria Morelos understood that peasant poverty was a product of Spanish and Creole rule. Hidalgo led the first wave of Mexico's revolt until he was executed in 1811. Father José María Morelos (1765–1815) then took command. He sought to displace the Spanish and creole elites, to abolish slavery, and, unlike Hidalgo, to revoke the special privileges and landholdings of the Church. The Spanish captured and executed Morelos in 1815. By the time Mexico won its independence in 1821, its revolution was controlled by its most conservative Creole elite. For two years Mexico was ruled as a monarchy, but in 1823 it was proclaimed a republic. Military leaders, businessmen, and foreign powers all struggled for control, and Mexico remained unstable for decades, although one of Morelos' goals, the abolition of slavery, was achieved in 1829.

Mexico's size was reduced by half. Following years of rebellions, Central American regions broke away from Mexico and formed a union, although it dissolved in internal regional antagonisms in 1838. With waves of immigrants entering from the United States, and encouraged by the United States government, Texas declared its independence from Mexico in 1836. Nine years later the United States annexed Texas, precipitating the Mexican–American war. In the peace settlement, America gained the territories of its current southwestern states.

Mexico, 1824–53. In 1821 the Viceroyalty of New Spain, with its capital in Mexico City, won its independence from Spain. By 1823, the Central American countries seceded, leaving Mexico with its current southern border. Then, piece by piece, the northern areas were lost to the United States: Texas through secession from Mexico (1836) and annexation by the U.S. (1845); some territories through warfare (1846–48); and some through purchase (1853).

boundary of Mexico 1824
independent republic of Texas 1836
ceded to Texas 1845
ceded by Treaty of Guadalupe Hidalgo 1848
Gadsden Purchase 1853
Mexico after 1853

Brazil. Brazil, the largest country in Latin America in terms of both geography and population, followed a different pathway to independence, and this helps to explain why it did not break apart after independence. When Napoleon invaded Portugal in 1807, the Portuguese royal family, assisted by Britain, fled to Rio de Janeiro and ruled the Portuguese Empire from the Brazilian capital for 13 years. King Dom João (John) VI (r. 1816–26) raised Brazil's legal status to equal that of Portugal and expanded Rio into a center of trade, administration, education, and cultural institutions.

In 1821 João returned with his court to Lisbon, but left his son and heir, Prince Pedro, in Rio. When the Parliament, or Cortes, in Lisbon attempted to cut Brazil and Rio back to size, the American-born Brazilian elite, the *mazombos*, counseled defiance. In 1822 Pedro declared Brazil independent, and Portugal did little to stop the move. Pedro was soon crowned "Constitutional Emperor and Perpetual Defender of Brazil," but the effective rulers of Brazil were its *mazombo* elites. Brazil was thus spared the warfare and disintegration characteristic of Spanish Latin America, but it was ruled by similar American-born descendants of Iberian families. While the former Spanish colonies became republics, Brazil became a monarchy under a member of the Portuguese royal family.

After Independence: Religious and Economic Issues

Many of the new nations of Latin America sought to increase their own power by breaking the authority and wealth of the Catholic Church. Many confiscated Church lands, refused to collect tithes to fund the Church, demanded a voice in the selection of clergy, and limited Church control over educational facilities. Many Native American Indians also wanted to reduce the power of the Church in favor of a greater appreciation of indigenous cultures, both outside of Christianity and in syncretic movements that joined existing indigenous beliefs and rituals with Christian practices. Mexico, which had a large Indian and mestizo population, was most eager to limit Church power, and its continuing struggles were the bloodiest. Over time, in each country, individual accommodations were made between Church and state, and to this day they continue to renegotiate their positions.

Economically, until at least 1870, Latin America remained overwhelmingly agrarian, with the *hacienda,* a kind of feudal estate, continuing as the principal institution for organizing production and labor. The vast majority of the *haciendados* were Creole, while the workers were overwhelmingly Indian and mestizo. Many Indians remained in villages, where their participation in any larger, external, national economy was marginal. Since ancestry counted so profoundly for each group, the ethnic and racial composition of its population, whether native-born or foreign-born, whether Indian, African, mestizo, or Caucasian, in large measure determined the fate and the culture of each colony.

As production for foreign markets increased, a new form of foreign domination, **neocolonialism,** arose. The principal new power was Britain, and its method was economic investment and control. By 1824, there were 100 British commercial firms, staffed by 3,000 British citizens, functioning in Latin America. Shipping to and from Latin America was carried primarily by British ships. Britain's economic domination of Latin American economies increased with the growing productivity and profitability of its Industrial Revolution at home.

In the mid-nineteenth century, Latin America was home to a mixed amalgam of philosophies and practices. From the United States and France, it inherited a legacy of revolution in the name of representative democracy and individual freedom. From Spain and Portugal it inherited a loyalty to more conservative, religious, hierarchical traditions. From Africa it inherited rich traditions of religion, food, music, and dance. From its own history of settlement it received a diverse mix of peoples from three continents, often in uneasy relationship with one another. From the international economy Latin America inherited a subordinate position, dependent on outside supply, demand, and control.

Early Evening Refreshment in the Praca do Palaccio, Rio de Janeiro, Jean-Baptiste Debret, 1835. **Lithograph.** The port and capital city of Rio has long been famous for its fun-loving life and for a modicum of racial integration. But Brazil did not abolish slavery until 1888. All three elements are suggested in this 1835 lithograph. (Bibliothèque Nationale, Paris)

KEY TERMS

hacienda A rural estate controlled by one person or family giving shelter and protection to many dependent workers. The owner was called a *haciendado.*

neocolonialism The control of one country by another through economic rather than political-military domination, a method frequently employed after the end of formal, political colonization.

SOURCE

An Epic Verse History of Latin America

In many parts of the world, historical traditions are kept alive not only in formal historical writing, but also in art, music, and poetry. Some of Latin America's most distinguished authors work in this tradition. The Chilean writer Pablo Neruda (1904–73), a recipient of the Nobel Prize for Literature in 1971, advanced a critical and disillusioned vision of Latin America in its first century of independence. In *Canto General* (1950), Neruda's epic poem of Latin American history, he paints the Spanish settlement of the land as a harsh and tawdry process.

> The land passed between the entailed estates,
> doubloon to doubloon, dispossessed,
> paste of apparitions and convents
> until the entire blue geography was
> divided into haciendas and encomiendas.
> The mestizo's ulcer, the overseer's
> and slaver's whip
> moved through the lifeless space.
> The Creole was an impoverished specter
> who picked up the crumbs,
> until he saved enough
> to acquire a little title
> painted with gilt letters.
> And in the dark carnival
> he masqueraded as a count
> a proud man among beggars,
> with his little silver cane …

The *conquistadores* of the sixteenth century had been expelled by the *libertadors* of the early nineteenth century, but the infrastructure of shopkeepers, clergy, administrators, and hangers-on that had become established in Latin America remained in place as the real inheritors of the revolution. Neruda scowled:

> Soon, undershirt by undershirt,
> they expelled the conquistador
> and established the conquest
> of the grocery store.
> Then they acquired pride
> bought on the black market.
> They were adjudged
> haciendas, whips, slaves,
> catechisms, commissaries,
> alms boxes, tenements, brothels,
> and all this they called
> holy western culture.

Neruda singles out the petty businessmen as the new, but unworthy, elite of Latin America. In more enterprising regions bigger businessmen and investors occupied the leadership positions. These men of practical affairs combined with craftsmen on the one hand, and with government policymakers on the other, to introduce limited industrial development in the twentieth century.

Political Revolutions: What Difference Do They Make?

Charles Dickens opened *A Tale of Two Cities*, his novel set against the background of the French Revolution, with the famous passage: "It was the best of times. It was the worst of times … it was the season of Light, it was the season of Darkness, it was the spring of hope, it was the winter of despair." Having examined the unfolding of this period of political revolution we can better understand Dickens' paradoxical characterization. All of the revolutionary movements were filled with ironies. The English revolutions succeeded in establishing constitutional government that slowly expanded to include ever larger segments of the population, and to include freedom of religion among its guarantees. But, less than a century later, the government that emerged from those revolutions refused to grant to its American subjects the rights enjoyed by Britons, provoking the American War for Independence. It did abolish the slave trade and slavery, but only in the early nineteenth century, and by that time, as we shall see in Chapter Seventeen, Britain had captured extensive, non-settler colonies overseas.

The *philosophes* spoke of human perfectibility and advocated human reason. They provided rationales that inspired revolutions in America, France, and Latin America, yet many preferred benevolent despotism, which they considered more efficient than democracy. One of the greatest *philosophes*, Rousseau, has been interpreted from many perspectives, as espousing government alternatives from radical democracy to totalitarian dictatorship. Later experience throughout the world, to our own day, continues to test the limits of the power of rationality in governing human affairs.

KEY TERM

libertador Literally, "liberator." Term applied to leaders of the independence revolts against Spanish rule in Latin America. Especially applied to Simón Bolívar, but given to others.

The War for Independence in North America freed Britain's 13 colonies and created the United States. The new nation introduced a limited democracy that nonetheless sanctioned attacks on Native Americans and permitted slavery. The most profound of all the revolutions of its time, the French Revolution, ended in class antagonism, with the monarchy restored, after much of Europe had been convulsed in more extensive warfare than it had ever seen before. In the course of his conquests, Napoleon abolished feudal privileges throughout Europe and introduced new codes of law and bureaucracies recruited on the basis of merit, but he established imperial governments, often in the hands of his own blood relatives, which provoked new anti-French nationalism among the peoples he conquered. In Haiti, in response to the slave revolt, Napoleon reversed France's stated opposition to slavery, and lost tens of thousands of soldiers to battle and disease. Haiti's successful slave revolt became a successful war for independence, but foreign opposition to Haiti's new government, and an internal lack of competent economic leadership, left the country impoverished. Wars for independence in Latin America freed that continent from direct, political control from overseas, but power was seized by Creole and *mazombo* elites who lorded it over the Native American multitudes. In addition, the new nations soon fell into economic dependence on their former colonizers.

Of all these revolutions, the French Revolution's legacies are the most ambiguous. Many scholars have looked to the radical Terror as a precursor to twentieth-century totalitarianism. Other scholars, however, have examined the revolution in terms of what it accomplished rather than what it failed to do. The French Revolution ended religious discrimination, and France went much further than England in allowing worshipers of all faiths, including Jews, to become full citizens. Though Napoleon reversed the decision, the National Convention abolished slavery, making it clear that distinctions of color and race should not matter in civic life. Still others have recognized that, while class antagonisms remained, the French Revolution established legal equality for most males, including freed slaves, who inhabited the country. Finally, the French Revolution in many ways legitimized the notion of revolution as a means of achieving political and social change. It inspired the Russian Revolution of 1917 and the later Chinese student movement, which staged a revolutionary parade at Tiananmen Square, Beijing, in support of French revolutionary ideals on the bicentenary of the storming of the Bastille on July 14, 1789. In short, the ideas of the French Revolution remain a powerful inspirational force today.

Asking Questions

- What is the difference between a political revolution and a simple change of political administration?
- What were the characteristics of the "Democratic Revolutions"?
- At the celebration of the 200th anniversary of the French Revolution in 1989, the British prime minister Margaret Thatcher remarked that the earlier British revolution had accomplished all that the French Revolution had accomplished— without the violence. Do you agree with her assessment?
- What are the differences between a revolution against a foreign colonial government, as in the revolution of the 13 American colonies against Britain, and a revolution against an indigenous government, as in France?
- What was the importance of the Haitian Revolution?
- Why did many of the leaders of the revolutions in Latin America feel disillusioned despite their accomplishments?
- To what degree is Wikipedia a modern equivalent of Diderot's *Encyclopedia*?

Suggested Readings

PRINCIPAL SOURCES

Burns, E. Bradford and Julie Charlip. *Latin America: A Concise Interpretive History* (Englewood Cliffs, NJ: Prentice Hall, 8th ed., 2006). The most recent edition of a standard work, especially strong on Brazil.

Craveri, Benedetta. *The Age of Conversation* (New York: New York Review Books, 2006). From the seventeenth century, aristocratic women hosted the salons that led into the French enlightenment of the eighteenth century.

Englund, Steven. *Napoleon: A Political Life* (Cambridge, MA: Harvard University Press, 2004). Adds to the literature on Napoleon in the mind of the French.

Furet, François. *Interpreting the French Revolution*, trans. Elborg Foster (Cambridge: Cambridge University Press, 1978). A masterful summary by one of the leading experts.

Galilei, Galileo. *Discoveries and Opinions of Galileo*, trans. Stillman Drake (New York: Anchor Books, 1957). Galileo's own observations and statements, fresh and clear, with helpful commentary.

Hobsbawm, Eric. *The Age of Revolution 1789–1848* (New York: New American Library, 1962). A personal, magisterial, interpretive summary, from a somewhat Marxist perspective. Excellent introduction to the period and issues.

Hochschild, Adam, *Bury the Chains: Prophets and Rebels in the Fight to Free an Empire's Slaves* (New York: Houghton Mifflin, 2005). Traces the activities of the men who established the British abolition movement. Very well written. Inspirational.

James, C.L.R. *The Black Jacobins* (New York: Random House, 1963). A stirring account of the activities and significance of the Haitian revolution.

Knight, Franklin W. "The Haitian Revolution," *American Historical Review* 105:1 (February, 2000), pp. 103–15. A review of the most recent scholarship on the revolution.

Kuhn, Thomas S. *The Copernican Revolution* (Cambridge, MA: Harvard University Press, 1957). A case study of the methods of science in working through received interpretations and developing new ones through the experiences of Copernicus.

——. *The Structure of Scientific Revolutions* (Chicago, IL: University of Chicago Press, 3rd ed., 1996). A generalized assessment of the methods through which scientists revise and sometimes discard older theories and develop new ones.

Lefebvre, Georges. *The Coming of the French Revolution*, trans. R.R. Palmer (Princeton, NJ: Princeton University Press, 1947). A classic

Marxist interpretation of the revolution.

Nash, Gary B., *et al. The American People: Creating a Nation and a Society* (White Plains, NY: Longman, 7th ed., 2006). Leading textbook account.

Palmer, R.R. *The Age of the Democratic Revolution* (Princeton, NJ: Princeton University Press, 1959). A lucid, standard, comprehensive interpretive account of the revolutions covered in this chapter.

Thompson, E.P. *The Making of the English Working Class* (New York: Vintage Books, 1966). Cultural as well as economic factors that inspired working people to see themselves as a class and to struggle for rights.

Williams, Eric. *Capitalism and Slavery* (Chapel Hill, NC: University of North Carolina Press, 1944). Williams portrays capitalism as promoting slavery when it is in the economic interests of slave owners, and as working for abolition when these interests change.

ADDITIONAL SOURCES

Abernethy, David B. *The Dynamics of Global Dominance: European Overseas Empires, 1415–1980* (New Haven, CT: Yale University Press, 2000). Traces and analyzes the expansion and contraction of empire, and evaluates its legacy. Thoughtful, lucid, and engaging.

Andrea, Alfred and James Overfield, eds. *The Human Record*, 2 vols. (Florence, KY: Wadsworth Publishing Co., 6th ed., 2008). Excellent selection of documents and visuals.

Boorstin, Daniel. *The Discoverers* (New York: Random House, 1983). Lucid, engaging account of the work of specific scientists and explorers and their impact on events.

Cohen, I. Bernard *Revolution in Science* (Cambridge, MA: Harvard University Press, 1985). Analyzes 450 years of major scientific revolutions and their interaction with the larger society. Magisterial yet lucid.

Columbia College, Columbia University. *Contemporary Civilization in the West*, Vol. 2 (New York: Columbia University Press, 3rd ed., 1960). Outstanding sourcebook with lengthy excerpts from highly influential thinkers and actors.

Curtin, Philip. *The Rise and Fall of the Plantation Complex* (New York: Cambridge University Press, 1989). Excellent analysis of the plantation itself and its significance to world trade and politics.

Davis, David Brion. *The Problem of Slavery in the Age of Revolution, 1770–1823* (Ithaca, NY: Cornell University Press, 1975). Analyzes the tensions between the idea of freedom and the practice of slavery.

——. "Looking at Slavery from Broader Perspectives," *American Historical Review* 105:2 (April, 2000), pp. 452–66. Global, comprehensive review of the literature.

Drescher, Seymour. *Econocide* (Pittsburgh, PA: University of Pittsburgh Press, 1977). Argues that the abolition of slavery was an economically costly decision, taken, primarily, for moral reasons.

Drescher, Seymour. *The Problem of Slavery in Western Culture* (New York: Oxford University Press, 1966). Explores the tensions between slavery and the ideals of individual freedom and democracy.

Fick, Carolyn E. *The Making of Haiti* (Knoxville, TN: University of Tennessee Press, 1990). A recent, comprehensive, cogent account.

Fogel, Robert William and Stanley L. Engerman. *Time on the Cross*, 2 vols. (Boston, MA: Little, Brown, 1974). A controversial, influential assessment of the economics of slavery.

Genovese, Eugene. *From Rebellion to Revolution* (Baton Rouge, LA: Louisiana University Press, 1979). A study of slave revolts and their significance to abolition.

Halévy, Élie. *England in 1815* (New York: Barnes and Noble, 1961). A classic account of a society successfully avoiding revolution.

Hammond Atlas of World History, ed. Geoffrey Parker (Maplewood, NJ: Hammond, 5th ed., 1999).

Hanke, Lewis and Jane M. Rausch, eds. *People and Issues in Latin American History* (New York: Markus Weiner, 3rd ed., 2006). A useful reader.

Hobbes, Thomas. *Selections*, ed. Frederick J.E. Woodbridge (New York: Charles Scribner's Sons, 1958). Primary sources.

Hobsbawm, Eric. *The Age of Empire 1875–1914* (New York: Vintage Books, 1987). Excellent, comprehensive account.

Hughes, Robert. *Goya* (New York: Knopf, 2003). Thoughtful, thorough, provocative, well-illustrated interpretation of the man and his art in their time.

Kolchin, Peter. *American Slavery 1619–1877* (New York: Hill and Wang, 1993). Comprehensive treatment, even after 1865, with comparisons to slavery in other societies.

Locke, John. *The Second Treatise on Government* (Arlington Heights, IL: Crofts Classics, 1982). Primary source.

McClellan III, James F. and Harold Dorn. *Science and Technology in World History* (Baltimore, MD: Johns Hopkins University Press, 1999). Outstanding coverage of science and technology from various parts of the world.

Márquez, Gabriel García. *The General in His Labyrinth*. trans. Edith Grossman (New York: Knopf, 1990). Fictionalized account of the end of the life of General Simón Bolívar.

Metcalf, Barbara D. and Thomas R. Metcalf. *A Concise History of India* (Cambridge: Cambridge University Press, 2002). Especially strong on issues of identity and the importance of Muslims and of women.

Nehru, Jawaharlal. *Glimpses of World History* (New Delhi: Jawaharlal Nehru Memorial Fund and Oxford University Press, 1982). Nehru wrote this socialistic account of world history from jail as a series of letters to his daughter.

Neruda, Pablo. *Canto General*, trans. Jack Schmitt (Berkeley, CA: University of California Press, 1991). A personal, critical assessment of Latin American history in verse by a master poet.

Nicholls, David, "Haiti: Race, Slavery and Independence (1804–1825)," in Archer, ed., *Slavery*, pp. 225–38. On the relationship of slavery to race in Haiti.

Patterson, Orlando. *Freedom in the Making of Western Culture* (New York: Basic Books, 1991). Slavery and racism conflict with the promise of freedom and democracy.

Rousseau, Jean-Jacques. *The Social Contract*, trans. Maurice Cranston (New York: Viking Penguin, 1968). Primary source.

Smith, Adam. *The Theory of Moral Sentiments* (Charlottesville, VA: Lincoln-Rembrandt Publishers, 6th ed., 1986). Primary source.

Smith, Adam. *The Wealth of Nations*, Books I–III (New York: Viking Penguin Classics, 1986). Primary source.

Thompson, Vincent Bakpetu. *The Making of the African Diaspora in the Americas 1441–1900* (New York: Longman, 1987). A view that transcends the experience of individual countries to see the comprehensive picture.

Tocqueville, Alexis de. *The Old Regime and the French Revolution*, trans. Gilbert Stuart (Garden City, NY: Doubleday Anchor Books, 1955). Classic analysis that locates precipitating factors in the revolution, and indicates that many endured long afterward.

Turner, Frederick Jackson. *The Frontier in American History* (New York: Henry Holt, 1920). Classic interpretation of the significance to America of huge, frontier spaces in the west.

White, Richard Alan. *Paraguay's Autonomous Revolution, 1810–1840* (Albuquerque, NM: University of New Mexico Press, 1978). A controversial study presenting Paraguay as attempting to create a more democratic government that is suppressed by its neighbors.

Wilentz, Sean. *Chants Democratic: New York and the Rise of the American Working Class, 1788–1850* (New York: Oxford University Press, 1984). Important contribution to working-class history.

PEARSON

For quizzes, flashcards, primary sources, interactive maps, videos, and other activities related to this chapter please go to

www.myhistorylab.com

CHAPTER SEVENTEEN

The Industrial Revolution

A Global Process

1700–1914

One of the key indicators of human progress has always been the improvement in the quality and quantity of the tools that we use and in the ways in which we organize production. Today we usually associate advanced industry with the Western world, but the most advanced civilization of premodern times was China of the Song dynasty (960–1279). China earned its reputation not only for its neo-Confucian high culture—its painting, poetry, and classical education—but also for its agricultural progress with new crops and more efficient harvesting. It produced armaments on a massive scale, including gunpowder and siege machines. The Song imperial government issued paper money and constructed extensive river and canal networks, which commercial ships navigated profitably. Under the Song, China was technically innovative, inventing the compass, improving the technology of silk production, ceramics, and lacquer, and vastly expanding printing and book production. China's advances in iron manufacture were so extensive that deforestation became a problem in parts of the north. (Until coal took its place, wood was used to smelt the iron ore.) The iron improved the strength and durability of tools, weapons, and the construction of major building projects, especially bridges. Other parts of the world lagged behind China's innovations in trade, commerce, and industry.

Beginning in the eighteenth century, however, Western Europe, and especially Britain, caught up with and surpassed China, and the rest of the world, in economic power and productivity. In Part Five, we surveyed some of the changes that enabled regions of Western Europe to emerge from their singular concentration on agriculture as the basis of their economy; to increase their concern with commerce, trade, and exploration; to develop new technologies; and to make a general commitment to financial success and the pursuit of profit. Slowly these new economic interests led to the creation of new tools: better ships; new and improved commercial instruments and organizations, such as the joint stock company; and even the adoption and adaptation of some of China's earlier inventions, including the compass, gunpowder, and movable type for printing. Businesspeople in Western Europe pursued new economic possibilities with a vigor and flexibility that were sometimes admirable, as in the search for new technologies, and sometimes morally reprehensible, as in the use of millions of slaves in the creation of vast sugar plantations in the Caribbean basin and in the extraction of gold and silver from New World mines through coerced labor for the benefit of European businessmen. All these economic initiatives—innovation at home and exploitation overseas—paved the way for the Industrial Revolution, which began in the eighteenth century.

KEY TOPICS

- The Industrial Revolution in Britain, 1700–1860
- Industrialization— Stage Two, 1860–1914
- Industrial Society
- Labor Movements and Socialism
- New Patterns of Urban Life
- The Industrial Revolution: What Difference Does It Make?

International Exhibition, World's Fair, South Kensington, London, 1862. At its core, the Industrial Revolution substituted inanimate power for human and animal energy. Before the Industrial Revolution, Western Europe had lagged economically behind China and India. New machinery dramatically altered that balance.

AT A GLANCE: INDUSTRIALIZATION IN THE WEST

DATE	BRITAIN	REST OF EUROPE	NORTH AMERICA
1760	• James Watt improves Newcomen's steam engine (1763) • James Hargreaves introduces spinning jenny (1764)		
1780	• Combination Act forbids workers to unionize (1799); repealed 1824		• Eli Whitney invents cotton gin (1793)
1800	• Luddite riots (1810–20) • Peterloo Massacre, Manchester (1819)		
1820	• George Stephenson's locomotive Rocket (1829) • Factory Act forbids employment of children (1833) • Chartist movement calls for universal male suffrage (1838)	• Invention of photography in France by Louis Jacques Mandé Daguerre (1839) • Worker revolts in Paris, Prague, Vienna, and Russia (1830)	• First transatlantic steamship lines in operation (1838) • Revolver invented by Samuel Colt (1836)
1840	• Sir Edwin Chadwick issues report on the Poor Laws (1842) • Friedrich Engels, *The Condition of the Working Class in England* (1845) • Repeal of the Corn Laws (1846) • Bessemer steel converter (1856) • Samuel Smiles, *Self Help* (1859)	• Year of Revolutions—in France, Austria, and Prussia (1848) • Marx and Engels, *The Communist Manifesto* (1848)	• Invention of the sewing machine (1846)
1860	• Under Prime Minister Gladstone, Liberal government begins to provide universal state-supported education (1870) • Liberals under Gladstone and Tories under Disraeli compete for workers' votes • Trade Union Act guarantees right to strike (1871)	• Siemens-Martin open-hearth steel production, Germany (1864) • Growth of chemical industries (after 1870) • Massacre of the Paris Commune (1871) • Bismarck unifies Germany (1871) • Germany's SPD is first working-class political party (1875)	• American Civil War (1861–65) • Richard Gatling invents the machine gun (1861) • Thomas Edison invents early form of telegraph (1864) • Invention of the typewriter (1867) • Canada becomes unified Dominion (1867) • Edison establishes private industrial development lab (1876)
1880	• London Dock strike (1889)	• Labor unions legalized in France (1884) • May 1 recognized in France as annual "Labor Day" (1890)	• American Federation of Labor founded (1886) • Kodak camera (1888) • Homestead Steel strike (1892)

This modern **Industrial Revolution** began with simple new machinery and minor changes in the organization of the workplace, but these initial changes were only the first steps. Ultimately, the Industrial Revolution multiplied the profits of the business classes and increased their power in government and public life. It broadened and deepened in its scope until it affected humanity globally, transforming the locations of our workplaces and homes, the size and composition of our families and the quality and quantity of the time we spend with them, the educational systems we create, the wars we fight, and the relationships among nations. As a global process the Industrial Revolution restructured the procurement of raw materials in the fields and mines of the world, the location of manufacture, and the range of international market-places in which new products might be sold. As the masters of the new industrial productivity adopted this global view of their own economic activities, their ventures became imperial in scope. They marshaled the powers of their governments to support their global economic capacities. Reciprocally, the governments relied on the power of industrialists and businesspeople to increase their own international strength politically, diplomatically, and militarily. The balance of wealth and power in the world shifted, for the first time, toward Europe, and especially toward Britain, the first home of the Industrial Revolution.

The Industrial Revolution in Britain, 1700–1860

The Industrial Revolution began in Britain around 1700, and although it is called a "revolution," it took more than 150 years to be fully realized. During this period, Britain created and mechanized a cotton textile industry, which soon became the world's most productive; created a railway network, which transformed the island's transportation and communication systems; and launched a new fleet of steam-powered ships, which enabled Britain to project its new productivity and power around the globe. Economic historians agree, however, that the industrial changes were possible because agriculture in Britain—the basis of its preindustrial economy—was already undergoing a process of continuing improvement. The transformation was so fundamental that it is called an agricultural revolution. (This agricultural revolution in the use of new tools and implements in producing new crops for market profit was actually a second agricultural revolution. As we saw in Chapters One and Two, the first occurred about 15,000 years ago, when nomadic peoples began to domesticate crops and animals and settle into villages.)

A Revolution in Agriculture

Britain (along with the Dutch Republic, as the Netherlands was known until 1648) had the most productive and efficient commercial agriculture in Europe. Inventors created new farm equipment and farmers were quick to adopt it. Jethro Tull (1674–1741), as an outstanding example, invented the seed drill (which replaced the old method of scattering seeds by hand on the surface of the soil with a new method of planting systematically in regular rows at fixed depths); a horse-drawn hoe; and an iron plow that could be set at an angle that would pull up grasses and roots and leave them to fertilize the land. New crops, such as turnips and potatoes from the New World, were introduced. Farmers and large landlords initiated huge irrigation and drainage projects, increasing the productivity of land already under cultivation and opening up new land. The word "**agronomy**," the systematic concern with field crop production and soil management, entered the English language in 1814.

As noted in Chapter Sixteen, governments revised dramatically the laws regarding land ownership in order to stimulate increased productivity. In Britain and the Netherlands peasants began to pay landowners commercial rents that fluctuated with market conditions, rather than paying fixed, customary rents and performing compulsory labor services. Moreover, lands that had been held in common by the village community and used for grazing sheep and cattle by shepherds and livestock owners who had no lands of their own were now parceled out for private ownership through a series of enclosure acts.

Seed drill, 1701. Jethro Tull (1674–1741) is a key figure of the eighteenth–century agricultural revolution, which saw new technology harnessed to farming techniques. Tull's machine drill employed a rotary mechanism that sowed seeds in rows, permitting cultivation between the rows and thus reducing the need for weeding.

Spinning and Weaving Wool,
Isaac Claesz Swanenburgh,
c. 1600. Oil on wood. This image
shows the steps involved in
spinning wool for the textile
industry in the Dutch Republic.
(Stedelijk Museum, Leiden)

Enclosures had begun in England in a limited way in the late 1400s. In the eighteenth century the process resumed and the pace increased. In the period 1714–1801, about 25 percent of the land in Britain was converted from community property to private property through enclosures. The results were favorable to landowners, and urban businessmen began to buy land as agricultural investment property. Agricultural productivity shot up; landowners prospered. But hundreds of thousands of farmers with small plots and cottagers who had subsisted through the use of the common lands for grazing their animals were now turned into tenant farmers and wage laborers. The results were revolutionary and profoundly disturbing to the society. Peasant riots broke out as early as the middle of the sixteenth century. In one uprising, 3,500 people were killed.

The process continued throughout the period of the early Industrial Revolution as many of the dispossessed farmers turned to rural or domestic industry to supplement their meager incomes. Later, rural workers left the land altogether and headed for new industrial jobs in Britain's growing cities. The capitalist market system transformed British agriculture and emptied the countryside, providing capital and workers for the Industrial Revolution. The economist Joseph Schumpeter (1883–1950) called capitalism a process of "creative destruction." In the agricultural revolution and the Industrial Revolution we see evidence of both: the often painful destruction of older ways of life and the creation of new, uncharted ways.

A Revolution in Textile Manufacture

The first important commercial product of the Industrial Revolution in England was cotton textiles. Until the mid-eighteenth century, the staple British textile had been woolens, woven from the wool of locally raised sheep. By then, however, European traders in India realized that the cotton cloth of India was far more comfortable and far easier to clean. As they began to import these light, colorful, durable cotton textiles, the Indian fabrics began to displace woolens in the British market. The British government responded by manipulating tariffs and import regulations to restrict Indian cotton textiles, while British inventors began to produce new machinery that enabled Britain to surpass Indian production in both quantity and quality. The raw cotton would still have to be imported from subtropical India (and later from the southern United States and Egypt), but the British could create at home their own manufacturing processes that turned it into cloth, increasing British jobs and profits, and cutting back on the purchase of finished cloth in India, thus undercutting jobs and profits there.

Merchants organized much of the early industrial production through the putting-out system (see p. 428). They would drop off raw cotton at workers' homes where women would spin it into yarn, which men would then weave into cloth, which merchants would later pick up. The spinning wheel, which had been in existence for centuries, allowed women to produce fairly uniform yarn. Men wove the yarn on looms that required two men sitting across from each other, passing the shuttle of the loom from left to right and back again. In 1733, John Kay (1704–64) invented the "flying shuttle," which allowed a single weaver to send the shuttle forth and back across the loom automatically, without the need of a second operator to push it. The spinners could not keep up with the increased demand of the weavers until, in 1764, James Hargreaves (d. 1778) introduced the "spinning jenny," a machine that allowed the operator to spin several threads at once. The earliest jennies could run eight spindles at once; by 1770, 16; by the end of the century, 120. Machines to card and comb the cotton to prepare it for spinning were also developed.

Thus far, the machinery was new, but the power source was still human labor, and production was still concentrated in rural homes and small workshops. Then a series of inventions led to the mechanization of the cotton industry. In 1769, Richard Arkwright (1732–92) patented the "water frame," a machine that could spin several cotton strands simultaneously. Powered by water, it could run continuously. In 1779, Samuel Crompton (1753–1827) developed a "spinning mule," a hybrid that joined the principles of the spinning jenny and the water frame to produce a better quality and higher quantity of cotton thread. Unfortunately, he was too poor to patent it, but he sold designs for it to others. Now British cloth could rival that of India. Fascinated by Arkwright's water frame, Edmund Cartwright (1743–1822)

James Hargreaves' spinning jenny. Named for his daughter, Hargreaves' invention was a spinning machine that prepared natural fibers for weaving. It thus made possible the expanded production of cotton cloth. The Industrial Revolution was built on relatively simple innovations like this jenny and the even earlier "flying shuttle" of John Kay, 1733. Compare the picture opposite to see how much more machine intensive/labor free is the production process of the spinning jenny.

The Industrial Revolution.
In the early nineteenth century the Industrial Revolution spread throughout the trading nations of Western Europe (and enmeshed their colonies, which provided both raw materials and markets). The earlier use of water power gave way to steam engines; coal became the power source. Canal transportation was superseded by railways, driven by steam. The density of the rail network and of the coal and iron fields in England reflects that country's lead in early industrialization.

believed he could make a fortune by applying the principles of the technology to weaving. After some experiments, he patented the power loom in 1785, with water power harnessed to drive the shuttle.

Meanwhile, in the coalfields of Britain, mine owners were seeking more efficient means of pumping water out of mine shafts. The key development was the steam engine. By 1712, Thomas Newcomen (1663–1729) had mastered the use of steam power to drive the water pumps. In 1763, James Watt (1736–1819), a technician at the University of Glasgow, was experimenting with improvements to Newcomen's steam engine, when Matthew Boulton (1728–1809), a small manufacturer, provided him with the capital necessary to develop larger and more costly steam engines. By 1785 the firm of Boulton and Watt was manufacturing new steam engines for use in Britain and for export. In the 1780s, Arkwright used a new Boulton and Watt steam engine instead of water power. From this point, equipment grew more sophisticated and more expensive. Spinning and weaving moved from the producer's home or small workshop adjacent to a stream of water to new steam-powered cotton textile mills, which increased continuously in size and productivity. Power looms, such as Cartwright's, invented to cope with increased spinning capacity, became commercially profitable by about 1800. Increasingly, in the 1800s, power looms became one of the most important technologies of the Industrial Revolution.

The new productivity of the machines transformed Britain's economy. It took hand spinners in India 50,000 hours to produce 100 pounds of cotton yarn. Crompton's mule could do the same task in 2,000 hours. Arkwright's steam-powered frame, available by 1795, took 300 hours; and automatic mules, available by 1825, took just 135 hours. Moreover, the quality of the finished product steadily increased in strength, durability, and texture. Cotton textiles became the most important product of British industries by 1820, making up almost half of Britain's exports.

Prior to this mechanization most families had spun and woven their own clothing by hand; thus the availability of machine-made yarn and cloth affected millions of spinners and weavers throughout Great Britain. As late as 1815 owners of new weaving mills continued the putting-out system, providing home-based weavers with cotton thread and paying them for the finished, woven product. When cutbacks in production were necessary, the home workers could be cut. Thus the burden of recession could be shifted to the shoulders of the home producer, leaving the mill owners relatively unscathed. In 1791, home-based workers in the north of England burned down one of the new power-loom factories in Manchester. Machine-wrecking riots followed for several decades, culminating in the Luddite riots of 1810–20. Named for their mythical leader, Ned Ludd, the rioters wanted the new machines banned. Soldiers were called in to suppress the riots.

The textile revolution impacted economies around the world, devastating some, energizing others. India's industrial position was reversed. Its markets for hand-manufactured textile were undercut by Britain's new industrial production, and India, ironically, became the textbook example of a colonial economy, supplying raw cotton to Britain and importing machine-manufactured cotton textiles from Britain.

The United States, on the other hand, prospered, but its prosperity gave a new birth to slavery. Britain's new machine-operated mills required unprecedented quantities of good-quality cotton. Raw cotton was oily and full of seeds. It was impossible to process the cotton into yarn without first cleaning it or removing the seeds from the raw cotton. In the United States, the invention of the cotton gin by Eli Whitney (1765–1825) in 1793 enabled workers to clean 50 pounds of cotton in the time it had previously taken to clean one. This solved part of the supply problem. The plantation economy of the United States revived and expanded, providing the necessary raw cotton, but, unfortunately, it also gave slavery a new lease on life.

MAJOR DISCOVERIES AND INVENTIONS 1640–1830

Year	Discovery/Invention
1640	Theory of numbers: Pierre de Fermat
1642	Calculating machine: Blaise Pascal
1650	Air pump: Otto von Guericke
1656	Pendulum clock: Otto von Guericke
1665–75	Calculus: Isaac Newton and Gottfried Leibnitz (independently)
1698	Steam pump: Thomas Savory
c. 1701	Seed drill: Jethro Tull
1712	Steam engine: Thomas Newcomen
1714	Mercury thermometer: Gabriel Fahrenheit
1733	Flying shuttle: John Kay
1752	Lightning conductor: Benjamin Franklin
1764	Spinning jenny: James Hargreaves
1765	Condensing steam engine: James Watt
1768	Hydrometer: Antoine Baumé
1783	Hot air balloon: Joseph and Étienne Montgolfier
1783	Parachute: Louis Lenormand
1785	Power loom: Edmund Cartwright
1789	Combustion: Antoine Lavoisier
1793	Cotton gin: Eli Whitney
1800	Electric battery: Alessandro Volta
1807	Steamboat: Robert Fulton
1815	Miner's safety lamp: Humphry Davy
1818	Bicycle: Karl von Sauerbrun
1823	Digital calculating machine: Charles Babbage
1824	Portland cement: Joseph Aspdin
1825	Electromagnet: William Sturgeon
1826	Heliography (pre-photography): Joseph Niépce
1828	Blast furnace: James Neilson
1829	Steam locomotive: George Stephenson

Interior of Crystal Palace, designed by Joseph Paxton for the Great Exhibition of 1851 in London. This glass-and-iron exhibition hall, a landmark of early modern architecture, was a celebration of the powerful Victorian economy and an expression of British technological accomplishment and imperial might.

American cotton production rose from 3,000 bales in 1790 to 178,000 bales in 1810, 732,000 bales in 1830, and 4,500,000 bales in 1860. Almost all of the cotton was produced by slave labor. The industrialization that had begun in Britain was reshaping the world economy.

The Iron Industry

The textile industry began with a consumer product that everyone used and that already employed a substantial handicraft labor force; it mechanized and reorganized the process of production and relocated it from homes and small workshops to large factories. Other industrial innovations created new products. Britain's iron industry, which had been established since the mid-1500s, at first burned wood to heat iron ore and extract molten iron, but by about 1750 new mining processes provided coal, a more efficient fuel, more abundantly and cheaper. About 1775, the iron industry relocated to the coal and iron fields of the English Midlands. A process of stirring the molten iron ore at high temperatures was introduced by Henry Cort (1740–1800) in the 1780s. This "puddling" encouraged the use of larger ovens and integrated the processes of melting, hammering, and rolling the iron into high-quality bars. Productivity increased dramatically. As the price of production dropped and the quality increased, iron was introduced into building construction. The greatest demand for the metal came, however, with new inventions. The steam engine, railroad track and locomotives, steamships, and new urban systems of gas supply and solid and liquid waste disposal all depended on iron for their construction. Britain's world market share of iron multiplied from 19 percent in 1800 to 52 percent in 1840—that is, Britain produced as much manufactured iron as the rest of the world.

With the new steam engine and the increased availability and quality of iron, the railroad industry was born. The first reliable locomotive, George Stephenson's

George Stephenson's locomotive Rocket, 1829, from a chromolithographic cigarette card of 1901. On October 14, 1829, the Rocket won a competition for an engine to haul freight and passengers on the Manchester–Liverpool Railway. The success of Stephenson's invention stimulated a boom in locomotive construction and track laying around the world.

WILL'S CIGARETTES.

GEO. STEPHENSON'S ROCKET, 1829.

HOW DO WE KNOW?

Why did the Industrial Revolution Begin in Britain?

Historians have long debated the origins of the Industrial Revolution. The term itself was used at least as early as 1845, in the opening of Friedrich Engels' *The Condition of the Working Class in England*:

> The history of the English working classes begins in the second half of the eighteenth century with the invention of the steam engine and of machines for spinning and weaving cotton. It is well known that these inventions gave the impetus to the genesis of an industrial revolution. This revolution had a social as well as an economic aspect since it changed the entire structure of middle-class society. (p. 9)

Arnold Toynbee (uncle of a twentieth-century historian with the same name) was apparently the first professional historian to use the term. In a set of lectures delivered in 1880–81, Toynbee identified 1760 as the beginning of the process. He chose this date in recognition of the inventions discussed in this chapter. In 1934, John Nef, economic historian at the University of Chicago, argued that because the iron industry had already been in place by the mid-sixteenth century, that date was a more appropriate choice. More recent historians, such as Fernand Braudel, have also seen the roots of industrialization stretching back for centuries. They have stressed the underlying economic, political, social, intellectual, and scientific transformations that we have discussed in the last few chapters. All these processes coalesced in the British economy in the late eighteenth century to create the Industrial Revolution:

- increasing productivity in agriculture;
- new merchant classes in power, and the evolution of a capitalist philosophy of economics that justified their power;
- a powerful state that supported economic development, despite the capitalist doctrine of laissez faire, which called for the state to stay out of business;
- the rise of science, with its new, empirical view of the world, and of technology, with its determination to find practical solutions to practical problems;
- a social structure that allowed and even encouraged people of different classes to work together, especially artisans, who worked with their hands, and financiers, who provided capital;

- more intense patterns of global trading for buying raw materials and for selling manufactured products;
- an expanding population that increased both the labor supply and the demand for more production;
- slave labor in plantation economies, which brought more than a century of exceptional capital accumulation;
- the discovery of massive deposits of gold and silver in the New World, which also increased capital accumulation; and
- "proto-industrialization"—that is, early forms of industrial organization that introduced new skills to both management and labor, paving the way for large-scale factory production.

This question of the origins of the Industrial Revolution is not purely academic. The debate carries serious implications for planning industrial development in today's world. As many newly independent nations with little industry seek to industrialize, they ask: Does industrialization mean simply the acquisition of machinery and the adaptation of advanced technology? Or must a nation also experience a much wider range of agricultural, economic, philosophical, scientific, political, and social changes? How, and under what terms, can it raise the capital necessary to begin? What are the tasks confronting a government wishing to promote industrialization? We shall examine these twentieth-century questions in the final chapters of this book. Those countries that have achieved high levels of industrialization—mostly the countries of Europe and their daughter civilizations overseas; Japan; and now some of the countries of East Asia (see Chapter Twenty-two)—have experienced a wide range of fundamental changes, akin to many of those experienced by Britain.

- Among the characteristics that made the Industrial Revolution possible, do some seem to you more important than others? Which ones? Why?
- Which processes that we usually include in the "Industrial Revolution" are changes in machinery and equipment? Which are changes in the social structure of the society?
- Which of these processes seem to be continuing to the present and continuing to influence contemporary economics?

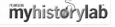

Rocket, was produced in 1829. It serviced the Manchester–Liverpool route, reaching a speed of 16 miles per hour. By the 1840s, a railroad boom swept through Britain and Europe, and crossed the Atlantic to the United States, where it facilitated the westward expansion of that rapidly expanding country. By the 1850s most of the 23,500 miles of today's railway network in Britain were already in place, and entrepreneurs found new foreign markets for their locomotives and tracks in India and Latin America.

SOURCE

Conflicting Images of Early Industrial Life: The English Romantic Poets

In the century 1750–1850, Britain was transformed by industrialization. Factories, cities, and the working classes all multiplied. One response to the turmoil created by these changes was Romanticism, a new international movement in literature and the arts, which opposed the rationalism of the Enlightenment and glorified emotion. Romantic poets in Britain, such as William Wordsworth (1770–1850) and Samuel Taylor Coleridge (1772–1834), turned away from the belief in modern progress through science and rational knowledge toward nature, history, and their own inner feelings. They saw a great vision of a new aesthetic beauty emerging. Wordsworth's view of London's natural glories represents this Romantic perspective.

Upon Westminster Bridge, September 3, 1802
Earth has not anything to show more fair:
Dull would he be of soul who could pass by
A sight so touching in its majesty;
This City now doth, like a garment, wear
The beauty of the morning; silent, bare,
Ships, towers, domes, theatres, and temples lie
Open unto the fields, and to the sky;
All bright and glittering in the smokeless air.
Never did sun more beautifully steep
In his first splendour, valley, rock, or hill;
Ne'er saw I, never felt, a calm so deep!
The river glideth at his own sweet will:
Dear God! the very houses seem asleep;
And all that mighty heart is lying still!

William Wordsworth

Others, such as the poet William Blake (1757–1827), who were closer to the lives of working-class people, saw the great suffering caused by industrialization. Devoutly religious and nationalistic, Blake nevertheless condemned the British people, the government, and the Church of England for tolerating "a land of poverty" in the very midst of "a rich and fruitful land." While Wordsworth looks over London from the vantage point of a bridge, Blake walks its streets and looks into the faces of its inhabitants.

London
I wander thro' each charter'd* street,
Near where the charter'd Thames does flow,
And mark in every face I meet
Marks of weakness, marks of woe.

In every cry of every Man,
In every Infant's cry of fear,
In every voice, in every ban,
The mind-forg'd manacles I hear.

How the Chimney-sweeper's cry
Every blackning Church appalls;
And the hapless Soldier's sigh
Runs in blood down Palace walls.

But most thro' midnight streets I hear
How the youthful Harlot's curse
Blasts the new-born Infant's tear,**
And blights with plagues the Marriage hearse.

William Blake (1792)

*charter'd = licensed by the government, controlled, owned
**the infant is blind at birth, from venereal disease transmitted by the parent

No matter how upsetting Blake's view of London may be, the even more lacerated heart of the Industrial Revolution was actually in the Midlands and north of England, around the cities of Manchester, Birmingham, and Liverpool.

The new locomotives quickly superseded the canal systems of Britain and the United States, which had been built mostly since the 1750s as the favored means of transporting raw materials and bulk goods between industrial cities. Until the coming of the steam-powered train, canals had been considered the transportation means of the future. (The speed with which the newer technology displaced the older is one reason historians resist predicting the future. Events do not necessarily proceed in a straight-line process of development, and new, unanticipated developments frequently displace older patterns quite unexpectedly.)

Steamships, using much the same technology as steam locomotives, were introduced at about the same time. The first transatlantic steamship lines began operation in 1838. World steamship tonnage multiplied more than 100 times, from 32,000 tons in 1831 to 3,300,000 tons in 1876. With its new textile mills, iron factories, and steam-driven transportation networks, Britain soon became the "workshop of the world."

Industrialization—Stage Two, 1860–1914

Between 1860 and the outbreak of World War I in 1914, a "second industrial revolution" further transformed world productivity, the ways in which humans lived their lives, and the power balances among the major nations and regions of the world. The principal technological advances came in steel, chemicals, and electricity.

The Steel and Chemical Industries

New technologies soon allowed iron ore to be converted to steel cheaply and abundantly. Iron is produced in blast furnaces and can be of high quality, but the final product contains some impurities. Steel production involves removing the impurities first and then adding carbon to the iron ore to create a much stronger and more versatile product, which can be shaped into bars, plates, and other structural components, such as girders. Germany, united as a country in 1871 under Otto von Bismarck, quickly forged ahead. By 1900 it was producing more steel than Britain, 6.3 million tons to 5 million tons; in 1913, on the eve of World War I, Germany's lead had grown to 17.6 million tons against 7.7 million tons. Germany also led in the invention of a number of additional new technologies, especially the internal combustion engine, the diesel engine, and the automobile.

Chemical industries grew, especially after 1870, as synthetic substances, notably derivatives from coal, began to augment and replace the earlier reliance on natural substances from vegetables, such as alkalis and dyes. Synthetic aniline dyes were made from coal tar. Both fertilizers and explosives could be made from synthetic nitrogen and phosphates. Artificial fertilizers added to a revolution in agricultural productivity, while explosives helped in the construction of engineering feats, such as the new tunnels through the Alps in Europe, the Suez Canal in North Africa, and the Panama Canal in Central America. Soda, made from the coal by-product of ammonia, was used in manufacturing both soap and glass. New drugs and insecticides enhanced the quality of human life, while perfumes and cosmetics made their way to the marketplace, as many middle-class and some working-class women, such as department store clerks, sought luxury goods to add a touch of romance to their lives. Plastics, produced from coal tar acids, became available in the late nineteenth century.

A canal connects two oceans.
The construction of the Panama Canal in 1905, linking the Atlantic and Pacific Oceans, ranks as one of the greatest engineering feats of all time. The task involved removing about 175 million cubic yards of earth as well as sanitizing the entire area, which was infested by mosquitoes that spread yellow fever and malaria.

Electrical Inventions

Electrical inventions sparked one another throughout Europe and across the Atlantic to the United States, as well. In 1831 Michael Faraday (1791–1867) in Britain first demonstrated the principle of electromagnetic induction by moving a metal conductor through a magnetic field to generate electricity, a process repeated regularly today in high-school classrooms. By 1850, several companies were producing simple electric generators. In the 1860s, in Germany, Ernest Werner von

Siemens (1816–92) developed a practical dynamo. In the United States in the 1880s, Nikola Tesla (1856–1943) invented methods to transmit power effectively over long distances, patenting the alternating current generator in 1892.

The best-known inventor of the age was the American Thomas Alva Edison (1847–1931), who acquired more than 1,000 patents for his innovations, 225 of them between 1879 and 1882, for incandescent light bulbs, fuses, sockets, switches, circuit breakers, and meters. More important than any single invention, however, was Edison's establishment in 1876 of probably the world's first private industrial development laboratory in Menlo Park, New Jersey, a rural area halfway between New York and Philadelphia. Until this time, invention had been largely an individual achievement, based on the skills and luck of the individual inventor. Edison's new research facility institutionalized the process of invention, and encouraged research and development and the commercialization of products such as the phonograph.

New Products and New Producers

The second Industrial Revolution corresponded to the era of big business. In Germany, the rising power in Europe, large **cartels**, collaborative business associations, were formed to produce electronic equipment and chemicals. For steel production, each major producing country had its own giants: Krupp in Germany, Schneider-Creusot in France, Vickers-Armstrong in Britain, and, largest of all, the United States Steel Corporation. These huge corporations integrated the entire process of production from raw material to finished product. They owned their own coal mines and iron works, produced steel, and manufactured such final products as ships, railway equipment, and armaments.

Industrial concentration displaced the artisan in favor of mass production and mass consumption. In these mass-market innovations, the United States was frequently the leader, producing the sewing machine (invented by Elias Howe in 1846); the typewriter (1867); clocks and watches, the everyday timekeepers of the new office and factory routines; the telephone, phonograph, and cinema; and small arms, such as the revolver, invented by Samuel Colt in 1836, and the repeating rifle, designed by Christopher Spencer in 1860. The machine gun, invented by Richard Gatling in 1862, was improved several times. In 1883 it took on the name of the Maxim gun, for the American Hiram Maxim, who created a gun that had a range of almost 1½ miles and could shoot 11 rounds per second.

Warfare and industrialization went hand in hand. In the United States, for example, the Civil War (1861–65) not only restored a political union but also marked the victory of the industrializing, urban, free-labor north, over the rural, plantation economy, slave-holding south. Wars of white immigrants against Native Americans accompanied the construction of new crosscontinental railroads. Wars against Mexico completed the borders of the contiguous United States, and wars against Spain brought the United States its first overseas colonies.

Machine shop, West Lynn works, U.S., c. 1898. The United States led the way in mass production of household goods. In the nineteenth century, people immigrated to the big cities from rural America and from overseas to work in factories—often for low pay, with long hours and in hot, noisy conditions. The factory system expanded hugely after 1913 when Henry Ford introduced assembly-line technologies to motor-car production. Compare with a factory in India, p. 654.

Worldwide Effects of the Second Stage

Profits from all these businesses, civilian and military, spilled over into finance capital, the purposeful reinvestment of capital into new business to reap new profits. Financiers sought new opportunities in far-flung regions of the world. The industrial development of the Americas offered huge opportunities, and Britain became the largest investor. From the 1840s, for example, the railway networks of both North and South America were in large part financed by British investors. The availability of such investment capital made the task of industrial and urban development easier in the Americas, because the necessary sums could be borrowed and repaid later.

These borrowings, and the industrialization and urbanization that came from them, encouraged the immigration that helped increase the population of North America from 39 million in 1850 to 106 million in 1900, and that of South America from 20 million to 38 million in the same period. The United States absorbed these investments without losing political control of its own internal development and became the most industrialized of all countries. South America, however, became an early example of neocolonialism, in which foreign economic control leads to indirect foreign political control.

Canada enjoyed internal self-government within the British Empire from 1840 and, in 1867, became a unified dominion that included Ontario, Quebec, Nova Scotia, and New Brunswick. It attracted increasing immigration and investment, especially after the United States' frontier was filled in with its own immigrants. Nova Scotia and New Brunswick had joined the original provinces of Quebec and Ontario on condition that a railroad be built to link them with Quebec. More dramatically, the Canadian Pacific Railway was completed in 1885, spanning Canada from east to west. Between 1900 and 1916, 73 million acres of land were planted with wheat and other commercial crops. Four hundred million dollars per year were invested in this sector and in the mining of coal, gold, lead, zinc, nickel, and copper.

In Russia and the Ottoman Empire, the largest investments came from France. For the six decades leading up to World War I, Russia's industrial output grew at the rate of 5 percent per year. It produced more steel than France, Italy, or Japan, and by 1914 it had 46,000 miles of railroad track and was the world's fourth largest industrial power. It could not, however, keep up with the industrial advances of the United States and Germany. Similarly, Russia's railway mileage seems less adequate when the immense expanse of the country, by far the largest in the world, is considered. The proportion of Russian industrial production remained at about 8 percent of the world total from 1880 to 1914, and most of its heavy industry was owned by foreigners.

MAJOR DISCOVERIES AND INVENTIONS 1830–1914

Year	Discovery/Invention
1831	Dynamo: Michael Faraday
1834	Reaping machine: Cyrus McCormick
1834	Photography: Louis M. Daguerre; William Henry Fox Talbot
1836	Revolver: Samuel Colt
1837	Telegraph: Samuel Morse
1839	Vulcanized rubber: Charles Goodyear
1852	Gyroscope: Léon Foucault
1853	Passenger elevator: Elisha Otis
1856	Celluloid: Alexander Parkes Bessemer converter: Henry Bessemer Bunsen burner: Robert Bunsen
1858	Refrigerator: Ferdinand Carré Washing machine: Hamilton Smith
1859	Internal combustion engine: Etienne Lenoir
1862	Rapid-fire gun: Richard Gatling
1866	Dynamite: Alfred Nobel
1876	Telephone: Alexander Graham Bell
1877	Phonograph: Thomas Edison
1879	Incandescent lamp: Thomas Edison
1885	Motorcycle: Edward Butler Electric transformer: William Stanley Vacuum flask: James Dewar
1887	Motorcar engine: Gottlieb Daimler/Karl Benz
1888	Pneumatic tire: John Boyd Dunlop Kodak camera: George Eastman
1895	Wireless: Nikola Tesla X-rays: Wilhelm Roentgen
1896	Radioactivity: Antoine Becquerel
1897	Diesel engine: Rudolf Diesel
1898	Submarine: John P. Holland Radium and polonium: Pierre and Marie Curie
1902	Radio-telephone: Reginald Fessenden
1903	Airplane: Wilbur and Orville Wright
1905	Theory of relativity: Albert Einstein
1911	Combine harvester: Benjamin Holt
1914	Tank: Ernest Swinton

Overall global investments were immense, with Britain far in the lead. By 1914 Britain had invested some $20 billion, France about $8.7 billion, and Germany about $6 billion. The global age of **finance capital** was in full swing.

Industrial Society

So far we have concentrated on the immense new productivity of industrialization, and on the abundance and the wonders of new products. But how did the workers fare? What were the conditions of life for those who worked the machines that produced this new wealth? Reports from the early years in Britain, the birthplace of the Industrial Revolution, relate with horrifying regularity the wretched conditions of the working class. Popular literature, including the novels of Charles Dickens (1812–70); official government reports; political tracts; and the cries of labor organizers all echo the same theme: In the midst of increasing national wealth, workers suffered wracking poverty and degradation. However, by the end of our period (1914), the condition of working-class people in Western Europe and the United States, at least, was becoming comfortable. What had changed? How? What was the significance of the change? These questions remain important today as increasingly sophisticated machines continue to produce more abundant and more sophisticated products—and more anxiety in the life of workers.

Population Growth and the Industrial Revolution

Many demographic studies suggest that levels of population and industrialization increased together. The population of Europe almost doubled between 1750 and 1850, from 140 to 265 million, and then jumped to 400 million by 1900. At the same time, emigration carried an additional 50 million people outward from Europe, especially to the Americas, Australia, and South Africa. At first demographers attributed most of the gains to industrialization, but much of this population increase occurred before the introduction of machinery, and the increase seems to have been world-wide: China's population multiplied four times between 1650 and 1850. Historians now believe the main cause of the overall population growth was the availability of new foods, such as maize, provided by the Columbian Exchange, but the Industrial Revolution had important effects on the specific patterns of growth and migration.

Demographers note two waves of change that followed the Industrial Revolution. First, death rates fell as people ate better and kept cleaner, and as public health measures increased the safety of the water supply, improved the sanitation of cities, combated epidemics, and taught new standards of personal hygiene. Second, parents began to realize that improved health increased the likelihood that their children would live to adulthood, and that it was not necessary to produce numerous children to ensure that two or three or four would survive. Urban birth rates went down as parents began to practice family planning. The old "**iron law of wages**" had argued that as income increased people would simply use the surplus to have more children; this did not happen. After years of rapid growth, by about 1900 the populations of industrial areas began to stabilize.

Winners and Losers in the Industrial Revolution

New entrepreneurs, men creating successful new industrial enterprises, often profited handsomely in this era. Their literary representative was Samuel Smiles (1812–1904), whose *Self Help*, published in 1859, advocated self-reliance as the key to "a harvest of wealth and prosperity." Smiles described the careers of many of these self-made new men—the "industrial heroes of the civilized world"—for example, Josiah Wedgwood, a potter, the son and grandson of potters, who created a new form of pottery that still bears his name. Wedgwood transformed the British pottery industry, earning great profits for himself and providing employment in his factories for 20,000 workers. As industries of all sorts expanded, each nation had its own examples of "captains of industry"—for example, in Germany, four generations of the Friedrich Krupp family, manufacturers of steel and weapons; in the United States, Andrew Carnegie, also in steel manufacture, and J. Pierpont Morgan, in investment banking.

The lives of the entrepreneurial elites provided inspiration to some, but they were obviously not representative of the majority. In Britain, the economic and political power of the inherited nobility declined. Their wealth, based on land ownership, diminished as that of the new industrial class grew. More to the point, handicraft workers were displaced by the new mechanization. In 1820 there were 240,000 handloom weavers in Britain; in 1840, 123,000; by 1856, only 23,000. Some of these workers found jobs running the new power looms, but many could not make the transition and fell into poverty. While attending his father's cotton mill in Manchester, Friedrich Engels (1820–95) compiled devastating accounts of *The Condition of the Working Class in England* (1845). His description of the St. Giles slum in London demonstrates his moral outrage:

> Heaps of garbage and ashes lie in all directions, and the foul liquids emptied before the doors gather in stinking pools. Here live the poorest of the poor, the worst paid workers with thieves and the victims of prostitution indiscriminately huddled together … [T]hey who have some kind of shelter are fortunate in comparison with the utterly homeless. In London fifty thousand human beings get up every morning, not knowing where they are to lay their heads at night. (pp. 34–38)

Government reports, although more restrained in tone, sustained these horrific views. Official committees studied conditions in the factories and neighborhoods of Britain's growing industrial cities and in its mines. In 1831, an investigation into the conditions of child labor in cotton and linen factories found children beginning work at the age of six, usually for 12- and 13-hour days. They were often given food so wretched that, despite their hunger, they left it for pigs to eat. Workplaces were cramped and dirty all year long, and were especially damaging to health during the long nights of winter, when gas, candles, and oil lamps added their soot and smoke to the air of the factory. Still worse conditions were revealed by the Committee on the Conditions in Mines in 1842. Children worked underground for 14 hours each day. Legally, they could work from the age of nine, but parents needing extra income frequently brought even younger children to work.

Putters or trolley boys, from *Mines and Miners* by L. Simonin, early nineteenth century. Until the reforms of the 1870s, owners of factories and mines were able to force children as young as five and six to work up to 16 hours a day—often in hazardous conditions. Orphans and pauper children were especially vulnerable since capitalists merely had to keep them fed and sheltered in return for their services. The resulting disease, industrial injury, and illiteracy tended to make poor families even poorer.

Investigations led to remedial legislation. The Factory Act of 1833 prohibited the employment of children under the age of nine in textile mills and provided for paid inspectors to enforce the legislation. Parliament passed a new Poor Law in 1834, which provided assistance just adequate to sustain life. The Poor Law required that recipients live in government workhouses and participate in government-created work projects, but these provisions were not usually enforced. An 1842 law prohibited the employment of women, and children under the age of ten, in coal mines. The Ten Hour Act of 1847 extended this ruling to cover factories and limited women's work hours. In practice, men's hours were also soon reduced.

Sir Edwin Chadwick (1800–90), an investigator for the Royal Commission on the Poor Laws, issued his Inquiry into the Condition of the Poor in 1842 after taking abundant testimony from workers in factories and mines, homes and workplaces. Chadwick noted that the British government had already begun legislating the conditions of child labor and of tenement construction. He now urged further legislation to provide for sewerage, drainage, sanitation, and a clean water supply. His report suggested that not only the poor workers but also their employers, the community, and the government would benefit. Chadwick's report helped inspire broad public support for the Public Health Act of 1848 and the creation of a Board of Health.

Redefining Gender

By creating factories, the Industrial Revolution drove a wedge between the home and the workplace that dramatically affected both. Wives who had been accustomed to working alongside, or at least in proximity to, their husbands on the farm or in the shop now found that the major source of employment was away from home. The Industrial Revolution forced redefinitions of identities. What should the woman's role and place be now? How should motherhood and work be balanced? In a world that expected most females to be under the protection of males, how were single women to define, and fend for, themselves? In what voice should the feminist movement address these complex issues?

As the Industrial Revolution began in semi-rural locations, its labor force was drawn primarily from young, (as yet) unmarried women, frequently daughters of local farmers. Some of the early factory owners built boarding houses for the women and treated them protectively, as young wards. Francis Cabot Lowell (1775–1817) built mills at Waltham, Massachusetts, on this principle. He promised the women hard work, with pay adequate to help their families and to save toward marriage. After his death, his partners extended his example by establishing a new town, Lowell, with the largest cotton mill built to that date. By the 1840s, about half the mills in New England followed this model. Factory work had its demands of order, discipline, and the clock, and the dormitory-boarding houses were somewhat crowded, but labor historian Alice Kessler-Harris quotes approvingly the very warm assessment of the Lowell experience from one of its workers in the 1830s: It was "the first field that had ever been open to her outside of her own restricted home … the first money they earned! When they felt the jingle of silver in their pocket, there for the first time, their heads became erect and they walked as if on air."

As new machinery became heavier, as factory work became more prevalent, and as a five-year-long economic depression beginning in 1837 pressed down on both the American and British economies, the workforce shifted. Men, often farmers and immigrants, moved into the factories, displacing the women. The men demanded higher pay, which factory owners had previously hoped to avoid by hiring women. The culture of the industrializing world of that time, primarily in Britain, called for men to support their families. A young, unmarried woman might earn just enough for herself and that would be considered adequate. A man required a "**family wage.**" The rising productivity of constantly improving machinery made this family wage possible, and it became the baseline standard for industry, although workers had to struggle for it for decades. Women were thus displaced from factory work and brought back to the home.

By the second half of the nineteenth century, "**domesticity**" became the desired norm for middle- and even working-class women and their families. Most middle-class women spent a great deal of time caring for their families and homes, and the new urban domesticity increased their level of security and comfort. Life expectancy, a basic index of well-being, rose rapidly for women in Britain, slightly more than for men. It increased from 44 years in 1890, to 52 in 1910, to 60 in 1920. Living standards began to rise and generally continued to rise into the twentieth century. New systems of ventilation, heating, lighting, indoor plumbing, and running hot and cold water contributed to domestic comfort and made life easier for those who could afford these services, although they often did not reach working-class neighborhoods.

Urban conditions made children less of an economic benefit, as they had been on family farms, and more of an economic burden. Family planning increased. Childbearing became less frequent, freer from infection thanks to antisepsis, less painful with the use of anesthesia, and safer with the professionalization of the practice of medicine. The presence of children in the home also decreased as free, compulsory education, beginning as early as the 1830s and 1840s, began to take them to school for several hours each day.

With more time freed from traditional domestic responsibilities, some women began to enter into the array of **white-collar jobs** that were opening. The most respectable jobs provided satisfying work that also fit the culturally approved role of women as caregivers and nurturers: teaching in the new school systems and nursing in the new hospitals. Other women worked as sales personnel in the new department stores (where they also shopped), and as secretaries and clerks in the new offices, although this was primarily a male occupation in the nineteenth century. A very few went into the professions: medicine, law, journalism, and business.

While domestic concerns and new technological wonders engaged the middle classes, and were desired by the working classes, for a great number of people they were out of reach. The 15–20 percent of adult females who had to work as principal breadwinners for themselves and their families confronted more basic problems of earning a living. The value placed on domesticity as the proper role for females, and the concomitant view that men should earn a "family wage" but that women needed only supplementary income, made the plight of the working woman doubly difficult. These women, often immigrants, desperately poor, and without male support, were no longer seen, as the first industrial women workers had been, as proud and independent, but as unfortunate objects of sympathy and pity.

They found jobs where they could. Domestic service was most common, employing two to three times as many women as industry, even in industrialized countries. On the margins of society, other women earned a living through prostitution. In the

"The New Machine for Winding up the Ladies," Anon., English cartoon, c. 1840. Upper-class English women wore corsets, devices made of whalebone that constricted the waist painfully, making it appear as tiny as possible and, by contrast, accentuating the hips, buttocks, and breasts. The corsets were often so tight that they interfered with women's ability to breathe properly and encouraged "swooning." The cartoonist mocks these practices.

KEY TERMS

family wage A wage, usually earned by a male head-of-household, adequate to support a family. The concept suggested that a woman's place was in the home and that the male husband-father was the family breadwinner.

domesticity An ideal that valued the woman who stayed at home, raising children, keeping the home as comfortable as possible, and making it a safe haven to which her husband could return after his daily work earning a family wage.

white-collar jobs Professional and clerical jobs; office work; clean work. This kind of work became more prevalent as the Industrial Revolution also created these kinds of urban, service jobs.

second half of the nineteenth century, censuses in the largest cities, London and Paris, routinely reported tens of thousands of prostitutes walking the streets, serving in brothels, or, occasionally, employed in more comfortable settings by more prosperous clients. These women were condemned by more conventional society, but they often found this job the only one that paid enough to enable them to support their families. Most of them worked only until about the age of 25, by which time they usually found other work or were married, a rosy picture painted by the middle classes, but often contradicted by working-class experience.

Economic and Political Reform

Britain's growing urban, industrial population demanded political and economic change. The government, recognizing that industrialization was transforming Britain away from its aristocratic and agrarian traditions and fearful of the consequences, responded initially by trying to repress the movement for reform. The Peterloo Massacre at St. Peter's Fields in Manchester in 1819 demonstrated the government's position. A huge but peaceful demonstration by some 80,000 people called for universal male suffrage, the annual election of the House of Commons in Parliament, and the abolition of the **Corn Laws**. The Corn Laws had raised the tariff on grain to levels that effectively banned importation, thus keeping the price of basic foodstuffs high, favoring landowners and farmers at the expense of the growing urban, industrial population. Mounted soldiers, brandishing their swords, charged into the crowd of demonstrators, killing 11 and wounding some 400. The government applauded the soldiers and passed further legislation to restrict free expression.

By 1832, however, partly because of revolutions on the European continent, and partly because of riots in Britain, the mood in Parliament had changed. The Reform Bill of 1832 expanded Parliamentary seats for urban constituencies and increased the number of voters by about 60 percent, though voters still totaled only about 800,000 in all of Britain. (England, Scotland, and Wales took their first official census in 1801 —an important mark of an industrializing society—and registered a total population of about 10.5 million. Ireland was not included.) A far greater proportion of the

The Peterloo Massacre, published October 1, 1819 by Richard Carlile. Colored etching. By the early 1800s, Britain was becoming more urban and more industrial. New constituencies demonstrated for new laws, such as universal male suffrage, and cheaper imported food (corn). On August 16, 1819, the government dispatched mounted soldiers to St. Peter's Fields, Manchester, to break up a protest of 80,000 people, killing 11 and wounding 400. The etching suggests that the protestors were not rabble, but respectable urbanites. Lines were now drawn between old, rural aristocrats and these newly rising urban interest groups.

new voters, however, were professionals rather than industrial workers. In 1835 Parliament enacted a Municipal Corporations Act, which reformed elections and administrations in large cities, enabling them to cope more successfully with the problems of growth and industrialization.

On some fundamental issues Parliament moved slowly, and sometimes it refused to move at all. It rejected, overwhelmingly, the petitions submitted between 1838 and 1848 by the Chartists, a national working-class organization calling for universal male suffrage, an end to property qualifications for members of Parliament, and equal electoral districts. Parliament feared that universal suffrage would bring an end to the sanctity of property and the capitalist economic system.

In 1846, however, Parliament did repeal the Corn Laws. With this victory of the urban constituencies and the triumph of free trade, Britain gave up its policy of self-sufficiency in food and entered fully into the international trade system to purchase its food and sell its manufactured goods. A second Reform Bill in 1867 doubled the electorate to about two million, about one-third of all adult males. The Bill enfranchised many urban working men, although it continued to exclude most of those agricultural and industrial workers who lived in the countryside.

The two major political parties competed for the votes of the working classes. The Liberals, under William Gladstone, began to provide universal, state-supported education (1870), and legalized labor unions (1871). The Tories, under Benjamin Disraeli, extended the acts regulating public sanitation, conditions of labor in factories and mines, and housing for the poor (1876–80). In 1884, under Gladstone, a third Reform Bill doubled the electorate again. (Britain adopted universal male suffrage for men 21 and older in 1918.)

Women's Suffrage. While women finally gained the right to vote in both Britain and the United States after World War I, it was not without a long and often violent struggle. The Chartists had peacefully demanded that women obtain the right to vote, without success. Women's suffrage committees were formed, but legislators in Parliament rejected most of their demands. The failure to win suffrage through peaceful means led Emmeline Pankhurst and her daughter Christabel to form suffragette organizations, which became increasingly violent. Though many abhorred the violence, many more grew sympathetic to giving women the right to vote. The participation of women

WOMEN'S EMANCIPATION 1790–1928

c. 1790	Olympe de Gouges writes the polemical *Declaration of the Rights of Woman and the Citizen*
1792	Mary Wollstonecraft writes *A Vindication of the Rights of Woman*, regarded as the first manifesto of the women's movement in Britain
1794	Condorcet writes of the desirability of establishing equality of civil and political rights for men and women in *Progrès de l'esprit*
1829	*Sati* (ritual suicide by Hindu widows) is banned in India
1848	Elizabeth Cady Stanton and Lucretia Mott organize the first women's rights convention at Seneca Falls, New York
1850	Beginnings in Britain of national agitation for women's suffrage
1857–72	Married Women's Property Acts allow British women to keep their own possessions on marriage
1866	Mott founds American Equal Rights Association
1868	First public meeting of women's suffrage movement held in Manchester, England
1869	In Britain women ratepayers may vote in municipal elections; Cady Stanton is first president of U.S. National Woman Suffrage Association
1890	Footbinding beginning to die out in China
1903	Emmeline Pankhurst founds Women's Social and Political Union
1906	Pankhurst and her daughters launch militant campaign in Britain
1913	Suffragettes protest in Washington, DC; International Women's Peace Conference held in the Netherlands
1914–18	Women assume workplace responsibilities outside the home during World War I
1918	British women householders over 30 years granted the vote
1919	Constance de Markiewicz is the first woman elected to Parliament in Britain
1920	19th amendment to the Constitution gives U.S. women the vote
1928	British women over 21 years granted the vote

Emmeline Pankhurst with her daughter Christabel, 1908. This mother and daughter team founded the Women's Social and Political Union (1903), the most renowned of Britain's suffrage movements. Their campaigns were militant and disruptive. They set fire to public buildings, smashed windows, sabotaged mailboxes, slashed paintings in London's National Gallery, and pelted government officials with eggs. Emmeline was jailed repeatedly, and force-fed when she went on hunger strikes.

in the national effort in World War I softened opposition, and in 1918 the vote was extended to British women aged 30 and over, provided they were married to householders, or met other qualifications of income and education. In 1928 the Representation of the People Act gave British women voting rights equal to those of men.

In the United States, women turned to conventions and voluntary associations to promote suffrage. One of the most important conventions was held in Seneca Falls, New York, in 1848. This convention called not only for the right to vote but also for increased educational and employment opportunities for women. Other conventions followed. Women first gained the right to vote in local and school board elections in some western states and finally gained national voting rights with the ratification of the Nineteenth Amendment to the U.S. Constitution in August, 1920.

Labor Movements and Socialism

Like women, who organized to obtain political rights, the working class organized to improve labor conditions. Social historian E.P. Thompson identifies the London Corresponding Society, founded in 1792, as perhaps "the first definitely working-class political organization formed in Britain." Workers were forbidden to unionize under the Combination Act of 1799, but in 1824 this law was repealed. Small trade unions took root, usually finding their greatest success among the better-off "aristocracy of labor"—the machinists, carpenters, printers, and spinners. Sometimes they would go on strike; politically they organized for suffrage campaigns; and some helped organize cooperative enterprises. The right to strike was recognized officially with the Trade Union Act of 1871. Unskilled workers began increasingly to join unions,

The Great Procession, June 18, 1910. Not only women campaigned for their right to vote: in this procession of the WSPU, a hunger-strikers' banner is hoisted aloft by male supporters.

with miners and transport workers usually in the lead. By 1914, four million Britons held membership in trade unions.

Karl Marx and the Workers' Revolution

In Britain, workers first created their own organizations, which then gained the support of political party leaders. Elsewhere, political leaders and theorists took the lead in organizing small groups of workers. Foremost among the theoreticians was the German Karl Marx (1818–83). A well-educated journalist of Jewish ancestry, Marx called for a worker-led revolution. He organized revolutionary **socialists** through active campaigning, wrote polemical tracts calling for revolution, such as *The Communist Manifesto* (with Friedrich Engels), and produced three volumes of scholarly analysis and critique of the capitalist system, called *Das Kapital*.

Marx began his studies in Berlin at a time when Western and central Europe were alive with revolutionary sentiments—both of workers seeking new rights and of nationalists seeking greater political representation. Marx moved to London, where he spent the rest of his life, much of it in active scholarship in the British Museum.

He believed that wealth is produced not so much by capitalists, who control the wealth, but by the **proletariat**—the laborers—who do the actual physical work of production. Because employers do not generally accept this point of view, workers do not receive proper compensation for their contributions. Violent revolution is the only recourse "to raise the proletariat to the position of ruling class, to establish democracy." In a stirring call to this revolution, Marx and Engels created the Communist Party and prepared its manifesto, concluding:

> Let the ruling classes tremble at a Communist revolution. The proletarians have nothing to lose but their chains. They have a world to win. Workingmen of all countries, unite! (*The Communist Manifesto*, p. 44)

Until the revolution would take place, Marx and Engels called for many shorter-term legislative goals, including: "a heavy progressive or graduated income tax … free education for all children in public schools … and … abolition of child factory labor in its present form." Many other labor groups shared these goals, and they were subsequently adopted in almost all industrialized countries.

Marx and Engels called for the establishment of a powerful, worker-led government to assume control of the economy, and they looked forward to a still later time when the state would be unnecessary and would "wither away." They identified the state as "the organized power of one class for oppressing another," so when workers ruled the state there would be no need for further oppression and the state would vanish. Marx and Engels gave no further description of this utopia, but it would be based on their most central and most radical tenet:

> The theory of the Communists may be summed up in the single sentence: Abolition of private property. (p. 23)

Their theory included a view of history that saw class struggle as perpetual: "The history of all hitherto existing society is the history of class struggles." The current form of the struggle was **bourgeoisie** vs. proletariat. The bourgeoisie themselves had created the proletariat by organizing the new factories that employed and exploited them. Marx condemned the sexual ethics of the bourgeoisie. Despite their official reverence for the family, Marx accused them of sexual abuse of their workers, economic perpetuation of prostitution, and wife-swapping among themselves: "Our bourgeois, not content with having the wives and daughters of their proletarians at their disposal, not to speak of common prostitutes, take the greatest pleasure in

KEY TERMS

socialist Socialists all believed that too much wealth was going into the hands of the owners of property and industry and too little to the workers who actually produced the wealth. The socialists divided sharply among themselves about the precise definition of the problem and the appropriate paths of struggle for change.

proletariat A collective noun designating the working class that produces wealth. The singular is "proletarian."

bourgeoisie A collective noun designating the class that owns and directs the means of production. In Marxist thought, the bourgeoisie and the proletariat need each other, but they are also always in conflict over the distribution of wealth.

Statue of Marx (left) and Engels, Statue Park, Budapest, Hungary. During the Cold War, when the USSR dominated the politics of Hungary, this statue sat in the capital city of Budapest. After the Cold War, and the end of Russian domination, the government of Budapest collected most of the statues of communist and Russian heroes from within the city and reassembled them in Statue Park, on the suburban fringe, as a museum of a time that had, thankfully, passed.

seducing each other's wives." Marx heaped scorn on religion, charging the bourgeoisie with using it as an "opiate" to divert the proletariat from its fundamental economic concerns. Marx was a materialist, arguing that economics is the basis of life; ideas and intellectual life are based on economic status: "Man's consciousness changes with every change in the conditions of his material existence, in his social relations and in his social life ... The ruling ideas of each age have ever been the ideas of its ruling class."

Marx wrote of the conflict between the roles of mother and of worker. With Engels, Marx condemned the "double oppression" of women by both capitalism and the family, but he praised capitalism for freeing women from being regarded as property. He encouraged women in their struggle for citizens' rights and economic independence. In *The Origins of the Family, Private Property, and the State*, Engels argued that the form of the family was not fixed. It had evolved substantially in the past, and he proposed further, revolutionary change:

The peculiar character of the supremacy of the husband over the wife in the modern family, the necessity of creating real social equality between them and the way to do it, will only be seen in the clear light of day when both possess legally complete equality of rights. Then it will be plain that the first condition for the liberation of the wife is to bring the whole female sex back into public industry, and that this in turn demands that the characteristic of the monogamous family as the economic unit of society be abolished. (Engels, pp. 137–38)

In retrospect, some of the most enduring criticisms made by Marx and Engels have been cultural rather than economic. They identified five critical areas of social-cultural tension during the height of the Industrial Revolution. Many of them still exist:

- the problem of coping with rapid change. *The Communist Manifesto* observed: "all that is solid melts into air";
- the alienation of factory workers from their work, as they became insignificant cogs in great systems of production;
- the alienation of workers from nature, as farmers left the countryside to find jobs in urban industries;
- the dominance of the husband over the wife in the modern family and the ending of earlier conditions of equality; and
- the economic competition that drove workers as well as owners to subordinate their own humanitarian and personal goals to the unceasing economic demands of the capitalist system.

Labor Organizations

The year 1848, when *The Communist Manifesto* was published, saw political and economic rioting across much of Europe. In part, people were reacting against the three decades of political conservatism that had reigned over Europe since the end of the

Napoleonic wars. In part, the working classes were beginning a long, sustained revolt against the hardships of the new industrial system. In the United States, too, workers protested and organized. 1848 was not so much the turning point here; 1865, the end of the U.S. Civil War, was more significant. The struggles in Europe, and especially France, were far more violent, but America, too, saw blood in the streets.

Austria and Germany. In central Europe, protesting students and workers briefly took control of Prague and Vienna in 1848 and then were suppressed in both cities by regular forces of the Austrian army at the cost of thousands of casualties. In Prussia, in the same year, worker demands for more democracy and more worker rights joined with demands for a new constitution that would lead toward the creation of a new nation of Germany from the merger of Prussia with the many small German-speaking states of the former Holy Roman Empire. At first it appeared that the Prussian king, Frederick William IV (r. 1840–61), would grant these demands. A Constituent Assembly was convened in Frankfurt to write a new German constitution. In the end, however, the king reasserted his divine right to rule and rejected the constitution. Under these circumstances, the smaller states refused to join in a unified government. Conservative forces remained in control of central Europe.

A new wave of labor unrest and strikes swept across the region in the late 1860s and early 1870s, signaling the growing strength of labor. In the newly created Germany, chief minister Otto von Bismarck (1815–98) pursued diverse and sometimes conflicting strategies to keep working people allied to his government. He extended universal male suffrage to the North German Confederation in 1867 and then to all of Germany when he unified the country in 1871. But he limited the power of the legislature and diluted the power of the vote so that government ministers remained responsible to the king, not to Parliament. When Germany's opposition Social Democratic Party (SPD) became Europe's first political party based on the working classes, in 1875, Bismarck sharply restricted its organizational activities. On the other hand, declaring, "I too am a socialist," he passed legislation providing workers' disability and accident insurance and, in the 1880s, the first compulsory social security system in Europe. This legislation, however, covered only male industrial workers, not women or children. The SPD created a separate organizational structure for women, which had enlisted 174,751 women members by 1914, the largest movement of women in Europe. However, the number includes not only women seeking independent expression, but also women who sought to ally themselves with their husbands as members of the party. Working women's organizations were undercut by the opposition of male unionized workers, who feared that the women would take away their jobs or, at least, increase the labor pool and thus drive down wages. Even so, thanks to government policies, worker militancy, and the example of Britain's painful experiences, Germany did not repeat the worst conditions of child and female labor, and of the excessive hours and brutal conditions of industrial work.

France. Worker revolts broke out repeatedly in France, many of them inspired by the French revolutionary tradition and others by the low wages and poor working conditions that characterized French industry. Skilled artisans, displaced by new industries, often organized these revolts. Even before the Industrial Revolution took root, worker and artisan revolts played a leading role in the French Revolution—and were crushed along with it. They boiled over again in 1848, first in a revolt against the monarchy of Louis Philippe (r. 1830–48). In response, a provisional republic was proclaimed, followed by the establishment of government-sponsored workshops to provide employment for the poor. A new, far more conservative government was elected, however, and it closed the workshops in Paris. The poor people of the city

Massacre of the Paris Radicals, **Edouard Manet.** The slaughter meted out to the Paris Commune of 1871 is graphically depicted by the post-Impressionist painter Manet. Left-wing urban leaders tried to set up their own state-within-a-state, but the communards were put down brutally by the national government. At least 20,000 were summarily executed and over 40,000 were taken prisoner. (Museum Folkwang, Essen)

barricaded city streets, and the army was called out. More than 10,000 people were killed or injured in the ensuing street riots.

Later in the century, the revolts were increasingly dominated by industrial workers. In 1871, much of the potential leadership of a workers' movement was once again wiped out. The French national government killed at least 20,000 people and exiled another 10,000 in the Paris Commune, an uprising of urban leaders in Paris.

After the 1848 revolt, Napoleon III commissioned Baron Haussmann (1809–91) to redesign the city of Paris to break down older, smaller neighborhoods, in which revolt had incubated, and to replace them with the large, glorious, easily policed boulevards of the modern French capital. After 1871, that project expanded. Ironically, the revolts resulted in the deaths of tens of thousands of the poor and oppressed and the stunning urban redesign of one of the most beautiful cities in the world.

A decade later, some of the exiles from the Paris Commune returned and organization began again, this time with greater success. In 1884 *syndicats*, or labor unions, were legalized. Two competing federations were formed, one calling primarily for mutual help, the other for political action. Together, they numbered 140,000 members in 1890, a figure that more than quadrupled to 580,000 by the end of the century. By 1909, an umbrella group, the Confédération Génerale de Travail, numbered nearly a million. In 1890, May 1 was recognized as an annual "Labor Day." French politics, however, was dominated by the wealthier business leaders. Industrial workers organized, but they commanded less influence than farmers, shopkeepers, and small businessmen.

The United States. In the United States, labor began to organize especially with the industrialization that began after the Civil War (1861–65). A number of craft unions joined together to form the National Labor Union in 1866, which claimed 300,000 members by the early 1870s. The Noble Order of the Knights of Labor, founded as a secret society in 1869, grew into a mass union, open to all workers, with 700,000 members in 1886. America's most successful labor organization was the American Federation of Labor, a union of skilled craftworkers, founded in 1886 by Samuel Gompers (1850–1924). Its membership grew to a million by 1900 and two million by 1914. Women were not allowed to join, but in 1900 the International Ladies Garment Workers Union, which organized male and female workers who made women's clothing, was formed—with men dominating its leadership.

A series of strikes in America throughout the 1890s led to violence, sometimes in response to falling wages, often in response to poor working conditions or to the excessive control of workers' lives by managers and owners. Hired detectives, local police, and even soldiers attacked strikers and were attacked in return. Steel workers near Pittsburgh lost the Homestead Steel strike in 1892, when the governor of Pennsylvania sent in 8,000 troops. A strike at the Pullman Palace Car Company in Chicago ended when a court injunction forced the workers back to their jobs. In the ensuing violence, scores of workers were killed. In resolving a 1908 strike of hat-makers, the United States Supreme Court ruled that trade union members were personally liable for business losses suffered during strikes. Until this ruling was reversed in the 1930s, militant unionism was virtually dead.

The United States did develop powerful labor organizations, mostly in the twentieth century, but, in contrast with Britain and other European nations, it never produced a significant political party based primarily on labor. Historians cite several reasons: Labor organization in the United States was fragmented into craft-specific unions. In this nation of immigrants, workers also held multiple identities; their ethnic identities frequently inhibited them from building union solidarity with those of other ethnic groups. Many immigrants came to America to earn money and return home; these workers did not usually develop a commitment to active unionization. Pay scales and working conditions in the United States were significantly better than in Europe, further muting worker grievances. Finally, the capitalist ideology of the country discouraged class divisions, and the government restricted labor organization.

Workers in the Nonindustrialized World

Wherever they reached, the new industrial products displaced old handicraft industries and workers. The craftsmen could not compete with the speed, consistent quality, and low price of the machine-made products. Many of them were ruined. The Indian cotton textile industry provided the most striking example. In 1834–35, the highest-ranking British official in India lamented, "The bones of the cotton weavers are bleaching the plains of India." Lord Bentinck's remark was especially true in Bengal, in eastern India, a region that had participated heavily in the export trade, but to some degree it rang true throughout India. And as a general observation on the fate of handicraft workers, the comment correctly captured the problem globally. Many of the displaced workers were pushed into agricultural work, especially as their countries could no longer compete as exporters of (hand-) manufactured goods and were transformed into exporters of raw materials and importers of finished manufactures. Some could find jobs in other crafts, not yet overtaken by the new industries. Some could continue their old crafts by cutting back farther and farther on their meager profits and incomes in order to try to compete with the machines. A few could produce fine handicrafts for the specialized luxury market. In the industrializing world, too, artisans were also displaced, but the rapidly expanding industries could absorb many of them. The craftspeople mourned the devaluation of their handicraft skills. The cold, standardized rhythms of the machines wore down

SOURCE

Tariffs, Wealth, and Poverty: Reflections on America and India by Pandita Ramabai

Pandita Ramabai (1858–1922) traveled in the United States for three years, 1886–89, and on her return home published a travelogue in Marathi. Translated literally as *The Peoples of the United States*, it has recently been published in English as *Pandita Ramabai's American Encounter*. In India, Ramabai was a pioneering reformer for women's education. American women impressed her for their public accomplishments individually and in the groups that they often organized. Indeed, the whole country impressed her favorably. One of the areas in which America compared most favorably with India was in its control of its own tariff policy. American industry did so well, Ramabai argues, because it closed its markets to imports that might be competitive. She criticizes the Indian people for not similarly excluding foreign competitive goods, but she does not give any indication of recognizing that America was free to set its own exclusionary tariffs; India, under British colonial rule, had no such freedom. Her audience, however, would surely have understood that. Or was Ramabai urging her fellow Indians simply to boycott foreign goods voluntarily—to just say no—even without formal tariffs? Some Indian nationalists of her time were beginning to argue for that position, and by the early twentieth century, this would be the official position of the Indian National Congress, as we shall see in Chapter Twenty-two.

The goods which come into this country from foreign countries are charged a heavy customs duty … The people here take great precautions to prevent the domination of foreign countries in trade and in other matters, and to prevent their becoming slaves of others … This is worth remembering by the people of our country who look to England for everything, who rely entirely on England, and who use English goods to the detriment of native industries and trade. The American said that drinking the tea and wearing the clothes imported from England harms the industries of his country; therefore he would never drink such tea or wear English clothes, but would content himself with whatever good or bad clothes were available in his own country. And he also acted accordingly. That is why this country has reached such prosperity today. And what have we achieved? We have given our gold and bought pots of pewter in return; we have shut down our handlooms and started wearing cheap English clothes. Like the Indians of North America, we have succumbed to the lure of shiny, colored glass beads; and we have sold our precious gem-studded land to foreigners in return for glass beads and glass bottles filled with wine. Now we are screaming because the wine has started to claim our lives, and the fragments of broken glass have made gaping wounds in our feet. This is why our country is in such a wretched state! This clearly shows that the United States and India are on opposite sides of the globe! (Ramabai, p. 227)

their spirits. But they had jobs and, as industrialization increased productivity, their incomes rose. Countries without much industrialization fared much worse.

Indentured Labor. In some of the poorest countries—most notably India and China—indentured labor (see p. 489) away from home became an alternative to unemployment for a wide range of peoples. Between 1831 and 1921, about two million people made their way from India and China and, to a lesser extent, from Africa, the Pacific Islands, and Japan, as indentured laborers to work primarily in sugar plantations around the world. Four factors encouraged this mass migration. First, the end of slavery forced a search for alternative labor sources. Slavery did not end all at once, with the British ban on the slave trade in 1807, nor with Britain's outlawing slavery in its colonies in 1833. It continued in the United States until 1863, in Cuba until 1886, and in Brazil until 1888; illegally, slavery continues today in many locations and in many different forms. After the formal end of slavery, many slaves continued to labor in conditions of semi-slavery. Nevertheless, the system was finished and a new source of labor was needed to supplement the quasi-slave population that continued. Second, the production of sugar increased globally, and dramatically, throughout the nineteenth century, from 300,000 tons in 1790 to ten million tons in 1914. Laborers were required even beyond the number of slaves previously employed in its cultivation and harvest.

Third, imperial reach connected far-flung regions of the world, making possible this international flow of labor. Indian indentured laborers traveling to the West Indies, or Mauritius, or Fiji remained within a single imperial system, with relatively similar laws, a single language of rule, and established systems of transportation and communication. One and a third million of them made the move. Similarly, indentured laborers from France's West African colonies migrating to the French Caribbean, or to Réunion in the Indian Ocean, moved within a single system. The 387,000 Chinese who emigrated under terms of indenture—the majority of them to Cuba and Peru—were less tied into a single empire, but they were part of the global economic system that the Europeans had developed. This was also true for the 65,000 Japanese who migrated to Hawaii. The fourth element in the indentured traffic was the technological capacity to move so many people around the globe, forth and back, because the indentures of the servants were for limited time periods, usually five to seven years, after which they might go "back home." Sometimes they were encouraged to return, sometimes not.

The indentured laborers were not displaced persons in the industrial system as the craftsmen were. Most were farm laborers to begin with, but it was the industrial system that created the mechanisms of the indenture system. Many observers compared the conditions of gang labor on sugar plantations to the rigors and routinization of the factory floor. The overwhelming majority of the servants were male, although the absence of females was probably tempered by the knowledge that after five or seven years the servants might return home to establish family life. Many observers thought that the women who did sign on as indentured laborers were mostly prostitutes. Some were, but most, like the men, recognized that even the low pay of the overseas indentured laborer was at least double that of the Indian or Chinese agricultural worker. They signed on in order to try to improve their situation. Although indentured servitude had some of the attributes of temporary slavery, it had a limited time frame, and thus the prospect of freedom at the end of years of indenture. For many it was a trap. For some it was an escape.

Chinese Cheap Labor, published in the July 29, 1870 edition of *Every Saturday*. Wood engraving. The engraving depicts workers on the Milloudon Sugar Plantation, Louisiana. As slavery was abolished, region by region, around the world, plantation owners often attempted to replace the now-freed slaves with cheap indentured laborers, especially from India and China. By 1870, some 2,000 Chinese were working in the cotton fields of Mississippi and Arkansas, and on plantations and shrimp farms in Louisiana. Although hundreds of thousands of indentured laborers came to areas like the Caribbean, altering local population balances in significant measure, in the U.S. the experiment failed as workers and employers clashed over rights and pay.

587

New Patterns of Urban Life

The core habitat of industrialization was the city. During the eighteenth century, cities began a period of growth that has continued without break until today. In the largest cities, by the late 1800s this process began to include middle-class suburbanization, which was made possible by the new railroad transportation systems for goods and passengers. In the early twentieth century, automobiles, buses, and trucks enlarged the system to ever-greater dimensions.

Much of the urban growth in the nineteenth century was a direct result of industrialization. The steam engine, which could be constructed anywhere, made the location of industries more flexible. Factories sprang up near port facilities, at inland transportation hubs, in the heart of raw materials resource centers, such as the Midlands of England, Silesia in central Europe, Hubei Province in China, Bihar in India, and near large concentrations of consumers, such as the great cities of Paris, London, Buenos Aires, and São Paulo. New industrial metropolises dotted the map.

Immigrants streamed into the new cities for jobs, as the balance between urban and rural populations tilted continuously cityward. Farmers became factory workers and so did the children of artisans. All found the new industrial city shocking. As they exchanged the lifestyles of farm and workshop for regimes of routinization, standardization, and regulation, they discovered that the skills they had previously mastered were of little use. At the same time, opportunities beckoned: cultural, educational, recreational, social, and, most important, economic. In the early years of the Industrial Revolution, conditions of labor and of public health were abysmal;

SOURCE

Diverse Perspectives

Like the proverbial elephant that appeared different to each person who approached it from a different perspective, the industrial city signified something different to each observer. Wordsworth and Blake (see box p. 570) saw early nineteenth-century London very differently. From the middle of the century, poets from other cities provide still different views.

Charles Baudelaire (1821–67) presents the hard-working people of Paris—indeed the city itself—as just struggling to get by at the break of a new day.

Parisian Scenes: Daybreak

The crow of a rooster, far off, cuts through the hazy air.
A sea of fog bathes the buildings.
Men in agony in the workhouses
Heave their dying breath in undignified gasps.
The debauched return home, broken by their work.
The shivering dawn robed in pink and green
Advances slowly along the deserted Seine,
And somber, aging, Paris, rubbing its eyes,
Picks up its tools, and goes back to work.

Charles Baudelaire

While Baudelaire anguished with his city's lonely despair, in the United States, Walt Whitman (1819–92) sang rapturously of the dynamism of his own Manhattan, New York:

Mannahatta

The down-town streets, the jobbers' houses of business, the houses of business of the
ship-merchants and money-brokers, the river-streets,
Immigrants arriving, fifteen or twenty thousand in a week,
The carts hauling goods, the manly race of drivers of horses, the brown-faced sailors,
The summer air, the bright sun shining, and the sailing clouds aloft,
The winter snows, the sleigh-bells, the broken ice in the river, passing along up or down
with the flood-tide or ebb-tide,
The mechanics of the city, the masters, well-form'd, beautiful faced, looking you straight in the eyes,
Trottoirs throng'd, vehicles, Broadway, the women, the shops and shows,
A million people—manners free and superb—open voices— hospitality—the most
courageous and friendly young men,
City of hurried and sparkling waters! City of spires and masts!
City nested in bays! My city!

Walt Whitman

Back Queen Street, Deansgate, Manchester. As this *Illustrated London News* drawing of housing conditions of the Manchester cotton operatives in 1862 shows, accommodation in this city could be spartan. Manchester, in particular, with its high mortality rate, desperately needed the attentions of voluntary agencies that were attempting to better the living conditions of those who had been drawn to work in the new industries. Despite the fact that many workers emigrated to the United States or to British colonies overseas, the population continued to grow at a great rate, with adverse consequences for public health and housing.

later, as productivity increased, workers organized, employers and governments paid heed, and conditions started to improve. "City lights" began to be more attractive. The nineteenth century began the age of global urbanization.

The Nature of the City

Philosophical and sociological speculations on the nature of the city flourished. In Germany, Max Weber (1864–1920) analyzed the modern industrial city as a new creation. He contrasted, negatively, its freewheeling life and amorphous institutions against the close-knit guilds and political and religious associations of earlier self-governing European cities, especially medieval cities (see Chapter Thirteen). Weber concluded that the sprawling industrial city—open to any immigrant who wished to come and embedded within a nation-state that controlled its life and politics—was quite different from the self-contained city of earlier times. Europe, at least, was living in a new era.

Many observers agreed, apprehensively. To them the openness of the new industrial city and the lack of institutional ties among its citizens seemed to be leading to breakdowns of both the social fabric and the individual personality. The division of labor was turning the individual into a specialist concerned only with narrow interests; the sense of personal or community wholeness was lost. And the sheer multitude of people and experiences in the city was also forcing the individual to retreat even further into a small, private niche. The urban dweller, they felt, was evolving into a person swift of intellect to achieve his own needs, but lacking concern for and integration with the larger community.

Some observers claimed to see the negative effects of urban individualism as part of an historical process that would ultimately lead to disaster. Oswald Spengler (1880–1936), a German philosopher of history, declared that the enormous "world-cities" of his day were inevitably destroying the spirit of the folk peoples that had built them. Such attacks on urban life perpetuated the centuries-old cultural struggle between the cosmopolitan city of businessmen and the (perhaps imagined) homogeneous countryside of the common folk.

Many scholars believed that quantitative statistical studies would enable both residents of the industrial city and their observers to understand most clearly the processes through which they were living and to make plans for future directions. Just as accurate measurement and assessment had helped bring in the industrial era, so they helped in its evaluation. Two men—Adna Ferrin Weber, an academic researcher, and Charles Booth, a businessman who wanted to understand the problems of urban poverty in order to combat them—launched quite different, exemplary, quantitative studies of the city that inspired public action as well as further research (see box opposite). With studies such as these, the new academic discipline of sociology, the formal study of humans in society, grew in importance.

Living in the City

In the United States, with millions of immigrants streaming into its cities in search of industrial jobs, urban diversity was accepted, even valued, and certainly studied. Scholars at the University of Chicago examined their own city, the world's fastest-growing industrial metropolis of the day, studying neighborhoods as well as the metropolis as a whole.

The "Chicago School of urban ecology" argued that urbanites did not live their lives downtown, as so many previous scholars had implied, but in local neighborhoods, each of which had its own characteristics. Within these neighborhoods, people's lives were not so disconnected, isolated, or alienated as they might appear superficially. At the end of the day, most people went back to their own homes in their own neighborhoods, places where they had a strong sense of self and community. The variety of social and economic lifestyles multiplied with the size

Paris, a Rainy Day, Gustave Caillebotte, 1876–77. An Impressionist's-eye-view of life in an urban setting. Although a number of studies suggest that the burgeoning urban development of the turn of the century ground down the lives of the poor, for the bourgeoisie, with leisure time on their hands, cities provided a backdrop for pleasure. (Musée Marmottan, Paris)

Quantifying the Conditions of Industrial Urbanization

"The most remarkable social phenomenon of the present century is the concentration of population in cities." These words open Adna Ferrin Weber's *The Growth of Cities in the Nineteenth Century*, published in 1899, the first comprehensive quantitative study of the subject. A century later it remains an invaluable introduction to the central issues. In the rivalry between city and countryside, Weber generally paid tribute to the role of the city:

> In the last half-century [1848–98], all the agencies of modern civilization have worked together to abolish this rural isolation; the cities have torn down their fortifications, which separated them from the open country; while the railways, the newspaper press, freedom of migration and settlement, etc., cause the spread of the ideas originating in the cities and lift the people of the rural districts out of their state of mental stagnation. Industry is also carried on outside of the cities, so that the medieval distinction between town and country has lost its meaning in the advanced countries. (pp. 7–8)

Apart from their cultural contributions, cities and industry were needed to absorb the surplus growth of rural population. In most of Europe, except France, he writes, "the rural populations, by reason of their continuous increase, produce a surplus which must migrate either to the cities or foreign lands" (p. 67). Without cities and industrial jobs, what would happen to this surplus population? This rhetorical question implied by Weber continues to our own day.

Weber began with a statistical summary and an analysis of levels of urbanization in his own time, and traced it back through the nineteenth century. As part of his research, Weber attempted global coverage and he gathered his data from official government publications as well as unofficial population estimates from around the world. In general, he found industrialization the main reason for city growth. England and Wales, 62 percent urban, were by far the most industrialized and the most urbanized regions on earth. The next closest were Australia, at 42 percent, and various parts of Germany, at about 30 percent. In general, the largest cities were growing fastest. London, the world's largest city in 1890, held 4.2 million people; New York, the second largest, 2.7 million. The least industrialized countries were the least urbanized—below ten percent—but most of these countries did not maintain statistical records.

In contrast to the gloom of poverty and oppression pictured by Marx and Engels a half-century earlier, Weber radiated optimism about the direction of urban life, including increasing levels of longevity and personal comfort. Describing conditions that only the wealthiest could enjoy, he wrote:

> Consider the conveniences at the disposal of the *fin de siècle* [end of the century] housewife: a house with a good part of the old-fashioned portable furniture built into it, e.g., china

cabinets, refrigerators, wardrobes, sideboards, cheval glasses [full-length, swivel mirrors], bath tubs, etc.; electric lights, telephones and electric buttons in every room, automatic burglar alarms, etc. … [Weber then quotes another urban advocate:] Thus has vanished the necessity for drawing water, hewing wood, keeping a cow, churning, laundering clothes, cleaning house, beating carpets, and very much of the rest of the onerous duties of housekeeping, as our mothers knew it. (pp. 218–20)

A judicious scholar, Weber did not omit the many negative aspects of city life at the end of the nineteenth century. Although death rates in the city had been declining steadily, urban death rates in 1899 remained higher than rural ones in most countries. In one of the worst examples, during the decade 1880–90, when the expected length of life at birth for all of England and Wales was 47 years, in Manchester, one of the greatest centers of the early Industrial Revolution, it was 29. Industrialization exacted its costs. Nevertheless, Weber reviewed the public health measures such as water and sewerage systems and the provision of clinics that had already been effective in other places, strongly advocated more of them, and remained optimistic about the urban future—if urbanites could cooperate for the common good.

Weber's pioneering statistical work gives us one flavor of industrial urbanization at the end of the nineteenth century. Charles Booth (1840–1916) gives quite another. Booth led a team of researchers in London, which produced the 17 volumes of *Life and Labour of the People in London*. Between 1886 and 1903, Booth and his colleagues systematically visited thousands of homes throughout London, interviewing workers to discover how the working people of the metropolis labored and lived. They concentrated their efforts in East London, the most industrialized, and most distressed, area of the city. The researchers asked questions about such critical issues as occupations, levels of income and consumption, housing size and quality, quantity and quality of amenities. They began with these statistical questions and then proceeded to qualitative discussion of the neighborhoods and their character. They concluded by asking what was being done, and what could be done, to improve conditions, especially through religious institutions.

- For Weber and for Booth, what was the relationship between formal, quantitative study of the city, and action to deal with its problems?
- How might Weber's global research be integrated with Booth's local, community research? How might the research of one influence the research of the other?
- Based on other readings from this chapter, what, if anything, is surprising about the research findings of Weber and Booth?

Guaranty Building in Buffalo, New York, designed by Louis Henry Sullivan, 1894–96. Sullivan's designs for steel-frame construction of large buildings—made possible because steel was now readily available and the elevator had been invented— were the forerunners of today's skyscrapers. A glance at the skyline of almost any large American or European city will confirm that Sullivan greatly influenced twentieth-century architecture, particularly in the United States. Sullivan's working principle that form follows function applied to the tall buildings (up to ten stories in the late nineteenth century) that he designed. It was important to maximize the limited space in city centers, and the idea of carrying buildings upward instead of outward met the need.

of the city and the diversity of its functions. Neighborhoods reflected this diversity.

A comprehensive perspective on the city would have to take account of neighborhoods as well as business districts. These commercial areas themselves were quickly increasing in size, complexity, and facilities. By the 1870s, department stores, coffeehouses, pubs, and restaurants had added urbanity to the central business district, attracting retail shoppers, window shoppers, and people with some leisure time. Theaters, concert houses, museums, the press and publishing houses, libraries, clubs, and a multitude of new voluntary associations provided culture and entertainment. They also created a "public sphere"— a setting in which citizens form and circulate their most influential civic ideas, goals, and aspirations. Here was the modern analogue of the ancient Greek *agora*.

A new transportation system made possible this specialization of commercial, cultural, industrial, and residential neighborhoods within the city. London opened its first underground railway system in 1863, the first major subway system in the world, and others followed. From the 1870s, commuter railways began to service new suburbs, and electric trolleys came into service after 1885. The availability of steel at commercial prices made possible the construction of skyscrapers, and the invention of elevators made them accessible. The first skyscrapers rose in the 1880s, beginning with ten-story buildings in Chicago.

Urban Planning

Out of the many examinations of urban living, town planning as a profession was born. One of the central problems of the industrializing city of the early nineteenth century was crowding. Poor ventilation, inadequate sanitation, polluted water, alienation from nature, and poor health—especially tuberculosis—resulted as densities in urban cores reached, and even surpassed, 100,000 people per square mile. By the last decades of the century the electric trolley cars and commuter railways offered the means to reduce population densities through suburbanization, and the city expanded in area as never before. At first the densities in the center did not appear to diminish, for the stream of new immigrants to the city matched and even exceeded those who were suburbanizing.

By the late 1800s, town planners began seeking comprehensive solutions to the new problem: How to provide space for population increase, allow for geographical expansion, yet continue to provide green space, while fostering participation in both the local community and the metropolis as a whole? The British reformer Ebenezer Howard (1850–1928) proposed a "Group of Slumless Smokeless Cities": a provocative concept of a region of 250,000 people on 66,000 acres. This would be far too miniature to cope with the problems of a London or a New York. Its intense control over the planning process also demanded political decisions that might not be possible within a participatory democracy. Nevertheless, the **garden city** concept of a core city ringed by separate suburbs, each set in a green belt, linked to one another by rapid transit, provided provocative, creative, somewhat utopian thinking for the new urban problems dawning with the new century.

The Industrial Revolution: What Difference Does It Make?

By the beginning of the twentieth century, the Industrial Revolution had brought unprecedented wealth and power to those who had mastered its technologies—especially the rulers and elites of the nations of Western Europe and the United States. Applying inanimate power, where previously there had been only humans and animals, had brought new productivity. Agriculture changed first, through enclosures and new agricultural practices, becoming both more intensive and more extensive, so that fewer farmers could feed more people, freeing—and forcing—many of their fellow workers to leave their farms for urban, industrial jobs. In the cities, steam power and, later, electrical power enabled factories and the new goods they produced to multiply. Families were restructured in the new urban, industrial settings, with changing relationships between husbands and wives, and more formal schooling for children. Women raised their voices, demanding an equality that they had felt on the family farm and were in danger of losing on the factory floor and in the urban household, with its smaller family groups, greater longevity, and proportionately fewer years spent in raising children. Railway tracks and steamship lines girdled the earth, and the oceans were connected by canals. Electricity lit up the night, provided the bright lights of the city, powered telephones and telegraphs, and supplied energy to factories and homes in remote areas. With a feeling of self-satisfied triumphalism, the masters of this industrializing world conquered much of the land surface of the globe and made it their colonial possession, thus bringing remote areas into the web of the industrial world, whether they wished to be there or not.

In the industrialized countries, the earlier years of poverty, insecurity, filth, and high death rates for industrial workers seemed to be passing as increasing productivity provided more material benefits, unions provided representation, and governments began to legislate in their favor—although the battles for workers' welfare were far from over. Antagonism between captains of industry and their workers continued. New kinds of social relationships formed among industrial workers as they arrived in new urban neighborhoods, with opportunities and constraints quite different from those they left behind in their rural homes. They were living in a world transformed, and now they were transforming themselves by building new kinds of communities along with their neighbors, friends, and coworkers.

Millions of migrants were on the move, from village to city, from country to country, and from continent to continent. Most traveled as free immigrants, but almost ten million people from poorer countries traveled as indentured laborers to supply the still-flourishing plantations of the world in the aftermath of the abolition of slavery. The condition of many of the "free" migrants, too, was often precarious. All of these groups formed new kinds of communities in their new homes. The study of sociology was born and flourished.

The Industrial Revolution restructured the world profoundly, as thoroughly as the agricultural revolution had done some 15,000 years earlier. Today we speak of living in a postindustrial world. Our sources of energy, our means of transportation and communication, our international and intercontinental connectivity, our cities, our political institutions, our levels of technical and professional education, our family and gender relationships are in many respects different from those at the height of the Industrial Revolution, yet they are all built on the transformations of that era. Those of us who live in countries that went through the Industrial Revolution as it unfolded still live with its infrastructure. Those of us who live in countries that did not directly experience the full weight of that revolution—in large parts of Africa and

KEY TERM

garden city A self-contained planned town combining work, residential, agricultural, and recreational facilities, and surrounded by a rural belt.

Asia, in particular—are now trying to understand which parts of it we must recreate in order to cope with the modern world, and which parts we may "leapfrog," finding a new way of achieving some of the benefits of that revolution without going directly through it; establishing networks of cell phone communication, for example, and using that technology, without ever establishing a network of land lines, with all of their infrastructure and expense; connecting remote areas by air without ever establishing a network of railway lines. While one group is emerging from the Industrial Revolution, another may be attempting to bypass it.

Asking Questions

In answering the first five questions, you may wish to specify different perspectives for different countries and time periods.

- What would you identify as the key social changes introduced by the Industrial Revolution?
- To what degree do you see rural people benefiting or losing out as a result of the Industrial Revolution?
- How are industrialization, urbanization, and immigration related to one another?
- In which ways do you see women benefiting from the Industrial Revolution? In which ways to you see them losing out?
- What were the new political problems raised by the Industrial Revolution?
- To what degree do you think we can consider the world today as still living in a period of industrial revolution? To what degree do you think that period is past?

Suggested Readings

PRINCIPAL SOURCES

Adas, Michael, ed. *Islamic and European Expansion* (Philadelphia, PA: Temple University Press, 1993). Excellent anthology of historiographical articles that introduce modern world history. Several articles on the period of the Industrial Revolution and its effects on men and women.

Headrick, Daniel R. *The Tools of Empire* (New York: Oxford University Press, 1981). The Industrial Revolution gave to Europeans the tools to create empire: weapons, steamships, and quinine.

Marx, Karl and Friedrich Engels. *The Communist Manifesto* (New York: International Publishers, 1948). The great critique of the evils of industrial capitalism and a revolutionary agenda to overthrow it.

Stearns, Peter N. *The Industrial Revolution in World History* (Boulder, CO: Westview Press, 1993). Excellent introduction to the background, development, and significance of the Industrial Revolution in global scope and historical time depth.

Thompson, E.P. *The Making of the English Working Class* (New York: Vintage, 1966). Thompson taught us to see the working class not only in

Marxist terms but also in cultural terms, to understand their lives as more than just revolutionary fighters.

ADDITIONAL SOURCES

Andrea, Alfred and James Overfield, eds. *The Human Record*, Vol. 2 (Boston, MA: Houghton Mifflin, 6th ed., 2008). Excellent anthology for world history.

Bairoch, Paul. *Cities and Economic Development*, trans. Christopher Braider (Chicago, IL: University of Chicago Press, 1988). Heavily quantitative assessment of cities' role in economic development.

Bell, Susan Groag and Karen M. Offen, eds. *Women, the Family, and Freedom: The Debate in Documents*, Vol. 1, *1750–1880* (Stanford, CA: Stanford University Press, 1985). Excellent selection of documents on the feminist movement, with insightful commentary.

Braudel, Fernand. *Civilization and Capitalism 15th–18th Century: The Perspective of the World*, trans. Sian Reynolds (New York: Harper and Row, 1984). Excellent, sweeping background to the Industrial Revolution.

Davis, Lance E. and Robert A. Huttenback. *Mammon and the Pursuit of Empire* (Cambridge: Cambridge University Press, 1989). Stresses the importance of economic interests, private and public, in the creation of empire.

Engels, Friedrich. *The Condition of the Working Class in England*, trans. W.O. Henderson and W.H. Chaloner (Stanford, CA: Stanford University Press, 1968). *The* explication of the horrors of early industrialization in England, written by a young businessman who became a communist because of what he saw with his own eyes.

——. *The Origins of the Family, Private Property, and the State*, ed. Eleanor Burke Leacock (New York: International Publishers, 1973). Condemns the contemporary (1884) status of women and urges fundamental restructuring.

Hobsbawm, Eric. *The Age of Capital 1848–1875* (New York: Vintage Books, 1975). This series by Hobsbawm provides an excellent overview of the period of the Industrial Revolution. Global, but strongest on Europe. Critical of capitalism.

——. *The Age of Empire 1875–1914* (New York: Vintage, 1987).

Kennedy, Paul. *The Rise and Fall of the Great Powers* (New York: Random House, 1987). Great empires since 1500 have been built and preserved by careful attention to the balance between guns and butter, military expenditure, and a thriving civilian economy.

Landes, David. *The Unbound Prometheus: Technological Change and Industrial Development in Western Europe from 1750 to the Present* (Cambridge: Cambridge University Press, 2nd ed., 2003). Landes has mostly praise for the European initiative, creativity, and hard work that created the Industrial Revolution.

Lenin, V.I. *Imperialism, the Highest Stage of Capitalism* (Beijing: Foreign Languages Press, 1965). The classic view that industrial nations seek empires as marketplaces for buying raw materials and selling finished products because home markets alone are insufficient.

Perrot, Michelle. *Workers on Strike; France, 1871–1890*, trans. Chris Turner with Erica Carter and Claire Laudet (Leamington Spa: Berg, 1987). Useful study of labor organization in industrial France.

Ramabai Sarasvati, Pandita. *Pandita Ramabai's American Encounter: The Peoples of the United States* (1889), trans. and ed. Meera Kosambi (Bloomington, IN: University of Indiana Press, 2003). A rare travelogue by an Indian woman, concerned with economic, social, and political development in America with special attention to women's progress.

Revel, Jacques and Lynn Hunt, eds. *Histories: French Constructions of the Past*, trans. Arthur Goldhammer *et al.* (New York: New York Press, 1995). How French historians understand the significance of their nation's history. New interpretations for new times.

Sennett, Richard, ed. *Classic Essays on the Culture of Cities* (Englewood Cliffs, NJ: Prentice Hall, 1969). An excellent selection of classical sociological essays.

Wallerstein, Immanuel. *The Modern World-system 1: Capitalist Agriculture and the Origins of the European World-economy in the Sixteenth Century* (San Diego, CA: Academic Press, 1974). The fullest exposition of the theory of core-periphery exploitative development, with Europe and the U.S. as the core and Asia, Africa, and Latin America as the periphery.

Weber, Adina Ferrin. *The Growth of Cities in the Nineteenth Century: A Study in Statistics* (Ithaca, NY: Cornell University Press, 1963). A dissertation that became a key to the quantitative understanding of urban growth worldwide.

For quizzes, flashcards, primary sources, interactive maps, videos, and other activities related to this chapter please go to

www.myhistorylab.com

CHAPTER EIGHTEEN

Nationalism, Imperialism, and Resistance

Competition among Industrial Powers
1650–1914

French armies marching across Europe under Napoleon in the early 1800s imposed their imperial governments and their legal systems on the nations they conquered. The new message seemed clear: A nation organized for war and administration could enter regions outside its own borders to fight, conquer, legislate, rule, and tax. Military and political catastrophe awaited those without this power. The Industrial Revolution, beginning in England in the eighteenth century and sweeping across the globe, demonstrated similar force in its new forms of economic organization and power. When a single national government could combine military and industrial power together, it wielded the power to build a global empire. Britain's takeover of India, for example, marked not only a political victory but also an economic conquest. The political and the industrial revolutions, when fused together as they were in France and England, demonstrated that empires could be far more powerful than nation-states. Inspired and frightened, acquisitive and defensive, other regions joined in the competition to create unified nations and empires. In this chapter we will look at successful attempts at nation-building and empire-building, and at some unsuccessful attempts as well. We will examine the role of women, who had important roles in the building and administration of empire, usually behind the scenes. Power, gender, and sexuality often went hand in hand. We examine also anticolonial revolts, successful and unsuccessful. We close with a case study of Japan, which saw the threat of colonial conquest and reorganized itself to maintain its independence. Japan provides a textbook case of successful national resistance to foreign colonial domination, which ultimately resulted in the construction of a new empire in Japan that raised its own challenge to the empires of Europe.

KEY TOPICS
- Nationalism
- Failed Nationalisms and Delayed Nationalisms
- The European Quest for Empire
- European Competition and Cooperation: Empire-building in Africa
- Gender Relationships in Colonization
- Anticolonial Revolts
- Japan: From Isolation to Equality
- Nationalism and Imperialism: What Difference Do They Make?

Nationalism

Nationalism, an appreciation of belonging to one's country and a commitment to serve on its behalf, has two faces. As a positive force, it promises to unite and empower the masses of a nation to work together for a common good. It views other nations as potential allies or as friendly competitors. As a negative force, it threatens to force the masses to serve the state and to turn one nation against another in destructive warfare.

In several of the cases we study here, the first goal of nationalism was to create a modern, independent nation where none existed. Independence movements within the Ottoman Empire fought to free their regions from imperial control; the American

The Sino-Japanese War in Korea, Kobaysgu Kiyochika, 1894. Engraving. Japanese forces are shown firing down on their Korean enemy as a journalist makes notes in the foreground. Contrast the modern uniforms and weapons of the soldiers with the those of the traditional samurai warrior, p. 692. (Victoria & Albert Museum, London)

nationalism A positive feeling of belonging to a particular nation, often including a desire to serve the nation, based on such elements as birth and ancestry, later choice and naturalization, acceptance of a common future, and/or material and cultural benefits of membership in the nation. In a negative form nationalism may lead to suppression of difference at home, and warfare against others abroad.

millet **system** The Ottoman Empire's system of rule through religious communities. Legal issues among members of individual *millets*, or religious groups, were administered by the group itself, and taxes were also collected by the *millets* on behalf of the empire. *Millets* kept in close contact with their coreligionists in other countries, sometimes undermining the power of the Ottoman government.

colonies fought to create a new nation, independent from England. In Italy and Germany, national movements built a larger nation out of smaller fragments. National movements have also created the reality of a modern nation out of a historical memory, as was the case of Zionism.

Nationalism in the Ottoman Empire

As powerful nations set out to build empires by conquering other peoples, they often met resistance in the form of anti-imperial **nationalism**. In their fierce competitions, rival empires sometimes found that they could weaken their adversaries by encouraging this anti-imperial nationalism in their conquered territories. Western European nations employed this strategy against the Ottoman Empire throughout the nineteenth and early twentieth centuries, ultimately detaching huge territories from Ottoman control.

In southeastern Europe, revolts against the Ottomans broke out in the Balkans from 1815 onward in the name of individual nationalities. With British and French diplomatic and military support, Greece won its independence in 1829. The Western European powers also supported successful movements for greater autonomy and limited self-government in Serbia and in Wallachia and Moldavia (in present-day Romania), diminishing the power of the Ottoman Empire while increasing their own. In the aftermath of these imperial defeats, Muhammad (Mehemet) Ali seized his opportunity to make Egypt effectively independent of the Ottomans in 1832. The Saud family had already won similar autonomy for parts of Arabia in the early nineteenth century. The French began their occupation of Algeria in 1830. The Ottoman Empire was unable to hold on to its territories.

The Ottoman Empire was especially vulnerable to nationalistic revolts from within that were supported by resistance from without. The Ottomans had organized their conquered peoples in the *millet* **system**, which differentiated subjects by religious communities. Each *millet* had a religious leader responsible for enforcing its religious laws and customs and for collecting taxes on behalf of the imperial government. This opened the door to Western, industrializing powers to enter into Ottoman politics. Different religious groups within the empire looked outward to their coreligionists in other countries for protection, if they felt their rights and privileges were under attack. The Greek Orthodox community, in particular, looked toward Russia, Roman Catholics looked to France, and Protestants looked to Britain. Religious missions from these countries received special privileges within the Ottoman Empire, and often served as bases for trade and intelligence-gathering as well. Foreigners trading within the empire were permitted the right to trial by judges of their own nation.

The Ottoman theory and practice of government through religious communities was thus quite different from that of Western Europe, where the nation-state was becoming the norm. In addition, the Ottomans had not kept up with the industrial development of the rest of Europe. Because of its weaknesses, Western Europeans began to call the Ottoman Empire "the sick man of Europe." On the one hand, the other European empires welcomed and exploited Ottoman weakness. On the other it frightened them, because it threatened to embroil them in imperial adventurism, and in competition and conflict with one another.

Between 1839 and 1876, Sultan Abdul Mecid I and his successor enacted the *Tanzimat* (Restructuring) reforms to bring the Ottoman legal code and its social and educational standards into closer conformity with those of Western European states. The reforms were limited, and ultimately reversed, by the sultans' reluctance to give up too much power. They did, however, create a new, Western-oriented elite that

AT A GLANCE: THE WORLD BEYOND THE INDUSTRIALIZED WEST

DATE	OTTOMAN EMPIRE	INDIA, SOUTHEAST ASIA, CHINA	AFRICA
1800		• Sir Stamford Raffles establishes Singapore for the British (1819)	• British forces drive Napoleon from Egypt (1801); Muhammad Ali assumes rule (1807) • Shaka seizes leadership of Zulu kingdom near Cape Colony (1816)
1820	• Greece wins independence; Serbia, Wallachia, and Moldavia gain autonomy (1829) • French gain control of Algeria from empire (1830) • Muhammad Ali renders Egypt effectively independent (1832)	• Java War, Dutch vs. Indonesians (1825–30) • Dutch introduce cultivation system in Indonesia (1830) • First Opium War (1839–42): China cedes Hong Kong to the British	• Great Trek north by the Boers (Afrikaners) (1834–41) • French invade Algeria (1830); warfare with al-Qadir (1841)
1840	• Crimean War (1853–56) • Westernization encouraged in the Hatt-i Humayun edict (1856)	• Taiping Rebellion begins (1850); suppressed 1864 • "First War for National Independence" in India (1857) • Russians seize Amur River region (1858) • Second Opium War (1856–60): Beijing occupied by French and British	• David Livingstone lands along Angola coast for first African expedition (1841)
1860	• Young Turks go into exile (1876) • Russian attack through the Balkans reaches Istanbul (1877)	• Russians seize Maritime Provinces (1860) and Ili valley in Turkestan (1871–81)	• Suez Canal opens (1869) • Diamonds and gold discovered in the Cape Colony region • Egyptian *khedive* forced to add Europeans to his cabinet (1878)
1880		• France seizes all of Indochina (1883–93) • Germany annexes Eastern New Guinea and the Marshall and Solomon Islands (1880s) • Japan defeats China in warfare (1894–95) • Boxer Rebellion (1898–1900)	• Bismarck's Berlin Convention apportions Africa among competing powers (1884) • General Kitchener retakes Sudan in Battle of Omdurman (1898) • Rhodesia (now Zimbabwe and Zambia) named after Cecil John Rhodes (1898) • Boer War (1899–1902) • Ethiopia defeats Italian forces at Adowa (1896)
1900	• Italy takes Libya from weakened empire (1911)	• India's first steel mill at Jamshedpur, Bihar (1911) • Subcontinent has 35,000 miles of railroad track (1914)	• Maji-Maji revolt against German rule in Tanganyika (1905–07) • Belgian Parliament takes over control of the Congo (1908) • British form Union of South Africa (1910) • Natives Land Act closes 87 percent of South African land to African ownership (1913)

threatened traditional government and its administrative and military officials. After 1876, the Young Turks, as these reformers were called, were forced into exile.

Meanwhile, the Crimean War of 1853–56 revealed the perils of Ottoman weakness in the face of European imperial competition. France and Russia sought mutually conflicting concessions from the Ottomans for control over the Christian Holy Land. France based its claims on its protection of resident Roman Catholics and their interests, Russia on the protection of the Eastern Orthodox. In a further attempt to wrest more land from the Ottomans, in 1851 Russia also occupied regions of present-day Romania and Bulgaria, along the Danube River. The Ottomans proved unable to recover their territory, lost their fleet in warfare with Russia in 1853, and seemed vulnerable to still further losses. Britain and France came to their assistance, declaring war on Russia in 1854. The Italian regions of Sardinia-Piedmont, hoping to gain recognition for their attempts to unify Italy, also contributed troops to the British–French alliance. Although Austria remained neutral, its threats of joining the anti-Russian coalition weighed heavily in the Russian decision to abandon its hold not only on Romania and Serbia, but also on the Crimean peninsula, which it had taken from the Ottomans.

A new Russian attack through the Balkans reached Constantinople itself in 1877 and Britain threatened to counterattack. An international conference in Berlin

HOW DO WE KNOW?

What is Nationalism?

For most people in today's world, nationality is an important part of personal identity, and historians find nationalism to be a central concern of the past two centuries. Some stress the significance of particular forms of nationalism, others argue that national identity is, and can be, constantly shaped and reshaped. In this sense historians of national identity are similar to historians of gender identity: They not only wish to understand where we have been, they also want to use these explorations of the past as a means to search for alternative futures.

One of the first historians and philosophers of nationalism, the Frenchman Joseph-Ernest Renan (1823–92), captured the twofold nature of nationalism in his 1882 lecture, "What is a Nation?" It looks both backward and forward in creating a unified vision. Nationalism requires a fundamental shared history in the lives of the citizens, but the past alone is not enough for constructing a nation. That task requires also a vision of what the nation might become and a political commitment to constructing such a future. More dramatically, in considering the nation as a "spiritual principle," Renan asserted his belief that in his time nationalism was displacing religion as a central concern:

> A nation is a spiritual principle, the outcome of the profound complications of history; it is a spiritual family not a group determined by the shape of the earth. We have now seen what things are not [by themselves] adequate for the creation of such a spiritual principle, namely, race, language, material interest, religious affinities, geography, and military necessity. What [else] then is required? …
>
> A nation is therefore a large-scale solidarity, constituted by the feeling of the sacrifices that one has made in the past and of those that one is prepared to make in the future. It presupposes a past; it is summarized, however, in the present by a tangible fact, namely, consent, the clearly expressed desire to continue a common life.

More recently, anthropologist Benedict Anderson has referred to the nation as an "imagined political community," stressing the importance of human imagination, creativity, and persuasion—all expressed through the public media—as the means by which the idea of the nation is created, refined, and disseminated. "It is imagined because the members of even the smallest nation will never know most of their fellow-members, meet them, or even hear of them, yet in the minds of each lives the image of their communion" (Anderson, p. 15). For Anderson, as for Renan, the nation is not so much an entity existing in nature as it is an institution created by leaders who are successful in gaining acceptance for their idea of the nation.

In addition to Renan's "spiritual principle," modern nationalism comprises two additional elements. First, at least since the French Revolution, the modern nation exists in a world of other nations, frequently competitive with one another. To some degree, each nation defines itself in its relationship with others. Second, at least since the French Revolution and the Industrial Revolution, the nation has been the vehicle for the spread of trade networks and capitalism throughout the world. The significance of the nation in achieving economic goals has given great power to national identity.

- How well does Renan's concept of the nation as a "spiritual family" fit the nationalism expressed in the American Constitution? How well does it fit the nationalism of the various Italian and German spokesmen?
- How might a nation express its desire to continue a common life? How might it reject that desire?
- How does Renan's concept of a "spiritual family" compare with Anderson's idea of an "imagined community"? Are they actually referring to the same relationship but with different words, or are their concepts different?

The Kanûn-i Esâsî, the first constitution under Ottoman rule, 1876. Turkish postcard, 1895. As the Ottoman Empire grew weaker, and ever more dangerously under attack from foreign powers, a group of advisors prevailed upon Sultan Abdülhamid II to issue a constitution. Here the Sultan (to the woman's right), the Grand Vizier, and representatives of the *millets*, the parliamentary representatives of the major religious and social groups in the country, grant freedom (represented by a woman without any Islamic veil) to Turkey. Above flies an angel carrying a banner, written in Turkish with the motto "Liberty, Equality, Fraternity." In reality, the Sultan kept all significant power. The parliament created by the constitution was dissolved within a year of its establishment, and the empire continued to weaken.

resolved the conflict for the moment, but tensions ran high. The mixture of Ottoman weakness, aggressive expansionism on the part of other European countries, assertive nationalism in the Balkans, and increasing militarization with increasingly powerful weapons threatened to precipitate a larger war. It arrived in 1914.

American Nationalism

American nationalism and imperial expansion, set apart geographically from the Old World by vast oceans to the east and west, seemed to express a different political philosophy. Foreign observers, like France's Alexis de Tocqueville (1805–59), commented on the newness of America and its lack of history. A substantial proportion of America's institutions, and of its population, was drawn from the British Isles, but immigrants came from all over the world. Some, including Native American Indians, who had arrived thousands of years before the Europeans, African-American slaves, and women, were excluded from full citizenship. But the pattern for future inclusion was also being set. The United States Constitution declared that a nation is not necessarily comprised of people who share a common history, geography, language, race, ethnicity, religion, and language. A nation could be formed on the basis of a new vision of the present and future and adherence to a common law. Many (though not all) new immigrants could join this nation, and, after slaves were freed, so could they, although racism remained a powerful force of exclusion and discrimination. Native Americans remained torn between allegiances to Indian nations and the American nation. Despite these divisions, the American Constitution illustrated the degree to which a nation was constituted by the will of its people, and especially of its leaders, rather than by primordial historical legacies.

In 1861, 85 years after its establishment, the American nation was faced with a struggle for survival when the 11 Confederate States of America seceded from the Union. The Confederacy claimed greater rights for constituent states, especially the right to sanction slavery, and it favored agrarian rather than industrial economic policies.

Some 500,000 men died in the Civil War that followed. Immediately following the war, the victorious central government instituted generous policies favoring reconciliation (often at the expense of the recently freed ex-slaves), although later these policies became more punitive. After the war, with unity secure, and northeastern business leaders asserting great powers, the industrial and economic expansion of the United States set a pace exceeding that of any other nation.

The New Nations of Italy and Germany

In the heart of Europe, nationalism grew in hard soil. The great powers of Austria, Prussia, Russia, France, and Britain suppressed national uprisings by peoples within their empires. When they drafted the peace settlements at the Congress of Vienna in 1814–15, after the Napoleonic Wars, they set limits on national movements in central Europe. A generation later, led by Prince Clemens von Metternich (1773–1859), foreign minister of Austria, conservative leaders of the major European powers successfully quelled powerful nationalistic uprisings in Poland, Prussia, Italy, and Hungary between 1846 and 1849. (Belgium did gain national independence, from the Dutch, in 1830.) Only in the 1850s did nationalism win major victories in lands under these empires. Then Italy and Germany began successfully to unite their several divided regions to form new nations. In each country, cultural nationalism preceded political mobilization.

The unification of Italy and Germany. The middle years of the nineteenth century saw popular forces drawing together the disparate territories of central Europe into modern nation-states. In Germany the political, military, and economic strength of Prussia had been growing for over two centuries, and Bismarck's wars with Denmark (1864), Austria (1866), and France (1870) eventually secured the union. In Italy the expansion of Sardinia-Piedmont into Lombardy, Venetia, and Rome, and Garibaldi's march through the south, united the nation.

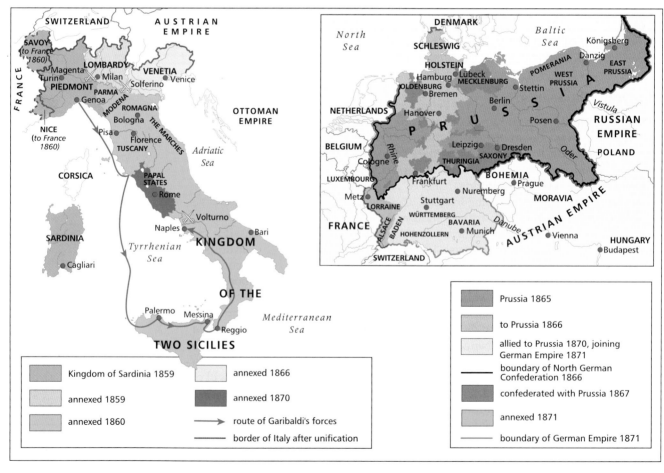

Before 1870, neither Italy nor Germany existed as the unified nations we know today. Each was divided up into many petty states under the control of different rulers. In Italy, the largest single state was the kingdom of Sardinia-Piedmont, but other states were controlled by other rulers. The area around Venice was controlled by Austria, and the region around Rome by the pope. Most of the small states of Germany had been included within Charlemagne's empire, founded in 800 C.E., and then within its successor institution, the Holy Roman Empire. Each of these states had its own ruler and even its own system of government. The largest, Austria, was in itself a significant state. The smallest had only a few thousand inhabitants. In addition, to the east lay Prussia, a powerful state that was beginning to think of itself as the leader of the German-speaking peoples.

As nation-states formed in Western Europe and demonstrated the economic, political, military, and cultural power that came from unity, regional leaders in Italy and Germany also sought unification for themselves. A common language and clearly demarcated geographical borders were considered vital elements in national unity, and were helpful to Italy in consolidating its peninsular nation. Germany, however, lacked clear natural geographic boundaries and faced the question as to which German-speaking states would be included within the new country and which would not.

Giuseppe Mazzini (1805–72) provided a prophetic vision for Italy. In 1831 he founded Young Italy, a secret association urging Italian unification and independence from foreign control by the French, Austrians, and Spanish. Mazzini's *On the Duties of Man* expressed his nationalistic, democratic, and humanistic views:

Statue of Giuseppe Garibaldi by Urbano Lucchesi in Lucca, Italy, nineteenth century. Giuseppe Garibaldi led a small army that conquered various independent regions of Rome and brought them under the unified rule of King Victor Emmanuel II. By 1860 virtually all of modern Italy had been brought together, except the Papal States centered on Rome, which were conquered—all except Vatican City—and annexed in 1870. Virtually every city and town in Italy has a statue of Garibaldi on prominent display.

> O my brothers, love your Country! Our country is our Home, the House that God has given us, placing therein a numerous family that loves us, and whom we love; a family with whom we sympathize more readily, and whom we understand more quickly, than we do others; and which, from its being centered round a given spot, and from the homogeneous nature of its elements, is adapted to a special branch of activity. (Columbia University, p. 570)

When Mazzini's cultural view was joined to the political organization of Camillo Cavour (1810–61), prime minister of Sardinia-Piedmont in 1852 under King Victor Emmanuel II, the nationalist movement was poised for political victory. Cavour formed a brief alliance with Napoleon III of France against Austria. This enabled the king to annex Lombardy. The adjacent regions of Parma, Modena, and Tuscany joined the kingdom in 1860 following a plebiscite, or popular vote. In the same year, the charismatic military commander Giuseppe Garibaldi (1807–82) led 1,150 followers, wearing red shirts, into the south Italian Kingdom of the Two Sicilies, which collapsed and subsequently joined Piedmont after a plebiscite. Venetia, the region around Venice, was added after a war in which Italy allied with Prussia against Austria. Finally, Rome was annexed in 1870 after French troops, which had protected the papal territories, were withdrawn to fight against Prussia. Through the various contributions of Mazzini, Cavour, Garibaldi, Victor Emmanuel II, Napoleon III, war, and popular votes, Italy had become a unified nation.

BISMARCK

« Je l'ai saisi ; j'ai mis l'écriteau sur ton front ;
et maintenant la foule accourt et te bafoue. »

French cartoon portraying Prince Otto Eduard Leopold von Bismarck, Prime Minister of Prussia, 1870. Political figures have traditionally been treated irreverently by cartoonists, but this caricature is savage. The French were outraged by Bismarck's ambitions to have the Prussian Prince Leopold on the Spanish throne—a key factor in the war between the two countries in 1870–71.

At about the same time, Prime Minister Otto von Bismarck of Prussia (1815–98) was unifying the multitude of small German states into a single German nation under William I (king of Prussia 1861–88, emperor of Germany 1871–88). The cultural basis of German unity was solidly established. The brothers Jakob and Wilhelm Grimm, founders of the modern science of linguistics, had analyzed the various German dialects and collected fairy tales from all parts of the region, publishing them in 1812 as a unifying folklore for the nation. And just as Mazzini had done in Italy, German historian and philosopher Heinrich von Treitschke (1834–96) urged Germany to fulfill its natural destiny as a unified, authoritarian, imperial power.

From 1828 a customs union, *zollverein*, that created a free trade area throughout many of the German states, had established an economic foundation for unification. Increasing industrialization provided the financial and military underpinnings for it. Now Bismarck instituted a policy of **blood and iron**. Two wars were the key. In 1866, Bismarck defeated Austria and formed the North German Confederation, excluding Austria. In 1871, he defeated France, annexing Alsace and Lorraine. In light of these victories the southern states of Germany—Bavaria, Baden, and Württemberg—also joined the newly formed nation.

The Rise of Zionism in Europe

One of the last of the nationalist movements to arise in nineteenth-century Europe was Zionism, the movement to recreate a Jewish homeland. Jews had been dispersed into Europe even during the time of the Roman Empire. By the beginning of the twentieth century, their principal European locations were in central and eastern Europe, in Poland, Russia, and Ukraine, although Western Europe also held important Jewish communities. Through the centuries Jews had prayed for a return to Zion, their ancestral homeland in modern Israel. In the second half of the nineteenth century, under the influence of various European nationalist movements, some philosophers proposed going beyond prayer. They looked forward to the establishment of a political state.

The move from prayer to political organization took concrete form towards the end of the nineteenth century. Suffering from **pogroms** in the Russian Empire and discrimination in much of the Austro–Hungarian Empire, Jews felt increasingly persecuted. On assignment in Paris to report on the trial of Alfred Dreyfus, a Jewish officer in the French army unjustly accused of treason, the Viennese Jewish journalist Theodor Herzl (1860–1904) encountered fierce anti-Semitism. Shocked to find such ethnic and religious hatred in the capital of the liberal world, where Jews had gained citizenship during the French Revolution, Herzl concluded that Jews could be free, independent, and safe only in a country of their own. In 1897, he founded the Zionist movement. Because Palestine, the goal of most of the early Zionists, was already the home of 600,000 Arabs, Jewish nationalism simultaneously, if unintentionally, took the form of a colonizing movement originating in Europe. Not all Jews embraced Zionism, although as discrimination and persecution increased in the twentieth century, the Zionist dream became an increasingly desirable alternative to remaining in Europe.

Failed Nationalisms and Delayed Nationalisms

Historians usually record the accomplishments of successful nationalist movements. These create states whose histories demand attention and, sometimes, admiration. But many nationalist movements fail, perhaps most of them. They never generate enough enthusiasm to bring their wishes to fruition, especially as they often face enormous obstacles: Smaller regions within larger states, perhaps with their own languages and cultures, reject membership in the larger political structure and undercut its nationalism in favor of their own. These smaller regions may succeed in creating their own, smaller states. On the other hand, if a proposed state is too small or too weak, it will not succeed in winning a place against the opposition of larger states or empires that wish to swallow it, or at least to carve it up into still smaller units that the larger states can control.

Sometimes nationalisms are suppressed and defeated for very long periods of time but then emerge successful, in the form of new, or reborn, political nations. These long-delayed successes serve as inspirations to proponents of other nationalisms to continue their struggles even when they seem to be defeated. They keep hopes alive.

The Disappearance of Poland

Take, for example, Poland. In the mid-eighteenth century, civil war and Russian territorial grabs so weakened the government of Poland that it could not resist partition and the further loss of territory. In 1772 Poland's neighbors, Russia, Prussia, and Austria, divided among themselves about one-third of Poland's land and half of its population. By 1791, Poland was regaining strength, but then confrontations over a new, liberal constitution led the conservatives to seek Russian assistance in national politics. Both Russia and Prussia intervened, dispatching troops, which dismembered the country in a second partition, with the Russians again taking the lion's share. The Poles revolted against these losses in an armed struggle led by Tadeusz Kosciuszko. They were crushed by Russia and Prussia. The victors combined with Austria in a third partition of Poland in 1797. This time nothing was left. The nation of Poland disappeared from the map of Europe, to return only in 1918, recreated by the peace treaties following World War I.

Africa, West and East: The Rise and Fall of States

In Africa, a series of religious movements for the purification of Islam led to the establishment of new, religion-based states, and even empires, in the eighteenth century. By about 1900, however, these states came into confrontation with expanding European colonialism, which defeated and dismembered them.

In the Sahel, the dry, semi-desert area immediately south of the Sahara, stretching from the Atlantic Ocean to the Red Sea, political and religious movements of Islamic revival flourished. Most of them were directed at keeping Muslims loyal to the faith and bringing polytheistic Africans under Muslim rule. They were not aimed at confronting Christianity. Some historians do believe, however, that the movements drew some of their inspiration from the knowledge among the Muslims that the regional balance of political power was shifting from an increasingly weak Muslim Middle East and Africa to an increasingly powerful Christian Europe. The formation of states, and sometimes empires, would help in monitoring religious behavior among Muslims and in resisting Christian inroads.

KEY TERMS

blood and iron Bismarck's policy of using warfare against enemies as a means of unifying his new nation. Subsequently the term has been used to designate the policy of any government committed to foreign warfare as a means of internal unification.

pogrom A murderous attack on a group of people—usually based on their ethnicity or religion—that is sanctioned by the government, either officially or unofficially.

In West Africa three movements stand out for special attention. They began in states founded in the eighteenth century by the Fulani peoples. In Hausaland, modern northern Nigeria, Usman dan Fodio (1754–1817), a prominent sufi teacher, condemned the rulers for corruption, sacrilege, persecution of true Muslims, and polytheistic practices. For years dan Fodio organized his opposition, gathering supporters from nearby groups. Frustrated by the inconsistent responses he received from the Hausaland rulers, dan Fodio urged his followers to arm themselves for coming conflict. The outbreak of hostilities began when a new sultan attacked a group of dan Fodio's followers in 1804. More a religious leader than a general, dan Fodio called on his son and his brother to lead the military campaigns that ultimately brought all of Hausaland under his control from the new capital at Sokoto. The Sokoto empire tended to favor Fulani people over Hausa, even though not all of the Fulani were Muslims. For the most part, however, it encouraged both Fulani and Hausa to unite in a single Islamic empire. Sokoto carried on commerce with the British, agreeing to a trade treaty in 1853 and conceding further privileges in 1885. In 1903, however, British forces assaulted Sokoto, defeating the kingdom and incorporating it into their own administration. The descendants of dan Fodio continue on today, however, primarily in religious roles, as nominal sultans of Sokoto and leaders of the Islamic community of the region.

Other *jihads*, or holy wars, were smaller in geographical and military scale. They were usually concerned with purifying the Islamic faith and practices of rulers and subjects. These included *jihads* in West Africa in the small states of Futa Toro, Futa Jallon, and the somewhat larger Massina. In Massina, al-Hajj Umar (*c.* 1794–1864), having returned from a pilgrimage to Mecca, and having visited Sokoto, gathered followers and armed them. ("Al-Hajj" or "el-Hajj" is the title earned by someone who has completed the *hajj* pilgrimage to Mecca.) Umar captured the kingdom of Massina and made it the center of his empire. He attempted to gain support from the French on the coast of West Africa, but they were unwilling. When he subsequently attacked French river traders, perhaps seeking to capture their guns, the French-controlled armed forces repulsed his attack.

Another leader who built an empire in the name of Islam, Samori Toure (*c.* 1830–1900), organized Mandinka and Diola ethnic groups under his military leadership. Although at one point he declared himself *almami*, or leader of the faithful, his devotion to Islam was sometimes compromised by battles against fellow Muslims and his murder of Muslim scholars in his capture of the town of Kong. Toure's empire, just south of the bend of the Niger River, as well as the empire founded by al-Hajj Umar, was situated in the path of French imperial conquest eastward from the Atlantic. In 1893–94, both were defeated and brought under French control. Although Toure's record is marred by his raiding for slaves (in order to barter them for guns), by his scorched-earth policy of retreat before the French, and by his destruction of Kong, the town to which he transferred his capital as he retreated, he is nevertheless credited by most historians as a guerrilla leader who held off the French for two years in his original empire and for two more in his second empire. In 1898 the French captured him and exiled him to Gabon, where he died in 1900.

In East Africa, near Khartoum, a religious leader named Muhammad Ahmed declared that he was the Mahdi, a messiah figure who would bring a new age that would restore the true religion. In 1881, he began to build a state in the Sudan. The Mahdi began his movement in opposition to the Egyptian government, but in 1882 the British reentered Egypt, seized Cairo, and claimed the Nile valley as effective rulers of the region. The British and the Mahdi were on a collision course. At first the Mahdi and his military leadership were victorious. In 1885, they defeated an Egyptian force commanded by British General Charles Gordon at Khartoum. Later that year the Mahdi died, leaving his state to a successor who, though Muslim, was far less militant than the founder. For some time Britain did not respond to this new state and its political and military successes. A decade later, however, it sent another force under General Horatio Herbert Kitchener to retake the Sudan for Egypt and to avenge Gordon's defeat and death. At Omdurman, Kitchener's army destroyed the Mahdists, killing 11,000 men and wounding 16,000 in a single battle on September 2, 1898, while losing just 40 of its own soldiers. Such was the power of the Maxim machine gun against an army that believed that their religious faith would make them impervious to bullets. Kitchener then proceeded to reclaim Khartoum. The total imbalance of military force and strategy between the British and the Muslim forces could not have been more clear, and neither could the willingness of the African Muslims to fight and die for their cause and their religion.

Egyptian Loss of Independence

Egypt, of course, is part of Africa, but, unlike the Islamic states just discussed, its experience in state-building came far more from its involvement with Europe. It tried to model its nationalism on what it learned from Europe. It failed to carry through its plans for modernizing its economy and politics, however, in large part because of European manipulation. As a result, it lost its independence to European colonialism.

Napoleon's invasion of Egypt in 1798 was influential, but very brief. Egyptian nationalists, backed by Ottoman and British military forces, drove them out by 1801. Two years later, the British also withdrew their troops. To lead the battles against the French, the Ottoman sultan had called in a troop of Albanian cavalry. After the fighting, its commander, Muhammad (Mehemet) Ali (1769–1849), took over the rule of Egypt, although he served nominally as a viceroy of the Ottoman Empire. Muhammad Ali introduced some new industries and then decided to concentrate on the cultivation of cotton as a cash crop for Europe's booming textile industry. To enable year-round cultivation, he built extensive new irrigation works. He also encouraged the development of Egypt's own textile mills. For the most part, he kept this economic modernization in the hands of the state rather than private entrepreneurs. He streamlined the administration and built a system of secular state schools to train administrators and officers, especially by training students in Western scholarship. He introduced a government printing press, which in turn encouraged translations of European books into Arabic.

A professional soldier, Muhammad Ali modernized the army and marched his newly equipped forces up the Nile, captured the Sudan, and established his capital in the city of Khartoum, in 1830. He also gained control of the holy cities of Mecca and Medina in Arabia to counter the power of the militantly Islamic Wahabi movement there. Fundamentally secular in outlook, Muhammad Ali attempted to reach accommodation with the moderate Islamic forces in Egypt rather than attack them or bring them around to his own perspectives. Muhammad Ali's son, Ishmail, succeeded him and commissioned a French firm to build the Suez Canal, which was opened in 1869. His grandson expanded Egyptian territorial holdings both eastward along the coast of the Red Sea and southward, inland, toward the headwaters of the Nile.

Muhammad Ali's modernization program brought mixed results. Egypt entered the international economy based in Europe, but soon was spending more on imports, military modernization, and beautification projects in Cairo than it was earning in exports. In addition, Egypt adopted an economic policy of encouraging monoculture, specializing in a single crop for export, in this case fine-quality cotton. This decision left the country vulnerable to the instability of international price

607

fluctuations on this single crop. As Egyptian debts rose, European creditors pressured their governments to force the *khedive* (the title given to Muhammad Ali and his successors) to appoint European experts as Commissioners of the Debt in 1876. In 1878 the *khedive* was forced to add French and British representatives to the cabinet. In 1881 the European powers went further. They had the Ottoman sultan dismiss the khedive, Muhammad Ali's grandson. When an Egyptian military revolt then seized power, Britain sent in its forces, primarily to protect the Suez Canal. They stayed on as the power behind the throne until the 1950s. For Egypt, entanglement with Europe proved a two-edged sword. It spurred economic and political nationalism, but then subverted and crippled it.

The European Quest for Empire

Nationalism triumphed in creating powerful modern nation-states, but at the cost of fierce and violent competition among them. Similarly, the emergence of a global capitalist marketplace was also based on sharp competition, much of it between joint stock companies, backed by their home governments. The Industrial Revolution intensified the competition, first between industrialized and nonindustrialized countries, such as Britain and India, and later among the newly industrializing nations and their industrialists.

European imperialism, to 1870. By the middle of the nineteenth century, revolutions had brought independence to most of the Americas. With Africa largely impenetrable, European imperialists focused on Asia. Russia had spread across Siberia to the Pacific, and the United States extended from the Atlantic to the Pacific, while Britain controlled India, South Africa, Australia, and New Zealand. In 1867 Canada achieved "dominion" status, virtual political independence.

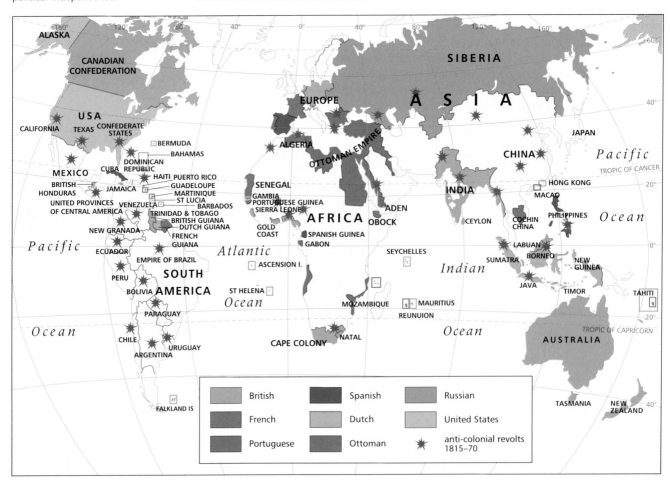

The greatest competition for imperial power took place overseas, beyond the borders of Europe. Empires were not new, of course, but advanced technology and new strategies of financial and economic dominance multiplied their power. By 1914, peoples of Europe and of European ancestry had settled and were ruling, directly or indirectly, 85 percent of the earth's land surface: Canada, the United States, most of Latin America, Siberia, Australia, New Zealand, and substantial parts of South Africa by invasion, settlement, and conquest; most of India, Southeast Asia, and Africa

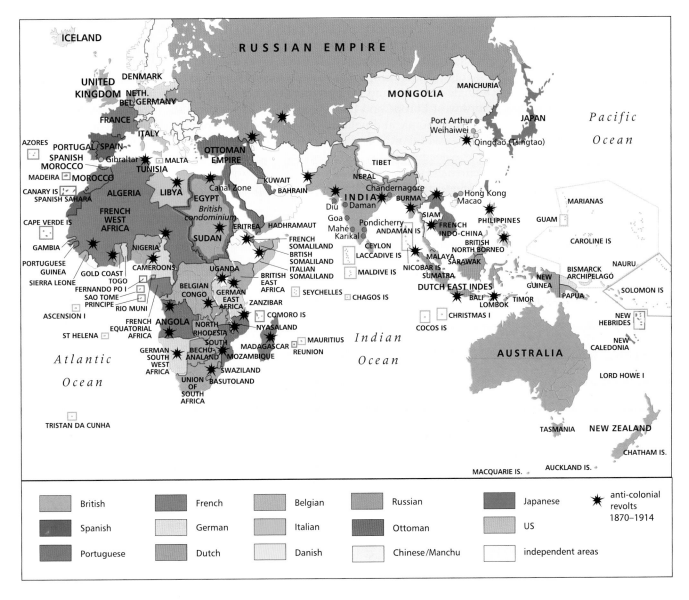

European and other empires in 1914. By the beginning of World War I, European imperialism had reached its zenith, with four-fifths of the globe under the direct political control of Europeans or people of European ancestry. Only Antarctica remained unclaimed. Although this power was sustained by technological, naval, and military superiority, insurrections were widespread and increasingly well organized. Imperial trade established a global economic system and spread European cultural values. Japan consciously pursued the European modern of imperial expansion by conquering Korea and Taiwan. China was under the control of the Manchus, who had invaded from the north in 1644 and ruled through the Qing dynasty.

world system A theory held by some social scientists concerning the political and economic organization of the world in modern times. According to world system theory, a few countries, the "core," dominated most of the others, "the periphery," and exploited them. During the period of imperialism this dominance was both political and economic. Afterward it was mostly economic, taking the form of neocolonialism.

social Darwinism A theory popularized by Herbert Spencer, based on a misreading of Charles Darwin's theory of the survival of the fittest. Darwin argued that those plants and animals best suited to a particular environment survived best in that environment. Spencer took this to mean that whichever creatures were dominant *ought to be* dominant. For example, the rich and powerful deserved to be rich and powerful; conversely, the poor and powerless deserved their low status.

White Man's Burden A concept, based on the title of a poem by Rudyard Kipling, that white man was superior to people of color, and that it was their duty to rule over them, serve them, and improve them. The concept was often invoked to justify a colonial system that was, in fact, hugely exploitative, a situation not mentioned in the poem.

by direct rule over indigenous populations; China mostly by indirect rule. The map on p. 609 indicates the holdings of each major imperial power in the eastern hemisphere. British holdings were so widespread—from India, to Australia and New Zealand, to Africa—that it was said that "the sun never sets on the British Empire." The French dominated West Africa, beginning with regions directly across the Mediterranean from France itself, and important parts of Southeast Asia.

Many regions of the world, such as Latin America, were nominally independent, but in fact their economies were controlled by European financial investors and their governments, especially the British. Some states, such as Russia and the Ottoman Empire, were dominated in large part by capital from northwestern Europe, although they also, in turn, held their own colonial areas. An important school of political thought, led by Immanuel Wallerstein, gives the term "**world system**" to these newly emerging relationships that brought together many different areas of the world into a single economic and political framework of inequality. According to this viewpoint, northwest Europe and the United States had become the core regions, dominating world economic and political power, while most of the rest of the world, excepting Japan, was subordinated into their periphery.

The leading states of Western Europe—especially Britain, France, and the Netherlands—had achieved their power through their "dual revolutions," political and industrial. Politically and socially they had achieved, or seemed to be in the process of achieving:

- consolidated nation-states;
- parliamentary democracies;
- bureaucratic administrations;
- freedom of the press, assembly, and religion;
- freedom from wrongful arrest and torture; and
- increased levels of literacy and general, public education.

Economically and industrially, they had achieved or seemed to be in the process of achieving:

- high levels of productivity;
- competence in new methods of science and technology;
- relatively high levels of health and of medical care;
- an integrated world economy;
- powerful weaponry;
- high levels of trade and international exchange; and
- high levels of economic entrepreneurship and legal protection of property.

Western Europeans began to define themselves as people who had mastered these qualities, in contrast to the peoples whom they were colonizing and dominating, who lacked them. Misinterpreting Charles Darwin, some believed that their power was a phenomenon of nature. Charles Darwin (1809–82) shook much of the Christian world when he published *On the Origin of Species* in 1859. In this work he suggested that the various forms of life on earth had developed over millions of years through the mechanism of natural selection, which allowed some species to survive while others died out (see Chapter One). Soon after Darwin's work appeared, the philosopher Herbert Spencer (1820–1903) (mis)represented Darwin's concept of "survival of the fittest" as a doctrine that explained and justified the rule by the strong over the weak. Spencer's "**social Darwinism**" argued that those who were strong deserved their superiority, while those who were weak deserved their inferiority. Spencer also believed that Europeans belonged to particular races and that these races were more advanced than those of other regions. He thoroughly approved of the existing social-political order that confirmed wealthy, powerful, white, male Europeans in positions of dominance. Rudyard Kipling's "The **White Man's Burden**," published in 1899, set these beliefs in verse:

> Take up the White Man's burden—
> Send forth the best ye breed—
> Go bind your sons to exile
> To serve your captives' need;
> To wait in heavy harness,
> On fluttered folk and wild—
> Your new-caught, sullen peoples,
> Half-devil and half-child.

Kipling argued that Europeans had an obligation to bring their civilization to those they conquered, although he saw this civilizing mission as a thankless task. Kipling's poem, perhaps naively, perhaps self-righteously, perhaps sarcastically, cites only the moral burdens of colonization without any references to its economic and political profits for the colonizer.

The British in India

The British East India Company had come to India in the seventeenth century to buy spices and hand-made cotton textiles in exchange for bullion, wool, and metals. The Mughal government of India granted the Company permission to trade, and through the seventeenth century it established trading posts, called factories, in crucial port locations, first at Surat on India's west coast, and then at Madras (now Chennai) (1639), Bombay (now Mumbai) (1661), and Calcutta (now Kolkata) (1690). During the eighteenth century, the Mughal imperial government began to weaken. Mughal overexpansion in south India drained the empire of funds and manpower, and alienated rural landlords whose taxes were increased. In addition, Emperor Aurangzeb (r. 1659–1707) imposed special taxes on non-Muslims, which his predecessors had not done, provoking rebellions in several regions of his Hindu-majority country. As the empire weakened, various regional contestants for power sought alliances with the British in their well-fortified trading outposts.

The British were not the only European power active in India. The French, too, controlled fortified trading posts along the coasts and entered into alliances with regional Indian powers. The general warfare that engulfed the two nations elsewhere (1744–48) pulled them into conflict in India as well. Led by brilliant military strategists, Joseph Francis Dupleix for the French and Robert Clive for the English, each side won significant battles, but ultimately Clive proved victorious and the French decided to cut back their Indian commitments. When warfare resumed in India, as a result of the Seven Years War (1755–63), a global struggle between Britain and France, the British easily defeated the French to emerge as the principal European power in India.

As Mughal central authority weakened, several rebellious leaders in the provinces sought alliances with the British to break free of Mughal control. They offered the British a share in their tax collections and political authority. In several regions the British accepted these invitations to alliance and, beginning in Bengal with the Battle of Plassey (1757), they soon gained control of large areas of the country. The British East India Company itself became the instrument of rule, since it was the institutional representative of the British in India. In London, the British Parliament established a Board of Control to oversee the activities of the Company, but in large measure this joint stock trading company had become the political master of large, and increasing, regions of Indian territory.

The Company in Charge. As a commercial enterprise, the Company's principal motive was the acquisition of profits, and now, as rulers, they adopted two policies to maximize them. First, they increased tax collection, both by raising rates and by increasing the efficiency of collection. Second, they manipulated tariffs, lowering them in India so that British manufactures would have easy access to Indian markets, and lobbying to raise them in Britain in order to block the import of Indian textiles. The beginning of Britain's Industrial Revolution and of the Company's establishment of control over large regions of India occurred at approximately the same time, in the second half of the eighteenth century. Colonial control thus immediately protected and facilitated the development of British industry, while effectively blocking Indian competition.

India was transformed into the model colony, importing manufactured goods from Britain's industries and exporting raw materials to its factories and distribution centers: raw cotton, which the British manufactured into cloth; jute for making sacks; leather; and enormous quantities of tea, as India displaced China as the leading provider of tea to Europe. Throughout the second half of the nineteenth century and the first years of the twentieth, two-thirds of India's imports from Britain were machine-manufactured textiles. Iron and steel goods came second. India became a lucrative destination for overseas investment, and about 20 percent of all overseas British investment in the late nineteenth century was in India.

Indian Industry. India's own taxes, however, paid for the building and maintenance of the Indian railway system, one of the most extensive in the world, with some 35,000 miles of track by 1914. The railway system in India made possible a range of diverse activities: the widespread deployment of colonial troops, increased commerce that benefited both Indians and British businessmen, the relief of famine through the shipping of food from areas of surplus harvests to areas of shortfall, the geographical spread of political dissidence, and pilgrimage visits to religious shrines throughout the country. Demonstrating the power of colonial rule, the British manufactured all of the components of the system—engines, cars, tracks—in Britain. Thus, even though the financing was drawn from Indian taxes, the profits of the manufacture, the

Victoria Terminus Railway Station, Bombay. Named in honor of the British Queen and Empress of India, and opened on the date of her Golden Jubilee, 1887, it is now renamed Chatrapati Shivaji Station, Mumbai. Built in Gothic style as the headquarters for the great Indian Peninsular Railway, the station resembles St. Pancras Station in London. British architecture in India often copied models from the home country, especially in buildings dedicated to modern industry and transportation.

SOURCE

"The Attack of King Industry"

Communities in India that were already active in business provided many of the new industrialists. Indian financiers became industrialists by importing the new industrial machinery ready-made from Europe. In Ahmedabad, the capital of Gujarat, local businessmen, led by an administrator with close ties to British entrepreneurs, followed Mumbai (Bombay) in establishing a local cotton textile industry in 1861.

A few years earlier Dalpatram Kavi, a local poet and intellectual leader, had called on his fellow countrymen to recognize the importance of industry to their future. His Gujarati poem, "Hunnarkhan-ni Chadayi" ("The Attack of King Industry"), presents a far-reaching agenda for reform centering on industrial change and proposes social restructuring as well. It suggests that the British had brought much of value to India and that Indians were prepared to absorb and implement some of this legacy, but without the British imperial presence and its costs.

Fellow countrymen, let us remove all the miseries of our country,
Do work, for the new kingdom has come. Its king is industry.

Our wealth has gone into the hands of foreigners. The great blunder is yours
For you did not unite yourselves—fellow countrymen.

Consider the time, see for yourselves. All our people have become poor,
Many men of business have fallen—fellow countrymen.

Put away idleness. Fill the treasuries with knowledge.
Now awake and work new wonders—fellow countrymen.

With kith and kin keep harmony. Do not enter into debt.
Limit the dinners for your caste—fellow countrymen.

Introduce industry from countries abroad and master the modern machinery.
Please attend to this plea from the Poet Dalpat—fellow countrymen.

(trans. Chimanbhai Trivedi and Howard Spodek)

expertise in engineering, and the industrial plant that built the railway industry went to Britain rather than to India.

Under British colonial rule, India began its own industrial revolution with cotton textiles, primarily in Bombay. This textile industry was started mostly by local Gujaratis, inhabitants of the western Indian region of Gujarat, who had long family histories of involvement in business. The need to found new industries to compete with the British found expression even in local poetry, as "The Attack of King Industry" makes clear (see box above). (In Calcutta, where jute textiles were produced, industry was largely pioneered by British investors.) Mining began in the coal fields of Bengal, Bihar, Orissa, and Assam, and in 1911 the Tata family of Bombay—a Parsi family, descendants of immigrants from Persia who had come to India in the eighth century—built India's first steel mill at Jamshedpur, Bihar. At the start of World War I, factory employment in all of India had reached about a million (out of a total population of about 300 million). While employment in large, mechanized factories was increasing, many hand craftsmen were being displaced, so the actual percentage of people earning their living by manufacturing of all sorts stayed approximately the same, at about ten percent of the workforce (and has continued about the same until today).

British Imperial Rule. In 1857 Indians revolted against rule by the British East India Company. The British called this a "mutiny" of army troops, but later scholars have shown it to be a more geographically widespread and more general opposition to British rule. Although some nationalist historians have called it "India's First War for National Independence," the revolt lacked unified leadership and direction. The British crushed the revolt, and from then onward they ruled India directly, imposing their influence throughout the administrative and educational systems of the country.

A map of the town and environs of Singapore, from an actual survey by G.D. Coleman, 1839. Singapore was not an indigenous town that gradually grew up around a bustling port; it was purposely founded in 1819 on the site of a fishing village by Sir Stamford Raffles, who saw its potential as a trading center. The British actively encouraged immigration to the new port, and divided the thriving city into separate areas for the different ethnic groups that lived and worked there. The divisions can be seen clearly on the map.

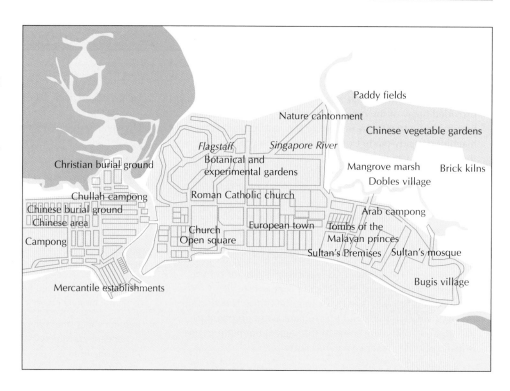

Concepts based on European political revolutions were introduced directly and indirectly through the formal secondary and post-secondary education system, the law courts, the press, and even through very limited elections. English replaced Persian as the official language of government. As a result, imperialism confronted its internal contradiction: How could an imperial power preach and teach the values of self-rule and democracy while maintaining its own foreign rule?

The British in Burma, Malaya, and Singapore

Although India was the "jewel in the crown" of Britain's colonial possessions, Burma and Malaya had their importance as well. Neighboring Burma was annexed in a series of wars, in 1826, 1852, and 1885, and administered by the British from its Indian headquarters until 1935. The British turned the colony into a major exporter of rice, timber, teak, and oil and developed the port of Rangoon to handle the trade. Further east, in Malaya, the British established a settlement at Penang in 1786; took Malacca from the Dutch in 1795; and established Singapore in 1819 as their major port in the region. They developed commercially profitable methods for extracting and exporting Malayan tin and turned Malaya's rubber plantations into the world's largest producers. They built up their port at Singapore into one of the largest and most geopolitically important ports in the world. Malaya and Burma, like India, became classic colonies, exporting raw materials to the colonizers and importing finished products from them.

Europeans in China, 1800–1914

Colonialism in China was different. To discuss colonialism in this period in China, we must begin not with the Europeans but with the Manchus, who established the Qing dynasty (1644–1911) and were enthusiastic colonizers. Even before they invaded and ruled China, the Manchus had established a state in their homeland of Manchuria, made Korea a vassal state, and controlled Inner Mongolia as a dependency. After establishing their rule in China, the Qing dynasty expanded westward, annexing new lands equal to the size of China itself (see Chapter Fifteen). They also conquered Taiwan and subordinated the peoples of Southeast Asia into tributary relationships.

		areas of influence
Qing (Manchu) Empire in 1850	other 19th-century revolts	Russian
British attacks during Opium War 1839-42	treaty ports	Japanese
area of Taiping rebellion 1850-64		French
area of Nien rebellion 1853-68		British
area of Boxer uprising 1900-01		German

The decline of the Qing dynasty. During the course of the nineteenth century, the authority of the Qing (Manchu) dynasty in China was undermined. Beset by the aggressive actions of European colonial powers, the Qing granted extensive trade and territorial concessions. Internally, a series of increasingly violent rebellions, both within the Chinese heartland and in the western (often Muslim) regions, brought the dynasty to the verge of collapse by the turn of the century.

The steamer *Nemesis* destroying 11 Chinese junks at Cherpez, Canton, China. E. Duncan, 1843. The two separate wars fought between Britain and China in the 1840s and 1850s began when the Chinese government tried to prevent British merchants from illegally importing opium. The British responded militarily, precipitating the Opium Wars (1839–42). (National Maritime Museum, Canada)

Revolts broke out against Manchu rule, but until 1800 they occurred mostly at the periphery of the empire and posed no serious threat to the dynasty.

The very size, power, and historical eminence of China created a sense of invulnerability. But China's leaders were not keeping up with changes taking place in the outside world that would soon intrude upon them. In 1793, for example, the Emperor Qianlong sent a letter to King George III of England, dismissing his request to open trade relations between the two countries: "There is nothing we lack … nor do we need any more of your country's manufactures" (Teng and Fairbank, p. 19). Although the emperor may have been exaggerating his independence for his own propaganda purposes, as some historians argue, the Chinese willingness to learn from the outside world was quite limited.

Meanwhile, by the early 1800s China faced a range of internal problems that demanded attention. A continuously rising population put pressure on resources and government administrative capacity. The 100 million people of 1650 had tripled to 300 million by 1800 and reached 420 million by 1850. More land was needed. Developing Manchuria seemed a suitable reply to the problem, but the Manchus would not permit Chinese settlement in their homeland. Nor did the Manchus increase the size of their bureaucracy to service the rising population, preferring to delegate administrative responsibilities to local authorities, a response that was inadequate.

One strength of the Chinese economy was the sale of tea, silk, and porcelains to the West in exchange for silver and gold. The Europeans trading with China, however, wished to staunch this outflow of bullion. Discovering that China would accept opium in place of precious metals, the British encouraged the growth of opium in their Indian colony and shipped it to China. The centuries of paying for Chinese exports with silver and gold came to an end. By the 1820s China was purchasing so much opium that it began to export silver!

The Opium Wars. Fearing for the health of both its people and its treasury, China banned the import of opium in 1839. It was too late. Proclaiming the ideology of "free trade," the British rejected the Chinese demand. When the incorruptible Imperial Commissioner Lin Zexu tried to confiscate and destroy the British stores of opium, British shipboard cannon shelled Chinese ships and port installations in the harbor at Guangzhou (Canton). This Opium War of 1839–42 was no contest; the Chinese emperors' lack of interest in Western science and technology meant that China lacked both modern cannons and steamships. In defeat, China ceded to Britain the island of Hong Kong as a colony and opened five treaty ports in which foreigners could live and conduct business under their own laws rather than under the laws of China. France and the United States soon gained similar concessions. Foreign settlements were established in the new treaty ports and became the centers of new industry, education, and publishing. The focus of international trade began to relocate from Guangzhou to the foreign settlements at Shanghai, at the mouth of the Yangzi River, a more central location along the Chinese coast.

Still China refused to establish the formal diplomatic recognition and exchange that European powers demanded. A second set of wars in 1856–60 led to the occupation of Beijing by 17,000 French and British soldiers and the sacking of the imperial Summer Palace. More treaty ports were opened, including inland centers along the Yangzi River, now patrolled by British gunboats. Europeans gained control over the administration of China's foreign trade and tariffs. The opium trade continued to expand. Christian missionaries were given freedom to travel and proselytize throughout China. The Chinese government was powerless to resist, and some Chinese worked actively with the foreigners as intermediaries in business and administration.

The Taiping Rebellion. As the Manchu government weakened in the last decades of the nineteenth century, revolts broke out, foreign powers continued to seize parts of the country and its tributaries, and there were more calls for internal reform. (The Chinese situation showed similarities with events in the Ottoman Empire at about the same time.) The greatest of the internal revolts, the Taiping Rebellion, began in 1850 and was led by Hong Xiuquan, a frustrated scholar who claimed visions of himself as the younger brother of Jesus Christ. The main demands of the Taiping leaders, however, were quite concrete: an end to the corrupt and inefficient Manchu imperial rule, an end to extortionate landlord demands, and the alleviation of poverty. Beginning in the southwest, the Taiping rebels came to dominate the Yangzi valley and established their capital in Nanjing in 1853. The imperial government was unable to respond effectively, but regional military leaders, equipped with more modern weapons, finally defeated the revolt with the help of the "Ever Victorious Army," a mercenary force composed of American and European soldiers, winning more power for themselves. By the time the Taiping Rebellion was suppressed in 1864, some 20 million people had been killed. At about the same time, additional rebellions broke out among tribal peoples near Guangzhou, among the Miao tribals in Guizhou, and among Muslims in Yunnan and Gansu. The largest of all the rebel groups, the Nien, controlled much of the territory between Nanjing and Kaifeng. Collectively, these rebellions cost another 10 million lives.

With the central government fully occupied with these internal revolts, foreign imperialists began to expand their territorial claims.

The Taiping Rebellion. Chinese history is filled with peasant revolts. The Taiping Rebellion (1850–64) was one of the largest. It almost toppled the Qing dynasty, and before it was suppressed some 20 million people died. Here, at the end of the revolt, regional, loyal troops are pursuing and defeating the rebels in their last stand at Nanjing. The representation of the Taiping here as a ragtag group of fleeing rabble is a view from the victors' perspective. It does not suggest just how powerful, and dangerous, these rebels had been.

Russians seized border areas in the Amur River region (1858), the Maritime Provinces (1860), and, for ten years, the Ili valley in Turkestan (1871–81). France defeated Chinese forces in a local war and seized all of Indochina (1883–93). Most humiliating of all, Japan, having embraced Western technology and imperialist ambitions, defeated China in warfare in 1894–95. China ceded Taiwan to Japan, granted it the right to operate factories in the treaty ports, and paid a huge indemnity. Korea also passed to Japanese control, although formal colonial rule did not follow until 1910. The historic relationship of China as teacher and Japan as disciple, which dated back at least to 600 C.E., had been abruptly reversed. The new industrial age had introduced new values and power relationships.

The Boxer Rebellion. By the last years of the nineteenth century, China was in turmoil. In Beijing, a group of nationalists, called "Boxers" by the Europeans because of their belief that martial arts rendered them invincible in struggle, were enraged by foreign arrogance in China. They burned Christian missions, killed missionaries, and laid siege to the foreign legations for two months. The imperial powers of Europe and the United States put down this revolt and exacted yet another exorbitant indemnity. The Europeans and Americans did not, however, wish to take over the government of China directly. They wanted to have a Chinese government responsible for China. They wanted to preserve China as a quasi-colony, and so they supported the Manchus in the formalities of power, even as they steadily hollowed out the content of that power.

Boxers on the march. The mostly poor peasants who formed the Boxer Rebellion of 1898–1900 blamed hard times on foreign interference and Christian missionaries. Renowned for the ferocity of their attacks, the rebels terrified Western residents as they marched into Tianjin (pictured). A 20,000-strong force, comprising soldiers from different colonial powers, finally crushed the revolt in Beijing.

Marble boat in the gardens of the Summer Palace, Beijing. In the last years of the nineteenth century Chinese reformers clamored for industrial, military, and administrative reform. They were incensed when the dowager empress of China built not a navy but a marble boat for entertainment in her Summer Palace.

The implementation of colonialism in China was often a joint enterprise. The colonizers cooperated in suppressing the Boxer revolt and in administering the colonial port cities, such as Shanghai. In these cities, the British, French, American, and Japanese governments each governed its own colonial neighborhood-settlement, each with its own cultural and architectural style. These settlements were mostly adjacent to one another and they coordinated their administrations. A group of Chinese modernizers began to organize new industries, beginning with textiles, later developing Western weapons and steamships. However, the government, now in the hands of the aging dowager Empress Cixi, who controlled the heir apparent until she died in 1908, blocked their reforms. Frustrated nationalists called for revolution. Their leading organizer was Sun Yat-sen (Sun Yixian), a Cantonese educated in Honolulu, where he became a Christian, and in Hong Kong, where he became a doctor. Sun called for a twofold anticolonial revolution: first against the Manchus and then against the European, American, and Japanese powers. Only after the first revolution succeeded in overthrowing Manchu rule in 1911 did Sun begin to push against the Western powers and Japan. The story of that struggle is told in Chapter Twenty-two.

The French in Algeria and Southeast Asia

We have already seen that weaknesses in the Ottoman Empire gave foreigners the opportunity to prey on its possessions in the Balkans and in Egypt. In North Africa, the French led the scavengers. By the late seventeenth and early eighteenth century, both Tunis and Algiers were only nominally under Ottoman rule. Both regions profited from piracy and were finally invaded by seafaring nations, Algeria by the French and Tunis by the Americans. (The phrase "to the shores of Tripoli" in the American Marine Corps hymn comes from this expedition.) The French attack on Algeria in 1830 began as a campaign against piracy, but relations between the ruler of Algiers and the French government spun out of control, and ultimately the French demanded and got his surrender and control over his possessions.

Algiers was politically fragmented, however, and the French found themselves at war with other regional leaders, especially Abd al-Qadir, son of the head of one of the most important Muslim brotherhoods, or religious/political organizations, in the Middle East. Resistance swelled under al-Qadir, and he began to build a small state with its own administration and a modernized army of 10,000 men trained by European advisers. At first, the French avoided confrontation with al-Qadir, who stayed south of their holdings, but in 1841 warfare broke out. Before the French won, they had committed 110,000 troops (a third of their army) to the war and had attacked neighboring Morocco to block reinforcements to their enemy. Revolts continued to simmer. The last and largest repressed in 1871, with 3,000 French soldiers reported killed. Since the French resorted to a policy of destroying the crops of al-Qadir's army, reliable estimates put Algerian casualties as high as one-third of the total Algerian population. French armies seized rural areas, opening them for French military occupation and settlement.

During the years of fighting and thereafter, tens of thousands of Europeans came to settle in Algeria, some in connection with the military, some in search of economic opportunity. About half were French, but all began to adopt French language and culture and to think of themselves as French people living in Algeria. By the 1850s there were 130,000 of them and by 1900 more than a half-million, about 13 percent of the population. Christians (and Jews after 1870) were deemed to be citizens of France; Muslims were legally subjects. After a change of government in France in 1870, Algeria was formally annexed to France, and French citizens—but not subjects—in Algeria received the right to vote for members of the French National

Assembly in Paris. Through official land transfers and sales, the best land came into French hands and was developed into commercial agriculture, while Algerian farmers were generally left with small, under-capitalized holdings. Algerians had been deprived of their best lands, and left out of the middle and upper reaches of the administration and of commercial enterprises. Algeria was governed for the French.

Because it was a settler colony and geographically so near to France, Algeria marked the beginning of French colonialism in North Africa—but only the beginning. In the later 1800s, France captured all the vast expanse of French West Africa, which included parts of sub-Saharan Africa (see map p. 623). France administered French West Africa from Dakar, Senegal, an Atlantic port on the westernmost point of Africa, which had been one of France's earliest points of contact and trade—especially slave trade—going back to the mid-1600s.

French colonialism conquered Southeast Asia much later than North Africa. Invading Vietnam in 1857, the French claimed to be avenging the murder of several French missionaries and Vietnamese Christians some two decades earlier. They were also seeking overseas markets and a French share in the colonization of Asia. In a series of wars and occupations, the French took possession of all of French Indochina (see map p. 615) by 1887. They reserved all but minor positions in their administration for French officials. They built public works—railroads, highways, bridges, canals, port facilities—all to benefit the French and facilitate the export of raw materials, such as rice, coal, and rubber, and the import of finished products. A few wealthy, landowning Vietnamese who collaborated with the French administration did well, but most of the peasantry saw their standard of living, and the amount of food they had to eat, decline under French colonialism.

The Dutch in Indonesia

The Dutch in Indonesia are much less well represented in historical literature than are the British and French in their colonies, probably because of the linguistic difficulties of studying the subject. Dutch is not much used outside the Netherlands, and Bahasa Indonesia and other Indonesian languages are not used much outside Indonesia. Nevertheless, the subject is of great interest and importance.

As we saw in Chapter Fourteen, the Dutch East Indies Company had been active as a trading company in Indonesia since the beginning of the seventeenth century. It went bankrupt in 1799, however, due to poor management and the (often illegal) competition of private traders. After 15 years of French and then British rule during the Napoleonic Wars, in 1815, the Dutch government took over direct rule of its Indonesian holdings. Prepared to assert their renewed control, the Dutch ruled through especially high levels of violence and cruelty. The Java War, 1825–30, reflected many background economic and political grievances, and it finally erupted when the Dutch built a highway through property housing the tomb of a Muslim saint. In the brutal combat that followed, 15,000 government soldiers were killed, including 8,000 Dutch. On the other side, some 200,000 Javanese died in the war and in the famine and disease that followed.

In 1830 the Dutch introduced a new, particularly exploitative economic policy called *Kulturstelsel*, "**the cultivation system**." The Indonesian peasants were forced to devote 20 percent of their land to the production of cash crops, especially coffee, sugar, and indigo, to be turned over to the Dutch for export to the Netherlands as a kind of taxation. From 1840 to 1880 the estimated profits sent back to the Netherlands equaled 25 percent of the total budget of the Netherlands. By 1870, however, complaints reached Amsterdam both from within and outside Indonesia against this system, which deprived Indonesians from growing the food they needed. The Dutch

KEY TERM

the cultivation system A system of Dutch rule over Indonesian agriculture that forced peasants to devote 20 percent of their land to cash crops for export. This policy took away the peasant's right to determine his use of his own fields and diminished the production of food.

government implemented a new "Liberal Policy" permitting capitalist investment in Indonesia from the Netherlands and lifting the harsh, restrictive regulations imposed on agriculture, and on cultivators, by the cultivation system. Plantations and industries began to flourish, their profits surpassing those of agriculture. Rubber, copra (dried coconut meat, from which coconut oil is extracted), tin, and oil became even more valuable export products than coffee, sugar, tea, and tobacco. At the same time, the government, determined to control all of the outlying islands, also expanded its political administration outward from its center on the island of Java. These more aggressive and intrusive political and economic policies, often referred to by historians as the "new imperialism," were typical also of the colonial expansion of the British and the French in their colonies at about the same time.

By 1901, reevaluations of the Liberal Policy declared it, too, to be too harsh and exploitative. The government declared a new "Ethical Policy," designed to improve the health and education systems of the islands. The results were not pervasive, but they did help to raise up a small, new group of leaders, educated in Western forms, who came to challenge Dutch rule, and ultimately bring it to an end (in 1949).

European Competition and Cooperation: Empire-building in Africa

When European traders arrived in India and China they found huge countries governed by powerful empires. Sub-Saharan Africa was quite different. It was much larger and more diverse, an entire continent, second only to Asia in size, with many states and with even more areas under the control of local families, clans, and ethnicities. Each area had its own history, and the experience of each different European group also varied in each different region.

In sub-Saharan Africa, the early European experience was mostly limited to the shoreline of the west coast, as the Europeans sought a shipping route to Asia. The European traders found that they could buy the slaves they wanted in the port towns they established along the coast, without going inland themselves: African rulers and merchants captured, collected, and brought the slaves to them for sale. The Europeans for the most part accepted this commercial arrangement as economically efficient. It saved them from conflict with local African rulers, and it did not endanger their health by bringing them into contact with diseases against which they had no immunity. Even from their coastal enclaves, the Europeans were able to make a considerable mark on Africa, purchasing and transporting ten million slaves to the New World over a period of four centuries.

In this coastal trade, the European sailors and commercial agents were often competitive, and some coastal enclaves were seized first by one group of Europeans and then another. The fortress at El Mina, for example, in today's Ghana, was built by the Portuguese in 1482, seized by the Dutch in 1637, and then by the British in 1871. But the coast was long, the trade extensive and open, and the sailing expeditions often cooperative with one another. European port towns along the coast were always more Afro-European than European, since the Europeans stayed only briefly while their mixed-race descendants remained, along with a much larger number of slaves. Saint Louis, for example, in modern Senegal, was home in 1810 to about ten Europeans, 500 Afro-Europeans, 500 free Africans who had absorbed European culture, and about 2,200 slaves. The British outlawed the slave trade in 1807, and attempted to end it by forcefully seizing slave ships of all nations. Nevertheless the trade continued for decades, suggesting that the slave ships were cooperating with one another to avoid the British anti-slavery patrols at sea.

European expansion in Africa. Steamboats, machine guns, and quinine (to combat malaria) all gave Europeans new access to the interior of Africa in the later nineteenth century, and they intensified their nationalistic competition. The British pursued the dream of linking their possessions from Cape Town to Cairo, while France seized much of North and Central Africa. Bismarck's Berlin Conference of 1884 tried to apportion the spoils among all the competing powers.

The Competition for South Africa

In the settlement of South Africa, cooperation gave way to competition and warfare. The Dutch established the first substantial European colony in sub-Saharan Africa in 1652 at the Cape of Good Hope on the southern tip of the continent. The settlement grew steadily, and immigrants from other European countries—especially Britain—joined it.

European expansion at the Cape had disruptive effects on local populations. As the Dutch and then the British set out to the rural areas to farm, they displaced the Khoikhoi people who had been resident in the area. The Khoikhoi chiefdoms dissolved in the face of warfare, displacement, and catastrophic smallpox epidemics that decimated their numbers. Some of the Khoikhoi, along with other African peoples, were taken as slaves to fill the labor needs of the Europeans. In 1708 the population of the Cape was about 1,700 free citizens and 1,700 slaves. By 1800 it

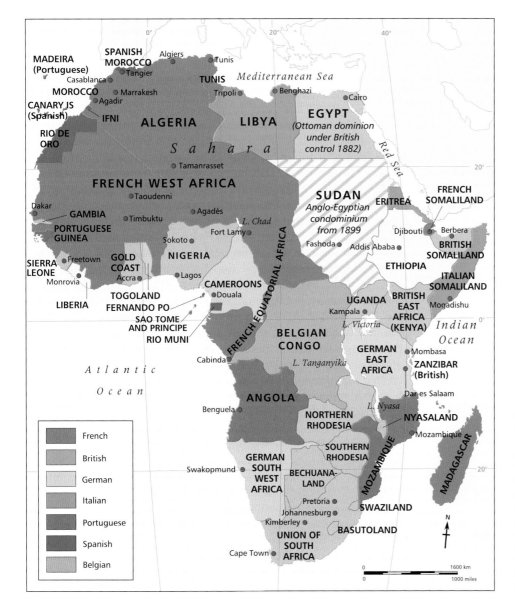

Africa in 1914. By the end of the nineteenth century, Africa presented European imperialists with their last chance to claim a "place in the sun." In a scramble for territory, Belgium, Germany, and Italy joined Spain, Portugal, Britain, and France in carving up the continent, riding roughshod over native concerns with brutal insensitivity. Conflict between the colonists was common, the war between the British and Dutch in South Africa being the most bloody.

totaled about 75,000, of whom one-third were free and two-thirds were slaves, mostly African but some of mixed race.

As a result of the Napoleonic Wars, military and legal control of the Cape Colony passed from the Dutch to the British. British laws and social practices were instituted, including the development of limited representative government, the abolition of the slave trade, and, in 1834, the abolition of slavery throughout the British Empire. Nevertheless, Europeans controlled the best land of the region. Their former slaves could aspire only to be wage workers rather than landowners and farmers. Property restrictions on voting effectively kept Africans removed from political power, and the Masters and Servants Act of 1856 limited the freedom of black workers, especially their freedom of geographical movement.

For the 8,000 people of Dutch descent, however, these limits on black freedom were not enough. They declared their opposition to the more liberal British customs of the colony, especially the abolition of slavery. They decided to separate themselves from the British and, in search of new land for farming, they departed on a march, or **Great Trek**, northward in the years between 1834 and 1841. These people, usually called Boers (meaning "farmers" in Dutch), or Afrikaners (for the African dialect of Dutch they spoke), ultimately founded two new republics, the Orange Free State and the Transvaal (see map p. 622). Meanwhile, the Cape Colony expanded eastward, partly to keep out the Boers. As they migrated, the Boers fought, conquered, displaced, and restricted to reservations the African peoples they encountered. Seeking labor to work the land, they often captured and virtually enslaved Africans living around them.

This geographical expansion of the European Cape Colony further destabilized a region already passing through a *mfecane*, or time of troubles. In 1816, Shaka (*c.* 1787–1828) seized the leadership of his small Zulu kingdom just to the north and east of the Cape Colony. He organized a standing army of 40,000 soldiers, trained them rigorously, housed them in stockades separate from the rest of the population, and armed them with newly designed short, stabbing spears, enormously effective in hand-to-hand combat. He instituted new battle formations, similar to those used by the ancient Greeks, with a massed center and flanks that could encircle the enemy and cut off its rear. By 1828, when Shaka was assassinated by two half-brothers, his kingdom had expanded, forcing local peoples to flee their lands. Some moved into the Cape Colony, but the vast majority turned north and east, traveling hundreds of miles into present-day Mozambique, Zimbabwe, Zambia, and Tanzania, and displacing other peoples in turn. All of these movements combined—the Boer trek, Shaka's Zulu expansion, and the migration of peoples fleeing before both of these advances— created the *mfecane* in southern and eastern Africa. Cape Colony itself, however, remained relatively tranquil, continuing to serve as a port in transoceanic trade.

When the Suez Canal restructured the shipping routes between Asia and Europe in 1869, ending the need for the long voyage around Africa, South Africa might have become a quiet colonial backwater. But in the 1870s diamonds were discovered at Kimberley, and in the 1880s the world's largest known deposit of gold was found at Witwatersrand. Competition for this new wealth intensified the general hostility between the Boers and the British into full-scale warfare. The British army of 450,000 men finally defeated the Boer army of 88,000 in the three-year South African War, which the British called the Boer War (1899–1902). In 1910, the British consolidated their own two colonies (Cape and Natal) with the two Boer republics

The Rhodes Colossus. Cecil John Rhodes became one of the main champions of British rule in southern Africa, promoting colonization "from Cape Town to Cairo." The statesman and financier divided his time between diamond mining and annexing territories to British imperial rule. Rhodesia (now Zimbabwe and Zambia) was named for him in 1894.

THE RHODES COLOSSUS
STRIDING FROM CAPE TOWN TO CAIRO.

into the Union of South Africa, which became a self-governing country. After 1913 whites in South Africa had the same sorts of political institutions and rights as in the British Dominions of Australia and Canada. Because of the European domination of the life of the colony, South Africa was considered a white settler colony despite its overwhelming black majority.

Sierra Leone and Liberia: Havens for Former Slaves

British, Americans, and Africans, working together, responded to the abolition of the slave trade and slavery, in part, by establishing two new colonies, Sierra Leone and Liberia, as refuges for freed slaves, and by founding new businesses, mostly based on tropical agricultural products, to replace slave trading in the export economy.

Freetown, in Sierra Leone, was founded in 1787 to serve as a haven for freed slaves. At first these were mostly black Americans, freed by the British during the American Revolution, and rebels from Jamaican slavery. After the abolition of the British slave trade in 1807, increasing numbers were slaves recaptured at sea by the British navy and set free. Between 1807 and 1864, the British Navy brought more than 50,000 recaptured slaves to Sierra Leone and granted them freedom. To cope with these numbers, the British reorganized Sierra Leone in 1808 as a formal British colony and promoted Christianity and Western culture among its residents. Some of the freed slaves, especially the Yoruba, used Sierra Leone as a staging point from which to return inland to the societies from which they had been taken. Most, however, remained in Sierra Leone, which continued to grow. The ex-slaves had come from very different regions of West Africa and missionaries attempted to unify them into a single Christian nation by providing them with a common education. In 1827 the Anglican Church Mission Society founded Fourah Bay College, an important institution for training African clergy. One of its first graduates, Samuel Crowther, became the first African bishop of the Anglican Church. The overwhelming majority of Sierra Leone's population were Africans who joined the colony on their own.

Following the example of Sierra Leone, the American Colonization Society received a charter from the United States government in 1816 to found a site on the West African coast for the repatriation of freed American slaves. In 1822, the first settlers arrived at the site that later became Monrovia, named for American President James Monroe. In 1847, when Monrovia held about 5,000 settlers, it formally declared its independence from the United States government. Nine years later it joined with its surrounding settlements to form the country of Liberia as an independent state, although it was still heavily reliant on American assistance. Americans supported Liberia for diverse reasons: Some saw it as a haven for former slaves, others saw it as a dumping ground in which America could rid itself of ex-slaves. As in Sierra Leone, the population of freed slaves always formed a small minority of the total population. Even today, descendants of repatriated slaves, known as Americo-Liberians, form only 2.5 percent of the total population of about 3.2 million.

Cooperation among Africans and Europeans

Europeans and Africans had cooperated for centuries in the slave trade. As that trade ended in the North Atlantic, both Europeans and Africans sought new export commodities. British schemes to develop cotton plantations on the Niger River failed disastrously as European personnel succumbed to tropical illnesses against which they had no resistance. French schemes for plantations in the Ivory Coast and Gabon similarly failed. Foreigners did establish some economic enterprises inland—and often the same person served as the representative of government and the representative

KEY TERMS

Great Trek Between 1834 and 1841 the Dutch settlers in the British Cape Colony left the British-dominated areas to the south to establish their own control in the north. The Dutch felt that the British were too liberal in their treatment of blacks.

mfecane Literally "time of troubles," the period in southern Africa from about 1816, when Shaka took control of the Zulu kingdom, until about 1841, when the Dutch completed their great trek. The expansion of the Zulus and of the Dutch dislodged local kingdoms and peoples, increasing political instability throughout the region.

of European business interests. Most of the basic agricultural and animal commodities, however, were produced and transported by Africans. Ivory—much in demand in the West for piano keys and billiard balls—continued as a staple throughout much of the continent. New market crops included palm nuts and kernels, peanuts, timber, dyes, wax, honey, and redwood. As steamships started to ply Africa's rivers, bulkier crops were added: cotton, coffee, sugarcane, and sugar products. Rubber came in the 1870s. In the area around the Congo River, cassava, citrus fruits, tobacco, and maize were introduced. Despite the abolition of the slave trade in the British Empire, the slave trade flourished throughout most of the nineteenth century in the south Atlantic and throughout Africa. The increase in commercial cropping, ivory harvesting, and copper and metal mining and production required labor. Often "freed" slaves were forced into labor on the new plantations and in the expanding caravan trade, especially in East Africa. Arab caravan leaders impressed slaves into the ivory trade in great numbers and with high mortality rates.

The transport networks within Africa were for the most part run by Africans themselves. In the east, Arab traders sometimes also conducted caravans from the coast to the Lake District. The Arab traders were backed financially and militarily by the Arab planters of Zanzibar with their rich harvests of cloves. The profit to be made from cloves in Zanzibar and from coordinating caravan transportation in East Africa was so great that the Arab ruler of the Oman Empire, Sayyid Said, moved his capital from Muscat in Oman to Zanzibar in 1840.

During most of the nineteenth century, the Afro-Europeans did well in business, education, and local public affairs in a relatively open environment. Commercial profit became more important than political power. Beginning with the 1880s, however, Europeans in larger numbers arrived to take over direct political and economic power and impose increasingly racist polices. Steamboats penetrated more deeply into the continent, upriver from the ports. Many of the African transport workers were displaced from their jobs, and some European commercial and administrative officials took up positions inland. Europeans also owned and managed some of the great plantations and industries in the interior: rubber in the Congo, coffee plantations in East Africa, and diamonds and copper in the Congo and South Africa. Joseph Conrad's great novel, *Heart of Darkness*, captures the remote setting and the foreboding mood of that transformation to European overlordship.

The Scramble for Africa

Many adventurers were drawn to Africa in the late eighteenth and early nineteenth centuries, further opening the interior of the continent to outsiders. The best known was David Livingstone (1813–73), a Scottish missionary and able scientist, who began his career in South Africa in 1841, intent upon establishing a missionary station and providing medical assistance to Africans. He returned home briefly in 1852, but by 1853 he was back in Africa. For three years he crossed and recrossed the continent. Livingstone was distinguished for learning African languages, treating Africans with respect, and constantly campaigning against the slave trade that was endemic in the African interior. Two subsequent, grueling adventures of exploration in equatorial Africa lasted a total of 13 years. Livingstone died in 1873 in what is today Zambia. In accordance with his wishes, his heart was buried in Africa, under a tree near the place where he died.

In 1871, when premature rumors of Livingstone's death reached Europe, the *New York Herald* newspaper dispatched the explorer Henry Morton Stanley (1841–1904) to try to find him. Not only did Stanley locate Livingstone, he carried out expeditions of his own—traveling with an armed retinue that resembled a military expedition or a slave caravan. On Stanley's return through Europe, Leopold II, King of the Belgians (r. 1865–1909), engaged him to establish trading stations along the Congo River. The colonization of central Africa was beginning. Stanley, representing the king, negotiated treaties with hundreds of local chiefs. The treaties gave Stanley himself the power to establish a Confederation of Free Negro Republics, an estate of some 900,000 square miles, which functioned as a kind of slave plantation within Africa for the personal economic benefit of King Leopold. The brutality of Stanley's treatment of Africans was perhaps the worst in the annals of European colonialism in Africa.

The Berlin Conference. As European powers explored and colonized Central Africa, they came into direct competition with each other. Fearing the consequences of this competition, Germany's chancellor, Bismarck, convened a conference for the European powers and the United States to establish ground rules for fixing borders among European colonies in Africa. The **Berlin Conference** (1884–85) assigned the administration of the Congo—a region named for the Congo River and for the now-defunct, historic Kingdom of Kongo—for example, to Leopold II personally as a kind of fiefdom. The Congo became, in effect, Leopold's private estate, 80 times larger than Belgium itself. Its economic purpose was, first, the harvesting of natural rubber from vines in the jungles and, later, the exploitation of the area's rich mineral reserves, especially copper. Laborers were forced to work as slaves at the point of a gun. Workers could be killed or have their hands cut off for failing to make quotas. Company agents killed and maimed workers who resisted. Ten million Congolese died as a result of the king's rule. In 1908, recognizing both the cruelty and the economic losses of the Congo administration, the Belgian parliament took over control of the colony from the king, but the Congo remained one of the most harshly administered of all the African colonies.

The Berlin Conference also divided up the lands of Africa on paper, generally apportioning inland areas to the European nations already settled on the adjacent coast. These nations were then charged with establishing settlements in those regions, and they quickly did so, dispatching settlers in a "**scramble for Africa**." Backed by their new weapons, especially machine guns, and their new steamboats, European governments forced one-sided treaties on African chiefs who often did not understand the significance of the documents they signed. The chiefs frequently became, in effect, the agents of Europeans for recruiting labor and collecting taxes. In exchange, the Europeans protected the chiefs from resistance and rebellion. As the chiefs ceded power to the Europeans, they gained power over their own people.

On the occasions when Africans resisted these agreements, Europeans responded with force. The Germans crushed perhaps the greatest of the unsuccessful rebellions, the Maji-Maji revolt of 1905–07 in Tanganyika. Led by Kinjikitile Ngwele, who claimed to have magic water (*maji*) that would make his followers invulnerable to wounds, the rebels refused to perform forced labor on the cotton plantations. The uprising ended with 70,000 rebels dead, including those who succumbed to disease and malnutrition. Other less spectacular revolts were similarly suppressed with violence.

KEY TERMS

Berlin Conference Convened by Bismarck of Germany to settle European disputes over territory in Africa peacefully.

scramble for Africa The rush of European nations to colonize the parts of Africa that were assigned to them in the international negotiations at the Berlin Conference.

Congolese plantation workers. For decades the Congo was administered as a private estate of King Leopold II of Belgium. Its rubber plantations and copper mines brought immense wealth to him and his country, but he treated the Congolese with sadistic brutality. Workers were killed and maimed for failing to reach the production quotas set for them. In 1908, following an investigation of the cruelty of the system, the Belgian government took control of the colony, but treatment of the Congolese people remained harsh.

African Musician, Aloysius O'Kelly, c. 1880. Oil on canvas. As European artists painted African scenes they often portrayed people of striking beauty and strength against exotic backgrounds. The musician may have been a *griot*, a bard whose songs and chants preserved the history of his people. (Taylor Gallery, London)

Europeans and Labor Relations in Africa

Throughout Africa, Europeans confronted the problem of finding labor for their new farms and enterprises. By confiscating African land and redistributing it among themselves, Europeans took farms away from Africans and produced a new wage-labor force. The 1913 Natives Land Act of South Africa closed 87 percent of South African land to African ownership; the small percentage that remained was the most marginal land. The newly displaced labor force was especially vital for the new coffee plantations in the highlands of East Africa. In the farming areas of Kenya, northern Rhodesia, Nyasaland, and Angola a system of tenancy without wages developed, a kind of share-cropping system. Within their colonies in Angola and Mozambique, the Portuguese used intimidation to coerce labor, but the Africans often fled or otherwise subverted the plans of their colonizers. The British colonies, which used the carrot of (low) wages, seemed more successful in eliciting production. Along the African coast, indentured laborers from India, China, and Southeast Asia were imported by the thousands to work in the sugar plantations.

The greatest problem was finding labor for the South African diamond and gold mines (and later for the great copper mines in the Congo as well). European colonial governments imposed taxation, which had to be paid in cash, forcing all Africans to find some way of raising the money. Jobs in the mines were one alternative. Because the Europeans feared the revolutionary potential of a stable African labor force in the mines, they usually recruited workers on contracts for only one or two years at a time. They split up families, housing the male workers in barrack-like accommodations near the mines while exiling their families to distant reservations, where the women and children carried on limited farming and craft production. Because the mine owners did not pay the workers enough to support their families, the farming and handicrafts of the women in effect subsidized the salaries of the workers in the mines.

Trade unions in the mines organized only the white skilled workers and kept Africans out of these jobs. In 1906, when the mines employed 18,000 whites, 94,000 Africans, and 51,000 Chinese indentured laborers, the white skilled workers went on strike to protest their being squeezed out by the Chinese and blacks. Owners brought in Afrikaner workers to break the strike, but ultimately the Chinese miners were repatriated and the skilled jobs were reserved for whites. Race thus trumped both the free markets of capitalism and the solidarity of labor unions.

Gender Relationships in Colonization

The Europeans who traveled overseas to trade beginning in the sixteenth century were almost invariably males, and they frequently entered into sexual liaisons with local women. As the men stayed longer, these relationships became increasingly important for business and administration as well as for social and sexual pleasure. In the Senegambia (present-day Senegal and Gambia), as the Senegal Company forbade its traders to marry locally, the French men found *signares*, concubines or

Why did Europeans Colonize the World?

The Industrial Revolution in Western Europe and the United States ushered in an era of imperialism that brought most of the world's land under European political control. Why did the industrializing nations assert their powers in this way? To some extent, the answer seems obvious: They relished the power, wealth, and prestige that apparently came with imperial possessions. They also claimed to welcome the opportunity to serve others. Further, the industrial system that they were building took on a life of its own, requiring ever-increasing sources of raw materials and more markets in which to sell. But why was trade alone not enough? Why did the industrialists feel it was necessary to take political control as well? Were there additional motives behind imperialism? And did the results of imperialism match the aspirations of the imperial rulers?

We cannot answer all these questions fully, but a review article by Patrick Wolfe in *The American Historical Review*, "History and Imperialism: A Century of Theory, from Marx to Postcolonialism," helps us to review and sort out some of the most prominent explanations.

Karl Marx deplored the exploitation of colonialism, but, as a European, he valued some of its contributions. Britain, he emphasized, brought to India a new economic dynamism, with railroads, industrial infrastructure, and communication networks. Ultimately this transformation would lead to capitalism and then socialism. Marx wrote in 1853: "Whatever may have been the crimes of England, she was the unconscious tool of history in bringing about that revolution" (Marx and Engels, *The First Indian War of Independence 1857–1859*, p. 21).

J.A. Hobson, a British economist writing in 1902, and V.I. Lenin, the leader of the communist revolution in Russia (see Chapter Nineteen), writing in 1916, agreed that the desire to control raw materials and markets drove imperialism. Hobson pointed out that the profits of the imperial system went mostly to the rich. He believed that if imperialism were ended overseas, a concentration on investment and industry at home would provide greater opportunities to the working classes in Europe. M.N. Roy, a founder of the Communist Party of India, disagreed with Hobson, arguing that the profits of imperialism did provide economic gains to European workers and that they would therefore support the system. The revolt against the imperial, and capitalist, system would have to begin among the workers in the colonies who were more exploited.

Several analysts have tried to grasp the imperial system as a whole, understanding the impact of colonizer and colonized upon one another. Some, like Marx, saw the system introducing valuable modernization into the colonies. Most, like Immanuel Wallerstein and the American economists Paul Baran and Paul Sweezy, argued that the imperial power would always seek to keep the colonies in a position of dependency and underdevelopment. The imperial rulers might introduce some technological innovations, such as railways that were necessary for their trade, but they had no interest in enabling the colonies to become economic and technological rivals. Indeed, one reason for imposing imperial domination was to prevent the colony from taking control of its own economic policies.

Ronald Robinson and John Gallagher, British historians writing in the 1960s, and French philosopher Louis Althusser, writing in the 1970s and 1980s, stressed the need to evaluate imperialism on a case-by-case basis. British imperialism in Egypt, for example, was quite sophisticated and benign compared with the raw cruelty of Belgian imperialism in the Congo. Even within individual colonies, imperialists treated different regions and groups differently, for example incorporating educated urban groups into the administration while treating plantation workers almost like slave labor. Imperial rule also varied considerably depending on the administration in power in the imperial country and also on the local imperial representatives on the scene. All three scholars eschewed generalizations and emphasized the complexity of the imperial enterprise.

Finally, some of the most recent scholarly analyses of imperialism—often referred to as postcolonial analyses—have stressed the cultural impact of imperialism on both colonized and colonizer. Imperial rulers usually drew a sense of pride from their conquest and exalted their own culture for possessing colonies. Colonized peoples, on the other hand, often suffered a sense of inferiority. They had to reexamine their historic cultural traditions and identities in light of the fact that they had been conquered by foreigners. The postcolonial literature that analyzes this cultural confrontation has expanded rapidly, with contributions by literary critics such as Edward Said, Homi Bhabha, and Gayatri Chakravorty Spivak. Indeed, as industrialization has brought peoples of the world into ever closer contact, and political philosophies have collided with one another, questions of personal and group identity have increased everywhere.

- Among the scholars who argue that economics is the main force behind imperialism, there are differences of opinion. What are these differences? Which point of view seems most persuasive to you?
- Some scholars have argued that political gain has been the main force behind imperialism. What evidence do you see to support this viewpoint?
- Many contemporary scholars argue that the colonizing countries have been influenced by colonialism culturally just as much as the colonized have been. What examples of this influence can you cite?

Nautch dancers, Hyderabad, 1860s. Observing and enjoying Nautch dancing (a redundancy, since *nautch* means "dance") was one of the pleasures of Indian princely courts, and Europeans soon developed a taste for the art. Photographers, too, were attracted by the elegance of the dance and the dancers, as this picture from Hyderabad by Willoughby Wallace Hooper and George Western suggests. The languid beauty of these dancers hints, correctly, that sometimes the women might have been prized—by Indians and Europeans alike—for other talents in addition to the dance. (British Library, London)

mistresses, among the local peoples. These women helped the men to negotiate local languages, customs, and health conditions.

In India, the **nabobs,** the successful traders and administrators who often became wealthy, were not forbidden to marry local women. They fathered Anglo-Indian children who came to form a small but important community of their own, especially in the large port cities of Bombay, Madras, and Calcutta.

As Europeans began to establish colonies, and as women began to travel to these colonies, usually with their husbands, sometimes in search of husbands, European women discouraged such relationships. More rigid sexual boundaries were established. In both India and Africa the relationships between colonizing men and colonized women became fewer and more distant. New guidelines for interracial behavior restricted not only sexual but also social relationships. As these relationships between men and women became less free, so, too, did the informality among the men across ethnic lines.

Earlier historians attributed this increasing social distance between Europeans and the peoples they colonized to the restrictive attitudes of the European women, who blocked their husbands from mixing with the local women. More recent, feminist scholarship has attributed the responsibility for the increased distance to both husband and wife. Both exhibited racism. Whatever may have been the differences of opinion between European men and women concerning the relationships between European men and the colonized women, almost all Europeans wished to restrict local men from having intimate contact with European women. As colonial settlements increased in size and stability, each family tended to view itself, somewhat pompously, as representative of the rulers, a colonial outpost in miniature.

Did the colonizing women form a solidarity with their colonized sisters? Most contemporary historians think not. The colonizers tended to focus on flaws, as they saw them, in the gender relations among the colonized peoples, and then set out to introduce reforms. In India the British outlawed *sati*, the practice of widows burning themselves to death on their deceased husbands' funeral pyres; they introduced a minimum age of marriage; and they urged widow remarriage despite upper-caste Hindu resistance. In Africa they sought to end polygamy. In each case, the colonial government emphasized the superiority of its own practices and the good fortune of the colonized to have the Europeans there to save them from themselves. The European colonizers pointed to their interventions in gender relations to justify and praise their own colonial rule. The colonizing women did the same.

The colonial presence did introduce new patterns of gender relations into the colonies, based on the European models. At least some of the colonized peoples chose to move toward a more European style of gender relations. They wanted more education for women, more freedom of choice in marriage, more companionate marriages, and an end to *sati* in India, to polygamy in parts of Africa, and to foot binding in China. Sometimes people adopted new customs because they seemed to be improvements over local practices, sometimes because the new behavior won favor for the colonized peoples with the colonizing masters.

Later, as nationalism took root, local peoples began to reject at least some of the foreign practices because of their colonial associations. Some women who had welcomed the aspirations of Western feminist freedoms, such as equal educational opportunity, the right to work outside the home, setting limits on family size, owning property, and equal rights under law, began to feel that these "freedoms" contradicted traditional family values in their own society, and they came to reject them. Such local women also looked more critically at the relationships between European men and women, and often found them fraught with tension and anxiety. They caricatured at least some of the colonial intrusions into their family and gender relationships as "white men saving brown women from brown men."

Christmas in India, a sketch by E.K. Johnson, *The Graphic*, 1881. Just as, for the most part, European men did not usually socialize or form a solidarity with the men whose country they had colonized, so, too, the women kept themselves apart and their lives centered on their families and their European friends. The wife would oversee the running of the household as she was accustomed to doing at home. Here an *ayah* looks after the youngest child in much the same way that a nanny would have back in England.

Anticolonial Revolts

Conquest by European colonial powers generally evoked anxiety and resentment among the colonized. Not for everyone, of course. Some of the conquered people found new jobs, education, business opportunities, and professional opportunities. Some praised the imperial powers for imposing peace among otherwise warring factions and imposing a rule of law that limited the arbitrary rule of local officials. New medical and technological systems raised the standard of living.

For the most part, however, the conquered peoples were resentful—or they became resentful. They might see some benefits to early colonial rule, but they also saw the looting of local treasuries and the imposition of confiscatory taxes. They cringed at the insults to indigenous rulers who were rudely displaced. Sometimes, in some places, where colonizers confirmed and protected local leaders in their power, their subjects were infuriated because now those leaders were impervious to local complaints. Later, as new systems of administration were introduced, they saw the "glass ceilings" that kept qualified local people out of its higher level jobs. Even when new colonial businesses offered new opportunities, the bulk of the profits was sent back to the colonizing country. The new educational, legal, and administrative systems undermined local traditions, culture, and religion. The use of a foreign language in public life—the norm in colonial situations—further inhibited the development of indigenous cultures. At least as significant as any of these more tangible frustrations were the racism and disrespect colonized peoples experienced from most of the colonizers, and which they deeply resented. Sooner or later, most colonized people wanted their independence. In region after region they rose in revolt against colonial rule.

Many of the early revolts looked backward, to restoring the institutions that had preceded colonialism. The 1857–58 revolt in India and the Mahdist uprising on the upper Nile, 1881–98, fit this pattern. So did a revolt of an Islamic mystical brotherhood, led by Shamil, "ruler of the righteous and destroyer of the unbeliever," against Russian rule in the Caucasus Mountains, 1834–59; Emilio Aguinaldo's revolt against United States colonial rule in the Philippines, 1898–1902; and continuing peasant revolts against Dutch rule in the islands of Indonesia, 1881–1908.

Later, armed revolts and nonviolent political movements against colonial rule became more forward-looking. Their leaders sought not a simple return to the past

KEY TERMS

han In Japan, a territory or feudal estate controlled by a feudal lord, or *daimyo. Han* were abolished in 1871.

Eastern Ethics; Western Science The watchword of Sakuma Zozan in Japan, urging acceptance of Western science and technology, but rejecting Western culture and ethics in favor of those of Japan. This position was found in many countries colonized by Europeans.

Revere the Emperor; Expel the Barbarian A much more conservative position, urging rejection of almost everything coming from Western colonization.

but a newly restructured nation, usually incorporating significant elements of the past with new goals based in part on innovations introduced by colonial powers. In India, the Indian National Congress, founded in 1885, proposed a pattern of parliamentary democracy for India, often with an admixture of Hindu reformism. In 1907, in Egypt, the reformist People's Party, led by Saad Zaghlul (1857–1927) became the core of the nationalist Wafd party after 1919. The Young Turk party, formed in 1878 in patriotic anger against the Ottoman defeats in the Balkans, grew into a revolutionary party by 1908. Indonesia's first nationalist association was formed in 1908, South Africa's in 1912, and Viet Nam's in 1913.

Each of these organizations had a conception of the future nation it was constructing, modeled in part on European military, economic, political, and administrative forms, but also incorporating its own cultural, religious, and social dimensions. Perhaps the most comprehensive of all these responses was that of Japan. By the mid-1850s, Japan had witnessed foreigners colonize and humble the ancient and venerable Chinese Empire. When American warships entered Japanese waters in 1853, the Japanese feared that a similar fate awaited them. They took dramatic action to insure that they would not fall victim to colonial rule.

Japan: From Isolation to Equality

Japan was unified in its ethnicity, with accepted legends of its national history; a single dynasty of emperors that related back to the founding of the nation in the seventh century B.C.E.; a single national language; an integrated national political structure; and an island-based geography. Japan's insular nature was intensified in the early 1600s when the government closed the country to foreign, especially European, contact. Faced with military attack from Western nations in 1853, however, and aware of recent Western invasions of China, Japan recognized the need to transform its institutions and its society. The history of Japan after 1853 charts its extraordinary move from isolation to full, prominent participation in the world of nation-states.

The End of the Shogunate

By 1639, as we saw in Chapter Fourteen, Japan had shut down commerce and contact with the European world. The exception was a Dutch outpost, virtually quarantined on Deshima Island in Nagasaki harbor, which was allowed to receive one ship each year. The Japanese also permitted the Chinese to trade at Nagasaki, but only under severe restrictions. Some trade could also pass to China through the Ryukyu Islands, under the guise of "tribute," and Korea could trade through the islands of Tsushima. Otherwise, Japan was isolated. In the late 1700s and early 1800s, European ships would occasionally attempt to establish contact, but the Japanese turned them away.

In 1853, however, the United States dispatched Commodore Matthew Perry (1794–1858) with a small squadron, including three steam frigates, to force Japan to open to trade, as China had been opened in the Opium War a decade before. Japan lacked the means to resist the Americans and the European powers that soon followed, and over the next few years, under pressure, the country opened more ports, at first on the periphery, but then at Nagasaki, Kobe, and Yokohama. Japan opened Edo (Tokyo) and Osaka to foreign residents, and then granted the foreigners extraterritorial legal rights. Foreigners were permitted to determine Japan's tariff policies. In 1863 and 1864, in the face of firing on their ships, British, French, Dutch, and American naval forces demolished Japanese coastal forts and supplies and forced Japan to pay an indemnity. Like China, Japan seemed headed toward control by foreigners.

Unlike China, however, young, vigorous leaders seized control of the government of Japan, forcing a dramatic restructuring of the nation's politics, administration, class structure, economy, technology, and culture. These leaders, for the most part young samurai warriors in the *han* (feudal estates) of Choshu and Satsuma at the southern extreme of Japan, recognized that Japan's current government was not capable of coping with the European threat. Great diversity of opinion flourished among the approximately 250 different *han* in Japan, but the most powerful regional leaders felt that the shogun, or military governor, who ruled Japan in the name of the emperor, should be removed and the emperor himself should be restored as the direct ruler of Japan. The young samurai, members of Japan's hereditary military elite, would then formulate the policies of the new administration in his name.

The samurai were able to employ some of the technological information introduced by the Dutch from their station in Nagasaki harbor. Indeed, in 1811 the shogunate had established an office for translating Dutch material, and it was expanded into a school for European languages and science in 1857. Some of the *han*, including Satsuma, Choshu, and Mito, did the same. By 1840, some Japanese were already casting Western guns and artillery. Sakuma Zozan (1811–64), one of the advocates of adopting Western military methods, coined the motto "**Eastern Ethics; Western Science**." Japan could adopt Western technology, he counseled, especially military technology, while still maintaining its own culture.

Sakuma believed that opening the country was both necessary and beneficial. Not everyone agreed, however, and in 1860 a group of samurai from the conservative *han* of Mito argued a contrary position: "**Revere the Emperor; Expel the Barbarian**." The lines of conflict were sharpening. Political violence increased as exponents of the opposing positions attacked each other. Mito loyalists assassinated Sakuma and

SOURCE

Fukuzawa Yukichi: Cultural Interpreter

Born into the lower levels of the feudal aristocracy in Kyushu, Fukuzawa Yukichi (1834–1901) had a thirst for knowledge that took him to Osaka, Nagasaki (for Dutch learning), to the United States in 1860 with the very first Japanese official mission (and again in 1867), and to Europe in 1862. Fukuzawa rejected government office, the usual alternative, in favor of private life as a journalist and teacher. He earned a reputation as the foremost interpreter of the West to Japan; his books describing the West as he understood it sold in the hundreds of thousands to a nation hungry for such observation and interpretation. He founded a school in Tokyo that later became Keio University, the training ground of many of Japan's business leaders. The following excerpts are from Fukuzawa's *Autobiography*, published in 1899. He states his goal of interpreting the West fairly, even though he knows that he will face opposition.

> The final purpose of all my work was to create in Japan a civilized nation, as well equipped in both the arts of war and peace as those of the Western world. I acted as if I had become the sole functioning agent for the introduction of Western culture. It was natural then that I would be disliked

by the older type of Japanese, and suspected of working for the benefit of foreigners … I regard the human being as the most sacred and responsible of all orders, unable in reason to do anything base … In short, my creed is that a man should find his faith in independence and self-respect. (p. 214)

He investigates the style of Western institutions:

> For instance, when I saw a hospital, I wanted to know how it was run—who paid the running expenses; when I visited a bank, I wished to learn how the money was deposited and paid out. By similar first-hand queries, I learned something of the postal system and the military conscription then in force in France but not in England. A perplexing institution was representative government. … For some time it was beyond my comprehension to understand what they [political parties] were "fighting" for, and what was meant, anyway, by "fighting" in peace time. "This man and that man are 'enemies' in the House," they would tell me. But these "enemies" were to be seen at the same table, eating and drinking with each other. (p. 134)

another reform leader in 1864 and then committed ritual suicide. Attacks on foreigners taking up residence and conducting business in Japan also increased.

In 1868, the forces of Choshu and Satsuma, joining with those of several other more remote *han*, seized control of the emperor's palace in Kyoto and declared the shogunate ended, the lands of the shogun confiscated, and the emperor restored to imperial power. Most of the fighting was over by November, although naval battles continued into early 1869. The **Meiji restoration** ended the power of the shogunate forever and brought the *daimyo* and their young samurai to power in the name of the Emperor Meiji (r. 1867–1912). The emperor assumed the throne at the age of 14 and reigned over a national transformation of astonishing scope and speed.

THE MEIJI RESTORATION AND INDUSTRIALIZATION IN JAPAN

1853	Commander Perry sails into Edo Bay, ending 250 years' isolation
1854	Treaty of Kanagawa gives U.S. trading rights with Japan
1860s	Series of "unequal treaties" gives U.S, Britain, France, Russia, and Netherlands commercial and territorial privileges
1868	Tokugawa shogun forced to abdicate. Executive power vested with emperor in Meiji restoration
1871	Administration is overhauled; Western-style changes introduced
1872	National education system introduced, providing teaching for 90 percent of children by 1900
1872	First railway opened
1873	Old order changed by removal of privileges of samurai class
1876	Koreans, under threat, agree to open three of their ports to the Japanese and exchange diplomats
1877	Satsuma rebellion represented last great (unsuccessful) challenge of conservative forces
1879	Representative system of local government introduced
1884	Western-style peerage (upper house) is created
1885	Cabinet government introduced
1889	Adoption of constitution based on Bismarck's Germany
1889	Number of cotton mills has risen from three (1877) to 83
1894–95	War with China ends in Japanese victory
1895	Japan annexes Taiwan and Pescadores Islands
1902	Britain and Japan sign military pact
1904–05	War with Russia ends in Japanese victory
1910	Japan annexes Korea
1914	Japan joins World War I on side of Allies

The Meiji Restoration

Japan's new leaders began to search the world for new political, economic, and military models that might be adapted to Japan's needs. A two-year overseas goodwill mission set out in 1871 to deepen relationships with the heads of state of the treaty powers, to discuss future treaty revisions, and to enable Japanese leaders to experience the West at first hand. Fifty-four students accompanied the mission. A ministry of education was established in 1871, and its first budget included funds for sending 250 students abroad to study. Many of these students became leaders in the new Japan. Foreign instructors were also brought to Japan. The late shogun's government had employed some foreigners in industrial enterprises. The Meiji rulers imported far more: American experts to introduce large-scale farming practices; German doctors to teach medicine; Americans to teach natural and social sciences.

Restructuring Government. The emperor was brought from his home in Kyoto to Edo, the former capital of the shogun, which was renamed Tokyo ("Eastern Capital") in 1868. In 1869, the *daimyo* of four of the most important *han* turned over their estates to the emperor, setting the pattern for other *daimyo* to follow and to unify the country. The *daimyo* retained certain rights of tax collection, which kept them financially well off, and stipends were paid to the samurai to avoid outright revolt. For a decade, revolts did simmer until the largest of them—40,000 troops in Satsuma under the reluctant leadership of Saigo Takamori—was crushed in 1877. Japan's national government held firm.

Following years of discussion, and study of European and American constitutions, in 1889 a constitution was promulgated, creating a bicameral, elected parliament, called the Diet. Democracy, however, was restricted. Only the nobility voted for the House of Peers. Only about one percent of the population, only males, could vote for the House of Representatives. The Diet could vote on important legislation, but only the executive could introduce it. The Constitution was presented not as the victory of a popular movement imposing limits on an autocratic government, but as a gift bequeathed by the emperor to his people. The emperor retained, at least in theory, all executive powers, including the right to make war and peace, and to conclude treaties. Despite all these limitations, Japan's Diet of 1890 was the first parliamentary form of government in Asia.

The core of the central government's new army was established in 1871. Money was invested in modern equipment, much of it manufactured in Japan. An army staff college began to train an officer corps following a German model, while the navy adapted a British model, often purchasing its ships from Britain. Service in the armed forces introduced Japanese conscripts to new ways of life, some travel, reading and writing, Western-style uniforms and shoes, nationalism, and reverence for the emperor. Japan was becoming the most powerful nation in East Asia.

Restructuring the Economy. Recognizing an economic principle that underlay the Industrial Revolution in Britain, Japan first built up its agriculture. It needed the profits, and it needed the food and manpower that an effective agriculture would make available for urban industry. New seeds, fertilizer, and methods were introduced throughout the islands, and agricultural colleges spread the new techniques and information. In the 1880s, agricultural production went up by about 30 percent, and from 1890 to 1915 by 100 percent. This production included not only food crops but also tea, cotton, and silk, mostly for the export market. The profits did not go to the peasants but to the landlord, who invested them in commerce or

KEY TERMS

Meiji restoration The reforms effected in Japan in the name of the emperor Mutsuhito (r. 1867–1912), who was known as the Meiji emperor. During his reign constitutional changes restored the emperor to full power, displacing the militarily powerful shogun, and Japan adopted many Western innovations as it became a modern, industrial, militarized state.

daimyo The feudal lords of Japan, who, by the sixteenth century, controlled almost the entire country.

Advertisement from the Mitsui dry-goods store (later Mitsuoki Department Store), Tokyo, c. 1895. Retail outlets were obvious signs of the drive to embrace industrialized Western culture, as this "before" and "after" picture aptly demonstrates. The traditional first floor (bottom), with its legions of clerks haggling over material, has been augmented by the newfangled second floor (top), where a more serene atmosphere and slick glass display cases proclaim a new style of consumerism.

Ginza District, Tokyo, about 1930. A general view showing the heart of the "new" Tokyo, sometimes known as Japan's Broadway. As Japan became more Westernized, its cities, and especially Tokyo, adopted the architectural and urban design patterns, as well as the transportation patterns, of the West. The Nippon Bridge was considered the center of the Japanese empire. All distances were computed from this point.

industry. Poorer peasants were squeezed off the land by high rents, and all peasants were heavily taxed to fund the large expenses of industrialization and militarization.

In large-scale industrialization, the government was the entrepreneur. It built the first railway line, between Tokyo and Yokohama, in 1872. In two decades about 2,000 miles of track followed. The government financed coal mines, iron mines, a machine-tool factory, cement works, glass and tile factories, wool and cotton textile mills, shipyards, mines, and weapons manufacture. However, the industry that contributed the most, silk, which accounted for more than 40 percent of all of Japan's exports, was developed largely by private entrepreneurs.

Cultural and Educational Changes. Under the Tokugawa shogunate, 1603–1867, each *daimyo* had his own capital (see Chapter Fourteen). As a result, Japan had a rich array of administrative towns and cities spread throughout the country. During the Meiji restoration, they provided the network for the diffusion of new cultural patterns. Some cities stood out: Kyoto, the home of the emperor, was the center of traditional culture; Osaka was the most important business center; and Edo (Tokyo) was, by the mid-1800s, the largest and most flourishing of the major cities, with a population of a half-million to a million people.

Tokugawa urban culture had mixed strains. At the center of business life were merchants dedicated to making money. Yet they liked entertainment and found it outside their homes. Homes were for wives, children, and household duties. The amusement quarters of the city were for restaurants, theater, artistic culture, the female companionship of geisha entertainers, and prostitutes.

Social networks based on neighborhoods, shrines, guilds, and civic needs, such as firefighting, provided a sense of community, and cities grew relatively slowly in the first generation of the restoration. By 1895 only 12 percent of Japan's population of 42 million lived in cities. Industrialization in large factories had barely begun. In 1897 only 400,000 workers in all of Japan were working in factories employing more than five workers. By the turn of the century, however, the institutional and economic changes of the Restoration were taking effect, and urban populations multiplied.

Western cultural styles, both superficial and profound, proliferated in Meiji Japan. The Gregorian calendar and the seven-day week, with Sunday as a holiday, were adopted in 1882, and the metric system in 1886. Samurai men began to prefer Western haircuts to the traditional shaved head and topknot. The military dressed in

The expansion and modernization of Japan. Responding to the threats of foreign gunboats, Japanese samurai leaders overthrew the long-established Tokugawa shogunate and restored imperial power under the Emperor Meiji in 1868. Within 50 years, industrial development, growing international trade, and territorial expansion made Japan a world power. Initially asserting its control of neighboring islands, and then taking advantage of Manchu decline, its victories over China (1894–95) and Russia (1904–05) established Japanese control over Taiwan, Korea, and Karafuto (southern Sakhalin), and its dominant influence over Manchuria and even parts of mainland China.

Meiji classroom scene, c. 1900.
The Meiji rulers saw education as critical to Japan's modernization. The Charter Oath declared that "Knowledge shall be sought throughout the world." Even before the Meiji, educational standards had been high; under the Meiji they approached 100 percent literacy.

Western-style uniforms, and in 1872 Western dress became mandatory at all official ceremonies. Meat eating was encouraged, despite Buddhist ethics, and *sukiyaki*, a meat and vegetable dish especially cooked at the table, was developed as part of Japanese cuisine.

Japanese readers turned avidly to Western texts. Philosophers of the Enlightenment drew attention to individual rights. Herbert Spencer's emphasis on the survival of the fittest, derived from Darwin's theory, proved attractive as a justification for Japan's assertion of its growing power and coming imperialism. Scottish author Samuel Smiles' popular text, *Self Help,* advocating pulling oneself up by the bootstraps, also found a receptive readership.

Tokugawa Japan had valued formal education. Samurai had attended Confucian-based schools run by the *han*; commoners had studied in schools located in Buddhist temples. At the time of the Meiji restoration, an estimated 45 percent of adult males and 15 percent of adult females could read and write, about the same proportions as in advanced European countries. Building on this base, the government introduced a highly centralized system of education and then mandated compulsory attendance. By 1905, over 90 percent of both boys and girls of primary school age were attending school. The schools were recognized for high quality, for providing public education superior to private schools, and for helping move Japan from the feudal, hierarchical society of Tokugawa Japan to a more egalitarian system than that of most European countries. At the university level, a series of excellent institutions was established throughout Japan, beginning with Tokyo University in 1886.

Gender Relations. The Meiji restoration opened up entirely new arenas of public life and achievement for Japanese men. For a few years before marriage, some Japanese women, too, found new opportunities in education, in factory employment, and in a handful of new cultural venues. For the most part, however, women's public options were restricted. As the emperor's position was restored, so was male dominance in the home reinforced. Women and minors were prohibited from joining political organizations and from holding or attending meetings in which political speeches or lectures were given. (The vote was granted to women in Japan only after World War II.)

The 1898 Civil Code reinforced patriarchy within the family, granting the male head of the family unquestioned authority. Women had few legal rights. At marriage, control over a woman's property passed to her husband. Fathers held exclusive right to custody over children. Concubinage was abolished in 1880, but society sanctioned prostitution and the discreet keeping of mistresses. As high school education was extended to women, the Girls' High School Law of 1899 declared its goal to create "**good wives and wise mothers**." Within the home, women held great authority and respect, but they were allowed virtually no place in the public life of Japan.

Equality in the Family of Nations. From the beginning of the Meiji restoration, Japan sought to end the demeaning provisions of **extraterritoriality**, which required that foreigners charged with legal crimes in Japan be tried by foreign courts rather than by Japanese courts. Japan also sought to regain control of its own tariffs. These goals provided the rationales for introducing new legal systems that were more consistent with those of Western countries. If Japan's laws were in accord with those of Europe, there would be no justification for continuing extraterritoriality. The British relinquished extraterritoriality in 1899 when the new legal codes took effect. Other nations followed suit, and Japan reciprocated by allowing foreigners to establish residences outside the treaty ports. Additional treaties returned full control over tariffs to Japan in 1911.

War and colonization also seemed important to full membership in the European community of nations. Japan had forced the establishment of a legation in Korea in 1876. As political leaders in that country divided over policy issues, some sought support from more conservative China, others from more progressive Japan. When fighting between the groups broke out in 1894, both China and Japan sent in troops, and war began between the two powers. Japan defeated the Chinese fleet, captured Port Arthur, the naval base in southern Manchuria, and the port of Weihaiwei on the Shandong peninsula. Peace negotiations gave Japan Taiwan and the Pescadores Islands, and Japan supplanted China as the dominant nation of East Asia. Korea was formally recognized as independent, but Japan held sway there nonetheless.

In the first years of the twentieth century, two further engagements with the West ratified Japan's arrival among the powers of the world. First, in 1902, Britain and Japan signed an alliance, the first military pact on equal terms between a European and a non-Western country. It brought together the most powerful navies of Europe and of East Asia. The treaty blocked Russian aspirations and further secured Japan's semi-colonial control over China. Second, in response to continuing Russian penetration of Manchuria and increasingly hostile diplomacy, Japan attacked the Russian fleet in Port Arthur in 1904. Fighting far from the center of their country, the Russian army was defeated. A Russian fleet dispatched from the Baltic was intercepted and annihilated by the Japanese in 1905 as it crossed the Straits of Tsushima.

An Asian power had defeated a European power for the first time since the victories of the Ottomans in eastern Europe in the seventeenth century. In Russia, the defeat precipitated a revolution against the government in 1905. The American President Theodore Roosevelt convened a peace conference—for which he was awarded the Nobel Prize for Peace—which gave Japan a protectorate over Korea, predominant rights over southern Manchuria, and control of southern Sakhalin Island. In 1910, with no European power protesting, Japan formally annexed Korea. Japan had reached the international status it had desired—less than a half-century after embarking on its quest. The values of nationalism, technological innovation, and imperialism had become as supreme in Japan as they were in Europe.

Nationalism and Imperialism: What Difference Do They Make?

Nationalism inspired existing nations with pride in their past and aspirations for their future. It gave them a sense of their potential strength and power. It often united people together in collective efforts and encouraged a greater sense of equality and common purpose among them. This was part of the message of the British, American, and French Revolutions. For regional groupings that were not political nations, such as Italy and Germany, the spirit of nationalism often inspired action toward unifying their divided regions into unified nations. For groups that felt themselves denied their national identity by a larger power that had colonized them—the Greeks, Romanians, and Bulgarians under the Ottoman Empire, and much of the world under European colonialism—nationalism offered the promise of autonomy and control over their own affairs. At its best, nationalism encouraged nations to learn from one another, as each had something unique to contribute.

Nationalism also inspired competition among nations that sometimes evoked greatness, but has also frequently led to warfare, conquest, and colonialism. It led to disputes among groups claiming national identity and national geographic borders that are difficult, if not impossible, to resolve. It accompanied, and sometimes encouraged, racism and arrogance. It created and perpetuated economic systems of great inequality in which the terms of trade were set by the powerful for their own benefit, often causing great suffering to the weak. All these aspects of nationalism, positive and negative, continued into the twentieth century—in ways that we shall explore in Part Seven—and remain powerful today.

The political and industrial revolutions of the eighteenth and nineteenth centuries bound nations and peoples together more tightly than ever before. Historically great nations like China and Japan, which had lived mostly within their own regions, were pulled into greater participation in the global economy, politics, and culture. New political and industrial relationships raised questions about the goals and the proper functions of the international economy: Is its purpose to create business profits or to provide for overall human welfare? Can it do both? How? Can the benefits of international competition be encouraged and its powers of destruction limited?

In this chapter we have seen European nations, and later Japan and the United States, backed by the power of their industrial revolutions, assert their control over most of the globe. Imperialists usually claimed that they were benefiting the peoples they ruled and cited statistics on new transport lines, new health clinics, new schools, and new political institutions. The conquered peoples usually pointed to evidence to the contrary: economies devastated, politics suppressed, cultural traditions undermined, and populations divided and turned against one another. These legacies continued into the twentieth century, and they continue today as former colonizers and former colonies adjust their economies, cultures, and foreign relations to one another. Consciously and unconsciously the world proceeds against a background in which some nations conquered and lorded it over others. The sensitivities of those relationships are still quite raw, as we see today when powerful nations attempt to exert their will politically, economically, and culturally over weaker ones—and the weaker choose to accept these conditions, to modify them, or to resist.

Asking Questions

- How do you define nationalism? Would a strong nation and a weak nation use the same definition?
- Give examples of nations that formed by bringing together groups and regions, and give other examples of nations that formed by breaking apart from larger powers.
- In what ways were the colonization of India and China similar to each other? In what ways were they different?
- What benefits did colonialism bring to late nineteenth-century colonies? Please cite specific examples. What benefits did it bring to colonizers? Please consider economic, political, and cultural aspects of colonialism. What were its negative effects on both colonizer and colonized?
- What do you believe to be the most important results of the coming of large numbers of European women to the colonies?
- What were the principal steps in Japan's actions to stave off colonial control?

Suggested Readings

PRINCIPAL SOURCES

Abernethy, David. *The Dynamics of Global Dominance: European Overseas Empires, 1415–1980* (New Haven, CT: Yale University Press, 2000). Presents European expansion through a series of phases, notes its extraordinary power in reshaping the world, but sees it as ultimately self-liquidating. Comprehensive.

Bayly, C.A. *The Birth of the Modern World 1780–1914* (Malden, MA: Blackwell, 2004). A masterpiece of synthesis, combining political, economic, social, and cultural history in a global, interactive framework, by a master historian.

Cooper, Frederick and Ann Laura Stoler, eds. *Tensions of Empire: Colonial Cultures in a Bourgeois World* (Berkeley, CA: University of California Press, 1997). Excellent selections on the effects of colonialism on the identity of colonizer and colonized. Several essays on feminist perspectives.

Curtin, Philip, *et al. African History from Earliest Times to Independence* (New York: Longman, 2nd ed., 1995). Masterly study, especially good on the combination of history and anthropology. Four authors bring specialization across regions, disciplines, and styles of understanding. The narrative sometimes wanders among them.

Davis, Mike. *Late Victorian Holocausts: El Nino Famines and the Making of the Third World* (New York: Verso, 2001). Brings together many classic arguments about imperial exploitation of colonies, and emphasizes the cruelty of this exploitation at the time when major famines were also devastating colonial economies.

deBary, William Theodore, ed. *Sources of Japanese Tradition Volume 2: Parts 1 and 2* (New York: Columbia University Press, 2nd ed., 2006). Outstanding collection of primary sources, especially on the cultural leaders and philosophies of Japan, from earliest to modern times.

deBary, William Theodore and Richard Lufrano, eds. *Sources of Chinese Tradition*, Vol. 2 (New York: Columbia University Press, 2nd ed., 2000). Outstanding source book, especially on cultural issues, from the Qing dynasty to the present. Vol. 1 carries the earlier history.

Hay, Stephen, ed. *Sources of Indian Tradition*, Vol. 2, (New York: Columbia University Press, 2nd ed., 1988). Superb anthology of primary sources, especially strong on the religious and cultural bases of modern India and their influence on its politics, about 1500 to the present. Vol. 1 carries earlier periods.

Hobsbawm, Eric. *The Age of Capital 1848–1875* (New York: Vintage Books, 1975). This series of Hobsbawm's books provides a well-written narrative sweep of world history through this period, from a leftist perspective. Often uses examples from popular culture, especially music.

——. *The Age of Empire 1875–1914* (New York: Vintage, 1987).

——. *The Age of Revolution 1789–1848* (New York: New American Library, 1962).

Hochschild, Adam. *King Leopold's Ghost* (New York: Houghton Mifflin, 1998). Narrates the horrifying story of the king's rule of the Congo, and the shipping agent who discovered and exposed it.

July, Robert J. *A History of the African People* (Prospect Heights, IL: Waveland Press, 4th ed., 1992). Clearly written survey, especially good on political history.

Morris-Suzuki, Tessa. *The Technological Transformation of Japan* (Cambridge: Cambridge University Press, 1994). Follows the technical and managerial decisions that brought Japan to parity and even superiority in economic and technological modernization.

Said, Edward W. *Culture and Imperialism* (New York: Vintage Books, 1993). Said's various books emphasize the ways in which imperial powers used their own interpretations of culture to assert their supremacy over the countries they dominated and, often, to get the colonized people to believe them.

ADDITIONAL SOURCES

Adas, Michael, ed. *Islamic and European Expansion* (Philadelphia, PA: Temple University Press, 1993). Still the best collection of introductory historiographic essays on the period 1000 to 1914 in world history.

Anderson, Benedict. *Imagined Communities* (London: Verso, 1983). Stresses the importance of the vision of nationalists in creating new nations, and the critical role of commercial publishing (print capitalism) in popularizing these visions.

Andrea, Alfred and James Overfield, eds. *The Human Record*, Vol. 2 (Florence, KY: Wadsworth Publishing Co., 6th ed., 2008). Superb collection of primary documents on modern history.

Bayly, C.A. *Origins of Nationality in South Asia* (New York: Oxford University Press, 1998). Seeks to discover how Indians developed the concept of a modern nation from their own cultural materials as well as from new conceptions brought from the West.

Bose, Sugata. *A Hundred Horizons: The Indian Ocean in the Age of Global Empire* (Cambridge: Harvard University Press, 2009). Seeks the unities in the Indian Ocean basin in the nineteenth and twentieth centuries. Densely written.

KEY TERMS

nationalism see p. 598

millet **system** see p. 598

blood and iron see p. 605

pogrom see p. 605

world system see p. 610

social Darwinism see p. 610

White Man's Burden see p. 610

the cultivation system see p. 620

Great Trek see p. 625

mfecane see p. 625

Berlin Conference see p. 627

scramble for Africa see p. 627

nabob see p. 630

han see p. 632

Eastern Ethics; Western Science see p. 632

Revere the Emperor; Expel the Barbarian see p. 632

Meiji restoration see p. 635

daimyo see p. 635

good wives and wise mothers see p. 638

extraterritoriality see p. 638

Braudel, Fernand. *The Identity of France*, trans. Sian Reynolds (New York: Harper and Row, 1988). Fascinating discussion of the process by which the various, disparate regions of France were unified into a single nation.

Briggs, Asa. *A Social History of England* (New York: Viking Press, 1983). Standard, well-written, well-illustrated history, stressing social conditions and change more than politics or economics.

Burns, E. Bradford. *Latin America: A Concise Interpretive History* (Englewood Cliffs, NJ: Prentice Hall, 6th ed., 1993). Excellent survey from a slightly leftist and critical perspective.

Burton, Antoinette. *Burdens of History* (Chapel Hill, NC: University of North Carolina Press, 1994). Sees European women adopting positions sympathetic to imperialism as a means of showing that they deserved the same rights as men because they shared the same political perspectives.

Cheng, Pei-kai and Michael Lestz with Jonathan Spence, eds. *The Search for Modern China: A Documentary Collection* (New York: W.W. Norton, 1999). Excellent selection, very well annotated. Designed to accompany Spence's textbook of the same name, but also stands alone.

Chatterjee, Partha. *The Nation and Its Fragments* (Princeton, NJ: Princeton University Press, 1993). Analyzes some of the movements by which India began to come together as a nation. Thematically notes the importance of religion. Geographically stresses the Bengal region.

Collcutt, Martin, Marius Jansen, and Isao Kumakura. *Cultural Atlas of Japan* (New York: Facts on File, 1988). Superb introduction with fine text, maps, and illustrations that all work well together.

Columbia College, Columbia University. *Introduction to Contemporary Civilization in* the West, Vol. 2 (New York: Columbia University Press, 3rd ed., 1960). Outstanding sourcebook with lengthy excerpts from highly influential thinkers and actors.

Conrad, Joseph. *Heart of Darkness* (Mineola, NY: Dover Publications, 1990). A classic, brief novel on the cruelty and corruption of the "ruler" of a European outpost in the Congo interior.

Cooper, Frederick. *Colonialism in Question: Theory, Knowledge, History* (Berkeley, CA: University of California Press, 2005). Excellent review of recent scholarship on "the cultural turn" in the study of imperialism.

Dalpat-Kavya Navnit. *Selections from Dalpat the Poet*, in Gujarati, ed. Deshavram Kashiram Shastri (Ahmedabad: Gujarat Vidyasabha, 1949). Dalpat's poetry expressed his beliefs that Indians in the mid-nineteenth century had much to learn from the British, including the methods of industrialization.

Davis, Lance E. and Robert A. Huttenback. *Mammon and the Pursuit of Empire* (Cambridge: Cambridge University Press, 1989). Argues that imperialism did not pay, at least not financially, at least not after the beginning phases. A careful economic analysis.

Eley, Geoff and Ronald Grigor Suny, eds. *Becoming National* (New York: Oxford University Press, 1996). Excellent analysis of several major Western theories on the meaning of nationalism.

Engels, Friedrich. *The Origins of the Family, Private Property and the State*, ed. Eleanor Burke Leacock (New York: International Publishers, 1973). Engels saw the exploitation of women as the first kind of economic exploitation that ultimately led to its fullest expression in the capitalist system.

Fujimura-Fanselow, Kumiko and Atsuko Kameda, eds. *Japanese Women* (New York: Feminist Press, 1995). Twenty-seven essays on many aspects of women in public and private life, their changing status, including men's views of the change.

Gluck, Carol. *Japan's Modern Myths: Ideology in the Late Meiji Period* (Princeton, NJ: Princeton University Press, 1985). Analyzes not only the formal ideologies, but also how they were received and perceived by the Japanese public.

Haldane, Charlotte. *The Last Great Empress of China* (Indianapolis, IN: Bobbs-Merrill, 1965). A portrait of the powerful woman who effectively ruled China at the end of the nineteenth century and opposed reform.

Hanke, Lewis and Jane M. Rausch, eds. *People and Issues in Latin American History* Vols 1 and 2 (New York: Markus Wiener Publishing, 3rd ed., 2006). Standard historical survey often presented through biography.

Headrick, Daniel R. *The Tools of Empire* (New York: Oxford University Press, 1981). Steamships, guns, and quinine were among the prerequisites of the European conquest of Africa.

Hertzberg, Arthur, ed. *The Zionist Idea* (Philadelphia, PA: Jewish Publication Society, 1997). Still the best primary source introduction to early Zionist thought and its evolution, with a 100-page introduction.

Hirschmeier, Johannes. *The Origins of Entrepreneurship in Meiji Japan* (Cambridge, MA: Harvard University Press, 1964). Sees the economic transformation of Japan as the key to its development and demonstrates how it developed under government guidance.

Hutchinson, John and Anthony D. Smith, eds. *Nationalism* (New York: Oxford University Press, 1994). Survey of source materials on the meaning and significance of nationalism by nationalist leaders from around the world.

Kennedy, Paul. *The Rise and Fall of the Great Powers* (New York: Random House, 1987).

Kennedy's discussion of what makes empires powerful and what weakens them is engaging and provocative.

Lenin, V.I. *Imperialism, the Highest Stage of Capitalism* (Peking: Foreign Languages Press, 1965). Perhaps the strongest argument ever for the importance of the capitalist competition for markets, both for raw materials and for finished goods, as the basis for imperialism.

Magraw, Roger. *France 1815–1914: The Bourgeois Century* (Oxford: Oxford University Press, 1983). Useful survey stressing the importance of the middle classes.

Marx, Karl. *The First Indian War of Independence 1857–1859* (Moscow: Foreign Languages Press, n.d., *c.* 1960). As a journalist covering this war, Marx took a pro-European, imperialist position: British rule in India was a benefit that would bring the colony into the modern world. Surprising?

Metcalf, Barbara and Thomas R. Metcalf. *A Concise History of Modern India* (Cambridge, MA: Cambridge University Press, 2nd ed., 2006). Fast paced. Especially interesting on Muslims, women, cultural reinterpretation, film, and architecture.

Moore, Barrington, Jr. *The Social Origins of Dictatorship and Democracy* (Boston, MA: Beacon Press, 1966). A classic of comparative history analyzing especially the role of the peasantry in revolutions from England to China.

Murphey, Rhoads. *A History of Asia* (Upper Saddle River, NJ: Prentice-Hall, 2008). Useful survey.

Oliver, Roland. *The African Experience: From Olduvai Gorge to the 21st Century* (Boulder, CO: Westview Press, 2nd ed., 2008). Sensitive, thoughtful, brief survey of African history by a master of the field.

Perdue, Peter. *China Marches West: The Qing Conquest of Central Asia* (Cambridge, MA: Harvard University Press, 2005). Brilliant, comprehensive study of Chinese imperialism in central Asia.

Renan, Joseph-Ernest, "What is a Nation?" in Eley and Suny, *op. cit.*, pp. 42–55. A classic essay.

Restoring Women to History (Bloomington, IN: Organization of American Historians, 1988). Set of historiographic essays covering what we know of women's history around the world. Dated, but still useful.

SarDesai, D.R. *Southeast Asia Past and Present* (Boulder, CO: Westview Press, 6th ed., 2009). Useful survey text.

Schirokauer, Conrad. *A Brief History of Chinese and Japanese Civilizations* (Fort Worth, TX: Harcourt Brace Jovanovich, 2nd ed., 1989). Useful survey text.

Seagrave, Sterling, with Peggy Seagrave. *Dragon Lady: The Life and Legend of the Last Empress of China* (New York: Knopf, 1992). Biography of the woman who ran China's politics for her young son, and actively opposed modernization.

Spivak, Gayatri Chakravorty, "Subaltern Studies: Deconstructing Historiography," in Ranajit Guha and Gayatri Chakravorty Spivak, eds. *Selected Subaltern Studies* (New York: Oxford University Press, 1988), pp. 3–32. The subaltern scholars set out to reveal the importance of the little guy who had been left out; Spivak notes that the scholars left out women.

Strobel, Margaret, "Gender, Sex, and Empire," in Adas, *op. cit.*, pp. 345–75. Excellent introduction to issues of gender relations in imperial settings.

Teng, Ssu-yu and John K. Fairbank. *China's Response to the West: A Documentary Survey*, 1839–1923 (New York: Atheneum, 1963). A superb, standard source book.

Vickers, Adrian (2005). *A History of Modern Indonesia* (Cambridge, MA: Cambridge University Press, 2005). From the arrival of the Dutch to the present. Lively. Engaging.

Waley-Cohen, Joanna. *The Sextants of Beijing: Global Currents in Chinese History* (New York: W.W. Norton, 1999). A somewhat revisionist recounting of China's extensive contacts with the outside world, attacking the concept of Chinese isolation.

Wallerstein, Immanuel. *The Modern World-system 1: Capitalist Agriculture and the Origins of the European World-economy in the Sixteenth Century* (San Diego, CA: Academic Press, 1974). Wallerstein's perspective on the core countries' dominance over the periphery is classic, but Eurocentric, problematic, and densely argued.

Wilentz, Sean. *Chants Democratic: New York City and the Rise of the American Working Class, 1788–1850* (New York: Oxford University Press, 1984). What was special about the American working class? Why did it not form a working-class political party? Wilentz's answers are cogent and lucid.

Wolf, Eric R. *Europe and the People without History* (Berkeley, CA: University of California Press, 1982). Historical anthropologist Wolf looks at the systems of domination in modern history from the viewpoint of the colonized and the worker.

Wolfe, Patrick, "Imperialism and History: A Century of Theory, from Marx to Postcolonialism," *American Historical Review* CII, No. 2 (April 1997), pp. 388–420. Enormously useful survey.

Yukichi, Fukuzawa. *The Autobiography of Yukichi Fukuzawa*, trans. Eiichi Kiyooka (New York: Columbia University Press, 1966). Yukichi's nineteenth-century views of the West are insightful.

For quizzes, flashcards, primary sources, interactive maps, videos, and other activities related to this chapter please go to

www.myhistorylab.com

The Olympics and International Politics

Organized, competitive athletics reflect the world around them. When, where, by whom, in front of what audiences, and for what stakes sports are to be "played" are questions decided through political, economic, and cultural negotiations. In the most famous of all competitions, the modern Olympic Games, these external forces appear clearly and repeatedly. The ups-and-downs of the Olympics reflect the ups-and-downs of the world outside the arena.

The reopening of the Olympic Games in Athens in 1896 was due to the enthusiastic promotions of a Frenchman, Baron Pierre de Coubertin. As a founding member of the International Olympic Committee (IOC), Coubertin had struggled for many years to revive the Olympic Games of ancient Greece, last staged in 393 C.E. Although Coubertin stressed his love of athletics, he succeeded in part because of the rampant nationalism of his age. Nations were eager to compete against one another, and sports provided a welcome, nonviolent format. The competition among athletes also became a competition among nations. In 1896, 13 nations of Western Europe and the United States participated; by 2008, some 200 nations from all over the world took part.

The decision to hold the first revived Olympic Games in Greece was in part meant to reconnect with the home of the original Olympics, but it was designed also to deliver a political message to the Ottoman Empire, Greece's former colonial ruler and hostile neighbor: that Greece had revived as an independent nation, and that other regions of the Balkans were also seeking their independence.

Women were not allowed to compete in the ancient Olympic Games, and they were barred from the first modern Olympics as well. Women competed in the Olympics for the first time in 1900, in lawn tennis and golf, and they participated in track and field events in the 1928 Amsterdam Olympics. This breakthrough in gender relations mirrored more wide-ranging victories for feminism in society at large, most especially the right to vote, which was accorded to women in several European countries and the United States in the decade just after World War I.

Germany staged the 1936 Berlin Olympics as a showcase for Adolf Hitler and his National Socialist (Nazi) Party. Leni Riefenstahl's documentary film, *Triumph of the Will*, produced for the government,

Fireworks over the Bird's Nest Stadium, Beijing, 2008. Winning the right to host the Olympic Games is a coveted mark of international status. Japan in 1964, Mexico in 1968, Russia in 1980, Korea in 1988—each country put on a display of national pride worthy of the honor. China's introductory ceremony in 2008—with its take-your-breath-away architecture, choreography, and fireworks—announced to the world that this ancient, venerable country had returned as a powerful, modern, dynamic nation.

LEFT Women racing in the 100 meters, Olympic Games, Amsterdam, 1928.

RIGHT A member of the International Olympic Committee talks with a masked PLO terrorist, Munich Olympics, 1972.

captured the intensely nationalistic spirit evident in parades and demonstrations for the occasion. In the end, however, the African-American athlete Jesse Owens delivered a great slap in the face to Hitler's racial theories of Aryan supremacy by winning the gold medal in the 100- and 200-meter races, the long jump, and as part of the 400-meter relay race. Altogether, American track-and-field teams, which included several African-American athletes, won 12 gold medals.

The right to host the Olympics has been a mark of national accomplishment. The first 13 summer Games were hosted by cities in Western Europe and the United States. The fourteenth Games, held in Melbourne, Australia, in 1956, were the first departure from that pattern. From that time hosting of the Games became far more international. By according Japan the right to host the sixteenth Games in 1964, the IOC recognized Japan's reentry into the community of nations after World War II. In subsequent years, additional nations sought and

received the right to host the Olympics as a badge of their significance in international affairs: Mexico in 1968, Moscow in 1980, Korea in 1988. China, host in 2008, mounted the most spectacular introduction in the history of the games, and more than four and one half billion spectators around the world witnessed at least some part of the Beijing Games.

The dark as well as the bright side of international politics has spilled over into the Olympic Games. During the 1972 Munich Games, eight Palestinian terrorists brought the warfare of the Middle East to the Olympics. They invaded the Olympic Village, where athletes live during the Games, murdered two Israeli athletes, and seized nine more as hostages. Negotiations between Olympics officials and the terrorists failed. All the Israeli hostages, one West German policeman, and five of the Palestinians were killed.

In 1979, the USSR invaded Afghanistan and U.S. President Jimmy Carter responded symbolically by refusing to allow America to compete in the 1980 Olympics in Moscow. In retaliation, the USSR refused to participate in the 1984 Olympics in Los Angeles. Despite the high aspirations of Baron Coubertin in 1896, Olympic competition could not be sealed off from international politics; on the contrary, they have always been tightly intertwined.

Turning Point Questions

1. Can you imagine an Olympic Games in which athletes compete as individuals rather than as part of national teams? How would this be different?
2. Do you agree that sports as public competition mirror world events? Give examples.
3. In 1936 most eligible nations attended Hitler's Munich Olympics. In 1976, the United States boycotted the Moscow Olympics because of the Soviet invasion of Afghanistan. Do you think either of these decisions was appropriate? Why?

Jesse Owens accepting the gold medal in the long jump, and signaling his defiance with an American salute, at Hitler's Berlin Olympics, 1936.

645

PART SEVEN
EXPLODING TECHNOLOGIES
1914–1991

Contested Visions of a New International Order

The twentieth century began with great promise. The political and industrial revolutions of the previous two centuries encouraged western Europeans to believe that they were mastering the secrets of securing a long, productive, comfortable, and meaningful life for the individual and the community. They believed that they were transmitting these benefits around the globe through their colonial policies, and that their colonial possessions would continue long into the foreseeable future. Polish poet Wislawa Szymborska captured the optimism:

> Our twentieth century was going to improve on others
> …
> A couple of problems weren't going to come up anymore:
> Hunger, for example, and war, and so forth.

World War I, global economic depression, World War II, the Cold War, and revolts throughout the colonial world shattered many of these European illusions. "Anyone who planned to enjoy the world is now faced with a hopeless task," Szymborska wrote. (For the complete poem, "How Should We Live," see p. 681.)

What had gone wrong? Technology can produce catastrophe as well as creativity. Optimists at the beginning of the century overemphasized its positive potentials and underestimated the problems of deciding its purposes, uses, and controls in a world of competition among nations, religions, ethnic groups, and ideologies.

The first half of the century saw technology put to use more in warfare than in peace (Chapters Nineteen and Twenty), but the second half brought a resurgence of optimism (Chapter Twenty-one): the United Nations emerged as a potential venue for conflict resolution and international bargaining, and the Cold War was contained as an armed truce, coming to an end almost without bloodshed (although many proxy wars had been fought in its name). Technology—especially information and communication technology and biotechnology—was once again promising beneficial revolutions globally and in everyday life.

The world had heard such promises before, and once again the voices of caution were loud and clear: prosperity and opportunity were not trickling down to billions of impoverished people, neither in rich nor in poor countries; ethnic and religious violence broke out repeatedly around the globe; issues of gender identity, growing increasingly sensitive throughout the twentieth century, continued to expose tensions in family and public life; and technologies of destruction continued to multiply side by side with technologies of productivity.

Atomic weapons test in the Marshall Islands, 1950.

CHAPTER NINETEEN

Methods of Mass Production and Destruction

Technological Systems

1914–1937

From the early years of the Industrial Revolution, people understood that the organization of human life would never again be the same. The neighborhood workplace and factory, the regional cities and towns, and the most intimate relationships among friends and family were transformed. At the global level, relationships between nations were realigned, as rapidly industrializing countries challenged each other for supremacy.

As advocates had feared and critics had warned, many of the results were horrific. World War I resulted from a small crisis, a single political assassination, that spun out of control. Ultimately, the crisis goaded the most powerful nations of Europe to attack each other with their new weapons, the most lethal ever: tanks, airplanes, and poison gas. In part because Russia could not keep up with the military technology of its neighbors—and because its citizens suffered grievously as a result—revolutionary leaders arose who took that country out of the Great War. The Soviet Union's new leaders promised to build up an industrial and military capacity second to none, even at the expense of the living standards of the common people: they chose "guns over butter," military expenditures over domestic consumption. Only a few years later, much of the world was plunged into a depression triggered by economic decisions that seemed to favor the rich over the poor, increasing an imbalance of wealth that ultimately undercut the welfare of both. Meanwhile, at the domestic level, new appliances that were at first luxuries soon became necessities in middle-class homes; families became smaller, cities larger, automobiles more numerous, and lives longer. The new technologies of the industrial age served the tasks their masters set for them—for construction as well as destruction.

Technology in the Twentieth Century

"Technology" refers not only to inventions but also to the systems that produce and sustain them. Thomas Hughes, a historian of science and technology, offers this comprehensive definition:

> In popular accounts of technology, inventions of the late nineteenth century, such as the incandescent light, the radio, the airplane, and the gasoline-driven automobile, occupy center stage, but these inventions were embedded within technological systems. Such systems involve far more than the so-called hardware, devices, machines and processes, and the transportation, communication, and information networks that

Modern Times, **1936.** In one of the greatest and most enduring comedic films, Charlie Chaplin takes aim at the capitalist industrial system, blaming it for impoverishing the world in the Great Depression of the time, and for driving the workers insane through the mind-numbing boredom of its production lines. Here, Chaplin satirizes the effects of the system on "The Little Tramp," his trademark character representing Everyman. Contrast this satiric, crazed view with the proud, even triumphal representation of industrialization on p. 560.

interconnect them. Such systems consist also of people and organizations. An electric light-and-power system, for instance, may involve generators, motors, transmission lines, utility companies, manufacturing enterprises, and banks. Even a regulatory body may be co-opted into the system. (Hughes, p. 3)

The power and the creativity of the technological enterprise became the most pervasive characteristic of the twentieth century. By 1914, when World War I began, many of the most important innovations were already in place, producing, or on the verge of producing, dramatic alterations in the world. Many of these innovations led to increased production of capital goods, such as machinery and steel, and many of them touched directly on the quality and style of life.

Transportation and Communication

By the early twentieth century, transport and communication networks made even the most distant places accessible and provided unprecedented mobility between them. In the cities, subways brought faster speeds and shorter waiting times. Commuter trains extended the new mobility further. Many urban workers who could afford the costs of commuting began to live in the suburbs. Industries, too, migrated to the suburbs, where they could adopt new, sprawling, single-story factory design.

In 1908, Henry Ford's automobile factory produced 10,607 Model T cars. In 1913, using the moving assembly line he had developed, Ford's factory turned out 300,000 cars—one car every 93 minutes. The Ford Motor Company made the automobile practical and cheap enough to be accessible to a mass market. Trucks were marketed at first in the hundreds and, by 1918, in the hundreds of thousands. Commercial bus operations began in Birmingham, England, in 1904 and in New York, Paris, and London in the next year. As automobiles, trucks, and buses multiplied, pressure mounted for road construction, and vast industries developed around the new vehicles: rubber for tires, glass for windows, steel for bodies and engines, and electrical systems for lights, starters, and, later, luxury equipment. Like electric power, automobiles provided both workhorses for industry and fantasies for private consumption, opening up new vistas of personal mobility and, for courting couples, new possibilities of privacy.

Airplanes developed swiftly from toys to commercial and military utilities. In 1903, the Wright brothers proved that heavier-than-air flight was possible, and by 1914, airplanes could fly at 60 to 70 miles per hour. Almost as soon as they were invented, planes were drafted for military service. In World War I, both sides used them.

Ships were certainly not new, and even steamships had existed for decades, but their design was improved. In 1907, the Lusitania crossed the

New farm technology. The American Burger tractor, invented in 1889, was the first to install an internal-combustion engine. With the introduction of automated farm machinery huge tracts of land around the world were brought under cultivation and food productivity soared. Here, in 1917, a woman from Vassar College in Poughkeepsie, New York, plows a field as part of the war effort.

Atlantic in five days. (In 1915, during World War I, it was torpedoed and sunk, as discussed below.)

Communication, too, took on new speed and reach. Virtually instantaneous radio telegraphy was in place across the Atlantic by 1901 and across the Pacific in 1902. By 1907, there were 6 million phone users in the United States alone.

Urban Life

New kinds of metropolises provided homes to massive populations served by trams, cars, buses, trucks, highways, and new systems for water, sewage, lighting, and public health. Cities constructed or bought electrical grids to light up the night, replacing gas lighting. In addition to street lighting and domestic lighting, from the early twentieth century workshops and factories could operate in shifts, round the clock. Agricultural time, based on the alternating, natural rhythms of daytime, nighttime, and seasonal changes, gave way to mechanical clocktime and calendar-time. Particularly after alternating current (AC) was adopted over direct current (DC), the ability to transmit power over long distances freed entrepreneurs from earlier technical constraints in locating their factories. They no longer required a waterfront location. The human tie to nature, in time and space, was attenuated.

The growth of cities, in number, territory, population, and proportion of total population, continued as one of the most striking features of the ongoing Industrial Revolution in the early twentieth century. They expanded on the basis of technological change and immigration. The mechanization of agriculture drove people off the farms; new jobs in manufacture, bureaucracy, and service industries drew them to the cities, sometimes from nearby rural areas, sometimes from great distances. Rates of urbanization and of economic development were closely correlated. Countries with high rates of industrial and economic development had high rates of urbanization, and vice versa. Although many of the newcomers found city life disorienting, many others found it exciting and full of attractions, such as the new movie theaters and dance halls. Department stores offered fashionable displays to entice buyers. City streets themselves provided spectacle, where men and women could see and be seen.

Technology and Gender Relations

Changes in technology precipitated profound changes in gender relationships. The invention of new household appliances facilitated women's domestic work, though some historians have also argued that by making such work easier, they created a culture in which women actually did more of it. For example, instead of one annual "spring cleaning," women began to use their vacuum cleaners to clean the house more frequently.

Automobiles gave adolescents new opportunities for the exploration of their sexuality out of the sight of parents. As further stimulus to exploration, Hollywood films introduced risqué themes and featured the best of American technology as props. Many individuals believed that films sold a culture of sex, which needed to be combated, hence the censorship of the Hays Code of the 1930s. Technology made birth control easier. Family size in England and Wales, for example, declined from 6.16 children in the 1860s to 2.82 children in 1910–14. But not everyone was pleased with the changes. Many people continued to believe that a woman's role was to raise children. Margaret Sanger in the United States, Marie Stopes in Britain, and Theodore van de Velde in the Netherlands published manuals emphasizing the enjoyment of sex by both men and women in marriage and, at the same time, advocating family planning. Sanger was arrested for sending her magazines through the mail, then for opening the first "family planning" clinic in New York in 1916. Police booked her as a "public nuisance." Only in 1936 did courts in the United States decide that information on birth control was not pornographic and give doctors the right to discuss it with their patients.

Scientific Research and Development

Educational facilities multiplied: basic education was provided to prepare workers for new job requirements; research laboratories were set up to incubate creativity and inventions; and institutes were established to concentrate on advances in scientific theory.

A revolution in chemistry multiplied productivity in agriculture and industry, changing the food that people ate and the clothing that they wore. Industrial chemists developed new filaments that made incandescent lighting commercially viable. They created purer and stronger steel. Organic chemists working with coal and coal tar developed a wide array of new synthetic products, beginning with dyes, and including a wide range of consumer products. Most notably, by 1909, Fritz Haber and his colleagues in Germany had invented a process for making ammonia (NH_3) directly from nitrogen and hydrogen found in the air, without the need of mineral products, paving the way to the massive inexpensive production of artificial fertilizers as well as explosives used in construction and poison gas used in war (see below).

In physics, the major discoveries were theoretical and were achieved by individual thinkers, who usually occupied research positions in universities and were in touch with the informal, but substantial, world society of scientists.

Albert Einstein. The most revolutionary of the theoretical physicists was the German Albert Einstein (1879–1955), whose theory of special relativity was published in 1905, when he was 26 years old. Practical applications implicit in this theory came decades later, but the philosophical significance (for those who could understand it) was immediate and revolutionary.

Einstein changed the way we look at the world. His special theory of relativity started from the postulate that the speed of light is constant and unchanging. If that is so, he argued, neither time nor motion is fixed. Both appear relative to the observer. For example, light from two stars may appear to arrive at the same time on earth, but the light has actually left each star at different times relative to earth because each star is a different distance from earth. In another paper published in 1905, Einstein set forth the principle that mass and energy are interchangeable, a relationship he expressed in the equation $E = mc^2$, energy equals matter times the speed of light squared. (The search for the atomic bomb was later undertaken on the basis of this formula, for the bomb represented the transformation of matter into enormous quantities of energy.)

Marie Curie and Pierre Curie. Nineteenth- and early twentieth-century women increasingly carved out places for themselves at the forefront of intellectual, scientific, and political life. The Polish-born French scientist Marie Curie, seen here in 1895 with her husband-collaborator Pierre, pioneered the study of radiation. Here, the husband-wife team appear to be riding bicycles for pleasure but, toward the end of the nineteenth century, bicycles also gave women more freedom by providing inexpensive personal transportation and encouraging more casual, comfortable dress styles.

In 1916, Einstein published his general theory of relativity, which explored the nature of gravity and gave a new explanation for it. Physical masses do not attract other masses; rather, they actually bend space toward themselves, so that objects roll toward them. Einstein thus overturned the basis of Newtonian physics, the intellectual structure on which physics had rested for two centuries. This indeterminacy in physics unsettled centuries of scientific thought and helped usher in a period of great indeterminacy in world affairs.

The Downside of Progress

Not all scientific and industrial progress was directed toward peaceful uses. The chemical, metallurgical, and electrical marvels of the early twentieth century were devoted to military as well as to civilian goals, and the peaceful competition in invention and production was matched by military competition. The competition between Britain and Germany was especially sharp, as Britain's share of world manufacturing output dropped while Germany's rose. (The greatest gains were actually made by the United States, but America was far away and was perceived by itself and by Europeans as relatively uninvolved in Europe's contests.) The British–German competition compelled attention. This was evident in the size of their armed forces. In 1914, on the eve of World War I, Germany's lead over Britain in terms of army and navy personnel stood at 891,000 against 532,000. (The United States had only 164,000 in its armed forces.) Both Russia, with 1,352,000, and France, with 910,000, had even more men under arms, but the Russians were not so well equipped, and neither could keep up with British and German sea power. Here Britain held a commanding lead, with 2,714,000 warship tons to Germany's 1,305,000 tons.

Most observers did not expect the competition to lead to war, however, because of the system of alliances the great powers had created to preserve the peace. The balance of power (see p. 548) between the Triple Alliance (Germany, Austria–Hungary, and Italy) and the Triple Entente (France, Russia, and Britain) was expected to keep each side aware of the potential costs of war and the benefits of peace. All these nations and empires understood that a miscalculation could embroil them in catastrophic war, but images of rationality and progress led political leaders to discount such fears—to their peril, as we shall discuss below.

Fritz Haber. The life of Fritz Haber (1868–1934) makes painfully clear, on a personal level, the irony, and tragedy, of intertwining technology for humanitarian benefit with the technology of warfare. In 1909, Haber synthesized ammonia from the nitrogen in the air, making possible the nitrogen fertilizers that have dramatically increased food production throughout the world. Haber was awarded the Nobel Prize for chemistry in 1918. In 1915, however, between the time of the invention and the award of the prize, Haber also developed and introduced the use of poison gas in World War I. An ardent German patriot, he developed the gas against the advice of many of his scientific colleagues, and his strenuous arguments for its deployment went against the spirit, although not the wording, of international agreements on the limits of warfare. His wife, Clara Immerwahr, also a brilliant scientist, and one of the first women in Germany to earn a Ph.D. in science, vigorously opposed Haber's obsession with chemical warfare. When the gas was first used on the Western Front, 5,000 Allied soldiers died and 10,000 were injured (see below). Ten days later Haber's wife shot herself to death. Biographers of both husband and wife agree that their quarrel over the gas was not the only factor in her decision, but apparently it did have a role. Nevertheless, and even after Germany's defeat, Haber continued to manufacture poison gas secretly, in violation of international treaties.

International Role Reversals

Since the Industrial Revolution began, inventions in Europe had challenged, displaced, and even destroyed traditional hand manufacture in the vast areas of the world that did not experience this revolution. As the pace of scientific invention and technological application increased, this displacement intensified, causing immense turmoil. In several cases, foreign colonial rule compounded the economic and technological disparities. Four examples—from India, China, Latin America, and the Ottoman Empire—reveal the process.

Before the Industrial Revolution, India had the largest textile industry in the world, and China manufactured fine silks, porcelain, and iron. When the Spaniards first entered Mexico City, they were awed by its advanced urban structures. The Ottoman Empire preserved much of the knowledge of the ancient world during the late medieval and early modern periods, and transmitted it to those Europeans interested in reclaiming it also for themselves. In many respects, culturally, and even economically, these Asian and American empires were more sophisticated than Europe. The Industrial Revolution reversed many of these relationships as Europe began to lead the world in scientific discovery and technological application. Some regions failed to recognize the new threats posed by European advances and were left behind. Many were intentionally prevented from responding as Europeans intervened with political and military power to sustain their growing industrial supremacy.

India

In the nineteenth century the hand spinners and weavers of India were superseded and impoverished by the mechanized spindles and looms of Britain. In the late nineteenth and early twentieth centuries, continuing invention in Europe destroyed still more of India's industries. In 1883, the German chemist Adolf von Baeyer determined the chemical structure of indigo and in 1897 his company made synthetic

Inside an Indian textile mill. The picture was taken in 1981, but the factory layout and the machinery are older, dating to the 1930s. Compare them with the American machine shop, c. 1898, on p. 572, and the Japanese factory of the 1930s on p. 691. Under British colonial rule, most industrial machinery in India had to be imported from England. Only after independence in 1947 did Indians begin to manufacture more of their own machinery.

indigo available commercially. At that time, Indian farmers were producing about 9,000 tons of indigo per year. By 1913, India produced only 1,000 tons and was importing synthetic indigo from Germany. Later developments—in plastics, for example—would similarly displace hand-manufactured goods and the jobs that went with them. Technological progress in one region caused economic dislocation and suffering in other regions, a process that continues to this day.

In 1911, Britain asserted its supremacy over India through the majestic symbolism of the *durbar*—a royal convocation—in Delhi, presided over by the King-Emperor George V, who traveled to India to make the first-ever appearance of a British monarch in the colony. The princes and the elites of India, dressed in their splendor, attended as his vassals (see illustration p. 517). The British proclaimed their power and enumerated their contributions to Indian progress, but in their hubris the British willfully overlooked the disruptions that their rule was causing and the rising resentment toward them on the part of the masses and of the elites who represented them.

The *durbar* was held in Delhi because Calcutta, the city that had served as the capital of British India for a century and a half, was seething with discontent against British rule. Indians were protesting not only Britain's economic and technological policies but also its political policies of control and its religious policies of **divide and rule**, which were designed to turn Hindus and Muslims against each other. The combined outcry against all of these policies forced the British government to transfer the capital itself. Indian leaders increasingly called for self-rule. Bal Gangadhar Tilak (1856–1920) summed up the Indians' growing demand: "Freedom is my birthright and I shall have it." Their struggle was yet in its early stages. It would take another decade, and new leadership, to consolidate an anticolonial political alliance between leaders and masses.

China

We have already seen, in Chapter Eighteen, the struggles that occurred in China in the last years of the nineteenth century over the proper policies for confronting Western domination. For the most part, the traditionalists defeated the reformers at the imperial court. China chose to strengthen its industrial capacities and restructure the official civil service examinations to put greater emphasis on science and technology, but the attempted reforms were too little and too late. In 1911, China had only one million industrial workers out of a population of 400 million. Most industry was on a small scale, much of it in textiles. Faith in the viability of the Confucian traditions, and in the government that implemented them, was dying out. After 70 years of military defeat, colonial subordination, peasant revolt, and intellectual contentiousness, China was ripe for revolution. The Mandate of Heaven was passing from the Manchu dynasty.

Revolution began in China in October 1911 with a bomb explosion in the Wuhan area that triggered a series of army mutinies and civilian revolts. Within a month, the Manchu government promulgated a civil constitution and convened a provisional national assembly. Yuan Shihkai (1859–1916), the most powerful military official in China, was elected premier. In January 1912, the boy emperor Puyi (r. 1908–12) abdicated, ending 2,000 years of China's imperial tradition, and Yuan received full powers to organize a provisional republican government. But he exceeded his mandate. In January 1916, Yuan took the title of emperor, provoking widespread revolt. Under severe military attack and critically ill, Yuan died in June of that year.

With no effective governing center, China entered a decade of rule by warlords, regional strongmen who had their own independent militias. Some of the warlords controlled whole provinces, others only a few towns or segments of railway line.

KEY TERMS

durbar A showy convocation of notables paying obeisance to, and receiving gifts from, the most powerful political leaders; a means of demonstrating and ratifying the relative position of each.

divide and rule A policy, usually unstated, by which a ruling power would encourage quarrels among its subjects so that they did not unite to challenge the ruling authority, and it could present itself as indispensable to keeping the peace. The rulers claimed that the divisions were inherent among the populations; anti-imperialists claimed that the rulers created them for their own purposes.

Founder of the GMD. Sun Yat-sen (Yixian), photographed here in western dress according to his custom, is considered the "father of the nation" even though he spent much of his life abroad and never achieved his own political ambitions. He was a revolutionary and helped to found the Guomindang. Although unable to stay in power himself, he influenced China's most important figures of the next generation: Chiang Kai-shek and Mao Zedong.

Some had formal military training, others were simply local strongmen. Some sought to play a role in forming a powerful national government, others wanted to continue China's division. Many were rapacious. Old, painful Chinese proverbs took on new reality: "In an age of chaos, don't miss the chance to loot during the fire," and "In the official's house, wine and meat are allowed to rot, but on the roads are the bones of those who starved to death."

The leading revolutionaries looked to Sun Yat-sen (1866–1925) as their mentor. Although raised in a peasant household, Sun received his secondary education in a missionary school in Hawaii and his medical training in Hong Kong. He spent most of his adult life in China's port cities or abroad.

In 1895, Sun had attempted a coup, but it failed and he was exiled. He was in the United States organizing for revolution when the 1911 uprising began. He returned to help found the Guomindang (GMD), China's leading revolutionary party. Sun was elected first president of the United Provinces of China, but a jealous and fearful Yuan exiled him in 1913. Sun returned to Guangzhou in the early 1920s and led his movement from that port city, but he never regained political office.

Sun's "Three People's Principles" included a heavy admixture of Western thought. The first, nationalism, called for revolution against foreign political control, beginning with the ousting of the Manchus from China, and against foreign economic control, which had rendered China

the colony of every nation with which it has concluded treaties; each of them is China's master. China is not just the colony of one country, but the colony of many countries. We are not just the slaves of one country, but the slaves of many countries … Today we are the poorest and weakest nation in the world, and occupy the lowest position in international affairs … other men are the carving knife and serving dish; we are the fish and the meat … we must espouse nationalism and bring this national spirit to the salvation of the country.

Sun's second principle, democracy, emphasized a predominantly Western political model: "Since we have had only ideas about popular rights, and no democratic system has evolved, we have to go to Europe and America for a republican form of government." (Andrea and Overfield, p. 350) He did, however, claim the separation of powers as an ancient Chinese tradition. Sun's third principle, under the heading "People's Livelihood," revealed his ambivalence toward Western technology and organization. He proclaimed the need for new technology:

First we must build means of communication, railroads and waterways, on a large scale. Second we must open up mines. Third we must hasten to develop manufacturing. Although China has a multitude of workers, she has no machinery and so cannot compete with other countries. Goods used throughout China have to be manufactured and imported from other countries, with the result that our rights and interests are simply leaking away.

But Western-style industrialization was not his chosen model. Fearing "the expansion of private capital and the emergence of a great wealthy class with the consequent inequalities" in China, Sun called for a different path: state ownership and "state power to build up these enterprises." He thought Marxism irrelevant for China: "In China, where industry is not yet developed, Marx's class war and dictatorship of the proletariat are impracticable." China's economic problem was not unequal distribution but lack of production.

Chinese of all political parties revered Sun, but they could not implement his plans. Sun, however, inspired the two leaders—Chiang Kai-shek (Jiang Jieshi) and Mao Zedong—who contested for dominance in China for a quarter century following his death in 1925. We shall read about their struggles in Chapter Twenty-two.

Latin America

Through the late nineteenth and early twentieth centuries, Latin America began to industrialize, largely with investments from overseas. At first, Britain was the principal investor, but after World War I the United States assumed that role. For the most part, economic and technological innovations were initiated by foreigners in search of profits. Most of the investments were concentrated in primary production—that is, farming and mining—rather than in industrial manufacturing. At the time of World War I, for example, the United States was buying about one-third of Brazil's exports, mostly coffee, rubber, and cocoa. (Half of Brazil's exports consisted of coffee.) Members of the Creole and *mazombo* elites, mostly descendants of the earlier settlers who had come from Spain and Portugal, saw that they too could share in the new earnings and win some acceptability among Europeans, and they joined in the new commerce. But for the most part the initiatives came from outside.

Most of the elites were content to treat their nations as private estates. Control and patronage mattered—money and profits were means to an end, not ends in themselves. In "Ariel", an essay written in 1898, the Uruguayan philosopher José Enrique Rodó (1872–1917) analyzed Latin America's trend in the direction of an industrial democracy on the United States model and rejected it. He saw that path as barbaric and inconsistent with the more leisurely, elitist, cultured world of the Creole rulers of Latin America. In the absence of democratic systems, most governments in Latin America were still in the hands of *caudillos*, military strongmen who governed on their own authority.

Not everyone was content with a system of control by local elites. Businessmen who were participating in the new commerce and industry began to think of new goals: more education, more industrialization, more independence from foreign investors, and more consistent government, with a larger, formal voice in politics for themselves. Toward the end of the nineteenth century, a huge influx of immigrants from Europe, especially Italy, brought with it ideas of industrial development and union representation, and by the early twentieth century, important labor unions were in place in the larger nations of Latin America. Another group advocating reform and national pride was the army, especially its junior officers. Often drawn from middle-class urban families and aware of modern technology through their knowledge of weaponry, army officers were more used to the importance of education, industrialization, business, and stable government.

In some countries these groups worked together and achieved their goals, but even the most progressive states, like Argentina and Uruguay, failed to undertake what might have been the most influential reform of all. They did not restructure the land-holding patterns that left wealthy landlords in charge of impoverished peasants. The reformers were urban people, and they were frequently related to the landlords; they had little practical sympathy for the agricultural laborers and no intention of sharing power or profits with them.

The Mexican Revolution, 1910–20. In 1910, in Mexico, urban and rural leaders rose up against the dictatorship of Porfirio Díaz (1830–1915), who had been ruling the country since 1876. At the age of 80, Díaz seemed poised to retire from the presidency. Under his leadership Mexico had seen the development of mining, oil drilling, and railways, in addition to increasing exports of raw agricultural products, especially henequen fibers, used in making rope. The middle-class urban Creole elite had prospered, but the salaries of the urban workers had declined, and rural peasants had fared even worse. Ninety-five percent of the rural peasantry owned no land, while fewer than 200 Mexican families owned 25 percent of all of the land of Mexico, and foreign investors owned another 20–25 percent. One single hacienda sprawled over 13 million acres and another over 11 million acres. Huge tracts of land lay fallow and unused while peasants went hungry. Finally, on a political level, no system of orderly succession had been worked out for Mexico. The reins of power rested in the hands of Díaz and his allies alone.

Democratic voting existed for a limited electorate, but when Díaz changed his mind and ran again for president, he imprisoned his principal challenger, Francisco Madero (1873–1913). Díaz won, but rebellions against his continuing rule broke out across Mexico, and he soon resigned and went into exile in Paris. Regional leaders then asserted their influence as Mexico erupted into civil war. The warfare was both personal and factional. It concerned differences in policy among the factions and the appropriate division of power between the central government and the states.

Many of the leaders who contested for power were mestizos, people of mixed race and culture, who demanded a dramatic break with the past control by the Creole elite. The two most radical, Francisco "Pancho" Villa (1878–1923) and Emiliano Zapata (1879–1919), advocated significant land reform, and implemented it in the areas they captured during the civil war. They attracted mixed groups of followers, including farm workers, agricultural colonists, former soldiers, unemployed laborers, cowboys, and delinquents. In November 1911, Zapata called for the return of land to Indian *pueblos* (villages). Tens of thousands of impoverished peasants followed him, heeding his cry of "Tierra y Libertad" ("Land and Liberty") and accepting his view that it was "Better to die on one's feet than to live on one's knees." Zapata's supporters seized large sugar estates, haciendas with which they had been in conflict for years. By including previously scorned groups and attending to their agendas, the revolution became more radical and agrarian.

Mexican revolutionaries. General Francisco "Pancho" Villa (center) and Emiliano Zapata (right, sporting his flamboyant moustache) sit together with their Mexican revolutionary army, men who had come from many different occupations and walks of life to join the ranks. The radical leaders hailed from different parts of the country, Zapata from south of Mexico City and Villa from the northern border, but they shared common goals.

With Díaz in exile, Madero became president, but he was removed by a coup and then assassinated in 1913. General Víctoriano Huerta (1854–1916) attempted to take over and to reestablish a repressive government similar to that of Díaz. Opposed by all the other major leaders, and also by President Woodrow Wilson of the United States, who sent American troops into Veracruz to express his displeasure with Huerta, the general was forced from power in March 1914. Another general, Alvaro Obregón (1880–1928), who made free use of the machine gun, won out militarily, but he agreed to serve under Venustiano Carranza (1859–1920), who had himself installed as provisional president.

The civil war continued, and control of Mexico City changed hands several times, but ultimately the more conservative leaders, Carranza and Obregón, forced out Villa and Zapata. Carranza became president in 1916 and convened a constituent assembly that produced the Mexican Constitution of 1917, promising land reform and imposing restrictions on foreign economic control. The new constitution protected Mexican workers by passing a labor code that included minimum salaries and maximum hours, accident insurance, pensions, social benefits, and the right to unionize and strike. It placed severe restrictions on the church and clergy, denying them the rights to own property and to provide primary education. (Most of the revolutionaries were anticlerical. Zapata was an exception in this, as the peasantry who followed him were extremely devoted to the church.) The constitution also decreed that no foreigner could be a minister or priest, vote, hold office, or criticize the government.

Enacting the new laws was easier than implementing them, but having the new constitution in place set a standard of accountability for government and served as a beacon for the continuing revolution. On the material level, not much changed at first. In 1920, Obregón deposed Carranza and became president. He distributed three million acres of land to peasants, ten percent of whom benefited. This redistribution helped to establish the principles of the revolution, demonstrating good faith on the part of the state and putting new land into production, although the state did not provide the technical assistance needed to improve productivity. Politically, Obregón began to include new constituencies in his government, including the labor movement, represented by a Labor Party, and the peasants, represented by a National Agrarian Party. The institutionalization of their presence in government promised new stability through wider representation. The representation, everyone recognized, was not only by social class but also by ethnicity and culture. *Mestizos* and even indigenous Indians achieved a place in government. Mexico's struggle against the threefold problems of racial discrimination against Indians, economic discrimination against the poor, and the denial of both problems behind a façade of political rhetoric was an inspiration throughout Latin America. It had come at a high price: one million dead out of a total population of about 15 million.

The Ottoman Empire

Unlike Mexico, which was generally dependent on European powers for its economic investment capital and initiatives, the Ottoman Empire retained its economic autonomy (although French capital was used to construct its major technological achievement, the Suez Canal). Unlike India, the empire did not lose its sovereignty, but like China, it lost many of the attributes of self-rule, while remaining formally independent. The Ottoman Empire fell behind the industrial and political developments in Western Europe and America, and it slowly disintegrated.

The process by which the Ottoman Empire became "the Sick Man of Europe" took more than a century. We have already reviewed the first stages, in which the

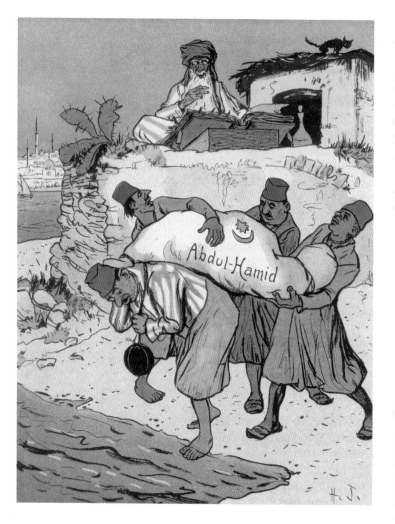

Ottomans lost control of Egypt, Greece, and most of its holdings in the Balkans. Despite its attempts at reform and reorganization, the empire was defeated by the Russians in war in 1878. In 1881, European bankers declared that the Ottoman Empire was not properly managing its finances and was defaulting on its debts. The Europeans demanded and got official representation in the offices of the Ottoman treasury. European powers also claimed rights to intervene in internal Ottoman affairs in order to defend the rights of Christian communities living in the Islamic Ottoman Empire. They stationed representatives of various Christian denominations in Constantinople to assert and represent those rights. Despite this foreign religious and political surveillance, the Ottoman government supported a series of attacks on the restless community of Armenian Christians in Anatolia, fearing continuing revolt from them, killing about 200,000 in 1895.

In 1908, a group of progressive army officers and liberal professionals—collectively called "Young Turks" (see Chapter Eighteen)—seized control of the government under the sultan. During these years, however, the dismemberment of the empire continued. Almost all of its remaining European and North African holdings were stripped away. Bulgaria declared its independence (1908) and Bosnia was annexed by Austria–Hungary (1908). Italy seized the North African territories of Libya and

Young Turks overthrowing the government of Ottoman Sultan Abdul Hamet in 1909. He had ruled since 1876, a period in which the Ottoman empire had grown steadily weaker and more out-of-touch with the Westernizing measures favored by the Young Turks. The Islamic scholar on the hill agrees that it is acceptable to dispose of the Sultan, although in reality the revolutionaries did not kill the Sultan; they merely deposed him.

the offshore Dodecanese Islands. Bulgaria, Serbia, and Greece aided Albania in gaining its independence in 1912.

A second Balkan war in the next year concerned the appropriate size of Bulgaria and control over Albania. Serbians, Greeks, Austrians, and even Italians were involved. The decision, favored by Austria, to make Albania an independent kingdom infuriated the Serbians, who wanted to control the region for its access to the sea, and agitated the Russians, who had backed the Serbians as brother Slavs. The economic and military competition among the great powers was embedded in these still larger issues of nationalism, a powerful force in early twentieth-century Europe.

People's reverence for their nation-states, and for their shared languages, history, ethnicity, and aspirations within those states, had grown so passionate that they were willing to fight and die for them. Cynics argued that the masses of the population were being manipulated into battle by industrialists in each country who stood to profit from war production, but the national feelings were powerful in themselves. Nationalism evoked just as much emotional commitment among the citizens of smaller, newer states with little economic base in military production—like the states in the Balkans—as it did among the great empires.

By 1914, the dismemberment of the Ottoman Empire, the resulting power struggle in the Balkans, and the constant warfare for control of the area created one of the most dangerous geopolitical regions of the world. Having fallen behind the industrial and military advances of its European rivals, the Ottoman Empire could no longer keep the peace in its region. Without effective Ottoman rule, the multitude of rival ethnic and religious groups encouraged strife and invited the intervention of the major powers of Europe. As noted, these powers were already deeply involved in competition for arms, markets, and prestige, and they were committed to mutually antagonistic military alliances, which, for decades, had preserved the peace through a balance of power.

On the one hand, peace and progress appeared to be the hallmarks of the era. On the other hand, international relations were tense and in a state of flux. Peripheral areas had become central. Historically great powers had become colonies and pawns in the hands of relative newcomers. Ethnic tensions and nationalisms of various sorts seemed to appear everywhere, especially in the Balkans. From one point of view, the status of world politics and economics appeared rosy and optimistic; from another, it was tense and potentially explosive.

The end of the Ottoman Empire.
The last decades of the nineteenth century saw the Ottoman presence in Europe decline as Austria–Hungary, Russia, and several aspiring new nations challenged Ottoman power. Arab revolt and internal dissent, combined with the Turkish defeat in World War I, brought to an end 600 years of Ottoman domination. Turkey was the core residual state, while several other regions were mandated to British and French control.

661

World War I

World War I. European rivalries for political and economic superiority, within Europe and throughout its imperial holdings, erupted in 1914. A fragile system of alliances designed to contain the ambitions of Germany and Austria–Hungary (the Central Powers) collapsed, resulting in a conflict of horrific proportions. Turkey joined the Central Powers. In France and Belgium a stalemate war of attrition developed. In the east a war of thrust and counter thrust caused enormous popular dissent and exhaustion, eventually bringing the collapse of the Turkish, Russian, and Austrian Empires alike. In all, 20 million people died.

On June 28, 1914, a Serbian nationalist assassinated Archduke Franz Ferdinand, heir to the Austro-Hungarian throne, and his wife. The assassin was outraged because the Austro-Hungarian Empire had seized Balkan territories with heavily Serbian populations. His bullets were the matches that lit the spark of World War I (called the Great War until World War II surpassed it in magnitude). One month after the murder, Austria–Hungary declared war on Serbia, triggering a domino effect. Under the system of alliances that had been built up over the preceding three decades, countries now came to the aid of one another. Russia mobilized its armies to defend Serbia and to take up positions on the borders of Germany. Fearing attack, Germany declared war on Russia and its ally, France. Intending to strike France quickly and decisively, and envelop its forces in a pincer movement, Germany sent massive forces across Belgium, violating an international treaty guaranteeing Belgian neutrality. Britain declared war on Germany on August 4, as did Britain's geographically remote

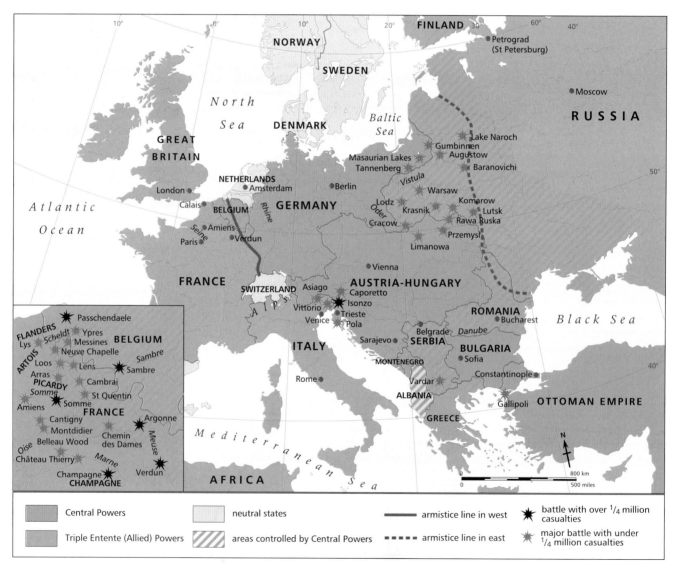

ally, Japan. The alliance system, which had been expected to prevent war among the highly competitive and nationalistic states of Europe, had instead drawn all the major powers into what had begun as a regional conflict in the Balkans. The lack of any organized system for preserving international order was clearly exposed. Within one week, all the major powers of Europe were at war. In November, the Ottoman Empire joined Germany and the Austro-Hungarian Empire in an alliance called the Central Powers. On the other side the British, French, and Russians, joined by the Italians in 1915, formed an alliance called the Allied Powers (the Allies).

War: A Stalemate from the Start

Europe had not faced continent-wide warfare since the end of the Napoleonic wars a century earlier. Despite all their armaments, neither side was prepared militarily or psychologically for the years of devastating trench warfare of the western front. Germany, attacking France through Belgium, expected a quick victory, but the French line held, and meanwhile the Russians opened an eastern front with unexpected speed, forcing the Germans to divide their troop strengths. Once the German troops had lost the momentum of their opening offensive, fighting bogged down into a costly stalemate that lasted for years.

The Battle of the Marne River, in northeastern France, fought to a draw between September 5 and 12, set the pattern. Each side continuously extended its battle lines outward until the enemies faced each other over a 400-mile front that stretched from the North Sea to Switzerland. Each side hunkered down in trenches for a kind of siege warfare, armed with machine guns and artillery, and protected by barbed wire. Attacks by either side, going "over the top" of the trenches, were met by devastating machine-gun fire. In addition, Germany later introduced poison gas, leading to subsequent international bans against its use (although many nations today continue to store poison gas in their armories). In the first month alone, each side suffered more than a quarter-million casualties and used up quantities of ammunition that they thought would last for any future war. Erich Maria Remarque captured the horrors of this trench warfare in his 1929 novel *All Quiet on the Western Front*. Soldiers lived in mud and knew that it could be deadly to leave their trenches. Disease killed many. Altogether millions were killed in battle and millions more were wounded, often with horrendous injuries. A new industry of prosthetics developed to replace absent faces and lost limbs. Generals called for any new weapons they thought might change the course of war, and the use of new technologies—such as aircraft and aerial bombing—generally only brought more loss of life.

Major campaigns to overwhelm the opponent by sheer numbers in direct infantry charges resulted in catastrophic losses. In February 1916, the Germans attacked at Verdun, near the confluence of the borders of France, Belgium, and Germany. The battle ground on for six months, with casualties of about 350,000 on each side, before the Germans gave up their attack. In July 1916, the Allies opened their own attack at the Somme River, some 50 miles to the north. The French were still bogged down at Verdun, but the British brought in heavy artillery and even some of their new tanks,

Life in the trenches. World War I became notorious for its trench warfare, in which combatants dug themselves into positions but made few territorial gains. The horrifying drudgery, the cold, the wet, the shelling, the machine gun fire, the nervous tension, the smell of corpses and mustard gas lasted for years. By the end of the conflict in 1918, 8.5 million soldiers had lost their lives.

which could penetrate the barbed wire and the trenches to knock out enemy machine guns. There were, however, few tanks, and the main strategy of the generals on both sides was simply to throw waves of attacking men at one another, directly into the machine-gun fire of the enemy. The costs in lives were almost unbelievable. In four months, the Germans lost a half-million men, the British 400,000, and the French 200,000. On the Western Front the war was essentially a stalemate from this time until the end.

In the east, the Germans defeated the Russians repeatedly, yet the ill-equipped, ill-fed, ill-commanded Russians continued to fight. In 1914, in the first months of the war, 225,000 Russian troops were captured by the Germans at the Battles of Tannenberg and the Masurian Lakes. In 1915, the Germans and Austro-Hungarians launched major offensives against Russia, killing, wounding, or taking captive two million Russians, many of whom fought with their bare hands. To send relief to Russia through the Black Sea, the British, French, Australians, New Zealanders, and Indians (under British command) landed some 450,000 troops on the Gallipoli Peninsula, at the entrance to the Dardanelles and the Black Sea. In the course of almost a year of fighting, 145,000 of these men were killed or wounded, and the operation was terminated.

In June 1916, Russia launched its own counteroffensive, but by 1917 the war had alienated the Russian people almost entirely. In March 1917, troops in St. Petersburg mutinied. The tsar abdicated, and although the new provisional Russian government attempted to continue the war, the armies collapsed. In November a revolutionary government captured power and sued for peace, withdrawing Russia from the war. (The Russian Revolution, one of the most significant consequences of the war, is discussed in detail below.)

The British opened another front against the Ottoman Empire by siding with the Arabs of Arabia and Palestine in their struggles against Ottoman imperial rule. Colonel T.E. Lawrence, "Lawrence of Arabia," took charge of this insurrection and, with his support, the emir Husayn of Hejaz (the west coast of Arabia, including Mecca) declared himself king of the Arabs. Thanks to this pressure of Arabs against Turks, General Edmund Allenby was able to push through Turkish lines and capture Jerusalem and Damascus in a series of battles remembered for their tactical brilliance and their use of armed cavalry and air support. Faced with this combination of Arab revolt and British military victories, the Ottomans sued for peace in October 1918.

In Africa, British and French forces seized the German colonies of Togo, Cameroon, South West Africa, and Tanganyika (now Tanzania)—vowing that the Germans should never come back. Similarly, in East Asia and the Pacific, Japan, an ally of Britain, declared war on Germany in 1914 and quickly took over the German concessions in China and the German-held Marshall and Caroline Islands. In 1915 it presented China with a list of "Twenty-one Demands" to which the Chinese had to accede, against their wishes. China felt it was being turned into a colony of Japan.

In the Atlantic, both Britain and Germany disregarded the accepted law of the sea permitting the shipment of cargo unrelated to military equipment and supplies. The British, whose navy was by far the most powerful, regularly stopped all ships bound for Germany and other enemy states and confiscated their cargo. The Germans, with a smaller navy, were less able to carry out such a policy. Instead, they directly attacked shipping headed for England and France, torpedoing and sinking ships, especially in the waters surrounding the British Isles. The largest of these ships, the *Lusitania*, was torpedoed off the Irish coast in May 1915, and 1,200 passengers, including 118 Americans, drowned as the ship sank.

America had been slow to enter the war, both because it preferred the peace of neutrality and because it saw no overriding virtue in one side over the other in this war of contending imperial powers. The sinking of the *Lusitania* inclined the Ameri-

HOW DO WE KNOW?

War Experiences Subvert Colonialism

Colonial powers employed their colonial armies in fighting both world wars, transporting them from one battle front to another. Military service overseas often transformed the soldiers, making them skeptical of the advantages of European civilization. Some European soldiers came to realize that at least some of the people they colonized did not respect them but rather feared and hated them. A young journalist from India, Indulal Yagnik, serving briefly as a World War I correspondent in Iraq, wrote of his growing realization of the resentment Arabs felt for British colonization. He saw Arab women in particular transmitting their resentment by asserting their religious and cultural conventions. He began to understand more fully the opposition to colonialism shared by Indians and Arabs:

> We understood … that in the entire region Arabs regarded the English as their enemies. Bitter antagonism dripped from their eyes. They moved about like lost undertakers, joking among

themselves but stopping the moment they saw the British. They talked with the foreigners mechanically, speaking only when it was completely unavoidable. They took their few cents in pay, and otherwise behaved like defeated and dependent enemies. Their dignified women hid themselves in burkhas, which covered them from head to foot. The white soldiers must have sensed their independent temper, however, and therefore their military superiors issued strict orders not to talk with the local women. (Yagnik, p. 262, translated from the Gujarati by Devavrat Pathak and Howard Spodek.)

- How did Yagnik's experiences in Arabia strengthen his anticolonial viewpoint?
- How important was Arab women's behavior in convincing Yagnik and the British that the Arabs were anticolonial?
- Does the evidence suggest that Arab women were more anticolonial than the men?

myhistorylab

cans to the side of the Allies—reaffirming also a basic preference for more democratic Britain and France over more autocratic Germany and Austria–Hungary—but it took another two years and additional provocations for America to join in the conflict.

In January 1917, Arthur Zimmerman, Germany's foreign minister, sent a secret telegram instructing the German ambassador in Mexico City to offer the president of Mexico "an understanding on our part that Mexico is to reconquer her lost territory in Texas, New Mexico, and Arizona," if Mexico joined in an alliance with Germany against the United States. The telegram was intercepted, translated, and published in the United States, astonishing and inflaming public opinion against Germany. At about the same time, at the end of January 1917, Germany announced to the Americans that it would begin unrestricted submarine warfare, sinking on sight all merchant ships around the British Isles and in the Mediterranean.

The United States, which had remained neutral, declared war against Germany and the Central Powers in April 1917. This decision sealed the fate of the combatants, all of whom were thoroughly exhausted by four years of relentless, enervating, disastrous warfare. The American contribution was smaller, and much briefer—only about four months of actual combat—than that of the major European countries, but it came at a decisive time. By the end of the war, a year and a half later, the United States had four million soldiers and sailors under arms—two million of them in France and another million on the way—had lent $10 billion in military and civilian assistance, and had set its farms and factories to producing record amounts of food and supplies. Shipping capacity multiplied from one million tons before the war to ten million by the end. Consumer production facilities in the United States were restructured to provide military equipment and supplies. Sugar and other consumer commodities were rationed. (Eight thousand tons of steel were saved in the manufacture of women's corsets.)

Once the United States began providing its abundant supplies and fresh troops, the Allied victory was secure. In the spring and summer of 1918, the German high command made a last attempt at an offensive, but they could not withstand the Allied counterattack. Germany sought an armistice. It took effect at 11 a.m. on

Colonial troops in battle, World War I. More than a million soldiers from Europe's African and Asian colonies served in World War I alongside French, British, American, and other troops on the Western Front, in the Middle East, and in Africa. More than 100,000 died in battle. After fighting on behalf of others, the troops returned from war inspired to demand greater freedom from colonial control for their own homelands.

November 11—11/11/11. Russia, Austria–Hungary, Turkey, and Bulgaria had already withdrawn from battle. The war was finally over.

The cost in life defied imagining. Some 70 million armed forces were mobilized. Most were European, but there were also 1.4 million from India who served in the Middle East, East Africa, and France; 1.3 million from the "white" dominions; and 134,000 from other British colonies. The French recruited 600,000 soldiers from their colonies in Africa and Southeast Asia; 40,000 of the Africans died fighting for the liberation of France. Another 200,000 came to work in factories in France. Almost ten million soldiers had been killed and 20 million wounded. England lost one million; France one and a half million, Germany almost two million, Russia one and three-quarters, the Austro–Hungarian Empire somewhat more than one million, Italy a half-million, the Ottoman Empire 325,000, and the United States 115,000.

Postwar Expectations and Results

After the bloodshed, destruction, and chaos of the war, it was clear that the world was in for major changes. Defeat forced the end of four historic empires: the Ottoman, the Austro–Hungarian, the German, and the Russian. The British Empire survived, but it had made wartime promises to India of increasing self-government that might limit Britain's imperial power. Internal revolution had brought the 2,000-year-old Chinese Empire to an end shortly before the war began, and Japanese wartime conquests in China suggested that Chinese sovereignty might also be in danger.

In addition, promises had been made during wartime that raised aspirations around the globe. Perhaps the most utopian and celebrated of all these promises issued from Woodrow Wilson. The American president had declared that the goal of the Allies was to "make the world safe for democracy." Allied war aims, as expressed by Wilson in his Fourteen Points, called for:

> A free, open-minded, and absolutely impartial adjustment of all colonial claims, based upon a strict observance of the principle that in determining all such questions of sovereignty the interests of the population concerned must have equal weight with the equitable claims of the Government whose title is to be determined. (cited in Hofstadter, pp. 224–25)

As leader of the country that had swayed the balance of victory, and as an intellectual in politics, Wilson commanded attention. Colonized peoples, and minority groups within many different nations, responded to his apparent message that all peoples should have a voice in their own governments. Millions of people in the colonies had contributed to the war effort of their colonizers. They expected— and sometimes they were explicitly promised—political rewards after the war.

The Arab regions of the Ottoman Empire, for example, understood Wilson's agenda to include independent states for them. They had fought alongside the British against the Ottoman Empire, and they expected that this wartime contribution would be rewarded. Moreover, in 1915, the British high commissioner (ambassador) in Egypt had privately told Mecca's leading official, Sharif Husayn, that Arabs would receive some kind of independence if they fought against the Ottoman Turks. In addition, and just before the Armistice was signed in 1918, Britain and France declared as their goal: "the complete and definitive liberation of the peoples so long oppressed by the Turks and the establishment of national governments and administrations drawing their authority from the initiative and free choice of indigenous populations."

Jews also looked forward to important changes. Had not the British government promised them "the establishment in Palestine of a national home for the Jewish people" if the Ottoman Empire was conquered? This declaration, issued by Britain's foreign secretary, Lord Balfour, in 1917, may have been issued primarily to enlist Jewish support for Britain against the Ottoman Empire, which held Palestine at the time. It captured the imagination of Jews around the world, especially those who had already emigrated from eastern Europe to settle in Palestine and those left behind in conditions of discrimination and persecution. The Arabs, however, noted that the same Balfour Declaration promised that "nothing shall be done which may prejudice the civil and religious rights of existing non-Jewish communities in Palestine." They believed these two promises to be incompatible.

India, which had contributed not only 1.4 million men, but had also paid £100 million in 1917 and some £20–30 million each year toward Britain's wartime debts, had also received a promise in 1917. The secretary of state for India, Edwin Montagu, declared Britain's goal to be "the increasing association of Indians in every branch of government, and the gradual development of self-governing institutions, with a view to the progressive realization of responsible government in India as an integral part of the Empire."

Many linguistic and ethnic minorities scattered among the nations of eastern and central Europe, in particular Czechs, Slavs, Estonians, Latvians, and Lithuanians, also looked forward to gaining independent states of their own. The Chinese anticipated the return of some colonial territories, at least those of Germany, which had been seized during the war by the Japanese. Africans in Africa, almost entirely under colonial rule, and in the African diaspora, often suffering from crippling discrimination, also took heart. Wilson's pledges appealed, for example, to the brilliant African-American scholar and activist, W.E.B. DuBois, and the Pan-African movement that he headed. Although they had no official status, a group of 58 delegates from Africa and the African diaspora convened in Paris at the time of the conference,

Pan-African Congress, Brussels, 1921. The first Pan-African Congress convened in Paris at the time of the peace conference, 1919, to press "for the international protection of the natives of Africa," direct supervision of colonies by the League of Nations, a right to education for colonized people, the global abolition of slavery, and an end to capital punishment for plantation workers. In 1921, representatives from the Americas, the Caribbean, Europe, and Africa met again to survey their (lack of) gains and to reaffirm their agenda. Some leaders, like W.E.B. DuBois of the United States (second from right), stressed the need for joint action among the races.

demanding equality for all people, an end to a kind of internal colonization of blacks in the United States, and the colonization of Africa by European powers.

One issue—women's suffrage—demanded attention at the national level by individual sovereign governments. In several major states the vote was granted. Before the war, only a few nations and regions had granted women the right to vote: Norway, New Zealand, and some of the states in Australia and in the western United States. The suffrage movements elsewhere had not won their objectives. With the end of the war, however, populations and their legislatures, grateful for the contributions of women to the war effort—in the armed services, in factories, and at home—reconsidered. In 1918, Britain granted the vote to women over the age of 30 and in 1928 extended that right to women over the age of 21. Germany granted women's suffrage in 1919 and the United States in 1920.

The Paris Peace Settlements

Thirty-two states were invited to the peace conference convened in Paris in 1919 and many unofficial delegations arrived as well. They met amid optimistic hopes and high expectations. In the end, the American, British, and French delegations were the most critical to the negotiations. (Communist Russia, which had just undergone its revolution, and was still fighting a civil war, was not invited.) Political borders across Europe and the Middle East were redrawn, punishing the states that had lost the war or, in the case of Russia, had withdrawn from it. Four great empires—Russian, Austro-Hungarian, Ottoman, and German—were destroyed by the war, its attendant revolution in Russia, and its peace settlement in Paris.

From territories of the former Russian empire four new states were carved out: Poland, Estonia, Latvia, and Lithuania. Finland had already claimed its independence in 1917. The Austro–Hungarian Empire was dissolved. Austria–Hungary itself was reduced in territory and population and divided into two separate states. Czechoslovakia and Yugoslavia, both of them weak and insecure, were created from its former territories.

The Ottoman Empire also disappeared; its core region in Anatolia and the city of Istanbul became the new nation of Turkey. Turkey itself was marked for further dismemberment into spheres controlled by France, Italy, and, most provocatively, by Greece, the centuries-old Christian enemy of the Muslim Turks. An independent Armenian state was to be established in eastern Turkey on the shores of the Black Sea, and an independent Kurdistan just to the south of it. Only the armed resistance of Turkish forces led by General Mustafa Kemal (1881–1938) prevented implementation. Musafa Kemal, later called Atatürk, Father of the Turks, drove out the foreign troops stationed in Turkey and preserved the geographical and political independence of his state until Turkey's full sovereignty was recognized by the 1923 Treaty of Lausanne. From the remainder of the Ottoman Empire's European territories, Romania and Greece were expanded. From its Middle Eastern regions, four new nations, predominantly Arab in population, were created—Syria, Lebanon, Iraq, and Palestine.

Germany, too, lost its status as an empire as Emperor William II fled to the Netherlands in the last days of the war and, in 1919, Germans voted to establish a democratic government. At the peace convention, Germany was severely punished by the victors. In the west, Alsace-Lorraine was ceded to France, large areas in the east went to Poland, and small areas were portioned out to Lithuania, Belgium, and Denmark. Germany was additionally ordered to pay heavy, seemingly unlimited, reparations for the cost of the war, although in practice not much was actually collected. Most galling for Germany, it was forced officially to accept total responsibility for causing the loss and damage of the war. Germany signed the Treaty of Versailles and left Paris humiliated and resentful, but, despite the loss of lands and the financial reparations, potentially still powerful.

All four of these great empires had held vastly diverse ethnic, religious, and cultural minorities within their borders. The Paris negotiators intended that the new states and new borders they carved out would give some of the larger minorities their own states and protect hostile ethnic groups from each other and from external domination. Minority rights and legal safeguards were also legislated into the constitutions of the new states and the remaining cores of the old empires. In accord with the principle of national self-determination, ten new states were born (or reborn), and 14 states were specifically charged with protecting racial, religious, and linguistic minorities within their borders, assuring those minorities of equal rights with all citizens, including the right to primary school instruction in their mother tongue. These measures were viewed as inherently fair and as removing the kinds of nationalistic provocation that had led to the recent war.

The new postwar nations.
In the wake of World War I, old empires fell and new states and colonies (euphemistically called mandates and protectorates) were created. The Austro–Hungarian and Ottoman Empires were eradicated. A belt of nation-states was established throughout central and Eastern Europe; some had brief lives and were soon annexed by Russia. The core of the Ottoman Empire became Turkey, while other segments were mandated to Britain and France as quasi-colonies.

The League of Nations

The Paris Peace Conference was not only supposed to resolve issues emerging directly from the war, it was also to find a way out of the use of war as a means of solving conflict. Paris was intended to ensure that "the Great War" would also become known as "the war to end all wars." Thus the Paris Peace Conference was also dedicated to creating an international organization to preserve peace. Inspired primarily by Wilson, the delegates created a League of Nations in 1920. However, the League, crippled by three congenital defects, never met its goals. First, its principal sponsor, the United States, refused to join because of Congressional opposition, a humiliating repudiation of Wilson's dream. The world's most powerful technological, industrial, financial, and military power—also the power that had most inspired the League—withdrew back into the isolation of its ocean defenses.

Second, despite its rhetoric, the new states it created, and the new protection for minority rights that it advocated, the League failed to resolve the complex issues of national identities within Europe and of colonialism overseas. In central Europe, nationality groups were widely dispersed. Not only were some groups, such as Ukrainians or Croatians or Jews, considered too small to form nations, there were also many groups, which did have their own states, but also had many members dispersed as minorities in neighboring states, such as Germans in Czechoslovakia. The wishes of minority groups for national autonomy—for example, for the official use of their own languages within larger nations and language groups—could not be satisfied in any practical way, and many minorities continued to feel aggrieved.

Colonies Disappointed. Similarly, as colonial governments did not relinquish their powers, the antagonism of colonized peoples towards their rulers intensified. The Arab world, for example, felt itself betrayed by the British and the French. Prince Faisal, who had fought on behalf of the Arabs against the Ottoman Empire, alongside Lawrence of Arabia, represented the Arab peoples at the peace talks and was bitterly disappointed to discover that France and Britain had their own, secret plans for these Arab states. France and Britain had publicly promised self-government to Arab regions of the Middle East that fought with them against the Ottomans, but secretly, between themselves, they had actually signed an agreement in 1916 to divide these regions among themselves. The four new states were "mandated" to European powers for tutelage until they would be considered ready for independence. Although the term "mandate" was used, the reality was semi-colonial status. Britain received mandatory power over Iraq and Palestine and France over Syria and Lebanon. Faisal himself was designated king of Syria, briefly, when a group of Syrians declared an independent state in 1920, but he was deposed and exiled by the French four months later. The British, however, believed that Faisal could help them keep Iraq quiet under their mandatory rule. So they made him king of Iraq in 1921. He ruled, at least nominally, until his death in 1933.

Halfway around the world, Japan sought and was awarded control over the East Asian possessions of Germany that it had captured during the war. Some of these colonial possessions were in the Shandong Peninsula of north China, and the Chinese naturally claimed them for themselves. In Paris, Chinese protestors physically blocked the nation's delegates from attending the signing ceremonies that turned these lands over to Japan. China never did sign the peace agreements. Within China, student-led protests against the treaties began on May 4, 1919, initiating a bitter critique of China's international humiliation, of its cultural links to the West, and of the apparent bankruptcy of its own historical traditions. This "May Fourth Movement" also helped to sow the seeds of the Chinese Communist Party, founded in 1921.

In India, Britain fell short of its wartime promise to expand the institutions of self-government; on the contrary, it passed the Rowlatt Acts, which restricted freedoms of the press and assembly. At the start of the war, most Indians seem to have trusted that Britain would bring self-government back to India, even if the process seemed very slow. Mohandas Karamchand Gandhi (1869–1948), who was becoming the leader of the Indian national movement, had even attempted to recruit troops, unsuccessfully, for the British war effort. All this changed after the war as the British cracked down and the Indians protested. (We discuss India in more detail in Chapter Twenty-two.)

In Africa, Europeans continued to administer the colonies they had seized in the late nineteenth century. British settlers began to move into new settlements, especially in the highlands of Kenya and in Southern Rhodesia (today's Zimbabwe). Especially in the British colonies, African tribal leaders were incorporated into the ruling structures, following some of the policies of indirect rule first evolved in India.

The existence of the League of Nations and its mandate system did, however, begin to suggest that colonialism might be limited over time. In Egypt, the Wafd Party began demonstrations and riots that persuaded the British to grant Egypt nominal independence while still controlling its foreign policy and defense, and the Suez Canal. In 1921, Britain granted dominion status to a new state in southern Ireland, ending centuries of colonial oppression (but leaving Northern Ireland still a part of Great Britain). It granted Iraq nominal independence in 1932.

The final congenital defect of the League of Nations was that it had no armed forces. This lack limited its willingness to intervene in disputes and made it impossible for it to back up even the decisions that it was willing to take. The great powers signed the Kellogg–Briand Pact in 1928, agreeing to settle their disputes without warfare, but the pact proved meaningless. The League effectively died with its failure to counter Japan's invasion of China in 1931; with Italy's invasion of Ethiopia in 1935, which turned one of only two independent countries in Africa (Liberia was the other) into a colony; with Germany's rearmament through the 1930s; and with the outbreak of the Spanish Civil War in 1936 (see Chapter Twenty).

Poster commemorating "The Internationale," the rallying anthem of the Communist movement. Karl Marx (left) and Friedrich Engels (right), pictured in the banner at the top of this poster, collaborated in developing the theoretical principles underlying "scientific socialism" and in organizing a working-class movement dedicated to revolting against capitalism.

The Russian Revolution

The Great War ended three centuries of rule by the Romanov dynasty and brought to power in Russia a new form of government that most Western European nations and the United States found dangerous and threatening. Others, including some Americans, found it an interesting alternative to the decadence of the West. They saw it as a dream for a better world. The Russian Revolution of 1917 challenged the capitalist order by instituting communism, which advocates the abolition of private property and the control of a country's economic resources by the state, at least temporarily. Russia's new leadership argued that the Communist Party should spearhead this system, by the use of violence if necessary. Leaders of the party believed that Russia could telescope the development process and catapult itself quickly into the ranks of the wealthy and powerful nations.

The Communist Party, called the Bolshevik (majority) Party until 1918, asserted its dominance over Russia's politics, economics, and society. Through the worldwide organization of the Communist International, it proposed itself as a model for, and leader of, colonized and backward countries in overthrowing foreign control and capitalist economic development. It argued that poor nations had been intentionally "underdeveloped" by, and for, the rich. The new communist system established by the Russian Revolution endured through years of hardship and of war, both civil and international.

The Build-up to Revolution

Geographically and politically, Russia has one foot in Europe, the other in Asia. As we have seen, Peter the Great (r. 1682–1725) turned westward, founding St. Petersburg as his capital, port, and window on the west. Catherine II, the Great (r. 1762–96), further nurtured the European Enlightenment at the Russian court. Stunned by his defeat in the Crimean War (1853–56) at the hands of Britain and France in alliance with Turkey, Tsar Alexander II (r. 1855–81) adopted a more liberal policy. He freed Russia's serfs in 1861, instituted the *zemstvo* (rural council) system of local self-government in 1864, reduced censorship of the press, reformed the legal system, encouraged industrialization, and promoted the construction of a nationwide railway system. Tsar Nicholas II (r. 1894–1917) furthered heavy industrialization under two progressive ministers, Count Sergei Witte (1849–1915) and Peter Stolypin (1862–1911), and allowed the birth of some representative political institutions, but he rejected the democratic reforms demanded by intellectuals, workers, and political organizers.

Despite the industrialization introduced under Nicholas II, on the eve of World War I Russia lagged far behind the Western European countries economically and industrially. At 175 million, its population was about 75 percent larger than that of the United States, more than 250 percent larger than that of Germany, and 400 percent larger than that of Britain; but its energy consumption was 10 percent that of the United States, 30 percent that of Germany, and 25 percent that of Britain. Its share of world manufacturing was 8 percent compared with the United States' 32 percent, Germany's 15 percent, and Britain's 14 percent.

Nicholas II had made great strides in increasing industrial production. Energy consumption increased from 4.6 metric tons equivalent in 1890 to 23 million in 1913; railway mileage grew from 22,000 miles in 1890 to 46,000 miles in 1913; and the per capita level of industrialization doubled from 1880 to 1913. But during that same period, the United States' per capita level of industrialization quadrupled, Germany's rose three and one-half times, and France's, Italy's, Austria's, and Japan's all slightly more than doubled. In a rapidly industrializing world, Russia had to race much faster just to keep up. To obtain the capital to build its industries Russia invited foreign investment, but this opened the nation to foreign control. In 1917 foreigners held nearly 50 percent of the Russian national debt. Russia was Europe's largest debtor.

Russia's agriculture was unproductive and its technology was primitive. The aristocrats held enormous power over the land and the peasants who worked it. An exploited peasantry living in *mirs* (village collectives) had neither the economic incentive nor the technical training to produce more. The small parcels of land they farmed privately were subdivided into tiny plots, as sons in each generation shared equally in the inheritance of their fathers. Finally, the government forbade the sale of village land to outsiders. This prevented exploitation by absentee landlords, but it blocked the investment from outside the village that might have funded agricultural improvement through new technology. Productivity stagnated. The sharp class divisions between the peasants and the gentry persisted, marked by differences not only in wealth and education, but also in dress and manners. Moreover, the costs of industrialization and the repayment of foreign loans had to be squeezed out of the agricultural sector. The result was a mass of peasants impoverished, technologically backward, despised by the wealthy elite, and suffering under the weight of a national program of industrialization for which they were made to pay.

Lenin and the Bolshevik Revolution

Several revolutionary groups protested these conditions, each offering a different plan. The Social Democrats followed George Plekhanov (1857–1918), who saw the need for more capitalist development in Russia to create new urban working and middle classes, which Plekhanov's party would then organize to overthrow the bourgeoisie. Plekhanov was actually an orthodox Marxist thinker who believed that before a communist revolution could emerge, capitalism would first have to lay the foundations of industry and create a proletariat of industrial workers. A lawyer, Vladimir Ilyich Ulyanov (1870–1924), later calling himself Lenin, advocated a far more immediate and abrupt communist revolution, and he stressed the need for the Communist Party to provide leadership. In 1902, in a pamphlet entitled *What Is To Be Done?* Lenin underlined the need for an absolutely dedicated core of leaders to carry out the revolution: "Give us an organization of revolutionaries and we will overturn Russia!"

In January 1905, with revolutionary feelings running high, some 200,000 factory workers and others in St. Petersburg, led by a priest, Father Gapon, assembled peacefully and respectfully to deliver to the tsar a petition for better working conditions, higher pay, and representative government. On that "Bloody Sunday," January 22, the tsar was not actually in the city; but his troops fired on the demonstrators, killing several hundred and wounding perhaps a thousand. The government's lack of moral authority was unmasked. By the end of the month almost 500,000 workers were on strike, joined by peasant revolts, mutinies of soldiers, and protests by the intelligentsia of doctors, lawyers, professors, teachers, and engineers.

Before this domestic turmoil erupted, the tsar had committed Russia to war with Japan, but defeats at sea and on land further revealed Russia's inadequacies in both technology and government organization. The defeat in the Russo-Japanese War, domestic tax revolts in the countryside, and strikes in the industrializing cities forced the tsar to respond. Yielding as little as possible, he established the first *duma*, or parliament, representing peasants and landlords, but allowing workers only scant representation. The tsar limited the powers of the *dumas*, frequently dismissed

The Odessa staircase scene from Sergei Eisenstein's silent film *Battleship Potemkin*, 1925. In a film famous both for its artistry and its revolutionary message, Eisenstein presents the ruthlessness of the troops of the Russian Tsar in suppressing the revolt of 1905 that began in part with a mutiny on the battleship *Potemkin* in the Odessa harbor. The troops move forward, relentlessly shooting and clearing a crowd of thousands of civilians supporting the mutiny. A young mother, shot to death, falls against her baby's pram, sending it careering down hundreds of steps, presumably to the baby's death.

Vladimir Lenin and Joseph Stalin at Gorki, Russia, 1922. After Lenin's premature death in 1924, Stalin battled to eliminate his rivals and emerged as supreme dictator of the Communist Party in 1929. He soon abandoned Lenin's New Economic Policy in favor of a series of brutal five-year plans to enforce the collectivization of agriculture and industry.

them, sometimes jailed their members, and chose their class composition selectively to divide the principal revolutionary constituencies, workers and bourgeoisie. The *dumas* endured as a focus for democratic organization and aspiration, but they were unable to work cooperatively, and the tsar was able to stave off revolution for a decade.

Unable to match the new technological warfare of other European countries, Russia suffered two million casualties in World War I. These losses finally united the many forces of opposition and brought down the monarchy. In the midst of revolutionary ferment, in February 1917, 10,000 women in St. Petersburg marched to protest the rationing of bread and demanded the tsar's abdication. Ordered by the government to fire on the protesters, the army refused.

In the first revolution of March 1917, the *duma* forced the tsar to abdicate and established a new provisional government, but the war persisted. The turmoil of mutiny and desertion in the army, food shortages, farm revolts, and factory strikes ground on. More radical groups sought to seize control. Lenin, with the assistance of the German government, which wished to sow discord in Russia, returned from exile in Switzerland. With the motto "Peace, Land, Bread," he called for an immediate withdrawal from the war, land for the peasants, and a government-run food distribution system. Lenin organized an armed takeover of the government headquarters, the railway stations, power plants, post offices, and telephone exchanges. On November 7 (October 25 on the old, Julian calendar), this revolutionary coup succeeded. The provisional government of Alexander Kerensky (1881–1970) fell and the communists seized power. Confounding Marxist doctrine, the revolution had occurred not in one of Europe's most capitalistic and industrialized countries, but in one of the most industrially backward. In March 1918, by signing the Treaty of Brest–Litovsk with Germany, the new government took Russia out of World War I.

Civil war between revolutionary "Red" and antirevolutionary "White" forces enveloped the country. Contingents of troops from 14 countries (including a small number of Americans in the Baltic and 8,000 at Vladivostok on the Pacific) joined the Whites. The Bolshevik government took over ownership of land, banks, the merchant marine, and all industrial enterprises. It confiscated all holdings of the church and forbade religious teaching in the schools. It established the Cheka, or security police, and instituted a reign of "Red Terror" against its opponents' "White Terror." In Yekaterinburg, the local **soviet** executed the tsar, his wife, and their children. By 1920, the communists, as the Bolsheviks now called themselves, were victorious in the civil war. In 1921, they banned all opposition, even dissenting voices within their party, and made the Central Committee, now under Lenin's control, the binding authority in the government. Lenin began the pattern of imprisoning his opponents in labor camps—a policy that was later expanded under his successors into a huge network of camps for political opponents of the government.

World war and civil war, which were followed by even more devastating drought, famine, and economic dislocation, convinced Lenin of the need for economic stability and provided an incentive to produce. In 1921, he implemented the New Economic

Policy (NEP), which allowed peasants to sell their products on the open market and middlemen to buy and sell consumer goods at a profit. The central government, however, controlled the "commanding heights" of the economy: finance, banking, international trade, power generation, and heavy industry.

State Planning in Soviet Russia

Lenin sought Russia's industrial transformation. In 1920, as he established the State Commission for Electrification, he declared: "Communism is Soviet power, plus electrification of the whole country." Lenin invited German and American technicians to Russia to help the country improve productivity, harnessing capitalist means to communist goals. He took special interest in the system of scientific management and time studies in the workplace that had been introduced in America by Frederick Taylor.

Lenin's death in 1924 ushered in a bitter power struggle from which Joseph Stalin (1879–1953) emerged triumphant over Leon Trotsky (1879–1940). Trotsky, a brilliant, ruthless man, who had organized the Red Army, had argued that through careful but bold planning a technologically backward country like Russia could leapfrog stages of growth and, through the "law of combined development," quickly catch up to the more advanced nations. Having banished Trotsky (who was eventually assassinated in Mexico), Stalin now implemented Trotsky's program. He declared his driving nationalist passion that Russia must no longer lag behind the more developed nations.

> [T]hose who fall behind get beaten. But we do not want to be beaten. No, we refuse to be beaten! One feature of the history of old Russia was the continual beatings she suffered for falling behind, for her backwardness. She was beaten by the Mongol Khans. She was beaten by the Turkish beys. She was beaten by the Swedish feudal lords. She was beaten by the Polish and Lithuanian gentry. She was beaten by the British and French capitalists. She was beaten by the Japanese barons. All beat her— for her backwardness: for military backwardness, for cultural backwardness, for political backwardness, for industrial backwardness, for agricultural backwardness. She was beaten because to do so was profitable and could be done with impunity. ... That is why we must no longer lag behind. (Andrea and Overfield, p. 398)

Stalin's rhetoric appealed not only to his immediate audience in Russia, but also to a more global audience of poorer states and colonies beginning to protest against their subordination and to seek independence and development.

To achieve "combined development," in 1928 Stalin instituted nationwide, state-directed **five-year plans** that covered the basic economic structure of the whole country. In place of capitalism, in which market forces of supply and demand determine production goals, wages, profits, and the flow of capital, labor, and resources, Stalin instituted government planning to make those decisions, from the large-scale national macro-level to the small-scale local micro-level.

Where could Russia find capital to invest in industrial development, especially with most world capital markets closed to the communist state? Stalin turned to his own agricultural sector and peasantry. By artificially lowering the prices for agricultural products and raising the prices for agricultural tools and materials, Stalin used his planning apparatus to squeeze capital and labor out of agriculture into industry. But he squeezed so hard that agricultural productivity fell and peasants withheld their crops from the artificially deflated market. State planning was not working.

Nevertheless, in 1929 Stalin increased the role of the state still further. He collectivized agriculture: more than half of all Soviet farmers were now compelled to

KEY TERMS

soviet A council of workers, the primary unit of government in the Soviet Union at local, regional, and national levels, also adopted by other communist regimes.

five-year plans State-directed plans, frequently prepared by communist governments, to control the economy and to direct its growth. They contrast with capitalist, laissez-faire, free-market economies, in which the government allows the forces of supply and demand to guide the market.

give up their individual fields and to live and work instead on newly formed collective farms of 1,000 acres or more. The communist government increased the use of heavy machinery and large-scale farming operations, stipulated the goods to be produced and their sales prices, encouraged millions of peasants to leave the farms for work on the state's new industrial enterprises, and eliminated wealthier peasants and middlemen.

Although some farmers were living better in 1939 than in 1929, many others were not. The most industrious and talented farmers were killed or imprisoned. Hundreds of thousands of better-off peasants, **kulaks**, who refused collectivization, were murdered; millions were transported to labor camps in Siberia. Peasants who owned animals preferred to slaughter them rather than turn them over to collectives. There had been over 60 million head of cattle in the **USSR** in 1928; by 1933, there were fewer than 35 million. Initiative shriveled as the more entrepreneurial farmers were turned into a kind of rural proletariat. The government continued to collect high proportions of the agricultural production to pay for the imports of foreign technology and machinery for its industrial programs. Although few developing countries today are willing to reduce private consumption below 80 percent of the national product, Russia reduced it to little over 50 percent. Much of the difference went to industrial development. Again, a government chose guns over butter. The political coercion and chaos introduced by these policies, combined with bad harvests in southeast Russia, led to the tragic deaths of between two and three million peasants by 1932.

While the peasants suffered enormous hardship, industry flourished as never before. At first, Russia hired foreign technology and imported foreign machinery. Despite ideological differences with the United States, Stalin, like Lenin before him, saw the necessity of importing American materials, machinery, and even some organizational programming. In 1924 Stalin declared:

> American efficiency is that indomitable force which neither knows nor recognizes obstacles; which continues on a task once started until it is finished, even if it is a minor task; and without which serious constructive work is inconceivable. … The combination of Russian revolutionary sweep with American efficiency is the essence of Leninism. (Hughes, p. 251)

Meanwhile, the Russian government was training its own personnel and learning to construct its own massive industrial plants. At the falls of the Dnieper River, the communist state constructed the largest hydroelectric power station in the world in 1932. In the early 1920s, the USSR had imported tens of thousands of tractors, most of them Fords and International Harvesters from the United States. By the 1930s, however, Russia constructed a giant plant at Stalingrad to manufacture its own tractors. At Gorki (Nizhny Novgorod) the government built a plant based on the American Ford model at River Rouge, Michigan. At Magnitogorsk, in Siberia, they constructed a steel complex based on U.S. Steel's plant in Gary, Indiana.

From 1928 to 1938, the per capita level of industrialization nearly doubled. From 1928 to 1940, the production of coal increased from 36 to 166 million tons, that of electricity from 5 to 48 billion kilowatt hours, and that of steel from 4 to 18 million tons. The planners began to convert a nation of peasants into a nation of industrial workers, as the urban population of the country increased three and one-half times from 10.7 million in 1928 to 36.5 million in 1938, from 7 percent of the country's population to 20 percent. Stalin explained: "The independence of our country cannot be upheld unless we have an adequate industrial basis for defense." (Kochan and Abraham, p. 368.)

Most dramatically, the Soviet increases came when Western Europe and North America were reeling under world depression (see below). The communist system won new admirers in the west. The American political comedian Will Rogers commented: "Those rascals in Russia, along with their cuckoo stuff have got some mighty good ideas. … Just think of everybody in a country going to work." Journalist Lincoln Steffens wrote: "All roads in our day lead to Moscow." British political critic and historian John Strachey exclaimed: "To travel from the capitalist world into Soviet territory is to pass from death to birth."

Many political leaders of countries under European colonial control saw the Russian example—telescoped development, state planning, rapid industrialization, the transformation of the peasantry into an urban labor force, emphasis on education and health services, national enthusiasm in rebuilding a nation along scientific lines—as just what they needed. As a political prisoner in British India in July 1933, Jawaharlal Nehru, future first prime minister of independent India, wrote to his daughter:

> People often argue about the Five Year Plan. … It is easy enough to point out where it has failed. … [but] One thing is clear: that the Five Year Plan has completely changed the face of Russia. From a feudal country it has suddenly become an advanced industrial country. There has been an amazing cultural advance; and the social services, the system of social, health, and accident insurance, are the most inclusive and advanced in the world. In spite of privation and want, the terrible fear of unemployment and starvation which hangs over workers in other countries has gone. There is a new sense of economic security among the people … further … this Plan has impressed itself on the imagination of the world. Everybody talks of "planning" now, and of Five-Year and Ten-Year and Three-Year plans. The Soviets have put magic into the word. (*Glimpses of World History*, pp. 856–57)

Women in the Soviet Union

For women, too, the Soviet system led to great change, though perhaps less than promised. As elsewhere, World War I had brought women into factories, fields, and even the armed forces, and the civil war continued the pattern. Over 70,000 women served in the Red Army. In 1921, 65 percent of Petrograd's factory workers were women. In 1917, the first Soviet marriage law constituted marriage as a civil contract and provided for relatively easy divorce and child maintenance procedures.

The government ordered equal pay for equal work, but the provision was not enforced. To bring law into line with practice, and recognizing the lack of availability of effective birth control methods, abortion on demand was granted as a right; so was maternity leave with full pay. When the men returned from the war, they wanted their jobs back and their women at home, but Russian women retained most of the benefits they had won and "legally speaking, Russian women were better off than women anywhere in the world" (Kochan and Abraham, p. 337). Over the next decades Russian women entered professions so rapidly that they became the majority in medicine and teaching and a substantial minority in engineering, technical occupations, and law.

In practice, however, women bore the double burden of continuing the major responsibility for running their homes and caring for their families while working full time. With the introduction of state-planned heavy industrialization after 1929,

Russian poster for women textile workers, 1930. Despite the government's difficulties in enforcing "equal pay for equal work," women's rights improved markedly under the communist system. This poster appears to idealize full-time employment combined with raising a family. This art style of presenting work and workers in idealized form is called "Socialist realism."

677

the double burden on women increased. The factories invited their labor, while shortages of foodstuffs forced them to spend more time and energy in ration lines and in the search for food. Abortion became so common that it was once again outlawed for a time after 1936. The struggle to balance the new legal equality and protection with older social and family traditions continued.

Postwar America

America left World War I as the technological and financial leader of the world. The factories that had supplied war goods returned to producing domestic consumer products that made the American middle and upper classes the envy of many around the world. Automobile registration rose from about a half-million in 1910 to over eight million in 1920 and 23 million in 1930. In addition, in 1930, American farms employed some 920,000 tractors and 900,000 trucks.

In 1910, there were 82 phones per thousand Americans; in 1930, 163. Only in the early 1900s did wealthier people begin to introduce indoor flush toilets and cast-iron bathtubs. By 1925, America was producing five million enameled bathroom fixtures annually. Thanks to the efforts of labor unions, the work week was being reduced from 60 hours per week to 45. Paid vacations were becoming common, with 40 percent of large companies giving at least one week of paid vacation per year. Diet improved; sales of fresh vegetables increased 45 percent in the decade after World War I. Life expectancy increased by more than 12 years between 1900 and 1930, from 47 years to 60 years.

All of the technological innovations discussed earlier in this chapter were introduced in America early on, if not first. Electricity replaced steam as the major source of power. In 1929, 80 percent of all industrial power was produced by electrical generators, and two-thirds of America's homes were electrified. Electrical appliances became common. Commercial radio began broadcasting in 1920 and millions of homes soon had receivers, with many people building their own. Movies became the main mass entertainment, with the first "talkie," *The Jazz Singer*, released in 1927. In 1929, 100 million people attended the movies each week. Watching stars such as Charlie Chaplin, Gloria Swanson, Mae West, Greta Garbo, and Rudolph Valentino gave viewers new ideas—and new fantasies— for their own lives. The films also gave audiences around the world their own peculiar version of American life.

Women's lives changed in this decade. Although the sale and prescription of the means of birth control was illegal in most states, Margaret Sanger convened the first birth control conference in 1921 and traveled across the United States and around the world promoting birth control. The size of American families dropped from 3.6 children in 1900 to 2.5 in 1930. About 25 percent of all women of working age actually worked outside the home, especially in office jobs, teaching, and nursing. In 1920, American women were constitutionally granted the right to vote. Much of the image of postwar America is of

Civil aviation. A steward serves passengers on board a KLM Fokker F18 in 1932. In the 1920s, the popularity of aerial circuses and flying clubs, run by former World War I pilots, combined with rapid improvements in technology, heralded a new age of civil aviation. By the 1930s a worldwide network of commercial routes had developed. In these early years the high cost of air travel created an aura of glamour and exclusivity.

risqué flappers, increased recognition of the sexuality of women as well as men, illegal drinking in speakeasies (after prohibition was introduced by the Eighteenth Amendment to the Constitution in 1919), and a general flamboyance. This image may have been true for an urban, upper middle-class, white population, a small—if conspicuous—minority of the total population. For most of working-class and rural America, life was still quite difficult.

In addition, fear permeated some corners of America. The United States, with its great industrial, agricultural, and administrative power, engaged in international commerce. But it refused to join the League of Nations and generally withdrew from participation in international politics outside of Latin America, where it had substantial financial investments and repeatedly intervened with military force. It seemed to fear involvement outside its own hemisphere.

Internally, in the immediate postwar years, American industries suffered many worker strikes. A third of a million workers struck against U.S. Steel in 1919. In the same year the Boston police force went on strike. The home of the U.S. attorney general, A. Mitchell Palmer, was bombed. Coming as they did just after the Communist Party took over the government of Russia, the industrial and political turbulence triggered a "**Red Scare**," a fear that communists would take over the United States, and Palmer began to round up, jail, and deport thousands of people accused of being communists, anarchists, and radicals. Hundreds of aliens were deported. The Ku Klux Klan revived and resumed its terrorism of Catholics, Jews, and African-Americans, especially the black soldiers returning from war who might no longer "know their place." At its height, in the early 1920s, the Klan enrolled several million members. By the end of the decade, the fears and frenzies had abated, but new, perhaps greater fears were in store, as the stock market crash of October 29, 1929, following years of economic difficulties on America's farms, ushered in the Great Depression.

Worldwide Depression

Periods of economic depression were considered normal in a free-market economy, as the forces of supply and demand would periodically fall out of step and then come back into line. But the Great Depression, which destabilized domestic and international politics worldwide, but especially in Europe, was extreme in its extent and duration. On October 29, 1929—"Black Tuesday"—the New York Stock Exchange crashed. Investors had bid up the price of stocks far beyond their intrinsic value, and suddenly, recognizing an imbalance between price and value, many withdrew their investments. The decline continued for years. By 1933, stocks were worth 15 percent of their value in 1929.

While the stock market crash represents the most dramatic moment of the Great Depression, underlying agricultural problems had already created some of the preconditions, while government economic policies magnified the severity of the financial problems. Throughout the 1920s, farmers who had produced at record levels during the war, to help feed embattled allies as well as domestic consumers, had difficulty cutting back production, resulting in huge, unsold surpluses and a depression in agriculture. Faced with such economic difficulties, countries closed their borders to imports so that they could sell their own products internally without competition. But as each country raised its barriers, international markets contracted and economic anxiety rose.

Mass unemployment swept Britain, America, and Germany; the unemployment rate among industrial workers in Germany reached 30 percent in 1932. Latin

KEY TERM

Red Scare The fear that communists would take over the United States, especially powerful in the years just after the Communist Revolution in Russia, 1917.

The Great Depression, 1929. One of many bread lines that wove their way through New York City during the Great Depression. This one was at Sixth Avenue and 42nd Street.

KEY TERMS

welfare state A government that assumes responsibilities for the welfare of its citizens, including such necessities as education, old age pensions, health care, and unemployment benefits. A more capitalist state leaves these responsibilities to private initiative.

kulturkampf German, "struggle over culture" or "culture war." The struggle among proponents of different views of culture for recognition and for control over state policies. Such struggles are normal in any society, but in Germany between the world wars they became intense. They were waged philosophically and physically, and, ultimately, by banishing from the nation unwelcome cultural ideas, and those who held them.

American countries, notably Argentina, which had been approaching a European standard of living, found their economies devastated, turned away from European markets, and sought to salvage what they could through domestic development. The value of world trade in 1938 was 60 percent below what it had been in 1929.

In 1921 two million unemployed in Britain were collecting unemployment insurance, thanks to an act that had been passed a decade earlier. The government also provided an old age pension system, medical aids, and subsidized housing. But the Great Depression increased this unemployment to almost three million. Unemployment payments multiplied while tax collections dropped. The **welfare state** expanded and government remained stable, but the Depression ground on.

America, the country most dedicated to private enterprise and "rugged individualism," and therefore most reluctant to expand government social welfare programs, saw national income drop by half between 1929 and 1932. Almost 14 million people were unemployed. Elected in 1932 in the midst of national despair, President Franklin Delano Roosevelt rallied the nation with charismatic optimism, declaring that "The only thing we have to fear is fear itself." Roosevelt believed that America's private enterprise system was fundamentally sound, but that it needed short-term assistance from the government to weather the depression, and permanent safety nets, also provided by the government, to ensure that weaker individuals would not succumb to the pressures of an intensely competitive economy. In accord with this philosophy, FDR instituted social welfare programs as a means of preserving America's capitalist economic structure. He provided financial relief for the unemployed; public works projects to create construction jobs; subsidies to farmers to reduce production and eliminate surpluses; and federal support for low-cost housing and slum clearance. A Civilian Conservation Corps was established, ostensibly to promote conservation and reforestation, but mostly to provide some three million jobs to the young. The Tennessee Valley Authority created an immense hydroelectric program, combining flood control with rural electrification and regional economic development.

Roosevelt increased the regulation of business and promoted unions. The Securities and Exchange Commission, created in 1929, regulated the stock exchange. The National Recovery Administration encouraged regulation of prices and production until it was judged unconstitutional in 1935. The Social Security Act of 1935 introduced unemployment, old age, and disability insurance—policies already in place in parts of Western Europe well before World War I. Child labor was abolished. Forty hours of work was set as the weekly norm. Minimum hourly wages were fixed. Union organization was encouraged and union membership grew from four million in 1929 to nine million in 1940. The most capitalist of the major powers thus accepted the welfare state.

The economy of communist Russia developed separately from the capitalist economy of the United States and Western Europe. In 1928 Russia introduced centralized national planning, emphasizing heavy industrialization. Although agriculture was devastated and levels of private consumption plummeted, factories flourished, industrial employment rose, and Russia avoided the worst effects of the Great Depression.

In Germany, the Depression followed on the heels of catastrophic inflation. In the 1920s the government induced hyperinflation to pay the resented war reparations, thus wiping out the savings of the middle classes and amplifying further resentment over the punitive Versailles Treaty, including its emphasis on German war guilt and insistence on Germany's disarmament. By 1924 industrial production had recovered —but then the Depression wiped out the gains. Germany depended on loans from several nations, especially the United States, to pay its enormous bill for war reparations. Following the stock market crash of 1929, however, American financiers, who were suddenly strapped for cash, called in these loans, undercutting first the German economy, which could not afford the repayments, and then the economies of the countries to which Germany had been paying.

Germany's new government was perceived by many as a weak and precarious experiment in constitutional democracy in a nation accustomed to a military monarchy. Left-wing parties, often communist, and right-wing parties, finally Nazi, confronted each other at the ballot box, in the factories, and in violent street fighting, with thugs on all sides assaulting each other, and often physically attacking prominent citizens as well. Germany's *kulturkampf*, or battle over cultural values, began to be waged in the streets.

During the **Weimar** period, Germany's cultural life achieved extraordinary artistic creativity. In architecture, the **Bauhaus** movement of innovators such as Walter Gropius (1883–1969) and Mies van der Rohe (1886–1969) redefined the function of buildings and their architects; in music and drama Bertolt Brecht (1898–1956) and

KEY TERMS

Weimar The constitution of the new German government after World War I was written in the city of Weimar. That government espoused democracy and cultural creativity, but was attacked from communists on the left and Nazis on the right, and was taken over by Nazis in 1933. Since then Weimar has stood for a government democratic and idealistic, but weak and fragile.

Bauhaus A movement in architecture arising in Germany between the world wars. It was characterized by an emphasis on streamlined forms, and a rejection of ornamentation. It followed the motto "form follows function." Its work became controversial among political parties. When the Nazis took over Germany they destroyed the Bauhaus school and most of its masters fled the country.

SOURCE

How Should We Live?

The Polish poet Wislawa Szymborska, winner of the Nobel Prize for Literature in 1996, reflects upon the disillusionment of the twentieth century and assumes that life should and must go on nevertheless. "How should we live?" she asks at the close of one of her most poignant poems, written in the 1970s. In this poem, however, she offers no answers:

Our twentieth century was going to improve on the others.
It will never prove it now,
now that its years are numbered,
its gait is shaky,
its breath is short.

Too many things have happened
that weren't supposed to happen,
and what was supposed to come about
has not.

Happiness and spring, among other things,
were supposed to be getting closer.
Fear was expected to leave the mountains and the valleys.
Truth was supposed to hit home
before a lie.

A couple of problems weren't going
to come up anymore:
hunger, for example,
and war, and so forth.

There was going to be respect
for helpless people's helplessness,
trust, that kind of stuff.
Anyone who planned to enjoy the world
is now faced
with a hopeless task.

Stupidity isn't funny.
Wisdom isn't gay.
Hope
isn't that young girl anymore,
et cetera, alas.

God was finally going to believe
in a man both good and strong,
but good and strong
are still two different men.

"How should we live?" someone asked me in a letter.
I had meant to ask him
the same question.
Again, and as ever,
as may be seen above,
the most pressing questions
are naive ones.

Wislawa Szymborska

Kurt Weill (1900–1950), the creators of the *Threepenny Opera* and its antihero Mack, the Knife, created new forms in cabaret presentations that challenged social conventions; in "classical" music, atonal composers, such as Alban Berg and Arnold Schoenberg, rejected the conventions of the traditional seven-note musical scale; in literature, novelists, such as Erich Maria Remarque, with his antiwar novel *All Quiet on the Western Front*, and Hermann Hesse, with his musings on Buddhism, won universal attention and acclaim; filmmakers such as Fritz Lang, in *Metropolis,* pioneered futuristic, philosophical themes; philosophers explored the role of philosophy in a democracy. Weimar culture emerged from one war only to be destroyed, or exiled, by another. Its leading personalities were threatened and ultimately driven out of Germany. Totalitarian forces and political ideologies, and finally Nazism, backed by thugs on the streets, triumphed, at least temporarily, over aesthetic and cultural creativity.

Methods of Production and Destruction: What Difference Do They Make?

The early twentieth century taught us skepticism. The greatest triumphs of science and technology could be transformed into instruments of death. Principles of physics that had been accepted as laws for two centuries and more were found to be only fragments of larger principles. Public health measures and medicine extended life spans; world warfare cut them down. Nationalism inspired people to work for the betterment of their country and its people, but at the same time to compete with, and make war against, those in neighboring countries, and often to limit freedoms of minorities, even at home. Revolutions continued for a decade and more, benefiting many people, but not fulfilling their promises to the masses. Great empires, some of them hundreds of years old, one of them 2,000 years old, toppled and dissolved in civil warfare. A world war ended, but because the issues that had caused it remained unresolved, indications were that it would soon resume in some form. Perhaps most frightening of all, totalitarian governments came to power in parts of the world that had been considered among the most civilized, only to challenge and subvert the whole basis of modern civilization, as we shall see in Chapter Twenty. This chapter's stories of warfare, imperialism, economics, science, and technology were clearly unfinished. Many of them are still unfolding.

Asking Questions

- What did the poet Wislawa Szymborska have in mind when she wrote that in the twentieth century, "A couple of problems weren't going to come up anymore: hunger, for example, and war, and so forth"?
- In what way does the Mexican Revolution appear to be a product of the technological developments of the early twentieth century? What other conditions promoted this revolution?
- What were the chief causes of World War I, and why were the Balkans so important in its origins?
- What promises were made by colonial powers during that war that were not kept afterward?
- What were the most important actions of the Soviet Union in the first decade after the Communist Revolution?
- In what ways was the United States a world leader in the decade following World War I? In what ways was it not?

Suggested Readings

Adas, Michael. *Machines as the Measure of Man* (Ithaca, NY: Cornell University Press, 1989). Technologically inventive peoples have often presented themselves as morally superior as well.

Akcam, Taner (tr. Paul Bessemer). *A Shameful Act: The Armenian Genocide and the Question of Turkish Responsibility* (New York: Metropolitan Books, 2006).

Andrea, Alfred and James H. Overfield, eds. *The Human Record*, Vol. 2 (Florence, KY: Wadsworth Publishing Co., 6th ed., 2008).

Bulliet, Richard W., ed. *The Columbia History of the 20th Century* (New York: Columbia University Press, 1998). Excellent collection of essays.

Camus, Albert. *The Myth of Sisyphus* (New York: Vintage Books, 1959). *The* existential novel, counseling persistence even in the face of unyielding fate.

Chafe, William H. and Harvard Sitkoff, eds. *A History of Our Time* (New York: Oxford University Press, 3rd ed., 1991).

Crossley, Pamela Kyle, Lynn Hollen Lees, John W. Servos. *Global Society: The World Since 1900* (Boston, MA: Houghton Mifflin, 2004).

Freeman, Christopher. "Technology and Invention," in Bulliet, pp. 314–44.

Freud, Sigmund. *Civilization and its Discontents* (New York: W.W. Norton and Co., 1961). Theorizes a constant, universal struggle between the psychological forces of order and disorder, love and destruction.

——. *A General Introduction to Psychoanalysis* (New York: Pocket Books, 1952). The master's presentation of his revolutionary concepts.

Gandhi, Mohandas Karamchand. *Hind Swaraj* or *Indian Home Rule* (Ahmedabad: Navajivan Press, 1938). A radical critique of the modern, industrial, materialistic world.

Hemingway, Ernest. *For Whom the Bell Tolls* (New York: Scribner, 1940). A classic, semi-autobiographical novel from the Spanish Civil War.

Hofstadter, Richard, ed. *Great Issues in American History: A Documentary Record* (New York: Vintage Books, 1959).

Howard, Michael and William Roger Louis, eds. *The Oxford History of the Twentieth Century* (New York: Oxford University Press, 1998).

Hughes, Thomas. *American Genesis* (New York: Viking, 1989).

Hughes, Thomas Parke. *Networks of Power: Electrification in Western Society, 1880–1930* (Baltimore, MD: Johns Hopkins University Press, 1983). Fascinating, innovative history of American technology.

Inkster, Ian. *Science and Technology in History: An Approach to Industrialization* (London: Macmillan, 1991).

Keegan, John. *A History of Warfare* (New York: Knopf, 1994). Compares and explicates the history of warfare through styles of war rather than strict chronology. Themes are stone, flesh, iron, and fire.

Kennedy, Paul. *The Rise and Fall of the Great Powers* (New York: Random House, 1987).

Kochan, Lionel and Richard Abraham. *The Making of Modern Russia* (London: Penguin Books, 1983).

Kragh, Helge. *Quantum Generations. A History of Physics in the Twentieth Century* (Princeton, NJ: Princeton University Press, 1999).

Landes, David S. *The Wealth and Poverty of Nations* (New York: W.W. Norton, 1999). History of the Industrial Revolution, giving great credit to Western ingenuity.

Lewis, David Levering. *W.E.B. DuBois: Biography of a Race 1868–1919* (New York: Henry Holt, 1993).

MacMillan, Margaret and Richard Holbrooke. *Paris 1919: Six Months that Changed the World* (New York: Random House, 2003). Lucid account of the aspirations, deliberations, and (mostly) failures of the "peacemakers" following World War I.

Nehru, Jawaharlal. *Glimpses of World History* (New Delhi: Oxford University Press, 1982).

Pacey, Arnold. *Technology in World Civilization* (Cambridge, MA: MIT Press, 1990).

Remarque, Erich Maria (tr., A.W. Wheen). *All Quiet on the Western Front* (Boston, MA: Little, Brown, 1958). Tragic, classic novel set in World War I.

Rosenberg, Rosalind, "The 'Woman' Question," in Bulliet, pp. 53–80. Excellent discussion of feminism.

Stoltzenberg. Dietrich. *Fritz Haber: Chemist, Nobel Laureate, German, Jew: A Biography* (Philadelphia, PA: Chemical Heritage Foundation, 2004). Haber invented the chemical production of fertilizer, which increased human life, and poison gas, which destroyed it.

Szymborska, Wislawa. *View with a Grain of Sand* (San Diego, CA: Harcourt Brace, 1995). Poetry of the Nobel Prize-winning poet.

Williams, Trevor I.A. *Short History of Twentieth-Century Technology c. 1900–c. 1950* (Oxford: Oxford University Press, 1982)

Yagnik, Indulal. *Autobiography*, Vol. 1 (in Gujarati) (Ahmedabad: Ravaani Publishing House, 1955). An idealistic, eager, Gandhian, troubled young man recounts his youth, mostly in India, but with some travel, too.

KEY TERMS

durbar see p. 655
divide and rule see p. 655
soviet see p. 675
five-year plans see p. 675
kulak see p. 676
USSR see p. 676
Red Scare see p. 679
welfare state see p. 680
kulturkampf see p. 680
Weimar see pp. 681
Bauhaus see p. 681

PEARSON
myhistorylab

For quizzes, flashcards, primary sources, interactive maps, videos, and other activities related to this chapter please go to

www.myhistorylab.com

CHAPTER TWENTY

World War II

To Hell and Back
1937–1949

The Great War demonstrated levels of man-made devastation never seen before. Yet hope springs eternal; optimists believed that the League of Nations, created at the end of the war, would insure that this had been "the war to end all wars." Unfortunately, pessimists proved more prescient.

No sooner had the Paris peace treaties been signed than leading economists predicted disaster. In *The Economic Consequences of the Peace*, published in 1920, British economist John Maynard Keynes argued that the treaties would push Germany and Austria into starvation. Like all of Europe, these countries would suffer from the crippling disruption of coal and iron supplies, transport, and imports of food and raw materials. In addition, the treaties stripped Germany of her overseas colonies and investments and her merchant fleet. It imposed on her crushing financial reparations to be paid to the victor nations. Keynes blamed the leaders of Britain, France, Italy, and the United States for their short-sightedness in making these demands, and he warned that starving people "in their distress may overturn the remnants of organization, and submerge civilization itself in their attempts to satisfy desperately the overwhelming needs of the individual."

In the next year, from a very different perspective, the Irish poet William Butler Yeats added his own fears concerning a profound cultural sickness that he saw infecting all of Europe in the wake of the war and the Russian Revolution:

> Things fall apart; the center cannot hold;
> Mere anarchy is loosed upon the world,
> The blood-dimmed tide is loosed, and everywhere
> The ceremony of innocence is drowned;
> The best lack all conviction, while the worst
> Are full of passionate intensity.

Yeats held out no hope in rationality or in technological progress, although he professed a belief in some mystical religious experience that was yet to come:

> Surely some revelation is at hand;
> Surely the Second Coming is at hand. (Cited in Wilkie and Hurt, p. 1655)

A decade later, worldwide depression confirmed the fears and pessimism of Keynes and Yeats. Sigmund Freud, the Austrian psychoanalyst who pioneered profound studies of the human mind and spirit, wrote of even deeper anxieties. Freud questioned the direction of all civilized, technologically advanced societies and feared that they might all be destroyed:

KEY TOPICS
- The Rise of Fascism
- Optimism Revives, Temporarily
- The Descent Toward War
- World War II, 1939–45
- Assessing the War
- The Tortured Image of Humanity
- Out of the Rubble: The United Nations and Resettlement
- Remembering the War
- Two World Wars: What Difference Do They Make?

Nazi rally at Nuremberg, 1937. Nazi Party members fill a stadium at a party meeting in Nuremberg, 1937. The mobilization of an entire nation in unquestioning support of its government is often referred to as totalitarianism.

Men have gained control over the forces of nature to such an extent that with their help they would have no difficulty in exterminating one another to the last man. They know this, and hence comes a large part of their current unrest, their unhappiness and their mood of anxiety. (Freud, pp. 34–35)

The events of the next years, 1930–39, continued to feed the worst fears of the economist, the poet, and the psychoanalyst. The outbreak of World War II at the end of the decade confirmed their bitter and tragic predictions. The first half of the twentieth century was the most violent period in history. Because of the cause-and-effect relationship between World War I and World War II, many historians see the entire period as a single long war, with a pause of two decades, including a global depression, serving as an uneasy intermission between acts.

Some bright spots brought hope during the interwar period: The birth of the League of Nations; an agreement among major naval powers meeting in Washington to limit the size of their navies; the Kellogg–Briand Pact of 1928, signed in Paris by 65 nations, promising to renounce war as a means of resolving conflicts; and the return of some prosperity in the mid-1920s. The optimism proved evanescent. Especially after the Great Depression, uncertainty, insecurity, and fear ruled the hearts of individuals and nations. In response, political leaders arose, in several countries around the globe, who promised that they could return their countries to certainty, security, and potency, if only their people would turn over dictatorial powers to them. Often the people listened and agreed, and often those who did not were beaten, exiled, or murdered. Powerful leaders and powerful governments demanded allegiance and obedience, believing that they could sweep away all barriers, domestic and international, that stood in their way. Democratic government, with its trust in the collective wisdom of the people, its suspicion of too-powerful rulers, its protection of minority rights and of individual rights of expression, was put on the defensive. The three major powers that chose fascist government—Germany, Italy, and Japan—had had almost no experience with democratic forms of government, and for a time in the late 1930s and early 1940s they seemed to be successful in mobilizing their nations into war machines. Ultimately, however, these fascist dictatorships overstretched their power and brought destruction down upon their nations and peoples. But, along the way, they destroyed many others as well. At least 50 million people died in World War II.

By the end of the second stage of this 30 years' war, 1914–45, the image of humanity had been shattered. Yet, once again hope flickered in the ashes of destruction. In a renewed attempt to "save succeeding generations from the scourge of war," the United Nations Organization (UN) replaced the League of Nations. With the passage of time, people around the world also began to ask the historian's questions: What lessons should we draw from this experience? What is important for us to remember and how should we remember it? They argued profoundly over the answers.

The Rise of Fascism

Desperate times evoke desperate responses. We have already seen in Chapter Nineteen one of these desperate responses: the triumph of communism in the Soviet Union. In this chapter we shall continue to follow its development. First, however, we analyze the rise of **fascism** in Italy in the 1920s under Benito Mussolini (1883–1945), in Germany after 1933 under Adolf Hitler (1889–1945), and, to a lesser degree, in Japan, where military leaders took power under the authority of the emperor throughout the 1930s.

The term fascism derived from the Latin word *fasces*, the bundle of sticks carried by officials in ancient Rome as symbols of power. Mussolini used it to describe power of the group over the individual—individually weak, but collectively strong. Fascism exalted the nation over the individual. It called for centralized autocratic government, often in alliance with major business leaders, with tight control of the economy and social life of the nation. It demanded the suppression of all opposition through unofficial paramilitary organizations of thugs who often took to the streets to attack and eliminate their opponents physically and brutally. If and when fascists succeeded in capturing office, they used the armed forces of the government to suppress opposition. They glorified warfare as a positive virtue. Fascism vested the power of the nation in a supreme leader. In Italy Mussolini, who had himself referred to as *Duce* (pronounced doo-chay), or supreme leader, filled that function. Why people supported fascism is unclear. Some followers must have been attracted by the promise that violence could solve the nation's problems, many more by the belief that a dictatorship could deliver a more prosperous economy than could an irresolute, quarrelsome parliamentary government.

Fascism in Italy

Although it had been on the side of the victors after World War I, Italy suffered from wartime losses of people and property, economic depression, and the social unrest that beset much of Europe. Labor strikes and peasant unrest in the form of nonpayment of rents and occasional seizures of land spread throughout the country. Governments elected in 1919 and again in 1921 were not able to deal with the unrest effectively. Mussolini organized groups of men—mostly thugs—from among the war's former soldiers, calling them *fascio di combattimento*, groups of combatants, and dressed them in uniforms of black shirts. These "Black Shirts" were his core supporters. When his attempts at winning power through elections in 1921 brought him only about seven percent of the vote, he turned his men loose on the streets to beat up labor organizers, communists, socialists, and local officials belonging to communist and socialist parties. The fascists claimed proudly that they killed 3,000 opponents in Italy from 1920 to 1922.

Announcing that the nation had descended into chaos, Mussolini declared a "March on Rome" in 1922 and threatened to take over the government. King Victor Emmanuel III capitulated to the threat and asked Mussolini to govern for a year as prime minister with full emergency powers. In the next elections, in 1924, Mussolini's party—through the use of violence, intimidation, and fraud took more than 60 percent of the vote. Seizing control of the state, Mussolini abolished all other parties, took away the right to strike, destroyed labor unions, and sharply censored the press. He instituted his own propaganda wing within the government to indoctrinate Italians into endorsing his programs.

He organized the country according to 22 major economic categories. For each category he had fascist representatives of

Mussolini and Hitler. The two men constructed the European alliance, which, with Japan, formed the Axis powers of World War II. At first, Italy's Mussolini was the dominant member, having come to power in 1922, but Hitler, though he came to head the German government only after 1933, ultimately set the agenda. Both men believed in strong government, with almost unlimited powers to the head of state (themselves), and minimal individual rights. Both glorified warfare and Hitler, in particular, promulgated a racial hierarchy that condemned those at the bottom to extermination.

made the trains run on time
The boast of Mussolini—that he made the trains run on time—became the criticism of his democratic opponents. Both he and they saw the force of the police and military as the means of this accomplishment. For Mussolini it evoked pride; for his critics, despair and even ridicule. For them, the cure—excessive state police power—was greater than the problem: inefficiency. Nowadays usually used to caricature a government eager to achieve efficiency but unconcerned about the effects on individual freedom.

labor, employers, and government meet together to decide wages, prices, working conditions, and industrial policies. All of them were assigned to a government minister and brought into the parliament. In fear of Mussolini's power, organized labor toed the line. Mussolini built roads, drained several hundred thousand acres of swamp lands for wheat production and malaria control, and "**made the trains run on time**," as the government boasted. While communists, socialists, liberals, and labor union leaders had little appreciation for either the man or his methods, businessmen and others wanting a society that functioned with little public turmoil gave their approval.

They also took patriotic pride in the new colonial war that he led: in 1935, Mussolini attacked Ethiopia, and he completed its conquest in 1936. When the League of Nations demanded that Italy withdraw, Mussolini scoffed: Great nations should have colonies. The League did nothing of substance to punish him, much less expel him from his conquests. To the contrary, Mussolini withdrew Italy from the League.

Hitler Rises in Germany

Mussolini's fascism drew the admiration of the young Adolf Hitler in Germany. Born in neighboring Austria, Hitler dropped out of high school at 16 and went to the national capital, Vienna, at 19, supporting himself at odd jobs, especially painting pictures. Much in prewar Vienna offended him: the wealthy royalty and aristocrats of the court; the prosperous businessmen; the socialist workers; the easy internationalism of the artists and the intellectuals; and most of all the Jews, who had assimilated into Austrian society and often held high positions in business and the professions. Like many in Vienna, Hitler became a virulent racist, exalting the "pure" German "race" and disparaging all others in a hierarchy that stretched downward from northern Europeans to southern Europeans, to Africans, and finally to Jews, at the very bottom.

Hitler felt himself more at home in Munich, Germany, where he moved in 1913. When World War I broke out, he volunteered for military service—serving as a dispatch runner—and came to value warfare as a blood-stirring and liberating experience. After the war, he began to work against the communist influences that were spreading among workers. In 1919 he joined the anticommunist German Workers' Party and became its head. He transformed the party into the National Socialist German Workers' Party—abbreviated as "Nazi"—thus launching his political career. Following Mussolini's model, the Nazis built up a group of storm troopers, the SA—a paramilitary organization that often attacked its opponents violently in the streets—and gave them a uniform of brown shirts. The organization of these thugs was just one sign of Hitler's disdain for the democratic German government of his day, usually called the Weimar Republic for the city in which it had been founded. As in Italy, many people in Germany preferred the order imposed by these paramilitary groups to what they perceived as the weakness of parliament and the street demonstrations of communists and socialists. They feared, in particular, the spread of the influence of the communist revolution that had captured Russia, a historic adversary not far away from their eastern border. They perceived a struggle, often expressed in street-gang-warfare between two authoritarian forms of government, fascism and communism, and they preferred fascism as the lesser of the two evils. The Weimar democracy seemed feeble by comparison with either of these two.

The Weimar Republic, an elected government of both working- and middle-class membership, had succeeded the German monarchy, which withdrew from power at the end of World War I. Both the militant right wing, which wanted a more centralized and powerful government under more autocratic leadership—like the

Nazis—and the militant left wing, which wanted a socialist or even communist government and hoped for a revolution like that in Russia, had little respect for Weimar. Both saw the centrist government as too weak.

1923 was an especially difficult year. Germany could not keep up with its payments of war reparations. In response, France seized the highly industrialized Ruhr valley, provoking national outrage in Germany, a good part of it directed against the weakness of the Weimar government itself. In addition, extraordinary inflation completely eroded the value of the German mark, making it hardly worth the paper it was printed on, wiping out the savings of the middle class, impoverishing the lives of workers, and endangering the stability of the government. Among those who further inflamed public opinion against the government, Hitler attempted a *putsch*, a revolt, to overthrow it, in Munich in 1923. Some army officers had already attempted a *putsch* in 1920. Hitler also failed, and was imprisoned for nine months. But he gained greater popular attention and during his months in jail he wrote *Mein Kampf* (My Struggle), his political manifesto, filled with his denunciation of the government, strident nationalism, plans for a Germany restored to—and beyond— her former greatness, the subordination of eastern Europe to Germany, and bitter, all-consuming anti-Semitism. He blamed Jews for being allied on the left with the communists and on the right with the capitalists, as too foreign from the German mainstream and as too assimilated into modern German life. For Hitler, Jews had become the scapegoat he could blame for all of Germany's woes.

Recognizing and frightened by the dangers of an unstable Germany, the French conceded and withdrew from the Ruhr, and the former wartime allies (with the exception of the Soviet Union) rescheduled the reparation debts to make them less onerous. For a few years, prosperity returned to Germany, but then the international depression of 1929 swept the country back into poverty and renewed humiliation. Germany seethed in anguish. Communists on the left and Hitler on the right blamed German democracy and the Weimar government for the nation's troubles. Hitler's

Nazi Party rally. Over 750,000 Nazi Party workers, soldiers, and civilians greeted Adolf Hitler at the 1934 Nuremberg conference. The German chancellor proclaimed that the Third Reich would last for the next thousand years. Ironically, the trial of Nazi war criminals by the victorious Allied powers would take place in the same city 11 years later.

totalitarianism A totalitarian state is one that seeks total control of the economy, politics, media, and culture of the state, under a single dictator or party. It does away with individual rights, proclaiming the rights of the state—as defined by its dictator—superior to those of any individual or group.

lebensraum In German, "room for living." The claim was that Germany needed to expand and take over the land of its neighbors because its own land was overcrowded. Similar claims on neighbors' lands have been issued by many nations throughout history.

the big lie A propaganda technique, defined by Hitler as a lie so colossal that no one would believe the liar would dare to say it if it weren't true.

became the strongest voice in the opposition. In a series of national elections from 1928 to 1932, his Nazi party's proportion of seats in the German parliament, the Reichstag, went from about 2 percent to about 46 percent, although in the next election, later in 1932, it fell to just below 40 percent. He gained support not only from backers who approved his entire program, but also from many conservatives, including army officers and influential business people, who differed on many points from Hitler's crude nationalism and racism, but who saw him as their chief defense against communism, which they feared even more. In 1933, German political leaders turned to Hitler—the head of the largest single party in the Reichstag—to head a coalition government. Hitler became chancellor of Germany by entirely legal processes. In order to rule without the constraints of a coalition, Hitler called for another election later in the year. In a contest marked by the violence of the SA, suspension of freedoms of speech and press, and a fire in the Reichstag building that Hitler blamed on the communists (although many claimed the Nazis had actually set the fire), the Nazis gained 44 percent of the vote. This was not enough, so Hitler announced a national emergency and, again using his SA thugs to intimidate the opposition, got the votes of a majority of the Reichstag to rule as dictator.

Once in power, Hitler moved swiftly to establish the kind of state that is often called **totalitarian**—that is, a state in which the individual is subordinated to a centralized administration that controls the national economy, politics, media, and culture, usually under a single dictator or a small council. As Mussolini had himself called Duce, so Hitler had himself called *Führer*, or leader. In 1925, Hitler had created the SS, another paramilitary organization, dressed in black uniforms. Though initially subordinated to the SA, the SS rose in prominence. All political parties apart from the Nazis were abolished. On June 30, 1934, the "night of the long knives," Hitler had the SS murder many leading Nazis whom he viewed as opponents and rivals. He established a secret police force, the Gestapo, in 1936. Opposition leaders were killed or dispatched to concentration camps. Churches were forbidden to criticize the government, and they were encouraged to cut their ties with overseas branches of their denominations. By contrast, the government encouraged the worship of pre-Christian Teutonic gods. Strikes were forbidden and employers were granted new powers in dealing with workers. Policies were based on bogus "racial science:" Hitler declared that Aryans (meaning speakers of Indo-European languages), especially Germans and Scandinavians, were the most elevated of races, Jews the lowest. Jews were dismissed from public office, including university service and the civil service. No matter how high their position, or the history of their service to Germany, in 1935 all Jews were stripped of citizenship. By now, seeing the handwriting on the wall, many had begun to flee the country, including two Nobel laureates whom we encountered in Chapter Nineteen: the chemist Fritz Haber and the world's most distinguished theoretical physicist, Albert Einstein.

Why did Germans tolerate this new order? Some, of course, accepted totalitarianism as appropriate. Others, frightened by the prospect of chaos, poverty, and communism, saw it as a severely flawed, but better, alternative. In addition, Hitler commanded the use of force in the country, now not only through the thugs of the SS, but also through the officially legitimate use of the army, police, and secret police. Citizens could protest only at risk to their life and safety. Finally, Hitler's program for rebuilding the country economically and militarily had great appeal. So, too, did his emphasis on the need for *lebensraum*, space for living, an expansion of Germany's territory first into Austria and Czechoslovakia and then through Poland, the Ukraine, and Russia. The Nazi propaganda machine, orchestrated by Joseph Goebbels, indoctrinated the nation, often spreading "**the big lie**" because, as Hitler wrote in *Mein Kampf*, "in the big lie there is always a certain force of credibility."

Hitler set the nation to work on programs of public works, building housing and superhighways, draining swamps, and reforesting rural areas. In 1936, following the Soviet model, he introduced state planning, although unlike the Russian case, he worked within the framework of private property. He urged Germany to become economically self-sufficient, and its skilled scientists developed many artificial products, such as rubber, plastics, and synthetic fibers, that enabled it to reduce its imports. Germans went back to work, and Germany escaped the severe unemployment suffered in most European countries during the Great Depression. The most remarkable dimension of Hitler's rebuilding program, however, was the most dangerous and most threatening: In violation of the Paris peace accords, Hitler began rebuilding Germany's military, and soon he deployed these forces in missions that precipitated World War II.

Hitler's Germany shared many characteristics with Mussolini's Italy. Both had developed strong governments that brooked no opposition. Both pursued policies of militarism and glorified war. The leaders in both nations set themselves up as the unchallenged and unchallengeable rulers of their states. In October 1936, the two governments proclaimed an "axis" that bound them together in international affairs. In the next month, Germany signed an Anti-Comintern Pact with Japan, pledging mutual support against possible attacks from the USSR. The next few years would bring together Germany, Italy, and Japan, along with their allies, as the Axis Powers in World War II. (The British, French, Soviets, Americans, and their allies would call themselves the Allied Powers.)

Japan Between the Wars

During the Meiji restoration, Japan achieved an astonishingly rapid reorganization of its government, administration, economy, industry, and finances. As we saw in Chapter Eighteen, Japan followed Western examples in seizing colonies for itself and asserting a sphere of influence in China. Reversing its previous student–teacher relationship with China, it defeated China in Korea in 1895 and became the dominant

Workers winding induction regulator coils in a Shibaura Engineering Works plant, Tsurumi, Honshu, Japan, 1930. In the 1920s and 1930s the Japanese often borrowed from Western models by inviting foreign firms to establish Japanese branches; by obtaining licenses to produce foreign technologies; and by adapting those technologies to Japanese conditions. Their industries consequently "leapfrogged" ahead very rapidly.

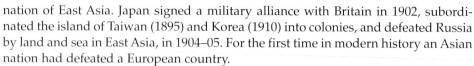

nation of East Asia. Japan signed a military alliance with Britain in 1902, subordinated the island of Taiwan (1895) and Korea (1910) into colonies, and defeated Russia by land and sea in East Asia, in 1904–05. For the first time in modern history an Asian nation had defeated a European country.

World War I profoundly affected postwar politics in East Asia. Japan was seated as one of the victorious Five Great Powers at the 1919 peace conference in Paris—the only non-Western nation accepted as an equal at the proceedings. It was assigned control over Germany's Pacific colonies, including the Liaotung Peninsula in north China, which Japan had seized in 1914. This led to the "May Fourth" movement of Chinese students in China, originally a student demonstration that metamorphosed into a broader movement for Chinese reforms at home and in international affairs (see Chapter Nineteen). In the end, China refused to sign the Versailles Treaty.

World War I presented Japan with an unprecedented economic opportunity. While other industrialized countries were occupied with war in Europe, Japan developed its industries relatively free from competition. Between 1914 and 1918 Japan's gross national income rose by 40 percent, and for the first time Japan exported more than it imported. Heavy industry showed particularly impressive growth. Manufacturing increased by 72 percent while the labor force expanded by only 42 percent, indicating the growing use of machinery to increase productivity. Transport increased by 60 percent. Between 1914 and 1919 Japan's merchant marine almost doubled, to 2.8 million tons. The production and export of consumer goods also advanced. In the first decades of the twentieth century, Japan's most important exports were textiles, primarily silk, 80 percent of which was produced by women.

As a latecomer, Japan could take advantage of technology already developed in the West (the "leapfrogging" path that Trotsky preached in Russia). Japanese industries practiced three different patterns in importing that technology. Some signed agreements with foreign firms to establish branches in Japan; some negotiated licenses to use the new technologies; and some practiced "reverse engineering," analyzing foreign machinery and reproducing it, with adaptations appropriate to Japanese needs. Adaptation produced innovations—for example, in applying chemical research to agricultural and even ceramics production. Private firms imported most of the foreign technology, but the government also encouraged research by funding state universities, laboratories, and the development of military technology.

Japan bridged the **dual economy**, the separation between large-scale and cottage industries that has inhibited growth in many countries. In a dual economy, one sector consists of large, highly capitalized, technically advanced factories employing thousands of workers producing modern products; the other sector includes small-scale workshops, with relatively low capitalization and less up-to-date equipment, often employing fewer than 30 workers, producing traditional goods. In most countries, the small-scale sector tends to shrivel as larger firms achieve economies of scale and put it out of business. Governments, too, often invest their resources in large

Samurai warrior. The ancient and proud warrior class of the samurai worshiped athletic prowess, swordsmanship, and fierce loyalty to the emperor. In 1877 the last 400,000 samurai were pensioned off to become *shizoku*, Japanese gentry, but their virtues lived on in the country's psyche. In times of crisis, the warriors' values turned Japanese nationalism into a potent force.

industries, neglecting the small sector. But in Japan, the smaller factories adopted appropriate scale, new technologies, and began to produce new goods needed by the larger industries. From the early years of the century, Japan evolved systems of sub-contracting between the large and small sectors, which made them interdependent and complementary.

Poor harvests in 1918 provoked a sharp rise in the price of rice, Japan's staple food. Massive riots broke out in hundreds of cities and towns, lasting 50 days, involving some 700,000 people, and resulting in 25,000 arrests and 1,000 deaths. The government responded by importing rice and other staples from its colonial territories in Korea and Taiwan. The riots represented the growth of Japan's urban voice as the urban proportion of the population rose from just over 10 percent in 1890 to close to 50 percent in the 1920s (to 66 percent by 2008). Labor was increasingly organized and the citizenry politicized. In 1925 all male subjects over the age of 25, 12.5 million people, were given the vote.

The riots also reminded Japan of its increasing dependence on its colonies for daily commodities. In the later 1920s, Taiwan and Korea provided 80 percent of Japan's rice imports and 66 percent of its sugar. For industrial raw materials, such as minerals, metals, petroleum, fertilizers, and lumber, Japan had to look farther afield, and this would lead it into fatal colonial adventures.

In the 1920s, industrial production increased by 66 percent. The *zaibatsu* (huge holding companies or conglomerates) came to control much of the Japanese economy and were very influential in politics. The four largest—Mitsui, Mitsubishi, Sumitomo, and Yasuda—were controlled by individual families, and each operated a bank and numerous enterprises in a variety of industries, ranging from textiles to shipping and machinery. A Mitsubishi mining company, for example, would extract minerals, which would then be made into a product by one of the Mitsubishi manufacturing companies. Next, this product would be marketed abroad by a Mitsubishi trading firm and transported in ships of another Mitsubishi affiliate. The whole process would be financed through the Mitsubishi bank.

The *zaibatsu* combined large size with an ability to shift production to meet demand. The *zaibatsu* families also held considerable influence in government, both through the money they controlled and their close family links with prominent politicians. The Major Industries Control Law of 1931, for example, encouraged large companies in key industries to join in cartels (see Key Term p. 572) to regulate production and prices.

International respect, growing wealth, rising urbanization, increasing industrialization, high rates of literacy, universal male suffrage (1925), and the institutionalization of political parties suggested that Japan was embracing liberal democracy. But the political power of the *zaibatsu* and the military undermined people's faith in democratic practice. The military, in particular, held extraordinary power, both under law and in popular opinion. In contrast to most democratic countries, in which the civilian government controls the military, Japanese law specified that the ministers of war and of the navy had to be active generals or admirals. Conversely, the formal powers of Japan's diet, or parliament, were restricted. In theory, the Japanese emperor held the ultimate political authority for the country and the political leaders who dominated public policy at home and abroad spoke in his name. The reality of power was ambiguous and historians debate how much power the emperor actually exercised himself and how much was exercised by others in his name. Japan's traditional Shinto religion emphasized the emperor's divinity and asserted the leading role of Japan's samurai warrior ethic.

Many of the samurai military elites began to claim expanded powers for the armed forces. They wished to protect Japan, a resource-poor island nation that was especially vulnerable to shifts in international trade and its regulation. The world

KEY TERM

dual economy An economy of two largely unconnected tiers: one tier of large-scale, modern, highly mechanized, highly capitalized businesses with large workforces; the other of small-scale workshops with little capital, limited mechanization, and a small workforce, producing traditional goods.

depression of 1929 shocked the Japanese economy as the value of exports dropped 50 percent between 1929 and 1931. Unemployment rose to three million, with rural areas hardest hit. Many civilians seemed to agree with the military: the future would look brighter if Japan could reorganize and control the economy of East Asia for its own benefit. Although the civilian government continued to criticize the military, generals increasingly gained control of the state and turned it toward military goals.

Scholars argue over the use of the term fascism in relation to Japan. Many prefer to term the Japanese experience "ultranationalism." Unlike the Italian and German cases, in which nationalism itself was new and the takeover of the state by fascist leaders using violence even newer, Japan had been nationalistic for millennia, with an emperor considered to be divine. Nevertheless, as Japan rebuilt in the early decades of the twentieth century, two generations after the Meiji restoration, it shared many of the fascist elements of Germany and Italy, which were to become its allies: A powerful military took over the principal tasks of government, using the symbolism of state authority—the emperor—to justify their actions; violent attacks by the military leaders silenced domestic opposition through beatings and murders; and an aggressive and expansionist foreign policy brought Japan's armies into war with its neighbors and annexed them.

Optimism Revives, Temporarily

The 1920s had appeared to usher in a time of peace. The League of Nations was founded in 1920. The League was not entrusted with peace-keeping missions, but it was expected to be a forum in which international conflicts could be managed through negotiations. It also carried out valuable humanitarian work in fighting epidemic disease in eastern Europe and in resettling political refugees—Russians fleeing the communism of the Soviet Union and Greeks and Armenians expelled from Turkey, for example. The League's Intellectual Cooperation Organization promoted cultural activities to bring together people from around the world. Among the members of its advisory committee were Albert Einstein of Germany, Marie Curie of France, composer Béla Bartók of Hungary, and novelist Thomas Mann of Germany. The organization's annual meetings in Geneva, Switzerland, attracted representatives not only from Western European countries and the United States, but also from Mexico, Venezuela, Brazil, Japan, China, Egypt, Poland, Czechoslovakia, Hungary, and India, even though it was still a colony of Great Britain.

Individual nations also pursued independent paths to preventing war and promoting peace. In 1921, a conference was convened in Washington to set limits on competition in naval forces. It achieved agreement on a 5:5:3 ratio in the total tonnage of large ships among Britain, the United States, and Japan respectively, with other World War I allies accepting lower limits. In 1925, the major powers, meeting in Locarno, Switzerland, signed a number of agreements designed to relieve some of the burden of guilt that Germany had been forced to accept for the war and to reintegrate Germany into the European diplomatic world. Germany accepted its western borders with France and Belgium unconditionally and agreed that it would use only diplomacy, and not force, in any attempt to alter its eastern borders with Poland and Czechoslovakia. To reinforce this agreement, France agreed to defend Poland and Czechoslovakia in case of any future attack. (Britain did not sign, arguing that its interests were not involved.) In 1928, 65 nations signed the Pact of Paris (known as the Kellogg–Briand Pact), agreeing to renounce war as a means of settling international conflicts. By 1928, optimism—and prosperity—had returned to the European world. By 1925, the index of manufacturing in Western and central

Europe surpassed that of prewar 1913. Russia, the worst hit of all world powers by the war, had returned to 70 percent, from a low of 13 percent in 1920. Lasting peace, too, seemed to have been achieved.

The Descent Toward War

Then came the Great Depression and its economic and political pressures. Most remarkably, as the democratic, capitalistic countries of Western Europe, the United States, and Latin America struggled with the world depression of the 1930s, the USSR, Germany, Italy, and Japan were thriving. Each of the four had adopted dictatorship, national planning, and militarization. Indeed, three of them—Germany, Italy, and Japan—launched military campaigns in the 1930s that would ultimately result in World War II, while the fourth, the USSR, built up a massive military force in anticipation of having to fight them off. The build-up of the militaries and the war campaigns fed on one another. The cost of maintaining the armed forces became so exorbitant that only war victories could pay for them, and to achieve war victories ever-increasing militarization was necessary.

The Steps to War

In 1931, strongly influenced by its wealthy business conglomerates, the *zaibatsu*, and by hyper-nationalist officers in the armed forces, Japan seized Chinese arsenals in Manchuria and began to take over the entire province. Japanese troops had been in place in Manchuria since their victory over the Russians in 1905. As justification for the takeover, they blamed China for the murder of a Japanese officer in Mukden, Manchuria, and for economic boycotts of Japanese goods. In 1932, Japan declared Manchuria an independent state, which it then ruled, establishing the last Chinese emperor, Puyi, who had been deposed in 1911, as a puppet head of government. The government was nominally Chinese but the Japanese pulled the strings. China, joined by several small nations, protested to the League of Nations. Japan quit the League, and, in any case, the League took no serious action. None of the other powers felt threatened. They did not want to commit troops, and the Western Europeans did not want to alienate Japan at a time when they felt the need for Japan as a partner in a quiet alliance against the Soviet Union. As noted, many in Japan opposed Japanese militarism, but, as in Germany, violent attacks stifled the opposition. Between 1930 and 1936, two prime ministers, one finance minister, and one important banker were assassinated. Speaking out against militarism in Japan was dangerous.

In 1935, Italy invaded Ethiopia. Despite the poignant speech of Ethiopian Emperor Haile Selassie before the

THE MARCH TO WAR	
1935–36	Italy conquers Ethiopia
1936–39	Spanish Civil War
July 7, 1937	Japanese troops invade China
September 1938	Appeasement in Munich; Germany annexes Sudetenland
September 1939	Nazi–Soviet Pact: Germany invades Poland; Britain and France declare war; Poland partitioned between Germany and Russia
March–April 1940	*Blitzkrieg*: German forces conquer Denmark and Norway
May–June	Italy declares war on Britain and France; German forces conquer France, the Netherlands, and Belgium
June 1940–June 1941	Battle of Britain; Britain holds firm against German bombing attacks
June 21, 1941	German forces invade USSR
December 7, 1941	Japanese bomb U.S. Navy, Pearl Harbor
January–March 1942	Japan conquers Indonesia, Malaya, Burma and the Philippines
June 1942	U.S. Navy defeats Japanese at the Battle of Midway
1942–43	End of Axis resistance in North Africa; Soviet victory in Battle of Stalingrad
1943–44	Red Army slowly pushes Wehrmacht back to Germany
June 6, 1944	Allies land in Normandy (D-Day)
February 1945	Yalta conference: Churchill, Roosevelt, and Stalin discuss postwar settlement
March 1945	U.S. planes bomb Tokyo
May 7, 1945	Germany surrenders
August 6, 9, 1945	U.S. drops atom bomb on Hiroshima, and then on Nagasaki
August 15, 1945	Japan surrenders

Guernica, Pablo Picasso, 1937. Painted as a protest over the German bombing of the little village of Guernica during the Spanish Civil War, this became one of the most famous of all antiwar paintings. Picasso refused to allow it to be moved to Spain from France until after Franco's death in 1975.

League of Nations, despite his revelation that the Italians were spraying chemical weapons from airplanes on his defenseless people below, despite his warning that all small nations were in danger of being swallowed up by larger and more powerful ones, despite his charge that some members of the League were supplying Italy with war materials, the League of Nations did nothing of substance to block the Italian annexation of Ethiopia. International faith in the League as a force for peace plummeted.

The Spanish Civil War. In 1936, civil war broke out in Spain. The country had been in turmoil as a relatively bloodless revolution deposed the king of Spain in 1931 and established a democratic Spanish republic. For five years, power oscillated between the conservative rightists, including members of the clergy, the military, and business elites, and the liberal leftists, including workers, socialists, communists, and anarchists. In elections in 1936, the leftists (republicans) won, and the rightists (nationalists), led by General Francisco Franco, began an insurrection that turned into a civil war. Many observers called this a "dress rehearsal" for World War II because Germany and Italy sent men (Italy sent 50,000 soldiers), money, and weapons to aid Franco and the rightists, while the Soviet Union sent technicians, political advisers, and equipment to bolster the republican government. The major democratic governments of Western Europe—including Britain and France—condemned Franco, but sent no support and prohibited the shipment of weapons. The United States declared its neutrality and declared an embargo on the export of arms to Spain. Privately, thousands of volunteers from the democratic nations went to Spain as volunteers to serve with the republican forces. American writer Ernest Hemingway immortalized this International Brigade in his novel *For Whom the Bell Tolls*. Hitler used the war as an opportunity to test the air force that he was building. Mostly he used his planes to transport Franco's troops, but on April 28, 1937, German air force squadrons supporting Franco bombed and destroyed the unprotected civilian town of Guernica, the capital of the Basque region of northern Spain. Spanish artist Pablo Picasso immediately painted *Guernica*, perhaps the most famous antiwar painting in history, depicting the anguish, pain, and suffering of men, women, children, and animals. The Spanish Civil War continued for three years; 600,000 people died. Franco's victory established a right-wing dictatorship that lasted four decades until he died in 1975. The League was not able to resolve the conflicting claims peacefully, and it commanded no armed forces of its own. Armed nationalism triumphed over unarmed internationalism.

Japan Invades China. On July 7, 1937, Japan invaded China. The pretext was an assault on Japanese troops near Beijing; the goal was the takeover of China. Within months, Japan gained control of most of the densely populated eastern half of the country, although the Chinese withdrew ever deeper into the interior and continued to fight until the very end of World War II. The League of Nations condemned Japan, but took no substantive action. The Japanese refer to this war as the "Pacific War." In global terms, the Japanese invasion of China is usually considered the beginning of World War II, although the war in Europe did not begin until September 1939.

Hitler's Early Conquests

After his appointment as chancellor in 1933, Hitler began almost immediately to expand Germany's military position despite the restrictions of the Paris peace treaties. In 1933 he took Germany out of the League of Nations and out of a disarmament conference that was taking place at the time. In 1934, Nazis in neighboring Austria assassinated the prime minister and demanded union with Germany. Hitler's proposed takeover of Austria at this time was prevented only by Mussolini, who declared his opposition to German troops occupying a neighboring country and stationed Italian troops at the Austrian border. In 1935, Nazi intimidation influenced voters in the rich, industrialized Saar region, on the border with France, to vote for annexation to Germany. Most provocatively, in 1935, Hitler began to re-arm Germany. In 1936 he sent his new troops into the Rhineland, German territory just west of the Rhine River, that had been designated a demilitarized zone. No one acted to oppose him. In March 1938, now with Mussolini's consent, German troops moved into Austria, declaring an *Anschluss*, or union, of Germany and Austria.

Next Hitler focused on Czechoslovakia, particularly the Sudeten area, where some three million Germans lived as a minority in the larger Slavic state. He threatened to invade the Sudetenland to annex it to Germany. As fears of war spread, the British prime minister, Neville Chamberlain, and the French premier, Edouard Daladier, flew to Munich to negotiate the fate of Czechoslovakia. They persuaded the Czechs to cede the Sudetenland to Germany, which left the rest of the country open to further German unilateral action. They had persuaded Czechoslovakia to sign its death warrant. They had bought off Hitler by offering up Czechoslovakia, not allowing themselves to realize that they had only delayed the war that was to come. The image of Chamberlain returning from Munich to London to proclaim that he had won "peace for our time" has, ever since, served as a symbol of the folly of appeasing aggressors. The Germans invaded and took over the remainder of Czechoslovakia in March 1939. In April, Italy took over Albania.

Russia had agreed to fight against Germany over the issue of Czechoslovakia, if only the French or British would join in, but they would not. Indeed, the British seemed to give more diplomatic attention to Germany, their potential enemy, than to the Soviet Union, their potential ally. On August 23, 1939, the USSR stunned the world by signing a nonaggression pact with Germany, its geopolitical archenemy and ideological rival. A secret protocol of the treaty was an agreement to divide up Poland between them if Poland's territory were ever conquered. For Hitler, the way was now clear. On September 1, German forces invaded Poland. On September 3, Britain and France finally declared war on Germany. The European theater of World War II had opened.

World War II, 1939–45

The early results were ominous. Implementing its strategy of *Blitzkrieg*, or lightning war, Germany sent one million troops into Poland, with armored forces in the front and air support overhead. Poland was not equipped to defend itself, and within a month organized resistance had ended. Germany incorporated western Poland into its new empire.

Meanwhile the Soviet Union invaded and seized eastern Poland, in accord with its nonaggression pact with Germany. The Soviets also stationed troops in the Baltic countries of Lithuania, Latvia, and Estonia and attacked Finland to seize part of its land. The League of Nations expelled the Soviet Union, but it got all the lands it claimed from the Finns.

Despite their declaration of war, France and Britain took no immediate military action against Germany. The lull through the winter of 1939–40 is often called the "phony war." In April 1940, however, Hitler resumed his strategy of *Blitzkrieg*.

The War in Europe

Germany invaded Denmark and Norway in April. In May, German armies invaded Belgium, Luxembourg, the Netherlands, and France. Nothing could stop them. The French had prepared an elaborate "Maginot Line" of defended trenches, underground bunkers, minefields, and barbed wire that they thought was impregnable. The Germans went around the line to the northwest and penetrated France. German tanks also entered France through Luxembourg and the Ardennes forest, which the French had thought impassable by tanks. Everywhere the Germans scored victories. With Rotterdam under air attack, the Netherlands surrendered. Belgium sued for peace. British, and some French, troops retreated to the French seaport of Dunkirk, and on June 4, leaving their armor behind them, they were hastily evacuated to England. On June 10, Mussolini joined in the attack on France, and soon invaded Greece as well. On June 13, the Germans occupied Paris, and on June 22, France surrendered. The country had been conquered in less than two months of fighting. Germany chose to administer the northern two-thirds of France directly. The southern third was administered from the town of Vichy by French officials who collaborated with the Germans. Some French joined General Charles de Gaulle with French forces in exile; some began guerrilla warfare against the Germans. Most acquiesced in the conquest and went about their daily life under German occupation.

Britain now stood alone against Germany, and Hitler attacked. He launched heavy bombing of London and other strategic cities in Britain throughout the summer and autumn of 1940. Winston Churchill, who had replaced Chamberlain as prime minister in May 1940, confronted the desperation of the situation directly and addressed his nation in rhetoric that stirred the blood and strengthened the backbone. Within a few days of assuming office, Churchill announced in Parliament: "I have nothing to offer but blood, toil, tears, and sweat!" And a month later:

> We shall go on to the end, we shall fight in France, we shall fight on the seas and oceans, we shall fight with growing confidence and growing strength in the air, we shall defend our island, whatever the cost may be, we shall fight on the beaches, we shall fight on the landing grounds, we shall fight in the fields and in the streets, we shall fight in the hills; we shall never surrender.

Despite heavy losses, including 20,000 dead in London alone, the British held firm, thanks to the Royal Air Force, the invention of radar, and success in cracking German

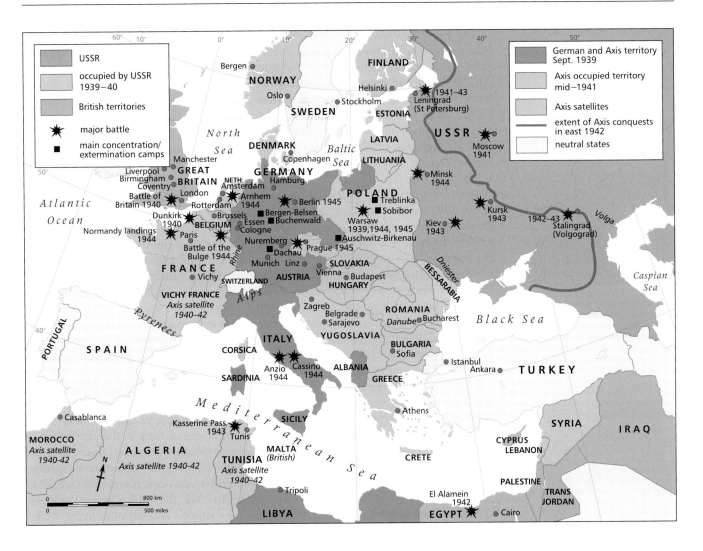

**Map legend (left):**
- USSR
- occupied by USSR 1939–40
- British territories
- ✷ major battle
- ■ main concentration/extermination camps

**Map legend (right):**
- German and Axis territory Sept. 1939
- Axis occupied territory mid–1941
- Axis satellites
- — extent of Axis conquests in east 1942
- neutral states

secret codes. By the end of 1940, Germany abandoned the Battle of Britain in the air, and gave up plans to invade the island by sea.

To the east, the Soviet Union, operating under cover of the nonaggression pact, had not only seized the eastern half of Poland and parts of Finland, and incorporated the Baltic States into its empire, it had also seized and incorporated parts of Romania that it had lost in World War I and began to target the Balkan states. Hitler moved first. He brought Romania, Bulgaria, and Hungary into the Axis, and occupied Yugoslavia and Greece. Then, in an unexpected, fierce attack, he turned his forces eastward, broke the nonaggression treaty, and invaded the Soviet Union on June 22, 1941, a date thereafter viewed in the USSR as its Pearl Harbor. A German army of three million men and some 3,500 armored vehicles, covered by the air support of the Luftwaffe (the German air force), invaded a 2,000-mile front in the USSR. The Soviets retreated from the central European lands they had taken, and moved hundreds of miles into the interior of their own country. They transported whole industrial plants deep into the interior as well. Finally, Stalin, who had been taken completely by surprise by the attack despite his years of preparation for warfare, counterattacked. The Soviet army, under General Georgi Zhukov, pushed the Germans back from their positions around the capital Moscow, relieving that city. The Germans, like Napoleon a century and a half earlier, retreated from Moscow in the face of the counteroffensive and the severe winter.

World War II in Europe. Fighting began in 1939 with a "*Blitzkrieg*," or lightning war, by Germany and her Italian ally. By late 1942 the Axis powers controlled most of Europe. But Germany's invasion of the Soviet Union in 1941 brought the power of that huge state into opposition and enmeshed Germany into exhausting land war. Britain held out defensively and then began to fight back, especially after the United States entered the war, bringing in air power and material support. By early 1944, the tide had turned.

The European war had another front in North Africa. In September 1940, the Italians, who held Libya, invaded Egypt, heading for the Suez Canal. To protect the canal, Churchill diverted troops and supplies from the Battle of Britain to North Africa. The British forces defeated the Italians in Egypt and Libya and even forced them out of Ethiopia. The Germans, however, under General Erwin Rommel, entered North Africa and battles raged back and forth between them and the British in 1941 and 1942. British lines, however, held at El Alamein, west of Alexandria, and the Suez Canal remained in British hands. Nevertheless, German submarines in the Mediterranean closed down transportation across that sea, and took a heavy toll on shipping across the Atlantic.

Hitler reorganized his Russian campaign in 1942, directing his troops to the south, in the direction of the rich oil fields of the Caucasus Mountains and the Caspian Sea. By the summer of 1942, Germany had taken all of the western possessions of the Soviet Union—the Baltic States, Byelorussia, Poland, and the Ukraine—and stood at the gateway to Leningrad. Holding its lines not far from Moscow, the German army besieged Stalingrad. Historians sometimes compare Hitler's position to that of Napoleon. Each man held approximately the same areas of Western Europe and each launched an assault into Russia that would devastate the country and force it into deep retreat, but would also leave Germany itself exhausted. To the west, each faced a determined Britain that responded to attacks with unexpected and ultimately victorious tenacity. The presence of the United States in World War II, however, would add a new ingredient to the balance.

From the beginning of the war in Europe, in September 1939, President Franklin D. Roosevelt had supported Britain and the Allies, but his support was limited by the isolationist feelings of many Americans. Roosevelt was able to lift the ban on arms sales, and in 1940, he sent a shipment of arms to England; later in the same year he added 50 destroyers in exchange for the right to establish military bases in some British possessions in the west. The United States also began military conscription, increased the size of its armed forces, and secured bases in Greenland and Iceland in order to protect American and Allied shipping. In 1941, the United States Congress introduced the Lend–Lease program to provide weapons and supplies to the Allied forces. Still, however, Roosevelt could not commit his country to war—until Japan attacked at Pearl Harbor in December. To understand this attack, we return to the Pacific theater of warfare.

The War in the Pacific, 1937–42

In 1937, a clash between Chinese and Japanese troops at the Marco Polo Bridge near Beijing had triggered the beginning of the Pacific War. The Japanese had not expected the fierce resistance of the Chinese. Planning to end the "China problem" with a single quick victory that would terrify the enemy into suing for peace, the Japanese army launched a full-scale attack on Nanjing. Japanese troops murdered, raped, and pillaged in what is now generally known as the Rape of Nanjing. Twelve thousand noncombatant Chinese were killed in the first three days after Nanjing was captured, and 20,000 cases of rape were reported in the first month. In the first six weeks some 200,000 civilians and prisoners of war were killed in and around the city. The atrocities set an ugly precedent for later Japanese cruelty toward many of the peoples they defeated throughout Asia during the war.

In the face of repeated Japanese advances, the Chinese government retreated to Chongqing, on the upper Yangzi River deep in the interior of the country. The Chinese, like the Russians retreating before the Germans, followed a **scorched-earth** strategy, leaving little in their wake that the enemy could use. The war in China

KEY TERM

scorched earth A strategy of defensive warfare, in which everything that might be of use to an invading army is destroyed by the defending army as it retreats.

became a stalemate. Even in 1945, when Japan itself was under attack, about a million Japanese soldiers were still fighting in China, and another 750,000 were in Manchuria. China's sheer persistence helped wear out the Japanese.

In September 1940, Japan signed the Tripartite Pact, formally aligning itself with Germany and Italy. But Axis plans were not well coordinated. Japan could have joined in the war against the USSR, opening a second front from Manchuria, as Germany wished. Instead, it signed a neutrality pact with the Soviet Union in April 1941 and turned southward to capture French Indochina, putting it on a collision course with the United States.

Isolationist pressure in America had thus far kept the United States out of armed warfare. However, the American government responded to Japanese aggression in China and Southeast Asia by placing an embargo on trade with Japan and by freezing its assets in July 1941. Resource-poor Japan, fearing for its supplies of oil and other raw materials, now had to choose between pulling back from China or confronting the United States in open warfare. Many Japanese resented American resistance to Japan's growing power as just another example of white man's colonialism. On December 7, 1941, Japan bombed the American Pacific fleet at Pearl Harbor, Hawaii. Attacking with more than 300 planes, the Japanese destroyed several battleships and seriously damaged three cruisers, three destroyers, and other ships. They also destroyed at least 180 airplanes. More than 2,000 people were killed and 1,000 were wounded. The attack severely crippled American sea power in the Pacific, though the Navy was able to repair some of the ships. The United States was also extremely fortunate that the three aircraft carriers attached to the Pacific fleet were training elsewhere at the time. America declared war the next day. In Britain, Winston Churchill immediately understood the consequences:

> Hitler's fate was sealed. Mussolini's fate was sealed. As for the Japanese, they would be ground to powder. All the rest was merely the proper application of overwhelming force. (Kennedy, p. 347)

The Japanese leaders who advocated the attacks—and many had opposed them—believed that they could defeat America if they struck before American industrial power and troop mobilization could move into high gear. So, on the same day as the attack on Pearl Harbor, Japan also attacked the Philippines, Hong Kong, Malaya, and other bases in Southeast Asia and the Pacific. By the middle of 1942, Japan had conquered the Philippines, the Malay Peninsula and Singapore, Indonesia, parts of New Guinea, Indochina, Thailand, and Burma. In the Pacific, Japan's attacks reached almost to Australia. Designating the conquests as the "Greater East Asia Co-Prosperity Sphere," Japan attempted to build an imperial system that would provide raw materials for its industries and markets for its finished products and that would willingly adopt Japanese cultural practices as well.

The plan did not work. The colonial economies could not produce and deliver the supplies that Japan wanted, and, more crucially, Japan could not absorb the

U.S. servicemen in the Pacific. Landing in Higgins boats from a base in Australia, American troops of the 163rd Infantry Regiment, 41st Division, hit the beach running during the invasion of Wadke Island, May 18, 1944. Two months earlier, the United States had begun firebombing Japanese cities.

agricultural products they could produce. Market structures based on the existing integration of world trade systems were not easily reorganized. Instead of implanting its culture, Japan's occupations evoked nationalistic opposition. Japan's treatment of conquered peoples and prisoners of war was notably harsh and earned it a reputation for cruelty. The brutalizing of thousands of Korean, Chinese, and Filipina women to serve as "sex slaves" for Japanese soldiers came to international attention half a century after the war was over.

Turning the Tide

By the end of 1942 the Allied counteroffensive had begun. The alliance of Britain, the Free French (an exile government based in London under the leadership of de Gaulle), the Soviet Union, the United States, and some twenty allied countries slowly evolved. Roosevelt already called them the United Nations. Roosevelt and Churchill, establishing a Combined Chiefs of Staff, decided to concentrate on the western and African fronts, leaving the main fighting against Japan for later.

In the Battle of the Atlantic, British and American navies successfully fought German U-boat (submarine) warfare and protected the ocean shipping routes. American troops could now be transported to Europe in relative safety. Under General Dwight Eisenhower, Allied forces launched a huge, surprise, amphibious invasion of Algeria and Morocco in November 1942 and pushed eastward. By the spring of 1943, they were met by British forces moving westward from Egypt under General Bernard Montgomery. By May 1943, North Africa was completely recaptured and the sea lanes of the Mediterranean were again safe for shipping.

The Soviets called on their allies to open a massive, land-based western front that would relieve the German pressure on the USSR. The Americans and the British deferred such an attack until they had made more thorough preparations, leaving the Soviets to rely on their own resources, and to doubt the commitment of the British and Americans to their Soviet allies. In the winter of 1942–43, the Soviet Union held out successfully against German troops at the Battle of Stalingrad, but at the cost of the lives of up to a half-million Soviet soldiers. More Soviets died in the Battle of Stalingrad, between September 1942 and February 1943, than Americans died in the entire war. The Axis powers lost fewer, about 150,000 killed and 90,000 captured. Stalingrad was the turning point in the eastern front. Once the siege was lifted, General Zhukov—already a hero for lifting the siege of Moscow in 1941—opened a Russian counterattack that began to push the Germans steadily westward. By now, also, food, supplies, and material were reaching the Soviet troops under the American Lend–Lease program. The millions of Soviet troops deployed in these waves of assault tied down millions of Axis troops, as in Operation Bagration, the USSR's massive offensive in the summer of 1944. In that year, the Soviet Union recaptured the Ukraine, Byelorussia, the Baltic states, eastern Poland, Romania, and Bulgaria. In early 1945 they entered Germany. Their battles on the eastern front also allowed the Allies to open fronts in Western Europe with greater safety.

In contrast to the large-scale warfare of the massed armies of the major belligerents, in many countries, **partisan** underground resistance also developed—sometimes against the Allies, especially against the Russians in eastern Europe, more frequently

Russian troops defending Stalingrad. In seven months of siege and warfare, July 1942 to February 1943, Russians and Germans suffered a combined two million casualties—killed, captured, and wounded—in the bloodiest battle in modern history. The Soviet victory turned the war around on the Eastern Front. The German offensive across Russia was halted and Axis troops were pushed onto the defensive, slowly but steadily retreating before Russia's armies.

against the Axis powers. Because warfare had become so mechanized and so overwhelming in its size and scope, the partisans usually had more social and psychological importance than military. In some cases, however, they were quite significant, even militarily.

Yugoslavia presented the most extreme case. It was captured by the Axis powers in April 1941 and was partitioned among them, with Germany and Italy taking the largest shares. From one part of the country an independent state of Croatia was created and placed in the charge of the Ustasa party, run by fanatical anti-Serbs. Even the Nazis were shocked at their virulence. Ustasa murdered hundreds of thousands—estimates run as high as two million—Serbs and other "undesirables" in 1941. Two groups of Serbian resistance fighters formed, one led by a Serbian officer in the Yugoslav army, the other by a communist named Josip Broz (1892–1981), who took the name Tito. Tito himself was not a Serb—he had a Croat father and a Slovene mother—but he fought on behalf of Yugoslavia as a leader of Serbian troops. The two leaders and their groups could not cooperate, so they fought separately against the Axis armies, and sometimes they fought against each other. Tito proved the more effective, and in 1943, after Italy withdrew from the Axis, Britain and America gave him direct support. By the end of the war, Tito commanded some 250,000 men and women and had emerged as the undisputed leader of Yugoslavia.

Bombers on a raid. By World War II aircraft of all kinds were poised for aerial combat. Here an SAAF/BAF Beaufighter fires three-inch RPs during an attack on German positions in the Yugoslavian town of Zuzemberg in 1945. The astronomical cost of bombs and aircraft contributed to the Allies' wartime expenditure of $1,150,000,000,000.

In the spring of 1943, the American and British air forces, from their bases in Britain, began bombing German cities. Unable to target military positions with accuracy, the air assaults became, in effect, attacks on civilians as well as on military objectives. In July 1943, the German city of Hamburg was mostly destroyed in firebombings, with far more civilian than military casualties. Some officers debated the morality of these attacks, but they continued and even increased. In February 1945, the Allies firebombed the German city of Dresden, leveling most of it and killing some 50,000 civilians. Since the city had no military or strategic value, the raids were widely condemned as purely punitive.

On July 10, 1943, the Allies invaded Sicily to begin their Italian campaign, moving quickly northward through the Italian boot. On July 23, Mussolini's government fell. In September 1943, Italy surrendered and switched sides in the war, joining the Allies. Fighting continued, however, as German armies invaded and held the capital, Rome, and northern Italy. Rome was liberated by Allied and partisan forces only in June 1944, the entire country in April 1945. Mussolini himself was captured and executed on April 29 by Communist Italian partisans as he attempted to escape to Switzerland. His body was taken to Milan, where it was suspended upside down at a gas station for public viewing.

The long-awaited land invasion of Western Europe began. **D-Day,** June 6, 1944, brought the largest amphibious military operation in history as Allied forces—American, British, and Canadian troops—invaded Normandy and began the push eastward. More than 4,000 ships carried the men; some 10,000 aircraft provided support. On the first day, 130,000 men landed by ship and parachute; within a month one million had landed. Although there were some disagreements over strategy

KEY TERM

D-Day Often used in the military as the day on which an important operation is to begin; more generally, signifies any date targeted for special action. Since the Normandy landing, June 6, 1944, the term "D-Day" has most often referred to that historic invasion.

among the Allied generals, the American Eisenhower and the British Montgomery, and some setbacks—as in the Battle of the Bulge, in the Ardennes forest of Belgium—the new offensive steadily pushed the Germans back. Paris was liberated in August. Allied troops entered Germany in September.

In the last few months of the war, however, new technologies of destruction were introduced. In September 1944, Germany launched V-2 missiles for the first time against Britain, ushering in an age of missile warfare. Because the guidance systems were not yet well developed, most of the V-2s missed their targets.

As the Allies conquered Germany in bitter combat—Russian troops invading from the east, American, British, French, and Canadian forces from the west—Hitler retreated to his bunker in Berlin. On April 30, with the Soviet armies closing in, he killed himself. Germany surrendered a week later, on May 7, 1945, and the war in Europe finally ended. The war in the Pacific continued for another three months.

The War in the Pacific, 1942–45

Even though the war in the Pacific received less Allied attention than the war in Europe, once America committed its industrial and technological strength to fighting Japan, the tide turned. Despite the losses of most of its Pacific fleet, in June 1942 American naval forces won their first battle at Midway Island. Then, from bases in Australia, they moved northwestward, "island hopping," taking Guadalcanal and New Guinea, recapturing the Philippines and the Pacific island chains. During the spring of 1945 they captured Okinawa after three months of brutal fighting. As early as March 1944, the Americans had begun firebombing Japanese cities. Japan had expected Americans to become tired of the war and negotiate a peace, but instead America demanded unconditional surrender.

The firebombing intensified. On a single day—March 9, 1945—83,793 people were killed, 40,918 were injured, and 267,000 buildings were destroyed in Tokyo alone. Burning and starving—caloric intake had dropped from a daily standard of 2,200 to 1,405 by 1944—Japan fought on. Finally, on August 6, 1945, America dropped the atomic bomb on Hiroshima. With the European war won, the USSR invaded Manchuria and Korea on August 8. On August 9, America dropped a

Summary executions in the Pacific. Japanese soldiers were notoriously brutal in their treatment of prisoners during World War II. British servicemen captured in the Pacific theater were forced to construct the Burma Railway and many died of starvation and disease in the process. Some were murdered in cold blood, as here, the imminent execution of three Allied fighters before open graves.

Legend:
- Japanese territory 1941
- Japanese offensives 1941-42
- Japanese territory July 1942
- Allied counter-offensives 1942-45
- Japanese territory August 1945
- atomic bomb attacks 1945
- major battle

World War II in the Pacific. Japan mounted combined operations in 1941 in East Asia, Southeast Asia, and across the Pacific, opening a war front from the borders of India to Hawaii. This supremely aggressive move was meant to secure the resources and markets needed to sustain the "Greater East Asia Co-Prosperity Sphere." It proved impossible to defend: Chinese resistance, a daring U.S. island-hopping campaign in the Pacific—culminating in the explosion of atomic bombs over Hiroshima and Nagasaki—and Soviet assaults on Manchuria defeated Japan completely.

A-bomb devastation. On August 6, 1945, the *Enola Gay* Super-Fortress aircraft released the first atom bomb ever used in warfare over Hiroshima, an important Japanese military base and seaport. About 70,000 people were killed instantly. By the end of 1950, a total of perhaps 200,000 had died from burns, radiation, and related illnesses. On August 9, a second nuclear bomb was dropped on Nagasaki. On August 15, Japan announced its surrender. Debates continue to rage as to the importance of the nuclear explosions in Japan's decision.

second atomic bomb, this time on Nagasaki. On August 15, 1945, Japan offered its unconditional surrender.

Japan lay in ruins. Some two million Japanese had died in the war, a fourth of Japan's national assets were destroyed, industrial production was at barely ten percent of prewar levels, millions of homes had been destroyed, and Japan had lost all its colonial holdings. Mass starvation was prevented only by food imported by the occupation authorities.

Assessing the War

World War II is often called a "total war" because it involved the entire populations and economies of the nations that fought it. The distinction between military and civilian disappeared. Noncombatants were bombed and killed on both sides. It is estimated that 50 million people died, 30 million of them civilians. The heaviest fighting was in the Soviet Union, which lost more people than any other country, about 20 million. (The devastation was so widespread, and so overwhelming, that some have estimated 40 million.) Japan lost two million people and Germany just over four million. Though there are no reliable statistics, well-informed estimates report from ten to 20 million dead in China. Britain and the United States each lostabout 400,000. Six million Jews died in Nazi concentration camps along with hundreds of thousands of Poles, gypsies, homosexuals, and handicapped persons.

Japan's early victories over European colonizers provided a double shock. Asians were able to defeat the most advanced European countries and the United States, at least for some time. As these victories enhanced the image of Japanese power, they undermined the image of the Europeans in Asia. After the war, when the European colonizers attempted to return—the British to Burma and Malaya, the French to Indochina, the Dutch to Indonesia—local nationalist groups rose in protest, sometimes armed, and eventually achieved independence. The Japanese victories helped pave the way toward ending European colonialism in the Pacific region.

ARMAMENTS PRODUCTION OF THE POWERS, 1940–43 (billions of 1944 dollars)		
	1940	1943
Allied combatants		
U.S.	(1.5)	37.5
USSR	(5.0)	13.9
Britain	3.5	11.1
Axis combatants		
Germany	6.0	13.8
Japan	(1.0)	4.5
Italy	0.75	—
		(Source: Kennedy, p. 355)

AIRCRAFT PRODUCTION OF THE POWERS, 1939 AND 1944		
	1939	1944
Allied combatants		
U.S.	5,856	96,318
USSR	10,382	40,300
Britain	7,940	26,461
Axis combatants		
Germany	8,295	39,807
Japan	4,467	28,180
Italy	1,800	—
		(Source: Kennedy, p. 354)

War and Technology

World War II witnessed a dramatic increase in the use of technology—tanks, submarines, and aircraft—as well as the number of troops. The sheer costs were staggering, and the forces that could spend more on armaments won the war. The productivity and availability of aircraft on each side represent their overall technological capacity.

Tanks, too, were vital weapons. In 1944, Germany produced 17,800; the Soviet Union, 29,000; the U.S., 17,500; Britain, 5,000 (Kennedy, p. 353). No wonder that after the initial shock and advantage of their first attacks, the Axis powers began steadily to fall behind the Allies. The technological and industrial capacity of the Axis powers simply could not keep up.

The Mobilization of Women

The military and industrial needs of World War II put new demands on the labor force, deeply affecting women's lives. The demands of keeping factories running at full blast during the war while putting millions of soldiers onto the battlefields required an unprecedented commitment of labor. Even during World War I, millions of women began to work outside the home for pay, and the stereotypes of "men's work" and "women's work" began to erode. This experience contributed to the achievement of women's suffrage in the United States (1920) and in Western European nations. Although South American countries were not much involved in World War I, many of them—Brazil, Cuba, Ecuador, El Salvador, and Uruguay—also granted female suffrage between 1929 and 1939 (Rosenberg, p. 67). The majority of women had not remained in the workforce after World War I ended, but after World War II unprecedented numbers of women continued to work in industrial and unconventional jobs.

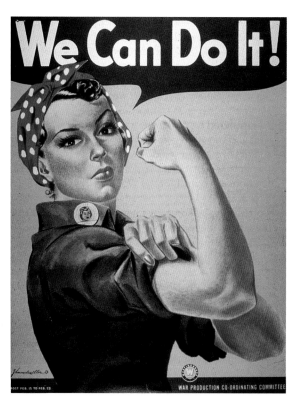

"Rosie the Riveter," symbol of World War II American women workers, on a poster from the War Production Coordinating Committee.

KEY TERM

gender The social attributes of being male or female, in contrast to the biological attributes of sex. Thus, bearing children is an attribute of the female sex, but caring for children can be done by males or females. If females are expected to care for children, that is an attribute of gender, not sex, since both males and females are capable of doing it.

The mobilization of women was, however, culturally specific. Different combatant countries followed different family and gender policies. The largest of the Allies—the United States, Britain, and the USSR—generally encouraged women to join the wartime workforce. "Rosie the Riveter," a woman working in an American munitions factory, became the recognized symbol of women's contribution to factory work in these Allied countries. The Axis powers, on the other hand, did their best to keep women at home despite the needs of the war. Hitler offered women "emancipation from emancipation." He offered marriage loans to married women who left their jobs, and then cancelled 25 percent of the repayment of the loan in exchange for the birth of each child. The Nazis banned abortion and closed sexual counseling clinics. Mussolini excluded women from government office, doubled the fees of female students in secondary schools and universities, and tried to prevent rural women from relocating to cities. In China, while the communists encouraged women to join in the struggle directly, the nationalists kept them at home.

As the troops returned from war to their old jobs, women tended to return from factory and military service to the home, both by choice and because of social pressure. However, gender relations could not remain unaffected by wartime experience. After the war, feminism found new voices. Simone de Beauvoir published *The Second Sex* in France in 1949, advancing the argument that while sex is biological, **gender**, the behavioral traits associated with each sex, is learned. As she wrote: "One is not born, but rather becomes, a woman." In the United States, Betty

SOURCE

Women as Spoils of War: Japan's Comfort Women

From earliest recorded history, stories of warfare include accounts of soldiers abusing women and of victors seizing women as their reward for victory. The story of Japan's "comfort women" during World War II carries these stories to an unusually cruel extreme. From 1932 to 1945, thousands of women—estimates vary from a few thousand to 200,000—were rounded up and forced into sexual slavery by the Japanese military as "comfort women" serving in "comfort stations"—that is, as captive sexual slaves in brothels administered by the Japanese armed forces. Although the situation was widely known in the military and was the subject of a Japanese novel in 1947, later made into a movie, the facts were generally swept under the rug. In 1990, the Korean Council for the Women Drafted for Military Sexual Slavery by Japan began to collect and publish the stories of many Korean women who had been taken by the Japanese and who were willing to talk publicly, 40 years after the events.

The Korean women were especially badly treated since the Japanese historically have looked down on Koreans. Subsequently, the Japanese government was called upon to apologize and pay reparations to the women. It has officially refused, although it has encouraged private Japanese donations to the women and has given some payments without acknowledging official responsibility. The government of Japan has frequently argued that the women were simply sex workers who sold their services to soldiers.

The testimony of Kim Young-shil, interviewed in North Korea in 1992, tells not only of sexual slavery but also of racial cruelty:

There was a girl next to my cubicle. She was younger than I, and her Japanese name was Tokiko. One day an officer overheard her speaking to me and accused her of speaking Korean [which had been forbidden]. He dragged her out to a field and ordered all of us to come out there. We all obeyed. He said, "This girl spoke Korean. So she must die. You will be killed if you do too. Now, watch how she dies." He drew his sword. Horrified, I closed my eyes and turned my face away. When I opened my eyes, I saw her severed head on the ground.

On Sundays we were made especially busy. Soldiers stood in line in front of our cubicles. They got ready for their turn by undoing their puttees from their legs, rolling them up and holding them in their hands. They shamelessly exhibited their lust like animals in heat. Many of them could not control themselves and shouted, "Madaka? Hayaku! Hayaku! [Not finished yet? Hurry! Hurry!] Some even came into my cubicle even before the act was finished.

I was totally exhausted. I could keep neither my sense of humiliation nor my dignity. I felt like a living corpse. When soldiers came to my room and did it to me one after another, it was done to a lifeless body. Again. And again. And again.

(Schellstede, pp. 50–51)

Friedan's *The Feminine Mystique* (1963) challenged women of the postwar generation to ask if life as homemaker in suburbia was fulfilling, to consider working outside the home, and to advocate for equal conditions in that work.

In Europe and the United States the new feminism became a powerful, if controversial, force. In other parts of the world, the concept of new roles for women outside the home and community was more disputed. Often the very fact that new concepts of gender relations came from the West, from colonial powers, influenced their reception, making them more attractive to some, more suspect to others.

The War's Horrors

Two horrors distinguished World War II from all other wars that came before. Massive warfare was not new. Military leaders from Alexander the Great to Chingghis Khan to Napoleon had attempted world conquest. But the atomic bombs dropped by the United States on Japan— a weapon capable of destroying all life on earth—changed both the nature of war and peace as well as humanity's conception of itself. And the policy of the Nazis to obliterate an entire people—the Jews—from the world, without any ostensible economic or territorial goal, and to mobilize the full resources of the state against this unarmed opponent, constituted a new goal, executed by new technology. It was later given a new name, **genocide**.

The Holocaust. Anti-Semitism was not new in Europe, but the Nazi program was unprecedented. First, it reversed the trend of acceptance and civic equality for Jews advanced a century and a half earlier by the French Revolution. Second, it targeted Jews as an ethnic or racial group rather than as a religious community. This was not a policy for conversion or even for exile. Anyone with a Jewish grandparent was considered Jewish under Nazi laws and marked for death. Third, the Nazi program put the entire weight of the nation into the task of wiping a people off the face of the earth, using all the technological and organizational skills at its disposal to carry out the mission, and continuing with it even when it was clear that the larger war was lost.

Hitler had made clear his beliefs in racial hierarchy—with Jews at the bottom. Once in power he set out to enslave and later to exterminate these "lesser peoples." He built concentration camps where prisoners were used as slave labor before being gassed and cremated. Millions of Jews were brought to the camps by a railway network specially constructed for this purpose. Even in the closing days of the war, when Germany had clearly been defeated, Hitler ordered the trains and the crematoria to continue operations. By 1945, some six million Jews, accompanied by millions from other "inferior" races, especially gypsies and Poles, joined also by homosexuals and handicapped people, had been murdered. The Holocaust, as this butchery was named, made World War II into a conflict of good versus evil even in the eyes of many Germans after the war. The moral crisis and the appalling devastation of the Holocaust are impossible to fully comprehend, but the writing of survivors such as Elie Wiesel (see pp. 712–13) helps us to understand them.

The liberation of Belsen.
Shocked British soldiers liberating Belsen concentration camp in northwestern Germany, in 1945, found 60,000 Jews and other victims of the Holocaust dying of starvation, typhus, and tuberculosis. 100,000 had already died in the camp, half of them Soviet prisoners of war. Many prisoners had been used for medical experiments. Framed by an open grave, a Dr. Klein is shown speaking to Movietone News. His experiments included injecting benzine into his victims to harden their arteries. He was responsible for thousands of deaths.

KEY TERM

genocide The act of murdering an entire people. Originally used for the Nazi attempt to exterminate the Jewish people, it has been used since then to indicate the attempt to murder a substantial segment of a designated population.

The Milgram Experiment and the "Final Solution"

How could people carry out acts of such inhumanity as the genocide against the Jews? Perhaps the leaders of Nazi Germany were insane—unrepresentative of normal people. But what about the ordinary Germans who said that they were simply following orders? To what extent do people just follow orders more or less blindly even if they know they are inflicting pain? In 1961, Yale psychologist Stanley Milgram set up an experiment to find out. He solicited volunteers from in and around Yale University. He brought them to a laboratory and explained that the experiment would test the effects of punishment on learning. The volunteer, who was to play the role of "Teacher," was briefly introduced to the "Learner," who was to learn pairs of words read aloud by the Teacher. Each time the Learner failed to learn properly, the experimenter would instruct the Teacher to inflict punishment by delivering an electric shock. The first time, the shock was 15 volts. The second 30, and each successive shock would add 15 additional volts up to a maximum, on the thirtieth failed attempt, of 450 volts.

The Teacher was told that the experiment would test the efficacy of the shocks in promoting learning. In fact, the experiment was to test how much voltage the Teacher would apply to the Learner. Teacher and Learner were sent to separate rooms, but the Teacher could see the Learner through a window. As the Learner made mistakes the experimenter told the Teacher to apply the voltage shocks. At the tenth shock, 150 volts, the Learner—who was an actor playing the role—demanded to be let out of the experiment. But this was not permitted. At this point only ten of the Teachers refused to give any more shocks. Seventy continued applying greater voltage for each wrong answer, in accordance with the experimenter's orders. The Learner continued moaning, shrieking, and demanding to be let out of the experiment. By the time the twentieth shock—300 volts—was administered, the Learner said that he refused to give any more answers. By this point, 21 of the volunteers stopped administering shocks despite the commands of the experimenter. At the twenty-first level, the Learner screamed out in sheer pain and gave no answer. Five more volunteers stopped their participation. From the twenty-third shock onward, the Learner remained silent, perhaps unconscious, perhaps dead. Nevertheless, most Teachers continued applying the shocks on command. Of the 80 volunteers, 51 continued to administer the shocks all the way to the top level—450 volts—long after the Learner appeared to be unconscious, if not dead. Milgram concluded that, at least within the confines of this narrowly bounded experiment, "normal" people follow orders in inflicting pain, even to the point of murder, so long as they believe that the person in charge, the experimenter, has the authority and the expertise to give the orders.

- Do you think Milgram's experiment is a valid way to research the question of why apparently normal people followed orders in wartime and the Holocaust? Why or why not?
- If you were the Teacher in the experiment, at what level do you think you would quit? Do you think you are different from the majority here? Why or why not?
- Were you surprised at the results of Milgram's experiment? Why or why not?

PEARSON
myhistorylab

The A-Bomb. The atomic bomb was tested for the first time on July 16, 1945, just weeks before it was used in Japan. As the fireball rose over the testing grounds at Alamogordo, New Mexico, J. Robert Oppenheimer, the bomb's architect and director of the $2 billion Manhattan Project that produced it, quoted from the Hindu *Bhagavad Gita*: "I am become Death, the destroyer of worlds." Of the 245,000 people living in Hiroshima on August 6, 75,000 died that day, another 100,000 thereafter, while still others suffered radiation poisoning, cancer, and genetic deformation. Three days later, a second bomb was dropped on Nagasaki, and five days after that, on August 14, Japan surrendered unconditionally. Today, despite years of continuing efforts toward arms control, there are tens of thousands of nuclear bombs and warheads on missiles, submarines, and airplanes capable of destroying human life many times over. Several nations that do not yet possess nuclear weapons are at work trying to develop or buy them. Most recently, fears have increased that terrorist individuals or groups might gain access to small nuclear devices.

Debate has raged over the wisdom and purpose of using the atomic bomb to end the war in the Pacific. Critics see the act as racist, pointing out that this weapon was not used in Europe (in fact the bomb had not yet been prepared at the time Germany surrendered in May 1945). Cynics suggest that its real purpose had less to do with defeating Japan than with demonstrating United States power to the Soviet

Union. Those who justify the use of the bomb suggest that losses of life on both sides would have been higher had the Allies invaded Japan's home islands. The use of the bomb certainly saved Allied lives, and it may even have saved Japanese lives. The casualties in the battles for Pacific islands had been in the hundreds of thousands, and war in Japan itself might have cost a million Allied troops and even more Japanese. Finally, the advocates argue, in a war of such scope and brutality, combatants inevitably use the weapons that are available. The question of why a second bomb was dropped at Nagasaki, three days after Hiroshima, remains an additional issue.

Some of the war technology, however, had by-products of use to civilians. Nuclear energy itself could be employed under careful supervision for peaceful uses in power generation and medicine. Radar, which Britain developed to protect itself from Germany in the Battle of Britain in 1940, was valuable in commercial aviation. Drugs, such as sulfa and penicillin, entered the civilian pharmacopoeia. But the technology of warfare drew the lion's share of the scientific and technological budgets of many nations, including the largest industrial powers, the United States and the USSR, and of many developing countries, as well.

The Tortured Image of Humanity

Until World War I, the Western idea of human progress through rationalism, science, and technological progress had been widely accepted. There had been no war between the great European powers since the 1870–71 conflict between France and Germany, and even that had been relatively small and contained (although 250,000 people died). Democracy seemed both progressive and ascendant. Life expectancy and quality seemed to be improving steadily.

The colonial dominance of Europe over ancient Asian and African civilizations had the effect of reaffirming Europeans' belief in the supremacy of their technology and political systems. Students from all over the world were coming to Europe's universities to study Western sciences and arts. If machines were "the measure of man," European civilization measured best of all, and was steadily gaining ground.

Some contrary voices, however, were already breaking through the self-congratulation. Mohandas Gandhi (1869–1948) of India, writing in 1906 in *Hind Swaraj* or *Indian Home Rule*, caricatured and reevaluated Western accomplishments from a different perspective.

> Formerly when people wanted to fight with one another, they measured between them their bodily strength; now it is possible to take away thousands of lives by one man working behind a gun from a hill. This is civilization. Formerly, men worked in the open air only as much as they liked. Now thousands of workmen meet together and for the sake of maintenance work in factories or mines. Their condition is worse than that of beasts. They are obliged to work, at the risk of their lives, at most dangerous occupations, for the sake of millionaires. Formerly, men were made slaves under physical compulsion. Now they are enslaved by temptations of money and of the luxuries that money can buy. … This civilization takes note neither of morality nor of religion. Its votaries calmly state that their business is not to teach religion. Some even consider it to be a superstitious growth. Others put on the cloak of religion, and prate about morality. … Civilization seeks to increase bodily comforts, and it fails miserably even in doing so. (Gandhi, p.36)

Gandhi concluded: "This civilization is such that one has only to be patient and it will be self-destroyed."

At about the same time, in Vienna, in the heart of central Europe, Sigmund Freud (1856–1939) developed the new art of psychoanalysis. Freud ascribed humanity's most profound moving force not to rationality, the pride of European science and technology, but to sexuality. He argued that people did not understand their own deepest drives; these were hidden in the unconscious. He, too, questioned the ability of European civilization to survive:

> There are two tenets of psychoanalysis which offend the whole world and excite its resentment. … The first of these displeasing propositions of psychoanalysis is this: that mental processes are essentially unconscious … [the] next proposition consists in the assertion that … sexual impulses have contributed invaluably to the highest cultural, artistic, and social achievements of the human mind. … Society can conceive of no more powerful menace to its culture than would arise from the liberation of the sexual impulses and a return of them to their original goal. (Freud, pp. 25–27)

New, nonrepresentational, or abstract, art also seemed to question the significance of rationality. The most innovative and honored of its creators, Pablo Picasso (1881–1973), drew from African "primitive" art to create new forms of his own. Through these African-inspired innovations, he demonstrated that the West had much to learn from the naturalism and spirituality of cultures that it dominated politically, economically, and militarily.

Voices of despair multiplied. Even the end of war did not bring renewal. T.S. Eliot's "The Waste Land" (1922) depicts, among its many gloomy scenes, the impending reunion of a wife with her husband, a soldier returning from World War I. The anticipation is grating and crude, even foreboding, rather than romantic, as the poet warns the wife:

> Now Albert's coming back, make yourself a bit smart.
> He'll want to know what you done with the money he gave you
> To get yourself some teeth. He did, I was there.
> You have them all out, Lil, and get a nice set.
> He said, I swear, I can't bear to look at you.
> And no more can't I, I said, and think of poor Albert,
> He's been in the army four years, he wants a good time,
> And if you don't give it to him, there's others will, I said.

She replies, with some venom:

> Oh is there, she said. Something o' that, I said.
> Then I'll know who to thank, she said, and gave me a straight look.

Eliot (1888–1965), perhaps the most influential English language poet of his generation, captures an arid, spiteful, loveless individual relationship and suggests that the same empty bitterness pervades the entire society.

With the far greater destruction of World War II and its atomic bombs and genocide, literature reflected humanity at rock bottom, estranged from itself and from the universe. In 1941, at the age of 12, Elie Wiesel had immersed himself in the practices of Hasidic, orthodox, devotional Judaism in Sighet, Hungary. In reply to the question, "Why do you pray?" he had said, "Why did I pray? A strange question. Why did I live? Why did I breathe?" But in 1944, after three years in a Nazi ghetto, he arrived in Birkenau, adjacent to Auschwitz, the hungriest of the concentration camps.

> Not far from us, flames were leaping up from a ditch, gigantic flames. They were burning something. A lorry drew up at the pit and delivered its load—little children. Babies! Yes, I saw it—saw it with my own eyes … those children in the flames. (Is it surprising that I could not sleep after that? Sleep had fled my eyes.)

So this was where we were going. A little farther on was another and larger ditch for adults. I pinched my face. Was I still alive? Was I awake? I could not believe it. How could it be possible for them to burn people, children, and for the world to keep silent? No, none of this could be true. It was a nightmare. (Wiesel, p. 16)

Wiesel soon becomes aware of someone reciting the Kaddish, the Jewish prayer for the dead.

For the first time, I felt revolt rise up in me. Why should I bless His name? The Eternal, Lord of the Universe, the All-Powerful and Terrible, was silent. What had I to thank Him for? (Wiesel, p. 22)

Long-cherished images of humanity and of the gods it had held sacred perished in the Holocaust. Yet Wiesel found the courage to make of his experiences in the death camps the stuff of literature and the basis of a new morality:

Never shall I forget that night, the first night in camp, which has turned my life into one long night, seven times cursed and seven times sealed. Never shall I forget that smoke. Never shall I forget the little faces of the children, whose bodies I saw turned into wreaths of smoke beneath a silent blue sky.

Never shall I forget those flames which consumed my faith forever.

Never shall I forget that nocturnal silence which deprived me, for all eternity, of the desire to live. Never shall I forget those moments which murdered my God and my soul and turned my dreams to dust. Never shall I forget these things, even if I am condemned to live as long as God Himself. Never. (Wiesel, pp. 41–43)

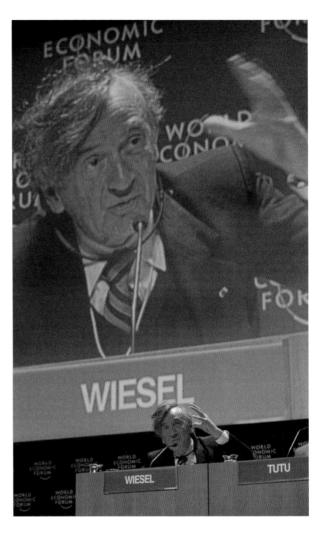

The Nobel Peace Prize winner Elie Wiesel at the World Economic Forum, 1998. Wiesel survived the Holocaust and devoted his life to alerting the world to its horrors, so that it might never happen again. Unfortunately, other "smaller" Holocausts continue to occur without effective external intervention.

To transmit this horrible personal history, to warn humanity of its own destructiveness, and to proclaim the need to preserve life became Wiesel's consuming passion. The award of the Nobel Peace Prize in 1986 recognized his mission.

From Japan, which suffered the world's first and (so far) only nuclear explosions in warfare, came similar meditations of anguish and despair, followed later by a commitment to prevent such catastrophe in the future. A student in Hiroshima Women's Junior College, Artsuko Tsujioka, remembered the atomic attack on her city in which 75,000 people were killed instantaneously and tens of thousands lingered on to die later or to be misshapen and genetically damaged from the persistent radiation:

It happened instantaneously. I felt as if my back had been struck with a big hammer, and then as if I had been thrown into boiling oil. ... That first night ended. ... My friends and the other people were no longer able to move. The skin had peeled off of their burned arms, legs and backs. I wanted to move them, but there was no place on their bodies that I could touch. ... I still have the scars from that day; on my head, face, arms, legs and chest. There are reddish black scars on my arms and the face that I see in the mirror does not look as if it belongs to me. It always saddens me to think that I will never look the way I used to. I lost all hope at first. I was obsessed with the idea that I had become a freak and did not want to be seen by anyone. I cried constantly for my good friends and kind teachers who had died in such a terrible way.

My way of thinking became warped and pessimistic. Even my beautiful voice, that my friends had envied, had turned weak and hoarse. When I think of the way it was then, I feel as if I were being strangled. But I have been able to take comfort in the thought that physical beauty is not everything, that a beautiful spirit can do away with physical ugliness. This has given me new hope for the future. (Andrea and Overfield, pp. 417–19)

HOW DO WE KNOW?

The Decision to Drop the Atom Bomb

Because nuclear weapons have so thoroughly changed the nature of war, peace, and diplomacy, and have even changed the way we think about the future of life on earth, attitudes toward them continue to change. Since Hiroshima and Nagasaki remain the only wartime deployment of the bomb, the decision to use it has received intense scrutiny. Even as the Manhattan Project was developing the bomb, at least one of the scientists central to its development counseled against using it. Leo Szilard wrote, "A nation which sets the precedent of using these newly liberated forces of nature for purposes of destruction may have to bear the responsibility of opening the door to an era of devastation on an unimaginable scale" (Rhodes, p. 749). President Truman nevertheless chose to drop the bomb, not just once, but twice. In the immediate aftermath of the explosions and Japan's surrender, an overwhelming proportion of Americans approved the decision. Even then, however, "Pacifist groups, a number of atomic scientists, some religious leaders and organizations, and a scattering of political commentators, both liberal and conservative, condemned the atomic attacks because of their indiscriminate killing of civilians and/or the failure of the United States to give Japan an explicit warning about the bomb before Hiroshima" (Walker, p. 98).

The United States Strategic Bombing Survey, published in July 1946, concluded that "certainly prior to 31 December 1945, and in all probability prior to 1 November 1945, Japan would have surrendered even if the Atomic bombs had not been dropped" (Walker, p.100). Such a "counterfactual" judgment, however, cannot be proved or disproved.

In 1961, former State Department official Herbert Feis, in his book, *Japan Subdued*, agreed that the Japanese would have surrendered by the end of the year, even without the bomb and even without an invasion. Nevertheless, he wrote, "the impelling reason for the decision to use [the bomb] was military—to end the war victoriously as soon as possible" (Walker, p. 104). He also noted that had there been an invasion, American casualties would probably have been in the thousands rather than the hundreds of thousands.

Gar Alperovitz, first in his dissertation and then in his book, *Atomic Diplomacy*, concluded on the basis of diplomatic sources, and especially the diary of Henry Stimson, Secretary of War, that Truman used the bomb more to impress the Russians and improve his bargaining position with them than to subdue the Japanese. Secretary of State James Byrnes, for example, told the

American ambassador to the Soviet Union, Joseph E. Davies, that American possession of the bomb "would have some effect [on the Soviets] and induce them to yield and agree to our position" (Walker, p. 64). Through the 1970s and 1980s scholarship responding to new documents tended to confirm a composite account: the bomb had been used both to end the war quickly—although the Japanese would have surrendered even without the bomb and without an invasion—and to intimidate the Russians.

J. Samuel Walker, who summarizes these debates in his book, *Prompt and Utter Destruction*, adds three more arguments that have been suggested as reasons for the use of the bomb. "Justifying the costs of the Manhattan Project" was one. How could the government spend $2 billion, and employ the efforts of 600,000 workers, and then not employ and demonstrate the results? As Henry Stimson put it when he heard that the first test bomb had been successful: "I have been responsible for spending two billions of dollars on this atomic venture. Now that it is successful I shall not be sent to prison in Fort Leavenworth" (Rhodes, p. 686). Also, there was a "lack of incentives not to use the bomb." As Stimson wrote, "I believe that no man, in our position and subject to our responsibilities, holding in his hands a weapon of such possibilities for accomplishing this purpose and saving those lives, could have failed to use it and afterwards looked his countrymen in the face." Finally, Truman believed he was dealing with an enemy that was "a beast." Loathing of Japan as a cruel and bitter enemy enabled Truman to use the bomb with a clear conscience. In questioning charges of racism, Walker adds that Truman might have used the bomb against Germany as well, but Germany had surrendered by the time the bomb was ready.

Questions concerning necessity and morality remain with us. They surround not only the use of the bomb in the past, but also its potential use in the future.

Indeed they surround all decisions concerning the use of massive force in warfare.

- In light of these assessments, would you have chosen to use the bomb on August 6, 1945? Would you have used it again on August 9? Why or why not?
- Which reasons would you consider appropriate for using the bomb? Which would you consider inappropriate?
- What have been the bases for different scholars arriving at different conclusions about the reasons for the decision to drop the bomb?

myhistorylab

On a national scale, Japan's peace parks at both Hiroshima and Nagasaki record the nuclear destruction as well as subsequent commitments to seeking international peace. Since World War II, Japan has been committed to keeping nuclear arms out of Japan and has been intensely involved in the efforts of the UN to work for peace. Its increased wealth and potential military power in the Pacific, however, put stresses on Japan's antimilitaristic patterns in the early twenty-first century.

The French existentialist author Albert Camus (1913–60), perhaps the most influential voice in European literature in his time, wrote in 1940, the year France fell to Germany:

> There is but one truly serious philosophical problem, and that is suicide. Judging whether life is or is not worth living amounts to answering the fundamental question of philosophy.

Perhaps, however, rock bottom had been reached, or perhaps hope is part of human nature, even in conditions of apparent hopelessness, for Camus answered his own question in *The Myth of Sisyphus* (1942) with an affirmation, which he repeated in 1955:

> This book declares that even within the limits of nihilism it is possible to find the means to proceed beyond nihilism ... Although *The Myth of Sisyphus* poses mortal problems, it sums itself up for me as a lucid invitation to live and to create, in the very midst of the desert. (p. 3)

Out of the Rubble: The United Nations and Resettlement

Out of the rubble of the war, both victors and losers had to restructure new relationships. The creation of the UN represented one of their most hopeful responses.

The United Nations

President Roosevelt first used the term "United Nations" publicly on New Year's Day, 1942, when he issued a joint declaration of war aims with Britain, the USSR, China, and 22 other countries. Planning for a permanent organization began in 1944, culminating in the Charter of the UN, which was signed in San Francisco by 50 countries on June 26, 1945 (and by Poland, also considered a founding member, in October of that year). The main purpose of the organization was "to save succeeding generations from the scourge of war," and its major institutions were designed to respond to threats to the peace. The UN General Assembly, in which every member country was represented and had a vote, provided a forum for the discussion of the major issues threatening world peace. The Security Council, with five permanent members (the United States, the USSR, Britain, France, and China), and several others elected for fixed terms by the General Assembly, could dispatch peace-keeping forces. An International Court of Justice was created to decide disputes among member states. In 1946, the League of Nations was formally dissolved and the UN took on many of its missions, such as promoting public health through the World Health Organization (WHO), and educational, economic, and cultural activities through the United Nations Economic, Scientific, and Cultural Organization (UNESCO). In its early years, the peace-keeping function of the UN was stymied by the mutual hostility of the United States and the Soviet Union. As permanent members of the Security Council, each had the right to veto major policy decisions of the UN, leaving the organization mostly powerless to resolve key conflicts between these two postwar superpowers. Nevertheless,

SOURCE

Preamble to the Charter of the United Nations

We the peoples of the United Nations determined

- to save succeeding generations from the scourge of war...
- to reaffirm faith in fundamental human rights, in the dignity and worth of the human person, in the equal rights of men and women and of nations large and small...
- to establish conditions under which justice and respect for the obligations arising from treaties and other sources of international law can be maintained...
- to promote social progress and better standards of life in larger freedom.

And for these ends

- to practice tolerance and live together in peace with one another as good neighbors...
- to unite our strength to maintain international peace and security...
- to ensure, by the acceptance of principles and the institution of methods, that armed force shall not be used, save in the common interest...
- to employ international machinery for the promotion of the economic and social advancement of all peoples...

Have resolved to combine our efforts to accomplish these aims.

its service as a forum for discussion, and its humanitarian activities ensured the place of the UN in the new, emerging international order. Its role increased in significance through the years. (We will discuss the UN at greater length in Chapter Twenty-one.)

Postwar Resettlement

Almost 100 million soldiers served under arms during the war, many of them in foreign lands. Some 20 million of them were killed. Millions more were captured as prisoners of war and required repatriation, resettlement to the areas from which they came. Millions of civilians had also been resettled or imprisoned by conquering armies that feared revolt among their newly subject populations. In addition, Germany and Japan had fought, in part, for *lebensraum*, more living space. They had dispatched millions of their civilians to new homes in newly conquered territories. These civilians, too, had to return to their original homes—or, at least, to new homes. Additional millions had been displaced by the warfare, fleeing as best they could from approaching armies. National borders were redrawn as a result of the war, especially in central and eastern Europe, and nationals of various countries often chose, or were forced, to move in accord with the new national geographies. Finally, millions also traveled in the hope of finding lost family members and in search of food.

During the war, for example, millions of Germans moved, as soldiers or civilians, into Eastern Europe and the Baltic countries. The Soviets also exiled about 500,000 Germans to Siberia. They deported some two million Poles and 180,000 Balts to Siberia, and replaced them with about equal numbers of Russians and Ukrainians.

In the years immediately following the war, some 15 million Germans who had been living or fighting in Eastern Europe returned to Germany. Four and a half million Poles, most of whom had fled the Nazis or the communists (or both), returned to Poland. The Soviets continued to enforce population exchanges, exiling almost two million Ukrainians and central Asian peoples to Siberia, along with some 300,000 more Balts to eastern Russia and Siberia. Here, too, they replaced them with about equal numbers of Russians and Ukrainians regarded as loyal to the new communist administration. Some 300,000 Balts fled westward to escape their new masters. Hundreds of thousands of other, smaller groups—Hungarians, Slavs, and Finns—also moved. Some 320,000 Jews, survivors of the Holocaust in Europe, emigrated to join the effort to create a new Jewish homeland in Palestine.

Similar migrations occurred in East Asia as some five and a half million Japanese returned home. Most were demobilized soldiers, but hundreds of thousands were civilians who had established homes in Korea and Taiwan over several decades of Japanese colonization. In Manchuria and North Korea, Soviet troops, who had entered the war in Asia only in its last few days, seized about a half-million Japanese soldiers and relocated them to labor camps in Siberia where they worked on construction projects. Thousands of others were murdered by Chinese taking revenge. Of the Japanese prisoners of war in Siberia, about ten percent died. Almost all of the rest were repatriated to Japan between 1946 and 1949.

All these movements were quite different from the return home by millions of victorious American troops. 400,000 American soldiers had been killed, but the American mainland had been essentially untouched, and the troops were repatriated in more or less orderly fashion to their own homes. Moreover, in gratitude for their service and in eagerness to reintegrate the troops peacefully and productively into civilian life, the U.S. government instituted new programs such as the G.I. Bill of Rights, which enabled millions of the veterans to go to college, an aspiration that might otherwise have been beyond their means. The booming wartime and postwar economy of the United States made these veterans' benefits financially possible, and soon the addition of millions of more highly educated veterans increased the productivity of the country's workforce still further. The postwar period in the United states—and elsewhere—brought a baby boom, a rapid rise in the birthrate as the country, and much of the world, recovered from a decade and a half of economic depression and world war.

Remembering the War

Remembering and representing World War II has proved contentious. The devastation was so painful that, at the time, many survivors wanted simply to forget and to get back to rebuilding their lives. Historian Tony Judt believes that forgetting may have been the best alternative, in the short run. If individuals and nations had turned immediately to reliving and revenging their memories, Judt asserts, the world might not have been able to move on. Judt writes only about Europe, but his evaluation may hold for East Asia as well. He argues that while there is a time to remember, there is also a time to forget. Later, however, will come a time to remember. Here we consider six different memorials of the war, the messages they were designed to convey, and some of the disputes over those messages.

The Nuremberg Trials, Germany, October 1945. After the war, the Allies put 22 of the most notorious Nazis on trial for crimes against humanity. Some critics called this "victor's judgment," but others thought it established new and better standards of international accountability.

The Nuremberg Trials

The stated goal of the trials at Nuremberg, Germany, in 1945 and 1946 (convened by the U.S., the Soviet Union, Great Britain, and France) was to demonstrate that crimes against humanity would be punished under international law in trials administered through public, systematic procedures. Individual leaders, not just nations, could be found guilty of war crimes. The trials also provided an opportunity for the world to grasp more fully the reality of the war's atrocities and especially of the Holocaust, with its concentration camps and gas chambers. Twenty-two of the most powerful surviving Nazi leaders were brought to trial for crimes against humanity, including: planning, initiating, and waging of wars of aggression, in violation of international treaties; mass murder; and genocide. Twelve were sentenced to death, seven to lengthy prison terms; three were acquitted.

Some critics argued that the trials simply administered "victor's justice," judging people for crimes that had not been classified as crimes at the time they were committed. Cynics noted that the men who were brought to trial had been on the losing side. Would they have been prosecuted for these crimes had they won? Nevertheless, the exposure of the evil of the war crimes and the appearance of the accused on trial had a cleansing effect for the war's victims as well as its witnesses. It served, at least in theory, as a warning that might curb the worst excesses of political leaders in the future.

Memorial Museums and Exhibitions

There have been many memorials to World War II in the form of museums and public displays. Here we consider five, two of them created to remember the Holocaust, two to remember Hiroshima, and one to consider the war's significance as a whole.

The Terror House. Hungary had been allied with Germany during the first part of the war. In 1944, when Hungary considered withdrawing from the alliance, the Nazis occupied the country. After the war, Hungary was occupied by Soviet troops until 1989. Both Germany and the Soviet Union treated Hungary as captured territory and exploited the land and its people for their own benefits. Each, in turn, used the same mansion in the center of Budapest as the headquarters for its secret police. Here the occupying governments held, questioned, tortured, and murdered Hungarian prisoners. In 2002, the now independent government of Hungary opened this house as a museum of the horrors of both occupations, a "Terror House."

The Terror House implicitly compares the Nazi occupation with that of the Russians. It presents the Russian occupation as longer, more pervasive, and perhaps more destructive. Critics of this perspective point out that the Nazis killed far more people. They accuse the museum of playing politics with history, since many currently active political leaders have old ties to these foreign governments. Several walls of the museum display pictures of perpetrators of political crimes and some of these pictures are of men and women active in contemporary Hungarian politics. The Terror House museum argues that the past is still living in Budapest and that political criminals—especially from the more recent communist era—are still at large and still powerful.

Memorials to Hiroshima. Two other museums, one in Hiroshima itself, the other in Washington, demonstrate the continuing battles over the representation of the atomic bombing of Hiroshima. Japan opened the Peace Memorial Park and Museum at Hiroshima in 1955 "as reminders of the past and contributions to a future of lasting peace." The museum's exhibits of photographs and artifacts from the atomic blast of August 6, 1945 display the devastation of nuclear weapons. The museum projects the message that such weapons of mass destruction should be banned. Critics of this museum note that the exhibit presents the nuclear attack in isolation. While it does not present Japan simply as an innocent victim, neither does it suggest any link between the use of the bomb and the Japanese attack on Pearl Harbor and the subsequent war in the Pacific. The display is about the deadly power of the A-bomb, not about the significance of the war in which it was used and the Japanese role in that war.

Criticism from a reverse direction forced the reorganization of an American museum display intended to commemorate the heroism of the flight of the *Enola Gay*, the plane that dropped the atomic bomb on Hiroshima. In 1995, the Smithsonian Institution prepared a major display at the National Air and Space Museum in Washington, D.C., to commemorate the fiftieth anniversary of the bombing. By this time, many critics had already declared that the bomb had not been necessary to victory over Japan, and that the use of the bomb had been, at best, a mistake and, at worst, a war crime. These critics suggested that victorious nations have the same responsibility as defeated nations to consider questions of morality and proportionality in their choices regarding war and peace. (See box p. 714.) The Smithsonian had intended to include some of this criticism in its exhibition, but so many groups across the United States protested the very idea of an exhibition dedicated to commemorating the *Enola Gay* that the entire exhibit was scaled back and presented in a different context. The *Enola Gay* protest underlined the gap that persisted, after half a century, between the critical views of some American scholars and the generally more approving views of the general American public as to the necessity and the morality of the use of nuclear weapons.

Remembering the Holocaust. Finally, disputes over Holocaust memorials indicate that different audiences understand this event differently. Auschwitz, the concentration camp in Poland where between one and one and a half-million people were killed, has become the name almost synonymous with the Holocaust. The

Holocaust Memorial, Berlin, inaugurated 2005, architect American Peter Eisenman. Constructed after years of political debate and architectural competition, a field of 2,711 concrete slabs fills about two square city blocks in the center of Berlin. (The Reichstag, Germany's Parliament building, is visible a few blocks away.) The slabs rise in height from a few inches at the edges to almost 16 feet in the center. Meanwhile the ground slopes irregularly downward from the edges to the middle, creating an interactive experience designed to be disorienting, representing a supposedly ordered system that has lost touch with human reason. Although Eisenman purposely did not put names on the slabs, so that the field would not feel like a cemetery, it does.

camp, along with Birkenau, about two miles away, was established as a museum in 1947. The Auschwitz–Birkenau State Museum has become a major tourist attraction, with many tour buses arriving daily.

Ninety percent of those killed at Auschwitz were Jews, and the exhibits in the museum now reflect that proportion. But the earliest prisoners under the Nazis were Polish nationalist leaders, mostly Catholic, and a substantial segment of the museum is set in the context of nationalism, memorializing the suffering of the Polish people under Nazism and the bravery of the Polish armed forces, who continued to fight in guerrilla warfare from within Poland, and in other countries as well, even after their defeat by the Nazis. Another segment of the museum is devoted to the thousands of Soviet prisoners of war who were also held in the camp, especially in the war's early years. From the end of the war until 1989, the period of Soviet occupation of Poland, the government gave most attention to these segments of the camp. Only after 1989 were the Jewish segments expanded. Still later, other exhibits were added, dedicated to the tens of thousands of gypsies who were killed in the two camps.

Not only did each group of Nazi victims receive attention in different sections of the museum, but even the signage was different from section to section, depending on the expected audience: always in Polish and English, often in Hebrew; in the memorial to the gypsies, in German. Auschwitz recalls the suffering of many different groups of people, and, in many respects, it considers them separately. Critics of the museum suggest that its organization has encouraged different groups to engage in comparative victimhood, as each points out ways in which it has suffered more than the others.

In 2005, in the very heart of Berlin, a few minutes' walk from the Reichstag building where the parliament meets, Germany opened its Memorial to the Murdered Jews of Europe. Spread over four and one half acres, the memorial is a field of gravestones, of uneven height, short and shallow at the edges of the field, higher and dug deeper into the ground toward the center. Visitors who enter the field become participants in the display, walking deeper and deeper into the sunken earth pathways, becoming more and more overwhelmed and disoriented by the unmarked gravestones rising ever-further above their heads. Specific information on the Holocaust is available at an underground information point, but the field of unmarked gravestones remains an open enigma for each "participant" to engage and to interpret individually. Critics of this exhibit have claimed that Germany already has enough memorials to the war and the Holocaust, and that the country needs no further reminders of this part of its history. Periodically, swastikas (the Nazi symbol) have desecrated the stones. Nevertheless, the government of Germany has plainly made a commitment to confront its past with this enormous, personal memorial in the very center of its capital city.

Two World Wars: What Difference Do They Make?

So many lives around the world were so deeply affected by these events that their interpretation continues to be contentious today. Genocides have continued and racial hatred persists, even as Holocaust memorials cry out, "Never again." Nuclear weapons have been reduced, but tens of thousands continue to menace civilization, and more nations and terrorist groups seek them out.

The end of World War II also saw the rise of two "superpowers," the United States and the Soviet Union, which came into their own through their victories in the war and the weakened conditions of Europe's former imperial powers. They then began a new contest for power, a "Cold War," which divided the world into two spheres of influence and struggle.

Nevertheless, the two world wars also brought enormous changes for the good. New technologies that had been developed especially for wartime, such as radar, aeronautics, communications, and antibiotics, found applications in peacetime. The UN proved to be more durable, more flexible, and more effective than the League of Nations. Europe developed new institutions that transformed that continent in mostly peaceful and productive ways.

Colonized countries, arguing that European powers could no longer claim to be models to follow, demanded and received their independence. Many argued that it was time for the formerly colonized countries to help Europe find its way out of its 30 years of hatred and destruction. The Senegalese poet and statesman Léopold Sédar Senghor held out the promise that Africa, finding its freedom and voice anew, could help Europe to return to health after a generation of destruction:

> The Africa of the empires is dying, see, the agony of a pitiful princess
> And Europe too where we are joined at the navel.
> Fix your unchanging eyes upon your children, who are given orders
> Who give away their lives like the poor their last clothes.
> Let us report present at the rebirth of the World
> Like the yeast which white flour needs.
> For who would teach rhythm to a dead world of machines and guns?
> Who would give the cry of joy to wake the dead and the bereaved at dawn?
> Say, who would give back the memory of life to the man whose hopes are smashed?
> They call us men of coffee cotton oil
> They call us men of death.
> We are the men of the dance, whose feet draw new strength pounding the hardened
> earth. (Okpewho, p. 134)

After 30 years of the worst warfare and destruction ever known, who could predict what new vistas lay ahead?

Léopold Sédar Senghor (1906–2001) poet, professor, philosopher, statesman. Born in Senegal, Senghor studied, and later taught, at universities in France. He helped found the philosophical movement of "Negritude," asserting the importance of ways of thinking and feeling that he considered distinctively African. For several years, under colonialism, Senghor represented Senegal in the French Assembly, and, after Senegal became independent in 1960, he became the first president of the new nation, 1960–80.

Asking Questions

- How did the depression of 1929–39 affect the recovery from World War I? Discuss the effects on different countries, such as Germany, the U.S., the USSR, and Japan.
- How important were thugs in the rise of fascism in Italy and Germany? What roles did they play? Why did people decide in large numbers to follow them?
- Compare fascism and communism (discussed in Chapter Nineteen) in terms of: (1) power of the state; (2) power of the leader; (3) role of private property; (4) value put on warfare; (5) willingness to enter international, diplomatic relations with other nations as an equal; and (6) individual human rights.
- Warfare affected the role of women, but the effect was different in different countries. Discuss these differences and similarities in the U.S., the USSR, Germany, and Japan.
- Elie Wiesel reports losing his faith not only in his fellow humans but also in God as a result of his experiences in the Holocaust. How does this compare with other responses to this disaster and to the atomic bombing of Japan?

Suggested Readings

KEY TERMS

fascism see p. 686

made the trains run on time see p. 688

totalitarianism see p. 690

lebensraum see p. 690

the big lie see p. 690

dual economy see p. 693

scorched earth see p. 700

partisans see p. 702

D-Day see p. 703

gender see p. 708

genocide see p. 709

PRINCIPAL SOURCES

Conot, Robert E. *Justice at Nuremberg* (New York: Harper and Row, 1983). A full account of the trial, and of many of the crimes and their perpetrators. The book was the basis for the absorbing film of the same name.

Dower, John. *Embracing Defeat.* Superb account of Japan under American occupation, 1945–52.

Freud, Sigmund. *Civilization and its Discontents* (New York: W.W. Norton and Co., 1961). Freud explains the battle between love and war. He is not sure which will win out.

Judt, Tony. *Postwar* (New York: Penguin Press, 2005). Marvelous, magisterial account of postwar Europe. Elegantly written.

Kennedy, Paul. *The Rise and Fall of the Great Powers* (New York: Vintage Books, 1989). Very good on the human and economic costs of war.

Rhodes, Richard. *The Making of the Atomic Bomb* (New York: Simon and Schuster, 1986). A comprehensive study of the Manhattan Project, including the science, administration, and politics of the production of the first nuclear weapon.

Straus, Ulrich. *The Anguish of Surrender: Japanese POWs of World War II* (Seattle, WA and London: University of Washington Press, 2003). Rich exploration of the psyche, and impact, of Japanese soldiers who chose to surrender and were imprisoned.

Weinberg, Gerhard. *A World at Arms: A Global History of World War II* (Cambridge: Cambridge University Press, 1994). Massive, one-volume history of the war, in all theaters, examining the use of both force and diplomacy.

Wiesel, Elie. *Night* (New York: Bantam Books, 1962). Terrifying personal account of Wiesel's youth in the concentration camps.

Yoshimi, Yoshiaki (trans. Suzanne O'Brien). *Sexual Slavery in the Japanese Military During World War II* (New York: Columbia University Press, 1995). A comprehensive, academic account of the sexual slavery of the "comfort women" and their relatively recent demands for reparations from the Japanese government.

ADDITIONAL SOURCES

Alperovitz, Gar. *The Decision to Use the Atomic Bomb* (New York: Knopf, 1996). Examines the entire range of debate by both decision makers and later commentators.

Andrea, Alfred and James H. Overfield, eds. *The Human Record,* Vol. 2 (Boston, MA: Houghton Mifflin, 3rd ed., 1998). Excellent collection of primary documents.

Bosworth, R.J.B. *Mussolini* (London: Oxford University Press, 2002). The most recent and important biography of Mussolini.

Browning, Christopher. *Ordinary Men: Reserve Police Battalion 101 and the Final Solution in Poland* (New York: Harper Collins, 1992). An excellent analysis of ordinary people involved in the Holocaust.

———. *The Path to Genocide: Essays on Launching the Final Solution* (Cambridge: Cambridge University Press, 1992). An analysis of Nazi Jewish policy.

Bulliet, Richard W., ed. *The Columbia History of the 20th Century* (New York: Columbia University Press, 1998). Excellent selection of academic articles tracing the key themes of the twentieth century.

Cook, Haruko Taya and Theodore F. Cook. *Japan at War: An Oral History* (New York: New Press, 1992). Japanese civilians and soldiers recall their own experiences.

De Grazia, Victoria. *How Fascism Ruled Women: Italy, 1922–1945* (Berkeley, CA: University of California Press, 1992). An examination of the ideas of womanhood under fascism in Italy.

Eliot, T.S. *Collected Poems 1909–1962* (New York: Harcourt Brace Jovanovich, 1936). Includes "The Waste Land." Eliot's poetry, with its startling imagery, irony, and often despairing search for meaning in the midst of a barren culture, defined modernism in literature.

Friedan, Betty. *The Feminine Mystique* (New York: Dell, 1963). Argued that American women were living unfulfilling lives at home after their children were grown. They should be participating more in public life outside the home.

Gandhi, Mohandas Karamchand. *Hind Swaraj* or *Indian Home Rule* (Ahmedabad: Navajivan Press, 1938). The Mahatma's classic denunciation of the materialism of Western civilization.

Hilberg, Raul. *The Destruction of the European Jews*, three vols. (New York: Holmes and Meier, 1984). Comprehensive analysis of the Holocaust.

Hitchcock, William. *The Bitter Road to Freedom: A New History of the Liberation of Europe* (New York: Free Press, 2008). Remarkable account of the tribulations of returning to normality after the war. Assiduously researched; written with flair.

Keegan, John, ed. *The Times Atlas of the Second World War* (New York: Harper, 1989). Indispensable for following and understanding the unfolding of the war.

Kershaw, Ian. *The 'Hitler Myth': Image and Reality in the Third Reich* (London: Oxford University Press, 2001). A collection of essays attempting to explain why people followed Hitler.

Keynes, John Maynard. *The Economic Consequences of the Peace* (New York: Harcourt Brace Jovanovich, 1920), pp. 211–16. Highly influential critique of the terms of the peace agreements as setting the stage for renewed warfare.

Lee, Lloyd E. *World War II* (Westport, CT: Greenwood Press, 1999). Somewhat sketchy coverage of major issues and campaigns of the war, useful chronology, primary documents,

biographies, and bibliography, especially of films and electronic sources.

Marrus, Michael. *The Holocaust in History* (London: Plume Books, 1988). An assessment of literature on the Holocaust.

Morris-Suzuki, Tessa. *The Technological Transformation of Japan.* (Cambridge: Cambridge University Press, 1994).

Okpewho, Isidore, ed. *The Heritage of African Poetry* (Harlow, Essex: Longman Group, 1985). Remarkable anthology with interesting discussions.

Overy, Richard. *Why the Allies Won* (New York: W.W. Norton, 1995). An assessment of the economic, strategic, political, and moral balance between the combatants.

Peukert, Detlev, J.K. *The Weimar Republic* (New York: Hill and Wang, 1993). An excellent social and political history of the Weimar Republic and the conditions that led to the rise of Hitler.

Rosenberg, Rosalind. "The 'Woman' Question," in Bulliet, pp. 53–80. Superb, brief survey of the major issues.

Schellstede, Sangmie Choi, ed. *Comfort Women Speak: Testimony by Sex Slaves of the Japanese Military* (New York: Holmes and Meier, 2000). The "comfort women" tell their own stories. Includes photographs of the women today, and a United Nations report on the situation.

Slater, Laura. *Opening Skinner's Box: Great Psychological Experiments of the Twentieth Century* (New York: W.W. Norton, 2004). One of the experiments presented and discussed is Stanley Milgram's.

Speer, Albert. *Inside the Third Reich: Memoirs* (New York: Macmillan, 1970). An insider's account of Nazi administration and wartime operations.

Spiegelman, Art. *Maus: A Survivor's Tale*, 2 vols. (New York: Pantheon Books, 1996). Astonishing. A son's deeply affecting account of his father's Holocaust experience told in comic book (graphic novel) form with mice for Jews and cats for Nazis. Pulitzer Prize-winning literary breakthrough.

Walker, J. Samuel. *Prompt and Utter Destruction: Truman and the Use of Atomic Bombs against Japan* (Chapel Hill, NC: University of North Carolina Press, 1997). Discusses the pros and cons of the decision to bomb, in light of the knowledge that policymakers had at the time.

Wilkie, Brian and James Hurt, eds. *Literature of the Western World,* Vol. 2 (New York: Macmillan, 1984). Excellent anthology. Gives complete works.

For quizzes, flashcards, primary sources, interactive maps, videos, and other activities related to this chapter please go to

www.myhistorylab.com

CHAPTER TWENTY-ONE

Cold War, New Nations, and Revolt Against Authority

Remaking the Post–World War II World
1945–1991

Two issues dominated the years following World War II. The first was the Cold War. Two powers, the Soviet Union and the United States, previously at the periphery of Europe's dominance, now surpassed Europe in military and political influence. In competition to establish their own new power in the postwar world, they challenged each other politically and threatened each other militarily, insisting that the peoples of earth choose sides between them. Few political, economic, or cultural events of this period escaped their intense competition.

The USSR and the U.S. competed to develop the most advanced forms of technology, especially for warfare: nuclear weapons, intercontinental ballistic missiles to deliver them, and the control of space, symbolized in the race to put satellites into orbit and to send astronauts to the moon. One of the great surprises of this period in history, however, is that throughout 45 years of armed-to-the-teeth confrontation, the two nations never attacked one another directly. They did, however, recruit other nations as surrogates and battlegrounds for their competition. Many of these arenas of their conflict were newly independent states.

The achievement of independence by more than 50 European colonies was the second great event of the years following the war. Each of these newly independent nations sought its own road to development. Many sought to cooperate with like-minded, friendly nations for their mutual support, and almost all were solicited by the two new **superpowers** to take sides in their global competition.

The two global transformations intersected. The U.S. and the USSR courted, and infiltrated, the new nations, seeking to win them over as allies politically and to exploit their resources economically. The superpowers sought to sell some of their weaponry to the new nations both as a means of gaining allies and of earning profits. On the other hand, many of the new nations developed their own low-tech military strategies. On battlefields around the world each of the superpowers found itself pinned down by guerrilla warriors seeking to establish their own independence of foreign control.

In the most dramatic examples, guerrilla warfare bled America in Vietnam and the USSR in Afghanistan, ultimately helping to bring down governments in both countries. Later military strategists would refer to battles between these unequal, contrasting military technologies and strategies as **asymmetrical warfare,** with outcomes not always obvious to predict. Even at the time, however, China understood the superpowers' dilemma, especially America's. The United States was unwilling to use its nuclear weapons to combat guerrilla warriors, and it was often unable to combat them effectively with its conventional

KEY TOPICS

- The Cold War: U.S. vs. USSR
- 1968: Revolt Against Authority
- The Cold War and the Emergence of New Nations
- The Emergence of the Third World
- The End of the Cold War: The Soviet Union Dissolves
- Pursuing Peace through Negotiation
- Legacies of the Cold War, Decolonization, Economic and Social Development: What Difference Do They Make?

Zhou Enlai, Bandung Conference, Indonesia, 1955. Zhou Enlai (center) arrives at the Bandung Conference along with many third world leaders to articulate a postcolonial world order.

superpower The term ascribed to both the U.S. and the USSR in recognition of their power, especially their military power, far greater than that of any other country in the world at the time.

asymmetrical warfare Warfare between groups armed and equipped very differently, and often using different strategies, usually between lightly armed guerrilla warriors and conventionally equipped armies of powerful states. Terror tactics and disinformation are also considered tactics of asymmetrical warfare. The term came into wide use in the 2000s, but it is also applicable to earlier guerrilla warfare.

paper tiger The mocking comment of the Chinese toward the Americans, who had vast arrays of conventional and nuclear weaponry, but could not cope with simply armed warriors, often guerrilla warriors, fighting for their homelands in Korea, Vietnam, and elsewhere.

Pax Americana Literally, "American peace," a Latin phrase derived by analogy from *Pax Romana* (the peace enforced within the boundaries of the Roman Empire by Roman rule) to designate the relative tranquility established within the American sphere of influence immediately after World War II.

Marshall Plan An American program of economic assistance for rebuilding noncommunist Europe after World War II, proposed by U.S. Secretary of State George Marshall.

military strategies and technologies. China mocked the United States as a "**paper tiger**" despite its weaponry.

While the Cold War and the emergence of new nations took center stage in the first decades after the war, three other developments also merit consideration. First, some nations sought to minimize the risk of future war and to reduce its destructive potential. France and Germany, in particular, the most powerful European countries at the end of World War II, initiated programs of mutual economic cooperation meant to create a different, peaceful future. Japan renounced entirely the use of nuclear weapons. Both Japan and the countries of Europe resolved to seek peaceful conflict resolution rather than further warfare. They rejected the belligerence of the Cold War. Both, however, relied heavily on the American military as a shield for their own defense against potential enemies, especially against the Soviet Union in Europe and China in Asia.

Second, nongovernmental organizations (NGOs)—which Americans have more commonly called volunteer organizations—carried out many significant tasks of economic development and social welfare, often supplementing government programs. NGOs offered private citizens the opportunity to work on vital problems of development that the government did not, or could not, address adequately.

Finally, apart from the political and economic concerns of the postwar period, cultural patterns, too, were shifting, sometimes dramatically. The United States and Europe, in particular, were shocked by the vigor of youth revolts aimed at ending the war in Vietnam, restructuring educational institutions, and opening new freedoms in sexuality, dress, speech, and self-expression. 1968 was a year of cultural confrontation; it encouraged revolts against authority everywhere, including the factory workplace and the university campus.

The Cold War: U.S. vs. USSR

From the middle of the nineteenth century, many leaders of the United States believed in its "manifest destiny." They believed that America had a message to spread about proper governance in the world, first by setting an example, and, second, by actively taking its message to other nations. Woodrow Wilson had done the latter with his Fourteen Points during World War I, as had Franklin Roosevelt in his Four Freedoms address and the Atlantic Charter (with Winston Churchill) during World War II. These extroverted missions often alternated with introverted periods of isolationism, but after World War II the extrovert United States prevailed. It emerged from the war victorious and by far the richest, most powerful, and most industrially productive country in the world, and it acted with a vigorous sense of optimism, but, at the same time, with a fear that its prominence was threatened by the rising power of the USSR.

In the first years after the war, the United States promoted a **Pax Americana**, a worldwide peace dominated by American power and enforced by American arms and wealth. As one of its first missions, it sought to help rebuild the economies of war-torn countries, especially in Western Europe and Japan, and to keep communist influences out. Through its $12 billion investment in the **Marshall Plan** it encouraged the reconstruction of Western Europe along democratic and mixed capitalist–socialist patterns. It paid special attention to Germany, attempting to reestablish its brief experience with democracy and to rebuild its economy. It paid even more attention to Japan, which it occupied militarily and politically for seven years. Although they had been devastated by war, both of these defeated nations retained important industrial plants that were still in operation, and their skilled workers and

Postwar Europe. Western and eastern bloc competition, following their alliance in crushing Nazi Germany, crystallized in the Cold War. The Soviet Union annexed territories in the Baltic states and eastern Poland and set up a string of puppet communist states later known as the Warsaw Pact alliance, from East Germany to Bulgaria. The Western Allies formed the countervailing NATO alliance. The stalemate continued for 40 years.

entrepreneurs had not forgotten their skills. Within a decade Germany (and Western Europe in general) and Japan had recovered economically to prewar levels and were beginning to experience an economic miracle that would make them still more prosperous. They were once again becoming powerhouses of the global economy.

American assistance provided a margin that helped them to speed this recovery, and, ironically, to institute social welfare measures more comprehensive, and more socialistic, than those of the United States. America also extended financial and political assistance to political parties and NGOs that struggled to establish themselves against communist challenges. America's involvement in the political life of its allies was usually public, but occasionally it was more secretive, as it backed parties it considered friendly and opposed others. America was especially active in France and Italy, where communist political parties regularly attracted upward of 25 percent of the vote and communist labor unions were capable of leading millions of workers on strikes against capitalist enterprises and conservative government policies.

The Soviet Union had a similar sense of mission for extending its power territorially and ideologically. In 1919, just two years after the success of their own revolution, Soviet leaders had established the Comintern (Communist International) to encourage communist parties and revolutionaries throughout the world. Under Joseph Stalin, the Comintern continued to dispatch agents around the world to promote communist revolution. To some nations that had been devastated by World

sphere of influence The geopolitical region in which one external power is considered dominant and other powers keep hands off.

iron curtain Term introduced by Winston Churchill to describe the division of Europe by the Soviet Union spreading its areas of control in central and Eastern Europe from Western Europe.

containment The postwar policy of the United States, advocated by diplomat George Kennan, to encircle and contain the Soviet Union within limits, through militant confrontation that would stop short of war. Containment advocated a balance of force.

War II, and to others just emerging from colonialism and seeking a model for rapid modernization, the Soviet Union's government-sponsored industrial successes were attractive (see Chapters Nineteen and Twenty). The USSR's ability to survive ferocious punishment in World War II, fight back, and triumph, despite untold material damage and the deaths of some 20 million people, earned its people and its government great respect in the world community. In the postwar period, the USSR appealed to those who looked with suspicion on America's overwhelming power and sought to restore some balance in international affairs. Some nations also preferred a socialist, or even communist, alternative to American capitalism. In addition, as a country with no overseas colonies, the USSR could easily position itself as a leader in the fight against colonialism.

The Cold War in Europe

Postwar agreements among the Allies provided some hope that the United States and the USSR would find a way to accommodate their different philosophies and compromise on their goals. Unfortunately, this did not happen. Agreements signed in the closing months of the war by Roosevelt, Churchill, and Stalin at Yalta, on the Black Sea, and at Potsdam, Germany (with President Harry Truman replacing Roosevelt, who had died just weeks before), gave the USSR latitude to expand its **sphere of influence** in Eastern Europe. Between 1945 and 1948 the USSR imposed communist governments, controlled from Moscow and backed by Soviet troops, on eastern European nations, and then organized the economies of these satellite nations to serve its own economy. Despite its anti-imperial rhetoric, the Soviet Union had kept control of the tsar's land-based empire and was now adding to it. Observing the Soviet takeover of central Europe in 1946, Britain's Winston Churchill observed ruefully, "An **iron curtain** has descended across the continent."

Moreover, in 1949, the communist revolution, which had been gestating in China through three decades of civil war, finally won control of that huge country. (We will discuss China in the next chapter.) Americans, who had supported the opposition armies in that civil war, could hardly believe the news. America had "lost" China! The opposition was forced off the mainland to the island of Taiwan. The largest country in the world in terms of population had now joined the largest country in the world in terms of land area in a communist alliance against America in the Cold War.

Meanwhile, the Russians viewed America's actions around the world with equal apprehension. They judged American economic assistance to Western Europe and Japan as an attempt to form alliances against the USSR. American support to the Turkish government helped keep Soviet troops out of that country. British and American assistance to the Greek government helped it to win its struggle against a communist guerrilla insurgency. In announcing its assistance to the Greek government, the U.S. issued the Truman Doctrine (1947), offering "to help free people to maintain their institutions and their integrity against aggressive movements that seek to impose upon them totalitarian regimes." America was implementing a policy of **containment**, a policy of keeping the USSR bound within acceptable limits, short of confronting it in direct warfare. The Soviet Union correctly read all of these American actions as attempts to restrict and encircle it. But would the United States stop short of war? This the Soviet Union could not predict. It did know, however, that at the end of the war, America alone had the atomic bomb, and had used it. From the Soviet perspective, this made the United States the most dangerous nation on earth.

Each side feared and provoked the other. The first open test of will came in Germany. Following World War II, the Allies had divided Germany into four zones

The Yalta Conference, 1945. At Yalta in February 1945 Stalin (right), Roosevelt (center), and Churchill (left) planned their postwar positions in Europe. Misunderstandings between them later led to Cold War tensions and recriminations.

for administrative purposes. The United States, Britain, and France held three zones in the western sector, and the USSR held the east. The former capital, Berlin, was divided into the same four sectors, but geographically the city lay deep inside the Russian-held eastern sector, about 100 miles from the western sectors. Despite this distance, in 1948 the western powers decided to integrate the economy of West Berlin more fully into the economy of West Germany. The Russians responded by blockading the access routes to West Berlin, challenging the ability of the western powers to maintain control over their sectors of the city. The Americans and the British chose a creative response, short of war, by airlifting supplies and personnel into West Berlin on a continuous, round-the-clock schedule until, almost a year and a half later, in September 1949, Russia gave up on its blockade. Nevertheless, Germany remained a divided country, and Berlin a divided city.

Nuclear weapons were the most terrifying arena of competition. Just as the Soviet Union had trembled when the United States exploded the world's first atomic bomb in 1945, so America reverberated in shock when the USSR followed with a bomb of its own in 1949. The American monopoly on nuclear weapons had lasted only four years. In 1952, the U.S. thought it was once again gaining nuclear supremacy as it exploded the world's first hydrogen bomb, a weapon many hundreds or thousands of times more lethal even than the atomic bomb, but, to America's consternation, the USSR matched this accomplishment in the very next year. In both cases, the Russians had attained this parity through the help of American spies, further shocking the Americans.

Driven by their mutual hostility, the two superpowers created military organizations of their allies. With its Western European allies and Canada, the United States created the North Atlantic Treaty Organization (NATO) in 1949, a military alliance that included democratic countries with capitalist, socialist, and mixed economies (see map of NATO and Warsaw Pact nations, p. 727). In response, the USSR formally established the Warsaw Pact in 1955 among the eastern European nations that were under its control. Four decades of Cold War standoff had begun.

Even the heavens became a field of contest. Here the Russians took an early lead, putting the first space satellite, the *Sputnik*, into orbit in 1957, followed by the first manned satellite in 1961. Embarrassed, President John F. Kennedy (1917–63) vowed that America would be the first to land a man on the moon, within a decade, and in 1969 that mission was accomplished.

The Tail Wags the Dog: Client States Draw the Superpowers to War

The superpowers boasted of their technological dominance expressed in bombs, missiles, Sputniks, and men on the moon, and of their political dominance over their dependent, or **client states,** as well. However, these dependent nations could also manipulate the superpowers for their own purposes, and sometimes even defeat them militarily, in asymmetrical warfare. Consider first the example of the Korean War in 1950. Later in this chapter, we will consider the Cuban Missile Crisis of 1962, the Vietnam War of 1964–75, and the Afghanistan War of 1978–88. These three wars, and the Cuban near-war, had political and cultural consequences even more significant than their military results.

The Korean War, 1950–53. Korea actually represents an early example of a country emerging from colonial control, finding itself caught between the conflicting claims of the U.S. and the USSR, and charting a course of its own. The Korean peninsula had been a colony of Japan from 1910 until 1945. At the end of World War II, control over the peninsula was at first divided at the Thirty-eighth parallel between the Soviets to the north and the Americans to the south, with the prospect of unification under Korean self-government left for future negotiations. On June 25, 1950, the armed forces of communist North Korea invaded South Korea. The North Koreans attacked with the approval of their two enormous communist neighbors, the USSR and China, and with some support in the form of training and equipment as well. North Korean armies drove all the way to the southernmost part of the peninsula before American troops, sent as part of a UN force, drove them back to North Korea by September, and then kept pushing them farther north, toward the border with China.

In response, China entered the war, sending in hundreds of thousands of troops in wave after wave of assaults, compensating with human numbers for what they lacked in equipment. In addition to their other weapons, the Americans and their allies deployed helicopters extensively to convoy troops, to stage aerial attacks, and to ferry wounded soldiers to mobile army surgical hospitals [MASH] units (later made famous by the long-running *M*A*S*H* TV series and film of the same name).

China crossed the border into the south, capturing the South Korean capital of Seoul for a second time, until additional United States and UN forces pushed them back to the Thirty-eighth parallel. Here the military and political situation ground to a stalemate that continued, with battles and negotiations, until the border of 1950 was reimposed with some modifications to reflect the military lines of the armistice. By war's end in 1953, 37,000 American soldiers had died along with about 200,000 South Korean soldiers and upwards of a half-million civilians. (North Korea did not release statistics, but estimates are approximately comparable.) China announced about 150,000 military dead, although the U.S. gave an estimate of four times that number.

The Korean War increased the American feeling of threat from communism, since China was now involved. The war strengthened the reputation of the Chinese, who had held the mighty Americans to a military standoff. Mao repeated his charge that America was a "paper tiger" despite its nuclear weapons. He believed that, after Hiroshima and Nagasaki, America could never again use the arsenal of nuclear weapons that it possessed; the Korean War seemed to confirm his view. Ironically, the war poisoned the atmosphere between China and Russia as well, because Stalin had at first offered to support China if it went to war with America, and then withdrew the pledge. In the end, the USSR did lend some support, but Stalin's equivocation left the Chinese leadership feeling betrayed.

The war brought some prosperity to Japan, which served as a manufacturing base for United States war supplies and a prime location for rest-and-relaxation for U.S.

troops. Personal contact between Americans and Japanese, especially between GIs and Japanese women, increased and the United States began to see Japan as its new ally in the Pacific. The United States terminated its occupation of Japan in 1952, and, reversing its earlier wish that Japan remain unarmed, encouraged that country to create some armed defense forces.

The Korean War drove a wedge between the United States and many of its European allies. They had supported the early war effort to repulse the North Korean attack but felt that America's continuing push across the border into North Korea was unnecessarily belligerent and costly, and had provoked the Chinese response and the long, grinding years of war that followed. In addition, several European nations, which had so recently been at war with Germany, were apprehensive about America's new strategy of rearming its former enemy as a military ally in the fight against communism.

The Cold War and U.S. Domestic Politics

The international struggle between the United States and the Soviet Union appeared to some as a struggle for land and empire, to others as an almost religious war between the ideologies of democracy and capitalism on one side and communism on the other. Everyone saw it as a bitter and consuming struggle. The international struggle overflowed into domestic policies as well.

McCarthyism and the Red Scare. Americans reacted badly when Russia, in 1949, broke the U.S. monopoly on the atomic bomb. How had this happened? Spies were suspected—and found—in the government and the scientific community in the United States. In response, U.S. Senator Joseph McCarthy (1908–57) unleashed a hunt for spies, communists, and fellow travelers—people sympathizing with communist perspectives—in a mixture of serious investigation and paranoia that threatened freedom of expression in the United States for several years. Public proclamations at this time also emphasized the importance of participation in organized religion in American life and contrasted it to the official atheism of the Soviet Union.

The success of the communist revolution in China in 1949, the Chinese commitment of millions of troops to the war in Korea in 1950, and America's inability to gain a clear victory in that war further fed American fears of communist power. This "Red Scare" and **McCarthyism** gained renewed strength in 1953, when Russia exploded a hydrogen bomb of its own. (The U.S. had tested one the year before.) Many government bureaucrats, artists, film producers, writers, and university professors suspected of present or past membership in the Communist Party of the United States, or of expressing views considered overly critical of the United States, lost their jobs and were blacklisted. Investigations of such people were carried out by a Congressional committee called the "House Un-American Activities Committee." This nibbling away at freedom

"A giant leap for mankind…" Edwin ("Buzz") Aldrin, the second man on the moon, clambers down the ladder of the *Apollo II* lunar module "Eagle" in July, 1969. Neil Armstrong had set foot on the moon moments earlier. The race for supremacy in space between the superpowers was fueled by the Cold War.

DEFENSE EXPENDITURE (in billions of current dollars)

	U.S.	USSR	China	Germany	UK	Japan
1930	0.699	0.722	–	0.162	0.512	0.218
1938	1.13	5.43	–	7.41	1.86	1.74
1950	14.5	15.5	2.5	–	2.3	–
1970	77.8	72.0	23.7	6.1	5.8	1.3
1987	293.2	274.7	13.4	34.1	31.5	24.2
1997	273.0	64 (Russia)	36.6	33.4	35.7	40.9

Defense expenditure. Fueled by the conflict and the Cold War, massive expenditure by the U.S. and USSR on military hardware kept them neck and neck. After 1960, the rapid militarization of the developing nations increased expenditures. After the fall of the Soviet Union, 1989–91, they decreased. (Sources: Paul Kennedy, *The Rise and Fall of The Great Powers* and *New York Times 2000 Almanac*)

of speech in America was not comparable to the almost complete suppression of it in the Soviet Union, but it did reflect a fear that pervaded America and threatened some of its core values of freedom of expression and of association.

The Military–Industrial Complex. In his 1961 farewell address as president of the United States, Dwight Eisenhower (1890–1969), a five-star general who had served as Supreme Commander of Allied Forces in Europe during World War II, warned his nation against the dangers of the "military–industrial complex," the combination of military and industrial leaders who might find it in their mutual interests to promote warfare.

> We must never let the weight of this combination endanger our liberties or democratic processes … Only an alert and knowledgeable citizenry can compel the proper meshing of the huge industrial and military machinery of defense with our peaceful methods and goals, so that security and liberty may prosper together.

The financial costs of the military-technological competition of the Cold War were astronomical. In 1960, in peacetime, the governments of the world spent nearly $100 billion on military expenses. But Eisenhower's warning went unheeded. The military build-up continued, as did the confrontations between the U.S. and the Soviet Union and its allies.

The Soviet Union and the Cold War

The USSR was changing, too. Joseph Stalin, who had dominated the nation with tyrannical powers for three decades, died in 1953. At the Twentieth Party Congress in 1956, Communist Party General Secretary Nikita Khrushchev (1894–1971) exposed the extent of Stalin's tyranny and began to relinquish some of the coercive powers of the communist state. In the ensuing period of "de-Stalinization," Khrushchev released a number of political prisoners of conscience, permitted the publication of many politically banned works, and moderated Stalin's plans for heavy industrialization in favor of greater production of consumer goods. The Soviet government itself gradually began to portray Stalin as a political monster, as Khrushchev also began to open more of the record, publicly revealing Stalin's atrocities:

> Arbitrary behaviour by one person encouraged and permitted arbitrariness in others. Mass arrests and deportations of many thousands of people, executions without trial and without normal investigation created conditions of insecurity, fear, and even desperation. (cited in Kochan and Abraham, p. 447)

Alexander Solzhenitsyn: Reporting on the Gulag. In the new climate of openness, Russian novelist Alexander Solzhenitsyn (1918–2008) was able to publish *A Day in the Life of Ivan Denisovich* (1962), a realistic novel depicting conditions in one of the Soviet prison labor camps. Khrushchev fell from power in 1964, however, and Solzhenitsyn's next two novels had to be smuggled out of the USSR. Internally his writings circulated illegally in *samizdat* ("self-published"), privately copied, formats. In 1970, the novelist was awarded the Nobel Prize for Literature. He did not travel to Stockholm to receive the award, however, fearing that he would be denied reentry to the Russia he loved despite its political problems.

Solzhenitsyn courageously took his exposés beyond *Ivan Denisovich*. In the three volumes of his *Gulag Archipelago* (1973–38), he revealed the full extent of the **gulag**, the nationwide archipelago of prison labor camps spread throughout the country, most of them in cold, vast, remote Siberia. As many as eight million citizens were imprisoned at any given time, and some 20 million may have died in the camps through torture and harsh living conditions, which Solzhenitsyn described at length. After the publication of the *Gulag Archipelago* in 1973, Solzhenitsyn was stripped of his Soviet citizenship and exiled. For 15 years he lived in the United States, until the Soviet government restored his citizenship in 1990. He returned to Russia to live in 1994. When he died, in 2008, Russia's president attended his funeral.

The USSR under Khrushchev. Under Khrushchev, the Soviet Union continued to attempt to catch up to the west militarily and economically—and in some competitions even to surpass it, as it did with the Sputnik space satellite in 1957. Khrushchev tried, unsuccessfully, to develop more of the "virgin lands" of Kazakhstan and Siberia, but agriculture continued to lag. The USSR seemed on a par with the United States militarily and industrially, but it did not even attempt to keep up in the production of consumer goods. The two sides differed in their interpretation of the significance of consumer goods in the lives of their citizens.

The "kitchen debate." In an astonishing, impromptu moment at an American exposition in Moscow in 1959, Khrushchev and American Vice President Richard

KEY TERM

gulag The acronym of Glavnoye, Upravleniye Ispravitelno Trudovykh Lagerey, the "Chief Administration of Corrective Labor Camps," a department of the Soviet secret police founded in 1934 under Stalin. It ran a vast network of forced labor camps throughout the USSR to which millions of citizens accused of "crimes against the state" were sent for punishment.

Moscow power parade. At the height of the Cold War, the arms race against the West saw Russian leaders Khrushchev and Brezhnev pouring colossal sums of money into military hardware, trying to keep pace with the American military machine. This parade shows tanks moving through Red Square, Moscow, to mark the 66th anniversary of the 1917 October Revolution. Lenin keeps watch.

Nixon debated their nations' ability to provide butter as well as guns. While walking through a model of a middle-class American home, Nixon called Khrushchev's attention to some of the appliances—TV in the living room, washing machine in the kitchen. These "make life more easy for our housewives," Nixon boasted. To which Khrushchev replied that the USSR did not have "the capitalist attitude toward women" and spoke of the "gadgets" as inconsequential.

This informal debate over the systems touched not only military and economic power, but also domestic life, gender relations, equality, and standards of living. American media regularly scoffed at the unfashionable, frumpy appearance of the wives of even the highest Soviet officials. The Soviets, on the other hand, stressed the strong representation of women in the professions, such as medicine and higher education (although not in high government positions). And while Americans praised the success of their system for the middle classes, Russian criticism pointed out America's racial and ethnic segregation, homelessness, and social inequities as the product of competitive capitalism. As Khrushchev argued in the "kitchen debate:" "In Russia all you have to do to get a house is to be born in the Soviet Union. You are entitled to housing … In America, if you don't have a dollar you have the right to choose between sleeping in a house or on the pavement."

Each side sought to win over the world's newly independent nations, as well, to its view of the appropriate life (discussed below). But for how long could the relatively backward economy of the USSR continue to support its one-sided investment in heavy military industries, and restrict the production of consumer goods? The Soviet government saw no alternative. It felt surrounded and threatened by the United States and its allies, and saw no choice but to continue preparing its defenses—guns over butter—mirroring Stalin's defensive policies with regard to Germany in the 1930s.

In foreign affairs, Khrushchev was as aggressive as Stalin. He maintained the USSR's domination of eastern Europe. He crushed the Hungarian uprising of 1956. He allowed the East Germans to build a wall through the heart of divided Berlin in 1961 in order to close escape routes to the West. And he stationed nuclear-tipped missiles in Cuba.

Confrontations in Cuba, 1961–62. The most frightening moment of the Cold War took place in 1962. In Cuba, an island nation only 90 miles off the coast of Florida, a revolution led by Fidel Castro (b. 1926) had overthrown the American-backed dictator Fulgencio Batista in 1959. Although Castro denied that he was a communist and did, for a time, try to negotiate agreements with the United States, he soon established close military and economic ties with the Soviet bloc, threatening America's hold over Latin America. In the Cold War environment of the time, the United States viewed Castro as a communist. When three multinational oil refineries refused to process oil brought to Cuba from the USSR, Castro expropriated the refineries. In response, the United States ended Cuban sugar imports to the U.S. In December 1961, Castro openly announced his allegiance to Marxism-Leninism. From that time, Cuba became dependent on the Soviet Union, reversing Batista's earlier dependence on the United States.

Castro, victorious, *en route* to Havana. Fidel Castro embraces a child amongst a crowd of well-wishers shortly after taking power. In January 1959, Cuban dictator Fulgencio Batista was ousted by Castro and his popular revolutionary army. The revolutionaries had been hiding in the mountains since December 1956, fighting against Batista's regime. Their fight to overthrow the dictator was called the "26th July Movement," after the date of their first insurrection against Batista.

Castro then proceeded to expropriate or confiscate foreign assets, including $1 billion in North American property and investments in Cuba. He collectivized farms, which took land away from peasants, and centralized control of the economy in the hands of the government. He took human development issues seriously, and devoted money and energies to health, education, and cultural activities. Education and all medical services were provided free to all citizens.

The living standards of most Cubans improved sharply. Nevertheless, most of the elites—hundreds of thousands of people, critical of Castro—fled, with the acquiescence of the government, which was pleased to have them gone. These exiles were received with open arms in the United States, where they formed a large community, centered in Miami, which lobbied heavily for the United States to take action against Castro. Meanwhile Castro and his close associate Ernesto "Che" Guevara dispatched advisers throughout Latin America and Africa to promote guerrilla wars against imperialism and **neocolonialism.**

Two confrontations between Cuba and the United States followed. The American government agreed to arm a group of about 1,500 Cuban exiles who planned to invade the island on the assumption that Cuba's people would join them, welcoming the opportunity to overthrow Castro. When the exiles did invade, on April 17, 1961, at the Bay of Pigs, they were met not by a popular uprising but by Cuban armed forces, who immediately defeated them.

In the next year, Cuba was the focus of the most direct confrontation of the Cold War between the United States and the Soviet Union. The Soviets had positioned nuclear missiles in Cuba. Although they denied the existence of these missiles, American reconnaissance aircraft obtained photographic evidence. President Kennedy demanded that the missiles be withdrawn, even threatening nuclear war over the issue. As the world watched, terrified, in fear of imminent Armageddon, Russian leader Nikita Khrushchev announced that the USSR would remove the missiles in exchange for American promises not to invade Cuba again and to remove its own missiles from Turkey.

Recent scholarship on the Cold War sees here also a confrontation between a superpower and a client state. In withdrawing the missiles, the USSR acted against the wishes of Castro, who was willing to push the nuclear challenge to the Americans even further to the brink. From this point onward, the two superpowers pulled back from such direct confrontation. The Soviet Party leadership, considering Khrushchev too reckless, removed him from power in 1964. He was followed by almost two decades of bureaucratic stagnation under Leonid Brezhnev (1906–82).

The Brezhnev Doctrine. In the spring of 1968, Czechoslovakia tried to escape Russian control and establish an independent government. Brezhnev ended the hopes of this **Prague Spring** by declaring that the Soviet Union would intervene in the affairs of its satellites to prevent counterrevolution, a policy later named the **Brezhnev Doctrine**. Soviet troops crushed the Czech revolt.

When Poland began to revolt in 1980 Brezhnev cracked down again. Here the Roman Catholic Church remained a powerful voice critical of communist rule, and when Karol Wojtyla, the Polish cardinal of Krakow, was elected pope in 1978, dissidents throughout Poland took heart. Millions turned out to welcome him on his visits back to Poland. Although their country, under communism, was officially atheistic, they now had a symbolic leader at the pinnacle of religious authority in Rome who could address their spiritual longings and provide a beacon of hope for independence from Soviet control. Lech Walesa (b. 1943), a shipyard worker in Gdansk, began to organize what ultimately became Solidarity, an independent trade union federation with a membership of more than ten million industrial and agricultural workers.

KEY TERMS

neocolonialism The assertion of power by one country over another, usually through economic dominance, but without formal political authority. A common relationship between countries that had previously been in a formal colonial relationship.

Prague Spring The period in the spring of 1968 when it appeared that Prague, and all of Czechoslovakia, would achieve greater freedom of expression and greater independence of control by the USSR. This hope was crushed by military intervention by the Soviets.

Brezhnev Doctrine In 1968 Leonid Brezhnev, head of the USSR government, declared that the USSR would intervene militarily to prevent any of its satellite countries from claiming independence. Issued when Czechoslovakia sought independence.

KEY TERM

domino effect The belief, held by many American policymakers, that if one country in a region became communist, others would follow, one after the other.

Solidarity demanded not only lower prices and higher wages, but also the right to strike, freedom for political prisoners, an end to censorship, and free elections. At Moscow's bidding, the Polish government jailed Walesa and other Solidarity leaders and declared martial law. The pope supported Solidarity, and the United States imposed economic sanctions on Poland, but Brezhnev remained unmoved. Brezhnev found that he could implement his doctrine because, in effect, NATO and the Warsaw Pact powers had tacitly agreed to respect each others' spheres of influence. When the USSR crushed democratic revolts in East Germany (1953), Hungary (1956), Czechoslovakia (1968), and Poland (1981), NATO protested but did not intervene.

In 1982, after Brezhnev died, martial law ended, and Walesa was freed. In 1983 he was awarded the Nobel Peace Prize. Demands for more freedom continued to build in Poland and throughout the Soviet Union.

The Mice that Roared: Debacles in Vietnam and Afghanistan

The 1959 film, *The Mouse that Roared*, brought fame to its lead actor, Peter Sellers, and laughs to its amused audiences. The film's premise was that a tiny, impoverished nation would declare war on the United States in order to lose immediately and then receive enough foreign aid to revive its economy and even flourish. (As the satire unfolds, the tiny nation wins the war!) The film, and even its title, became the ironic symbol of small nations successfully embroiling large nations in their own affairs for their own benefit. The United States fell into this trap in Vietnam, the USSR in Afghanistan.

The United States and the Vietnam War. After World War II, the French attempted to reestablish their colonial rule in Vietnam. They met armed opposition and guerrilla warfare led by Ho Chi Minh, the leader of the communist Vietminh, or Independence League. The Vietminh had established themselves in 1939 to fight against French colonialism. Then they fought the Japanese occupation. Now they were once again fighting the French, and this time they won. In May 1954 the French signed an armistice agreement with the Vietminh that partitioned the country at the Seventeenth parallel. The Vietminh governed the north. In the south, the French transferred full sovereignty to a new anticommunist government and withdrew their troops. Civil war engulfed the south. The north, under a communist government, called repeatedly for the reunification of the country and supported communist insurgents, the Vietcong, against the government of the south. America, tragically misreading this essentially nationalist civil war as a Cold War battle and unskilled in fighting guerrilla warfare, committed increasing numbers of its own troops to supporting the government of the south in an ultimately doomed cause. American policymakers feared a **domino effect**: they believed that if South Vietnam fell to the communist north, other countries of the region would follow one after the other.

President Kennedy first committed American advisers to South Vietnam in 1961. President Lyndon Baines Johnson (1908–73) expanded the American commitment to full-scale warfare. By 1968, more than a half-million U.S. troops were fighting in support of South Vietnam. More than 58,000 American armed forces died in Vietnam during the war; 200,000 South Vietnamese

Children fleeing from Trang Bang, South Vietnam, June 8, 1972. The children were fleeing from a napalm attack ordered by the American military. This Pulitzer Prize-winning photograph, taken by photographer Nick Ut, became an instant antiwar plea and helped turn American opinion against the war in Vietnam.

SOURCE

Guerrilla Warfare

With the success of Mao's communist, agrarian revolution in China and Castro's in Cuba, and continuing peasant uprisings around the world, including Vietnam, the 1960s were especially alive with rural guerrilla warfare. Usually led by young, vigorous, brave, and single-minded revolutionaries, the guerrilla movements had a powerful mystique, and a number of successes. They demonstrated the potential of very simple conflict techniques against the most sophisticated modern weapons.

One of the most charismatic of the guerrilla warriors was Ernesto "Che" Guevara, who was born in Argentina in 1928 and who was captured and killed while organizing a guerrilla movement in Bolivia in 1967. He participated in Castro's revolution in Cuba and was later appointed head of the national bank. But Guevara chose life as a full-time revolutionary, helping to establish guerrilla *focos*, revolutionary outposts, in many locations. His speeches and writings, like Mao's, were a bible to guerrilla warriors.

Nuclei of relatively few persons choose places favorable for guerrilla warfare, sometimes with the intention of launching a counterattack or to weather a storm, and there they begin to take action. But the following must be made clear: At the beginning, the relative weakness of the guerrilla fighters is such that they should endeavor to pay attention only to the terrain, in order to become acquainted with the surroundings, establish connections with the population, and fortify the places that eventually will be converted into bases. The guerrilla unit can survive only if it starts by basing its development on the three following conditions: constant mobility, constant vigilance, constant wariness …

We must carry the war into every corner the enemy happens to carry it—to his home, to his centers of entertainment: a total war. It is necessary to prevent him from having a moment of peace, a quiet moment outside his barracks or even inside; we must attack him wherever he may move …

Our every action is a battle cry against imperialism, and a battle hymn to the people's unity against the great enemy of mankind: the United States of America. Wherever death may surprise us, let it be welcome, provided that this, our battle cry, may have reached some receptive ear and another hand may be extended to wield our weapons and other men be ready to intone the funeral dirge with the staccato singing of the machine gun and new battle cries of war and victory.

(Sigmund, pp. 370, 381)

military, more than a million South Vietnamese civilians, and 5,000 other allied forces also died. North Vietnam claimed 1,100,000 military deaths. Estimates of civilian deaths in the north were between one and two million. The war displaced more than six and a half million people in South Vietnam alone. The American effort failed.

The Vietnam War intruded deeply and divisively into U.S. domestic life. In the 1960s and early 1970s, the civil rights and feminist movements coalesced with the nationwide protest against the war in Vietnam, creating a vibrant, creative, colorful, shrill, and sometimes violent culture conflict that convulsed the country with its excesses on both sides (see section on "1968," below). Publicly and privately, within millions of families, citizens struggled with questions about the legitimacy of draft-dodging this unpopular war, the use of drugs, sexual freedom, and the appropriate limits of self expression and hair length. Johnson, buffeted by a failing war abroad and hostile antiwar protests at home, declined to run for a second term. His successor, Richard Nixon (1913–94), could do no better against the Vietnamese guerrillas. America signed a peace agreement in 1973 and evacuated its last troops in ignominious defeat in 1975. Vietnam was reunified in 1976 under the rule and administration of the North Vietnamese.

The USSR in Afghanistan. In 1979, the USSR once again applied the Brezhnev Doctrine, invading Afghanistan to maintain its alliance. The invasion ultimately brought the USSR its own Vietnam.

In 1978, a pro-Soviet coup took over Afghanistan. In 1979 the USSR sent in troops and supplies to put down anticommunist, Islamic revolts against the new government, and sponsored a second coup in favor of an even more pro-Soviet government. More than 100,000 troops helped the new government secure the cities, especially the capital, Kabul, but the Muslim rebels, supported by assistance from the United States, controlled the rural areas. (The rebels receiving aid from the U.S. included a group of militant Muslims called the Taliban, and among them was a young Saudi guerrilla fighter named Osama bin Laden.)

The USSR lost some 15,000 soldiers in a decade of fighting in Afghanistan, which led to intense criticism of the Soviet government back home. The UN brokered a peace agreement in 1988 that called for the withdrawal of all foreign troops, and the Russians went home discredited and in disarray. Afghanistan itself was thoroughly destabilized and descended into continuing civil war, with the Taliban generally taking command, but with no group firmly in control of the entire country.

1968: Revolt Against Authority

Broadway musical *Hair: The American Tribal Love-Rock Musical. Hair* opened off-Broadway in 1967, and on Broadway in 1968, at the height of the Vietnam War. It captured the American rebellious counter-culture of peace movements, draft dodging, and hippie lifestyles expressed in long hair, colorful but tattered dress, indulgent sex, and illicit drugs. It celebrated the "make love not war" spirit of the time. In this scene, most of the hippies burn their draft cards. Claude, who does not, ultimately is sent to Vietnam and dies in the war. A Broadway revival in 2009 won numerous awards.

"1968" has become a shorthand designation for a series of revolts against authority that briefly shook established governments and institutions, and then seemed to dissipate, but ultimately transformed some of the most intimate aspects of life, as well as some of the cultural attitudes of a new generation.

We have already encountered some of the manifestations of "1968." In Czechoslovakia in 1968, cultural leaders like Vaclav Havel (b. 1936) challenged the moral authority of the USSR, and the Soviets responded with a massive invasion of tanks and troops, and jail terms for the dissidents. In the United States, anti-Vietnam War protests brought the presidency of Lyndon Johnson to an end. Student revolts challenged the moral and academic authority of major universities. They seized college buildings and demanded changes in curriculum, in faculty-student relationships, and in student representation in university decision making. College and high school students experimented with drugs and new fashions in dress and personal style. Proclaiming "Make love, not war," young people expanded freedom of expression in music, theater, and literature. The Beatles traveled to India to study meditation with Maharishi Mahesh Yogi, and young people from Canada to Japan followed suit.

Leaders of third world revolution such as Mao Zedong of China and "Che" Guevara of Argentina (by birth) and Cuba (by choice) earned the reverence of irreverent youth around the world.

In Western Europe, too, 1968 brought revolt, beginning with student protests over a constricted, outdated, and unresponsive university establishment and continuing with massive strikes by millions of factory workers. The numbers of students in European universities multiplied in the postwar period, partly as a baby boom generation came to university age, partly as more of them sought university education for the new age. West Germany had about 100,000 university students in 1950, and 400,000 by 1970; the number of university students in France by 1967 was about equal to the number of high school students 12 years earlier (Judt, p. 394). University expansion did not keep up with the new demographic demands, not in buildings, nor in faculty, nor in curriculum. Students, perhaps inspired by other protests around the world, took their frustrations to the streets, especially in Paris, where in May 1968 they rioted and occupied the streets around the Sorbonne, the University of Paris. Soon factory workers joined in their own, much larger protests against their working conditions. In France, as many as ten million workers went on strike that month. In Italy the strikes came a little later, but were more sustained: 5.5 million workers on strike in the fall of 1969; 4.5 million in 1972; 6.1 million in 1973. In addition to the usual demands for shorter hours and more pay, the strikers wanted more say in the management of the factories.

Governments in France and Italy, particularly, felt threatened—but only temporarily. Not all the citizenry was sympathetic to the revolts. Many felt that the protesters and strikers were asking for too much. Indeed, in subsequent elections, more conservative leaders won new mandates: Nixon in the United States and de Gaulle in France in 1968; Giulio Andreotti in Italy in 1973. Some student and worker demands were met, others not. Although many issues remained unresolved, the turmoil dissipated with the passage of time, the end of the Vietnam War, and, especially in eastern Europe, with government repression.

The evaluation of "1968" has therefore been mixed. The most intense forms of cultural explosion passed relatively quickly, but from this time onward, cultural authority became more open and more flexible. Older rigidities of control, often viewed as stifling, had cracked open, and would not be put back together again.

The Cold War and the Emergence of New Nations

The Cold War was one of the great postwar reconfigurations. The collapse of colonialism and the emergence of more than 80 new nations from colonial control to independence was another. This process of decolonization was in large part a legacy of the world wars and the global depression. These cataclysms, continuing for 30 years from 1914 to 1945, depleted the colonizers of manpower, financial resources, and moral authority. They no longer had the power to hold on to their colonies, especially as many of the colonies began to assert their right to independence. The colonized peoples, and many of the colonizers themselves, no longer believed in the "white man's burden" of civilizing the non-Western world. The almost unimaginable devastation of the wars exploded the myth of the superiority of the civilization of the colonizers.

Leaders of anticolonial movements had already been disillusioned once, when promises of self-government were broken at the end of World War I. By the time of World War II they no longer believed the word of their colonial masters. Famously, when the British offered to give India self-government at the end of World War II in exchange for India's participation in the war effort, Mohandas Gandhi declined, mocking the offer as "a postdated check on a failing bank." Following World War II, the demands for independence intensified throughout the colonial world. In the words of Kwame Nkrumah of Ghana:

> It is only when a people are politically free that other races can give them the respect that is due them. It is impossible to talk of equality of races in any other terms. No people without a government of their own can expect to be treated on the same level as peoples of independent sovereign states. It is far better to be free to govern or misgovern yourself than to be governed by anybody else. (Nkrumah, p. 9)

The anticolonial nationalists gained important new allies as the United States and the Soviet Union both added their voices. The Soviet Union had from its inception declared its opposition to overseas colonialism, although its holdings in central and Eastern Europe and central Asia looked like its own form of colonialism close to home. The United States, too, especially under Presidents Roosevelt and Truman, spoke out for an end of colonialism. These anticolonial stands had some effect. Britain's Winston Churchill, for example, moderated his pro-colonial positions, especially in regard to India, in deference to his wartime colleagues.

In the long run, Churchill's increased moderation wasn't enough. The British voted his party out of office at the end of the war. The voters felt that Churchill was the right man for the war, but not for the peace. They wanted new directions at home and abroad. They began to see British imperial holdings as economically and militarily costly in the face of renewed colonial resistance, and perhaps as morally inappropriate as well. They called for terminating the imperial enterprise. The combination of increasingly resistant colonized nations and colonizing powers no longer able, or willing, to repress them led to the conferring of independence.

The Middle East Breaks Free

The British- and French-mandated territories in the Middle East were the first to gain their freedom. Iraq had been granted formal independence from Britain in 1932, as a kingdom. British troops were called in, however, when coups attempted to overthrow the monarchy. In 1958, a leftist coup did succeed in overthrowing the king, breaking the ties to Britain and reorienting the country's foreign policy toward the USSR. Jordan gained independence from Britain in 1946, as did Lebanon (1943) and Syria (1946) from France.

In 1947 the UN passed a resolution agreeing to partition the British-mandated land of Palestine between its bitterly antagonistic Jewish and Arab populations. In 1920, only about 60,000 Jews were living in Palestine, about one-tenth the number of Arabs. Jewish immigration and settlement increased between the two world wars, driven in part by the increasing persecution of Jews under the Nazis in Germany and its conquered territories. Arab resistance to this new stream of immigration from Europe led to repeated armed clashes between the two groups. To reduce tensions, the British severely restricted Jewish immigration. In the face of the Holocaust, however, the Jewish people felt a desperate need for a safe haven and they continued to immigrate illegally.

In 1947, the UN declared its partition plan, and the British prepared to leave. Arabs and Jews armed for battle. David Ben-Gurion (1886–1973), as political head of the Jewish community, declared the establishment of the State of Israel in 1948, triggering an immediate armed attack from its neighbors. The new state survived the war, even expanding its borders slightly, but no peace treaties were signed, only agreements to cease fire. Since no new government had yet arisen to claim sovereignty over the Arab segments of Palestine, the king of Jordan asserted his country's control of that territory. The area was generally referred to as "the West Bank" of the Jordan River. The entire situation remained volatile.

Asian Nations Declare Independence

In Southeast Asia, the Japanese had driven out the European colonial powers during World War II. At the end of the war, when the Europeans tried to return, they faced nationalist opponents who wanted no more of colonialism. In Indonesia, the largest of these countries, Achmed Sukarno (1901–70), who had been imprisoned by the

Dutch and freed by the Japanese, declared independence in 1945, before the Dutch tried to return. The Dutch did return the next year and, with the help of the British, attempted to reestablish their rule through force of arms. In 1949, however, after four years of fighting, and after the United States threatened to cut off Marshall Plan aid to the Dutch, they withdrew, recognizing Indonesian independence.

The Japanese had also seized Vietnam during World War II. When the French attempted to reestablish colonial rule, they met armed opposition and guerrilla warfare. As we have seen above, a sequence of military struggles—against the French; against the southerners, who tried to remain a separate nation; and against the United States—finally ended with the unification of Vietnam in 1976.

India, the largest of all the colonies, finally won its independence from Britain in 1947, although the subcontinent was partitioned on religious grounds into two nations, India and Pakistan. Because of its size and importance, India will be discussed at greater length in Chapter Twenty-two.

In China, the communist revolutionaries, fighting for two decades under the leadership of Mao Zedong, captured the government in 1949, closed down the foreign holdings in the treaty ports, and asserted China's control over its own destiny. Again, because of China's size and importance, its history of revolution and reconstruction as a communist state will be told in Chapter Twenty-two.

African Struggles for Independence

Most African countries obtained independence between the end of World War II and the 1970s, in some cases after long struggles, in others quite abruptly. Although nominally independent since 1922, Egypt gained full sovereignty over the Suez Canal only in 1956. In 1957, Ghana became the first black African country to win its independence, from Britain. Most of the French colonies gained their independence in 1960. Dozens more followed these precedents in the next decade.

The new nations faced many challenges. European colonizers had drawn the boundaries of their African colonies for their own convenience, without regard for tribal and ethnic differences. After independence, these differences came to the foreground, often resulting in civil wars. In claiming independence, national leaders proclaimed such diverse ideologies as bourgeois democracy, workers' socialism, Islamic resurgence, and indigenous nationalism, in various combinations. These ideologies were often in conflict with one another. Most of all, the countries had not been prepared for independence by their colonial rulers and they struggled to achieve stability. Their educational facilities, economic enterprises, and physical infrastructures were minimal. They were caught up in the Cold War struggles of the U.S. and USSR. They were too weak to bargain effectively with the international businesses that came to exploit their natural resources. Their leaders often sold out to foreign political and economic interest groups.

Egypt. In 1952, a group of Egyptian army officers, among them Gamal Abdel Nasser (1918–70), overthrew the government, forced King Farouk to abdicate, and asserted Egypt's independence from British control. In 1956, the British withdrew their troops from the Suez Canal and Egypt nationalized the waterway.

Ghana's independence. Prime minister (later president) Kwame Nkrumah waves to a celebrating crowd as the Gold Coast colony becomes the newly independent country of Ghana on March 6, 1957, the first colony in sub-Saharan Africa to gain its independence. Nkrumah formed a one-party state in 1964. His regime was ended by a military coup in 1966 during his absence on a trip to China.

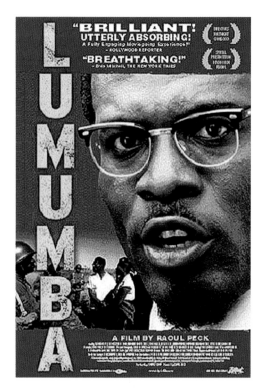

"BRILLIANT! UTTERLY ABSORBING! A Fully Engaging Moviegoing Experience!" — HOLLYWOOD REPORTER

"BREATHTAKING!" — Elvis Mitchell, THE NEW YORK TIMES

A FILM BY RAOUL PECK

Patrice Lumumba, Congolese nationalist and first prime minister of the Congo after independence, 1960. Partly because of his anti-Belgian, anticolonial speech at the independence celebrations, Lumumba was viewed as a potential ally of the Soviet Union in the Cold War. As the Congo divided along tribal lines, and the wealthiest province seceded, the Congolese opposition, supported by Belgium and the United States, had Lumumba assassinated. The 2000 film, by Haitian filmmaker Raoul Peck, portrays Lumumba as a Cold War martyr whose spirit of independence and bravery live on.

Israel, which had been suffering guerrilla attacks across its border from Egypt, reached an agreement with Britain and France jointly to retake the canal, put an end to cross-border attacks, and change the governing policies of Egypt. At the end of October, Israeli forces attacked Egypt, and a few days later Britain and France bombed Egypt and air-dropped troops to join in the fighting. U.S. President Eisenhower, blind-sided and infuriated by this neocolonial aggression by his own allies, put pressure on them to withdraw from Egypt and the canal. As a result, Nasser's reputation reached heroic heights throughout the Arab world as a man who had confronted the Western powers, divided them, and got rid of them.

In 1958, Nasser concluded an agreement with the Soviet Union accepting its assistance in building the Aswan High Dam on the Nile River, one of the greatest engineering and hydroelectric projects of the day. Nasser died in 1970, and his successor, Anwar Sadat (1918–81), expelled all Soviet advisers, once again demonstrating that politics were mercurial in former colonies, and could cause problems for their former colonizers. Sadat was assassinated, but his successor, Hosni Mubarak (b. 1928), continued his policies of keeping the Soviet Union at a distance, and maintaining collegial diplomatic relations with the United States.

Congo. The "Congo crisis" of 1960 demonstrated again the cross-cutting interests of the Cold War superpowers, international business groups, and the competitive regional and ethnic groups within a newly created nation. The Congo is rich in diamonds, copper, coffee, and crude oil. It has 70 percent of the world's known reserves of cobalt. In earlier days it was also known for its natural rubber, before the general use of its synthetic alternative. For the profits of these products, Leopold II, king of the Belgians, had first taken the Congo as his personal colony in 1885. Because of the extraordinary cruelty of his rule, the Belgian government itself took control in 1908, but violence and autocracy remained characteristic of Belgian rule.

Political devolution to limited self-rule began only in 1957. A small group of educated Congolese, who saw the preparations for independence in other African colonies, began to assert their own demands. Joseph Kasavubu (c. 1910–69) was an early advocate of independence, but his focus was primarily on his own ethnic group, the Bakongo people. Patrice Lumumba (1925–61) provided a more national and more militant leadership. Antigovernment rioting began in January 1959. In January 1960, Belgium convened a Round Table Conference in Brussels and, with breakneck, unrealistic speed, declared that the Congo would be independent on June 30, 1960. Belgium had not prepared the Congo to function as an independent state. The nation had some 4,000 senior administrative posts to fill but only 30 university graduates.

At the independence celebrations, Lumumba, the newly elected prime minister, delivered a bitter speech revealing his deep-seated, festering rage toward the Belgians:

We are no longer your monkeys ... We have known the back-breaking works exacted from us in exchange for salaries which permit us neither to eat enough to satisfy our hunger, nor to dress and lodge ourselves decently, nor to raise our children as the beloved creatures they are.

We have known the mockery, the insults, the blows submitted to morning, noon, and night because we were nègres [blacks]. We have known that our lands were despoiled in the name of supposedly legal text which in reality recognized only the right of the stronger ... And, finally, who will forget the hangings or the firing squads where so many of our brothers perished, or the cells into which were brutally thrown those who escaped the soldiers' bullets—the soldiers whom the colonialists made the instruments of their domination? (Andrea and Overfield, pp. 507–08)

Within days of independence, the army mutinied; Kasavubu, the new president, dismissed Lumumba; Lumumba, in turn, dismissed Kasavubu; Moise Tshombe (1919–69), a pro-Western political leader of Katanga, the Congo's richest region, declared that region independent under his leadership; the Belgians supported Tshombe's move; and both Kasavubu and Lumumba appealed to the UN for assistance. Lumumba wanted the UN peace-keeping force to bring Katanga, with its rich mineral wealth, back into the Congo, but Kasavubu did not. Their dispute paralyzed the UN forces. Lumumba called on the USSR for assistance, placing the Congo in the middle of the Cold War struggles. Lumumba was captured by Kasavubu, escaped, was recaptured, turned over to the Katanga secessionists, and murdered, apparently with the complicity of the Belgian government and the assistance of the American Central Intelligence Agency (CIA). UN forces defeated Katanga and its mercenary armed forces only in 1963. By this time, however, other provinces of Congo also revolted against the central government and were subdued with the help of European mercenary troops. Most surprisingly, in the movement to restore the authority of the central government, Moise Tshombe—who had been the leader of secessionist Katanga—became prime minister.

Continuing disputes between Tshombe and President Kasavubu opened the way for a military coup led by Joseph Mobutu (1930–97; later Mobutu Sese Seko). With help from Morocco, France, and the United States, Mobutu held out against invasions and continuing attempts at secession. Mobutu ruled with dictatorial powers, changed the name of the country and its principal river from Congo to Zaire, and transferred much of the wealth earned by Congo's exports to his own overseas accounts—knowledgeable observers guessed their total value at $4 to 5 billion—until he was forced from office and into exile in 1997.

Congo is an especially stark example of the troubles of a weak new nation, rich in natural resources but under-developed economically and technologically, deeply divided among its various ethnic groups, caught up in the politics of the Cold War and the lures of the international marketplace, and ultimately captured by a kleptomaniac, tyrannical dictator for his own purposes.

Algeria. Algeria won independence in 1962 after a long and bitter struggle that threatened to plunge France itself into civil war. France had been the colonizing power in Morocco, Algeria, and Tunisia. Independence for Morocco and Tunisia came relatively easily and peacefully in 1956 through negotiations with France. Algeria won its independence, however, only through violence and civil war.

Algeria had the largest European settler community in North Africa. The French in Algeria numbered one million, about 12 percent of the total population, but they held one-third of all the cultivable land. These settlers had become

Charles de Gaulle visits Algiers in June, 1958. Algeria had been agitating for independence since 1954, and in 1956, Ben Bella, one of the main Algerian leaders, was arrested. Two years later a political crisis in France, precipitated by continuing Algerian frustration and pressure for independence, put General de Gaulle, the commander of the free French forces during World War II, into office as the new president of the Republic. De Gaulle maintained French rule in Algeria as long as possible, while he prepared the French people for the inevitable shift in power. Finally, in 1962, Algerians achieved independence and the French withdrew.

prosperous and comfortable. For them, Algeria was home. By the early 1950s, 80 percent of them had been born in Algeria. Officially, Algeria was not a colony but an integral part of France, with constitutional representation in the French National Assembly. In addition, through the 1930s, the Algerian elite were French-educated and saw themselves as more French than Algerian. By the 1940s, however, reformists were moving

HOW DO WE KNOW?

Evaluating the Legacies of Colonialism

As the colonial era ended, historians divided sharply in assessing the impact of colonial rule. Leften Stavrianos, who spent most of his career at the University of California, San Diego, presented a Marxist, primarily economic, critical perspective. Colonial rule created "an unprecedented increase in productivity" in commerce and industry, but no corresponding increase in pay for the workers nor in distribution of wealth to the colony. In many colonies, white settlers and plantation owners seized the best lands. Rural communities were disrupted as

> private property arrangements displaced the former communal ownership and cultivation of land … Land now became a mere possession, food a mere commodity of exchange, neighbor a mere common property owner and labor a mere means of survival. (Stavrianos, p. 9)

As the Industrial Revolution matured into industrial capitalism, exploitation became more severe. The results were unfortunate and long-lasting:

> All these global economic trends combined to produce the present division of the world into the developed West as against the underdeveloped Third World. But underdevelopment did not mean nondevelopment; rather it meant distorted development—development designed to produce only one or two commodities needed by the Western markets rather than overall development to meet local needs. In short, it was the familiar Third World curse of economic growth without economic development. (Stavrianos, p. 11)

Theodore Von Laue, who studied Westernization, on the other hand, said very little about economic inequalities. Deeply influenced by Judeo-Christian perspectives, he emphasized the cultural upheavals of colonialism and the paradoxical introduction by force of Western values of freedom:

> The world revolution of Westernization, in short, carried a double thrust. It was freedom, justice, and peace—the best of the European tradition—on the one hand; on the other hand (and rather unconsciously) raw power to reshape the world in one's own image.

The transformation to Western values was not complete, however:

> Underneath the global universals of power and its most visible supporting skills—literacy, science and technology, large-scale organization—the former diversities persist. The traditional

cultures, though in mortal peril, linger under the ground floors of life. Rival political ideologies and ambitions clash head on. The world's major religions vie with each other as keenly as ever. Attitudes, values, life-styles from all continents mingle freely in the global marketplace, reducing in the intensified invidious comparison all former absolute truths to questionable hypotheses.

Von Laue looked forward to the day when all people

> Will be ready to fuse their personal egos with the egos of billions of other human beings, even in intimate matters like procreation and family size.

It would appear that the common values on that day would be the Western values of the Enlightenment.

Dipesh Chakrabarty questioned this assumption that Western values would be the governing ones. Born in India after independence, trained in Australia and the United States, and later teaching there as well, Chakrabarty argued that the greatest (self-)deception of the colonizers was to project European values as the appropriate goals for the entire world, and to see history moving in that direction: "First in Europe, then elsewhere." He rejected the idea that the rest of the world exists in Europe's "waiting room." He did appreciate European, Enlightenment values, but he did not think that they were the only valid ones, nor that they ought to or necessarily will become universal. Chakrabarty did not address economic issues. On cultural transformations brought by colonialism, however, he was not prepared to accept Von Laue's celebration of exclusively Western values, nor to look forward to the day when they alone would triumph.

- Which effects of colonialism do you think were more important, the economic and technological effects, or the cultural effects? Please be specific in the effects you are discussing.
- To the extent that the Cold War that lasted from the mid-1940s to the mid-1980s represents in part the values of the West, what values do you think colonized countries learned from the West?
- Do you think it is a good idea that some day the peoples of the world may share a similar set of values? Why or why not? If it is a good idea, then what should those values be? To what extent are they technological values?

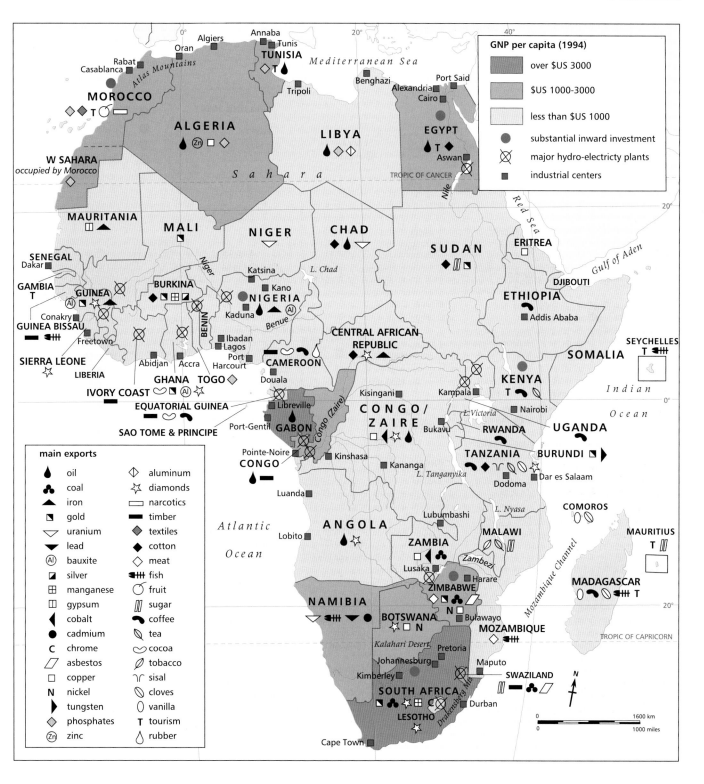

The economic development of Africa. The legacy of European colonialism has determined Africa's economic development, with a persistent reliance upon primary products, mainly mineral wealth and cash crops. Both are widely exploited by multinational franchises, bringing small benefit to local economies. Political instability, corruption, disease, and natural disaster combine with low investment in education and health to create a general condition of underdevelopment. However, some countries are growing more adept at exploiting their resources for the country's benefit, for example Nigeria with its oil wealth. The northern Arab states and South Africa stand out as wealthier than the center of the continent.

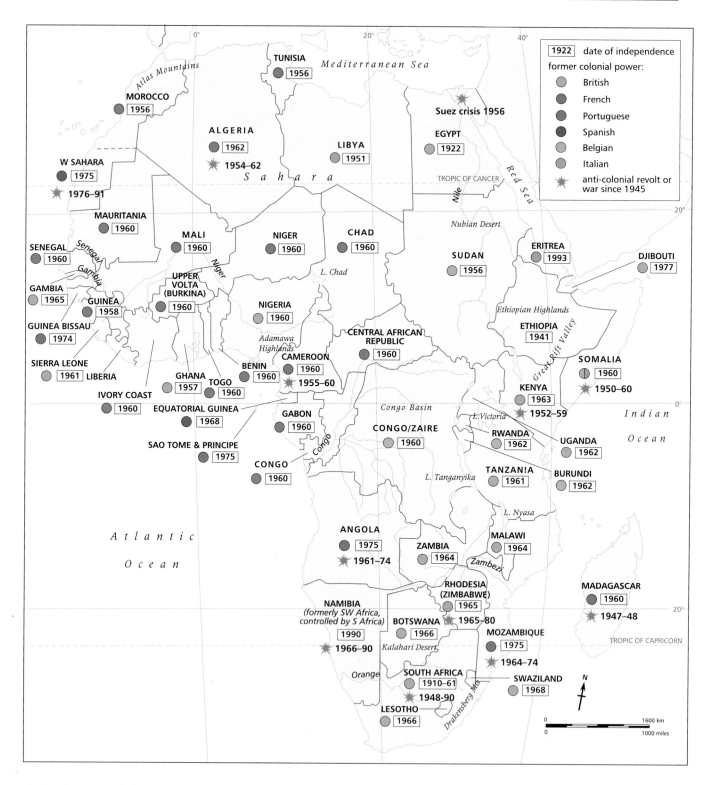

The decolonization of Africa. Ethiopia had been colonized only briefly by Italy, Liberia had been established as an independent state, and Egypt had nominal independence from 1922, but most African states gained their independence after World War II, first those in North Africa, and then, following Ghana in 1957, those of sub-Saharan Africa. Each colonial power had its own pattern for granting independence. The British and French hoped to establish amicable relations, generally, while the Portuguese and Belgians left in more bitter circumstances.

to create a more powerful Arab–Islamic nationalism, fostering social unity, a distinct national consciousness, and solidarity with other Arabs against European rule.

By the mid-1950s, an Algerian revolution against French rule led by the National Liberation Front was met by French repression. The two sides became increasingly entrenched. The violence ratcheted upward and spread not only throughout Algeria, but to France as well. The governmental system of France, the Fourth Republic, was weak, and it fell as civil war seemed to threaten. In this time of crisis, the French government asked the hero and leader of the French resistance in World War II, Charles de Gaulle (1890–1970), to take over as president of France under a new constitution. Despite an apparent mandate to continue the war, de Gaulle surprised his supporters by choosing to negotiate a settlement that finally granted Algeria independence in 1962, but only after 300,000 Algerians and 20,000 Frenchmen had been killed. Virtually all the one million European residents, many of whom had lived in the country for generations, left Algeria.

Of the Algerians, only 7,000 were in secondary school; in 1954, only 70 living, native Algerians had had a university education. The leaders of the new nation, hardened by their years of guerrilla warfare and ideologically committed to centralized control, took over the tasks of development. They instituted a four-year plan in 1969, and nationalized the petroleum and natural gas resources that had been discovered in 1956. They devoted much of the new oil revenues to industrialization. They increased education's share of the national budget from 2.2 percent of the gross national product to ten percent. The birth rate, however, remained very high. Rural migrants streamed toward the cities, and hundreds of thousands of Algerians emigrated to France in search of jobs.

Mozambique, Angola, and Guinea-Bissau. Portugal held on in Africa longer than any other major colonial power. Ruled by a dictator, Antonio Salazar, from 1932 to 1968, and then by Marcelo Caetano, Portugal was not about to give up control of its large African colonies of Angola and Mozambique, where many Portuguese had settled, nor even the much smaller colony of Guinea-Bissau. It governed harshly, with repressive labor policies that forced some 65,000 to 100,000 Mozambiquans to travel each year to work in the mines of South Africa. Each person had to keep an identification passbook at all times. The press was rigidly censored. The police were ruthless. Most of all, Portugal, alone among the European colonizers, believed that its current economy and its future greatness depended on continuing to control its African colonies. (Portugal was not even willing to cede its historic, but tiny, possession of Goa to India until, in 1961, the Indian government dispatched armed forces to seize the enclave.)

In the face of mounting international pressure against colonialism, Portugal maintained that Angola, Mozambique, and Guinea-Bissau were not colonies but "overseas provinces." In 1961, revolts broke out in all three. Supported by white-dominated South Africa, Portugal battled fiercely against anticolonial guerrilla fighters, but the warfare placed great strains on Portugal's economy and armed forces. Moreover, the three colonies were drawn into the Cold War as the USSR and Cuba dispatched troops to aid the guerrillas. Finally, in 1974, a military coup captured the government of Portugal and granted independence to all three colonies. Once again, resistance movements had triumphed over European colonial powers and, in the process, forced changes in the home government.

Even among the colonizers, colonialism was no longer considered an appropriate form of government, except in rare cases of geographically tiny dependencies, such as Caribbean or South Pacific islands, for example. As new countries became independent, however, the two contesting blocs of the Cold War tried to win them

third world Today, often refers to economically poor countries, often with ineffective governments, but historically the term referred to a group of newly independent countries that proposed strategies of development different from those of the U.S. and its allies, the first world, and the USSR and its allies, the second world.

nonaligned nations Those states, usually newly independent states, that chose not to take sides in the Cold War between the U.S. and the USSR.

over and often involved them in proxy wars, as we have seen, and will see further below. One reaction against such interference from the U.S. and the USSR was the formation of a third bloc of nations, unaligned with either of the superpowers.

The Emergence of the Third World

Today the term **third world** country is frequently used with a negative, and much resented, connotation to designate poor, technologically underdeveloped, inefficiently organized nations. When the term first came to be used in the 1950s, however, it carried more inspirational connotations.

The first and second worlds were bitterly and expensively polarized into two hostile, belligerent, heavily armed blocs, one led by the United States, the other by the USSR. Many of the newly independent nations wished to be **nonaligned**, to avoid taking sides. They felt that Europe and the United States regarded human life as cheap—as two world wars had demonstrated. These new nations urged disarmament, especially nuclear disarmament, at a time when the first two worlds were locked in an arms race. They advocated state investment in such basic human needs as food, clothing, shelter, medical care, and small, appropriate-scale technology, often through international assistance, rather than in the proliferation of weapons. They reminded the rest of the world that although they were "new nations" politically, many of them, such as India, Egypt, and Ethiopia, were ancient civilizations that took pride in centuries of traditional wisdom. And, although race was not usually mentioned overtly in third-world advocacy, almost all members of the third world were peoples of color, while the overwhelming majority of both first and second world groups were white. As they gained independence, these former colonies entered the UN, changing the size, complexion, and direction of that organization.

Third-World Countries Organize

In 1955, third world representatives convened by Jawaharlal Nehru (1889–1964) of India, Gamal Abdel Nasser of Egypt, and Marshal Tito (1892–1980) of Yugoslavia met to launch their collective entry into international politics. They convened an international conference of leaders of twenty nations of Africa and Asia in Bandung, Indonesia in 1955—the first such meeting of third word nations as a political bloc—to articulate a postcolonial agenda. They called for a global reduction in military expenditures and ideological confrontation, and an increase in expenditures for economic development, health, education, welfare, and housing.

The representatives at Bandung were not all from Africa and Asia—Tito, for example, represented Yugoslavia, a European, communist country. Nor were they all nonaligned—Zhou Enlai represented China at a time when his country was allied with the USSR. Nor did any permanent organization emerge. But for the first time, non-Western leaders assembled to articulate their own vision of a new world order. Further meetings of the nonaligned nations took place in Belgrade, Yugoslavia, in 1961; Cairo, Egypt, in 1964; and Lusaka, Zambia, in 1970.

An array of regional organizations also emerged to resolve regional problems and to present a united front in negotiations with other international organizations, such as NATO and the Warsaw Pact: the League of Arab States (1945); the Organization of American States (1948), although the OAS included the United States and was heavily influenced by it; the Organization of African Unity (1963); the Association of Southeast Asian Nations (1967); the Caribbean Community and Common Market (1973); and the South Asian Association for Regional Cooperation (1985).

In 1960 the Organization of Oil Exporting Countries (OPEC) was created primarily by the oil-rich states of the Middle East, but it also came to include oil-producing states in Africa, Indonesia in Southeast Asia, and Venezuela in South America. OPEC's original goals were economic, but in the 1970s it began also to actively support the political goals of its member states in confrontations with Western countries, especially on issues involving Israel and the Arab states.

Despite their poverty and political weakness, third world countries began to have powerful influences in the world, with effects that seriously unsettled the superpowers. In 1948, for example, Yugoslavia's Tito, who had led his guerrilla forces against the Nazis during World War II, rejected Soviet assistance, even though his country was communist in its politics and economics. He expelled Soviet advisers and, in turn, Yugoslavia was expelled from the Comintern.

In 1949, following their successful revolution, Chinese communist leaders signed a 30-year treaty of "friendship, alliance, and mutual assistance" with the Soviet Union. We have already seen the turmoil this caused in the United States: America refused to recognize the new government, and within a year China and the U.S. were at war in Korea. But the Chinese revolutionaries ultimately had a falling out with the Soviet Union as well. To the Chinese, the Soviets seemed far too restrained in their efforts to spread communism, and they refused to share their nuclear technology with China. In 1958, Mao Zedong expelled all his Soviet advisers, accusing them of arrogance. By 1960, the two communist titans were fighting in armed skirmishes over their mutual borders. The USSR cancelled its assistance to China, and China began to spread propaganda against the USSR.

Client States and Proxy Wars

Some nations were able to play both sides diplomatically to get whatever benefits they could from the Cold War competition, but many more were entrapped by it. Between 1945 and 1983, some 20 million people were killed in more than one hundred wars and military conflicts, almost all of them in the third world. About a third to a half of these conflicts were guerrilla wars, as peasants and urban workers fought armed struggles in small groups—often under the leadership of young intellectuals—against their exploitation by the rulers of their country. Frequently one superpower backed the government, the other the guerrillas. The superpowers themselves, however, usually stood in the background and let others fight and kill on their behalf.

In these localized wars the great powers could also sell or give away their older weapons systems and test the newer ones in countries whose leaders were only too eager to obtain them. Many of these **proxy wars** were fought in Africa, as we have seen in the cases of Congo, Angola, and Mozambique—sometimes with Cuban troops fighting very far from home. In the Middle East, Israel was widely viewed as a client state of the U.S., and, in response, many Arab states turned to the USSR for economic aid and military assistance. In guerrilla wars in the Americas—in Nicaragua, Guatemala, and Chile—the United States and the USSR supported opposing parties, and Cuba often supplied training to communist guerrilla fighters.

Nicaragua, Guatemala, and Chile were not "new nations" in the 1960s. They had become formally independent a century and a half earlier, but they remained poor, divided by social and ethnic differences, and economically dependent on other, wealthier countries, especially the United States, which claimed the Western hemisphere as its sphere of influence. They identified with the developmental issues of the third world.

KEY TERM

proxy war A war waged between dependent, client states of larger, more powerful states that do not become directly involved in the fighting.

An anti-American poster from the time of the Sandinista revolution, Nicaragua, 1979. Note the various drawings on the figure: military helicopters on the hat; a peace sign ("paz") among the little egghead representations of people massed together demonstrating; an ironic dollar bill with "In God we trust" on the leg. The final touch is the cowboy boot resting firmly on Uncle Sam's hat to keep him in check. Uncle Sam is even a sickly gray color in contrast with the brightly colored cowboy.

Nicaragua. Strains in the relationship between the U.S. and Nicaragua had deep roots. In 1909, to overthrow the Nicaraguan government, which had begun to grant economic concessions to governments other than the United States, the U.S. encouraged a revolt and dispatched marines to support it. The troops remained, with very few breaks, until 1933, training a Nicaraguan National Guard to join them in defense of U.S. interests. One Nicaraguan army officer, Augusto Cesar Sandino (1893–1934), rejected American hegemony and for seven years, 1927–33, fought a guerrilla war against the U.S. Marines and the Nicaraguan National Guard until he was deceived during peace negotiations, arrested, and murdered by officers of the guard under Anastasio Somoza Garcia (1896–1956). Somoza subsequently seized control of the national government and, with the support of the United States, turned the presidency into a family dynasty for his two sons after him.

In the 1960s, a revolutionary movement largely composed of students, naming itself the Sandinista Front for National Liberation, in memory of Sandino, initiated an armed guerrilla revolt. As the Somoza government became more rapacious, the resistance expanded and intensified, finally driving the government into exile. By the time the Sandinistas came to power in 1979, however, some 50,000 people had been killed in guerrilla warfare. The Cuban government, which had helped the guerrillas with training and equipment, now continued its assistance with advice to the new government, especially on programs for health and education.

American President Ronald Reagan (1911–2004), with almost fanatic zeal, attempted to destabilize the Sandinista government. He authorized the creation of a paramilitary force against them, based across the border in Honduras, trained and supplied by the United States. He mined Nicaraguan harbors, violating the laws and treaties of the United States and earning the condemnation of the World Court. When the American Congress refused to fund this clandestine war, the Reagan administration arranged to fund it secretly with the profits from equally secret arms sales to Iran, a country generally considered hostile to the United States at the time. An American congressional investigation finally uncovered the double scandal.

Eventually, several Central American governments negotiated a settlement of the civil war in Nicaragua, including an end to foreign military involvement and a call for honest elections. For his initiative in this effort to negotiate an end to the Nicaraguan conflict, Costa Rican President Oscar Arias was awarded the Nobel Prize for Peace. The nine years of warfare, 1981 to 1990, had cost approximately 60,000 deaths and another 28,000 casualties. Since 1990, Nicaragua has been ruled by democratically elected governments and relationships with the United States have normalized.

Guatemala. In Guatemala, the world's second largest producer of bananas, Jacobo Arbenz (1913–71) was elected president in 1951. (The term **"banana republic"** evolved to describe countries, like Guatemala, that were economically dependent on a single crop that they sold primarily to a superpower, and were helpless in the face of superpower political and military intervention.) At the time, the United Fruit Company, a private company owned mostly by citizens of the U.S., was Guatemala's largest landowner and held a monopoly on Guatemala's transportation infrastructure. To suppress banana production and keep prices high, the United Fruit Company left thousands of acres of arable land fallow. Arbenz proceeded to seize some 400,000 acres of fallow land. He offered compensation according to the value of the land declared for tax purposes by the United Fruit Company itself, but the company found this insufficient. Arbenz also wanted to build a highway from his capital to the Atlantic Ocean, thus breaking the company's transportation monopoly, and to build a hydroelectric power plant, freeing Guatemala from its dependence on a foreign supply. Finally, fearing an attack by exiles training in neighboring countries, Arbenz sought to buy arms from the United States. When the U.S. turned him down, he bought from Poland, a communist country. Almost immediately a small Guatemalan army-in-exile of some 150 soldiers, equipped by the United States, attacked from Honduras. The Arbenz government fell, virtually without defenders, in 1954.

Arbenz's successor, Carlos Castillo Armas (1914–57), returned the lands taken from the United Fruit Company, abolished several political parties, disenfranchised all illiterates (about half the adult population), and had those who opposed him jailed, tortured, exiled, or executed. Castillo Armas was assassinated in mid-1957, and soon Guatemala plunged into a civil war in which 100,000 people died before a negotiated resolution was achieved in the 1990s. In 1999, U.S. President Bill Clinton (b. 1946), speaking in Guatemala, "apologized for U.S. support of right-wing governments that killed tens of thousands of rebels and Mayan Indians in a 36-year civil war" (*New York Times Almanac*, 2000, p. 16).

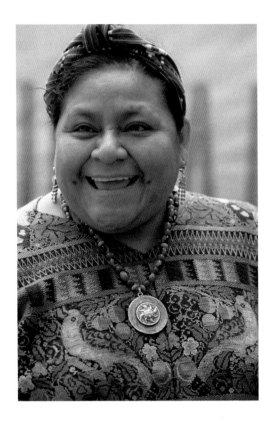

Rigoberta Menchu. Menchu, a Guatemalan Indian, won the Nobel Peace Prize in 1992. Her book, *I, Rigoberta Menchu: An Indian Woman in Guatemala*, was published in 1983 and became a bestseller. Although later challenged as exaggerated and "borrowed," this autobiography presents an accurate account of Indian oppression and suffering.

Chile. Chile began a program of agrarian reform and nationalized, with compensation, copper mines owned by American companies. The moderate government had good relations with the United States. In 1970, seeking more radical reform, the voters in Chile elected as president the socialist Salvador Allende (1908–73), whom the United States government and major transnational corporations opposed. Once in office, Allende confirmed their fears. He increased agrarian reform, purchased control of most banks, and continued the nationalization of the foreign-owned copper industry, which produced 75 percent of Chile's exports. Allende increased the salaries of government workers and expanded medical and housing programs. Allende ran up against the usual tension between the desire to improve economic and social benefits, on the one hand, and the problem of finding resources to pay for them, on the other. Shortages and inflation resulted. The United States government sharply reduced loans and aid to Allende's socialist government, and international banks cut back on loans. The CIA, with a mandate to overthrow Allende, covertly financed opposition parties and labor strikes. Finally, the middle class, and especially housewives, who found the resulting chaos and economic instability intolerable, persuaded the military to act. In September 1973, they attacked and bombed the presidential palace, killing Allende.

General Augusto Pinochet (1915–2006), who headed the new government, jailed more than one hundred thousand Allende supporters, men and women, and ultimately killed several thousand of them. Feared and hated for his violence toward the opposition, Pinochet was nevertheless effective in restoring the economy, with the aid of advisers from the United States. In a plebiscite in 1988, Pinochet was rejected by Chile's voters, and the government passed to the opposition. After 15 years of military rule, Chile had returned to democracy.

The End of the Cold War: The Soviet Union Dissolves

In the space of two years, 1989–91, after more than four decades of Cold War, intercontinental confrontation backed by nuclear weapons, and bitter competition to divide up the new nations of the world, the Soviet Union suddenly collapsed and disintegrated, the Cold War came to an end, and the ideological struggle between capitalist democracy and communism was brought to a halt, at least temporarily. The collapse and disintegration of the Soviet Union, and of the Communist Party that had created and administered it, shocked the political and cultural world of the late twentieth century and transformed identities around the globe.

The Soviet Union's Alternative Model

From the time of its establishment in 1917, the Soviet Union had offered alternative models to the capitalism, democracy, and individualism of Western Europe and the United States. Through the global depression, it had demonstrated that state planning could keep an economy—at least its industrial sectors—humming. In the 1930s, it alone had responded vigorously to the dangers posed by the rise of Nazism by building up a strong military defense, and throughout World War II it held the eastern front at enormous cost in Soviet lives and wealth. During the Cold War, the Soviet Union alone provided a balance against the overwhelming military power of the United States, and offered support and an alternative path for newly independent nations emerging from colonialism. At the same time, the totalitarian power of the communist government and the gulag of prison camps through which it enforced that power were crucial ingredients in the Soviet system. Its occupation of central and eastern Europe from 1945 made it an imperial, and dreaded, neighbor.

Individuals, institutions, states, and governments had looked to the Soviet Union as a model for seven decades—some with hope, others with fear and apprehension. With its collapse they lost a pole star in their map of their political universe. Political identities everywhere were reshuffled.

Gorbachev's Reforms, 1985–91

In the Soviet Union, two men guided the process that brought the Soviet Union to its end: Mikhail Gorbachev and Boris Yeltsin. Gorbachev (b. 1931) came to power in the USSR in 1985. He assessed the problems of the Soviet Union directly and bluntly. Its economy was neither producing nor distributing goods effectively. Its bureaucracy was bloated with Communist Party officials, while the growing professional classes protested restrictions on freedom. The churches continued to seek greater freedom of expression. Not only in the satellite countries of Eastern Europe, such as Poland, but in the non-Russian states of the USSR itself nationalist groups sought greater independence—especially the Baltic states, which had long chafed under Russian control, and the Muslim-majority states of central Asia, which were culturally, linguistically, and religiously different from Russia. In its haste to industrialize, the USSR had allowed technology to get out of control, as evident in the massive pollution of air and sea, most frighteningly in the Aral Sea, which was drying up. In addition, the ongoing war in Afghanistan was bleeding the country of lives, treasure, and spirit. Finally, the Soviet Union was engaged in an arms race with the United States that it could no longer afford.

In response to these problems, Gorbachev introduced his policies of *glasnost* (political and cultural openness) and *perestroika* (economic restructuring). *Glasnost*

SOURCE

Gorbachev at the United Nations, December 7, 1988

Gorbachev left two contrasting legacies. At home, he failed in his practical attempts to bring *perestroika*, the restructuring of the Russian economy, politics, and society. On the other hand, his vision of the future for the world inspired people everywhere. It underpinned his dismantling of the Soviet Union, its Communist Party, and its control over the satellite countries of central and Eastern Europe. The vision seemed utopian yet somehow, perhaps, achievable. Gorbachev's speech at the United Nations General Assembly in New York City on December 7, 1988, summarized his goals and aspirations. It called for global cooperation, tolerance for diverse social and political systems, protection for the globe's ecology, assistance for development in the poorer nations, and disarmament, which he pledged to begin immediately in the Soviet Union on his own initiative. This was quite a new agenda for the Soviet Union, and for the world. The speech drew enthusiastic, even ecstatic praise from statesmen and common people around the world.

> Further world progress is now possible only through the search for a consensus of all mankind, in movement toward a new world order … It is a question of cooperation that could be more accurately called "co-creation" and "co-development." The formula of development "at another's expense" is becoming outdated. In light of present realities, genuine progress by infringing upon the rights and liberties of man and peoples, or at the expense of nature, is impossible …
>
> It is evident, for example, that force and the threat of force can no longer be, and should not be instruments of foreign policy …
>
> The variety of sociopolitical structures which has grown over the last decades from national liberation movements also demonstrates this. This objective fact presupposes respect for other people's views and stands, tolerance, a preparedness to see phenomena that are different as not necessarily bad or hostile, and an ability to learn to live side by side while remaining different and not agreeing with one another on every issue …
>
> In the course of such sharing, each should prove the advantages of his own system, his own way of life and values, but not through words or propaganda alone, but through real deeds as well … Otherwise we simply will not be able to

solve a single world problem; arrange broad, mutually advantageous and equitable cooperation between peoples; manage rationally the achievements of the scientific and technical revolution; transform world economic relations; protect the environment; overcome underdevelopment; or put an end to hunger, disease, illiteracy, and other mass ills. Finally, in that case, we will not manage to eliminate the nuclear threat and militarism.

> Now about the most important topic, without which no problem of the coming century can be resolved: disarmament …
>
> Today I can inform you of the following: The Soviet Union has made a decision on reducing its armed forces. In the next two years, their numerical strength will be reduced by 500,000 persons … The Soviet forces situated in those countries [of central and Eastern Europe] will be cut by 50,000 persons, and their arms by 5,000 tanks.
>
> We would also like to draw the attention of the world community to another topical problem, the problem of changing over from an economy of armament to an economy of disarmament. Is the conversion of military production realistic? … We believe that it is, indeed, realistic … It is desirable that all states, primarily the major military powers, submit their national plans on this issue to the United Nations.
>
> We are talking first and foremost about consistent progress toward concluding a treaty [with the United States] on a 50 percent reduction in strategic offensive weapons … about elaborating a convention on the elimination of chemical weapons—here, it seems to us, we have the preconditions for making 1989 the decisive year; and about talks on reducing conventional weapons and armed forces in Europe. We are also talking about economic, ecological, and humanitarian problems in the widest possible sense …
>
> One would like to believe that our joint efforts to put an end to the era of wars, confrontation and regional conflicts, aggression against nature, the terror of hunger and poverty, as well as political terrorism, will be comparable with our hopes. This is our common goal, and it is only by acting together that we may attain it. Thank you.

meant, first of all, telling the truth about the communist state, and this included the truth about its past. Khrushchev had already revealed many of Stalin's atrocities. Under Gorbachev historians revealed even more: some 20 million people killed under Stalin and a similar number oppressed. *Glasnost* also extended to the present. Those who would have agreed with Solzhenitsyn's 1973 statement, "It has always been impossible to learn the truth about anything in our country," now heard directly about the depth of their nation's problems.

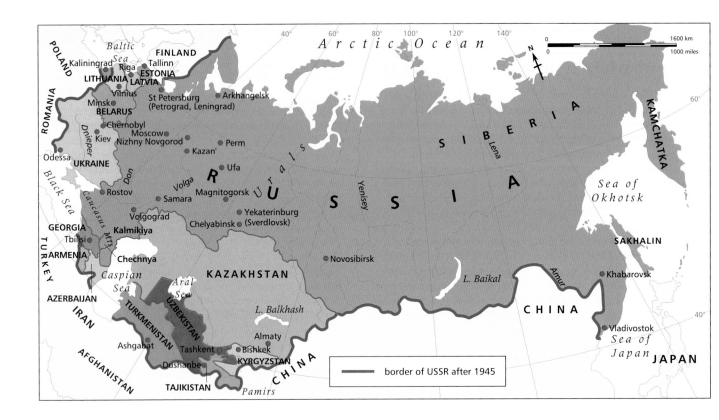

The break-up of the Soviet Union.
The Soviet experiment with Marxist ideology crumbled, after 70 years, at the end of the 1980s. President Gorbachev's policy of *glasnost* (1985) allowed the nations of Eastern Europe to move, largely bloodlessly, toward independence and economic reform, but in the Caucasus Mountains and central Asia reform was often accompanied by an insurgence of nationalism, organized crime, and power struggles. In 1991 these nations also became independent—except for Chechnya, where fighting continued for years.

Glasnost revealed the problems. *Perestroika* looked for solutions. Gorbachev tried to reduce the size of the bureaucracy, to increase the efficiency of agriculture and industry, and to trim the military budget. He appointed reformers to important government offices. He planned and began a more competitive economic system, though one still under state control.

Gorbachev was somewhat trapped by his own promises, for soon the reformers were criticizing him for moving too slowly and for an unwillingness to cut free of discredited communist economics. Under *glasnost*, ethnic groups throughout the length and breadth of the highly diverse Soviet Union began to voice their grievances. Riots between ethnic groups broke out in some areas, and full-scale independence movements began in the Baltic States. Others soon followed elsewhere. Meanwhile, the war in Afghanistan that Brezhnev had initiated in 1979 ground on, with 2,000 Russian soldiers dying every year and no evidence of Soviet gains.

In 1988, Gorbachev allowed multi-candidate elections and began to give the Supreme Soviet increased powers. In February 1990, he announced that non-Party candidates could stand for office. The monopoly of the Communist Party over the government ended. Gorbachev was willing to see the Soviet empire and the Communist Party disintegrate, and they did. His spokesman announced that he was replacing the Brezhnev Doctrine of massive intervention in rebellious satellite countries with the (Frank) Sinatra Doctrine of "My Way," allowing them to break free of the Soviet Union however they chose. Incredulous and ecstatic, Germans, using sledgehammers, pickaxes, and their bare hands, tore down the Berlin Wall, the symbol of their division into east and west. The date, November 9, 1989, became a new national holiday. Gorbachev continued his negotiations for arms reductions with U.S. Presidents Ronald Reagan and George H.W. Bush, and in December 1989, Gorbachev and Bush formally announced the end of the Cold War.

With the removal of Soviet armies, all six satellite nations in Eastern and central Europe became independent: East Germany, Poland, Hungary, Czechoslovakia (which, in 1993, divided into the Czech and Slovak Republics), Bulgaria, and Romania. Divided at the end of World War II, East and West Germany reunited. At first, Gorbachev resisted the right of constituent republics of the USSR to declare their independence and leave the union, but many now simply defied his wishes: the Baltic states of Estonia, Latvia, and Lithuania; the Eastern European Slavic states of Belarus, Ukraine, and Moldova; the Caspian Sea states of Armenia, Georgia, and Azerbaijan; and the Muslim majority states in central Asia: Turkmenistan, Uzbekistan, Tajikistan, Kyrgyzstan, and Kazakhstan. With government control uncertain, historic national and ethnic identities reemerged within and between these states. These identities were sometimes hostile to one another, and violent clashes, as well as celebration, marked the end of the Soviet empire.

Yeltsin Crushes the Coup. In August 1991, while Gorbachev was vacationing in the Crimea, diehard communists mounted a coup against him for moving too quickly. Boris Yeltsin (1931–2007), a reformer and the president of the Russian Federation, led public resistance to the coup, contacted political leaders across the country and around the world to gain support, and courageously went out to the streets and climbed atop an armored troop carrier to make his position clear. When the army refused to attack Yeltsin and his headquarters, the coup was finished. Gorbachev returned from the Crimea, but Yeltsin was the hero of the moment.

A few days later Gorbachev resigned as general secretary of the Communist Party and moved to dissolve it altogether. On December 24, 1991, the USSR formally dissolved itself into 15 independent states. The new states joined in a loose Commonwealth of Independent States as a mechanism for continuing cooperation. The USSR was no more; the Communist Party was reduced to a shell; the global political landscape was transformed. The nation that Gorbachev had ruled no longer existed. Yeltsin's Russia was by far its largest surviving state.

Perhaps the most amazing outcome of the Cold War was that, for the superpowers, it had remained mostly cold. Despite all the saber-rattling, all the expensive weaponry, all the conniving with client states, despite even the Cuban Missile Crisis, the United States and the Soviet Union had always pulled back from nuclear war. Although they fought proxy wars, they did not confront each other in direct warfare. Some observers speculated that the investment in the threat of nuclear war—in Mutually Assured Destruction, or MAD—had provided a ritualized pose of macho strength on both sides that allowed the superpowers to avoid actual warfare. In retrospect it appeared that for 45 years they had created their own form of an international balance of power.

Pursuing Peace Through Negotiation

While the United States and the Soviet Union were busy threatening each other, nations of Western Europe and Japan, having suffered grievously in World War II, sought new methods of peaceful cooperation, often in the area of sharing and developing technology. They were often critical of both the U.S. and the USSR for their emphasis on armed confrontation. The UN, often at the behest of newly independent nations, sought to minimize the polarization of the superpowers. It also undertook to monitor the effects of technology on the health of the globe, as in climate change and ocean pollution. And numerous NGOs throughout the world also tried to improve life on the planet through peaceful means.

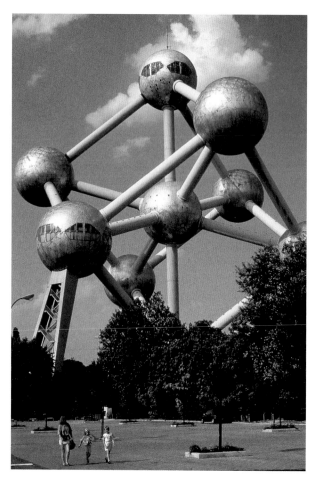

The Atomium, Euratom headquarters, Brussels. As European countries that had fought each other for centuries began to forge institutions of cooperation after 1945, collaboration in the peaceful development of atomic energy took on both practical and symbolic importance. The 1957 Treaty of Rome that established the European Economic Community (EEC) also created Euratom to create joint policies. The Atomium at Euratom headquarters in Brussels symbolized this new commitment.

Toward a Unified Europe

In 1947, Winston Churchill had described Europe as "a rubble heap, a charnel house, a breeding ground for pestilence and hate." But out of the wreckage came several economic miracles, many of them the result of cooperation between recent enemies. In 1950, French and West German officials agreed to form the European Coal and Steel Community with its own independent international authority. The ECSC was born in 1952 with the addition of Italy and the Benelux countries (Belgium, the Netherlands, Luxembourg). Its success led to the Treaties of Rome in 1957 that established the European Economic Community (EEC), or Common Market, to lower and ultimately remove tariffs among member countries; to foster the free movement of goods, labor, and capital; and to establish a single external tariff. The treaties also established Euratom to create common policies for the peaceful development of atomic energy.

In 1965, the Brussels treaty merged the ECSC, the EEC, and Euratom to create the basis of a unified West European economic administration. Additional nations were admitted, including Britain, Ireland, and Denmark in 1973, Greece in 1981, and Spain and Portugal in 1986. Western Europe was moving toward a new era, a "Europe without frontiers," and its economy flourished. The economies of Western European nations experienced extraordinary growth. Germany called it a *wirtschaftswunder*, an economic miracle. Others referred to it as their "golden years."

The successes of the golden years rested on wide international cooperation outside of Europe as well as within. Part of the institutional base was prepared in 1944 in Bretton Woods, New Hampshire. Representatives of 40 nations gathered there to plan a new global economy for the postwar period that would escape the catastrophic depression that had followed World War I. They created three new institutions: the International Monetary Fund (IMF), the International Bank for Reconstruction and Development (World Bank), and the General Agreement on Tariffs and Trade (GATT). The IMF provided short-term loans for countries that were having difficulty meeting their balance of payment obligations. These were designed for moments of extreme, but short-term, crisis. The first goal of the World Bank was to provide capital for rebuilding war-torn nations. By the late 1960s and 1970s, as European nations had recovered from the economic devastation of the war, the bank increasingly turned to the developmental needs of the third world, although not to their short-term needs for relief. The GATT was designed to promote world trade by bringing down tariffs among all member nations.

Until the 1980s all of these organizations were generally praised for their achievements among the capitalist nations of the world. The communist bloc—both the European nations in the Soviet sphere and China after its communist revolution—refused to participate because they did not trust the open market as a means of economic decision making. They rejected the capitalist laws of supply and demand in favor of state planning and therefore could not accept the Bretton Woods principles. In this sense, Bretton Woods helped to divide the world into opposing blocs, even as it proved successful for the West.

SOURCE

Rachel Carson's *Silent Spring*

American biologist Rachel Carson's *Silent Spring* (1962) exposed the devastating effects on humans, wildlife, and plants caused by the use of toxic chemicals—pesticides, fungicides, and herbicides—in everyday farming and insect control throughout the world. By virtue of its combination of scientific rigor and journalistic vividness, *Silent Spring* is frequently credited as the founding statement of the ecological movement in the twentieth century.

> The most alarming of all man's assaults on the environment is the contamination of air, earth, rivers, and sea with dangerous and even lethal materials. This pollution is for the most part irrecoverable; the chain of evil it initiates not only in the world that must support life but in living tissues is for the most part irreversible. In this now universal contamination of the environment, chemicals are the sinister and little recognized partners of radiation in changing the very nature of the world—the very nature of its life … Chemicals sprayed on croplands or forests or gardens lie long in the soil, entering into living organisms, passing from one to another in a chain of poisoning and death. Or they pass mysteriously by underground streams until they emerge, and through the alchemy of air and sunlight, combine into new forms that kill vegetation, sicken cattle, and work unknown harm on those who drink from once-pure wells. (Carson, pp. 23–24)

Carson's powerful voice evoked responses. For example, after she revealed that DDT, one of the most powerful chemicals used to combat mosquitoes and, thus, malaria, was also poisonous to humans, governments throughout the world generally banned its use. "Green" parties, with strong platforms on ecological issues, began to organize in many countries, especially in Western Europe, and more mainstream parties began to adopt some of their programs. Citizens founded organizations such as the World Wildlife Fund and Greenpeace in order to protect the environment. Some farmers began to use natural means of pest control in place of chemicals, and consumers began to seek out "natural" or "organic" foods raised without the use of chemical fertilizers and pesticides.

As Carson pointed out, the political issues, and their implications for the standard of living in each country, were thornier than the technological:

> The Earth is one but the world is not. We all depend on one biosphere for sustaining our lives. Yet each community, each country strives for survival and prosperity with little regard for its impact on others. Some consume the Earth's resources at a rate that would leave little for future generations. Others, many more in number, consume far too little and live with the prospect of hunger, squalor, disease, and early death. (Carson, p. 28)

Japan's Recovery

Just as startling as Europe's recovery after the war was the speed of Japan's recovery. Like Germany, Japan had the remains of an industrial infrastructure and a highly skilled workforce that could shift into production for peace. The U.S. occupation, 1945–52, improved Japan's competitive position by redistributing land; breaking up the *zaibatsu* holding companies that had controlled the economy; encouraging the growth of labor unions (until some of them began to become communist); and restructuring the educational system, opening up high school and college education for the first time to millions of Japanese students. The United States also encouraged Japan, as it had Germany, to join it in the Cold War struggle against the Soviet Union. Japan benefited both from U.S. investment and from U.S. reliance on the Japanese economy for supplies during the Korean War—and later during the Vietnam War—and for bases for American troops and for their rest-and-relaxation during these wars.

Japan did not, however, participate in these wars. Its postwar constitution forbade such overseas military actions. Article Nine of the Japanese constitution states, "The Japanese people forever renounce war as a sovereign right of the nation and the threat or use of force as means of settling international disputes." It also outlawed the presence of nuclear weapons on Japanese territory. The constitution declared that "land, sea, and air forces, as well as other war potential, will never be maintained." Even so, in 1954 the Japanese parliament established the Self-Defense Forces, which by the early years of the twenty-first century came to number almost 250,000 armed troops. Nevertheless, Japan's military spending as a proportion of its total national

AT A GLANCE: EUROPE AND THE UNITED STATES

DATE	POLITICS	SOCIETY AND CULTURE
1950s	• Korean War (1950–53) • Egypt nationalizes Suez Canal, establishing independence from Great Britain (1956) • Treaties of Rome (1957) lead to establishment of European Community • Ghana wins independence from Great Britain (1957)	• Contraceptive pill becomes available in the late 1950s
1960s	• Cuban Missile Crisis (1962) • Algeria wins independence from France (1962) • Group of 77 reforms (1964) • America involved in Vietnam War (1964–73) • Lyndon Johnson sponsors Voting Rights Act (1965) • U.S. Defense Department creates internet (1969)	• Rachel Carson, *Silent Spring* (1962) • Betty Friedan, *The Feminine Mystique* (1963) • Martin Luther King delivers "I Have a Dream" speech in Washington Mall (1963) • Stanley Kubrick, *Dr. Strangelove* (1964) • Malcolm X assassinated (1965) • *Apollo II* lands on moon (1969)
1970s	• Formation of OPEC (1973) • Watergate affair forces resignation of President Nixon (1974)	• UN conference on the Human Environment (1972) • Near meltdown of nuclear reactor at Three Mile Island, Pennsylvania (1979)
1980s	• "Star Wars" Strategic Defense Initiative, proposed by President Reagan (1981–88)	• World Wide Web created (1989)
1990s	• Maastricht Treaty (1991) • Bosnian War (1991–95) • Russia joins the Group of Seven, forming the G-8 (1997) • War in Kosovo (1998–99)	• UN "Earth Summit" in Rio (1992) • Around ten percent of the U.S. population are foreign-born (1997) • Internet connection worldwide rises from three million people in 1993 to 200 million in 1999 • Protests in Seattle, Washington, against the World Trade Organization (1999)

budget was relatively small, as it put its faith in the American military shield and invested its money in productive economic enterprises.

Between 1950 and 1973, Japan's gross domestic product grew at 10.5 percent per year. By 1980, Japan's per capita income, at almost $10,000 per year, rivaled America's at $11,400. Economists were beginning to speak of "Japan as Number 1" because of the efficiency and quality of its consumer products, especially its automobiles; its skill in overseas marketing; and its prospects for soon surpassing even the United States as the world's leading economy.

Japan's economic success also turned on its ability to bring together government advice and guidance with freely operating private enterprises. Its Ministry for International Trade and Industry successfully guided Japanese industries away from **sunset industries**, such as steel production, into **sunrise industries**, such as automobiles and computers, and helped them find financial investments and marketing opportunities. Several countries of East and Southeast Asia—especially Korea and Taiwan, Japan's former colonies—adopted this model of state guidance and private enterprise with great success. These two nations, along with the city-states of Hong Kong and Singapore, were often referred to as the "**Asian tigers**" for their aggressive and successful economic development along the Japanese model.

The UN: Growth and New Missions

Meanwhile, the UN was demonstrating some success as an arena for defusing international tensions, providing peace-keeping missions to global trouble-spots, and developing programs for international cooperation, including issues involving technology.

KEY TERMS

sunset industries Industries that are expected to be in decline in the near future.

sunrise industries Industries that are expected to be most profitable in the near future.

Asian tigers The countries in East and Southeast Asia that were doing extremely well economically in the last decades of the twentieth century. The list almost always includes South Korea, Taiwan, Singapore, and Hong Kong, and sometimes Indonesia and Thailand.

AT A GLANCE: THE SOVIET UNION AND JAPAN

DATE	SOVIET UNION	JAPAN
1950s	• At the 20th Party Congress Nikita Khrushchev officially exposes Stalin's tyranny (1956) • Khrushchev crushes Hungarian uprising (1956) • Soviet space program puts first rocket, *Sputnik*, into space (1957)	• Economic benefits from American participation in the Korean War (1950–53)
1960s	• Alexander Solzhenitsyn, *A Day in the Life of Ivan Denisovich* (1962) • Cuban missile crisis (1962) • Leonid Brezhnev puts down Czech revolt, the "Prague Spring" (1968)	• Admitted to Organization for Economic Cooperation and Development (OECD) (1964) • Bullet train inaugurated (1964) • Hosts Olympics (1964)
1970s	• Lech Walesa begins to organize independent trade union federation, or Solidarity, in Poland (1978) • Pope John Paul II visits Poland (1979)	• Economy hit badly by "oil shocks" (1973)
1980s	• Mikhail Gorbachev institutes policies of *glasnost* and *perestroika* on coming to power (1985) • Partial meltdown of Chernobyl nuclear power plant (1986)	• Trade frictions with United States and Europe • Equal Employment Opportunity Act (1986) • Death of Emperor Hirohito (1989) • Hit by recession (1989)
1990s	• Coup attempt against Gorbachev by die-hard communists fails (1991) • USSR dissolves into 15 independent states of which Russia is largest (1991) • Boris Yeltsin convenes Constitutional Assembly that produces new constitution for Russia (1993) • Russia accorded associate status in NATO (1997) • Yeltsin resigns as president (1999)	• Becomes world's largest donor of foreign aid—$14 billion (1994) • East Asian financial collapse (1997)

By the end of 1984 the membership of the UN had expanded to 159 sovereign states, the overwhelming majority of the world's nations. It provided a home in which the newly emerging nations could gain political recognition and representation. The diversity of states brought a diversity of ideologies, and UN decisions and activities were subjected to a constant stream of criticism from one point or another on the political spectrum. Yet within that highly politicized framework the organization went on with its work, providing a forum where nations could meet, discuss common goals, and negotiate agreements. It did not always succeed, but such a forum was invaluable. In the mid-1980s, Soviet leader Gorbachev called the UN a "unique instrument without which world politics would be inconceivable today," even though it lacked the sovereignty of a government and commanded only such powers as its members chose to vest in it. The UN helped to negotiate a resolution of the Cuban Missile Crisis, the Arab–Israeli war of 1967, and the Iraq–Iran war of 1988. It called for the first arms embargo against South Africa in 1963 and made it mandatory in 1972.

The UN dispatched "peace-keeping" armed forces, with military personnel drawn from many different countries, to police zones of potential conflict. These missions were not designed to fight wars, but to maintain the peace in cases in which antagonistic nations agreed that they would work for peace, but required an honest "police force" to maintain it. UN peace-keeping forces were first sent to the Middle East in 1948 to monitor the ceasefire between the new state of Israel and its Arab neighbors. A small force was sent to Cyprus in 1964 to maintain a buffer between the Greek Cypriots and the Turkish Cypriots who had been fighting for control of the island. They were also sent to Kashmir in 1972 to monitor the Line of Control

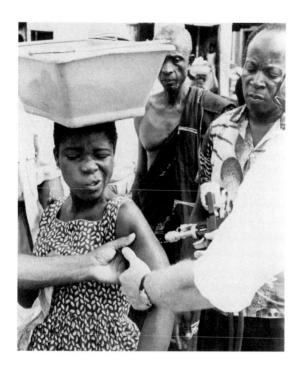

A girl vaccinated against smallpox, Nigeria, 1969. In 1979, in one of the great triumphs of international humanitarian organization, the World Health Organization declared that smallpox had been eradicated. Every human being on earth had been inoculated against it.

between India and Pakistan after the two countries signed peace agreements to end their 1971 warfare.

On a third level, the UN undertook many initiatives in organizing for the general welfare of the globe. The UN coordinated the first global census in 1953, monitoring critical demographic changes. It found that the world's population had multiplied from about 2.5 billion in 1950 to about six billion in 2000, with most of the increase coming in the poorer countries. At the same time, death rates were falling, leading to an increase also in the elderly population of the world, especially in the wealthier countries. People were also moving steadily from rural to urban areas. Estimates suggest that in 1950 about 30 per cent of the world's 2.5 billion people, about 750 million, lived in cities. By 1990, about 45 per cent of the world's six billion people, 2.7 billion, lived in cities. (In 2007 the figure reached 50 percent.) By 1990, more people lived in cities than had lived in the entire world in 1900. The most rapidly growing cities, and most of the largest of them, were in the poorer, less industrialized areas of the world, with the fewest resources for responding to the requirements of such immense populations, for example, São Paolo, Brazil; Mexico City; Mumbai (Bombay) and Kolkata (Calcutta), in India; Shanghai and Beijing (Peking) in China. Each had upward of ten million inhabitants. To direct attention toward the needs of these enormous populations, and especially of their poorest citizens living in slums, the UN inaugurated its Habitat program in 1978.

Recognizing that most social and economic problems affect men and women differently, in 1975 the UN sponsored a "Decade for Women," opening with the first World Conference on Women, in Mexico City. Later women's conferences followed in Copenhagen in 1980, Nairobi in 1985 and Beijing in 1995.

In 1979, the WHO declared that smallpox had been eradicated: every human being on earth had been inoculated against the disease. The WHO was only one of numerous international organizations working officially with the UN, many of them created by the UN itself. Others included the Food and Agriculture Organization (FAO), which works to increase the productivity of farms, forests, and fisheries; the International Atomic Energy Agency (IAEA), which monitors the nonproliferation of nuclear weapons and promotes the peaceful use of atomic energy; the International Labor Organization (ILO), which creates labor standards and promotes the welfare of workers everywhere; UNESCO, the UN's Educational, Scientific, and Cultural Organization, which promotes research and publication; and the World Bank, which extends loans to help poor countries in their development tasks.

Finally, the UN began a struggle against global ecological destruction with the UN Conference on the Human Environment meeting in Stockholm in 1972. Many concerns dominated the agenda, but the main ones were the depletion of the ozone layer; global warming and greenhouse gasses; deforestation, especially in the tropics, where at least 25 million acres of trees are cut down yearly; acid rain, the pollution of the atmosphere with airborne chemical pollutants; and the destruction of the marine environment through ocean dumping, ship pollution, and the absorption of chemicals into the water table. The UN established the first rules regulating the laws of the sea, including laws regulating ocean fishing (1970).

Agreement was emerging on the need for international cooperation in a stronger UN environment program, but the UN lacked sovereign power. It could gather information, carry out research, make recommendations, hold conferences, and provide counsel, but it had no powers of enforcement. Implementation depended on the decisions of member nations.

NGOs and Transnational Organizations

The UN was perhaps the most important of all the organizations acting on a global scale that were not themselves actual governments. The second half of the twentieth century saw an enormous growth in the number and power of **NGOs** devoted to more specific issues. These NGOs changed the way nations and economies carried out their work.

Normally, the term NGO does not include private businesses, but they too are in a sense NGOs, and, in the later years of the twentieth century, they created not only multinational corporations but even transnational corporations. Multinationals were companies headquartered in one nation but operating in several. By the late twentieth century, America alone had tens of thousands of such corporations.

KEY TERM

NGO Non-governmental organization. Broadly, any organization not controlled by the government, carrying out its own mission. Most commonly refers to voluntary organizations carrying out work of social and community service that the government cannot or does not do.

HOW DO WE KNOW?

The Social Setting of Technology

Even as the developed world created new products, established ever more efficient means for producing them, and designed advertising to convince people that these new products were necessary, a few people raised their voices to ask if this form of economic and technological development was "progress." One of the most prominent of these critics, E.F. Schumacher, declared as the title of his 1973 book: *Small Is Beautiful*. Schumacher, a British economist, served for 20 years as head of planning at the British Coal Board, but his economic philosophy stressed the small-scale rather than the large. He wanted an economics based in nature rather than in the subjugation of nature:

> In the excitement over the unfolding of his scientific and technical powers, modern man has built a system of production that ravishes nature and a type of society that mutilates man … The development of production and the acquisition of wealth have thus become the highest goals of the modern world in relation to which all other goals, no matter how much lip-service may still be paid to them have come to take second place … This is the philosophy of materialism, and it is this philosophy—or metaphysic—which is being challenged by events … It is of little use trying to suppress terrorism if the production of deadly devices continues to be deemed a legitimate employment of man's creative powers … Equally, the chance of mitigating the rate of resource depletion or of bringing harmony into the relationships between those in possession of wealth and power and those without is non-existent as long as there is no idea anywhere of enough being good and more-than-enough being evil.

Schumacher briefly explored the history of the economics profession to chart its transformation. The first professorship in political economy was endowed at Oxford in 1825, and from the beginning philanthropists and economists alike asked what should be its scope; many, including Schumacher, argued that economics should be subservient to ethics. In 1969, the Nobel Prize for "economic science" was established, suggesting that this discipline would not rank second to any other. Schumacher, however, argued that the earlier evaluation was more appropriate.

Arnold Pacey, a British physicist who became an historian, also argued that technological developments were most effective when they fit the society that was adopting them. Pacey was not directly arguing ethics, as Schumacher was, but his idea that inventions should fit the needs of society, and society's ability to absorb them, agreed with Schumacher that technological "development" should not proceed for its own sake, but rather for the sake of society. In an era of rapid technological development, when third world nations frequently wanted the same technology for war and for peace as the first world had, the moral principles expressed directly by Schumacher and indirectly by Pacey set up a challenge: What would be the appropriate scale for the technology to be adopted? The argument for appropriate-scale technology was made forcefully, in practical terms, by Mahatma Gandhi of India, as we shall see in Chapter Twenty-two.

- Was Schumacher correct that technological "progress" is pursued, at least some of the time, simply for the purpose of making a profit, whether or not new technology is needed? Please explain, with examples.
- Can you provide examples of technologies that seem appropriate for the people and societies that use them and examples of technologies that seem inappropriate?
- How important do you think it is to ask about the appropriate scale of technology? Can you give an example of such a question in your own life?

PEARSON
myhistorylab

Transnational corporations also operated in many countries, but had no clear headquarters. Sometimes, for financial purposes (often, to evade taxes), they placed much of their financial structure in small, relatively unregulated nations, like the Cayman Islands or Curaçao. Regulating and policing the transnationals was not easy. Also, while multinational corporations might finally have to balance their desire for bottom-line profits against the need to live within the laws and values of their home country, transnationals had no allegiances other than profit. Transnational business became more competitive, but less responsive to values other than profit.

At the same time, more conventional NGOs, much smaller to be sure, also took shape. The World Wildlife Fund (WWF), for example, founded in the 1950s, grew to more than five million members working in more than one hundred countries. It became the world's largest privately financed conservation organization working to conserve the world's biological diversity, advocate for the use of renewable natural resources in sustainable fashion, and promote the reduction of pollution and wasteful consumption.

Amnesty International also grew into a worldwide movement with over two million supporters dedicated to the protection and promotion of human rights. Amnesty took as its model the Universal Declaration of Human Rights. It acted to stop grave abuses of the rights of physical and mental integrity, freedom of conscience and expression, and freedom from discrimination. It campaigned to free prisoners of conscience, ensure fair trials for political prisoners, protect refugees, abolish the death penalty, and end political assassinations and torture. It sought to bring to justice those responsible for human rights violations. It publicized its findings in order to bring public pressure on governments, armed political groups, companies, and others in order to stop the abuses.

Oxfam, originally the Oxford Committee for Famine Relief, traces its origins to a group of Quaker intellectuals, social activists, and Oxford University academics who founded an organization to provide famine relief to Greece during World War II. In the immediate postwar years it directed its attention to European needs, but in 1951 it extended famine relief to people in India, and in 1953, following the Korean War, to the homeless, hungry, and orphaned in Korea. In the 1960s, Oxfam turned primarily to the needs of the third world. It focused less on famine relief and more on supplying the tools by which people could improve their living standards. Oxfam also prepared educational materials to explain to the first world the root causes of poverty and suffering, the connections between the first and third worlds, and the role that first world people could play in improving the physical conditions of life in the third world.

These three well-known organizations are only a few of the thousands of multinational and transnational NGOs. Many of the larger ones are organizations of trade unionists, religious groups, sports enthusiasts, and artists. The Soviet Union dissolved, for example, in part because of international labor support for Lech Walesa's Solidarity

UN AGENCIES

The primary focus of attention in the UN has been on peace and war, but its various programs and agencies, many concerned with technology, have provided forums for the resolution of other issues and the promotion of international welfare. Key agencies include:

- International Court of Justice (World Court), has dealt with issues such as territorial rights, territorial waters, rights of individuals to asylum, and territorial sovereignty
- Food and Agricultural Organization (FAO), monitors information for improving food supply and distribution
- World Trade Organization (WTO), oversees international trade, settles trade disputes, and negotiates trade liberalization
- World Bank, provides financial assistance to developing nations
- United Nations Educational, Scientific, and Cultural Organization (UNESCO), sponsors research and publication
- United Nations Children's (Emergency) Fund (UNICEF), establishes programs for family welfare
- World Health Organization (WHO), monitors and researches health conditions
- International Labor Organization (ILO), promotes employment and seeks to improve labor conditions and living standards
- World Intellectual Property Organization, protects the interests of the producers of literary, industrial, scientific, and artistic works
- Commission on Human Rights, gathers information and formulates policy on the rights of persons belonging to national, ethnic, religious, and linguistic minorities, including indigenous peoples

movement and because the Polish Cardinal Wojtyla was elevated to the position of pope in the Roman Catholic Church.

Wealthy private foundations that carry out humanitarian work formed another cluster of NGOs. For example, the Rockefeller Foundation sponsored the work of agricultural scientists who discovered and disseminated new strains of wheat and other grains that increased food productivity by as much as five times through the 1960s and 1970s. The **green revolution** they created saved the world from mass starvation in the face of continuing population growth. Norman Borlaugh, who directed these efforts, won the Nobel Peace Prize in 1970 for his work.

Nevertheless, NGOs were frequently criticized for escaping full public scrutiny. For example, many political observers feared that the Rockefeller-financed green revolution, which did so much to increase food productivity, would ultimately create tensions in society by making the rich richer and the poor poorer. The "miracle" seeds required new fertilizers and an abundance of irrigation water and pesticides. Richer farmers could afford to use them but poorer farmers could not, and these farmers often lost their land. In addition, over time the chemical fertilizers reduced the fertility of the soil. In the short run, the world needed the green revolution to feed its people; in the long run the unforeseen consequences might be devastating. Short-run obvious benefits outweighed long-run potential problems, and the search for new hybrid, high-yield crops soon expanded from wheat to rice and other global staples.

Amnesty International protest. Amnesty International is a worldwide movement of people who campaign for internationally recognized human rights for all. Founded in 1961, Amnesty now has more than 2.2 million members, supporters, and subscribers in over 150 countries and territories, in every region of the world. Amnesty campaigns to stop violence against women, abolish the death penalty, and free prisoners of conscience—people who have been jailed for exercising their right of freedom of speech.

Legacies of the Cold War, Decolonization, Economic and Social Development: What Difference Do They Make?

A healthy skepticism colors the transformations of the twentieth century. "Winners" gained more wealth, power, and convenience than had ever been known. Hundreds of millions of people, long colonized, won their political independence. Yet even the most fortunate often felt insecure, for the wars of the century were the bloodiest ever, the weaponry the most powerful and frightening, carrying the potential to destroy all human life. Governments had shown the power not only to fight wartime enemies but also to attack, imprison, exile, and destroy masses of their own citizens. Transportation and communication meant that almost no area of the world was unaffected by others. Serious questions arose as to the ability of the earth and the seas to withstand the pressures of the new technologies on planetary resources. Ecological sustainability became a new concern. Even for "winners," this was an age of anxiety.

For those less fortunate, poverty, servitude, ill-health, and hunger remained the common fate. Even though experts declared that new technologies provided the capacity to feed the entire, growing population of the earth, governmental policies, national and international, did not provide the necessary legal and technological means of distribution.

The postwar years, however, seemed to favor the optimists over the pessimists. Global wars stopped. Despite proxy wars, the nuclear weapons of the Cold War remained unused. Almost all colonies gained their independence. The UN offered

KEY TERM

green revolution The revolution in agricultural production brought about by the use of new hybrid seeds, with increased use of irrigation, fertilizers, and pesticides.

763

a global forum in which the peoples of the world could come together to address their common needs. The purview of the UN was continually extended to include not only conflict resolution, peace-keeping, and international law, but also issues of education, child welfare, the condition of women, labor relations, human rights, ecology, settlement patterns, and appropriate technologies. The world's economy—its production of food as well as of consumer goods—expanded more rapidly than its population. In historical retrospect, optimists could be justified in calling the postwar years of reconstruction, decolonization, economic expansion, and cultural regeneration a golden era.

Asking Questions

- What were the reasons for the Cold War competition between the U.S. and the USSR?
- Why did decolonization take place so quickly, once the initial process had begun?
- How did the superpowers and the new nations attempt to use one another for their own benefit? Please give examples.
- What function do voluntary organizations serve in a society? Give examples of how a voluntary organization has changed the policies of a country.
- Why did ecological issues rise to such great importance in the period 1945–85? Give some examples of the issues.
- Many observers have termed the period 1945–73, in Western Europe especially, a "golden age." Why? Would the same term hold for Africa, Asia, or Latin America in that period? Why or why not?

Suggested Readings

KEY TERMS

superpower see p. 726

asymmetrical warfare see p. 726

paper tiger see p. 726

Pax Americana see p. 726

Marshall Plan see p. 726

sphere of influence see p. 728

iron curtain see p. 728

containment see p. 728

client state see p. 730

McCarthyism see p. 730

gulag see p. 733

neocolonialism see p. 735

Prague Spring see p. 735

Brezhnev Doctrine see p. 735

domino effect see p. 736

third world see p. 748

nonaligned nations see p. 748

proxy war see p. 749

banana republic see p. 750

sunset industries see p. 758

sunrise industries see p. 758

Asian tigers see p. 758

NGO see p. 761

green revolution see p. 763

PRINCIPAL SOURCES

Applebaum, Anne. *Gulag: A History* (New York: Doubleday Books, 2003). A comprehensive scholarly account, stressing the economic importance of the Gulag and human relations inside it. Complements Solzhenitsyn's first-person, fictionalized account.

Bulliet, Richard W., ed. *The Columbia History of the 20th Century* (New York: Columbia University Press, 1998). Comprehensive and thoughtful collection of articles by theme rather than chronology.

Burns, E. Bradford and Julie Charlip. *Latin America: A Concise Interpretive History* (Upper Saddle River, NJ: Prentice-Hall, 2006). A standard text. Especially strong on Brazil.

Carson, Rachel. *Silent Spring* (New York: Penguin Books, 1965). An attack on the chemical and pesticide industries. The single most important book in launching the modern ecological movement.

Chakrabarty, Dipesh. *Provincializing Europe: Postcolonial Thought and Historical Difference* (Princeton: Princeton University Press, 2000). Sees the pattern of Western history as only one possible pattern. There are others.

Dower, John. *Embracing Defeat* (New York: W.W. Norton, 2000). A comprehensive, wonderfully readable story of America's occupation of Japan, 1945–52. Emphasizes the human contacts more than the institutional changes.

Fieldhouse, D.K. *Black Africa 1945–1980* (London: Allen and Unwin, 1986). An attempt to understand what has gone wrong in independent Africa, and why.

Friedman, Thomas. *From Beirut to Jerusalem* (New York: Farrar, Straus and Giroux, 1989). Presentation of the continuing Israeli–Arab hostility by a leading New York Times reporter.

Goncharov, Sergei N., John W. Lewis, and Xue Litai. *Uncertain Partners: Stalin, Mao, and the Korean War* (Stanford, CA: Stanford University Press, 1993). Reveals the bargaining and, ultimately, the hostility between the communist leaders.

Harden, Blaine. *Dispatches from a Fragile Continent* (Boston, MA: Houghton Mifflin, 1990). Washington Post bureau chief in sub-Saharan Africa calls it the way he sees it, and not much is very pleasant or elevating.

Hitchcock, William. *The Struggle for Europe* (New York: Anchor Books, 2003). Excellent, lucid history of postwar Europe, concentrating mostly on political history.

Judt, Tony. *Postwar: A History of Europe since 1945* (New York: Penguin Press, 2005). Comprehensive, masterly survey of the continent, 1945–2004.

Keen, Benjamin. *A History of Latin America* (Boston, MA: Houghton Mifflin, 7th ed., 2004). Good, standard comprehensive coverage. Now expanded into two volumes.

Kenez, Peter. *A History of the Soviet Union from the Beginning to the End* (Cambridge: Cambridge University Press, 1999). A study and evaluation of principal institutions and their impact. Thoughtful analyses and evaluations.

Kennedy, Paul. *The Rise and Fall of the Great Powers* (New York: Random House, 1987). Kennedy focuses on the balance between economic health and military preparedness.

Morris, Benny. *The Birth of the Palestinian Refugee Problem 1947–1949* (Cambridge: Cambridge University Press, 1988). A major revisionist historian indicts the Israelis for driving many Palestinians out of their homes.

Morris, Benny. *Righteous Victims: A History of the Zionist–Arab Conflict, 1881–1999* (New York; Knopf, 1999). Revisionist historian finds plenty of blame to go around for the continuing Arab–Israeli struggle.

Service, Robert. *A History of Twentieth Century Russia* (Cambridge, MA: Harvard University Press, 1997). The story told largely through the actions and statements of Russia's leaders.

Sigmund, Paul, ed. *The Ideologies of the Developing Nations* (New York: Praeger Publishers, 2nd rev. ed., 1972). Excellent selection of observations, analyses, and manifestos by leaders from throughout the third world in its heyday.

Solzhenitsyn, Alexander. *The Gulag Archipelago*, three vols. (New York: Harper and Row, 1974–78). The terrifying revelations of the prison system at the base of Soviet government control of its citizens.

Stavrianos, Leften. *Global Rift* (New York: Morrow, 1981). A left-wing interpretation of the divisions between the rich and poor nations.

Vogel, Ezra. *The Four Little Dragons: The Spread of Industrialization in East Asia* (Cambridge, MA: Harvard University Press, 1991). Korea, Taiwan, Singapore, and Hong Kong demonstrated that countries could leap from the third world to the first. Vogel shows how they did it.

Von Laue, Theodore. *The World Revolution of Westernization* (New York, Oxford University Press, 1987). Sees the Western world as leading the way for everyone to modernization.

Westad, Odd Arne. *The Global Cold War: Third World Interventions and the Making of Our Times* (Cambridge: Cambridge University Press, 2005). Focuses on the destructive connections between Cold War politics and new nations.

ADDITIONAL SOURCES

Andrea, Alfred and James H. Overfield, eds. *The Human Record*, Vol. 2 (Florence, KY: Wadsworth Publishing Col, 6th ed., 2008).

Avishai, Bernard. *The Tragedy of Zionism* (New York: Farrar, Straus, and Giroux, 1985). Covers the impact on the Arab world as well as the Jewish.

Black, Maggie. *A Cause for Our Time: Oxfam, the First Fifty Years* (Oxford: Oxford University Press, 1992). Recounts Oxfam's history, the tough decisions it has made, and its increasing influence in development planning.

Duus, Peter. *Modern Japan* (Boston, MA: Houghton Mifflin, 2nd ed., 1998). Excellent and comprehensive text.

Fanon, Frantz. *The Wretched of the Earth*, trans. Constance Farrington (New York: Grove Press, 1963). Classic statement of the psychological wounds of colonialism. Calls for anticolonial violence as a means of healing.

Hobsbawm, Eric. *The Age of Extremes: A History of the World, 1914–1991* (New York: Pantheon Books, 1994). The dean of living historians surveys the scene politically, economically, and culturally. Engagingly written.

International Institute for Environment and Development and the World Resources Institute. *World Resources 1987* (New York: Basic Books, 1987). Basic report with abundant quantitative information.

Johnson, Hazel and Henry Bernstein, eds. *Third World Lives of Struggle* (London: Heinemann Educational Books, 1982). Marvelous and touching selection of biographical and autobiographical sketches of people's lives with some poetry and interpretive articles as well.

Kochan, Lionel and Richard Abraham. *The Making of Modern Russia* (London: Penguin Books, 1983). Useful on the Khrushchev and Brezhnev years.

Nkrumah, Kwame. *Ghana: The Autobiography of Kwame Nkrumah* (New York: Thomas Nelson and Sons, 1957). Leader of the first black African country to achieve independence from British rule tells his story, up to 1957.

Nugent, Neill. *The Government and Politics of the European Union* (Durham, NC: Duke University Press, 5th ed., 2003). Dry but comprehensive, thorough examination of the major institutions and their significance.

Power, Jonathan. *Like Water on Stone: The Story of Amnesty International* (Boston, MA: Northeastern University Press, 2001). Recounts the struggles of this preeminent international human rights organization.

Schumacher, E.F. *Economics as if People Mattered* (New York: Harper Perennial, 1989). Schumacher's essays in "humanistic economics" are concerned with the human effects of economic systems and advocate for appropriate-scale technologies.

PEARSON
myhistorylab™

For quizzes, flashcards, primary sources, interactive maps, videos, and other activities related to this chapter please go to

www.myhistorylab.com

CHAPTER TWENTY-TWO
China and India
Into the Twenty-First Century

Home to some of the world's most ancient and influential civilizations, China and India are almost worlds in themselves. Both are vast and densely populated countries containing, together, more than a third of the world's population. Both were subject to European colonial domination in the nineteenth and early twentieth centuries. Both gained full political independence in the middle of the twentieth century and both were, and remain, predominantly agrarian countries. Nevertheless they followed very different paths of development. Because of their sheer size, the similarity of many of their circumstances, and the contrast in their decisions on development, we devote a full chapter to them.

China and India: A Comparison

At the turn of the twentieth century China, with 400 million people, contained about 25 per cent of the world's population. The India of the British Empire—which included today's Pakistan and Bangladesh—contained about one-sixth, about 285 million people. Both countries were overwhelmingly agricultural, with populations about 80 to 85 percent rural. Both were vast in territory and densely populated.

Politically, India was ruled as a colony of Britain until 1947. China was not administered directly by foreign powers, but Britain, France, Russia, Germany, and Japan had great economic and cultural control over the huge nation and directly ruled small portions of it. Under British rule, India had a single central administration, despite its diverse ethnicities, languages, religions, castes, and local princes. China, on the other hand, was without an effective central government through most of the first half of the century, suffering both civil war and invasion from Japan.

Both countries sought independence from foreign control. Both began these struggles as protest movements from within their modern sectors, envisioning an industrialized, bureaucratized future, led by professional men trained in modern administrative, educational, journalistic, legal, and military skills. As they began to gain success, however, leaders of the struggle for independence in both countries found this urban- and professional-based organization inadequate. They turned instead to mass movements of the peasantry and common people, who were the overwhelming majority of the population.

India and China attained independent statehood at about the same time. India won independence from Britain in 1947. In China, the communist revolution achieved victory in 1949 and unified almost the entire country (except for Taiwan,

Jawaharlal Nehru and Zhou Enlai, 1954. Prime Minister Nehru (right), accompanied by Chinese foreign minister Zhou Enlai, is cheered by crowds as he arrives on a state visit to Red China.

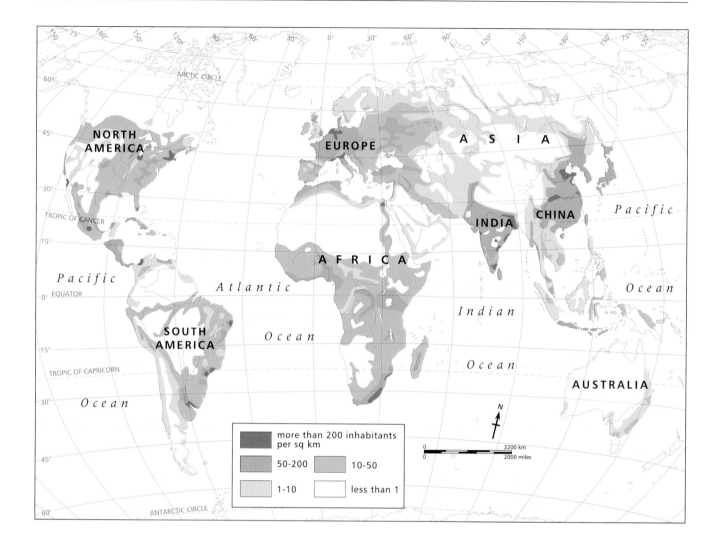

World population distribution 2000. While the bulk of the world's population lives, as always, in coastal regions or along river valleys, the rapid rise in urbanism over the last century has created enormous imbalances as cities attract economic migrants from their hinterlands and from abroad. Some areas, like Europe, are so urbanized that their entire surface has high densities; others, like China and India, are so packed that even rural areas house urban densities. The only areas with low densities are those ecologically difficult for human life—deserts, mountains, and frozen regions.

Hong Kong, and Macao) under its leadership. Then the two countries chose different strategies of development. Influenced by British colonial legacies and by its own heterogeneity, India chose democratic electoral politics and a mixed socialist–capitalist economy, with strong cultural ties to the Western democracies and some military links to the Soviet Union. In China, on the other hand, a victorious communist army asserted strong central control after years of warfare. At first China looked to the Soviet Union for advice and assistance, but soon came into conflict with these mentors on issues of ideology, policy, and national self-interest. Despite the central role of the peasantry in the struggles for independence, both countries quickly turned toward developing their cities and industries.

The large rural populations in both countries, however, made industrialization along Western lines, based on smaller populations and urban settings, difficult. They turned instead to models of technology that were appropriate for their populations and the rural conditions. Often relying on models of development that were different from those used in the West, both countries have become formidable competitors with Europe and the United States in the twenty-first century.

China's Revolutions

China fell into political and military chaos after the 1911 revolution that ended its 2,000-year-old empire. Two groups emerged from these divisions: the Guomindang (GMD, National People's Party), led first by Sun Yat-sen (1866–1925) and then by Chiang Kai-shek (Jiang Jieshi, 1887–1975), and the communists, commanded by Mao Zedong (1893–1976).

Chiang began as a military commander and later sought to build a government based on his GMD party. Mao began as a Communist Party organizer and later built an army, mostly of guerrilla warriors. Both leaders revered Sun Yat-sen and accepted his "Three People's Principles" as guidelines for their political and economic programs, but they interpreted Sun's teachings quite differently. Where Chiang emphasized the role of businessmen, international alliances, and individual initiative, Mao stressed the peasant farmer, community organization, and indigenous institutions. The two men and their parties fought for control in a bitter civil war that festered for a quarter century following Sun's death in 1925. Both learned that "in a country ruled and plundered by marauding warlord armies, it was naked military power that was crucial in determining the direction of political events" (Meisner, p. 21). In Mao's blunt words: "Political power grows out of the barrel of a gun."

Chiang Kai-shek and the Guomindang

Chiang had studied in a Japanese military academy, fought in the 1911 revolution to overthrow the Manchu government, and rose to command China's own new Whampoa military academy near Guangzhou, established with Soviet financing. After Sun's death, he succeeded to the leadership of the GMD.

Chiang courted diverse, apparently contradictory constituencies. A staunch advocate of the neo-Confucian New Life movement in the 1930s, Chiang wrote *China's Destiny* in 1943 to reaffirm the conservative virtues of China's indigenous, hierarchical, genteel culture. Yet he also became a Methodist, as Sun had. Also like Sun, Chiang married a Chinese Christian woman and valued the contributions of foreign Christians in China's economic modernization. He maintained a wide and diverse array of close personal, professional, and financial connections with Shanghai underworld figures, Soviet Comintern agents, Western businessmen, and Christian missionaries.

Foreign powers in the treaty ports monitored China's shifting fortunes with considerable self-interest. By 1931 foreigners had invested $3.25 billion in China. Foreign loans financed Chinese railways and heavy industry, and foreigners held 75 percent of all investments in shipping, almost 50 percent of the cotton spindles, and 80 to 90 percent of the coal mines. Through the early 1920s, the politicization and unionization of industrial workers encouraged many strikes; the employers, many of them foreigners, responded violently. These employers wanted a compliant government that would help them break the strikes and keep the workers in line. They believed Chiang to be their man and they provided large loans to keep his government afloat.

Foreign-based Christian missionaries and educational institutions also supported the GMD, attracted partly by Chiang's own Christian affiliation. The YMCA movement claimed 54,000 members in 1922. In the early 1920s some 12,000 Christian missionaries served in China. Christian and foreign colleges enrolled 4,000 of the 35,000 students in Chinese colleges in 1922. Nine percent of their students were women. China's universities incorporated the study of Western culture and literature, and Western academic luminaries (as well as the Nobel-laureate poet, Rabindranath Tagore of India) toured and lectured widely.

AT A GLANCE: CHINA AND INDIA

DATE	CHINA	INDIA
1900	• Boxer Rebellion against Western influence is suppressed by foreign troops (1900)	• Mohandas Karamchand Gandhi publishes *Hind Swaraj*, or *Indian Home Rule* (1909)
1910	• 1911 Revolution ends Manchu dynasty and 2,000 years of imperial rule • Yuan Shihkai elected premier (1911); dies 1916 • Warlords battle throughout China • May 4th Movement (1919)	• Gandhi returns from South Africa and establishes new ashram in Ahmedabad (1915) • Government of India Act creates dual British/Indian government (1919) • British crack down on freedom of the press and assembly in the Rowlatt Acts (1919) • Amritsar (Jalianwala Bagh) massacre (1919)
1920	• Chinese Communist Party formed (1921) • Sun Yat-sen dies (1925) • Guomindang (GMD) and Communists vie for power (1925–49) • Chiang Kai-shek captures Beijing (1927–28); rules from Nanjing • Mao's Report on Hunan Peasant Movement (1927)	• Non-cooperation campaign boycotts British interests (1920–22) • Gandhi fasts for 21 days to promote Hindu–Muslim unity (1924)
1930	• Mao Zedong leads Communists on the Long March, from Jiangxi to Yan'an (1934) • Japanese seize Manchuria (1931) and go on to invade China proper (1937) • Communists kidnap Chiang to gain cooperation in the war against Japan (1936)	• Salt March campaign (1930–32) • Gandhi outflanks socialists by persuading Jawaharlal Nehru to postpone land redistribution • Congress appoints National Planning Commission (1938)
1940	• Japan surrenders; civil war resumes (1945) • Foundation of the Communist People's Republic of China (1949) • Foreigners expelled (1949)	• "Quit India" campaign (1942) • Independence from Great Britain is accompanied by partition of the subcontinent (1947)
1950	• China invades and colonizes Tibet (1950) • Korean War (1950–53) • "100 Flowers Campaign" briefly permits some freedom of expression (1956–57) • Mao initiates "Great Leap Forward" experiment (1958–60)	• Policy of protective discrimination reserves jobs for untouchable castes (1955) • Hindu Marriage Act (1955) and Hindu Succession Act (1956) increase rights for women. Muslims are not affected
1960	• Diplomatic relations with Russia are severed (1961) • Sino-Indian border war (1962) • Cultural Revolution initiates party purges and reignites revolutionary zeal; formation of Red Guard (1966)	• Death of Nehru (1964)
1970	• China joins United Nations (1971) • Groundbreaking visit to China by President Nixon (1972) • Mao dies; "Gang of Four" arrested (1976) • Deng Xiaoping comes to power; economic liberalization (1979) • One family, one child policy (1980)	• Civil war leads to creation of Bangladesh on land of East Pakistan (1971) • Prime Minister Indira Gandhi asserts dictatorial powers during "Emergency Rule" (1975–77) • Policy of forced sterilization (1975–77)
1980	• China joins World Bank and the International Monetary Fund (1980) • Students demonstrating in Tiananmen Square are killed by soldiers (1989)	• Indira Gandhi assassinated (1984)
1990	• Hong Kong reverts to Chinese sovereignty after 155 years as a British colony (1997) • Macao returned to China by Portugal (1999) • China voted "most favored nation" trading status by U.S. (2000)	• Rajiv Gandhi assassinated (1991) • Prime Minister P.V. Narasimha Rao lowers tariffs and begins to welcome foreign investments (1991) • Pakistan and India test nuclear devices in violation of international treaties (1998) • Population reaches one billion (1999)

With the support of Western business and cultural leaders, and of the Soviet Comintern as well, Chiang undertook to defeat the warlords and reestablish a viable central government under his own control. Through the great northern expedition from Guangzhou, Chiang captured Beijing in 1927–28, established his own capital in Nanjing on the lower Yangzi River, and began to consolidate GMD power over China.

Mao Zedong and Peasant Revolt

Mao Zedong, Sun's other principal successor, shared his goals of a strong, united, independent China and the improvement of the people's livelihood, but his background was quite different from Sun's and from Chiang's.

First, even though Mao, too, participated in the 1911 revolution, it had ended by the time he was 18. Second, Mao's experience was limited to China. Although he read widely in Western as well as Chinese literature and philosophy, his first travel outside China, a visit to the Soviet Union, came only in 1949. Third, Mao had little experience of the Western business and missionary establishments in China. His own formative experiences were in the countryside and in formal educational institutions. Compared with both Sun and Chiang, Mao cared little for China's reputation in the West but much for the quality of life of the Chinese peasant. He had grown up on his father's farm in Hunan province, where he learned at first hand of the exploitation of the peasant. He viewed his father as one of the exploiters.

By 1919, Mao had come to study at Beijing (Peking) University, just as China's resentment against foreign imperialism was boiling over. The peace treaties of World War I assigned Germany's holdings in the Shandong Peninsula of north China to Japan rather than returning them to China. Enraged students created the "May 4th Movement," a powerful and enduring protest against China's international humiliation, the apparent irrelevance of its historical traditions, and its cultural links to the West. The May 4th Movement helped to sow the seeds of the Chinese Communist Party (CCP), which came to fruition in 1921. At the time, Mao was a participant in the Marxist study group of Li Dazhao, chief librarian of Beijing University and one of the founders of the CCP. In a statement quite unusual for a Chinese intellectual, Li had already proclaimed the importance of the peasantry and called on the university students to help them to mobilize:

> Our China is a rural nation and most of the laboring class is made up of peasants. If they are not liberated then our whole nation will not be liberated. … Go out and develop them and cause them to … demand liberation. (Spence, p. 308)

When Mao first joined the party he began organizing workers in the industrial plants of the Wuhan region, but in 1925 he was reassigned to peasant organization in his native Hunan. Despite the orthodox Marxist doctrines of the CCP's Comintern advisers, in Hunan Mao came to see the rural peasantry, rather than the urban proletariat, as China's revolutionary vanguard. He abandoned the emphasis on large-scale industrial planning and sought instead local solutions to local problems through locally developed, appropriate rural technologies. Mao's 1927 report on the Hunan peasant movement updated Li's rural emphasis, adding large doses of communist rhetoric:

> the broad peasant masses have risen to fulfill their historic mission … the democratic forces in the rural areas have risen to overthrow the rural feudal power. The patriarchal-feudal class of local bullies, bad gentry, and lawless landlords has formed the basis of autocratic government for thousands of years, the cornerstone of imperialism,

KEY TERM

soviet Chinese soviets, governing councils made up of peasants, were modelled in part on Russian examples, but they focused on rural, rather than urban, administration. Founded during the revolutionary movement, they also provided guerrilla warriors for the campaigns.

warlordism and corrupt officialdom. To overthrow this feudal power is the real objective of the national revolution … The leadership of the poor peasants is absolutely necessary. Without the poor peasants there can be no revolution. (de Bary, p. 869)

The peasants had to use their strength to overthrow the authority of the landlords. This revolution required violence.

While Mao was organizing rural peasants in the 1920s, Chiang was massacring the core of the revolutionary urban proletariat. As he completed the northern expedition and consolidated his control over the warlords, he turned, in alliance with the international business community, and without excessive objection from the Soviet Comintern, to murdering thousands of communist workers in the industrialized cities of Shanghai, Wuhan, and Guangzhou in the spring of 1927. In Changsha, local military leaders joined with the GMD and local landlords to slaughter thousands of peasants who had recently expropriated the land they worked from its legal owners. By the summer of 1928, only 32,000 union members in all of China remained loyal to the Communist Party. By 1929, only three percent of party members were proletarians. Mao's peasant alternative was, of necessity, the communists' last resort.

When the GMD put down the Hunan Autumn Harvest Uprising in 1927, Mao's core group retreated to the border area between Hunan and Jiangzi. Other communist leaders, driven from the cities, joined them in this rural area. They instituted **soviets**, local communist governments that redistributed land, introduced improved farming methods, and instituted new educational systems to spread literacy along with political indoctrination. They recruited and trained a guerrilla army. Mao himself formulated its tactics: "The enemy advances, we retreat; the enemy camps, we harass; the enemy tires, we attack; the enemy retreats, we pursue" (Spence, p. 375).

The guerrillas could exist only with the cooperation of the peasantry, whom they wished to mobilize. Mao therefore ordered them to treat the peasants with respect: "Be courteous and polite to the people and help them when you can… Be honest in all transactions with the peasants… Pay for all articles purchased" (Snow, p. 176).

Gender Issues in the Revolution

Feminism had begun to flourish in China by the 1920s with the formation of such organizations as the Women's Suffrage Association and the Women's Rights League. Their constituency was mostly Western-influenced urban intellectuals. These women and men read magazines like *New Youth*, which criticized Confucius for his emphasis on patriarchy and obedience to authority. They translated and published Henrik Ibsen's feminist play *A Doll's House* in 1918. Ba Jinn's novel *Family*, one of the key works of China's reformist New Culture Movement, transplanted Ibsen's advocacy of women's equality and independence into a modern Chinese setting. Margaret Sanger, the American advocate of contraception, toured and lectured throughout China in 1922. There were also some 1,500,000 women working outside their homes for pay in light industrial factories, mostly textiles, in China's cities. Women's rights were already advancing in China's coastal metropolises; Mao now refocused feminist attention on the countryside and the peasantry as well:

the authority of the husband … has always been comparatively weak among the poor peasants, because the poor peasant women, compelled for financial reasons to take more part in manual work than women of the wealthier classes, have obtained more right to speak and more power to make decisions in family affairs. In recent years the rural economy has become even more bankrupt and the basic condition for men's domination over women has already been undermined. And now, with the rise of the peasant movement, women in many places have set out immediately to organize the rural women's association; the opportunity has come for them to lift up their heads, and the authority of the husband is tottering more and more every day. (de Bary, p. 872)

Communist policies took two complementary directions. The first, and more effective, restructured the labor and military forces to give more scope and power to women. Building the Chinese soviets and fighting guerrilla battles required the support of every available resource. While women did not usually participate in warfare directly, the increased need for production and personnel brought them out of the house into new jobs, effectively raising their status.

The Long March and the Communist Triumph

Chiang sent five successive military expeditions against the Jiangzi soviet, beginning with 100,000 men and leading up to one million. By 1934, the communists could no longer hold out. Mao led some 80,000 men and 35 women out of the siege and began the Long March, a 370-day, 6,000-mile strategic retreat, by foot, under constant bombardment and attack from Chiang's forces, across rivers, mountain ranges, marshes, and grasslands, to a final new base camp in Yan'an. Some 20,000 men finally

The Long March, 1934–35. The Long March, actually a strategic retreat of some six thousand miles from Communist headquarters in southeast China to a new base in northwest China, provided the founding legend of the Chinese Communist movement, a tale of daring, resourcefulness, and guerrilla warfare. Along the route of the march, the leaders organized villagers into soviets, local government groups that redistributed land and set up educational and health facilities. Here leaders of the march address their followers in Shensi Province, towards the end of the march.

arrived in Yan'an, of whom about half had marched since the beginning; the rest had joined *en route*. The courage, comradeship, commitment, and idealism of this march, in the face of seemingly insurmountable natural obstacles and enemy harassment, were the formative experience of a generation of Chinese communist leaders. At the front, Mao now became the unquestioned leader of the movement, party, and army.

The Communist Revolution in China. Chinese communists and nationalists (GMD) united briefly to subdue the warlord factions that emerged after the collapse of the Manchu (Qing) dynasty, and to consolidate a national government. After 1927 Nationalist repression forced the communists to retreat to remote areas, focusing in the northwest after the Long March of 1934–35, where guerrilla warfare continued. With the Japanese invasion of China proper in 1937, China was torn by both international and civil war. After Japan's defeat in 1945, the communists turned to defeating the GMD as well.

The Yan'an Soviet. In remote, impoverished Yan'an, Mao established his capital and rebuilt his soviet structure, nurturing his army and inducting its soldiers into agricultural assistance work; redistributing land; encouraging handicrafts; and establishing newspapers and schools, an arts and literature academy, and medical programs for training paramedical **barefoot doctors**. The Chinese communist program developed more fully here: a peasant-centered economy, administered and aided by guerrilla soldiers, capped by a dictatorial but comparatively benevolent communist leadership, encouraging literacy accompanied by indoctrination in communist ideology. Tension built up, however, between the advocates of ideological goals and the proponents of practical implementation, between being "Red" and being "expert."

Cooperation with the GMD. Meanwhile, Mao wished to join forces with Chiang to unite China against the foreigner. By comparison, Chiang seemed less nationalistic. He appeared willing to compromise with the Japanese, and more eager to pursue the Chinese communists than to fight the foreign invaders. In the "Xi'an incident" of 1936, dissident generals kidnapped Chiang and threatened to kill him if he did not join more vigorously in the fight against the Japanese. Subsequently, Chiang moved toward temporary cooperation with the communists.

In 1937, the Japanese invaded China proper. At first, the Japanese hoped to rule China with the help of Chinese collaborators, as they had Manchuria, but their cruelty in the capture of Nanjing in December 1937 backfired (see Chapter Twenty). Instead of collapsing, the Chinese resistance became more resolute. The communists fought a rearguard guerrilla war from their northern base in Shaanxi, while Chiang led a **scorched-earth retreat** to a new headquarters far up the Yangzi River in Chongqing. Soldiers and civilians endured dreadful suffering.

The GMD Retreats to Taiwan. By the early 1940s, nationalist cooperation began to unravel as communists and GMD forces jockeyed for temporary power and future position. Following the defeat of Japan in 1945, full-scale civil war between the GMD and the communists resumed. The U.S. extended help to Chiang in training his troops, airlifting them to critical military locations, and delivering military supplies. The Soviet Union, fighting for its life against Germany, stayed out of the conflict against Japan until the last week of the war. Then it entered Manchuria, carrying off a great deal of that region's military and industrial equipment to the Soviet Union, while turning over some of it to the Chinese communists. As China's civil war continued after 1945, communist forces in many parts of the country, well disciplined and warmly supported by peasants, defeated the ill-disciplined and ill-provisioned GMD forces, whose rations and materials were often sold off for private profit, without ever reaching them. By the fall of 1949, the communists had driven the GMD completely out of mainland China to the island of Taiwan. Selfishly, the GMD occupied and took over houses and businesses of Taiwanese who already lived there. They claimed that their government in Taiwan was the true China. They dreamed of someday recapturing, reuniting with, and returning to the mainland.

The People's Republic of China

On the mainland, the new rulers surrounding Mao modeled much of their government on their experiences during the Long March and the Yan'an soviet. They returned to these experiences for inspiration in difficult times as long as they lived. Their principal fears were of foreign domination, internal chaos, and the lingering power of the wealthy urban classes and the large-scale rural landholders.

barefoot doctors Paramedical personnel trained in simple, basic levels of medicine and dispatched to work in rural areas, where virtually no professionally trained doctors chose to practice.

scorched-earth retreat A retreat in which everything left behind that might be useful to the enemy is destroyed.

Revolutionary Policies

Mao's policy goals for the new government included the redistribution of land;
protection of women's rights to hold land; implementation of appropriate technology;
the production and equal distribution of basic necessities for all; and universal literacy.
The government mobilized tightknit, local, social networks not only to suppress
such vices as opium addiction and prostitution but also to enforce rigid political
indoctrination and conformity. It encouraged family members to inform against one
another in cases of opposition to the new government and it employed psychological
coercion—"**brain washing**"—to extract confessions of political deviance.

Land redistribution was a top priority. During this class revolution, perhaps half
the peasantry of China received at least some benefits while as many as one million
landlords were killed. The communist government at first invited the cooperation
of businessmen, both Chinese and foreign. But policies changed abruptly as China
entered the Korean War in October 1950. Threats, expropriation, and accusations of
espionage—sometimes justified—against businessmen and Christian missionaries
forced almost all foreigners to leave China by the end of 1950. Numerous campaigns
against counterrevolutionaries; the confiscation and redistribution of private property;
thousands of executions; intensive public, group pressure to elicit confessions from
those perceived as enemies of the revolution; and regular confrontations between
workers and owners destroyed the capitalist sector in China. Pressured by the United
States, many countries refused to recognize the new government. The government of
the USSR, on the other hand, maintained a strong alliance.

Communist policies on urbanization and industrialization were ambivalent. The
communists had come to power as an anti-urban, peasant movement. The large
cities, especially Shanghai, had fostered the foreign enclaves, extraterritorial law,
and colonial behavior that flagrantly insulted the Chinese in their own country,
but they also housed China's industrial base, military technology, administration,
and cultural life. Although the government attempted to limit immigration to the
cities, newcomers from the countryside continued to arrive steadily, if slowly.

Trial of a landlord. Most such
trials ended with a confession and
a promise to reform; some ended
with a bullet for the accused. In its
first moves toward collectivization,
the communist government
instituted a number of land reforms
that gave the land to the peasants
who worked it and did away with
the landlords—literally.

China's population, which had been 10.6 percent urban in 1949, reached 17.4 percent urban in 1976, an increase from 57 million to 163 million people.

Militarily, the communists extolled the spirit of the guerrilla warrior over the power of high-tech weaponry. They taunted America, the world's most heavily armed country, as unwilling or unable to deploy its vast arsenal, especially its nuclear weapons, in combat. Nevertheless, China also bought, produced, or purloined up-to-date military technology. In 1964, it exploded its first atomic bomb; in the mid-1970s it followed with hydrogen bombs; in 1980 it tested missiles with a range of 7,000 miles; and, in 1981, it launched three space satellites.

"Let a Hundred Flowers Bloom." Economically, China adopted a five-year plan based on the Soviet model (see Chapter Nineteen). It called for multiplying the value of industrial output between 1952 and 1957 almost two and a half times, and claimed at the end to have overachieved the target by 22 percent. By the end of the plan, even democracy seemed a possibility. In 1956–57, Mao's call, "Let a hundred flowers bloom, let a hundred schools of thought contend," opened the gates to public expression and even criticism of government. In Beijing, students and others posted their thoughts on what became known as Democracy Wall. By late 1957, however,

KEY TERM

"Hundred Flowers" campaign An invitation by Mao Zedong to the Chinese people in 1956–57 to express their ideas freely and openly. At first viewed as an invitation to democracy; later, after many who spoke out were jailed and punished, it came to be seen as a well-laid trap.

HOW DO WE KNOW?

A Journalist–Activist Responds to the "Hundred Flowers" Campaign

When Mao introduced the **"Hundred Flowers" campaign**, journalist Liu Binyan praised him for his democracy. As he saw the reaction of the party, however, and the subsequent use of the campaign as a means of identifying and punishing critics of the government, Liu came to see the entire movement as a trap. Liu Binyan became one of the most prominent and most active of the opponents of the communist government of China. Not all historians agree with this assessment of Mao's motives, although the results were clear.

This excerpt is both a primary document, as the record of a participant, and a secondary document, as a later assessment of a previous event.

I do not remember a moment in my life more exhilarating than when Mao Zedong's February 1957 speech to the State Council was released. My estimation of him soared to sublime heights. At China Youth News the response was equally enthusiastic; it seemed as if we were at the beginning of a new era in China … In that speech, Mao announced that dogmatism should not be mistaken for Marxism; he reiterated his policy of letting "a hundred flowers bloom and a hundred schools of thought contend"; he advocated open criticism and reiterated that senior party leaders should not be exempt from criticism. As for strikes by workers and students— unprecedented since the founding of the People's Republic and now taken seriously for the first time—he said the right way of dealing with them was not by force or coercion but by overcoming bureaucratism.

These issues were exactly the unspoken ones that had been weighing on me for the last few years—special privileges with

party ranks, bureaucratism, and dogmatic tendencies. Now my disquiet had been dispelled as if by magic. The political climate in Beijing cleared up; the mood of intellectuals brightened, everything seemed to take on a rosy hue. Mao was virtually advocating more democracy and liberalization in matters of ideology; as a journalist and writer, I now felt I had a free hand in pursuing my vocation.

[Liu then describes meetings with local party officials that demonstrated that many did not interpret Mao's words as he did. They saw any approval of open expression to be very limited, at most.]

Thirty years later, I reread Mao's speech (the original version, not the one revised for publication) and realized that at the time I had been too preoccupied with his main drift to detect hints of other tendencies hidden between the lines. For instance, he did not mince words over Stalin's dogmatism, but then insisted that Stalin must be assessed on the "three-seven" principle—that is, seven parts merit to three parts fault. Again Mao considered "democracy" as basically a tool to mobilize the people for the Party's own ends. (Liu, pp. 69–70)

- Which of Liu's points make his document a primary source document? Which of his points make it a secondary source document?
- Why did Liu find Mao's campaign to let a "hundred flowers bloom," surprising?
- What led Liu to change his mind in assessing the purpose of Mao's "hundred flowers bloom" campaign?

Steel furnace, Shiu Shin, China, 1958. The French photographer Henri Cartier-Bresson traveled to Shiu Shin to capture and record the life of its communes. Some 310,000 inhabitants were divided into seven popular communes, or production units. Some were responsible for "backyard," very small-scale, local, steel furnaces. China's mobilization of its masses of rural population for undertaking industrial production was extraordinary, a continuation of the ethic of its Communist, rural revolution, but the quality of the steel was low.

fearing uncontrolled, growing protest, the government reversed its policies. It jailed protesters, sent them to labor camps, and exiled them to remote rural farms. Many observers felt the entire experiment had been a trap to expose and apprehend critics of the regime.

The Great Leap Forward. Increasingly threatened by an inability to feed its rapidly expanding urban populations, the government implemented the **Great Leap Forward**, "sending down" city people to work in villages, grouping almost all of rural China into communes, virtually shutting down whatever small private enterprises had survived, and attempting to downscale and disperse industry by establishing local, low-technology enterprises, referred to generically as "backyard steel mills." The idea was that committed communists could manufacture, in small-scale production units, goods normally produced only in large-scale factories. The enterprises generally failed. The Great Leap Forward, administered by powerful, distant government officials, who attempted to restructure the entire economy of the nation according to communist ideology, led to economic catastrophe, including millions of deaths by starvation.

The Cultural Revolution. In the face of these policy failures, Mao began to silence resistance. For a few years, the government had relaxed its economic and social controls, but in 1966 it reinstated even more extreme ideological and economic policies in the Great Proletarian **Cultural Revolution**. Mao sought through this revolution to purge the party of time-serving bureaucrats and to reignite China's revolutionary fervor. Those who responded most enthusiastically were the armed forces and the students, who, with Mao's encouragement, organized themselves into the Red Guard. Students denounced their teachers and party officials squelched freedom of expression. Professors and intellectuals were exiled to remote villages and forced to undertake hard manual labor.

The Long March was now 30 years in the past, yet nostalgia for its ideological zeal continued to motivate China's aging leaders. Mao was venerated as their last hope to restore the intensity of those early days of the revolution. Millions of copies of *The*

KEY TERMS

Great Leap Forward The policy of the Chinese communist government in the late 1950s of building China's economy on the basis of small-scale, localized production in rural communities.

Cultural Revolution The policy of the Chinese communist government, 1966–76, of basing its economy on rural productivity and quelling the intellectual and cultural life of the cities, subordinating freedom of thought completely in favor of communist ideology.

Quotations of Chairman Mao, often called the "Little Red Book" because of its size and the color of its cover, were published. These were circulated and read publicly throughout the country to audiences who were forced to listen. Economic chaos and starvation on the one hand and the total stifling and destruction of intellectual and academic life on the other brought China's economic and cultural life to a standstill.

Recovery. As the damage became clearly visible, China reversed its policy in yet another example of *fang–zhou*, "loosening up–tightening down." The People's Liberation Army was given the task of suppressing the Red Guards, the youth and student cadres who had wreaked chaos in the name of Mao. The government sought new international recognition, most dramatically through the normalization of relations with the United States in 1972. Domestically, attention refocused on restoring industrial productivity. "Between 1950 and 1977 industrial output grew at an average annual rate of 13.5 percent … the highest rate of all developing or developed major nations of the world during the time, and a more rapid pace than achieved by any country during any comparable period of rapid industrialization in modern world history" (Meisner, pp. 436–37). By 1980, China was producing more steel than Britain or France.

On the other hand, agriculture was upended, collectivized, and relatively neglected in terms of investment. The agonizingly slow growth of agriculture could barely keep pace with population growth. By the time Mao died in 1976, China was ready for a dramatic change in leadership and policies.

Women in the People's Republic of China

Throughout the revolution, Mao had stressed the rights of women. After the communist victory in 1949, the new government issued a new marriage law that forbade arranged marriages, prohibited marriage contracts for the purchase and sale of wives, and encouraged free choice of marriage partners. This law met strong resistance. Men who had already bought their wives objected; so did mothers-in-law, who ruled over each household's domestic labor force. The traditional Chinese family provided for old age security, child-care, medical facilities, and the production and consumption of food, clothing, and shelter. The new communist marriage law seemed to threaten this structure without providing any alternative. The law was not widely enforced. In addition, the leadership of the party remained conspicuously male.

Other laws in the new communist nation banned concubinage, footbinding, prostitution, and trafficking in women. A 1953 law gave women the vote. Beginning in 1955, the government emphasized the importance of family planning; this led, in 1979, to a policy of limiting families, especially in urban areas, to only one child. Liberation of women was also seen as a means of expanding the labor force. In 1949 only 7 percent of the workforce was female; by 1982 the figure had reached 43 percent. About 70 percent of women worked (although in an overwhelmingly rural society, where women have always worked, all these official figures must be interpreted with caution). Declaring that "women hold up half the sky," the communist government set out to wipe out centuries of exploitation.

Chinese woman with bound feet. From the early years of the twentieth century urban women had begun to leave the confines of home to work in light industry. The move from home to workplace gave women higher status, which was further strengthened by the reforms of the communist government when it came to power. The abandonment of foot binding in all but the most outlying areas of China did much to enhance the freedom of women.

In practice, the task was not so simple. Historic patterns of male dominance persisted. The overwhelming majority of communist officials were men, and while they legislated better conditions for women, it was they, not the women, who formulated and promulgated the legislation. Decisions to end patriarchy were made patriarchally, and therefore had limited effects in practice. Men continued to feel that they should make the major decisions in the household, the workplace, and the political arena. Women in the workforce found that they now had the double burden of a day job outside the home and housework inside the home; this housework was not equally shared. Sixty to 70 percent of the unemployed were women. In 1980 literacy among males had reached 78 percent; among females, it was 60 percent.

Most glaring of all the inequalities was the ratio of men to women. Already 108:100 in 1981, it rose to 110:100 by 2000 and 118:100 in 2005. In a situation where only one child was permitted, families were choosing to abort female fetuses, or to kill newborn female babies, or to allow young girls to perish through persistent neglect of their health needs, in preference to males.

The documentary film *Small Happiness*, directed by Carma Hinton and Richard Gordon in 1984, as one part of the *Long Bow Trilogy* on "One Village in China," presents perspectives on gender issues from just one village. Nevertheless, the conversations recorded among the women of the village provide profound insights. The oldest among them had her feet bound years before, but that procedure is now outlawed and defunct. Babies, whether male or female, are no longer killed because there is not enough food for them. Contraception is practiced universally. Agriculture is becoming more of a female occupation, as many men travel to cities in search of work. The men who remain do not do housework. The old proverb still endures: "To give birth to a boy is considered a big happiness. To give birth to a girl is a small happiness."

China's International Relations

In the first decade of communist rule, China's chief ally was the USSR, which helped the new communist state design its five-year plan, train and provision its armed forces, and build factories, transportation facilities, urban neighborhoods, and administrative centers. But in the mid-1950s, the two countries quarreled bitterly over ideology. Replaying the scenario of 1927, China once again found the USSR becoming too moderate politically. The two giant countries even contested their mutual borders in central Asia in armed skirmishes. In 1961, they severed diplomatic relations. Only after 1985 were relations between the two countries normalized. Still, the two powers remained wary and armed across thousands of miles of shared borders.

The United States. China's relations with the United States began in cold hostility and hot war. For almost two decades after 1949, America lamented and resented its "loss" of China. America continued to support Chiang's forces on Taiwan after 1949, mostly because it wanted to combat communism. The U.S. lobbied to keep the People's Republic of China out of the UN; the government of Taiwan, the Americans asserted, represented the Chinese people. From 1950 to 1953, America and China fought each other for control of the Korean peninsula, America in alliance with the government of South Korea, China in alliance with the North. America suffered some 27,000 war dead; estimates of Chinese dead ranged from 150,000 to 600,000.

In the 1970s, however, the bitter hostility melted. Mao and his new advisers, retreating from the economic catastrophe of the Cultural Revolution, sought assistance from abroad. Meanwhile, the United States, favoring more pragmatic

President Nixon meets with Communist Party Chairman Mao Zedong in Beijing, during his groundbreaking 1972 visit to China. Alarmed by aggressive Soviet actions in Czechoslovakia, China and the United States took steps to improve their diplomatic relations. Four years after the Sino–Western rapprochement, begun in 1971, foreign trade with China had tripled, and by 1980, China had joined the IMF and the World Bank.

policies, did not stand in the way of China's joining the UN in 1971. In 1972, President Nixon visited China. Full diplomatic relations were established between the two countries in 1979.

China's Neighbors. Within its own area of the world, China for 2,000 years has viewed itself as the dominant, central power, and has sought that recognition from its neighbors, with mixed success. In many of these countries, China was a feared and resented neighbor, not an uncommon relationship for a regional superpower. China invaded Tibet in 1950 and forced the Dalai Lama, its most important spiritual and temporal leader, to flee and to seek refuge in India in 1959. In Cambodia, it backed the murderous Khmer Rouge Party and its leader Pol Pot in the vicious civil wars through the 1970s, even committing troops briefly to combat.

On the other hand, the astonishing economic recovery of Japan after World War II challenged China's leadership position. Japan was advancing rapidly to become the world's second largest economy while China lagged far behind. China's authorities were forced to rethink their economic policies.

Moreover, in several nearby states, Chinese minorities were viewed with suspicion as possible subversive infiltrators for the Chinese nation and the Communist Party. In 1965, as Indonesian nationalism turned against them, thousands of Chinese were murdered in Indonesia, and hundreds of thousands more were exiled.

India. China's relationship with India has been complex. When India became independent in 1947 and China completed its revolution in 1949, the two nations chose dramatically different social, political, and economic paths. At the Bandung Conference of nonaligned countries, in 1955, both offered leadership to nations newly emerging from colonialism. China became a model for agrarian guerrilla

Ping pong diplomacy. China's ping pong team was invited to America by the National Ping Pong Association, U.S., April 1972. In this friendly match, a Chinese and an American ping pong player are on the same side, a symbol of the new friendship between China and America.

revolt throughout Southeast Asia and beyond, while India's nonviolent path inspired others, especially in black Africa.

India did not protest China's takeover of Tibet in 1950. It did, however, offer refuge to the Dalai Lama and his followers when hundreds of thousands of them fled a renewed communist crackdown in 1959. India consistently backed China's petition to enter the UN, even when differences over border demarcations led to open warfare in 1962. The Chinese decisively defeated Indian troops, penetrated through the mountain passes to within striking distance of India's heartland, and then withdrew voluntarily to the borders they had claimed. India's first test of nuclear devices in 1974 represented, in part, an attempt to catch up to the military power of her larger neighbor.

Postrevolutionary China

China demonstrated the inevitability of each huge nation of the world finding its own developmental path. China might for a time take guidance from one foreign ideology or another, and it might enter into alliances with various powers at one time or another, but finally it sought a path appropriate to its own size, geography, power, technology, and historical experience. Chinese at home and abroad, including many who disapproved of current government policies, took pride in the newfound unity, power, and independence of their nation. China might make mistakes, but they would be its own mistakes. Leaving behind a century of humiliating colonialism and devastating international and civil war, China sought to establish stability and ideological purity. Soon it would seek a larger place in the world.

India's Struggle for Independence

With the exception of the border war in 1962, India and China usually regarded each other as friendly rivals. Both were cautious in their approach to Western powers, their former imperial masters. Both set out to provide new models of development for countries emerging from colonial rule. These models differed because the countries' colonial experiences differed. Nevertheless, in India, as in China, the modern movement for independence began within the educated, intellectual, urban classes before expanding to include the peasantry. In India this expansion was led by Mahatma Gandhi, and focused primarily on the upper levels of peasantry.

First Steps Toward Self Rule

Established in 1885, at British initiative, as a vent for Indian nationalist criticism, the Indian National Congress led the resistance to British rule in the early twentieth century. The Congress' leadership was concentrated in the hands of men who were educated in British ways, through British-run schools, sometimes in Britain itself. More than a third of its members were trained in the legal profession. In 1835, T.B. Macaulay, legal adviser to the British government of India, had declared the intent of the government's educational policies to create a class "Indian in blood and colour, but English in taste, in opinions, in morals, and in intellect" (Hay, p. 31); the Congress leadership reflected the results. It approached government respectfully, proclaiming allegiance to the British monarchy, and framed its petitions—for representation on government councils, for example—in constitutional forms.

INDIAN INDEPENDENCE—KEY FIGURES

Rabindranath Tagore (1861–1941) Indian poet, painter, and musician from Bengal, who translated his own verse into English. He received the Nobel prize for literature in 1913. An ardent nationalist and advocate of social reform, he resigned his knighthood (granted in 1918) in protest against British repression in India.

Mohandas Karamchand Gandhi (1869–1948) Indian political and spiritual leader, who fought against anti-Indian discrimination in South Africa before returning to India in 1914. He became leader of the Indian National Congress in the 1920s. Gandhi maintained nonviolent ideals through civil disobedience campaigns and was imprisoned in 1922, 1932, 1933, and 1942 for anti-British activities. He played a crucial part in the negotiations leading to independence.

Muhammad Ali Jinnah (1876–1948) The founder of Pakistan. A member of the Indian National Congress, at first he advocated cooperation between Hindus and Muslims. Later, he transformed the Muslim League from a cultural to a political organization. In 1940, Jinnah demanded the partition of British India into separate Muslim and Hindu states. Jinnah achieved his goal, but he had to accept a smaller state than he had demanded. He became governor-general of Pakistan in 1947 and died in office.

Jawaharlal Nehru (1889–1964) Indian nationalist politician and prime minister, 1947–64. Before partition, he led the socialist wing of the Congress Party and was regarded as second only to Gandhi. Between 1921 and 1945, he was imprisoned by the British nine times for political activities. As prime minister he developed the idea of nonalignment (neutrality toward the major powers), established an industrial base, and sustained a parliamentary democracy based on the rule of law.

Subhas Chandra Bose (1897–1945) Indian nationalist leader (known as "Netaji"—"Respected Leader"), who called for outright Indian independence. Frequently imprisoned, he became president of the All-India Congress (1938–39). He supported the Axis powers (Germany, Italy, and Japan) during World War II and became commander-in-chief of the Japanese-sponsored Indian National Army made up of captured Indian soldiers. He was reported killed in a plane crash during his military career, adding to his stature as a martyr for his nation.

Congress leaders trusted British claims to be preparing India for democratic, responsible government. They welcomed a series of constitutional reforms establishing official councils with substantial Indian membership, elected by very limited elites, to advise the government. The Government of India Act, in 1919, expanded provincial and central legislatures and created a dual government, transferring powers over agriculture, public works, education, and local self-government to Indian elected legislators at the provincial level.

This half-way house proved unstable; Britain had trouble deciding whether it wished India to be a democracy or a colony. Each new issue revealed the contradiction. When Indian demands for political independence increased after World War I, the government responded with repression. Against the advice of all of the elected Indians on the Imperial Legislative Council, in 1919 the government passed the Rowlatt Acts, which cracked down on freedom of the press and assembly. When British troops shot point-blank into a peaceful crowd of protesters in Amritsar in the Punjab, killing 379 Indians and wounding 1,100, even Indian moderates could no longer justify British rule.

Mohandas Gandhi and Civil Disobedience

At this juncture Mohandas Karamchand Gandhi (1869–1948) emerged as a leader offering new political directions, new moral perspectives, and new programs of internal reform. Gandhi—called Mahatma, or "great soul," by his followers—inspired India to find strength and courage in its own village roots and spiritual traditions. His leadership had serious limitations, but virtually all political activity in India, almost until the present, would revolve around the Congress, which he now reconstructed into a mass movement.

SOURCE

Gandhi's First Experience with Racism in South Africa

Mahatma Gandhi published his *Autobiography* originally as a series of newspaper articles. Many of the episodes also carried a moral message for readers. The story of his first encounter with racism in South Africa implies that he had never experienced such severe discrimination, neither in colonial India nor during his law school days in London.

On the seventh or eighth day after my arrival, I left Durban. A first class seat was booked for me. ... The train reached Maritzburg, the capital of Natal, at about 9 p.m. ... A passenger came next, and looked me up and down. He saw that I was a "colored" man. This disturbed him. Out he went and came in again with one or two officials. They all kept quiet, when another official came to me and said, "Come along, you must go to the van compartment."

"But I have a first class ticket," said I.

"That doesn't matter," rejoined the other. "I tell you, you must go to the van compartment."

"I tell you, I was permitted to travel in this compartment at Durban, and I insist on going on in it."

"No you won't," said the official. "You must leave this compartment, or else I shall have to call a police constable to push you out."

"Yes, you may. I refuse to get out voluntarily."

The constable came. He took me by the hand and pushed me out. My luggage was also taken out. I refused to go to the other compartment and the train steamed away. I went and sat in the waiting room, keeping my hand bag with me, and leaving the other luggage where it was. ...

It was winter, and winter in the higher regions of South Africa is severely cold. Maritzburg being at a high altitude, the cold was extremely bitter. My overcoat was in my luggage, but I did not dare to ask for it lest I should be insulted again, so I sat and shivered. There was no light in the room. A passenger came in at about midnight and possibly wanted to talk to me. But I was in no mood to talk.

I began to think of my duty. Should I fight for my rights or go back to India, or should I go on to Pretoria without minding the insults, and return to India after finishing the case? It would be cowardice to run back to India without fulfilling my obligation. The hardship to which I was subjected was superficial—only a symptom of the deep disease of color prejudice. I should try, if possible, to root out the disease and suffer hardships in the process. (Jack, p. 29–30)

Gandhi and Nehru. Mahatma Gandhi, wearing his customary *dhoti*, loin cloth, and Jawaharlal Nehru are deep in conversation at the All-India Congress Committee Meeting in Bombay, July 6, 1946, where Nehru took office as president of the Congress. Gandhi and Nehru were the charismatic figures who led the Indian National Congress, a broad-based political organization which was the vehicle for the nationalist movement for independence.

Gandhi Develops *Satyagraha* in South Africa. Gandhi grew up in a prosperous, middle-class family—his father was an administrator in local government—and, like many of the leaders of the National Congress, he studied law in Britain. In 1893, as a young lawyer, he left India to work for an Indian emigrant business firm in South Africa. There, apparently for the first time, Gandhi suffered racial persecution personally and repeatedly (see box opposite).

Most of the Indians in South Africa had come as indentured laborers. The South African government wanted them to return home at the end of their service and instituted racist laws that made their long-term status untenable. Indians were required to carry identification cards at all times and to pay heavy head taxes. Most disturbing of all, in 1913, the government nullified all marriages not performed by Christian clergy, rendering illegitimate the children of almost all the Indian immigrants. Although he had arrived as the lawyer for a wealthy Indian Muslim client, Gandhi identified with the pain and humiliation of his less privileged countrymen and, indeed, suffered along with them. He was physically evicted from public facilities and threatened with beatings and even death for asserting his rights. Until now a rather private person, Gandhi began to organize a protest movement.

Instead of leaving at the end of his year's employment, Gandhi remained in South Africa for 21 years, from 1893 to 1914, formulating new methods of resistance through civil disobedience. Some of his strategies were based directly on Indian religious and moral principles, some were his own creative responses. He began with the principle of *ahimsa*, "nonviolence"—a basic tenet of the Jain religion and of several branches of Hinduism—insisting that those who accepted his leadership must reject the use of violence. Then he formulated the new strategy of *satyagraha*, or "truth-force." (Gandhi coined this word, from the Hindi *satya*, truth, and *agraha*, force, to describe his strategy of militant, nonviolent civil disobedience.) *Satyagraha* called for peaceful, even self-sacrificing, opposition to oppression through methods designed to force the oppressors to recognize the immorality of their own position and to relieve the suffering of their victims.

Those who followed Gandhi's path of civil disobedience had to be prepared to suffer willingly the legal consequences, including imprisonment, and frequently the extra-legal consequences, such as beatings by thugs. Often they "courted arrest," convinced that their imprisonment would expose the perversity of the laws they were opposing. Gandhi established a headquarters, modeled on the Hindu religious *ashram* (the headquarters of a religious sect), and founded a publishing house next door for spreading the principles of his movement.

Because he renounced violence, Gandhi called his methods "passive resistance," but there was nothing passive about them; they were actually systems of militant nonviolence. (Later he renamed them "civil resistance.") These techniques were later adopted by leaders of resistance movements around the world, from Martin Luther King (1929–68) in the U.S. to Nelson Mandela (b. 1918) in South Africa itself.

In 1909, Gandhi published *Hind Swaraj*, or *Indian Home Rule*. Banned in India, this short book championed India's own civilization, urged Indians to conquer the feelings of fear and inferiority that their colonial rulers had encouraged, and made a forthright attacked on British cultural, economic, and political hegemony.

We have hitherto said nothing because we have been cowed down ... it is our duty now to speak out boldly. We consider your schools and law courts to be useless. We want our own ancient schools and courts to be restored. The common language of India is not English but Hindi. You should, therefore, learn it. We can hold communication with you only in our national language ...

We cannot tolerate the idea of your spending money on railways and the military. We see no occasion for either ... We do not need any European cloth. We shall manage with articles produced and manufactured at home. You have great military resources ... You may, if you like, cut us to pieces. You may shatter us at the cannon's mouth. If you act contrary to our will, we shall not help you; and without our help, we know that you cannot move one step forward. (Jack, pp. 118–19)

Gandhi's success in South Africa was limited to short-term compromises with the government, but he earned the esteem of his countrymen in both South Africa and India. When Gandhi finally returned home and established a new *ashram* in Ahmedabad in 1915, his countrymen were eagerly awaiting his political initiatives for India itself. He did not disappoint them.

Gandhi and the Independence Movement

Gandhi soon demonstrated his organizational genius. Recognizing India's smoldering grass-roots anger against British rule, further inflamed by postwar economic hardship and political repression, Gandhi reconstituted the Congress from an organization of Western-educated elites into a mass organization with millions of dues-paying members from India's villages as well as its cities. He incorporated the vigor and boldness of current leaders like the fiery Bal Gangadhar Tilak (1856–1920), who proclaimed, "Freedom is my birthright, and I shall have it," and the milder-mannered Gopal Krishna Gokhale, who became Gandhi's political mentor in his first years back in India, as he was becoming reacquainted with his native land. Gandhi also mobilized India's enormous size and diversity by carefully cultivating personal and political alliances with a younger generation of regional leaders, including Rajendra Prasad (1884–1963), in Bihar, later the first president of independent India; Vallabhbhai Patel (1875–1950), in Gujarat, who became organizational "boss" of the entire Congress Party; and Jawaharlal Nehru (1889–1964) in Uttar Pradesh (then called United Provinces), who became the first prime minister of independent India.

SOURCE

Gandhi and Labor Relations

Most famous for his advocacy of the spinning wheel and his condemnation of mechanized industry, Gandhi was actually very pragmatic in his approach to technology. He recognized that the mechanized Indian textile industry gave jobs to hundreds of thousands of workers and produced yarn and cloth that Indian consumers desperately needed. Cynics added that the mill owners were among Gandhi's most generous financial supporters. Gandhi played a pivotal role in founding the Ahmedabad Textile Labour Association, one of India's most powerful labor unions, and he served as an adviser to several others. His advice to labor, and to management as well, reflected his view of the importance of harmony rather than conflict in industrial relationships, as in all human relationships.

> Two paths are open before India today, either to introduce the western principle of "Might is right," or to uphold the eastern principle that truth alone conquers, that truth knows no mishap, that the strong and the weak alike have a right to secure justice. The choice is to begin with the laboring class. Should the laborers obtain an increment in their wages by violence? Even if that be possible, they cannot resort to anything like violence, howsoever legitimate may be their claims. To use violence for securing rights may seem an easy path, but it proves to be thorny in the long run. Those who live by the sword die also by the sword …

> If, on the other hand, they take their stand on pure justice and suffer in their person to secure it, not only will they always succeed but they will also reform their masters, develop industries and both master and men will be as members of one and the same family. A satisfactory solution of the condition of labor must include the following:
>
> 1. The hours of labor must leave the workmen some hours of leisure.
> 2. They must get facilities for their own education.
> 3. Provision should be made for an adequate supply of milk, clothing and necessary education for their children.
> 4. There should be sanitary dwellings for the workmen.
> 5. They should be in a position to save enough to maintain themselves during their old age.
>
> None of these conditions is satisfied today. For this both the parties are responsible. The masters care only for the service they get. What becomes of the laborer does not concern them … The laborer, on the other hand, tries to hit upon all tricks whereby he can get maximum pay with minimum work.
>
> A third party [the union] has sprung up between these two parties. It has become the laborer's friend. (from *Young India*, June 1, 1921, reprinted in Homer Jack, pp. 157–59)

Gandhi adopted the nascent economic principle of *swadeshi*, the use of products of "one's own country," and organized nationwide boycotts of British imports. As he mobilized the nation in campaigns of mass civil disobedience Gandhi included the poor and the **outcaste**—those outside India's caste system—in order to achieve not only independence from the British but also social reform at home.

Cultural Policies. Gandhi was not opposed to the general concept of the caste system, seeing differences among people, conferred by birth, as a part of India's social reality, but he fought the designation of about 15 percent of the country's population as outcastes and "untouchables," literally not permitted to touch or be touched by people of upper castes. Declaring, "It has always been a mystery to me how men can feel themselves honored by the humiliation of their fellow beings," Gandhi coined a new name for the untouchables: *harijan*, "children of God." (This term later came to be considered patronizing and was replaced by *dalit*, "oppressed," the term most commonly used today.) He brought *harijans* into his movement and into his ashram. In his drive for a free India, Gandhi rejected the use of English in India's public life and schools, and urged the development of India's regional languages and literature.

Ascetic in his personal life, Gandhi led a temperance movement to ban alcoholic drinks. To identify with the poor and the villagers, he gave up his Western lawyer's suits in favor of the simplest loincloth, shawl, and sandals. Perhaps unintentionally, he became a kind of early patron saint of the "small is beautiful" movement, denouncing modern, highly-mechanized industry and arguing for small-scale,

KEY TERM

outcaste Refers to a person outside the caste system of India, usually also an outcast, rejected by the upper levels of society. Nowadays usually referred to as *dalits*, or oppressed persons.

alternative technologies, such as the spinning wheel. His reasons were both economic and humanitarian:

> Hunger is the argument that is driving India to the spinning wheel … We must think of millions who are today less than animals, who are almost in a dying state. The spinning wheel is the reviving draught for the millions of our dying countrymen and country-women … I do want growth. I do want self-determination. I do want freedom, but I want all these for the soul … A plea for the spinning wheel is a plea for recognizing the dignity of labor.

The Congress Party made the spinning wheel its emblem, handspun, handwoven cloth its dress, and the production of a daily quota of handspun yarn a requirement for membership.

Congress Campaigns for Independence. Gandhi led the Congress in three huge, nation-wide *satyagraha* campaigns. These campaigns fell far short of winning independence, but they demonstrated to the world that masses of Indians wanted the British out. They undermined any remaining British claims to moral authority to rule. They announced that India was becoming a cohesive political entity, ready to rule itself.

The Non-Cooperation campaign of 1920–22 boycotted British colonial schools, law courts, administrative positions, manufactures, and imports. A decade later, in the Salt March campaign of 1930–32, Gandhi drew world attention to India's freedom movement brilliantly by focusing on salt. He exposed the hardships created by the government's monopoly on the manufacture and sale of salt. Salt is necessary for life, even for the poorest person, but the British controlled its sale for their own profit. By marching to the sea and manufacturing salt from sea water, Gandhi demonstrated just how easy it is to extract salt from nature, for free, by anyone living along India's thousands of miles of coastline. By taking almost a month to march the 240 miles from his ashram to the seaside, Gandhi gave time for the news media of the world to cover the story. He shamed the British for forbidding this simple "manufacture" of salt, and for forcing people instead to buy their salt from a government monopoly. He put government officials in an awkward situation. If they

The salt march. Mahatma Gandhi begins the symbolic 240-mile, 27-day march from Ahmedabad to Dandi on the coast, where the participants collected sea salt and thus technically broke the salt law—the government's monopoly on salt production. Civil disobedience did not win independence immediately, but it did discredit the moral and political authority of the colonial government.

arrested him for breaking the law, they looked stupid, and perhaps cruel. If they didn't arrest him, they looked foolish and impotent. The government chose to enforce the law. It arrested tens of thousands of demonstrators at the seashore, and Gandhi himself a few days later. By extracting salt from the sea water, Gandhi had initiated a new nationwide campaign of civil disobedience. Once again he had challenged the moral authority of the colonial government in the eyes of most Indians and of world opinion. (*Time* magazine named Gandhi "Man of the Year" in 1931.)

Ten years later, the Quit India campaign of 1942 refused Indian political support to Britain's efforts in World War II until independence was granted. Most Indian leaders preferred the British over the Germans, but they refused to make a commitment to the war effort until their own country was granted its independence. (The Indian army, however, did fight loyally under British command.) By the time World War II ended, the British realized that they could no longer suppress Indian nationalism, certainly not at a cost they could afford. Almost 200 years after the Battle of Plassey made them a power in the country, the British prepared to leave India.

Gandhi's Leadership. Most Indians praise Gandhi as the father of the independent nation; some regard him as a saint. However, India's transformation into an independent state was not only a moral victory, but also an exercise in **realpolitik,** in the reality and importance of everyday politics. Gandhi's campaigns demonstrated India's resolve to resist colonial rule and undercut Britain's argument that Indians were not capable or worthy of self-government. If Britain wished to continue to hold India, it would have to expend immense resources in wealth and manpower. Following its losses in the Great Depression and World War II, Britain could not afford, and would not choose, this expenditure. Gandhi's mobilization of his nation had been effective. In a world battered by the murderous dictatorships of Hitler and Mussolini, Stalin and Mao, and by years of the most horrifying violence in human history, Gandhi had shown an alternative path. He had talked of means as well as ends. His method of *satyagraha* had not only made it impossible for Britain to continue to rule India, it had also pointed Indians in the direction of their own internal social reform.

Gandhi was not successful everywhere, however. Despite his three nationwide campaigns, beginning in 1920, the British did not finally concede independence until 1947. Some Indian leaders, like Subhas Chandra Bose (1847–1945) of Bengal, felt that violence would have achieved independence sooner. Many in Bose's socialist wing of the Congress also found Gandhi too compromising with business and landlord interests as he consolidated his power. They did not agree with Gandhi's view that class conflicts—between landowners and tenant peasants, for example—should be set aside until after independence was won. Perhaps Gandhi's most serious failure, the one that left him most disappointed, was his inability to capture vast numbers of Muslims for the Congress.

Independence and Muslim Interests. As early as 1906, long before Gandhi's return to India, a group of Muslims who feared that the Hindu majority would dominate the Muslim minority once the British left created the All-India Muslim League as an alternative to the Indian National Congress. At times the two organizations reconciled their differences, but as independence came closer they split irrevocably. Despite valiant efforts, Gandhi failed to persuade the most important Muslim leaders that Muslim interests would be safe in an independent, secular India. Mohammed Ali Jinnah (1876–1948), "the father of Pakistan," was one of the unconvinced. He called for a separate state for Muslims. Muslim cultural leaders, like the poet Muhammad Iqbal (1877–1938), also believed that Islamic culture could flourish only in an Islamic state. The closer independence came, the more militant the separatists became.

KEY TERM

realpolitik A German word meaning practical politics, that is, a policy determined by expediency rather than by ethical or ideological considerations.

Independence and Partition

At independence in 1947, the subcontinent was partitioned into Hindu-majority India, an officially secular country, and Muslim-majority Pakistan, an officially Islamic country. The Indian National Congress transformed itself into the National Congress Party and assumed the responsibility of running the country until elections were held. Then, Jawaharlal Nehru was elected independent India's first prime minister. Mohammed Ali Jinnah became Pakistan's first governor-general.

Hindu–Muslim Separation/Partition

Pakistan's peculiar geography, with two "wings," east and west, separated by some 800 miles of hostile Indian territory, reflected the distribution of Muslim majorities in the subcontinent. At partition an estimated 12 million people shifted their homes. Six million Hindus and Sikhs from East and West Pakistan moved into India; six million Muslims from India transferred to Pakistan. The transfer of population was bloody;

Political change in south Asia after 1947. At independence in 1947, British India was partitioned into secular, but Hindu-majority, India and Muslim Pakistan amid enormous violence and migration. Disputes over Kashmir continue until today. In 1971, the east wing of Pakistan fought, with Indian assistance, a war of independence against the west and became Bangladesh.

Mass migration. The partition of India at independence created an unprecedented transfer of population in two directions: Most Hindus and Sikhs fled Pakistan for the safety of India, while many Muslims living in India struggled to get safely over the border into the newly established Islamic nation. This packed train, groaning with refugees from Pakistan, arrives in Amritsar, just over the Indian border, on October 16, 1947.

between 200,000 and one million people were murdered. Gandhi, too, was murdered at about this time—by a Hindu fanatic who thought that he was too friendly to Muslims and their new state of Pakistan.

Most Indians rejected religion as the official basis of statehood. When East Pakistan revolted against the domination of West Pakistan and declared itself the independent state of Bangladesh in 1971, Indians rejoiced: their rival state was now broken in two, and they felt vindicated in their belief that religion alone should not, and could not, be the basis of national unity.

Few Hindus remained in Pakistan, but a sizeable Muslim minority, ten percent of India's population, remained in India. While Hindus and Muslims mostly cohabited the land peacefully, under a secular constitution, tensions between them remained and were sometimes exploited by political leaders, with increasing frequency after 1990.

One of the continuing flashpoints has been the region of Kashmir, bordering, and claimed by, both Pakistan and India. Kashmir was one of the regions of India that had been ruled by the British indirectly, through a local *maharajah*, or prince. He was a Hindu and, at independence, he asked to join his state to India. However, the great majority of the population of Kashmir was Muslim, and they have never been given the opportunity to express their opinion in a vote. Several wars have been fought for control of Kashmir; the region is currently divided roughly along the line of the military cease-fires. No political resolution has been reached.

Unifying the Nation

At independence, the Indian National Congress transformed itself into a formal political party. Jawaharlal Nehru became the first prime minister, a position he held until his death in 1964. Home Minister Vallabhbhai Patel convinced and coerced India's 562 princes, local rulers under British colonial authority, to declare their merger with India, ending the fear of a breakup of the subcontinent into numerous, separate, small states. Linguistic fragmentation was also averted. Gandhi had organized the Congress by linguistic regions, different from the administrative units employed by the British. After independence, following several regional disputes, the Congress government agreed to draw up the new state borders in accordance with these linguistic borders. Some powerful regional separatist movements emerged—in Madras (now Tamilnadu) in the 1960s, in the Punjab in the 1970s and 1980s, in Kashmir regularly, and in several of the distant and ethnically Mongoloid northeastern states—but a combination of political bargaining and armed force has maintained the unity of the country.

Democracy and its Challenges

The democracy proposed by British rulers became a reality in India after independence. Except for two years of "Emergency Rule," from 1975 to 1977, India has functioned democratically and constitutionally as a union of some 30 states and territories, with universal adult franchise and guaranteed freedoms of press, assembly, speech, and religion, and an independent judiciary. Despite imperfections, India takes pride in being the world's largest democracy.

Indian Politics

Within its democratic framework, communist governments have also been elected in India's individual states. In 1957, the state of Kerala chose the first freely elected communist government anywhere in the world. Indians have not, however, given strong support to militant communism. The reasons may include: India's generally religious orientation; skepticism about a philosophy and organization tied to foreign governments; recognition of communism's origin as a proletarian rather than a peasant movement; and state repression of revolutionary organizations.

Until 1991, laissez-faire capitalism fared even less well. Indians, including much of the business community, seemed to view capitalism as excessively individualistic and materialistic, based on a philosophy of self-interest, often seen as greed, and associated with colonialism in the past and the return of a neocolonial economic dominance in the present. Despite a large free-enterprise sector in the economy, especially in agriculture, most major Indian parties advocated socialism, on the grounds of its stated concern for the common good. Nehru, in particular, espoused "a socialist pattern of development." His policy continued in force for a generation after his death, despite widespread criticism that it led to excessive power—and corruption—concentrated in the state and in the bureaucrats who controlled access to business licenses and investment capital. Many of these views changed in 1991 when India was forced by regulations of the IMF to move toward a more free-market economy.

Through the first four decades of Independence, one party, the Congress, dominated India's democracy and the party's leadership was dominated by one family, the Nehru dynasty. Jawaharlal Nehru, prime minister from Independence until his death in 1964, was soon succeeded by his daughter, Indira Gandhi (her name by marriage; she was not related to the Mahatma), who was prime minister from 1967–77 and from 1980 until her assassination in 1984. She was followed by her son, Rajiv, 1984–89. After he was assassinated in 1991, many Congress leaders asked his widow, Italian-born Sonia Gandhi, to take his place as head of the party. Ultimately, she did.

Indira Gandhi. Indira Gandhi's reputation as a tough, determined leader grew when she ordered Indian troops to support East Pakistan in its 1971 civil war for independence from West Pakistan. Her support facilitated the creation of Bangladesh. In 1974, she ordered India's first underground test of an atomic bomb.

Her political manipulations, however, partially undermined India's democratic system. In 1975, facing the likely loss of political power, she had the president of

India declare an "Emergency." She jailed the leaders of the opposition, curtailed freedom of speech and of the press, and set quotas of people to be rounded up for forcible reproductive sterilization, largely in response to India's large population. These dictatorial excesses alienated most Indians; when Gandhi restored elections in 1977, she was voted out of office.

After a brief period in jail for election irregularities, Gandhi was voted back to power in 1980. She continued her political manipulations, alienating many Sikhs in the Punjab. Their opposition finally led to armed confrontation in which thousands died. Armed opposition leaders took refuge in the beautiful and sacred Sikh Golden Temple in the city of Amritsar. Gandhi ordered an army strike to dislodge them and the temple was badly damaged in the crossfire. In revenge, two Sikhs in Gandhi's bodyguard assassinated her in 1984.

Indira Gandhi, prime minister of India, inspects the guard at an Independence Day celebration, August 23, 1967. Mahatma Gandhi did much to encourage women's participation in public life during the years leading to independence. Although many women are well-educated, overall the literacy rate among females is only 54 percent (76 percent for males, according to the 2001 census).

Gender Issues

Indira Gandhi was only the most prominent example of women in Indian politics. Mahatma Gandhi had encouraged women's participation in the freedom movement, and many followed his call to come out of their homes into the public sphere for the first time. The poet Sarojini Naidu (1879–1949), who became president of the Indian National Congress, is the most famous. India instituted universal adult suffrage in 1950. In each national election approximately 55 percent of women voted, compared with about 60 percent of men. In 2005, women held 45 seats out of 542 in the lower house of Parliament and 28 out of 242 in the upper, indicating a slowly increasing proportion from 1950. State government ratios were similar. New constitutional amendments, passed in 1993, created new electoral institutions for local government, and called for 33 percent of their seats to be held by women. By 2003, these amendments had created some three million additional representatives in local government. One-third of them were women.

Legal Changes. The 1955 Hindu Marriage Act raised the age of marriage for Hindu women to 15 (18 for men) and assured Hindu women the right of divorce. The Hindu Succession Act of 1956 gave daughters equal rights with sons in inheriting their father's property. On the other hand, Parliament did not legislate new personal law for non-Hindus, so other religious communities continued under their traditional systems of family law. This exclusion disturbed many feminists, but they trod lightly here; many Muslims, even feminist Muslims, did not want the secular state to interfere in the religious law of their community.

Social Changes. Because family structures in India, especially north India, are both patrilineal and patrilocal—that is, inheritance and residence patterns follow the family of the male—the birth of a female child is often regarded as a financial and even emotional burden. Years of child-care and expense culminate in the girl's leaving home for marriage into another family, often somewhat distant and with limited ties to the family of origin.

The sex ratio in India in 2001, about 933 women to 1,000 men (106 men to 100 women), is one of the lowest in the world, although not so low as China's. It suggests the systematic neglect of females, especially young girls. As amniocentesis and sonograms became more widely available, allowing parents to know the sex of unborn children, abortion of female fetuses seemed to result. Laws were passed to ban the use of these tests for this purpose, but the laws were widely disregarded. At the other end of the life cycle, women tend to outlive men, and widows are especially vulnerable if their children choose not to support them. Suicide rates for Indian women are comparatively high, and isolated cases of *sati* (suttee), in which a widow immolates herself on her husband's funeral pyre, continue. In 2001, the literacy rate among females was 54 percent as compared with 76 percent for males; but this was up from 8 percent and 25 percent, respectively, in 1951. The treatment of women in southern India is widely regarded as more egalitarian than in the north, perhaps because of different local traditions, including the influence in a few localities of matrilineal and matrilocal systems that follow the female line in inheritance and residence.

Economic Changes. Disconcerting results from a 1984 anthropological study of a village near Delhi suggested that the position of poor, rural women was actually deteriorating as a result of increasing general prosperity in the new economic system and of increasing urbanization. Several factors were to blame. First, women who had worked in agriculture alongside their male kin were displaced when their husbands left field work to seek jobs in the cities. Second, women who traditionally worked in caste-based occupations as servants through *jajmani* (family patronage) systems could no longer find such jobs. Third, mechanization had replaced female labor in a variety of arenas. Finally, changes in cropping patterns had made female help in the fields less necessary. These factors all contributed to the marginalization of poor women, giving them less voice in their family and ultimately devaluing them (Wadley, in Wiser and Wiser, p. 287).

An encouraging contrary development has been the organization of working women into effective unions that provide both economic opportunity and political

New technology crosses gender lines. Power tillers provide a new technology more appropriate economically than either bullock-drawn plows or tractors in some areas of India. They are available through collaboration with Japan (Mitsubishi). In entering her new occupation, the driver has received financial and technical assistance from the Self-Employed Women's Association in Ahmedabad, one of India's most prominent organizations of poor, working-class women.

representation. In cities such as Mumbai, Madras, and Ahmedabad, voluntary organizations of tens of thousands of working women have begun to gain access to capital for working-class women who carry on their own small businesses; to form cooperatives, which help them secure raw materials and market finished products; to lobby government for workers' safety, health, insurance, maternity, and job protection in nonunionized, small-scale shops; to develop new educational models for job training; and to create new systems of health delivery, especially for women. One of the most important of these organizations is the Self-Employed Women's Association in Ahmedabad, a daughter organization of the Textile Labour Union, which had been founded with the help of Mahatma Gandhi. By 2008, SEWA claimed one million members across India.

Economic and Technological Development

At independence, 361 million people lived in India; by the mid-1980s, the population had more than doubled to three-quarters of a billion people; by 2000 it reached one billion. During droughts in 1964–66, mass starvation was averted only by the importation of 12 million tons of food grains each year, primarily from the United States. More recently, however, India has not only been able to feed itself, it has even sold food overseas (although millions of Indians do not receive adequate food even now).

Revolutions in Agriculture. A "green revolution" took root in India in the late 1960s. New strains of wheat, developed in Mexico under the auspices of the Rockefeller Foundation, increased India's productivity even faster than her population. Between the early 1960s and the late 1970s, rice production rose by more than 50 percent; wheat production tripled. Total grain production rose from about 50 million tons per year at independence, to about 150 million tons in the mid-1980s, to about 190 million tons in 2008.

Meanwhile, a "white revolution" in dairy production and distribution was also taking place. Dairy cooperatives were formed throughout India, enabling village farmers to pool and ship their highly perishable products to urban markets—as fresh milk in refrigerated train cars, and as processed cheese and dairy products in conventional shipping—thus providing incentives for increasing production.

These revolutions in agriculture were not without their problems. First, ecologically, questions were raised about relying so exclusively on so few new strains of "miracle wheat." Were too many seeds coming from too few genetic baskets? Would the massive new quantities of chemical fertilizers needed to support the new seeds ultimately ruin the ecology? Would India's water resources prove adequate as the use of these water-intensive seeds expanded? Second, economic growth increased disparities and tensions between haves and have-nots and between those who worked more entrepreneurially and those who did not. The new productivity benefited most those who already had the economic resources to afford the new seeds, fertilizers, pesticides, and irrigation water. The rich were getting richer— although the poor did not seem to be getting poorer—and social tensions increased. Similarly, disparities between richer and poorer states grew.

Challenges of Population and Poverty. Government implementation of family planning, rejected overwhelmingly in the wake of Indira Gandhi's program of forced sterilization in 1975–77, has been soft-pedaled ever since. Nevertheless birth rates fell from about 44 per thousand at independence to about 33 per thousand in 1985, to 22.7 in 2007, indicating great general interest in smaller, planned families. Life expectancy at birth rose from about 30 years at independence in 1947, to 56 in 1985, to 69 in 2007.

On the other hand, in 2007, the government of India reported that 46 percent of Indian children under the age of three were underweight or severely underweight, and 18 percent were malnourished: "India is home to the highest number of undernourished people in the world. And we are working hard to fight that fact."

Industrialization and its Consequences. Industrial productivity increased, but the structure of the workforce did not change—exactly the process Mahatma Gandhi had feared. New machinery produced more goods more efficiently, but it did not provide proportionately more jobs. Although industrial production multiplied almost five times between 1951 and 1980, the percentage of workers in industry essentially stagnated, from about 10 percent in 1951 to about 13 percent in 1980 and back to 11 percent in 2000. Unemployment was reported steady at about 8 percent.

Until the 1980s, industrial policy derived from Gandhi's and Nehru's conflicting philosophies. Gandhi had urged austere consumption levels, handicraft production, spinning wheels, and national self-sufficiency through import substitution. Nehru implemented socialism, central planning, industrialization, government control and development of the "commanding heights" of the economy—energy, steel, petroleum, banking and finance—and regulation of the large-scale capitalist sector. Despite their strong differences on the importance of large-scale industry and modern technology, both Gandhi and Nehru stressed domestic self-sufficiency in production.

HOW DO WE KNOW?

Technological Hazards and Questionable Accountability

Indian attitudes toward modern technology have fallen between the skepticism of Gandhi and the enthusiasm of Nehru. Some of the most biting critiques of India's technological policies on development came from a "modern intellectual," Ashis Nandy, who criticized the government for giving excessive power to the scientific-technological establishment. In particular he focused on India's nuclear establishment in the mid-1980s:

> Nuclear scientists were freed from all financial constraints. The budget of the nuclear program ... was routinely pushed through parliament without any scrutiny whatsoever. And the expenditures ... were never publicly audited. All data on performance ... failures, unsafe technology and insufficient regard for human rights ... were protected by law from the public gaze. And all enquiries made from outside the nuclear establishment were preempted with the help of a special act that made it impossible to mount any informed, focused, data-based criticism of India's nuclear programme. (Nandy, p. 5)

Further skepticism concerning winners and losers in the quest for industrial modernization resulted from a tragedy of poison gas leakage in a Union Carbide insecticide plant in Bhopal in 1984, the worst industrial accident of its kind in the world up to that date. Compounding the tragedy for the victims, the American-owned corporation resisted payment of compensation:

> Dreadful tragedy struck central India's Bhopal ... in December 1984 ... Deadly invisible gas from Union Carbide's insecticide storage tanks had escaped through defective valves to be blown by ill-winds over the slumbering bodies of thousands of poor innocents outside that giant plant's walls, less than 400 miles south of New Delhi. Within hours, 2,000 people were dead and hundreds of thousands of others had been injured by the worst industrial accident of recent history. Union Carbide was still American-owned, one of the few multinationals in India that had not been taken over by a majority of Indian shareholders and management ...
>
> Though hundreds of billions of dollars in damages were quickly claimed in thousands of lawsuits filed both in India and America, virtually nothing was paid to any of the actual victims for seven full years after the tragedy devastated Bhopal. Legal snares and questions of jurisdiction plagued the process, serving to thwart justice instead of expediting its realization. (Wolpert, pp. 421–22)

- Why do you think that India's nuclear development program had such independence of action without public political supervision? Do you approve of such secrecy in India? In the nuclear development programs in the U.S.? Why or why not?
- On what basis do you think Union Carbide resisted paying compensation to most of the victims of the leak? After you have made your guesses, you may wish to check Bhopal and Union Carbide on the web to see what answers you can find.
- In an overwhelmingly agrarian, poor, rural society such as India, what do you think is the proper place for modern industry, such as nuclear weapons? Peaceful use of atomic energy? Chemical insecticides?

PEARSON
myhistorylab

These policies were increasingly challenged by the new international political-economic wisdom of the 1980s, based on the economic successes of the East Asian countries and the political policies of the U.S. and Britain. Increased consumption spurred increased productivity, and a consumer society began to appear in India.

High-tech innovation for both home and foreign markets increased productivity, and India began to manufacture submarines, computer software (for which it had become a world center) and hardware, and machine tools, and even prepared to export nuclear power plants adapted to third world conditions. Its impressive scientific and technological establishment had the capacity to adopt and adapt the newest technological advances.

In part, these technological successes were possible because of an extraordinary imbalance in India's educational expenditures. The government strongly favored higher education while starving the primary schools. These policies, rooted in traditional hierarchical attitudes and interests, produced a skewed society in which the highly educated elites compared with the best anywhere in the world, but overall basic literacy was low, only about 65 percent even as late as 2000. Again, Gandhi's fears were coming true.

International Relations

India was the first major colony to win independence after World War II, and it served as a leader to other newly emerging countries. Nehru, in particular, provided articulate, innovative direction, and after independence India remained a model of democratic political stability and gradual economic growth in a society of unparalleled heterogeneity. Its international role, however, declined. It was defeated in its 1962 border war with China, and then it began to spend more on its armed forces. Military expenditure rose from $1.7 billion in 1960 to $9.8 billion in 1987 (in constant dollars, adjusted for inflation).

Decolonization throughout the world was virtually complete by the 1980s, and political colonialism was no longer a major global issue. The attention of new nations shifted to economic development. Japan and the highly successful "tigers" of East and Southeast Asia, with their more open, more liberalized, and more expansive economies, attracted them. More recently, China has been a model. In a world concerned with economic growth, the persistence of poverty and illiteracy made India a more problematic model for others. Its progress seemed too slow. It remained, however, a viable democracy and the dominant power in the south Asia region. And, as its economy grew in the early 2000s, so did its international reputation.

Comparing China and India: What Difference Does It Make?

At the end of World War I, India's demand for independence ignited a mass movement that bore many similarities to China's. With the vast majority of its population in rural areas, India, like China, was rooted in agriculture and the peasantry. Like China's Mao, India's Mahatma Gandhi mobilized this rural constituency. Both leaders created new social and economic institutions for greater equity and emphasized the need for new, simple technologies appropriate to their agrarian, impoverished societies. Both regarded their methods and solutions as models for others to copy.

The differences between the two mammoth countries were at least equally significant. Unlike China, which had no functioning central government between 1912 and 1949, and had been carved into numerous European and Japanese spheres of influence, India had a central government, which was under British colonial control until independence in 1947. While China suffered decades of civil warfare, political disputes in India were addressed through generally peaceful, constitutional processes. India's nationalist leaders, unlike those of China, welcomed businessmen and professionals along with the peasantry in their independence struggle. Unlike China, in its independence movement India pursued an extraordinary strategy of nonviolent mass civil resistance. It fought no civil war, nor did the battles of World War II significantly touch its borders. When independence came, relations with colonial Britain remained harmonious, and India retained membership in the Commonwealth of Nations, an association mostly of Britain's former colonies. Even the partition of the subcontinent into India and Pakistan in 1947 followed constitutional processes, although the subsequent transfers of population were enormously violent.

The 1971 creation of the independent country of Bangladesh on the land of East Pakistan was the product of civil war, in which India aided Bangladesh against West Pakistan. Naxalite movements of communist, agricultural guerrilla warfare (named for the village of Naxalbari, scene of their first revolt) broke out repeatedly, but mostly in somewhat remote eastern regions of *adivasi* populations of impoverished tribal peoples. Hindu–Muslim and high caste–low caste tensions sometimes also burst into violence, but the open violence of these confrontations was usually confined to local areas and short periods of time.

A generation after ending colonialism, both China and India could point to significant accomplishments, including cumulative and growing economic expansion—more rapid in China, slower in India; political cohesion; and social transformation in accord with their differing agendas. Both countries had moved from concentration on rural areas, a promise of their colonial struggles, to concern also with their cities and their industries. They shared a similar challenge: How to maintain a coherent national agenda after the unifying enemy of colonialism had been defeated?

By the late twentieth century, both countries had chosen to shift economic policies dramatically, in the direction of deregulation and capitalism. Mao's principal successor, Deng Xiaoping, chose to abandon Mao's state-controlled communist programs centered on the domestic market, for free-market laissez-faire policies oriented toward international trade. The result was something new in world history: a Communist Party-controlled politics coupled with a capitalist economy. The economic results were spectacular, with growth rates of ten percent per year for many years. In light of such economic expansion no one knew the degree to which the political system could remain under party control.

India was slower and less dramatic in its policy changes, but its choice to open its economy moved in a similar direction. The transformation began in the late 1980s, under Prime Minister Rajiv Gandhi, and increased in speed after 1991 as a result of economic deregulation imposed by the IMF as a condition for granting India desperately needed loans. India's growth rates were not as high as China's, about five percent annually, but still much higher than they had been under previous state regulations.

India confronted enormous, persistent challenges from both its own social structure and the colonial heritage: hierarchical caste divisions, including especially severe discrimination against ex-untouchables; conflict between religious communities, especially Hindus and Muslims, but Sikhs as well in and around the Punjab; tensions among regional and linguistic groups; renewed oppression of women; an economy of scarcity with widespread, persistent hunger and poverty; and continuing massive population growth. In these struggles, India followed policies of democratic political stability for development, including technological policies of great diversity.

Both China and India were aware of the technological and economic progress of Japan and the Asian tigers. For China this represented a galling challenge, since the

Japanese powerhouse dominated the economics of East Asia, displacing China from her historic position. India did not see itself in competition with Japan, but it recognized that the smaller countries of Southeast Asia, which had previously trailed India, had now surpassed it economically and in consumer technology. India, too, saw this as a model and a challenge.

By the end of the twentieth century, economic, social, political, and cultural change was taking place so rapidly in both India and China that we devote renewed attention to these two giants in the final section of this book, particularly to economic change in China in Chapter Twenty-three and to social and political change in India in Chapter Twenty-four.

Asking Questions

- Compare Mao and Gandhi in terms of both their personal experience with agrarian issues and their policies for dealing with them.
- Compare Mao and Gandhi in terms of their policies on the use of violence and nonviolence in attaining their political objectives. To what extent are the differences in their philosophies a result of differences in the political context in which they lived and worked?
- Compare the status of women in the philosophies of Mao and Gandhi.
- To what degree did the experiences of the Long March and the guerrilla war of the Chinese communist revolution provide good guidelines for government policy in governing China after 1949?
- To what degree did the experiences of the Indian independence movement provide guidelines for government policy in governing India after 1947?
- In the debate over the technology to be used in modern India, what do you think are the strong and weak points of Gandhi's position and of Nehru's position?

Suggested Readings

CHINA

Andors, Phyllis. *The Unfinished Liberation of Chinese Women, 1949–1980* (Bloomington, IN: University of Indiana Press, 1983). Feminist, antipatriarchal ideology was central to the Chinese communist program. Andors captures the ideology and the degree of implementation.

Blunden, Caroline and Mark Elvin. *Cultural Atlas of China* (New York: Facts on File, 1983). Another in the excellent Facts on File series. More than an atlas, it is a comprehensive approach to China, scholarly yet accessible.

deBary, W. Theodore, *et al. Sources of Chinese Tradition*, Vol. 2 (New York: Columbia University Press, 1999). An outstanding anthology of statements by China's intellectual and political leaders. The 1999 revision doubled the number of selections.

Ebrey, Patricia Buckley, ed. *Chinese Civilization: A Sourcebook* (New York: The Free Press, 1993). A very different selection from deBary's. Ebrey's selections capture the lives of common people. Illuminating and excellent.

Meisner, Maurice. *Mao's China and After* (New York: The Free Press, 1986). A thoughtful, rather pro-Mao account of the revolution. A scholarly, accessible standard.

Schell, Orville, ed. *The China Reader*, 4 vols. (New York: Random House, 1967–74). Tells the story of China's revolution from the end of the colonial era through the end of Mao's years through an exceptional array of documents.

Snow, Edgar. *Red Star over China* (London: Victor Gollancz, 1968). Journalist Snow visited Mao in Yan'an and brought back to the West the first detailed knowledge of the man and the movement. Inspiring from a very pro-Maoist viewpoint.

Spence, Jonathan D. *The Search for Modern China* (New York: W.W. Norton & Company, 1990). Clearly written, detailed yet highly accessible, excellent as an introduction to the subject and to further scholarly investigation. Reissued in paperback in 2000.

Spence, Jonathan D. *Mao Zedong* (New York: Viking/Penguin, 1999). Concise, readable, reasonably comprehensive biography.

KEY TERMS

soviet see p. 772

barefoot doctors see p. 775

scorched-earth retreat see p. 775

brain washing see p. 776

"Hundred Flowers" campaign see p. 777

Great Leap Forward see p. 778

Cultural Revolution see p. 778

outcaste see p. 787

realpolitik see p. 789

INDIA

Bayly, Susan. *Caste, Society, and Politics in India from the Eighteenth Century to the Modern Age* (Cambridge: Cambridge University Press, 1999). Accessible, highly scholarly introduction to the phenomenon of caste, the changing meaning of caste, and the changing economic and political significance of caste.

Brown, Judith M. *Modern India: The Origins of an Asian Democracy* (New York: Oxford University Press, 1984). Stresses the constitutional processes in achieving independence, and in the negotiations between the British and the Congress. Brown sees India's postindependence democracy as a result of that process.

Chandra, Bipan. *India's Struggle for Independence, 1857–1947* (New York: Penguin Books, 1989). Chandra stresses the popular, revolutionary side of the independence struggle, and sees Gandhi as the integrative force who encouraged it to take democratic directions.

Dalton, Dennis. *Mahatma Gandhi: Non-Violent Power in Action* (New York: Columbia University Press, 1993). Remarkably lucid account of Gandhi's theory and practice of *satyagraha*, and especially good on his fast in Calcutta, 1947.

Forbes, Geraldine. *Women in Modern India* (Cambridge: Cambridge University Press, 1998). Useful survey of women in education, cultural and social life, and reform, the nationalist movement, the economy, and recent political action. Especially interesting for shift from elite issues to the masses.

Guha, Ramchandra. *India after Gandhi* (London: Macmillan, 2007). Covers the challenges of independent India, with pride in its accomplishments and reservations about continuing problems.

Hay, Stephen, ed. *Sources of Indian Tradition*, Vol. 2 (New York: Columbia University Press, 2nd ed., 1988). Excellent selection of statements by Indian political and cultural leaders. Stresses the elites.

Nehru, Jawaharlal. *The Discovery of India* (Bombay: Asia Publishing House, 1960). A personal history, Marxist in orientation, written from jail by the prime minister of India, illuminating of the nation's history and of Nehru's understanding of that history.

Panagariya, Arvind. *India: the Emerging Giant* (New York: Oxford University Press, 2008). A comprehensive, thorough overview of India's economy since independence.

Rothermund, Dietmar. *An Economic History of India: From Pre-Colonial Times to 1991* (London: Routledge, 1993). Clearly written, succinct introduction to the subject.

Rudolph, Lloyd I. and Susanne Hoeber Rudolph. *The Modernity of Tradition* (Chicago, IL: University of Chicago Press, 1967). Still the clearest introduction to the idea that tradition and modernity are not opposites, but interact in the hands of creative leaders, such as Gandhi and, later, caste leaders.

Wiser, William H. and Charlotte Viall Wiser. *Behind Mud Walls 1930–1960* (including Susan Wadley, "The Village in 1984," "The Village in 1998") (Berkeley, CA: University of California Press, 2000). The Wisers kept revisiting a north Indian village and writing down their observations. A fascinating, very readable review. Make sure to get the latest edition, as Susan Wadley continues to update the Wisers' work.

ADDITIONAL SOURCES

Bouton, Marshall M. and Philip Oldenburg, eds. *India Briefing: A Transformative Fifty Years* (Armonk, NY: M.E. Sharpe, 1999). Every year or two, Oldenburg and a co-editor bring together an excellent, scholarly set of interpretive essays on current events in India under the title *India Briefing*. This edition covered the entire period from independence.

Brass, Paul. *The Politics of India Since Independence* (Cambridge: Cambridge University Press, 2nd ed., 1994). Another in the Cambridge series of comprehensive introductions to India. Brass is comprehensive, thoughtful, and, appropriately, quite skeptical of official rhetoric.

Drèze, Jean and Amartya Sen. *India's Economic Development and Social Opportunity* (Delhi: Oxford University Press, 1998). Sen won the 1998 Nobel prize for economics for his stress on the importance of education and health in development economics. Here he and Drèze bring that perspective to an analysis of India's record.

Fairbank, John King. *The Great Chinese Revolution: 1800–1985* (New York: Harper & Row, 1986). Until his death, Fairbank was one of the masters of Chinese history. This book is now dated, but very useful and interesting.

Frankel, Francine. *India's Political Economy, 1947–2004: The Gradual Revolution* (New York: Oxford University Press, 2005). To know how India said it was doing, and how it was actually doing in economic and political development after independence, this is a good place to begin.

Goldman, Merle and Roderick MacFarquhar, eds. *The Paradox of China's Post-Mao Reforms* (Cambridge, MA: Harvard University Press, 1999). Although focused on China after Mao, the contrast is illuminating.

Hardgrave, Robert L. and Stanley Kochanek. *India: Government and Politics in a Developing Nation* (Stamford, CT: Harcourt College Publishers, 1999). A standard, introductory text, continuously revised for three decades.

Hardiman, David. *Gandhi in His Time and Ours: the Global Legacy of His Ideas* (New York:

Columbia University Press, 2003). Bringing conflicting interest groups under his umbrella, Gandhi set an example to India and the world.

Jack, Homer, ed. *The Gandhi Reader* (New York: Grove Press, 1956). A comprehensive source book covering Gandhi's philosophies and activities in politics, economics, and moral life, mostly by Gandhi, some about him.

Jayakar, Pupul. *Indira Gandhi* (New York: Viking, 1992). A friendly, but critical biography by a friend and colleague.

Karlekar, Hiranmay, ed. *Independent India: The First Fifty Years* (Delhi: Oxford University Press and the Indian Council for Cultural Relations, 1998). A set of assessments of uneven quality, but many quite fascinating, of many aspects of India since independence. Written in India for Indians; may be somewhat dense for foreign readers.

Kennedy, Paul. *The Rise and Fall of the Great Powers* (New York: Random House, 1987). Kennedy looks at the great powers since 1500. He introduces China only in recent times. India doesn't make it. Interesting for his view of what counts in national greatness.

Liang, Heng and Judith Shapiro. *Son of the Revolution* (New York: Vintage Books, 1983). Liang's biography as a young man who survived the Cultural Revolution, but saw it destroy his parents, their marriage, his schooling, and his earlier belief that the revolution was benign.

Liu Binyan. *A Higher Kind of Loyalty* (New York: Pantheon, 1990). Exiled from China, journalist Liu Binyan writes from America incisive, angry criticism of the actions of the government of the country that he loves.

MacFarquhar, Roderick Timothy Cheek, and Eugene Wu, eds. *The Secret Speeches of Chairman Mao* (Cambridge, MA: Council on East Asian Studies, 1989). Mao's policies in his own words.

Nandy, Ashis, ed. *Science, Hegemony and Violence* (Delhi: Oxford University Press, 1988). Nandy is an oddity: a prominent, Western-educated intellectual who is quite skeptical of Western influences in India, including scientific and technological influences.

Pa Chin. *Family* (Garden City, NY: Doubleday & Company, 1972). This novel of the 1910s and 1920s presented a new, feminist vision of what a family might be in modern China.

Ramusack, Barbara, *et al.* *Women in Asia: Restoring Women to History* (Bloomington, IN: Indiana University Press, 1999). Product of a decade-long project of the Organization of American Historians to provide perspectives and bibliographies on the study of women in the non-Western world. Other volumes treat sub-Saharan Africa, the Middle East, and Latin America.

Schell, Orville and David Shambaugh, eds. *The China Reader: The Reform Era* (New York: Vintage Books, 1999). An excellent selection of essays and observations on the changes in China after Mao's death. Updates the earlier four volumes of China Reader noted above.

Weiner, Myron. *The Child and the State in India* (Princeton, NJ: Princeton University Press, 1991). In a very critical, down-to-earth assessment, Weiner asks why literacy rates and school attendance are so low, and child labor so extensive. Hierarchical values are a major culprit.

Wolf, Eric R. *Peasant Wars of the Twentieth Century* (New York: Harper & Row, 1969). A classic comparative study of the philosophies and strategies of modern guerrilla warfare. China figures prominently.

Wolpert, Stanley. *A New History of India* (New York: Oxford University Press, 8th ed., 2008). A useful, standard, sometimes rambling, highly readable text.

Wu, Harry. *Bitter Winds* (New York: John Wiley, 1994). One of the bitterest attacks on political repression in contemporary China.

PEARSON

myhistorylab

For quizzes, flashcards, primary sources, interactive maps, videos, and other activities related to this chapter please go to

www.myhistorylab.com

From Past to Present to Future

In this last Part, we sketch a view of the last 25 years or so in light of the thematic perspectives we have been developing throughout our study of world history. So far, we have explored seven themes; now we ask how well they help us understand the world of our own times. How well do earlier themes apply to today's conditions, and how much do they need to be modified?

For example, in our study of early evolution, we were considering a very small number of human beings. In those days, there were not many of us on the earth. We hardly created a "footprint." Today we are approaching seven billion, and we are profoundly altering the quality of the soil, water, and air of our planet. Some serious scholars fear that we may be making it unlivable. The accompanying picture of a segment of the Brazilian rain-

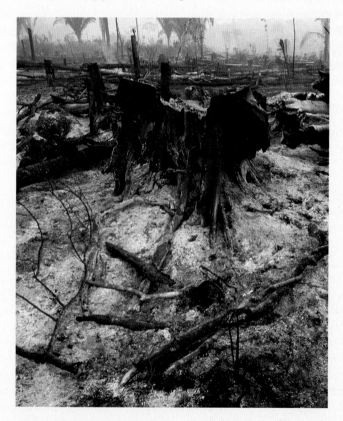

The Brazilian rainforest after logging and burning, 1985. Compare the destruction of a forest in the Czech Republic, as a result of acid rain, on p. 852.

forest after logging and burning provides inconvenient evidence of our ill-used power. A similar picture, on p. 852, of trees in the Czech Republic, destroyed by acid rain, adds further testimony. A chart on p. 885 identifies greenhouse gas emissions that are producing global warming. The study of evolution today must include, at least in part, the study of global ecology.

To understand the terrorist attack on the World Trade Center in New York in 2001, one of the traumatic events of recent times, along with the parallel attack on the Pentagon, and the apparently failed attack on America's political headquarters in Washington, requires an understanding of many of the themes we have explored: How did the attackers pervert a noble religious tradition to justify the murder of innocent civilians? How did a relatively small group of terrorists manage to plan and successfully execute this novel use of technology? What was their perception of the global economic, military, and political goals of the United States and of its power to achieve these goals? How did the attackers assess their own power in relationship to that of the semi-imperial United States?

On a more optimistic note, the theme of social change, also permeates the past 25 years and often presents a more praiseworthy picture of human accomplishment. Artistic communities, for example, banded together internationally to confront global social issues. In the face of hunger and starvation in Africa, dozens of internationally renowned musicians performed in a pair of huge concerts (Live Aid) in 1985 in London and Philadelphia, raising awareness of global poverty and collecting some £150 million (about $285 million) for direct assistance. Live 8, in 2005, saw more than 1,000 musicians performing in ten concerts, coordinated around the world, dedicated to urging governments to increase their aid to poor countries. The first Live Earth concert, organized by Nobel Prize winner and former U.S. Vice President Al Gore, was dedicated to raising awareness of global warming and took place in multiple locations in 2007.

The 2004 meeting of the World Social Forum in Mumbai (Bombay), India, brought together some 100,000 people to advocate for social change. The Forum began as an alternative to the meetings of the G8, the leading

Live Aid concert finale, London, 1985. From left are George Michael, Paul McCartney, Andrew Ridgeley, Freddie Mercury, David Bowie, and Bob Geldof. Another Live Aid concert was held in Philadelphia on the same day. Both concerts raised funds and awareness to combat global poverty.

industrialized powers of the world. The Forum has continued to grow as it has added to its agenda concerns for gender relations—including not only women but also gays, lesbians, bisexuals, and transgendered people; global ecology; and the dramatically unequal global distribution of political and economic power.

As you assess the usefulness of our themes in understanding contemporary history, we hope they will also help you consider the mark that you yourself wish to make in the unfolding of the world's history.

Turning Point Questions

1. What reasons were given by al-Qaeda leaders to explain the World Trade Center attack? What were the explanations offered by leaders of the United States?
2. Why has it been difficult to create an international consensus on a program to preserve the ecology of the globe?
3. Do you think that the musicians who performed in the Live Aid concerts would have been comfortable attending the World Social Forum? Why or why not?

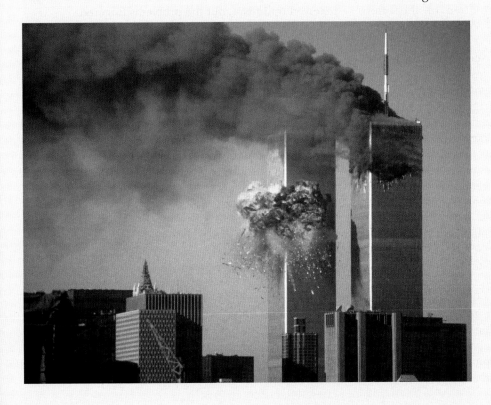

The attack by al-Qaeda on the World Trade Center, New York, September 11, 2001.

PART EIGHT

THE USEFULNESS OF HISTORY

Understanding the Present in the Light of the Past

From the outset, the argument of this textbook has been that knowledge of the major themes in world history helps us to understand not only the past but also the present. It asserts that history provides training in understanding the complexity of human life and affairs. It claims that certain themes are always present in human life. We have presented seven of them as major aspects of human life that appear and reappear in various combinations throughout history. Now, in Part Eight, we see how well the themes help us understand the world in its recent past and in its possible directions for the future.

The opening unit dealt with the evolution of hominids into homo sapiens and their very early social organization. We *homo sapiens* have changed physically only imperceptibly, if at all, in the past 100,000 years, but cultural evolution, and perhaps the evolution of the brain, showed new developments about 35,000 years ago.

In the 1950s, scientists discovered DNA (deoxyribonucleic acid), a chemical within the cells of each individual organism that carries the genetic instructions to make it what it is. DNA reaffirmed the scientific theory of evolution, and added information on genetic relationships among humans, between humans and animals, and even between humans and diseases, like AIDS. Our understanding of DNA has also given us the capacity to intervene in nature in daring enterprises never before charted, for example in the cloning and genetic engineering of crops and animals. Such constant technological innovation reminds us that to create new tools, even before the consequences can be evaluated, is human, and contentious.

Our second unit, dealing with settlement patterns, introduced themes concerning urbanization that have repeated throughout human history. Especially at the turning point of the Industrial Revolution, vast numbers of people left the countryside for industrial jobs in the big city. In the past generation, the cityward migration continued, but the conditions changed: the newest, biggest cities were in the developing world, most new jobs were in service industries; urban expansion was in

the suburbs, and a handful of metropolises seemed to dominate the entire global system of cities. By 2006, half the world's population lived in cities.

Our third theme, on politics in history, focused on the ancient empires of China, Rome, and India. The imperial theme remained critical, although at the end of the twentieth century the emphasis was on the fall of empire more than its rise. In 1991 the Soviet Union unexpectedly imploded. Its disappearance left the United States as "the sole superpower." But what did that mean? America seemed crippled: unable to apprehend the terrorists who attacked it, mired in protracted wars in Iraq and Afghanistan, failing to balance its international trade accounts, and finally witnessing its capitalistic marketplace sink into recession. The election of 2009 brought renewed optimism, but the problems lingered.

Meanwhile, around the globe other nations were on the rise. The European Union brought peace and unprecedented prosperity to its members. China achieved economic growth rates of ten percent per year for three decades. India grew more slowly, but with one billion people, nuclear weapons, and software expertise, it, too, gained in importance. By the early years of the twenty-first century, Russia, developing its immense oil wealth, was once again more assertive. More countries adopted democratic systems of government although others, most notably China, chose more dictatorial forms.

Our fourth unit introduced the theme of religion in history, focusing largely on the five most ancient, widespread, scripture-based religions: Hinduism, Buddhism, Judaism, Christianity, and Islam. The skepticism of the French Revolution and the atheism of the Russian seemed to undercut religion as a force in modern history, but in the late twentieth century religion reemerged as a powerful force in political life.

Revolution brought a theocracy to power in Iran in 1979 and ushered in an era of global Islamic political militancy. Christianity continued to take on a new complexion as it expanded, especially in Asia, Africa, and Latin

America, and revived in Russia. Protestant evangelicals, firm in their emotional faith, attracted new followers and introduced their religious principles into political contests throughout the Americas. Religious differences often embittered political relations, for example, between Jews and Muslims in Israel–Palestine and Hindus and Muslims in India. Chinese Communists suppressed Buddhists in Tibet and Muslims in Xinjiang as religion once again vied for center stage in global politics.

Trade, our fifth theme, rose to extraordinary importance. Truly global trade, initiated by the voyages of Columbus and da Gama, was in full sway by the turn of the twenty-first century. England and the United States reoriented their economies in the 1980s in the direction of free trade and, through their influence over the World Bank and the International Monetary Fund, they imposed policies of free trade on many of the poorer countries of the world, which usually found the conditions too harsh for their fledgling economies. The fastest growing national economies—China and the Southeast and East Asian "tigers"—embraced free trade and prospered by fashioning export-based economies. The World Trade Organization (WTO), the chief regulator of trade, became one of the most important institutions in international relations.

The victory for world trade, however, was far from total. The WTO was attacked by groups who believed that capitalistic competition would produce inhumane economies. Poor countries suspected that free trade would put them at the mercy of more developed economies and turn them into virtual colonies. Even the U.S., the staunchest advocate of free trade, wanted limits and regulations to protect its own economy.

Many of the social revolutions, which were the theme of our sixth unit, continued. In the aftermath of World War II, the United Nations promulgated an International Charter of Human Rights. High on the agenda were the rights of women. Each region of the world had its own issues: equal political and legal rights; equal pay for equal work; election to high political office; equal right to be born and nurtured and not to be aborted or neglected in favor of male children. Everywhere older cultural, religious, and sexual traditions concerning appropriate gender relations were reexamined and contested. As a corollary, gays and lesbians were also fighting against discrimination, often with considerable success.

The struggle against racism was at least equally important, equally widespread, and it, too, won significant victories: the apartheid government of South Africa dissolved into a one-person-one-vote democracy; political mobilization against caste discrimination created a social revolution in India; America elected an African-American president. The migration of peoples continued with greater numbers than ever before and virtually every large country in the world addressed the social and legal problems of migrant assimilation.

Around the globe millions of citizens organized themselves into non-governmental organizations (NGOs) to fight for the rights of women, minorities, and political dissidents and to struggle against poverty, to obtain food, water, shelter, health care, jobs, and other daily necessities for their constituents. Popular culture crossed national borders, creating a different kind of social revolution of its own: "fusion" in food, music, and the arts.

On the other hand, many people resisted social revolution out of a desire to preserve their cultures and languages unchanged. Others resisted for less noble motives of sexism, homophobia, racism, and a general antagonism toward "the other." Struggles among cultures continued as part of the human condition.

The seventh unit, with its theme of technological change, connects smoothly with social revolution, since rapidly evolving technology continued to inspire new opportunities and incite new turbulence. The rise of computerization and virtually instantaneous communication around the globe revolutionized the world. Information became available as never before. Containerization slashed the cost of shipping. New jobs were created, older ones terminated, and millions more transferred from high-wage countries to nations with lower labor costs.

Sources of power, however, grew increasingly problematic. Could the world continue to depend so heavily on fossil fuels? How long would they last? How much would they cost? How much of their pollution could the earth's environment tolerate before all human life was endangered? Perhaps most threatening of all was the continuing presence of nuclear weapons and, especially, the fear that they would fall into the hands of terrorists. Technologies of peace and war continued as technologies of blessing and curse.

Conclusion: The Search for Identity. The structure of this book suggests that individuals and groups are constantly confronting changes originating from the many themes of human life, from new understandings of our evolution to a bewildering array of changing technologies. As we absorb new experiences and information, individually and collectively we modify our sense of self, our sense of where we are coming from and where we might (like to) be going. Usually the modifications are incremental and small, but sometimes they demand major transformations in attitude and behavior. This study of major themes in human history is designed to help readers see how others in the past negotiated their encounters with these themes, and how we might embark on our own encounters, with as much satisfaction as possible, in the present.

CHAPTER TWENTY-THREE

Contemporary History: Evolution, Settlements, Politics, and Religion

Contemporary history is hard to understand because we are living through it. Usually historians form their judgments only after they know how things turn out, but in the case of contemporary history we don't know yet. Who will win the war? Which candidate will win the election? How will his or her policies work out in the long run? Which styles in music, art, or fashion will endure and which will perish quickly as mere fads? How can we form definitive conclusions when we are still in the middle of events?

In contemporary history, the history of the last 20 years or so, the results are not clear. Leaders change their policies. Sports teams that are winning go into slumps; so do national and international economies. New inventions and ideas render older ones obsolete, eliminating long-standing industries and jobs while creating new ones. Unpredictable events erupt, totally altering the course of events.

So what do we do? It is the argument of this book that a grounding in the central themes of history helps us grasp contemporary events. The themes do not tell us how current events will turn out—the past does not predict the future—but they alert us to possible outcomes that we might not have considered. They enlarge our awareness of what is important to consider.

In this chapter we review the themes of the first four units of the text—evolution, settlements, politics, and religion—and illustrate ways in which they continue to appear in our own time. In the process, we shall see how knowledge of the past enlarges our understanding of the present, and how being well-informed in the present enriches our appreciation of the past.

KEY TOPICS

- On Evolution
- On Settlements
- On Politics and Empire
- On Religion
- The Thematic Approach: What Difference Does It Make?

On Evolution

As we saw in Chapter One, long before the scientific discoveries of the process of evolution, most major cultural and religious traditions of the world had mythological tales of the creation of the world and of humans. Those mythological explanations endure because they frequently contain profound understandings of human nature. But scientific methods of exploration, data collection, and evaluation have led to more systematic ways of understanding the emergence of human life. Scientists today believe that humans evolved from hominids, over millions of years, through biological processes that increased their adaptability, sophistication, and power. In the mid-nineteenth century, British naturalist Charles Darwin formulated the biological hypothesis that a process of "natural selection" was responsible for the evolution of species. Since then

Protest against global warming, Pontianak, Indonesia, 2000. Due to forest fires that rage on unchecked, and to urban congestion, Indonesia is one of the most polluted places on earth.

the entire record of fossil discoveries has supported the Darwinian argument and, since the 1970s, the study of human DNA (deoxyribonucleic acid), the biological material that instructs all the cells within each individual, has added further confirmation.

In Chapter One, we also reviewed evidence for extensive cultural development, beginning with migration and adaptation to new geographical areas, increased capacity for speech and communication, and the fashioning and use of increasingly sophisticated hand tools. About 35,000 years ago, in quicker succession, came further cultural accomplishments: the creation of art, the domestication of plants and animals, and the association of humans in small bands for hunting, gathering, farming, and child-raising. It appears that further evolution of the human brain, though not of the rest of the body, made these later cultural developments possible.

The DNA Code and its Discoveries

Our study of biological and cultural evolution makes us more sensitive to a number of scientific developments in our own time. Consider, for example, the discovery of DNA and its functions. The unlocking of this secret of biological development, largely the work of James D. Watson and Francis Crick in the 1950s, based on data provided by Rosalind Franklin, has opened many new doors. Most recently, for example, some scientists, reading the DNA of selected individuals from around the world, have argued that they see evolution continuing within historical time periods. Individuals within some groups show genetic change in specific brain cells that normally produce somewhat larger brains. The lead researcher, Prof. Bruce Lahn at the University of Chicago, concluded, "the growth of brain size and complexity—is likely still going on." (*Science Daily*, Sept. 9, 2005 http://www.sciencedaily.com/releases/2005/09/050909221043.htm) Other scientists dispute these findings, partly because the test group is too small for statistical verification. But the subject of the speed of evolution is on the table as part of contemporary history.

In another development, stemming from the fact that the great apes and humans share 97 percent of the same DNA, two philosophers, Peter Singer of Australia and Paolo Cavaliere of Italy, founded the Great Ape Project in 1993:

> The idea is founded upon undeniable scientific proof that non-human great apes share more than genetically similar DNA with their human counterparts. They enjoy a rich emotional and cultural existence in which they experience emotions such as fear, anxiety and happiness. They share the intellectual capacity to create and use tools, learn and teach other languages. They remember their past and plan for their future. … The Great Ape Project seeks to end the unconscionable treatment of our nearest living relatives by obtaining for non-human great apes the fundamental moral and legal protections of the right to life, the freedom from arbitrary deprivation of liberty, and protection from torture. (http://www.greatapeproject.org/)

In 2007 the Project won a signal victory when the Spanish Parliament conferred these three legal protections on great apes.

Cloning and Genetic Engineering. Other new by-products of the cracking of the DNA genetic code have been the cloning of animals and the production of genetically modified foods. These processes, too, are subjects of contemporary history, for they are continuing day by day, acclaimed by some but opposed by others, both within and outside the scientific community. Genetic engineering has enabled scientists to make clones, genetically exact copies of living creatures. The first clone of a mammal, a sheep, was born in 1996. Cloned from a cell taken from a mammary gland, she was named Dolly, in honor of the singer Dolly Parton, and was a genetically exact copy of an already existing sheep. She gave birth to six sheep, born naturally. But from the age of five she suffered from arthritis, and she died of a lung infection at age six, about half the usual life span of a sheep. Geneticists wonder if her biological age matched that of the sheep from whose cell she was cloned rather than that of a conventional newborn. In addition, Dolly was the only sheep to survive out of 277 attempts at cloning up to that time. Subsequently, other mammals were cloned, including horses and bulls, but also with failure rates that bring into question the value of the technique.

The cloning of humans has been a subject of avid discussion and controversy. Cloning humans is illegal in most countries, both because the failure rate in cloning large, complicated animals is so high, and because the ethics of it are questionable. Should bereaved parents be allowed to clone a much-loved child who has died in an accident? Or is each individual unique and entitled to a unique genetic identity? Would you want to be cloned over and over again for centuries to come? Consider also that no one knows what, if any, biological changes may be inserted into the hereditary chain through cloning, and that any such changes would be irreversible.

This question of unknown long-term effects has especially dogged the acceptance of genetically modified foodstuffs. Here scientists mix genetic material, DNA, from different kinds of organisms to create new organisms that have never existed before. One of the most prevalent examples is the creation of seeds, through the grafting of recombinant DNA cells (DNA cells taken from different kinds of organisms and combined in the laboratory in new ways), which are resistant to specific plant diseases. Genetically modified seeds and plants have been widely accepted in the United States, but not in most parts of Europe. Trade battles over the issue continue. In the long view of history, this is a debate over the degree to which evolution is acceptable if it is human-made and artificially produces new organisms that could not form in nature. Once genetically modified organisms enter into the breeding patterns of the natural world, they cannot be removed. Will they prove to be safe?

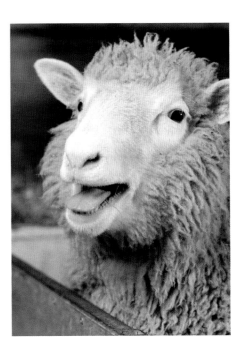

Dolly, the cloned sheep, 1997. Genetic engineering promised great hopes for increasing longevity, health, and food supplies, but it entered a new, unknown world of biological transformation that cannot be reversed.

The Evolution of Diseases

Evolution occurs not only in the world of humans, animals, and plants; diseases also evolve. Some disease microbes prove resistant to today's medications; their genes will survive in new generations. For this reason, medications that are effective today will sooner or later prove inadequate to treat resistant strains of diseases. Doctors caution that the overuse of antibiotic drugs will speed up the evolution of new forms of infection that the drugs will not be able to suppress. In this way, pharmacology becomes a footrace between the evolution of diseases, and the creation of new medical remedies.

Some new diseases appeared among human populations without prior indications. The most lethal was AIDS (Acquired Immunodeficiency Syndrome), which is believed to have crossed over from chimpanzees to humans in the mid-1900s in West Africa, perhaps transmitted by a bite or a cut or through the ingestion of chimpanzee meat. AIDS then spread among humans through sexual contact and the sharing of nonsterile injection needles, but it was identified as an epidemic only in 1981.

When HIV (Human Immunodeficiency Virus), the virus that causes AIDS, was first recognized as a health threat in the late 1970s, no drugs were available for treatment and the disease was deemed fatal. By 1996, however, a combination of drugs was found to be effective in inhibiting the development of HIV into AIDS, but the drugs are very expensive. In the third world, where 95 percent of HIV cases

AT A GLANCE: EVOLUTION, SETTLEMENTS, POLITICS, RELIGION

DATE	EVOLUTION	SETTLEMENTS (CITIES)	POLITICS	RELIGION
1968–1970s			• 1978 Deng Xiaoping heads Chinese government	• 1968 Latin American Bishop's Conference supports Liberation Theology • 1979 Iranian revolution
1980s	• 1981 AIDS epidemic identified	• 1980 Shenzhen, China, designated Special Economic Zone (SEZ) • 1980s sites and services programs for slum improvement	• 1989 Tiananmen massacre • 1989–91 Russia leaves Afghanistan; Soviet Union dissolves • 1983, 1993, 1995, 1996, 1998, 2000 Bombing attacks on US overseas military diplomatic posts	• 1989 *Fatwa* against Salman Rushdie
1990s	• 1993 Great Ape Project • 1996 Sheep (Dolly) cloned	• 1990s in-place, slum upgrading projects • 1992 Rodney King race riot, Los Angeles	• 1993 Formation of European Union (EU) • 1994 Chechnya declares independence from Russia • 1997 Hong Kong reverts to China • 1999, 2004, 2007–09 former USSR satellites join NATO and the EU	• 1990s Pope John Paul II criticizes Liberation Theology • 1990 Latin American Evangelical Pentecostal Commission (CEPLA) established; 75 million Pentecostals in Latin America (2005) • 1992 Militant Hindus raze Babri Mosque • 1992–98 civil war in Algeria; 100,000 die • 1992–95 civil war in Yugoslavia • 1999 Chinese government bans Falun Gong
2000s	• 2002 Discovery of Toumai skull and (2005) teeth and jaw fragments	• 2005 Immigrant riots in suburban Paris • 2006 Fifty percent of world's population urban	• 2003 US declares war on Iraq • 2005 Agreement in Northern Ireland for peaceful power sharing • 2008 China hosts Olympic Games	• 2000s Christian–Muslim battles in Nigeria • 2002 Gujarat, India: Hindu–Muslim killing, leaving 2000 dead

occur—60 percent of them in sub-Saharan Africa—the drugs are prohibitively expensive, although some drug manufacturers have negotiated to provide them at somewhat lower cost in poor countries.

By the end of 2007, approximately 25 million people worldwide had died of AIDS. In 2007 alone, an estimated 2.1 million people died of AIDS and related diseases; 33 million were affected with the HIV virus, 15 million of them women; and 2.5 million new cases of HIV were reported or estimated. Global spending on AIDS research, prevention, and treatment reached $10 billion in 2007, 30 times the spending in 1997. The new funds came in part from philanthropies such as the Bill and Melinda Gates Foundation; the Global Fund to Fight AIDS, Tuberculosis, and Malaria; as well as governments, such as the initiative of U.S. President George W. Bush to spend $15 billion, later increased to $30 billion, over five years in a global anti-AIDS program.

Gender Relationships

A third area in which the issues of evolution reappear is the debate over the significance of gender in human affairs. Although we do not know for sure, paleoanthropologists believe that gender roles must have been determined largely by biology, with women giving birth and nursing infants and as a result staying closer to home and being responsible for gathering food, and perhaps, later, for growing it. Men would have been more responsible for hunting and foraging at longer distances. Most believe that because of their greater physical strength, men must have claimed more authority within the family. In the early twentieth century, feminists asserted that physical strength should not determine political rights; women must have the vote. In the United States women gained the right to vote in 1920. By the mid-twentieth century, the feminist demand was for equality in the workplace and in the legal system. Feminists achieved many successes, especially in the Western world, but much remained to be achieved.

Gender relationships within the family were transformed in the second half of the twentieth century. Marriage rates declined, as more couples chose to live without a formal ceremony and more people chose not to pair off at all. Parents chose to have their children later in life, and to have fewer of them. Apart from the immediate post-World War II baby boom, birth rates generally declined everywhere. Increasingly, women worked outside the home. Throughout the world, gender definitions—the expectation of what men and women would do—changed markedly. And it changed differently for different groups of women. The feminist movement, never monolithic, splintered into far more groups than ever before. In the Western world, many women wanted to retain, or reclaim, the lives of mothers and housewives, while others wanted to assert their right to a creative career. Most wanted both. The decisions by governments and employers on whether or not to provide maternity leave and child-care facilities affected women's opportunities. These issues became important targets of feminist campaigns.

Especially in Europe, "essentialist feminism" argued that women must define themselves in their own way, not in terms of what men are or are not, but in terms of themselves. Ultimately, feminists asserted, this would also create the most rewarding form of female-male (and female-female) relations. In France, Luce Irigaray wrote in *This Sex Which is Not One*:

> How can I say it? That we are women from the start. That we don't have to be turned into women by them, labeled by them, made holy and profaned by them. That that has always happened without their efforts. And that their history, their stories, constitute the locus of our displacement. Their properties are our exile. Their enclosures, the death of our love. Their words, the gag upon our lips… Let's hurry and invent our own phrases. So that everywhere and always we can continue to embrace… (Irigaray, pp. 212–15)

In the non-Western world, feminists also felt that they had to create their own self-definitions, not only without reference to ways in which males might define them, but also without reference to the ways in which Western women would define them. Beginning with the essay by Chandra Talpade Mohanty, "Under Western Eyes: Feminist Scholarship and Colonial Discourses" (1991), third world women refused to be pigeon-holed by women in the first world. Mohanty declared that they would define themselves not as a single group, but in all their separate identities.

Gay Rights. Debates over the acceptability of homosexuality in Western cultures have turned on the question of what behaviors are natural in human sexuality. Like feminists, gays and lesbians rejected being defined by others, and claimed the right

Panamanian gays march to demand their rights in Panama City, Panama, June 25, 2005. Gay men and women are demanding that the government pass an anti-discrimination law. The struggle for legalizing gay rights, which began in the United States and Western Europe, has spread throughout the world. The sign reads "No more deaths because of homophobia."

to define their feelings and their behavior as normal and natural. They often joined with feminists in revolting against patriarchal definitions of sexual behavior and propriety. In general, the 1960s initiated a movement for sexual freedom and expression for everyone. Feminist and gay movements, along with smaller, parallel movements of bisexuals and transsexuals, were all parts of it.

The public assertion of gay rights took inspiration from the resistance to gay bashing in the United States. The forceful resistance by gays and lesbians to a police raid on the Stonewall Inn, a gay bar, in New York's Greenwich Village, on June 27, 1969, is often viewed as a turning point in public attitudes. In 1973, the American Psychiatric Association declassified homosexuality as a mental disorder, as did the WHO in 1992, the government of Great Britain in 1994, the Ministry of Health in Russia in 1999, and the Chinese Society of Psychiatry in 2001. What was at stake was the definition of what it means to be a healthy human being.

On Settlements

Since ancient times, people have gathered together, forming ever larger communities. In Chapter Seventeen we looked at urban settlements at the turning point of the Industrial Revolution. Vast numbers of people left agriculture for industrial jobs and cities began to absorb an ever-larger segment of the workforce. In the twentieth century this process speeded up. Service jobs replaced industrial jobs as the primary urban occupation and cities multiplied in population. In 1900, about one person in six lived in a city, a total of about 260 million people. By 2000, 47 percent of the world's population was urban, about three billion people worldwide. According to UN estimates the 50 percent mark was reached in 2006.

The Growth of Cities

Individual cities grew to enormous size. By the end of the twentieth century, nineteen had become "megacities," with populations of ten million or more. They expanded geographically to breathtaking proportions. The Los Angeles metropolitan region, for example, held a population of 12 million, spanned a diameter of 120 miles, included five counties and 132 incorporated cities, and produced a gross annual economic output of nearly $250 billion.

During the twentieth century, the geographical distribution of cities shifted in an unexpected way. The link between economic growth and urbanization, which had once seemed so logical and natural, was broken. In earlier times, cities had mostly arisen in wealthier regions, where their presence seemed to reflect the "pull" of urban economic growth and job opportunities. In the late twentieth century, cities became more characteristic of poorer regions of the world, where their growth seemed to reflect the "push" from an overpopulated countryside with a scarcity of jobs. In 1900, cities in the "economically developed world" held about 163 million people; those in the "underdeveloped world" about 97 million. By 2000, the developed world held 900 million urbanites, the underdeveloped world 2.150 billion.

The key economic functions of cities changed equally dramatically. The large-scale industrial manufacture of commodities, such as steel in Pittsburgh, automobiles in Detroit, and textiles in Mumbai, gave way to service industries, such as: information technology in California's Silicon Valley and India's Bangalore; the film industries of Hollywood and Bollywood; the pleasure palaces of Las Vegas and the somewhat more risqué Bangkok and Manila; the theme parks of the Disney empire in Florida, California, Paris, Tokyo, and Hong Kong; and the tourism of such holiday destinations as Cancun, Rio de Janeiro, and Cape Town.

A Single Global System

By the end of the twentieth century, shifts in international politics fostered the incorporation of cities into a single global system with an unprecedented density of interaction. After the two world wars, vast regions of Asia and Africa, which had been divided into separate spheres of colonial influence, became independent of colonial control. The countries of Latin America, under the quasi-colonial influence of the United States, also gained increasing power to chart their own paths. After the Cold War came to an end, the political forces that had carved up the world into the "first world" of capitalist democracy, the "second world" of Communist Party dominance, and the "third world" of mostly impoverished colonies gave way to a more thoroughly integrated global system of cities.

So extraordinary were the size, technological transformation, and global integration of twentieth-century cities, that many observers viewed this combination as a fourth turning point in world history, equivalent in its impact to each of the three earlier urban revolutions: the move from nomadic existence to settled village life, about 15,000 years ago; the establishment of the first full-fledged cities, about 5,000 years ago; and the industrialization of cities, about 200 years ago.

Systems of Cities

In the late twentieth century, the World Wide Web created an entirely new dimension in the historic networks of exchange of goods, people, and ideas. The internet, "the information superhighway," created for military purposes in the 1970s, and widely available to the general public beginning in the 1990s, transformed personal and institutional relationships as dramatically as the automobile had transformed them almost a century earlier. By reducing the cost of transmitting information to virtually zero, the internet increased the density, extent, and speed of communication and exchange of capital throughout the world system of cities. Improvements in browsing the internet led to the formalization of the World Wide Web in 1989. People understood the power of the Web immediately. By 1994, some three million had connected; by mid-1999, 200 million; and by the end of 2005, more than one billion.

The new technology of the Web and the new political economy of more open borders produced "globalization," the linking of cities and regions into global networks for the exchange of information, capital, commodities, and labor. The openness and diversity of the Web were revolutionary. Access was available, free of cost, to everyone, everywhere, who had access to a computer and an internet provider. Nevertheless, some urban centers remained dominant and even increased their dominance. Sociologist Saskia Sassen noted the persistent influence of New York, London, and Tokyo over the international economy, referring to them—and only them—as "Global Cities." At the other extreme, some regions were hardly touched by globalization. For example, only 13 million of sub-Saharan Africa's 765 million inhabitants, 1.7 percent, used the internet in 2005. By contrast, in the U.S., Japan, South Korea, Canada, Australia, and the Netherlands, about two of every three residents used an internet connection. (Statistics on usage available at www.internetworldstats.com)

With the Web and email providing inexpensive instantaneous communication everywhere in the world, it became easier for manufacturers to relocate production facilities to poorer areas where wages were lower. The United States alone lost 35 million jobs between 1969 and 1976, one-half of them from its "rustbelt" industrial heartland. (Bluestone and Harrison) Similar patterns appeared in Western Europe and in Japan. The economies of developed regions were shifting out of manufacturing into services.

China was the great exception, demonstrating continuous growth in urban manufacturing. China instituted four "special economic zones" to jumpstart development. The largest, the city and region of Shenzhen, contiguous to Hong Kong, grew from virtually no population in 1980 to 12 million in 2005. Manufacturing, trade, and services flourished. Directly across the Huangpu River from Shanghai, the government designated Pudong a "national project" in 1991, also with the status of a special economic zone. By the early years of the twenty-first century, Pudong held some 10,000 financial, commercial, and trade institutions from over 60 countries in over 100 high-rises, among them some of the world's tallest skyscrapers. China's urban population had risen from 16 percent in 1960 to 19.6 percent in 1980, then jumped sharply to 35.8 percent in 2000, and 40.5 percent in 2005.

Similar policies of urban development through state-aided capitalist enterprise were also adopted in communist Vietnam, especially in Ho Chi Minh City in the south, but also in Hanoi in the north. Cities in communist countries, which had been cut off from the global economy for decades, were now joining it and adopting urban bourgeois consumer styles, although the Party did not (yet) allow political democracy.

The Soviet Union remained committed to centralized state planning under a single-party state until 1989–91 when the system imploded and the USSR dissolved as a political entity. Centralized state planning under a single-party state came to an end. Russia's urban population reached 73 percent in 1990 and stabilized at that point. Ethnic diversity in the major cities, especially in Moscow, increased as Chechens and peoples from regions of the former Soviet Union, as well as immigrant Turks, Arabs, Chinese, and Vietnamese arrived in search of work. Ethnic competition sometimes broke out in violence.

Russian cities that had provided only minimal shopping facilities in the past began to see new shops open and private businesses flourish, quickly giving the cities more life and color. Billboards proliferated. Business services, a sector of the economy virtually nonexistent under communist rule, employed almost 10 percent of Moscow's workforce by 2000. Many of the members of this new class were young, just beginning to master the language, computer, and business skills of their new tasks. Often they arose from among former Communist Party bureaucrats, the people most experienced in administration and possessing the connections to buy the businesses, at bargain-basement prices, from the state, which was now withering away. Their prosperity inspired envy—and new commercial outlets to attract their disposable income. By 2005, Moscow was estimated to have 33 billionaires, more than any other city in the world, and about 30,000 millionaires. (*The Times* of London, 20 October 2005, www.timesonline.co.uk/article/0,,13509-1833619,00.html)

Cities as Systems

As cities gained access to the global system, albeit not on equal terms, to what degree did the internal structures of cities become more alike? To what degree did the global system of cities encourage similarities in the internal systems in cities everywhere?

One group of scholars claimed that Los Angeles was becoming the model of the emerging global city. A "Los Angeles School" of urban studies identified Los Angeles as the new "shock city" of the United States. Los Angeles more than doubled in population between 1950 and 1975, from just over four million people to just under nine million, easily leapfrogging Chicago to become America's second largest city and, the scholars asserted, also surpassing Chicago as the scene of the newest trends in urban development.

Many of Los Angeles' "shock" characteristics reflected trends globally: spatial and social fragmentation in a city with multiple geographical centers, many central business districts, no dominant social and economic group, and no normative cultural style. The urban agglomeration consisted of a vast hinterland of individual cities each with its own personality; vast social divisions and inequities among its ethnically diverse residents; high levels of immigration, both high- and low-skilled,

KEY TERM

gentrification The return of wealthier citizens to areas of cities that had become rundown, and their new investment in restoring and revitalizing the areas.

Los Angeles County 1990 House Values

- $130,000 or less
- $130,000–$260,000
- $260,000–$390,000
- $390,000–$520,000
- $520,000 or more

(County Median = $162,000)

Housing segregation by income level: median house values, Los Angeles, 1990. Towards the end of the twentieth century, large cities across the United States were experiencing housing segregation by income level. Large, older areas in the city centers became rundown and impoverished, providing housing for the poor, while areas on the periphery provided homes for the wealthy. There were exceptions. **Gentrification** occurred in some downtown pockets as wealthier citizens chose to return, and some older peripheral areas housed poorer people. But this map from Los Angeles captures the general, overall pattern. Data and cartography by Philip J. Ethington © 2009.

815

from several continents; a massive and lucrative film industry of illusion, fashion, and profit; high-tech industrialization, much of it based on industries for warfare, airplanes, missiles, and electronics; strong linkages to the global economy as America's leading port city on the Pacific Rim; a fast-growing economy with strong emphasis on consumption; challenging ecological problems (born of its semi-desert location in a kind of topographical bowl); and reliance on privately owned cars running on endless miles of freeways as the principal means of transportation.

In race riots, too, Los Angeles was a "shock" city. The riot in Los Angeles' Watts neighborhood in 1965 was one of the worst of America's many civil disturbances during that decade. In 1992, the most destructive urban rioting in the history of the United States erupted when a court exonerated white police officers, who had been captured on videotape beating Rodney King, an African-American.

The Impact of Immigration. Like Los Angeles, many global megacities had high rates of diverse immigration, fragmented social groups, and tense separations among classes. Third world megacities attracted migrants from all parts of their nation and beyond. Abidjan drew from all of the West African Sahel; Mexico City from throughout Central America; Shanghai from the entire Yangzi River basin. Oil-rich cities of the Persian Gulf attracted migrants from the surrounding Arabian Sea periphery in Africa and Asia. European cities received citizens from their former colonies; Paris, for example, from North and West Africa; London, from India, Pakistan, and the West Indies.

The immigrants did not always find the jobs they were seeking, and, as in Los Angeles, tensions came with the combination of diversity and inequality: "Large public housing projects in Paris and Amsterdam were increasingly populated by the structurally unemployed and their children, and—just as in their New York and London equivalents—violence was simmering just below the surface" (Hall, p. 459). Not all violence was based on immigrant diversity. In many countries, electoral contests and sports competitions evoked periodic outbreaks of violence. Urban riots across India in the 1990s and early 2000s pitted Hindus and Muslims against one another as social upheaval, religious tension, and political grandstanding combined to inflame both spontaneous mobs and organized rioters. (Brass) Violence among competing criminal gangs also flared up periodically in many cities around the world.

A set of studies of large cities around the world concluded that in the process of globalization the spatial divisions among classes, ethnic groups, racial groups, and lifestyle groups within the city increased and "hardened, sometimes literally in the form of walls that function to protect the rich from the poor" (Marcuse and van Kempen, p. 250). Patterns of social segregation were common from city-to-city and nation-to-nation. They resembled Los Angeles. In all of the cities, people could live out their lives almost completely within geographically self-contained divisions, with residence, work, recreation, and socialization all included within their quarters of the city. These quarters were also separated from one another according to their political outlooks and self interest. "Partially out of self-interest and partially simply because they do not see, meet and hear the others, decisions painful to others are easily made" (ibid.). The spatial divisions were increasing whether cities were industrializing or deindustrializing, whether they seemed to be on the leading edge of globalization or excluded from it.

Socially, the segregation of Asian and African immigrants in Europe had similarities to racial segregation in the United States. As African-Americans had migrated from the rural south to the urban north in the U.S., so migrants from poorer regions and nations came to the now-booming cities of Europe in search of jobs. Some came from the former imperial colonies: Indians, Pakistanis, and West Indians to London,

Birmingham, Leeds, and other British cities; Algerians, Tunisians, Moroccans, Senegalese, and Malians to Paris. There were millions of others without any imperial connections, especially from Yugoslavia, Turkey, and southern Italy. Millions of the migrants came from Islamic countries, introducing a new religious element into many European cities. By 2000, 15 percent of Paris's population, 15–25 percent of the population of Frankfurt, Stuttgart, and Munich, and 50 percent of the population of Amsterdam was made up of international migrants.

Reactionary political parties, such as that of Jacques Le Pen in France, *Front National* (the National Front), ran on platforms urging bans on immigration and the expulsion of those immigrants already present. At street level, fights between immigrant and native youths became frequent, sometimes leading to firebombings. In many European cities, nativist youths shaved their heads and, as "skinheads," went out seeking "foreigners," even those who had been in place for a generation and more. In England the phenomenon earned its own name: "Paki[stani]-bashing." In France, as the Muslim population coming from the former colonies in North Africa increased, cultural conflict took on additional religious overtones. In 2005, rioting shook the immigrant, relatively poor, suburbs of Paris and spilled over into other cities in France and even into the Netherlands and Belgium. Beyond the immediate need to restore law and order, local and national political leaders appeared stymied as to what course to take economically, culturally, and politically.

The Rise of the Urban Slum. In the poorer countries of Asia, Africa, and South America, urban slums continued to expand in size and population. An estimated "924 million people lived in slums worldwide in 2001, or about 32 per cent of the global urban population … with higher concentration in the developing world cities" (UN, p. 2). Cities and nations experimented with diverse strategies for coping with their slums. Until the 1960s, most government plans in the developing world advocated the construction of public housing to accommodate new urban immigrants. The cost, however, was prohibitive. By the 1980s programs of "sites and services" won favor. Governments would provide slum dwellers with space—a site marked off with individual plinths, or floors, often about 200 square feet—and the basic services of water, sewage, and electricity, which householders could not provide for themselves on an individual basis. The recipients of the plots would then construct their own housing from their own resources. Even this strategy proved expensive and it was difficult to decide which of the slum dwellers should receive the plots. In addition, after construction, the owner-builders often sold off their new homes to more middle-class buyers and returned to the slums, preferring the money to the home.

Generations of squatter settlements in Venezuela. Squatters migrate to cities in search of jobs, and often temporarily settle in shacks. If they succeed in finding employment, they upgrade and expand their shacks into more conventional homes. On this hillside in Caracas, Venezuela, several generations of squatters, acting collectively, have slowly improved and expanded their homes and their settlement. The picture does not make clear whether they have also received legal recognition. Many squatter settlements do succeed in achieving legal status, some do not.

By the 1990s a new strategy of upgrading the existing slums gained acceptance. Governments would retrofit slums with water and sewage lines and electric connections, and realign their street plans. Often they also provided deeds or security of tenure. These interventions improved the physical quality of life of the residents while maintaining the basic social structure and organization of the slum. In some cities, these structural improvements were supplemented with social, health, and educational services. As governments and NGOs gained experience, they created a wide array of partnership programs to work with—rather than just for—the slum dwellers. (Plummer)

Despite pessimistic accounts such as Mike Davis's *Planet of Slums*, not all situations were dismal. By the turn of the millennium, differences among the regions of the world were emerging clearly. Cities whose economies were generally improving, as in much of East and Southeast Asia, and those that implemented specific policies to improve the lives of slum dwellers, as in much of Latin America, showed progress. On the other hand, in Africa, the proportion of slum dwellers continued to rise rapidly (UN, p. 2). Because their settlements were often illegal, slum organizers had to negotiate deals with the police and the politicians. Squatters could maintain their toeholds in the city only through collective organization, and payoffs to authorities.

Global Research and Planning

With half the world's population urban, with metropolises sprawling for miles in all directions, and with the accessibility of the World Wide Web, the historic city, with its legally delineated boundaries, had become less distinct as a functional unit. The end of the Cold War broke down other regional boundaries as well. In 1976 the UN sponsored the first Conference on Human Settlements, called Habitat I, in Vancouver, Canada, followed by Habitat II in Istanbul in 1996, and Habitat III, again in Vancouver, in 2006. Urban research and study centers multiplied around the globe, some linked to government planning offices, some to universities, and some to NGOs. They addressed a wide spectrum of concerns including: physical planning, ecology, group relations, women's issues, youth organization, slum improvement, neighborhood planning, and the historic preservation of significant structures from the past. Cities were now firmly embedded in regional systems and global networks of communication, trade, and migration. Urban research and urban planning attempted to keep pace. It was easy to argue that the pattern of settlements around the world had indeed entered a fourth stage.

On Politics and Empire

The turn of the twenty-first century brought some abrupt and astonishing realignments of global power. The Soviet Union had recently collapsed, leaving Russia in search of a new, more modest role commensurate with its reduced sphere of influence, but taking into account its enormous oil wealth, powerful armaments, and desire for recognition. America, despite its "superpower" status, soon found itself embroiled in two wars, and then saw its economy fall into the deepest recession in almost a century. Although the Cold War was over, new forms of guerrilla warfare—including terrorist attacks by suicide bombers, willing to die in order to destroy their enemies—unleashed new uncertainties and fears. On the other hand, Europe was successfully expanding the membership and wealth of its steadily growing union. And China, riding the fastest economic expansion known in modern history, rose to new prominence and prestige.

The Former Soviet Union

We have already discussed in Chapter Twenty-one the shock that attended the collapse and disintegration of the Soviet Union and of the Communist Party between 1989 and 1991. In retrospect, the weaknesses of the USSR seemed quite apparent. Its economy was neither producing nor distributing goods effectively. Its bureaucracy was top-heavy with Party officials who limited the freedoms of the growing professional classes. Official atheism suppressed deep desires for religious freedom among the people. Resentments festered in the satellite countries of Eastern Europe and in the non-Russian states of the USSR against governments that had been imposed from Moscow by force of arms, and against Moscow itself. The Soviet Union's lands were an ecological disaster area. The huge Aral Sea was thoroughly polluted and had begun to dry up. In 1986, a nuclear power plant at Chernobyl, Ukraine, suffered a catastrophic meltdown. At first the USSR tried to deny the disaster, but as the waves of radiation poison spread outward, the nations of central Europe responded with anger and condemnation. An ongoing war in Afghanistan was ravaging the nation, with no end in sight. Finally, the Soviet Union could no longer afford its arms race with the United States.

President Mikhail Gorbachev, who presided over the dissolution of the USSR, won a reputation in the outside world for wisdom and courage, but inside the USSR many judged him a failure. His successor, Boris Yeltsin (1991–99), kept the country afloat with foreign loans. Meanwhile, the transition from communism to capitalism funneled immense wealth into the pockets of a few insiders who managed to buy state-run enterprises at throwaway prices. Corruption was rampant. Inequalities multiplied as the average worker lost the welfare protection formerly provided by the communist system. In addition to these domestic problems, the Muslim-majority republic of Chechnya declared its independence from Russia in 1994. Yeltsin put down the main revolt, after almost two years of fighting, but Chechen guerrillas continued the struggle, killing hundreds in numerous confrontations in Chechnya and within Russia itself, including attacks in theaters, schools, subways, and airplanes. The guerrilla warfare continues till today.

Yeltsin's successor, Vladimir Putin, formerly head of the Russian secret police, looked on his predecessors with scorn for their weakness and attempted to reassert the power of the Russian state. He imposed limits on the freedom of expression, jailing and even murdering opponents. He confronted the United States over the deployment of weapons systems. In 2008, he attempted to reclaim parts of the contiguous nation of Georgia, which had once been a part of the Soviet Union. Putin could assert renewed power on the basis of renewed exploitation of Russia's natural oil and gas deposits, and the immense profits from their international sales. Russia holds some of the world's largest natural gas and petroleum fields, and, under Putin, became the world's second-largest producer of oil, after Saudi Arabia. By 2007 oil and gas made up 65 percent of Russia's exports. The Russian economy became one of the fastest growing in the world, gave Russia renewed leverage internationally, and invested Putin with great popularity and power.

Theater siege, Moscow 2002.
In 1991, as the Soviet Union collapsed, Chechnya declared its independence. Russia responded with force and warfare followed, which continues sporadically until today (2009). Russia regained control of Chechnya, but only after tens of thousands were killed on both sides. Most of the fighting has been in Chechnya itself, but Chechen rebels have also attacked theaters, schools, subways, and airplanes in Russia. In 2002 Chechen guerrilla fighters—most of them women—seized a theater in Moscow and held some 800 people hostage for three days, until Russian troops recaptured the building.

Nevertheless, Russia was not seen as a serious rival to the United States, as the USSR had once been. For centuries, world politics had turned on a balance of power among the major nations. This was true even during the Cold War, when the two superpowers balanced one another. With the end of the Soviet Union, America remained as the sole superpower, able to project massive military, economic, and cultural power everywhere on the globe. At least, that was conventional wisdom. But what did it mean to be sole superpower?

The United States Stands Alone

In 1992 Francis Fukuyama argued in *The End of History* that the fall of Soviet communism had left just one viable political-economic system in the world, the capitalist-democratic system of the United States, its allies in Western Europe, and a few other countries. Indeed, even postcommunist Russia was now moving in this direction. This system had won, Fukuyama argued, because it was the best. There were some outstanding examples that seemed to support his point: Economically, the United States had recovered from economic difficulties in the 1980s, a period in which it had appeared that Japan—with its Toyotas and Hondas and array of high quality consumer products—might surpass it. In the early 1990s, however, the American economy, energized by innovations in communications technology and marketing, entered into a new phase of growth, one of the longest and steepest in the history of the nation (while Japan experienced significant difficulties, especially in the financial sectors of its economy).

Without the Soviet Union as an alternative, many nations turned toward America for assistance or advice. Almost all the former satellites of the USSR chose to move toward free-market economic policies, and the Czech Republic, Hungary, and Poland joined NATO in 1999, with Russia's full consent. Six other former satellites joined in 2004, again with Russian consent. Middle Eastern nations, with no Russian alternative to choose, now aligned their foreign policies toward America and relied on America to mediate the Arab–Israeli dispute. India, which was already democratic politically, added a set of economic policy changes to reduce the role of the state in the national economy and to convert to greater reliance on free markets. In the Caribbean, communist Cuba's economy, already weak, virtually collapsed as the Soviet Union could no longer buy its sugar crop nor supply subsidies. Economically crippled, the Caribbean island no longer had the strength to send guerrilla troops to other parts of Latin America nor to parts of Africa where it had been deeply enmeshed: Angola, Mozambique, and Ethiopia. America saw this as a victory over the island nation.

These examples seemed to support Fukuyama's thesis, but there were other perspectives. Because it regarded itself as the lone superpower, America sometimes chose to act unilaterally, projecting an arrogance that alienated friends as well as enemies. America imposed sanctions on Iran and Cuba and forced others to comply. It refused to ratify international treaties agreed upon by its closest allies, cut foreign aid, withheld dues to the UN and other international agencies, cut State Department funding, and abolished the United States Information Agency. It declined to sign the Kyoto Protocol, an international agreement on the reduction of greenhouse gases signed by 178 nations and recommended by all the major advocates of a healthy global ecology, and it offered no alternative vision. In supporting Israel's assassination attacks on Palestinian guerrilla leaders, which often also killed innocent civilians, and in not confronting Israel over its construction of settlements in the occupied West Bank, in contravention of international law, America stood aloof from most of the rest of the world. Many felt that America's unilateralism was making many important international problems worse.

Terrorism. Terrorist attacks on the United States and its interests at home and overseas dispelled any illusions that history had ended. One attack was from within, as Timothy McVeigh blew up the federal building in Oklahoma City in 1995, killing 168 people, in retaliation for the government's 1993 armed assault on the Branch Davidians, a small religious sect based in Waco, Texas. This, however, was seen as an isolated incident.

More typically, terrorist attacks occurred overseas and were part of a violent dialogue with Islamic militancy. In 1983, a suicide car bomb destroyed the U.S. embassy in Beirut, Lebanon, killing 63. Later in the same year, suicide bombers exploded a truck bomb at U.S. Marine headquarters at the international airport in Beirut, killing 241 Marines and sailors. (Minutes later another bomb killed 59 French paratroopers in their barracks, also in Beirut.) In 1993, a bomb delivered by Muslim terrorists exploded in a garage under the World Trade Center in New York, killing six. In Saudi Arabia, a bomb killed seven Americans at a military training installation in 1995, and another exploded at an American air force barracks in 1996, killing 19. In 1998, almost simultaneous explosions at U.S. embassies in Kenya and Tanzania killed 220 people. In 2000, a small boat sailed alongside the USS *Cole*, a U.S. Navy destroyer, in the harbour at Aden, Yemen, and bombed the ship, killing 17 sailors.

Terrorism is a strategy employed by the weak against the strong. It targets civilian noncombatants, in civilian locations, to terrify a general population into granting political concessions. Terrorism is not a new method of fighting. According to statistics compiled by the U.S. Department of State, from 1981 to 1991, terrorist attacks worldwide averaged more than 500 a year. From 1991 to 2001 there were never fewer than the 274 attacks of 1998.

Many countries had long experience with terrorism. The Irish Republican Army frequently launched attacks against civilians in Britain up to 2005, when it agreed to give up its arms in favor of an official agreement on the governance of Northern Ireland. Algerian terrorism against their French colonial rulers, both in Algeria and France, during their war for independence, 1954–62, brought France to the brink of civil war. The ETA armed revolutionaries, representing some of the Basque peoples in their quest for greater autonomy for their region of northern Spain, have killed some 800 Spaniards, about 350 of them civilians, since their founding in 1959. In eastern India, since 1967, "Naxalite" rebels (named for an Indian village where the movement began), proclaiming a communist–Maoist philosophy, have waged a guerrilla war in an attempt to turn the region communist. Tamil rebels, beginning as terrorists in the 1980s, seeking autonomy for their region of Sri Lanka, grew so numerous as to create a civil war in that country. Chechens in Russia, Uighurs in China, all used methods of terror in their campaigns for autonomy.

By contrast, the American mainland had not been touched. The attacks of September 11, 2001, on American soil shocked the nation out of its sense of invulnerability. Now America had joined the ranks of the stricken. But how would the United States react to these attacks? When George W. Bush declared a "war on terror" in response to these attacks, many wondered what form such a war would take, how it would be fought, and how one would know when victory had been achieved?

Torture at Abu Ghraib. Beginning in 2004, thanks to investigative reporting by the media, accounts of torture of prisoners held in the Abu Ghraib prison in Iraq began to surface. Powerful photographic evidence of physical and psychological torture, sexual abuse, and homicide were published. This macabre photograph of a prisoner, hooded, forced to stand on a small platform, and being tortured with electrical shocks was one of the *less* repulsive examples. America's use of torture shocked American citizens and diminished the nation's reputation around the world.

America's decision to strike back at Osama bin Laden, mastermind of the 9/11 attacks, and at the Taliban government who gave him shelter in Afghanistan seemed appropriate to observers abroad, especially those who had experienced terrorism in their own country. But the decision to launch a war against Iraq, in March, 2003, drew massive international condemnation, for America could not demonstrate any credible connection between Iraq and Osama bin Laden. America's impatience in not waiting for the results of a UN investigation into the claim that Iraq possessed "weapons of mass destruction" was also widely criticized. Later, America's decision to place hundreds of captive "enemy combatants" in a special detention center in Guantanamo Bay, Cuba, without charges, without trials, without benefit of legal counsel, and without even notifying anyone in the outside world of their imprisonment—effectively suspending the centuries-old tradition of **habeas corpus**—and using torture against these prisoners was also widely condemned.

In assessing America's actions following 9/11, Harvard Professor of Government Joseph F. Nye, Jr., considered three kinds of power: military, economic, and "soft" moral and cultural power. America still retained the strongest military power in the world, he said, but it had overstretched itself in its wars in Iraq and Afghanistan, had virtually no reserves capable of projecting American military power elsewhere, and had not succeeded in capturing bin Laden even several years after his attack. Its economic power was undermined by the costs of the war, challenged by the rise of new economic powers in the world, and compromised by its enormous trade deficits with the rest of the world (see below and Chapter Twenty-four). Most important of all, Nye claimed, America's "soft power—its ability to attract others by the legitimacy of U.S. policies and the values that underlie them" had eroded significantly.

> According to Gallup International polls, pluralities in 29 countries say that Washington's policies have had a negative effect on their view of the United States. A Euro-barometer poll found that a majority of Europeans believes that Washington has hindered efforts to fight global poverty, protect the environment, and maintain peace.
>
> Such attitudes undercut soft power, reducing the ability of the United States to achieve its goals without resorting to coercion or payment. (Nye, p. 16)

Meanwhile, around the globe new nations and groups were cultivating their own power.

The Unification of Europe

In the aftermath of two world wars, Western Europe devoted itself to regional cooperation and, finally, unification. Constitutionally, a major step was taken in 1993 at Maastricht, the Netherlands, when all 12 of its members committed themselves to transforming the European Economic Community into the European Union (EU). They agreed to work toward formulating a common foreign policy, a common defense policy, guidelines toward similar social policies, and policies for assistance from the wealthier members toward the poorer. They established common policies for agriculture, fisheries, and nuclear research projects. They also committed to creating a common currency. In 1998 they created a European Central Bank to monitor and coordinate financial activity, and by 2002, when the single currency, the Euro, was adopted in most of its member states, the EU had become the world's largest integrated market.

The EU brought rapid economic growth, increased cultural creativity, and a more prominent voice in international affairs to most of its member states. Following the collapse of the USSR in 1991, many of the nations of central Europe applied to join the EU. In 2004, seven of them were admitted—Lithuania, Latvia, Estonia, the Czech

SOURCE

The Continuing Rationale for European Integration

In 1995, François Mitterrand (1916–96), past president of France and an elder statesman both of his own country and of the EU, spoke passionately to the EU Parliament, summarizing the EU's great accomplishments in binding up the physical, emotional, and economic wounds of war-devastated Europe. He looked forward to even greater achievements in formulating and enhancing its collective cultural identity. Mitterrand asserted that the success of the EU as a whole would also enhance the cultural identity and creativity of each of its member states, just as the collective success of its economic policies had benefited the economies of the individual member nations.

> Our Europe must be embodied in something more than simply balance sheets and freight tonnages. I would go as far as to say ... that it needs a soul, so that it can give expression ... to its culture, its ways of thinking, the intellectual make-up of its peoples, the fruits of the centuries of civilization of which we are the heirs. The expressions of Europe's many forms of genius are rich and diverse; and, as in the past, we must share with the whole world—while not seeking to impose them, somewhat differently from in the past—our ideas, our dreams, and, to the extent that they are of the right kind, our passions. ...

The cultural identity of nations is reinforced by the process of European integration. The Europe of cultures, ladies and gentlemen, is a Europe of nations as opposed to a Europe of nationalism. ...

I was born during the First World War and fought in the Second. I therefore spent my childhood in the surroundings of families torn apart, all of them mourning loved ones and feeling great bitterness, if not hatred, towards the recent enemy, the traditional enemy. ...

My generation has almost completed its work; it is carrying out its last public acts, and this will be one of my last. It is therefore vital for us to pass on our experience. Many of you will remember the teaching of your parents ... will have felt the suffering of your countries, will have experienced the grief, the pain of separation, the presence of death—all as a result of the mutual enmity of the peoples of Europe. It is vital to pass on not this hatred but, on the contrary, the opportunity for reconciliation which we have, thanks—it must be said—to those who, after 1944–1945, themselves bloodstained and with their personal lives destroyed, had the courage to envisage a more radiant future which would be based on peace and reconciliation. That is what we have done.

(*Official Journal of the European Communities: Debates of the European Parliament*, 1994–95 Session No 4–456, pp. 45–51, excerpted in Hunt, p. 343)

Republic, Slovakia, Hungary, and Poland—along with the two island nations of Cyprus and Malta, and Slovenia, newly independent from the former Yugoslavia. In 2007, Romania and Bulgaria also joined, bringing the total EU membership to 27 nations. The dream of a unified, peaceful, prosperous, democratic Europe seemed fulfilled. Europeans shared a common market, without internal tariffs, and with unrestricted movement throughout the Union of goods, services, capital, workers, and tourists. Citizens of most of the member nations could travel throughout the EU with only a basic identity card, for the most part encountering no customs formalities, and they could live wherever they chose within the EU.

The EU, however, is not a conventional, unified state. It has no military. It provides neither welfare nor basic educational functions to its inhabitants. It does, however, finance EU-wide programs in science and technology, culture, and the environment, and it supports efforts to raise the economic status of its poorer member states. It sets standards for health and safety regulations, social security and working conditions, and agriculture. The EU today (2009) recognizes 23 official languages, and most major documents are translated into all of them. In practice, however, English has become the most common language for commercial, political, and cultural exchange throughout the EU, as it has throughout the world.

Many questions about the further empowerment of the EU remain. Low voter turnouts in elections to the European parliament and rejections by voters in several countries of steps toward further unification leave in question the degree to which the EU will be consolidated, and the pace at which further empowerment might take place.

An additional set of questions facing the EU concerns its reception of new applicants. The question of Turkey is the most pressing and problematic. Turkey's application has been pending since 1987. Officially, the EU is concerned as to whether Turkey is in compliance with EU standards for the administration of justice, for economic regulations, and for the resolution of a dispute with Greece over the sovereignty of the island of Cyprus. Beneath these official questions, however, are deeper issues: Should the EU add a nation that is geographically mostly in Asia, and which is religiously and culturally Islamic, although constitutionally secular? Many political leaders wish to preserve the EU as a union of nations of Christian heritage situated within the European continent. Turkey's EU application raises the question: How far is the EU willing to push the geographic and cultural envelope of "European" identity?

A second issue for the EU is its stance regarding immigration. Since entry into any one of the nations gives access to almost all, EU member states demanded that the requirements for first entry be formidable and their enforcement be strict. Potential immigrants from outside find increased difficulty in attempting to enter EU countries.

In addition to these increased barriers to immigration from outside, serious frictions have arisen also from immigration from one nation to another within the EU, especially from the poorer nations of southern and Eastern Europe to the wealthier nations of the north and west. The issue of immigration from poorer countries to richer ones, and the desire to limit this immigration was, in fact, a global issue, and we will discuss it at greater length in Chapter Twenty-four.

In assessing the relationship of the EU to the United States as superpower, we must look at three elements. In terms of armed power, the EU has no formal collective military power. The key institution for European powers to act together militarily is the North Atlantic Treaty Organization (NATO), which includes most EU members, and NATO is under American command. The United States' annual expenditure for its military in 2008 was $547 billion. Britain, which had the largest expenditure of any single nation in Europe, spent only one tenth of that, about $60 billion. All European nations collectively spent $293 billion. (Stockholm International Peace Research Institute: http://milexdata.sipri.org/result.php4) Militarily, America was in a class by itself.

In terms of economic power, the situation was quite different. In 2007, the EU generated an estimated gross domestic product (GDP) of $16.8 trillion, 30 percent of the world's estimated total. In 2005, the EU accounted for 18.1 percent of world exports and 18.9 percent of global imports, making it the world's main exporter and second biggest importer. Its principal partners are the other two major world trading blocs, the United States first, with a total of approximately $2.5 trillion, and China second, with a total of approximately $2 trillion. Trade among EU countries themselves represents two thirds of all EU trade. In short, in economic terms, the EU is now a competitor of the United States, and a rival for investment capital.

The degree to which the EU had become an alternate "superpower" became increasingly clear as the European currency, the Euro, became more valuable and the U.S. dollar less so in the 2000s. In 1999, when the Euro first came into use, its value relative to the U.S. dollar was US $1.18 = Euro 1.00. By 2002, the Euro had dropped to US $0.90 = Euro 1.00. In other words, the dollar became steadily stronger and more valuable than the Euro. However, from 2002 onward the values began to reverse, and by 2008, US $1.50 = Euro 1.00. The dollar in relation to the Euro was worth merely 60 percent of its value only six years before. Economically, America was no longer the sole superpower. (Federal Reserve Bank of New York: http://www.ny.frb.org/markets/fxrates/historical/fx.cfm) The dollar began to appreciate once again in late 2008, in the face of global recession; the dollar still seemed more reliable than the Euro.

Finally, in terms of soft power, Europeans were extremely proud of their newfound ability to bargain, negotiate, and find peaceful resolutions to problems that had plagued them for centuries. In a world of great conflict, this was its soft power contribution; it had developed a culture of effective compromise and conflict resolution. When the United States embarked on its war with Iraq in 2003, without waiting for UN sanction and with little international support except for that of Britain, two of Europe's most distinguished philosophers, Jürgen Habermas of Germany and Jacques Derrida of France, argued that America was losing its standing in the world. America was unnecessarily warlike, they said. Its use of torture and its sequestration of prisoners without charges and without trial diminished it even more. Moreover, America's high rates of violent crime, especially homicide, its high rates of imprisonment, high rates of citizens without medical insurance, increasing economic inequality, and its use of capital punishment shocked most Europeans. Europeans felt that their welfare states were more humane. America was losing its soft power advantage, while Europe was gaining. (Borradori *et al.*) The EU presented an alternative to America's status as a superpower by developing its own economic power, by crafting its own form of soft power, and by questioning the importance of military power. Europeans were asking: What does it mean to be a superpower?

China: An Emerging Superpower?

China's extraordinary economic progress after 1980 turned that huge nation into another alternative to America as a superpower. The speed and scope of China's economic growth was unprecedented in the history of the world. The takeoff occurred only after Mao's death in 1976.

By the end of 1978, Deng Xiaoping (1904–97) and his allies had gained control of the party and its agenda. They remained in control for the next two decades. Deng advocated **economic liberalism,** operating with minimal government intervention but within a state firmly controlled by the Communist Party. By the time of his death, Deng and his colleagues had sold off about half of the state's economic holdings leaving only 18 percent of the workforce in state employment, down from 90 percent in 1978. He welcomed direct foreign investment, which reached $42 billion in 1997 ($78 billion in 2008). Per capita income quadrupled. Deng also shifted more investment to agriculture, ended the failed policy of collectivization, and introduced a "private responsibility system," allotting land to private farmers for their own production for personal use and for market. These new policies unleashed enormous productivity gains of 9 percent a year in the early 1980s. The growth in China's total GDP led the world, averaging 11.2 percent per year, 1986–97. Health standards improved. Life expectancy reached 70 (72 in 2008).

As its population topped one billion, China acted aggressively to limit population growth. Government programs for "small family happiness," beginning in 1974, culminated in the 1980 policy of one family, one child. The party set maximum birth quotas for each county and city, established a nationwide system for distributing contraceptive devices, enforced regulations against early marriage, and provided incentives for having only one child and disincentives for having more. The bureaucracy monitored pregnancies and births carefully and abortions were frequently coerced (Rosenberg, p. 70). Fertility rates fell to 2.3 per hundred women in the 1980s (1.8 in 2008). The policy evoked widespread unrest, evasion—more easily accomplished in rural areas—and, in some case, female infanticide, as couples preferred their one child to be male. The smaller families, however, led to a dramatic reduction in the responsibilities of child-care and encouraged greater

KEY TERM

economic liberalism
This term has had various meanings at different times. Today it usually refers to a free-market, capitalistic economy, with minimum government intervention. Often referred to as neo-liberalism.

HOW DO WE KNOW?

The Force Behind China's Economic Growth: Capitalism or Socialism?

As Chinese productivity grew at record rates in the 1980s, and even faster in the 1990s and early 2000s, almost all commentators attributed the economic expansion to the capitalistic reforms promoted by Deng Xiaoping. They usually contrasted Deng's success to the failed communist policies that he discarded. See, for example, the very representative point of view presented in a fine, new history of the twentieth century:

> The Chinese state had established a Soviet-style command economy in the 1950s by nationalizing industry and foreign trade, setting prices and collectivizing agriculture; inefficiency and low growth resulted ... Living standards remained low, and most people lived in cramped, unmodernized housing ...
>
> After Mao's death in 1976, reformers gained more power and began more active restructuring of the economy. Deng Xiaoping, a masterly politician who became head of the Central Advisory Commission, slowly moved the party toward economic reform. Once they were allowed to contract out of their agricultural communes, peasants deserted them in droves, working as family units and selling their surpluses in private markets. Output and rural incomes rose, stimulating rural industry. As trading companies under local control multiplied, foreign contacts expanded and foreign investment poured into the country. Overseas Chinese returned to invest. ...
>
> a new private sector boomed in southern coastal areas ... Wages rose and so did demand for consumer goods. (Crossley et al., p. 476)

Nobel Prize-winning economist Amartya Sen might not disagree with the analysis of Deng's reforms, but he gives much more credit to the accomplishments of Mao's communist government in paving the way. His analysis of China's success comes as part of a discussion of the market-based economic policies that India began to adopt in 1991. Sen uses China's example to caution against the transition to capitalism before appropriate social policies have been set in place:

> While prereform China was deeply skeptical of markets, it was not skeptical of basic education and widely shared health care. When China turned to marketization in 1979, it already had a highly literate people, especially the young, with good

schooling facilities across the bulk of the country. In this respect, China was not very far from the basic educational situation in South Korea or Taiwan, where too an educated population had played a major role in seizing the economic opportunities offered by a supportive market system. In contrast, India had a half-illiterate adult population when it turned to marketization in 1991, and the situation is not much improved today [1999].

> The health conditions in China were also much better than in India because of the social commitment of the prereform regime to health care as well as education. Oddly enough, that commitment, while totally unrelated to its helpful role in market-oriented economic growth, created social opportunities that could be brought into dynamic use after the country moved toward marketization ... But the relevance of the radically different levels of social preparedness in China and India for widespread market-oriented development is worth noting even at this preliminary stage of the analysis. (Sen pp. 42–43)

Sen does credit Indian democracy with other advantages for development that are lacking under China's communist government. In general, however, he seems to turn upside-down Marx's view of the triumph of communism arising out of a base constructed by capitalists. In China he sees capitalism arising out of a base constructed by communists.

- Is Sen's account of the achievements of Chinese communism inaccurate, or is he simply giving credit to a human-welfare achievement that others are overlooking? Why is he giving this emphasis? Is he right to stress the importance of human welfare measures in economic development?
- According to Sen, why should Indian leaders be cautious in adopting for their own country the free-market policies that seem to work for China?
- To what degree should human welfare be considered in the assessment of the success of an economic system? Can an economic system be considered successful if education, health, and welfare standards of the general population are not rising?

myhistorylab

freedom for women in the home and greater equality and participation in work and public life outside.

After Deng's death, the transition of power occurred smoothly within the Communist Party-run government, with Jiang Zemin succeeding him as China's most important political leader, followed by Hu Jintao in 2002. In recognition of its position as a full participant in global trade, China was admitted to the World Trade Organization in November 2001. China continued to liberalize its economy further by selling off state-run enterprises to private owners. China's economy continued to set records for overall expansion, doing much to alleviate poverty among its masses.

The growth rate of the economy averaged about 9.7 percent for 30 years, from 1978 to 2008. In the same period, the overall rate of poverty dropped from about 65 percent of the population to about five percent. Total adult literacy reached 90 percent. Young women were attending school at the same rate as men, and the rate of literacy for females aged 15–24 was 99 percent.

Much of China's wealth came from its extraordinary success in world trade, a huge turnaround from the days of Mao, when foreign trade was discouraged. China's exports in 2006 were $974 billion; its imports $778, earning the country a trade surplus of almost $200 billion. China's trade with the United States was especially imbalanced. China earned a trade surplus of $233 billion, the difference between its exports to the U.S. of $288 against its imports of $55 billion. In 2008, this once impoverished country held foreign reserves of $1.5 trillion.

Although its economy was proportionately much smaller, in terms of sheer growth China was running rings around the United States, while its military expenditure was only $59 billion, about ten percent of the United States'. As a proportion of total economic productivity, China spent somewhat less than two percent on its military, while the U.S. spent somewhat more than four percent. China was becoming a world power, a counterweight to the United States' superpower, not by force of its military might, but through the organization of its economy.

As China's industrial economy continues to grow, the country uses more fuel, which it has been purchasing from more than 20 countries around the world, often in joint ventures with the host country to develop oil fields and transportation facilities. China has become the world's third-largest net importer of oil after the United States and Japan, and its oil ventures bring it into commercial enterprises in such countries as Saudi Arabia, Angola, Sudan, Kazakhstan, Russia, Iran, Canada, Indonesia, and Venezuela. China's fuel needs in gas and oil grew so rapidly that they drove up energy prices around the world in the late 2000s.

Poverty. China's combination of communist governance with capitalist economics nevertheless left the country with many problems. Despite the rise in the production of national wealth, distribution was a problem. China still had millions of people living in abject poverty on less than $1 per day. The estimates vary widely from 55 million to 300 million, although all agree that the poverty reduction has been extraordinary.

Although the poor are becoming richer, the divisions between rich and poor are also growing. These divisions are regional, between the wealthier coastal areas and the more impoverished inland areas, and between the wealthier cities and the more impoverished villages, and they are gender related, with women having less access to the better jobs. Especially in jeopardy are the villagers who come to the city to try their luck. These migrant workers provide the low-cost labor for China's growing economy—when they can find jobs—but their conditions are harsh. The World Bank reported 40 million workers unemployed in 2007 because of economic restructuring and 140 million rural migrant workers in search of jobs in China's booming cities. It further reports fewer women working in white-collar jobs than men; layoffs in urban industries affecting women more than men; and wage differences between men and women on the increase.

Recognizing these imbalances not only in income but also in access to education, health services, and employment possibilities, the government is attempting to real-locate resources toward inland areas, toward villages, and toward women. The usual course of capitalist development, however, is for already developed areas to move forward faster than those that are underdeveloped, so the government's programs must counteract the natural effects of the market. The results remain to be seen.

The Environment. Environmental degradation, including the pollution of air and water, has increased with China's industrialization. The rise of factories and cars and the use of artificial fertilizer have increased the level of pollution of land, air, and water in China. One of the most colossal projects will be the largest offender. The Three Gorges Dam on the upper Yangzi River, the largest hydroelectric project in the world, is scheduled to open in 2011. The dam is displacing more than one million residents, flooded out by the reservoir forming behind it. It is also pouring the industrial wastes that have been emptied into the river through the years into that reservoir of water that will be drunk downstream throughout central China. The cost of the dam is about $30 billion. The government justifies it as a project befitting China's status as one of the world's great powers, and one whose electricity generation will save China's air from the pollution that would otherwise have come through coal generation of electricity. But some government officials acknowledge the ecological problems.

The Three Gorges Dam, Hubei Province, China, 2003. By 10 a.m. each morning at the dam site, the Yangtze River rises 114 meters above sea level. Despite the criticism of the dam's impact on the ecology and residents of its region, the Chinese government views this as one of its most beneficial and spectacular technological accomplishments.

More recently, China's use of high-sulfur gasoline as a means of fueling its ever-increasing engines creates additional pollution. Sulfur levels in fuels are tightly regulated in the United States and Europe because of their high toxicity. China feels it cannot be so picky. Despite the fact that the sulfur pollutes the air, ruins the catalytic converters that have been designed to cut down on other pollutants, and burns at very low efficiency, it is cheap and available. China considers this a necessary alternative for a relatively poor, rapidly developing country.

Corruption. At higher levels of the economy, white-collar crime and corruption became major problems. As in Russia, as the government liberalized economically, state assets were often sold to the Party faithful at bargain prices. Meanwhile, the lure of new profits, a relaxation in law enforcement, and a rise in bribery created a new class of privately wealthy moguls. China witnessed a rapid recrudescence of quasi-illegal night spots, gangsterism, drug dealing, secret societies, prostitution, and gambling, much of it owned and operated by the police and military.

The Road to Democracy. Deng's government spoke proudly of its accomplishments in the "four modernizations" of agriculture, science and technology, industry, and defense. Critics, however, called for the "fifth modernization"—democracy. In 1989, tens of thousands of demonstrators, mostly students, assembled in Tiananmen Square, in central Beijing, demanding democracy as the antidote to a government ruled by old men, infested with corruption, and no longer in touch with the grass roots. The government called in the army to clear the square. In the process, several hundred (some say as many as 5,000) demonstrators were killed, and more injured. China was not prepared for protest, transparency, and democracy.

A few years later, further questions arose concerning Chinese toleration of democratic protest. In 1997 the island of Hong Kong, and the tiny strip of adjacent territories on the mainland, which had been a British colony since 1842, reverted to Chinese sovereignty. (Two years later Portugal returned tiny Macao to China.) Because of the last years of British rule, however, the people of Hong Kong had become accustomed to both capitalism and democratic elections. They feared possible suppression by Beijing and in July 2003, for example, an estimated 500,000 people demonstrated in Hong Kong against proposed laws that would have curtailed civil rights. Here the Chinese responded differently, scrapping the proposed laws. They recognized Hong Kong's value as an international port and window on the world, and were not willing to jeopardize those advantages in a political crackdown that would have alienated world opinion and Hong Kong entrepreneurs.

Tiananmen Square, June 5, 1989. Tanks traveling down Changan Boulevard, in front of the Beijing Hotel, are confronted by a brave Chinese man who pleads for an end to the killing of students demonstrating for greater freedom of democratic expression. This photograph came to symbolize the struggle of the Chinese people to reassert their dignity and gain democracy in the face of the huge and powerful communist regime.

On the other hand, in 1999 the government arrested thousands of members of the Falun Gong religious-meditation-exercise movement. Falun Gong combines elements of Buddhism, Taoism, and the martial arts. The group declared itself apolitical, but the government of China feared that any group of such size had political implications. Its membership of 70 million was larger than that of the Communist Party. In 1999 after 10,000 members of Falun Gong staged an unauthorized demonstration in Beijing, protesting government suppression of its activities, the government banned the sect entirely. Human rights reports claim that half of China's prison labor camp population are members of Falun Gong and that they are regularly subjected to torture. Critics claim that the Chinese government is subjecting Falun Gong members to organ harvesting, although the evidence is not certain. Falun Gong has millions of practitioners outside of China and they demonstrate regularly on behalf of their colleagues in China.

The Chinese government's difficulties with transparency were in evidence during its handling of the SARS health epidemic of 2002, which killed some 350 people in China. Anxious that news of the epidemic would cut into its international business and travel, China failed to report this previously unknown disease at first. As news did emerge, the WHO and others censured China for covering up news that could have enabled faster health responses throughout the world. From then on, China released news about the epidemic promptly and widely.

The greater emphasis on transparency seemed to continue in 2008, when Sichuan Province in southwest China suffered a massive earthquake, killing almost 70,000 people and leaving between five and ten million homeless. This time the government immediately released the details of the catastrophe, sent massive relief teams of its own to the area, and accepted rescue groups from countries such as South Korea, Japan, Singapore, Russia, and Taiwan. The international press praised this openness, but then it learned that the Chinese government was suppressing the news that some 7,000 schoolrooms had collapsed in the earthquake, burying thousands of students. As parents demanded an inquiry into the shoddy construction of these schools, the government attempted to silence them with offers of payment and threats of jail.

Tibetan protesters, 2008. China has often claimed Tibet as its own, and Tibet has always responded with claims of independent sovereignty. Most recently, in 1950, the Chinese government invaded and occupied Tibet and in 1959, under immense pressure, Tibet's most venerated leader, the Dalai Lama, fled the country. Revolts against Chinese rule flare periodically. As world attention focused on China during the 2008 Olympics, Tibetans took the opportunity to demonstrate again their opposition to Chinese rule.

The greatest test of Chinese openness came with the Olympic Games in Beijing in August, 2008. The awarding of the games to China signalled recognition of the nation's coming of age. The International Olympic Committee was concerned, however, over the issue of transparency, until it received China's pledge to allow journalists and visitors to the Olympics to report on China without limits. These pledges were not honored. Prior to the Olympic Games, Buddhists in Tibet, and their sympathizers around the world, used the run-up to the games to gain world attention for their campaign for autonomy for Tibet. In Tibet, the protesters were beaten and some were killed. China urged governments around the world to limit the attention the protesters received. China claimed to allow protesters, of all kinds, to petition for a few public spaces that were set aside for them in Beijing during the Olympics, but none of the petitions were granted, and some of the petitioners, including a few foreigners, were arrested. In a like manner, China restricted domestic news reporting and denied foreign journalists full access to the internet.

The Olympics of 2008 gave insight into China as an alternative power to the United States. Militarily, the Chinese could not compare, and did not seem interested in competing. It had no neighbors against whom it needed a substantial armed force. Its military was strong enough to suppress internal dissent. For the moment, it had the military it needed.

On the other hand, economically it had become a great power. Its ability to host the Olympics with new stadiums, trains, roads, hotels, and visitor facilities—some the best in the world—showcased that prosperity and vigor to the world. For a generation, China's economy had been the fastest growing in the world. It provided eight percent of the world's total of exports and 6.4 percent of its imports. Its trade balances and foreign reserves were astronomical and growing. Its investments in overseas markets made it a significant force in the domestic and foreign policies of countries around the world. For example, as China grew economically stronger, and the U.S. came to depend on Chinese credit to finance its deficit spending, China quietly gained influence over American policy. China was still emerging from a century of extreme poverty, and its villages and its interior were still very poor, so its economy trailed far behind America's, but its growth trajectory was the envy of the world.

In terms of soft power, cultural power, the Olympics were also a showcase of China's special position. It was not a democracy. It did not permit freedom of expression. It had reneged on its promises of openness to its own citizens and to visitors from overseas, and it suppressed protest, sometimes brutally. Yet it provided more access than had been available a few years earlier. Meanwhile its spectacular opening ceremonies, watched by more than two billion people around the world, and its athletes' excellence in winning more gold medals than any other country, revealed the potential accomplishments of authoritarian rule. China's "soft power," its cultural example to the world, repelled and attracted at the same time.

Unlike the United States, the superpower, and the EU, an alternative power—both of which were relative newcomers on the world stage—China could hark back to an ancient imperial past. In some ways it reclaimed that past as the dominant power in its area of the world, with an economy of astonishing energy, and with a cultural thrust inspiring wonder as well as apprehension. In some ways the new China was even more powerful than its ancient imperial predecessor. In earlier times China's role was essentially regional, with limited contacts to the outside world. Today's China was less of an empire, and not yet a superpower, but its economic power had achieved global reach.

On Religion

The five most widespread religions of the world are, in the Western world, Christianity, Islam, and Judaism (from which Christianity and Islam emerged), and, in the eastern world, Hinduism and Buddhism. In all five cases, the success of these religions in gaining followers and in expanding into new areas was directly dependent on their alliance with political power. Early Christianity gained the support of the Roman Emperor Constantine. Islam united political and spiritual power in the single person of Muhammad. Hinduism came to India through the waves of Aryan immigrants and later gained power through the sponsorship of the Gupta dynasty that ruled northern India. Buddhism gained ascendancy with the rule of the Emperor Asoka. Judaism for the most part failed to gain a political ally, and attracted relatively few followers. For a period of about 1,200 years, however, Jews established military and political rule over a small region on the eastern shores of the Mediterranean, approximately modern-day Israel, and during that time Judaism expanded.

We have noted in the discussion of the *philosophes* and the French Revolution (Chapter Sixteen), and of the communists and the Russian Revolution (Chapter Nineteen), the general belief from the eighteenth to the mid-twentieth century that religion was in decline as a force in history. New concepts of rationality challenged religion's otherworldly belief system, and new concepts of politics argued that state governments and organized religion should be kept separate. Important revolutionary groups, especially in France, Russia, and later China, actively and aggressively rejected organized religions, withdrew state support, and oppressed religious groups as a matter of state policy. By the early twenty-first century about 767 million people rejected organized religion (*Encyclopedia Britannica Book of the Year, 2006*), and another 150 million professed atheism, skepticism, or disbelief. These two groups total about one in six, or 16 percent, of the world's population.

One of the surprises of the later twentieth century was the reemergence of religious groups as powerful political forces. The past 20 to 30 years have provided abundant evidence of the power of religious faith to motivate public as well as private action. No one is entirely sure why. Many argue that the speed of change brought about by globalization threatened many people's sense of security. Religious leaders promised faith and security to fill the void and they attracted many new followers. Partly the attraction was philosophical and psychological. Partly it was the practical assistance that religious groups offered. Often, such groups sponsored social welfare programs and provided community support that governments did not. Followers came for the practical assistance and then stayed for the religious and political messages. This combination of practical assistance, community membership, and a message of comfort and cosmic acceptance has been a hallmark of religious attraction since earliest times.

In the late twentieth century, this combination was especially prominent in Islam, which has been the fastest growing world religion in recent years. Although many Westerners have come to see Islam as an aggressive and militant religion, especially after the 9/11 terrorist attacks in the United States, most Muslims would argue that they are not the aggressors, but the aggressed upon, and that Islam serves to sustain them in times of trouble. They assert that colonialism in the Middle East left behind underdeveloped economies and a history of personal insults and cultural disrespect. In Palestine, they claim that Israeli oppression is the cause of their economic stagnation and social disarray. In India, they claim that the Hindu majority restricts their opportunities, and even their rights. In Chechnya, they cite continuing Russian occupation and military intervention. Within the past 30 years, a sharp divide has emerged between the Muslim self-image as an oppressed religious group prepared at last to reassert its dignity and the views of some outsiders who see Muslims as potential terrorists.

Theocracy in Iran

In 1979 an Islamic revolution, led by the **Ayatollah** Khomeini, overthrew the government of the Shah of Iran and in its place established a Muslim **theocracy.** At the same time, the new Iranian government also successfully challenged the power of the United States, which had supported the Shah.

During World War II, the British forced the abdication of Iran's Shah Reza Khan in favor of his son, the pro-British Muhammad Reza Pahlavi. Meanwhile, the increased exploitation of Iran's oil resources had begun to bring new wealth to the kingdom. In 1951, Prime Minister Muhammad Mussadeq (1880–1967) nationalized the Iranian oil industry against the wishes of the Shah. In response, Britain and the United States conspired with the Iranian army in a coup that supported the Shah and overthrew Mussadeq.

Indebted to the West, the Shah joined America in a cold war military alliance directed against the Soviet Union. He invited additional Western oil investment, and proceeded to use Iran's oil wealth to fund deep and massive—but convulsive, erratic, and uneven—Westernization of the country. By the mid-1970s, about 150,000 foreigners had come to Iran to run the new high-technology industries and to live luxuriously in secluded residential communities. Rural people were also flooding into the cities, putting great strains on the urban infrastructure. Shortages of foodstuffs and other basic necessities resulted and corruption was everywhere: in the Shah's court, the government, the bureaucracy, and within the business community. Opponents of the Shah's system of forced modernization—including much of the student community—were pursued, jailed, and often tortured.

Opponents to the Shah's forced modernization included *ulama*, religious scholars, who lamented the suppression of traditional religion, along with many citizens who felt themselves squeezed economically and resented the loosening of what they felt to be the moral foundations of the society. In 1963, a Shi'ite Muslim religious leader, the Ayatollah Ruhollah Khomeini (1902–89), led an abortive uprising against the Shah. The army killed 15,000 of the rebels and exiled Khomeini. But, from

The Ayatollah Khomeini returns to Iran, 1979. Exiled in 1963, the Ayatollah Khomeini established himself in Paris but kept in touch with his supporters, opponents of the Shah, back home in Iran. When popular resentment against the Shah's policies of economic development undercut the ruler's power, Khomeini returned to the tumultuous welcome of millions of followers. In overthrowing the Shah, Khomeini's revolution, based on Islam and on his own interpretation of the Quran, demonstrated the enduring power of religious principles as guiding motives in national affairs, at least in Iran.

Paris, the Ayatollah kept in contact with dissidents in Iran via tape recordings and telephone, and in 1979 he returned to lead popular demonstrations of as many as five million people. He forced the Shah into exile. Islamic law, the *shari'a*, became the law of the land and Islamic government was introduced. Women were ordered to return to draping themselves in the *chador*, the combined shawl and headscarf many Muslim women wear, as Iran became a theocracy. Khomeini declared:

> No others, no matter who they may be, have the right to legislate, nor has any person the right to govern on any basis other than the authority that has been conferred by God … It is the religious expert and no one else who should occupy himself with the affairs of the government. (Francis Robinson, *Atlas of the Islamic World since 1500*, p. 171)

The religious fervor of the revolution astonished many Western observers who thought, mistakenly, that the Iranians had approved of the modernizing policies of the Shah and that the man and his government were popular.

Strategically located, rich in oil, religiously militant, and internally secure, Khomeini's revolutionary government frightened its neighbors and wreaked havoc on many others more distant. In its first two years, it executed 800 people and exiled thousands. When America offered asylum to the exiled Shah, who was suffering from cancer, Iranian students responded by seizing the American embassy in Tehran in November 1979 and holding 52 of its staff hostage. President Jimmy Carter failed to secure their release through negotiations. He then attempted a clandestine air rescue, which was aborted in humiliating failure. Carter's defeat in the 1980 presidential election was due in large part to these failures to cope with revolutionary Iran. The third world had again humiliated the government of a superpower. (The hostages were finally released on January 20, 1981, the date on which Carter's term came to an end, 444 days after their capture.)

Khomeini's militancy increased instability in the Middle East. It inspired religious dissidents to attack the Great Mosque in Mecca during the *hajj* pilgrimage period in 1979 in an attempt to trigger a revolt against the Saudi Arabian government. Three hundred people were killed. In Egypt, in 1981, Islamic militants linked to Iran assassinated President Anwar Sadat. In 1989, following the publication of the novel *The Satanic Verses*, Iranian clerics proclaimed Britain's Indian-born, Muslim author Salman Rushdie a heretic, and issued a *fatwa*, a religious decree, that marked him for execution. A bounty of $5 million was placed on his head, and he was forced into hiding under the protection of the British government for several years. In Beirut and other Middle Eastern centers, Western hostages were seized. Fearing that Iran's Shi'ite religious revolution would spill across the border, Iraq, under Saddam Hussein, with the quiet support of the United States, attacked Iran, precipitating eight years of warfare and hundreds of thousands of deaths.

Legal restrictions on women, based on interpretations of religious principles, continued in revolutionary Iran, calling for Islamic dress codes and Islamic legal authority over marriage, divorce, child custody, and the right to work. Most Iranian women accepted these restrictions willingly as a stand against Western culture and imperialism. Women's literacy rose to 59 percent (70 percent in 2002), with 95 percent of girls of primary school age attending classes. Birth rates dropped from 49 per thousand under the Shah to 39 per thousand under Khomeini (to 17 in 2008). The percentage of families using contraception rose from 3 to 23 in 1987 (*World Resources*, p. 257) to 73 percent in 1997 (UN data: http://www.un.org/esa/population/publications/contraceptive2005/WCU2005.htm). Feminism, nationalism, and religion in Iran were intertwined in a unique configuration that did not fit into any stereotype.

For about a decade after Khomeini's death in 1989, more moderate leaders administered Iran. Then, in 2005, Mahmoud Ahmadinejad was elected president.

Although the Iranian president's power is subordinate to the country's religious rulers, Ahmadinejad's public assertions denying the Holocaust, calling for Israel to be wiped off the map, and declaring that Iran would proceed with development of its own nuclear power led to further tensions with Western countries, especially the United States. In response the United States and Israel both threatened preemptive bombings of Iran's nuclear research facilities. In the meantime, Iran was repairing relations with Iraq, improving them with Syria, and maneuvering into a position of considerably more power in the Middle East. But a disputed presidential election in 2009, which kept Ahmadinejad in power, brought hundreds of thousands of protesters to the streets and challenged the legitimacy of Iran's government.

Islamic Militants in Afghanistan

In the same year as the Iranian revolution, 1979, a resurgent Islam confronted a Soviet invasion in Afghanistan. The government of Afghanistan was allied with the Soviet Union, an officially atheistic country. Large numbers of militant Muslim guerrilla fighters, called *mujahideen*, opposed this alliance. To support the government against the *mujahideen*, the Soviets dispatched more than 100,000 troops, along with tanks and aircraft. The war became a part of the Cold War, as the *mujahideen* drew support from several nations—the United States, Pakistan, Saudi Arabia, and other Islamic countries. (The United States boycotted the 1980 Olympics in Moscow to express its anger over the Russian invasion.) Many freelance guerrillas also came to Afghanistan to fight against the USSR. After a decade of warfare, having lost some 14,000 soldiers, the Russians withdrew in defeat in 1989. In Iran and Afghanistan Islamic militants had confronted and repelled both of the world's superpowers, America in Iran, the USSR in Afghanistan.

The Russian withdrawal left Afghanistan in civil war, finally won by the mujahideen in 1992. Four years later, however, another Islamic militant group, the Taliban, seized control of the government of the country, although many private militias continued to operate outside of its powers.

One of these was the private militia assembled by Osama bin Laden. Bin Laden had been born in Saudi Arabia in 1957, the seventeenth child and seventh son of a devout Sunni Muslim family that had become extremely wealthy in the construction business. He earned a degree in public administration in Jeddah in 1981. He had grown up in an atmosphere of militant **Wahabi** puritan interpretations of Sunni Islam, at a time when Islamic nationalism was growing, and he went to Afghanistan to join in the struggle against Soviet occupation. He created **al-Qaeda** ("the base") to obtain and organize war supplies and to lead troops in the field. When the Soviets withdrew from Afghanistan, bin Laden returned to Saudi Arabia, committed to a militant, politicized vision of Islam.

In 1991, Iraq invaded Kuwait and the U.S. replied with an invasion of Iraq. Saudi Arabia, also fearing Iraq, invited U.S. troops onto Saudi lands. Bin Laden was enraged by the Saudi cooperation with the Americans, and especially by the stationing of American forces on Arabian soil, so close to Mecca. Bin Laden returned to Afghanistan, only to find that it had collapsed into civil war. He proceeded to Sudan, then led by a militant Islamic government. In 1994, the government of Saudi Arabia revoked his citizenship and froze his assets in Saudi Arabia. Under pressure from Saudi Arabia and the United States, Sudan expelled bin Laden in 1996 and he returned to Afghanistan, now under the government of the Taliban, a group of seminary students with military experience.

In Afghanistan, bin Laden established the World Islamic Front for the Jihad against Jews and Crusaders, a headquarters for radical Muslim movements. He

KEY TERMS

Wahabi Wahabi Islam follows the very conservative teachings of Muhammad ibn Abd-al-Wahhab, an eighteenth-century scholar. It is the dominant form of Islam in Saudi Arabia.

al-Qaeda "The base." The militant Islamic group of guerrilla warriors mobilized by Osama bin Laden in Afghanistan, first to fight against Russian invaders, and later to attack the United States and its allies. Subsequently, a number of militant Islamic guerrilla groups in different parts of the world adopted the name al-Qaeda, some with ties to bin Laden's group, some without.

issued a *fatwa*, stating that it was the duty of Muslims to kill American citizens and their allies. In his camps, he trained jihadis for these tasks. In a spectacular attack on September 11, 2001, al-Qaeda members hijacked four airplanes. Suicide pilots flew two of them into the World Trade Center twin towers in New York City, in the heart of the Wall Street area, the symbolic center of the capitalist world, destroying both towers and killing almost 3,000 people. Another flew a plane into the Pentagon, the symbolic center of the American military, destroying one wing of the building. One plane crashed in central Pennsylvania, failing its apparent mission to attack the White House.

Shortly after the attacks of September 11, bin Laden broadcast the following message on the Arabic news channel al-Jazeera, declaring his view of the political mission of Islam and his opposition to American policies, militarism, confrontation with Iraq, and support for Israel.

Osama bin Laden appears on Al-Jazeera television, October 17, 2001. Bin Laden here praises the attacks of September 11 and defies the US in its threats to attack Afghanistan's Taliban government. The US overthrew the Taliban some days later, but this was not their end. The Taliban regrouped and, within a few years, were once again vying for power in Afghanistan.

What the United States tastes today is a very small thing compared to what we have tasted for tens of years. Our nation has been tasting this humiliation and contempt for more than 80 years.

One million Iraqi children have thus far died in Iraq although they did not do anything wrong. Despite this, we heard no denunciation by anyone in the world or a *fatwa* by the rulers' *ulema* [body of Muslim scholars].

Israeli tanks and tracked vehicles also enter to wreak havoc in Palestine, in Jenin, Ramallah, Rafah, Beit Jala, and other Islamic areas and we hear no voices raised or moves made.

They … instigated even those countries [a reference primarily to Saudi Arabia] that belong to Islam against us.

Neither the United States nor he who lives in the United States will enjoy security before we can see it as a reality in Palestine and before all the infidel armies leave the land of Mohammed, may God's peace and blessing be upon him.
(http://news.bbc.co.uk/1/hi/world/south_asia/1585636.stm)

Bin Laden's attack polarized the Islamic world. Although some approved, many Muslims condemned it as a terrorist attack on innocent civilians, which violated Islamic morality. Many Islamic countries, like Saudi Arabia, also condemned and felt threatened by the attack.

The response of the United States, however, polarized world opinion even further. In the immediate wake of the attack, the United States received the immediate sympathy of the world. The American attack on Afghanistan, in an attempt to bring bin Laden to justice and to displace the Taliban government which gave him protection, received broad, although not universal, support. But the subsequent American invasion of Iraq was widely condemned throughout the Islamic world, and in most parts of the rest of the world as well, as an attack on a nation that had nothing to do with bin Laden, al-Qaeda, or the terrorist attacks of 9/11. Most, though not all, nations of the world saw the United States using the al-Qaeda attack as a pretext for a war on Iraq for ulterior purposes, perhaps for control of Iraq's oil, perhaps to establish an Iraqi government subservient to America's wishes. If part of bin Laden's plan had been to turn the entire Arab world against the United States, then the United States had played into his hands. America's invasion of Iraq, its use of torture against Muslims, and its unqualified support of Israel, led much of the Islamic world to view America as fighting a war against Islam.

Islam, Secularism, and Christianity

Several Islamic-majority countries faced conflicts between groups that wanted more theocratic governments, headed by religious authorities, and those that preferred more secular governments, with more of a separation between mosque and state. In Turkey and Algeria secular armed forces intervened in elections throughout the 1990s to prevent Islamic political parties from coming to power. Algeria suffered all-out civil war, from 1992 to 1998, which killed at least 100,000 people, and continues to simmer until today. In 1981, in Egypt, members of the Islamic Brotherhood assassinated the relatively secular President Anwar Sadat, who had jailed many of their members and had made peace with Israel. They also attempted to assassinate his successor, Hosni Mubarak, who followed similar policies.

In some states of sub-Saharan Africa, armed conflicts broke out among followers of Islam, Christianity, and indigenous African religions who had usually coexisted peacefully. The trigger was often the attempt to impose Islamic legal systems on people who were not Muslims. Civil war broke out in 1966 in Chad, which is about 50 percent Muslim, mostly in the north, and 25 percent each Christian and followers of indigenous religions, mostly in the south. Since then, fighting has continued sporadically.

In neighboring Sudan, the people of the north, home to the 70 percent of Sudan's population that is Sunni and mostly Arab, have repeatedly attempted to impose Islamic law on the south, which is mostly black and mostly practices indigenous religions. The result has been protracted civil war in a country that is overwhelmingly poor and prone to famine. As many as two million people—mostly southerners—have died in wars and famines and millions more have been displaced from their homes. In 2004, forces in the north and south reached accommodations that seemed to allow peace and stability in the south.

By then, however, the people of the Darfur region of the western part of the country, claiming oppression, were at war with the central government and its local armed representatives, the Janjaweed. In Darfur, however, both groups were Muslim by religion. The issue seemed to be ethnic rather than religious, northern Arabs against western black Africans. The UN and several individual nations extended relief aid and considered military intervention to protect the people of Darfur. The issue became very complicated, as China supported the government of Sudan while much of the rest of the world supported the Darfur refugees. But China had become a very wealthy country, which could not easily be swayed, and it needed Sudan's oil. So Sudan got its way. The refugees of Darfur continued to suffer and their international advocates stewed.

In Nigeria, too, the attempt to impose *shari'a* law precipitated violence. Nigeria is by far the most populous African country, with 140 million people. Its population is about 45 percent Muslim, 45 percent Christian, and 10 percent followers of indigenous religions. In early 2000, some 2,000 people were killed in northern Nigeria when the regional government instituted *shari'a* law. In retaliation, several hundred Muslims were killed in the east and south, and many more migrated to areas where their religious group was dominant. In May 2004, Christians attacked a Muslim market town in central Nigeria, leaving many people dead. Muslims and Christians fled areas in which they were minorities. In the north, Muslims forced 20,000 Christians out of their homes, and President Obasanjo put the area under military command. Despite the hostility it engendered among non-Muslims, several additional northern states of Nigeria instituted *shari'a* law as the basis of their official legal codes.

Issues concerning the status of women in Islam have brought further unwanted international attention to Nigeria. In 2002, a young woman accused of adultery was to be stoned to death under *shari'a* law, but she appealed the case and was acquitted in 2003. Also in 2002, the Miss World Pageant was scheduled to be held in Nigeria until Muslim leaders decried the spectacle of women parading in scanty bathing suits as incompatible with Islam. Riots broke out, killing more than a hundred people, and the pageant was moved to London.

Religious Strife in Yugoslavia

One of the worst examples of religious strife occurred in eastern Europe, in the Balkans, where civil war raged from 1992 to 1995 and continued to sputter afterward as well. Hundreds of thousands of people died and many more were made homeless in the worst warfare in Europe since World War II. Here, Eastern Orthodox Christians, Roman Catholics, and Muslims were involved, with Muslims suffering by far the greatest number of casualties.

The Balkans is a region of divisive nationalisms, and although religion was not the only issue in the civil war, it was important. The multiethnic state of Yugoslavia was created after World War I. After World War II, ethnic hostilities within Yugoslavia were suppressed by the nation's leader Marshal Tito, and even after his death the communist government of the country continued his policies. After the Soviet Union dissolved in 1989, however, Yugoslavia followed its example and splintered into several regions. Three of them—Serbia, Croatia, and Bosnia–Herzgovina—soon locked in warfare. Although Yugoslavs were not especially zealous in their religious observance, especially after a half-century of communist rule, religion was one of the key elements in the division and here Christians were the aggressors.

Serbs were generally Orthodox Christian (65 percent), while most Croatians were Roman Catholic (77 percent). Bosnians were the most mixed, but with a plurality (40 percent) Muslim, 31 percent Orthodox Christian, and 15 percent Roman Catholic. Until 1989, intermarriage between religious and national groups was not uncommon. But as Yugoslavia split apart, religious identity seemed to inspire horrendous violence.

Serbia's president, Slobodan Milosevic, and the head of his military, Radovan Karadzic, rejected the new national divisions of Yugoslavia. They attempted to keep Croatia and Bosnia–Herzegovina under Serbia's control. Civil war raged for three years, 1992–95, as Serbia undertook a policy of "**ethnic cleansing**," a euphemism for genocide, attempting to kill or drive out the Muslim and Croat populations, especially from Bosnia. Milosevic employed rape and torture as instruments of policy. Hundreds of thousands of people died and many more were forced from their homes. The UN attempted repeatedly to broker a peace agreement, but each attempt was rejected or broken. Many observers faulted the EU, the United States, and the UN for their unwillingness to commit the military forces necessary to impose peace. In December, 1995, however, a U.S.-brokered peace agreement was signed in Paris by the presidents of Bosnia–Herzegovina, Croatia, and Serbia. The UN then committed 60,000 peace-keeping troops to oversee the agreement.

Ethnic map of Yugoslavia based on 1991 census data. The death of Marshall Tito in 1980 and the example of the dissolution of the USSR, 1989–91, weakened forces that had kept the disparate peoples and territories of Yugoslavia together from 1918. After 1991 the country dissolved into several constituent new nations, each with its own dominant ethnic group, several of which promptly went to war with one another. Tensions continued, and became especially intense when Kosovo declared its independence from Serbia in 2008. Kosovo's population, given as Albanian by ethnicity, is predominantly Muslim by religion.

None of the three new states was, however, internally homogeneous. Within the newly created nation of Serbia, one province, Kosovo, had a majority who were Albanian by ethnicity and Muslim by religion. Kosovo had enormous historical significance. In 1389, the conquest of Kosovo by the Muslim Ottoman Turks marked the Ottomans' triumph over Serbia and the destruction of the Serbian state for 600 years. Political leaders of both Bosnia and Serbia stoked lingering resentments of this historic battle in order to inflame current-day antagonisms. For example, on June 28, 1989, the 600th anniversary of the Battle of Kosovo, one million Serbs assembled to hear Milosevic recall the glories of Serbia's past.

In 1998, when the Albanian Muslims of Kosovo declared their intention to secede from Serbia and launched a guerrilla war, Milosevic responded with fury, driving some 700,000 ethnic Albanians from their homes in Kosovo and resuming his policies of ethnic cleansing. After months of inaction, in 1999 NATO began a 72-day bombing campaign. Serbia surrendered and gave up its claims to Kosovo. Milosevic accepted 50,000 UN troops as peace-keepers. Before the UN soldiers arrived, however, the remaining Albanian Muslim Kosovars and the returning refugees drove out the Serbian residents of Kosovo, implementing reverse ethnic cleansing. Hatred and revenge flowed in both directions. As peace was established and enforced, the Serbs were invited to return.

The next year, 2000, Milosevic was defeated in Serbian elections and the new government turned him over to the International War Crimes Tribunal in The Hague, the Netherlands, for trial as a war criminal for his actions in Kosovo. (The UN Security Council established the tribunal in 1993.) It was the first European invocation of such a trial since World War II. Milosevic died of a heart attack in 2006, before a verdict was reached.

The tribunal also indicted eight men for sexual assault, the first time that the systematic practice of rape had been condemned and prosecuted as a weapon of war and a "crime against humanity," and not just overlooked as "something that happens" during the stress of warfare.

Hinduism and Islam in India

At independence, India was partitioned into two new nations, India and Pakistan, as we saw in Chapter Twenty-two. Although Mahatma Gandhi, the leader of the freedom movement, Jawaharlal Nehru, India's first prime minister, and the Congress Party that they led declared themselves secular, a substantial group of Hindus regarded Muslims as second-class citizens, or, at an extreme, even as foreign invaders. These militant Hindus form the backbone of the Bharatiya Janata Party, Indian People's Party, or BJP, stressing "**Hindutva**," or "Hinduness." As a rallying cry, the BJP's goal has been to make Hindu identity the basis of national identity and thus to exclude non-Hindus from full membership in the Indian nation.

In the 1980s, the BJP began to capture more votes and, in 1990, L.K. Advani, the chief organizer of the BJP, launched a religious pilgrimage/political campaign across northern India. Advani led the procession in a Toyota van decorated as a war chariot of Lord Rama. This political/religious pilgrimage was to finish at the northern Indian town of Ayodhya, the home of a mosque built by the first Mughal emperor, allegedly on the grounds of a Hindu temple, which he destroyed and which was said to mark the earthly birthplace of the Hindu Lord Rama. Advani's ultimate goal was to destroy the mosque and rebuild the temple. His pilgrimage instigated rioting between Hindus and Muslims throughout its journey and hundreds of people, Hindus and Muslims, were killed across India. Actually the pilgrimage did not reach Ayodhya. The chief minister of the state in which Ayodhya is located arrested Advani and halted the pilgrimage on grounds of incitement to riot.

KEY TERM

Hindutva A political–religious slogan calling for the merger of the Hindu religion with the power of the Indian state. It is the rallying cry of several militant Hindu organizations.

Militant Hindus atop and around Babri Mosque, Ayodhaya, India, 1992. In December 1992 many thousands of Hindu extremists destroyed the 430-year-old Muslim mosque, claiming that it had been built on ground originally sacred to Hindus as the birthplace of the Lord Rama. This act unleashed rioting between Hindus and Muslims throughout India. Thousands of people were killed.

Two years later, in defiance of the government of India, and in violation of a pledge that he had made, Advani instigated the destruction of the Ayodhaya mosque. In response, even more serious riots broke out throughout India. In Mumbai 2,000 people were killed and bombs were exploded in the city's stock exchange. Nevertheless, the BJP's electoral totals continued to climb from one election to the next. Religious violence seemed to win victories at the ballot box. By the end of the decade, the BJP captured enough votes to elect a governing coalition. In office, the BJP leadership stressed "Hindutva," or "Hinduness" as the basis of their political identity.

In 2002, a group of militant Hindus were returning from a pilgrimage to Ayodhya. They apparently heckled some Muslim vendors on a train platform in one of the towns of Gujarat State. In response, Muslims apparently set fire to a part of the train, killing 59 pilgrims. (Later evidence suggested that the fire had started accidentally inside the train carriage, with no connection to any external attacks.) Across Gujarat State, attacks against Muslims followed, killing as many as 2,000 people and leaving some 140,000 homeless, in refugee camps. The attacks seemed organized, and the state police did little to stop them, bringing charges against the state government of complicity in the killing.

In the next election in the state, the ruling BJP party won a landslide victory, gaining its biggest majorities in areas where the attacks had been most deadly, and suggesting that the call of Hindutva and the attacks on Muslims were once again politically effective. Meanwhile, throughout India, wherever the BJP held power, school textbooks were rewritten to give prominence to stories of Hindu power and to depict Muslims as foreigners and unpatriotic. Muslims seemed to be under siege.

On the other hand, in the national elections of 2004, the BJP was badly defeated. Moreover, the head of the triumphant Congress Party was Sonia Gandhi, the Italian-born, Christian widow of the assassinated former prime minister, Rajiv Gandhi. Manmohan Singh became the first Sikh prime minister. And the president of India, filling a largely ceremonial position, was a Muslim. Despite the emotional appeal of Hindutva, most Indians seemed to appreciate the diversity of their composite identity.

Buddhists in Tibet

Buddhism, suppressed in the early years of the communist revolution in China, reasserted itself in a challenge to government authority, especially in Tibet. In 2008, public protests by Tibetan Buddhists demanded independence from the Chinese government, which seized control of the region in 1950, and drove out the Dalai Lama in 1959. Wanting no interference with the Olympic Games, which China was hosting proudly in Beijing, the Chinese government cracked down on the protesters. Nevertheless, outside of China, prior to the Olympic Games themselves, "Free Tibet" demonstrations followed the Olympic torch on its journey around the world. Even the authoritarian government of communist China could not squelch all these protests nor deny the continuing role of religion in national and international affairs.

Judaism

With the creation of the State of Israel in 1948, officially a Jewish state, Jews held sovereign power for the first time in almost 2,000 years, since the Roman Empire had conquered Judea and exiled its population. The new state was, however, surrounded by hostile neighbors. With some, Egypt and Jordan, Israelis reached political settlements and negotiated peace treaties. But with others, including Syria and Lebanon, they did not. The greatest hostility appeared between the Israelis and the **Palestinians**, Arab residents, mostly Muslim but also Christian, whose territory they had conquered in warfare in 1967.

As a result of the changed political status, Jewish political philosophy seemed to change. Previously, as weak, scattered, and dependent people, Jews had emphasized the biblical concept that they would live "not by might and not by power," but by God's spirit. Now, surrounded by hostility, many of them came to believe that only military might would enable them to survive. They built the most powerful armed force in the Middle East, almost certainly including nuclear weapons, and brandished their weapons and power in ways that appeared restrained and unavoidable to the Israeli government, but excessively brutal to many others.

Israel's dominance over the Palestinians, and the Palestinian response in the form of guerrilla attacks on Israelis, including numerous suicide bombings, has inflamed relationships between the Arab world and the United States, Israel's strongest supporter, and much of Europe as well. The issue is essentially political, and will be discussed in the next chapter in that context, but because of the difference in religion between Israelis and Palestinians, it has often been framed in a religious idiom.

Christianity

Christianity is by far the world's largest religion, with two billion people professing the faith in Europe, Latin America, Africa, Asia, North America, and Oceania. All the years of missionary proselytizing throughout the colonies of Europe reaped an abundant harvest.

Roman Catholicism. Half of this Christian population are Roman Catholics, and half of these live in Latin America. The election of Polish Cardinal Karol Josef Wojtyla as Pope John Paul II (1920–2005) in 1978 also reflects the international range of the Roman Catholic Church, for he was the first non-Italian pope since 1523. His career highlighted some of the connections between religion and politics in the late twentieth century. First, by elevating a cardinal from behind the "Iron Curtain" the Church gave moral support to the people under the control of the Soviet Union. The Soviet communist government was officially atheistic and suppressed religious freedom both in Russia, where Orthodox Christianity had been dominant for a thousand years, and in the Eastern and central European countries, where Roman Catholicism held sway. The Church saw the Cold War not only as a struggle between economic and political systems, but also as a struggle between atheism and religious faith.

In his first overseas trip, to Mexico in 1978, John Paul II stressed this theme to a crowd that some estimated at five million people, the largest crowd in human history. (In 1995, in Manila, four million are estimated to have attended the pope's mass.) In the year after his elevation to the papacy, John Paul II visited Poland to the enthusiastic welcome of millions of his countrymen, who saw him as a beacon of hope for greater freedom. Throughout the 1980s, as Lech Walesa organized the Solidarity labor movement in Poland against the government, the pope offered moral support. In his many travels abroad he stressed human rights and the importance of religious and national freedom everywhere. As communism collapsed by the end of the decade, many felt that John Paul II was giving a belated reply to Stalin's sarcastic question about the power of the pope, "How many divisions has he got?"

While he was an enemy of atheism and communism, John Paul II was no friend of capitalism, which he saw as exploitative of workers. In 1979, at Yankee Stadium in New York City, he denounced the rich of the United States, and of other wealthy countries, for neglecting their poor.

John Paul II demonstrated his openness to the world by his remarkable record of travel—to Mexico, the United States, Turkey, India, China, Cuba, the Philippines, Haiti, Egypt, Israel, and some 30 countries in Africa—about 100 overseas trips in all. He traveled a greater distance than all previous popes combined. He reached out to non-Catholics and non-Christians, especially Jews and Muslims, in his trip to the Holy Land in March 2000 and in his meeting with the chief Sunni cleric, the Sheikh al-Azhar, in Cairo. He called anti-Semitism a sin and referred to Jews as "our older brothers in faith." He visited Canterbury Cathedral in England, the most important cathedral in the Anglican faith, and Lutheran churches in Germany and Sweden.

This pope's positions were, however, quite complex. His conservative orientation of the Church had already appeared in his rulings on personal, family, and sexual issues. During the meetings of the Second Vatican Council, convened in Rome in 1962 by Pope John XXIII (r. 1958–63) to update several of the Church's teachings, the future John Paul II articulated his positions: opposition to abortion, birth control, the ordination of women as priests, and homosexual practices, and insistence upon clerical celibacy. Nevertheless, Catholics around the world practiced birth control to about the same extent as their non-Catholic neighbors, ignoring the Church's teachings on this issue. Meanwhile other Christian groups were liberalizing their attitudes. For example, the Church of England voted to ordain women as priests in 1994. The Episcopal Church in the United States ordained a female bishop for the first time in 1988 and the first openly gay male bishop in 2003. In 2006 a woman was named head of the Episcopal Church in the U.S.

John Paul II also took a conservative position on the means of combating poverty. In the late 1960s and 1970s a new school of thought, called **liberation theology**, took shape in Latin America. Identifying with Jesus' ministry to the poor, it established grass-roots organizations in poor neighborhoods of cities and in rural pockets of poverty. These communities combined religious study and prayer with efforts to identify, define, and actively solve the problems of their localities. They challenged local leaders to effect needed change. By the late 1970s, some observers estimated 80,000 such communities in Brazil alone.

As liberation theology threatened the state and the wealthy, it confronted powerful opposition forces that were willing to engage in violence if necessary. In March

KEY TERM

liberation theology
A movement within the Catholic Church, especially in Latin America, especially in the 1960s and 1970s, combining some of the social concerns of Marxism with those of the Christian gospel, focusing on serving the needs of poor people, and organizing them for confrontations against governments when necessary.

Radical religion. A priest holds hands with members of the Base Christian Community in Panama. Proponents of liberation theology, which originated in Latin America in the 1960s, typically aligned themselves with left-wing, revolutionary movements, such as the Sandinistas in Nicaragua. When influential priests and bishops espoused a Marxist view of society and argued that the Church's role was to assist the oppressed, they came into conflict with established Catholic authorities as well as political leaders.

1980, Archbishop Oscar Romero of El Salvador was assassinated as he was officiating at mass in a San Salvador chapel. The right-wing assassin had opposed the archbishop's message: "When all peaceful means have been exhausted, the church considers insurrection moral and justified" (Keen, p. 595). Romero, who had also advised soldiers that it was morally just to refuse to follow unjust orders, was only one of about 850 church leaders who had been assassinated since the assassination of Camilo Torres, a priest and sociologist in Colombia. An outstanding scholar and teacher, Torres gave up on peaceful reform and joined Colombia's communist-led guerrillas. He was killed in a battle with government forces in February 1966. In December 1980, three American nuns and a lay missionary who had gone to work with poor refugees in El Salvador were murdered by security officers of the state.

The advocates of liberation theology claimed to combine Christian ethics with Marxist politics. Pope John Paul II, raised in communist Poland, rejected this Marxist orientation. As new posts opened, he appointed mostly conservative priests, and as a result the clergy in Latin America were deeply split. About 20 percent aligned themselves with liberation theology, but the overwhelming majority, especially in Brazil, accepted the pope's orientation. Some critics claim that the pope's opposition to liberation theology helped open the door to the rapid growth of Protestant evangelical Christianity in Latin America. Meanwhile John Paul's successor, Pope Benedict XVI (r. 2005–), took much more interest in theological issues and in Europe, than in the political-social organization of the poor in the developing world.

Evangelical Christianity. Evangelical Christianity was giving a new face to the world's largest religion, especially in the Americas. In 1940 there were barely a million Protestants in all of Latin America; by 2004 there were some 50 million, 10 percent of the total population. About half of them lived in Brazil. About 80 to 90 percent of the Protestants were **Pentecostals**, appealing usually to the very poorest groups in society, and often to those who had been uprooted from rural areas. Pentecostals differ from other Protestants in their emphasis on direct, personal experience of God and revelation, rather than on the authority of scripture or of the Church hierarchy. Many of these Pentecostal groups were allied with North American churches and often received assistance from them. Pentecostal religion seems to appeal most to women in Latin America. It often refers to Jesus as Divine Husband and Father, emphasizes male responsibility and chastity, and calls for a "reformation of machismo" in family relationships. Poor women see Pentecostalism improving their lives and the lives of their families.

KEY TERMS

evangelical Christianity Those forms of Protestant Christianity that emphasize the literal truth and authority of the Bible, and salvation through the personal acceptance of Jesus Christ.

Pentecostals Christians who stress a direct, personal experience of God, Jesus, and revelation, rather than the authority of scripture or of the church hierarchy.

Religion in the United States

Throughout our period, America has been the most formally religious of all industrialized countries, as measured by the proportion of the population who are members of churches and attend them regularly. In the years of the Cold War, Americans proclaimed their religious belief as one of the characteristics that set them in opposition to "godless communism." In 1954, Congress added the words "under

HOW DO WE KNOW?

Perspectives on Religious Identity in the United States

Two recent studies of religious identity in the United States have painted contrasting pictures. Diana Eck celebrates an ever-increasing array of new and different religious communities. After noting the increasing diversity of their congregations and services in her Cambridge neighborhood, Eck sent her Harvard students to explore more systematically, first around Boston and then in their hometowns across America. In her book, *A New Religious America*, she reports the results of this Pluralism Project, exploring the extent to which "new" religions—especially Hinduism, Buddhism, and Islam—are appearing in America. She links her findings directly to the recent global migrations that are bringing about a million new immigrants to America every year:

> The immigrants of the last three decades … have expanded the diversity of our religious life dramatically, exponentially. Buddhists have come from Thailand, Vietnam, Cambodia, China, and Korea; Hindus from India, East Africa, and Trinidad; Muslims from Indonesia, Bangladesh, Pakistan, the Middle East, and Nigeria; Sikhs and Jains from India; and Zoroastrians from both India and Iran. Immigrants from Haiti and Cuba have brought Afro-Caribbean traditions, blending both African and Catholic symbols and images. New Jewish immigrants have come from Russia and the Ukraine, and the internal diversity of American Judaism is greater than ever before. The face of American Christianity has also changed with large Latino, Filipino, and Vietnamese Catholic communities; Chinese, Haitian, and Brazilian Pentecostal communities; Korean Presbyterians, Indian Mar Thomas, and Egyptian Copts. In every city in the land church signboards display the meeting times of Korean or Latino congregations that nest within the walls of old urban Protestant and Catholic churches.

Karen Armstrong's crosscultural study of militant fundamentalist movements in Islam in Egypt and Iran, in Judaism in Israel, and in Christianity in the United States, paints a very different picture. Armstrong spent seven years as a nun, then became a college professor, and during the past two decades has become one of the most respected writers on religious history, especially on Christianity, Islam, and Judaism and their relationship to one another. Her reflections on fundamentalist Christianity in the United States suggest very little flexibility, compromise, or openness to new religious groups:

> Fundamentalism is not going to disappear. In America, religion has long shaped opposition to government. Its rise and fall has always been cyclical, and events of the last few years indicate that there is still a state of incipient warfare between conservatives and liberals which has occasionally become frighteningly explicit. In 1992, Jerry Falwell, who still adheres to the old-style fundamentalism, announced that

with the election of Bill Clinton to the presidency, Satan had been let loose in the United States. Clinton, Falwell thundered, was about to destroy the military and the nation by letting "the gays" take over. Executive orders permitting abortion in federally funded clinics, research on fetal tissue, the official endorsement of homosexual rights, were all signs that America "had declared war on God."

How can we reconcile these very different perspectives on religious identity in contemporary America? Philip Jenkins, in his study of the global expansion of Christianity, suggests that we consider the demographics:

> The number of adherents of non-Christian religions in the United States is strikingly small. If we combine the plausible estimates for the numbers of American Jews, Buddhists, Muslims, and Hindus, then we are speaking of about 4 or 5 percent of the total population.

This proportion is not so different from Western Europe where non-Christians form about ten percent of the population of France, four percent of Britain, and five percent of Germany and the Netherlands. In many African and Asian nations, religious minorities make up 10 to 20 percent of the population, and in some cases even more. The same questions that attend religious diversity in many other countries of the world appear also in the U.S.

So, Eck's celebratory report is restricted to a very small, and perhaps not quite so remarkable, proportion of the population. On the other hand, Armstrong's fundamentalists also do not make up an American majority. In a 1984 poll, only nine percent of Americans identified themselves as "fundamentalists," although "44 percent believed that salvation comes only through Jesus Christ."

Religious identity is important to most people in America. Both new immigration and "old time religion" are having their effects on shaping it. The results of this amalgam are not yet clear. As Eck remarks, "diversity alone does not constitute pluralism … whether we are able to work together across the lines of religious difference to create a society in which we actually know one another remains to be seen."

- What other historical examples can you give of national religious identity changing under the influence of new immigrant groups?
- What other historical examples can you give of new religious identities clashing with older established ones?
- Do you think that demographics is the main reason for the differences in perception about American religious life as represented by Eck and Armstrong? What other reasons can you suggest?

God" to the pledge of allegiance to the flag, and in 1955 required the words "In God we trust" to be included on all American currency. President Eisenhower declared that "our government makes no sense unless it is founded in a deeply felt religious faith—and I don't care what it is." By 1960, 95 percent of Americans identified with some religious denomination. The center of gravity of American religion rested with the "mainline" churches—Baptists, Episcopalians, Lutherans, Methodists, Presbyterians—each with membership numbering in the millions, and established, formal organizational structures and forms of prayer. That center was expanding to include Roman Catholics, symbolized by the election of John F. Kennedy as president in 1960. Although generally associated with conservative, status quo politics, much of the American mainline religious community was also open enough to support the Reverend Martin Luther King, Jr., the African-American Baptist minister, who led the fight for equal rights for blacks and minorities in the 1950s and 1960s.

As American culture began to move in new directions in the 1960s and 1970s, the mainline religious groups were often willing to modify their conservative positions, to become more relativistic, and to tolerate, accept, and even embrace many of the new social forces swirling through the country: the anti-Vietnam War protests, the Civil Rights movement, the Women's movement, the increased immigration of Latin Americans and Asians, the revolution in sexual mores, the public expression of gay and lesbian lifestyles, and the development of a "counterculture," which embraced drugs, folk and protest music, provocative styles of dress and self-presentation, and freer sexual expression.

Many believing Christians, however, saw the social and cultural habits of America changing beyond recognition. They turned to their Bibles to rediscover the fundamentals of their faith, and decided that America was moving in the wrong direction. These fundamentalists began creating more of their own organizations and institutions. In 1979 a Gallup poll showed that one out of three American adults reported a "born-again" conversion, an experience of being touched and changed by a personal encounter with Jesus. Fifty percent believed that the Bible was an accurate account of history. One hundred and thirty million people reported listening to and watching 1,300 evangelical Christian radio and television stations. Evangelicals were an important constituency in presidential elections, and powerful voices in challenging the right of women to obtain legal abortions.

Sexuality and family relations surfaced as contentious religious issues. The Supreme Court's *Roe* v. *Wade* decision (1973) legalized abortion, but abortion clinics were attacked by people who viewed abortion as murder. Some doctors who performed abortions were murdered, and across the country Planned Parenthood offices and clinics hired armed security personnel for their safety.

Despite the continuing power of the mainline churches and of the rising visibility of the "born-again" fundamentalists, secularism and nonaffiliation also increased in the period 1990 to 2001. The percentage of adults who reported their religious identity as Christian dropped from 86 to 76. The number of adults who did not subscribe to any religion doubled from 14.3 million to 29.4 million, from 8 percent to 14 percent of the total population. This decline in religious affiliation, quite different from the pronouncements of the religious evangelists, suggested that perhaps, beneath the surface, America was moving in the direction of European countries, with their much lower proportions of religious affiliation.

New immigrants brought yet another, international dimension to American religious identity, increasing its diversity and cosmopolitanism. As Hindus and Sikhs immigrated from India, Muslims from the Middle East and Pakistan, Buddhists from Southeast Asia, and other religious groups from elsewhere, American religious identity broadened. The new immigrants and their native-born children sometimes encountered xenophobia, but they enriched and extended religious identity and ethnic identity in the United States. They made up about seven to eight percent of the total population, and with their mosques, temples, sanctuaries, and church announcement boards in non-European languages, they added a highly visible new dimension to American religious identity. That identity continues in flux.

The Thematic Approach: What Difference Does It Make?

Biological and cultural evolution, expanding urbanization, imperial projects, and religious devotion and conflict—themes around which we have structured this book from the beginning of human history—continue to serve as valuable touchstones for understanding the present. They are among the foundational building blocks of human society. Our study of history, as the study of change over time, gives us an important key to understanding them.

In our final chapter we continue with the last three of our themes—trade, revolution, and technology. We then bring our study to a conclusion with a consideration of the formation of individual and collective identity. The issue of identity formation has always been critical to human history, and it is receiving special attention among historians at present, because it offers an approach to integrating all our themes. We live in a world of swirling biological, cultural, regional, political, religious, economic, social, and technological changes. To live our lives fully, we try to make sense of these changes and find our individual and collective ways through them. In light of all these themes, our final chapter asks how individuals and groups synthesize their understanding of who they are in a world of constant global change.

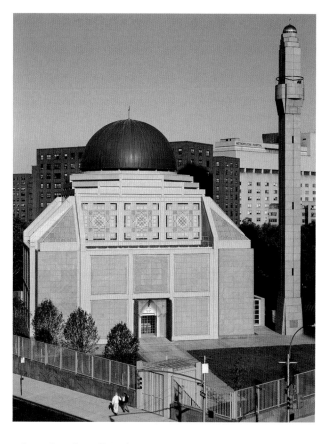

Islamic Cultural Center, New York City. Religions from around the world were finding new homes in America, often transplanted by new groups of immigrants and supplemented by native-born American converts.

Asking Questions

- The processes of cloning living beings and of developing genetically modified foods have both come about through the scientific manipulation of DNA in light of the insights of evolutionary biology. Please explain this statement.
- In what ways are the large cities of the early twenty-first century different from those of the early twentieth?
- What have been the principal strategies of the early twenty-first century for coping with slums? To what degree are the problems and solutions similar in the developing world and in the developed world?
- What is the relationship between the decline in American power and the increase in Chinese power in the early twenty-first century?
- How have the successes of the European Union in the early twenty-first century altered Europe's view of itself and its view of the United States?
- Some scholars argue that religious identification has increased because globalization has increased, and even that religious tensions have increased, in some regions, because globalization has increased. On what basis do they make these arguments? Do you agree with them?

Suggested Readings

In this chapter we are moving into contemporary times, and even into current events. In addition to newspapers and the popular news magazines, such as *Time* and *Newsweek*, and television and radio news programs, two publications are especially useful in tracking current events. The following serve an educated, but not specialized, readership:

The Economist, a weekly review published in London and providing extensive coverage of the United States and the entire world. Edited from a traditional liberal perspective—that is, favoring free markets and human rights as developed over the past centuries in Europe and the United States—*The Economist* covers the globe each week. Whatever one may think of its philosophical and political bias, the comprehensiveness and accessibility of its coverage cannot be matched in the English language.

The *New York Review of Books*, published bi-weekly, takes the form of a tabloid of book reviews, but its reviews are lengthy and extensive explorations of subject areas. The particular book or books under assessment serve as a springboard for wide-ranging, thoughtful, and careful discussions of the subject matter. The authors are leading scholars in their fields.

PRINCIPAL SOURCES

Ayres, Alyssa and Philip Oldenburg, eds. *India Briefing: Takeoff at Last?* (Armonk, NY: M.E. Sharpe, 2005). The most recent, as of 2009, of a series published every year or two, of outstanding summary articles on developments in contemporary India. Various articles on politics, economics, social life, the arts, and culture.

Crossley, Pamela Kyle, Lynn Hollen Lees, and John W. Servos. *Global Society: The World since 1900* (Boston, MA: Houghton Mifflin, 2nd ed., 2007). A fine, well-written history of the twentieth century, organized thematically rather than by nations or regions. Special emphasis on technology and useful references to websites for further research.

Das, Gurcharan. *India Unbound* (New York: Random House, 2000). A newspaper columnist and successful businessman reports on, and relishes, the opening of the Indian economy since 1991.

Gilbert, Mark. *Surpassing Realism: The Politics of European Integration since 1945* (Lanham, MD: Rowman and Littlefield, 2003). Step-by-step account of the building of the European Union with fascinating contemporary commentaries along the way.

Glenny, Misha. *The Balkans: Nationalism, War, and the Great Powers, 1804–1999* (New York: Viking, 2000). Comprehensive account of the Balkans and their somewhat unfortunate fate in the hands of the great powers, sometimes because of intervention, sometimes because of lack of intervention.

Human Development Report 2007/08: Fighting Climate Change: Human Solidarity in a Divided World (New York: United Nations Development Programme, 2008). A survey of the nations of the world with an abundance of statistical tables and numerous, brief, specific topical discussions.

Hunt, Michael H. *The World Transformed: 1945 to the Present: A Documentary Reader* (Boston, MA: Bedford/St. Martin's, 2004). An outstanding selection of primary documents with global scope and thematic breadth.

Jaffrelot, Christophe. *Hindu Nationalism: A Reader* (Princeton, NJ: Princeton University Press, 2007). Superb selections on the merger of religion and politics, covering almost 100 years.

——. *India's Silent Revolution: The Rise of the Lower Castes in North India* (London: Hurst and Company, 2003). Amazing, peaceful transformations in a hierarchical society.

Jaffrelot, Christophe, ed. *A History of Pakistan and Its Origins* (New York: Anthem Press, 2004). Excellent selection of scholarly articles on the complexities of Pakistan.

Kishwar, Madhu. *Off the Beaten Track: Rethinking Gender Justice for Indian Women* (New Delhi: Oxford University Press, 1999). The editor of one of India's leading feminist journals, *Manushi*, discusses the evolution of her thought in light of the possible and the ideal.

Meredith, Robyn, *The Elephant and the Dragon: The Rise of India and China and What It Means for All of Us* (New York: W.W. Norton, 2007). Chapter-by-chapter, point-by-point comparisons of the recent developments in these two giant nations.

Nafisi, Azar. *Reading Lolita in Tehran: A Memoir in Books* (New York: Random House, 2003). How an English professor and her students bucked the regime and studied literature as they chose.

Nugent, Neill. *The Government and Politics of the European Union* (Durham, NC: Duke University Press, 5th ed., 2003). Detailed exposition of the institutional workings of the EU, with very useful historical prelude and concluding perspectives on the future.

Rogel, Carole. *The Breakup of Yugoslavia and the War in Bosnia* (Westport, CN: Greenwood Press, 1998). Basic narrative supported by detailed chronology and primary documents to 1997. Critical of almost all participants and of NATO and the U.S. for years of appeasement.

Sassen, Saskia. *The Global City: New York, London, Tokyo* (Princeton: Princeton University Press, 2001).

Sen, Amartya. *Development as Freedom* (New York: Random House, 1999). Nobel Prize-winning economist stresses the significance of human development—health, education, and welfare—as the key issue in economic development, both as its cause and its result. Clearly and persuasively argued.

Tully, Mark. *India's Unending Journey* (New York: Random House, 2008). Tully was the BBC's revered and respected correspondent from New Delhi for 25 years. He is perceptive and direct about his observations, especially as India enters uncharted territory.

Ullman, Richard H., ed. *The World and Yugoslavia's Wars* (New York: Council on Foreign Relations, 1996). Explores not only the wars but also the (lack of) responses by the European Community, the United States, and the United Nations.

ADDITIONAL SOURCES

Bluestone, Barry and Bennett Harrison. *The Deindustrialization of America* (New York: Basic Books, 1982). Predicted dire consequences as a result of shoring of jobs and decline of manufacture in the U.S.

Borradori, Giovanna, Jürgen Habermas, Jacques Derrida. *Philosophy in a Time of Terror: Dialogues with Jurgen Habermas and Jacques Derrida* (Chicago, IL: University of Chicago Press, 2003). Evaluations of the United States, especially in light of the Iraq war, by several of Europe's preeminent philosophers.

Brass, Paul. *The Production of Hindu-Muslim Violence in Contemporary India* (Seattle, WA: University of Washington Press, 2003). Sees violence between the groups as a result of cynical political manipulation.

Cavalieri, Paola and Peter Singer, eds. *The Great Ape Project: Equality Beyond Humanity* (New York: St. Martin's Press, 1994). The book that underlies the campaign.

China Development Brief. *250 Chinese NGOs: Civil Society in the Making* (Unpublished Report: China Development Brief, 2001). Underlines the importance of NGOs to China's progress—economic as well as political—and outlines the mission and accomplishments of 250 of them.

Hall, Peter. *Cities of Tomorrow: An Intellectual History of Urban Planning and Design in the Twentieth Century* (Malden, MA: Blackwell, 3rd ed., 2002). Key developments in the history of urban planning in the twentieth century, with most, but not all, examples taken from Europe and the U.S.

Huang, Shu-Min. *The Spiral Road* (Boulder, CO: Westview Press, 2nd ed., 1998). Changes in a Chinese village through the eyes of a Communist Party leader.

Inman, Robert. *Making Cities Work. Prospects and Policies for Urban America* (Princeton, NJ: Princeton University Press, 2009). Collection of essays by leading experts on key issues.

Irigaray, Luce. *This Sex Which is Not One* (Ithaca, NY: Cornell University Press, 1985). An approach to finding gender equality through an acceptance of the complementary sexuality of women and men.

Mohanty, Chandra Talpade, Ann Russo, and Lourdes Torres, eds. *Third World Women and the Politics of Feminism* (Bloomington, IN: Indiana University Press, 1991). The issues of feminism are different in different parts of the world, as this academic selection makes clear.

Nye, Joseph F. Jr., "The Decline of America's Soft Power," *Foreign Affairs*, May/June, 2004, Vol. 83, No. 3 (pp. 16-21). Brief, to-the-point exposition of the importance of soft-power, that is, cultural power, in international relations.

Plummer, Janelle. *Focusing Partnerships: A Sourcebook for Municipal Capacity Building in Public-Private Partnerships* (London: Earthscan Publications, 2002). Gives best-practice examples from third world nations.

For quizzes, flashcards, primary sources, interactive maps, videos, and other activities related to this chapter please go to

www.myhistorylab.com

CHAPTER TWENTY-FOUR

Contemporary History: Trade, Social Revolution, Technology, Identity

This final chapter reviews the last three themes of the text—trade, social revolution, and technology—and assesses their significance in understanding today's world. In conclusion, we touch briefly one final theme. This theme of identity has become a central concern for historians in the past 20 years because it explores the ways in which people, groups, and institutions define themselves in eras of continual change and constant spin—eras like our own. It explores how they integrate in practice all the themes we have been discussing in the abstract. The theme of identity provides a conceptual viewpoint that helps us to integrate the past and present and even to anticipate the future. And with it, we close our study.

On Trade

Modern trade began its rise to global importance in the thirteenth century. The nations of Western Europe—first Spain and Portugal, later the Netherlands, England, and France—felt themselves isolated from the trade networks of the Middle East, the Arabian Sea, and the overland silk routes to eastern markets. To find a place in this global economy, Portugal dispatched Bartholomeo Dias and Vasco da Gama around the coast of Africa in search of the East Indies. Spain sent Columbus in the other direction, on his daring expedition across the Atlantic. As these voyages began to pay off, merchant communities in the Netherlands, England, and France began to participate in the trade and its profits, and later mounted ventures of their own.

Even China, approaching from the east, asserted its interests in the Indian Ocean trade by dispatching Admiral Zheng He on his seven voyages, some of which reached as far as the coast of East Africa. From western Africa, Mansa Musa, king of the gold-rich kingdom of Mali, entered into this trade as a by-product of his *hajj* pilgrimages to Mecca.

International trade, of course, was not new. Sumerians had traded westward to Egypt and the Nile Valley and eastward to India and the Indus Valley. Later, silk routes had facilitated trade between Han China, the ancient Roman Empire, and the empires of India. But the trade of the twelfth century and beyond, especially the trade initiated from Europe, introduced several new dimensions. First, from this time onward trade became the driving force in international relations, not merely a component of other kinds of relationships. Second, with improved navigation, trade networks became global; the oceans, no longer a barrier, became a bridge. Third, private merchant communities acquired influence within their home countries and

Israeli–Palestinian relations on the West Bank, 2000. An Israeli soldier is seen in discussion with two Palestinian women.

internationally, separate from government, but intertwined with it. Merchants and trade came to rival political leaders and government in their powers to determine the fate of nations.

In recent years, world trade has reached unprecedented levels, which keep rising almost every year. "Between 1990 and 2007, the global economy grew from US $22.8 trillion to US $53.3 trillion, and global trade increased 133 percent" (Zakaria, p. 20). This increasing interaction in commercial trade—and also in other kinds of international exchange—is called **globalization**.

Globalization has become a buzzword. With globalization, increasing communication technology, free market capitalism, and decreasing government regulation have come together:

> in a way that is enabling individuals, corporations and nation-states to reach around the world farther, faster, deeper and cheaper than ever before, and in a way that is also producing a powerful backlash from those brutalized or left behind by this new system. (Friedman, 1999, pp. 7–8)

Economically, globalization thrives on the new, inexpensive transportation and communication facilities of the later twentieth and early twenty-first centuries. Politically, it requires freedom of movement of goods, services, capital, knowledge, and people across borders, although the freedom of people to move is more restricted than the other categories. It makes possible the movement of billions of dollars of investment capital around the globe at the stroke of a computer key. It creates new institutions for negotiating across international borders, rules, and regulations. It increases the level of interaction of peoples, producing new and different social and cultural forms. Globalization means not only increased trade, but also increased travel and tourism, more world music and literature, and new dimensions of international economic investment. Because of these broad and deep influences, globalization evokes passionate responses, both for and against.

Although many advocates of globalization claim that its home is the entire world and its benefits are equally accessible to everyone, more critical observers see its contemporary origins in the United States, spread not only by America's businesses but also by its effective control over global financial institutions. They see globalization as just one more measure of the superpower status of the United States. Since about 2000, however, as the American role in the global economy has shrunk somewhat, and as the roles of China, Japan, and Europe have increased, the process of globalization appears more fully global, and America's leadership position significantly diluted and challenged.

The Institutions of Globalization

The principal financial institutions that facilitate the expansion of globalization—the IMF, the World Bank, and the GATT—were put in place toward the end of World War II (see Chapter Twenty-one). In 1995 the members transformed the GATT into the World Trade Organization (WTO). The new institution reflected the growth in world trade. From 1950 to 2000, global exports grew on average by six percent annually. At its inception, the GATT had 40 members; when it became the WTO, there were 128, and by 2008, the WTO included 153 members. The members negotiate, sign, and implement agreements that form the legal ground rules for international trade. These agreements are intergovernmental, but they are designed to enable producers, importers, and exporters—usually private businesses—to conduct business successfully. Should disputes arise over interpretations of the agreements, they are adjudicated by the WTO, which can enforce its decisions by invoking sanctions against violators.

The Internet, the World Wide Web, and Containerization. The WTO has provided the institutional organization to facilitate the expansion of global trade. The internet, the World Wide Web, and the improved transportation facility of containerization have provided the technology.

In 1994, some three million people worldwide were connected to the internet; by 2008, that figure had increased to 1.5 billion. The largest national group, 253 million, was in China (19 percent of its total population); the second largest was in the United States, with 220 million users (73 percent of the American population). About 30 percent of internet users claim English as their native tongue; about 20 percent claim Chinese (http://www.internetworldstats.com/stats.htm). Other electronic communications media expanded similarly, with almost unbelievable speed. In 1990 there were 11 million cellular phone subscriptions world wide; at the end of 2006 there were 2.6 billion, with the largest number, 481 million, in China. With the internet and World Wide Web, shopping, research, and accessing and transmitting documents can all be done while sitting in front of a computer at home, in an office, or on the road. E-mail and texting have made instantaneous global communication available at nominal cost.

Transportation played as large a role as communication. In his remarkable book, *The Box: How the Shipping Container Made the World Smaller and the World Economy Bigger*, Marc Levinson tells the story of Malcolm McLean's 1956 introduction of containers of standardized size that were sealed from shipper to receiver, even as they moved among different modes of transportation—trucks, railway cars, and ships. These standardized containers have dramatically reduced the need for human labor in loading and unloading freight at each of the transfer points along the way. Great cranes carry out the work. The sealed containers also cut the rate of pilferage and damage to goods. In 2005 about 18 million containers made over 200 million trips per year, carrying the overwhelming majority of shipping cargo, at a cost that

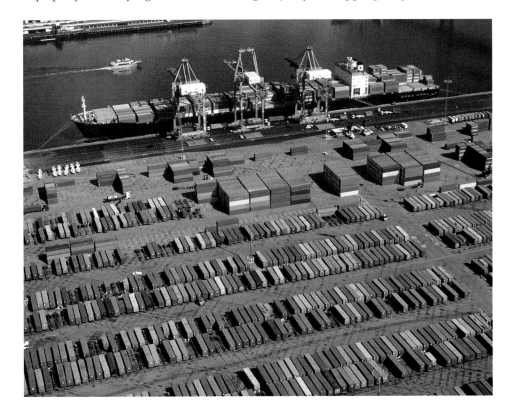

Shipping containers. Standard-size containers have been used on a limited basis for centuries. In the late 1950s, however, greater standardization in containers was achieved, first by the transportation industry and then through the regulations of the ISO (International Organization for Standardization). With standardization of size, freight could be shipped from original expediter to final consumer at relatively rapid speed and low cost, moving interchangeably from train to truck to ship, protected against pilferage. Containerization has facilitated the globalization of trade.

has become negligible. The reduced cost of shipping was one of the principal innovations that helped bring China, so distant from European and American markets, into the center of the world trade network:

> In 1956, China was not the world's workshop. It was not routine for shoppers to find Brazilian shoes and Mexican vacuum cleaners in stores in the middle of Kansas. Japanese families did not eat beef from cattle raised in Wyoming, and French clothing designers did not have their exclusive apparel cut and sewn in Turkey or Vietnam. (McLean, p. 1)

Evaluating Globalization

Given the constant development of new technologies and the creation of new institutions, it might appear that globalization is inevitable, and globalization does have its ardent advocates. But it also has fierce critics. In 1999, protesters gathered at the meeting of the WTO in Seattle, Washington, to demonstrate their apprehensions at the increasing tempo of world trade and their demands for more regulation by national governments and by the UN. The protesters feared that the quest for profits would overrun humanitarian concerns. They sought regulations to protect the environment, human rights, labor, and children's welfare.

Many of the protesters also feared that globalization would homogenize the world's cultures into a single "McDonald's" culture and even replace its many languages with a single, dominant global language, English. These protesters were not convinced that new communication networks would allow small, niche cultures, languages, and organizations to flourish, as advocates of globalization argued.

In 2001, an umbrella organization of protestors, the World Social Forum, held its first annual meeting in Porto Alegre, Brazil. By the time of the fourth meeting in 2004, in Mumbai, India, 100,000 people participated. At the seventh meeting in Nairobi, Kenya, in 2007, 66,000 people from 110 countries attended. In 2008, no centralized meeting was held, but regional forums around the world convened more localized sessions, although for 2009, the forum returns to a central location in Belem, Brazil.

Trees destroyed by acid rain, Sebestiana, Czech Republic, 1997. Acid rain is one of several pollutants produced by industry that threaten life and health on our planet. Compare the destruction of parts of a Brazilian rainforest as a result of logging and burning, p. 802.

Under its motto, "Another World is Possible," the Forum seeks alternative political and economic models to those that dominate the world today. The issues raised by the forum are not new, but their massive representation at the global level, including participation by UNESCO, is.

Disputes over the future of globalization are not surprising. Globalization increases economic dislocations. Some consequences are immediately evident and can be evaluated easily; others may not be discernible for decades. The process confers great benefits on the winners and exacts costly consequences from the losers. Because of the competitive nature of the capitalist system, the fundamental order on which globalization rests, those who are able to take advantage of the new possibilities gain much faster than those who cannot, or do not.

Global economic competition increases the speed of technological change, bringing new employment possibilities to some, but eliminating older jobs. Newer technologies are often capital-intensive, that is, they use a lot of expensive, "labor-saving" equipment, which does away with many jobs and may reduce total employment, at least temporarily. This kind of economic innovation brings an overall increase in productivity, but at the cost of lost jobs and worker income. Throughout the 1990s and 2000s, investors commonly regarded company layoffs of workers as moves toward efficiency. As companies laid off workers, the share prices of company stock went up. The economist Josef Schumpeter (1883–1950) famously remarked that capitalism was a system of "creative destruction." But those who benefited from the creativity and those who suffered from the destruction were usually different people.

The new technologies have increased the gap between those who keep up with the change and those who do not. Lagging regions do their best, but they have a very long way to go. The nations of sub-Saharan Africa increased their usage of the internet ten times between 2000 and 2008. Even so, they still have only 3.5 percent of the world's internet users (for 14 percent of the world's population). Because the new technologies are dependent on research laboratories, these facilities, especially in the United States, continue to attract talented, skilled persons, draining them from less technologically sophisticated nations.

On the other hand, to some degree, poorer countries are benefiting from the possibility of new employment opportunities. New, communications-related jobs are being **outsourced** to third-world countries where salaries are low. For example, Bangalore and Hyderabad, cities in India, have become miniature "Silicon Valleys" through the investments of multinational companies such as IBM, Texas Instruments, and Microsoft, and the entrepreneurship of local information technology experts who have started their own firms, such as Infosys, Wipro, and Tata Consultancy. Here, skilled personnel earn salaries far higher than most local jobs provide, although still substantially below those of the U.S., the EU, and Japan. These salary differentials produce a flow of investment capital, goods, and labor outsourcing around the globe, from wealthier countries to poorer ones.

As a result of the search for cheaper locations for production, inequalities among nations are actually decreasing, and the proportion of people living in absolute poverty is declining. Average living standards around the world have been improving. The proportion of people suffering from extreme poverty, living on less than the equivalent of $1 per day, fell from about 40 percent in 1981 to about 30 percent in 1990 and to 18 percent in 2004, in large part thanks to the improvements in China's economy. In China alone, 400 million people emerged from such abject poverty. But China was not alone. "Poverty is falling in countries housing 80 percent of the world's population" (Zakaria, p. 3). In 2006 and 2007, 124 countries grew at a rate of four percent or more, including 30 countries in Africa. (This evaluation was

KEY TERM

outsourcing Buying goods and services, including personnel, from sources far away from the place where they are to be used, usually from overseas locations. A major example is the establishment of overseas call centers in countries where labor is cheap to service customers in places where labor is expensive.

HOW DO WE KNOW?

Evaluating Globalization

Globalization—in the sense of global networks of economic, political, and cultural exchange—is not new. We have seen examples throughout this text going back thousands of years. The increasing sophistication of transportation and communication, especially the computer, the internet, and the World Wide Web, however, have given globalization far greater scope in the last two decades than ever before. As the power of globalization has increased over the past 15 years, its evaluations have become more careful and more nuanced.

Thomas Friedman, chief foreign political correspondent for the *New York Times*, introduced his highly influential *The Lexus and the Olive Tree* with a sense of the inevitability of globalization:

> I feel about globalization a lot like I feel about the dawn. Generally speaking, I think it's a good thing that the sun comes up every morning. It does more good than harm. But even if I didn't much care for the dawn there isn't much I could do about it. I didn't start globalization. I can't stop it—except at a huge cost to human development—and I'm not going to waste time trying. All I want to think about is how I can get the best out of this new system, and cushion the worst, for the most people. (p. xviii)

Joseph Stiglitz, Nobel Prize winner in Economics, served for a number of years as vice president and chief economist of the World Bank. Stiglitz came away from the experience appalled by the failures of globalization and the hardships it often inflicted, especially on the poor. His powerful critique, *Globalization and its Discontents*, differs sharply from Friedman's general acceptance of the system:

> I have written this book because while I was at the World Bank, I saw firsthand the devastating effect that globalization can have on developing countries, and especially the poor within those countries. I believe that globalization—the removal of the barriers to free trade and the closer integration of national economies—can be a force for good and that it has the potential to enrich everyone in the world, particularly the poor. But I also believe that if this is to be the case, the way globalization has been managed, including the international trade agreements that have played such a large role in removing those barriers and the policies that have been imposed on developing countries in the process of globalization, need to be radically rethought. (pp. ix–x)
>
> Today, few—apart from those with vested interests who benefit from keeping out the goods produced by the poor countries—defend the hypocrisy of pretending to help developing countries by forcing them to open up their markets

to the goods of the advanced industrial countries while keeping their own markets protected, policies that make the rich richer and the poor more impoverished—and increasingly angry. (p. xv)

By the beginning of 2009, a global recession of frightening proportions had reinvigorated criticisms of globalization. The International Labor Organization of the United Nations issued a report on income equality and inequality. With Stiglitz, it criticized excessive increases in inequality, but with Friedman, it felt that in the long run globalization would prove valuable.

> Partly through the lack of proper regulation or an adequate supervisory framework, the frequency of financial crises has increased in both developed and emerging economies as a consequence of financial globalization. Worldwide, systemic banking crises have been 10 times more likely throughout the 1990s than during the late 1970s, which was hardly a period of calm economic activity. Such increased instability has come at a steep cost to inequality, as low-income households have been particularly affected by repeated boom-bust cycles. There is also evidence … that financial globalization is associated with higher unemployment. From a longer term perspective, however, and at least as regards economic growth, the benefits of financial liberalization outweigh the costs of crises. (p. 39)

Enigmatically, the ILO did not explain when or how it expected the long-run benefits to overcome the short-term losses. Much seemed to depend on policymakers around the world acting in the future with far greater wisdom and discretion than they had in the recent past.

International Labor Organization: *World of Work Report 2008: Income Inequalities in the Age of Financial Globalization* (Geneva: International Labour Office; International Institute for Labour Studies, 2008).

- What experience has each author had in defining, evaluating, and implementing globalization?
- To what degree is each author dogmatic in his evaluation of globalization? What dogmas does he seem to accept or to reject?
- To what extent can you begin, on the bases of these authors' suggestions, to formulate your own values in evaluating globalization? On the bases of these introductions, which of the three evaluations do you think you would find most interesting? Most useful?
- How do the ideas of George Soros, discussed in our text above, compare with those of these authors?

written just as the world economy was plunging into a global recession at the end of 2008. That recession is reversing some of these successes, but it is too early to know the full extent of the losses.)

As global mobility of jobs and capital increases, differences of income have become less related to nationality, and much more to occupation and education. A well-educated person with a good job in China will be more similar in economic status to a colleague in Western Europe or the United States than to a fellow citizen of China with a poor education and a poor job. But income disparities among individuals, within countries and worldwide, have been increasing. Income inequality has increased most dramatically in poorer countries: "Over the past two decades [1983–2003] income inequality worsened in 33 of 66 developing countries with data" (*Human Development Report*, 2003, p. 5). At the turn of the twenty-first century, the richest five percent of the world's population received about a third of the total global income, about the same as that received by the poorest 80 percent.

Debates over globalization arise also because economists do not always agree on the mechanisms of economic change. While they are agreed on the huge decline in poverty in China, for example, they argue over the causes of that decline. The conventional view is that the increased trade brought by globalization increased the wealth of everyone in China, poor as well as rich. But World Bank data suggest a different interpretation. Not trade, expanding primarily in the 1990s, but earlier agricultural reform in the 1980s—decollectivization, egalitarian land reform, a readjustment of farm procurement prices—made the difference. In this huge agricultural country, the economic empowerment of hundreds of millions of farmers brought their living standards up above the poverty line. Amartya Sen, Nobel laureate in economics, takes this argument further: China's great economic advances in the 1990s and 2000s may have been achieved through participation in the globalizing, capitalist market, but this participation was possible only because of China's accomplishments in providing education and health care during the communist regime of Mao Zedong. In addition, Mao's policies of economic **autarky**, keeping China out of international markets, may have slowed growth, but they protected China's fledgling industries. Mao's protectionism, coupled with his social welfare policies, prepared the Chinese to participate successfully in the global economy once Deng Xiao Ping opened the gates, first by reforming agriculture, then by expanding trade.

China succeeded in becoming the manufacturing base not only for much of the developed world; it has also succeeded in capturing manufacturing jobs once held by countries like Mexico. China had not only cheap labor but also a base in education and infrastructure that enabled it to respond to opportunity. Countries that lacked this base did less well. For example, in 1994, ten years after Mexico entered into the North America Free Trade Agreement (NAFTA), liberalizing trade with the United States and Canada, that country's real wages were lower, and rates of inequality and poverty were higher, than they had been before. Nations had to be prepared for globalization; with proper institutional structures they could succeed brilliantly; without them they were in danger of moving backward.

Setting Goals for Globalization

By the early 2000s, the attention of the World Bank and many other institutions concerned with global economic development shifted from achieving equality, or even **equity**, to reducing, and ultimately ending, poverty. Following a "Millennium Summit" convened by the UN in September 2000, 189 nations accepted eight "Millennium Development Goals" (MDG) to be achieved by 2015. These include:

KEY TERMS

autarky An economic system based primarily on internal self-sufficiency with little participation in external trade.

equity A condition in which participants in a system believe that the system is fair and unbiased. Equity does not necessarily imply equality, a situation in which all participants have equivalent goods and rights, but it does require that participants share a sense of justice and fairness in the system.

- eradicating extreme poverty and hunger;
- achieving universal primary education;
- promoting gender equality and empowering women;
- reducing child mortality;
- improving maternal health;
- combating HIV/AIDS, malaria, and other diseases;
- ensuring environmental sustainability; and
- developing a global partnership for development.

In 2008, halfway to the target date of 2015, it appeared that the world was on course to achieve the MDG. This accomplishment, however, owed much to the progress in China, and to a lesser extent, in India. These giant countries, each with about a sixth of the world's population, pulled the data upward. Some other countries, mostly in Asia, also saw marked reductions in poverty. (The global recession, beginning in late 2008, threatened to undermine this progress as well.)

However, many smaller, poorer countries, especially in Africa, were not achieving the goals for their populations. A UN report issued in September, 2008, laid much of the blame squarely on the wealthier countries for failing to meet their commitments to provide aid to these poorest countries and to open their own markets more fully to the exports of these countries. In 2006, development assistance fell by 4.7 percent, and then dropped another 8.4 percent in 2007. Though industrialized countries made a commitment to raise their aid contributions to 0.7 percent of national income by 2015, the actual figure in 2007 was only 0.28 percent. Despite its pledges, the United States, one of the least generous of donor nations, contributed just 0.16 percent of its national income.

The issue of market access was equally contentious. Wealthier countries in Europe and the United States had numerous **protectionist** policies, restricting access to their markets for the raw materials and finished manufactures of impoverished third world countries. By imposing tariffs on imports and providing subsidies to their own producers, against the spirit and sometimes the letter of the WTO, wealthier nations captured business worth about $100 billion per year from their trade with the poorer nations of the world. Western political leaders often attended more to the protectionist voices of their internal lobbyists and producers than to the needs of the people of impoverished nations overseas.

Hazards in the Trade System

Since the late 1990s, the world trade system has faced two serious malfunctions that threatened the entire system. One involved East and Southeast Asia and then spread to much of the rest of the world before it was contained by combined action on the part of several nations. A second began in 2007 in the United States through malfunctions in the American system of issuing and insuring mortgages and then spread internationally to the multitude of institutional investors who held American, defaulting mortgages in their portfolios.

The countries of East and Southeast Asia experienced extraordinary growth between 1965 and 1996. While the average annual growth of the GNP for the world as a whole during these three decades was 3.1 percent, for East and Southeast Asian nations it averaged 6.8 percent. Then the currency of Thailand fell sharply, as investors recognized that the national economy was not expanding as rapidly as incoming investment and loans. The values of land and industry on which the loans and investments had been based had been artificially inflated, in a "bubble," and when they collapsed, the bubble burst, and so did the value of Thai currency.

KEY TERM

protectionism The policy of protecting domestic production from external competition by limiting or prohibiting imports from other countries.

Investments stopped abruptly and loans were recalled, first from Thailand and then from neighboring countries with similar financial problems. In the space of a few months entire national economies collapsed and others went into a deep recession. Japan, the world's second largest economy, suffered financial bankruptcies and the devaluation of its stocks and bonds.

What had happened? The Asian economies had been doing many things right. They had budget surpluses, low inflation, high rates of savings, and substantial exports. But they had taken on more loans, especially short-term loans, than their productivity justified, and as collateral they had presented real estate that was unrealistically overpriced. Beyond this, their internal financial systems were not **transparent**—that is, not open to external analysis and evaluation. Presumably they were hiding some important information. Corrupt politicians, bureaucrats, bankers, and organized crime leaders were siphoning off investment capital inappropriately, for their own benefit, and covering up their actions. Meanwhile investment money and loans poured in from overseas. The monies were misused, pocketed, or poorly invested in speculation, until finally the economies collapsed.

The governments, which had been so helpful as their economies had grown, were now not strong enough to bail out the failing banks and industries. The system of government direction, which had produced economic miracles, now left a wake of recession and depression. Those that had relied less on international funds and that had paid more attention to basic business fundamentals—like Taiwan and Singapore—had fewer troubles; those that had taken in the most foreign loans and investments and had invested them least prudently—like South Korea, Indonesia, and Thailand—were most affected.

The IMF came to the rescue in some of these countries with massive loans, but its very arrival frightened off private investors, who saw this as a sign of economic insolvency. In addition, the IMF was more concerned with recovering its loans and investments than with the economic health of the defaulting countries. It stipulated adherence to a collection of measures known as the "Washington consensus": opening the borders to international investment (although this was already in place and had caused some of the problems); lowering or removing tariffs against imports; **privatizing** government businesses; reducing government welfare programs; laying off government employees; and devaluing local currency. All these measures are the instruments of classical, conservative economic theory, although many economists argued that these measures had never been rigidly implemented in the economies of wealthy countries. The IMF virtually took over control of the economies of the defaulting countries. It demanded a regimen of economic austerity so severe that it jeopardized the health and welfare of the citizens of the country. This was the experience, for example, in South Korea in 1997, which accepted a bail-out loan of $58 billion, the largest ever in the history of the IMF.

Trillions of dollars in investment funds were swirling around the globe without guidance or tracking or common purpose. Capital markets had become global, but the national and international institutions for keeping them honest and transparent had not. Some regulation was needed at the international level. This was the great institutional deficiency now exposed by the experience of East and Southeast Asia. After several years of suffering and of economic restructuring, these countries mostly recovered their former economic health, and some, like Korea and Singapore, have pushed far ahead. Their experience, however, highlights the dangers of unregulated global capital movements and of wishful thinking.

By 2008, economic problems in the United States threatened also to infect the international economy. The economy of the United States, however, was so large that

KEY TERMS

transparency The quality of making public and clear the (financial) transactions of government or of private enterprise. Increasingly, transparency is highly valued as a necessity for successful development.

privatization The act of selling off government-owned enterprises to private business firms.

international bankers were willing to help stabilize it, lest failure in America pull down the entire international system.

In the 1990s, the United States had profited from globalization. Its domestic economy grew as computerization introduced new economies in both production and distribution. New markets opened with China and the former Soviet Union and its allies. With cheap labor available overseas, American businesses sent many enterprises offshore. Although American workers felt the loss of manufacturing jobs, the prices of imports were lower than domestic production had been, so inflation was under control and the dollar went further. Despite the complaint of labor unions that jobs were being lost, most Americans regarded globalization very favorably.

A very few years later, they were much less sure. In the spring of 2008, a *Los Angeles Times*/Bloomberg poll reported "that 50 percent of respondents said free trade hurt the economy, while only 26 percent said it helped" (*Newsweek*, Sept. 8, 2008, p. 66). The years since 2000 had been difficult. Real wages had gone down, and jobs were less secure, in large part because of overseas competition and the off-shoring of America's businesses, relocating them to other countries. America continued to buy overseas hundreds of billions of dollars more than it sold, amassing colossal trade deficits, especially with China. In the year 2006, the United States ran a trade deficit of $817 billion with the rest of the world. Of that deficit, $233 billion was with China, and $88 billion with Japan. America could afford this only because China and Japan took their profits and invested them back in American financial securities and business enterprises. Slowly China was gaining control over these securities and enterprises, as Japan had in the 1980s and early 1990s. American influence over the global economy diminished as others grew far faster than did the United States. In 2000, U.S. stock exchanges accounted for about half the value of global stock markets; at the beginning of 2008, they accounted for just 33 percent. Americans had one of the lowest savings rates in the world, and American businesses became increasingly reliant on foreigners for investment. Other nations, especially China and Japan, had the money to make these investments because they sold to America far more than they bought.

In 2008, failures in the United States' banking and mortgage systems caused numerous bankruptcies in smaller companies. Larger financial institutions were saved only by government intervention in the form of loans plus assistance in negotiations to have another company buy the failing firm. The mortgage crisis was more difficult. Newer financial institutions had been permitted to enter into issuing mortgages without the restraints of the regulations imposed on more traditional savings-and-loan institutions. Home buyers were tempted to take out mortgages larger than they could afford, on terms that they did not always understand, on houses that were overpriced and would soon drop in value. As the economy went into a downturn in late 2008, home buyers began to default. Then, as inflated home prices began to come down, the companies that had issued the mortgages suffered huge losses. The repossessed homes were worth less than the mortgages.

The losses were spread widely because financial institutions at home and abroad had bought up hundreds of billions of dollars worth of mortgages as securities, not realizing that the properties were worth less than what they had paid. Some weaker banks and financial companies around the world began to fail. At home, even the largest mortgage security companies of all, "Fannie Mae" (Federal National Mortgage Association) and "Freddy Mac" (Federal Home Loan Mortgage Corporation), which between them held $5.5 *trillion* dollars worth of mortgages, were in danger of collapsing as their stock plummeted in value. These institutions, however, were "too big to be allowed to fail," and the United States government backed them up, first with loan securities, later with billions of dollars worth of actual loans, and finally by directly taking over the management of the failing companies. A few weeks later,

AIG, the American International Group, an enormous insurance company, suddenly appeared to be on the verge of bankruptcy, which would affect not only policy holders in the United States, but also vast numbers of investors overseas. Again, the United States government rode to the rescue with a loan of $85 billion, in exchange for which it received 80 percent of the company's stock.

A few days later the government agreed to allocate up to $700 billion to buy up bad debts that were crippling major financial companies. Otherwise, it appeared that lending for commercial and private purposes was drying up. If that happened, the economy of the United States, and of the world, would come to a halt. In essence, the government of the country that had been the world's leading apostle of capitalism was bailing out some immense corporations, and picking up the debts of others, to save them from failure. In the globalized financial world of 2008, these government interventions were necessary not only to protect and reassure American homeowners and investors, but, perhaps more importantly, to insure that investors overseas did not stop investing in America. For if the Chinese, and the oil-rich states of the Middle East, stopped investing in American securities, or, even worse, began to withdraw the trillions of dollars they had already invested, the American economy would collapse. The size of America's financial problems was unprecedented in the history of the world's economy, and sober observers were not sure what would come next.

It was no surprise, then, that with many countries improving their economies through global trade, while America fell into increasing difficulties with its trade imbalances and endangered domestic economy, other countries were applauding globalization while Americans were beginning to have second thoughts. In 2008, all 24 countries included in the annual Pew Global Attitudes survey showed a majority agreeing that "increasing trade and interaction is a good thing for their countries." At the highest end were Nigeria, with 91 percent replying "good" or "very good"; India with 90 percent; Spain, 89; South Korea, 88; and China, 87. Registering last was the United States at 53 percent, still a majority, but down sharply from 78 percent in 2002. (http://pewglobal.org/reports/pdf/260.pdf) A student of history might begin to think back to the seventeenth century when Spain and Portugal, which had made fortunes from their colonies, especially in the New World, lost ground to the rising, more astute, more prudent northern European nations of the Netherlands, England, and France. Economic supremacy in one era did not necessarily carry over into supremacy in the next.

On Social Revolution

Revolutions in trade, politics, and industry in the sixteenth, seventeenth, and eighteenth centuries laid the foundations for the social revolutions in nationalism, anti-imperialism, and gender relations in the eighteenth and nineteenth centuries. The sequence at the turn of the twenty-first century was not so different. "Globalization" was an update on the earlier world trade expansion; the end of colonialism and the dissolution of the Soviet Union corresponded to the political revolutions two centuries earlier; and the digital revolutions in communication, science, and technology, and the transportation revolution in containerization, expanded on the breakthroughs of the original Industrial Revolution.

Not only was the context for social change similar to that of earlier times, but the specific social revolutions also related to and expanded upon earlier social revolutions. In the late twentieth and early twenty-first centuries, nationalism, regionalism, and transnationalism have flowered anew. Massive new waves of immigration have tested the abilities of governments around the globe to formulate effective policies.

The feminist movement has increasingly diversified as it has reached around the world. Homosexuality has won increasing public acceptability. National struggles against racism have advanced, in South Africa, for instance, aided by pressure from the international community. In a more conservative vein, widespread concern has arisen that local cultures might lose their integrity, overwhelmed by larger, more powerful waves of global culture. This fear has frequently inspired cultural backlash.

Nationalism

The buzz around 1990 was that nationalism was on its way out. Communication, transportation, business corporations, and NGOs all functioned transnationally. For more and more people and institutions, the nation seemed less and less relevant with each passing year. As the future unfolded, however, it appeared that the rumors of the death of nationalism were grossly exaggerated.

Already in 1990 Estonia and Lithuania declared their national independence, helping to precipitate the dissolution of the USSR. Latvia, Russia, Ukraine, and Belarus also soon declared their independence. The remaining 15 Soviet republics became independent states at the end of 1991 when the Soviet Union dissolved. Within Russia itself, the predominantly Muslim state of Chechnya began guerrilla warfare in hopes of becoming an independent republic. Eastern European nations, including Poland, Hungary, Bulgaria, and Romania, were equally jealous of their independence. Czechoslovakia divided into two in 1993, as political leaders of the Czech Republic and those of Slovakia thought that separation would produce two separate, more cohesive states rather than a single ethnically-mixed one. As East Germany became independent, East and West reunited in 1990 after 45 years of Cold War division.

As these newly independent states took their places in the UN and other international bodies, UN membership jumped from 166 in 1991 to 184 in 1993. The new states built new museums, including the Terror House in Budapest, Hungary, and the memorial at Checkpoint Charlie in Berlin, to commemorate foreign occupation, and to put it behind them.

Nationalists continued to wage war in the name of the state. When Yugoslavia broke apart into separate independent states in 1991, war broke out among some of the new states. At least 100,000 people were killed. Three states asserted their national prestige by testing nuclear weapons—India and Pakistan in 1998 and North Korea, on a more rudimentary level, in 2006. The willingness of the United States to go it almost alone in its war against Iraq in 2003, despite massive protests around the world, and without allowing time for UN inspectors to complete their investigations, and its unwillingness to sign up to various widely agreed-upon international accords, including the Kyoto Accords against global warming, and the establishment of the International Criminal Court in The Hague, demonstrated that unilateralist nationalism was alive and well in the U.S.

Nations protested and reinforced their borders against foreign commercial competition and against new waves of undocumented immigrants. The WTO was called on repeatedly to adjudicate disputes over trade tariffs as various countries, including the United States, sought to protect their internal markets from foreign imports, often in contravention of agreements for freer trade. Similarly, the barriers to immigration were an issue for almost all states. For example, the United States sought to limit migration from Latin America, Germany from Turkey, Italy from Romania, France from North Africa, India from Bangladesh, Japan from everywhere. Those who predicted the imminent demise of nationalism and the fall of national borders proved quite mistaken.

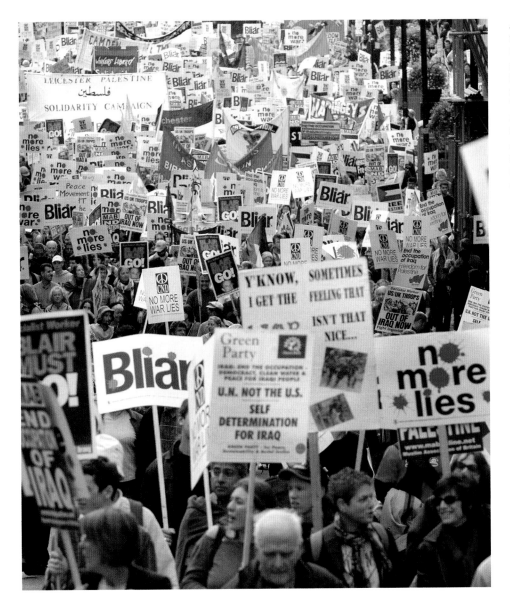

Antiwar protesters march through the streets of Piccadilly, central London, 2004. Up to 100,000 people from across the UK attended the march and rally, calling for troops to be removed from Iraq. The Campaign for Nuclear Disarmament, Stop The War Coalition, and the Muslim Association of Britain organized the event. Hundreds of thousands also marched in Rome, New York, and other major cities worldwide.

As some nations reveled in the sovereignty of their already independent existence, other groups asserted their right to revolt, to free themselves from their current "rulers," and to establish new independent states of their own. Chechens, we have already mentioned. Other independence movements included Basques in the north of Spain; Kurds in the north of Iraq, sometimes joined by other Kurds just across the borders in neighboring Turkey, Iran, and Syria; Tamils in Sri Lanka; Tibetans and Uighurs on the southern and western extremes of China. All of these groups, and many others, around the globe felt that their own nationalism was being suppressed by the nationalism of much larger states in which they were embedded, and from which they wished to escape.

Sometimes the desire for nationhood could lead to successful compromise. Northern Ireland provided an excellent example. Forty-five percent of its population chose to identify themselves as Protestant, most of them in favor of union with Great Britain; 40 percent identified as Roman Catholic, most of them favoring union with the Irish Free State. For decades Northern Ireland was torn by violence between the two groups. From 1921 it had significant autonomous power, under British rule, but this was revoked in 1972 because of continuing violence. Home rule, granting even more power, was promised once again in the "Good Friday Agreement" of 1999. In 2005 the Irish Republican Army, which had led the armed resistance to British rule, put down its arms, opening the way to implementation of power sharing in the elections of 2007. The British reduced their presence to 5,000 armed troops. Northern Ireland was relatively peaceful.

The Palestinian–Israeli Conflict. The unsatisfied national claim that most disturbed the peace of the world at the turn of the twenty-first century was that of Palestinians living under Israeli occupation in the West Bank of the Jordan River and the Gaza strip. Their grievances went back to 1948, when the UN partitioned Palestine into two areas, one for a Jewish state and one for Arab Palestinians. After the Holocaust, much of world opinion revisited the promise of Britain's Balfour declaration of 1917 (see Chapter Nineteen) and favored creating a Jewish homeland refuge. Angered by the proposal for a Jewish state in the very heart of the Arab world, Palestinian Arabs argued that they had not been responsible for the Holocaust, and they rejected the partition plan. Palestinian Arabs favored the armies of the surrounding Arab states when they attacked Israel at the time of its birth, attempting to obliterate the state before it took root. But Israel survived the war as a new state. Palestinian Arabs had made no plans for establishing a state on the territories apportioned to them, so the West Bank came under the administration of the government of neighboring Jordan. The Gaza strip was administered by Egypt.

Defeated in warfare, the neighboring Arab states nursed their grievances. In a second war, in 1967, they were defeated yet again, and this time Israel captured the West Bank and Gaza. Some Israelis wished to turn over these lands to the rule of the Palestinians themselves in exchange for a peace agreement. The majority of Israelis, however, wished to keep them, and did. On the Arab side, also, some wished to reach an accord with the Israelis, offering a peace treaty in exchange for the land. Others would be satisfied with nothing less than destroying the Israeli state.

The Camp David peace accords. In Maryland, September 1978, Israeli prime minister Menachem Begin, President Jimmy Carter, and Egyptian president Anwar Sadat relax during the historic Camp David peace talks that resulted in the 1979 treaty between Israel and Egypt. The Camp David Accords, documents signed by the leaders of Israel and Egypt, were a preliminary to the signing of the formal peace treaty between the two nations. The treaty returned the Sinai to Egypt.

The Middle East since 1945. The presence of oil and gas reserves, the establishment of a Jewish homeland state of Israel in Palestine (1948), the intervention of outside states, and the emergence of militant, armed, political Islam have stirred the region. In addition to Arab–Israeli confrontations, an eight-year conflict between Iran and Iraq, a war over Iraq's invasion of Kuwait, the American invasion of Iraq in 2003, and civil wars and revolutions have kept the region in turmoil.

Despite continued attempts to resolve the conflict over land and sovereignty, often brokered by outside political groups, extremists on both sides, though a minority on each side, have so far won the day. On the Israeli side, "settlers" from Israel moved onto the lands of the West Bank and Gaza, with the support of the Israeli government, despite the rulings of the UN that occupation of conquered lands is illegal. By 2008, about 200,000 settlers had staked out homes in parts of Jerusalem that had been Arab, and another

KEY TERM

intifada Colloquial Arabic: the act of shaking off; uprising, rebellion.

200,000 had built in other parts of the West Bank. The settlers have dominated these lands through often inhumane treatment of their Arab owners. In 1987 and again in 2000, Palestinians launched resistance movements, called **intifadas**, against Israeli occupation, using both peaceful and violent means to dislodge the Israelis from the West Bank and the Gaza strip, and, some wished, even from Israel itself. The violent means included "suicide bombers," people willing to blow themselves up as they delivered and detonated bombs to attack Israelis, and crude rockets fired into Israel from Gaza and Lebanon. These tactics brought worldwide attention to Palestinian claims, but they hardened the resistance of the Israelis.

In addition to these victories of the hard-liners on both sides, the leaders of the Israelis and of the Palestinians both knew that their lives were in danger from their own countrymen if they attempted to negotiate peace. Anwar Sadat, president of Egypt, negotiated a peace treaty between Egypt and Israel in 1979 and was

Israel and its neighbors. The creation, with Western support, of a Jewish homeland in Palestine in 1947 occurred at a time of increasing Arab nationalism. Israel's birth in 1948 was attended by a war and more followed in 1956, 1967, 1973, and 1982. Peace treaties exist only with Egypt, which regained the Sinai peninsula, and Jordan (1994). Beginning in 1987, an intifada (uprising) by Palestinians forced more attention on Israeli–Palestinian relations—an extremely vexed issue. In 1993, the Palestinian Liberation Organization and Israel began negotiations that would return land to Palestinian control and perhaps lead to a Palestinian state, while recognizing Israel's right to exist. So far these negotiations have proved fruitless and a second intifada began in 2000. Meanwhile some 400,000 Jewish settlers have established homes in East Jerusalem and other sectors of the occupied West Bank, complicating any efforts to trade land for peace.

Map legend:
- Jewish state after UN partition of Palestine 1947
- Israel after War of Independence 1948-49
- Israeli conquests after Six-Day War 1967
- Israeli border after Yom Kippur War 1973
- Israeli security zone in Lebanon from 1978
- areas of Palestinian self-rule from 1994

SOURCE

The Geneva Accords: A Nongovernmental Plan for Peace

Intense peace negotiations between Israelis and Palestinians at Camp David in the United States in 2000 and in Taba, Egypt, in 2001 failed to produce peace agreements. Nevertheless, some of the representatives decided to continue to pursue a detailed framework for a peace agreement as a model of what might be achieved and to prove that responsible leaders on both sides could be partners in the search for peace. At the end of 2003, the Israeli Yossi Beilin and the Palestinian Abed Rabbo unveiled the agreements they had reached in their secret meetings in Geneva. They distributed copies throughout Israel and the Palestinian territories, claiming that at least 40 percent of each population accepted their framework for peace. Meanwhile the second Palestinian *intifada* and Israel's harsh repression continued all around them, and a brutal war would follow in Gaza in 2008–09, on the one hand mocking their efforts as utopian and, on the other, demonstrating dramatically the need for peace.

> We, the undersigned, a group of Palestinians and Israelis, endorse, on this day, October 12, 2003, a model draft framework final status agreement between the two peoples. At this point in time, after the Palestinian government and the Israeli government have accepted the Road Map [an international plan especially favored by the Americans], which includes reaching a final status settlement by 2005,

based on a two-state solution, we consider it to be of utmost importance to present to the two peoples and the entire world an example of what such a final status agreement could include. This is proof that despite all the pain entailed in concessions, it is possible to reach an historical compromise which meets the vital national interests of each side. We present this model agreement as a package—which stands together as an integral whole.

In the near future we will launch a campaign whose goal is to convince both sides of the value of such an historical compromise in the spirit of this model framework agreement, designed to put an end to the protracted conflict …

The decision to complete and later present this model draft agreement was not easy for any of us, however, we have decided to pursue this path since we believe that action of this type can serve as a source of hope after a long period of suffering, killing, and mutual accusations, that it can help build trust and facilitate the removal of the walls between our nations. In the context of the Road Map process, this draft agreement signifies a mutually acceptable and realizable endgame—to be reached by 2005, and as an answer to the skeptics and supporters of endless interim agreements. This agreement will bring about the creation of a sovereign Palestinian State alongside Israel, put an end to the occupation, terminate conflict and bloodshed, and end all mutual claims.

subsequently assassinated by an Egyptian Muslim extremist. Yitzhak Rabin, prime minister of Israel, who was on the verge of reaching a peace accommodation with Palestinian leader Yasser Arafat in 1995, was assassinated by an Israeli extremist.

Samuel Huntingdon argued in 1996 that the world was witnessing what he called a "Clash of Civilizations" among the major religious-cultural groupings of the world: Christian, Muslim, Chinese, Japanese, and Indian. Martha Nussbaum's 2007 book, *The Clash Within*, argues, on the contrary, that the most difficult political struggles today are not usually between opposing civilizations, but rather between the extremists and the moderates on each side. The moderates, if left alone, might be able to find peaceful compromise, but the extremists seek to prevent this. They want victory and they sabotage attempts at compromise. This analysis holds especially clearly for the Israeli–Palestinian deadlock in which the moderates on both sides appear to be more or less in agreement on a two-state solution, with Israel and Palestine existing side-by-side in peace, while extremists on each side reject compromise and appear to wish to reduce their opponents to impotence, or to destroy them entirely.

Despairing of finding a negotiated settlement of the conflict, Israeli Prime Minister Ariel Sharon unilaterally removed Israeli settlers and troops from Gaza in 2005. The Palestinians then held elections, which were won by the extremist faction, Hamas. Despite this victory in democratic, fair elections, both Israel and the United States refused to recognize Hamas, citing Hamas's use of terrorist tactics in its fight against Israel and its refusal to recognize Israel's right to exist as a state.

The Israeli–Palestinian separation wall. Construction of this wall began in 2002. Israelis claim they built it to stop terrorists from entering Israel, and call it a security fence; Palestinians say that Israelis built it as a land-grab and an effort to separate Palestinians from their own lands, and call it an apartheid wall. The approximately 20 feet high concrete barrier makes clear the line of separation between Israel and the Palestinian territories, but it often runs on the Palestinian side of the 1967 prewar border. Debates over the appropriateness of the wall therefore concern not only the reasons for its existence, but also its geographical placement.

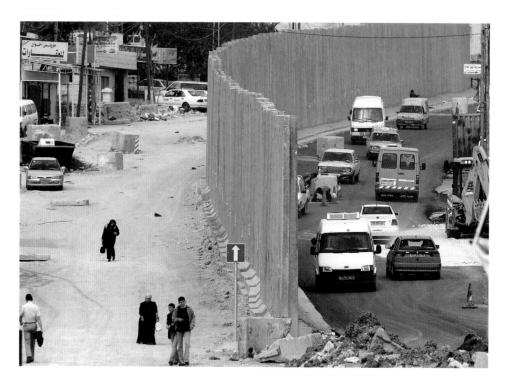

The struggle between Israelis and Palestinians attracted intense international interest because of the massive external forces arrayed on each side. The Palestinians drew the support of much of the Arab world, and even of the broader Islamic world, while Israel drew the backing of the United States and, to a lesser extent, allies in Europe. Israel's allies feared that pro-Palestinian terrorists would continue to attack targets around the globe. When Osama bin Laden struck the World Trade Center and other targets in the United States, for example, one of his stated objectives was to avenge the occupation of Palestine by Israelis. The persistent dangers of international terrorism led many nations to consider the Israeli–Palestinian conflict the most explosive of all the world's trouble spots.

The EU, especially, urged diplomacy in this conflict and European diplomats became increasingly involved in Middle East peace negotiations. In late twentieth-century Europe, nations that had fought bitter wars against each other throughout the first half of the twentieth century had entered diplomatically into agreement after agreement to create and extend the EU, to replace their former enmity with productive cooperation (see Chapters Twenty-one and Twenty-three). The EU boasted that its recent experience in peaceful resolution of ancient conflicts could serve as a model in the Middle East, and in other conflicts around the world.

Commerce, Business, and National Borders. Some political nationalists demanded the perpetuation of existing borders, others called for drawing new ones. The world of commerce and business suggested that national borders were significantly less important than before. Networks of finance and capital cut across and transcended national boundaries.

The international economy has changed dramatically since 1990 "as a result of privatization, deregulation, digitalization, the opening up of national economies to foreign firms, and the growing participation of national economic actors in global markets" (Sassen, p. XVIII). Today the management of information for highly specialized and interconnected services, and for global finance, requires more sophisticated facilities than ever before, and a very few cities, led by New York, London, and Tokyo, have grown to fulfill those functions. These cities claim an importance and power that go beyond their national borders. In terms we have encountered in Chapter Twelve, they are the hubs of the world's trade diaspora, although there are others with similar but less elaborate facilities, such as Frankfurt, Paris, and Sao Paolo. The highly skilled, highly sophisticated masters of the system of international finance dominate these global cities and draw spectacular pay checks, while those "lacking these attributes," those at the low-skills end, "are likely to get caught in the opposite cycle" (p. xxi). In the globalized society, the talented and well-educated in the realms of global finance may get rich, but for the rest, "There has been a generalized dismantling of a system that provided a measure of job security, health benefits, and other components of a social wage to a critical mass of workers" (Sassen, p. 339).

Gender Issues

In the late twentieth and early twenty-first centuries, role definitions and gender status had become global issues. Suffrage and political participation had always been an issue, so one useful index of gender equality was the proportion of women elected to national government. According to statistics gathered by the Interparliamentary Union, the global average of seats in national governments held by women was 18 percent. The variation ran from Rwanda with nearly 50 percent, Sweden with 47 percent, and Cuba with 43 percent, to Iran with 3 percent, Egypt with 2 percent, and Saudi Arabia with none. The United States ranked sixty-ninth, with 17 percent. (http://www.ipu.org/wmn-e/world.htm)

Different countries held diverse, and sometimes conflicting, perspectives on the significance of gender issues. The differences emerged clearly at the series of Conferences on Women hosted by the UN. The first, in Mexico City in 1975, inaugurated the UN Decade for Women. Five years later a conference in Copenhagen marked the midpoint, followed by a decade-closing conference in 1985 in Nairobi. Another conference followed in Beijing in 1995. These conferences led to commitments by the overwhelming majority of member nations to gathering data on women, helping to end their political and economic "invisibility," and working harder to insure women's education, health, and employment on an equal basis with men.

In addition to the governments, thousands of representatives of NGOs from around the world also participated. These representatives began to network, to seek solidarity, and to address problems that they saw as common, sometimes for the first time. For example, African representatives noted that when agriculture was oriented to subsistence farming, to feed individual families, women played a major role, but when agriculture was commercialized and became a money-making occupation, women were pushed out. Sometimes new programs were created. Several different groups

Micro-lending in Africa.
Micro-lending, providing very small sums of money as business loans to relatively poor people, has proved very effective in helping the borrowers to start very small enterprises and thus to escape from poverty. Micro-lending has been especially effective with poor women, perhaps because they have been almost completely excluded from normal banking channels, perhaps because they have been especially effective at banding together to guarantee each other's loans, and thus get lower interest rates. Here members of Opportunity International's 'Blessed Mary' Trust Group in Accra, Ghana, meet weekly to repay their loans and support each other.

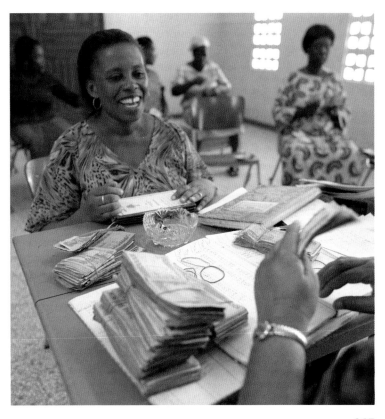

micro-finance or **micro-credit**
The provision of very small loans, often equivalent to $100 or even less, to very small-scale businessmen and women, people who would not usually have access to conventional commercial bank loans, because the banks do not deal in such small amounts, and because they would not usually recognize the relatively poor borrowers as "bankable." The loans are usually at below market rates, and are usually secured by the common bond among groups of borrowers that they will stand guaranty for one another.

that had begun to extend **micro-finance** to women, providing them with small loans to start their own small businesses, began to share ideas for cooperation. The **micro-credit** movement, now worldwide, has usually been most attractive to and widespread among women, perhaps because they have had the most difficulty in accessing loans through normal commercial banks, and because they have proved especially creative and responsible in bonding together to insure one another's loans, and thus to secure lower interest rates. Muhammad Yunus, of Bangladesh, won the Nobel Peace Prize in 2006 for his establishment in 1976 of the Grameen Bank, the world's leading micro-lender; about 95 percent of the bank's loans have been to women.

Reproductive rights for women, and health standards for women and children, became another focus. India and China mounted campaigns against the abortion or infanticide of unwanted female babies, a difficult struggle against the deeply rooted preference for boy children. In the Islamic world, interpretation of religious traditions took on central importance. Many feminist groups urged reinterpreting the Quran to discover and proclaim the pro-feminist viewpoints that can be found within the sacred scripture. Other Muslim women, however, proclaimed bluntly that in their view the classic Islamic texts were irreconcilably antifeminist and antidemocratic. For them, feminists would have to proceed in opposition to, rather than with the support of, the teachings of the Quran.

Sharp differences also emerged as to what were the most important goals for women. Often women in developed, richer countries stressed the need for opening new categories of jobs to women, equal pay for equal work, child care, and reproductive freedom of choice. In less wealthy nations the issues might be the right to own property, to be free from the control of male relatives, to have equal access to food, schooling, and medical care. Many third world women felt that first-world women chose to concentrate on the wrong issues. Too often first world women talked about the evils of veiling and of clitoridectomy (the surgical removal of the clitoris, sometimes incorrectly referred to as female circumcision), as if third world women had to be saved from the evils of their own societies. But in reality the most important problems were not these internal cultural issues, but rather structural issues in the global economy and politics. The feminist movement would be achieving its goals when it addressed these more fundamental issues. Egyptian feminist and author Nawal El Saadawi put it this way:

> The women's liberation movements have played a very important role since the 1970s in struggling against neocolonialism and the multinational companies, against wars, the arms race and nuclear armament, against racism and against discrimination based on race, colour, religion, or social class. (Saadawi, p. 4)

So sometimes women could come together for the common good across national borders, but sometimes they viewed each other only with suspicion.

Homosexuality, too, was seen differently in different locations. In many parts of the world laws against homosexuality were abolished. Armed forces accepted acknowledged homosexuals, as did some national intelligence agencies that previously feared that gay and lesbian operatives would be subject to blackmail. Some governments in North America and Europe legalized same-sex marriage: the Netherlands was the first in 2001, followed by Belgium, Canada, Norway, South Africa, and Spain. In the United States, three states have recognized same-sex marriage: Massachusetts, California, and Connecticut, although California's recognition was short-lived. (Several other states, and some nations, such as Britain, Croatia, and Mexico, have created legal unions for same-sex couples.) On the other hand, although it appeared that homosexuality was becoming accepted as a valid and legal sexual orientation, some nations deemed it shameful, if not sinful. In 2008, the president of Iran boasted that in his country there were no movements to protect the rights of homosexuals, primarily because Iranian society would not tolerate them.

Racial Equality

Racism, like gender discrimination, was generally in retreat. The achievement of South Africa in ridding itself of apartheid policies, through peaceful means, was an astonishing victory. The quiet revolution of low castes and ex-untouchables in India drew less attention, but affected far more people. And in the United States in 2008, Barack Obama's election as the first African-American president appeared as a triumph of progress in American race relations.

Apartheid in South Africa. Apartheid (segregation of the races) had been established by law in South Africa in 1948. About 20 percent of the population was white, descended from Dutch and British settlers, and this minority controlled the government, most productive farmland, all industry, and the upper reaches of the economy. Black Africans had no political freedoms and were subject to severe restrictions on where they could live, work, and study. Most indigenous Africans were effectively forced into service as landless laborers in white-controlled farming and industry. Blacks working in the cities could not legally establish residence there but had to commute long distances each day from government-designated black residential areas or else stay in dormitory settings, leaving their families behind in the villages.

Black African frustration, resentment, and anger at first expressed itself principally through independent Ethiopian churches as early as the 1870s and 1880s. The African National Congress (ANC) formed in 1912 as a constitutional party of protest

A new and democratic dawn for South Africa. South African president Nelson Mandela and second deputy president F.W. de Klerk address a huge crowd in front of the Union Building in Pretoria, after the inauguration ceremony on May 10, 1994. Only a few years earlier it would have been inconceivable that the imprisoned Nelson Mandela could ever attain high office in a country so firmly wedded to the policies of apartheid.

First-time voters, South Africa, 1994. Residents of the Western Transvaal queue to vote for the first time in South Africa's multiracial elections in 1994. After years of apartheid and oppression, black South Africans showed a respect and devotion to their new democracy that inspired citizens of democracies around the world who often took for granted their own right to vote and to participate in governance.

and grew steadily over several decades. In the 1950s, as other African nations began to win independence, European observers urged South Africa to liberalize its racial policies, but the government of South Africa stubbornly resisted. In 1960, in the town of Sharpeville, the government confronted unarmed political protesters, massacring 69 black Africans and wounding many others. The ANC shifted to strikes and armed protests, renouncing attacks on people and limiting itself to sabotage of property. The South African government continued to crack down. ANC leader Nelson Mandela (b. 1918), a brilliant and charismatic lawyer, was arrested, charged with plotting to overthrow the government, and eventually sentenced to life in prison. At his trial in 1964, Mandela declared his commitment to his country and his vision for its future:

> I have fought against white domination. I have cherished the ideal of a democratic and free society in which all persons live together in harmony and with equal opportunities. It is an ideal which I hope to live for and to achieve. But if needs be, it is an ideal for which I am prepared to die. (Edelstein, p. 73)

The ANC and the general movement for racial justice were crippled but not killed off by the government's repression. As Zambia and Zimbabwe, Angola and Mozambique won independence and majority rule in the 1960s and 1970s, world attention focused on South Africa as the last remaining bastion of white, minority rule. In addition, the newly independent nations bordering South Africa sheltered members of the ANC and other movements for majority rule, including some dedicated to guerrilla warfare. Following the massacre at Sharpeville, many nations gradually adopted sanctions against South Africa, restricting or stopping trade; "disinvesting" or withdrawing economic investments; and ending diplomatic, cultural, and sports exchanges. South Africa became a pariah nation, cut off from intercourse with much of the rest of the world until it moved toward racial equality.

Enforcing the sanctions proved difficult. South Africa was a regional economic powerhouse, with rich resources: 85 percent of the world's platinum; two-thirds of its chromium; half its gold; half its manganese; and substantial proportions of its gem-quality diamonds. Geopolitically, 90 percent of Europe's oil passed by its waters. Many large and powerful nations, including the United States and Great Britain, did not want to abandon their own economic interests in South Africa, and did not fully comply. They argued that "constructive engagement" through trade would be more effective in ending apartheid. Neighboring states also ignored the sanctions. They had tens of thousands of workers who subsisted only through jobs in the South African mines and industries; they continued surreptitious trade and diplomatic relationships.

Nevertheless, the sanctions did gradually exact their toll; isolation was painful, culturally and diplomatically as well as economically. The continuing expansion of independence among the African states brought black rule ever closer to South Africa's borders, and unrest within the country continued. In 1976 protests against government educational policies began in Soweto, a black township outside Pretoria, and led to nationwide riots in which 600 people were killed. Some liberalization was granted: black labor unions were legalized, the prohibition on interracial sex was abolished, segregation in public transportation ended. Finally, in 1990, the new government of President F.W. de Klerk (b. 1936) lifted its ban against the ANC and freed Nelson Mandela. He had spent 27 years in prison. De Klerk's National Party repealed apartheid laws and began wary and difficult negotiations with the ANC for transition to majority rule. In 1993, Mandela was awarded the Nobel Peace Prize, and in the 1994 South African elections, open equally to all races on the principle of one person-one vote, the ANC won 62 percent of the vote. Mandela was elected president.

The Truth and Reconciliation Commission. South Africans confronted the problem of establishing a new political and cultural identity for themselves after the collapse of apartheid government. For the first time in their history, the blacks of South Africa counted as political equals to the whites. But unlike many other colonial situations in which most white colonizers left the newly independent colony, in South Africa, the whites had been residents of the country for centuries. This was their home. They viewed themselves as Africans, and most of them had no intention of leaving. Even if they did, they had no other home to which to go. Thus 32 million mostly impoverished and until recently suppressed and persecuted blacks and eight million mostly wealthy and highly privileged whites had to find new ways of getting along together. One of their highly imaginative solutions was the Truth and Reconciliation Commission, which functioned from 1996 to 1998 in an effort to clear the air for further interracial cooperation in the future.

The commission was initiated by President Mandela and headed by Archbishop Desmond Tutu (b. 1931), the head of the Anglican Church in South Africa. Its goal was to bring the peoples of South Africa together by exposing the bitter and violent realities of the past and, through that exposure, enabling all of its peoples to see themselves as part of a single nation. The commission heard cases of some 20,000 people who had suffered gross human rights violations since the Sharpeville massacre in 1960 until the first democratic election in 1994.

Thousands of people from all corners of the country stepped forward to testify. Thousands were granted some measure of reparations from the state treasury. Most whites, unable to state publicly that they had benefited from apartheid, did not initiate the act of admitting their crimes. Some, however, did step forward, helping in the process of reconciliation. Many others came because of accusations of criminal activity brought against them. The proceedings of the commission were not equivalent to criminal trials, and amnesty could be granted to those who could demonstrate that they were carrying out the political policies of the state, rather than their own agendas, and were acting without sadism. In his concluding remarks,

HOW DO WE KNOW?

South Africa's Truth and Reconciliation Commission

Many observers of the commission's proceedings raised serious criticisms. Some felt that the granting of amnesty came too easily to defendants in these noncriminal proceedings. Defendants could plead that they were simply following orders of the government and that they had not acted sadistically, and receive amnesty. Dirk Coetzee, first commander of a counterinsurgency unit, and his team were convicted in criminal court for the murder of Griffiths Mxenge, a civil rights lawyer, but subsequently the commission granted them amnesty because they were simply carrying out their duties as policemen engaged in the government's struggle against the liberation movement. Griffiths' brother was disgusted with this decision for amnesty:

> My main objection is that amnesty promotes the interests of the perpetrators, as once they are granted amnesty they are not criminally liable and no civil action can be instituted against [them], and that is totally against the interests of the victims. It is totally unjust. (Edelstein, p. 113)

On the other hand, Josephine Msweli was more forgiving of the men who killed her sons:

> I want the people who killed my sons to come forward because this is a time for reconciliation. I want to forgive them and I also have a bit of my mind to tell them. I would be happy if they could come before me because I don't have [my] sons today … I want to speak to them before I forgive them. I want them to tell me who sent them to come and kill my sons. Maybe they are my enemies, maybe they are not. So I want to establish as to who they are and why they did what they did. (Edelstein, p. 154)

One member of the commission, Pumla Gobodo-Madikizela, a clinical psychologist, reaffirmed the healing power of public disclosure by victim and perpetrator alike: "If a memory is kept alive in order to transcend hateful emotions, to free oneself or one's society from the burden of hatred, then remembering has the power to heal" (Edelstein, p. 30).

She lamented, however, the inability of most whites, despite the commission, to recognize that they had benefited from the general violence of the system of inequality imposed by apartheid.

Despite its shortcomings, the commission brought truth to light, and most commentators believed that this truth allowed purification of the body politic. It allowed the true identity of the old state to be exposed so that a new identity could be formed.

Michael Ignatieff, director of the Carr Center for Human Rights Policy at the Kennedy School of Government, Harvard University, wrote:

> Any society that allows its torturers to retire with medals and pensions inevitably pays the price. The price of lies is immobilized nostalgia for tyranny … you cannot create a culture of freedom unless you eliminate a specific range of impermissible lies … The Truth Commission had rendered some lies about the past simply impossible to repeat. (Edelstein, pp. 20–21)

Ignatieff concluded that the Truth and Reconciliation Commission made it impossible for white South Africans to deny the violence of their society. They could no longer deflect blame by saying that any problems were caused by only a few rotten apples, but those were the exceptions rather than the rule. What the TRC uncovered was something very different indeed:

> not a few bad apples, not a few bad cops … but a system, a culture, a way of life that was organized around contempt and violence for other human beings. The truth, the cold core, of apartheid was the Sanlam building in Port Elizabeth where they threw you against radiators and beat you with wet towels. Every South African citizen was contaminated by the degradation, that deadness, that offence against the spirit. (Edelstein, p. 21)

Knowing the painful truth, however, would ultimately set the society free.

- President Nelson Mandela inspired the creation of the commission and Archbishop Desmond Tutu was its chairman. Based on the concept and workings of the commission, how would you characterize the politics and ethics of these two men?
- How would you interpret the key goals of the commission? Were they realistic? Do you think they correspond to human nature as you understand it?
- Ignatieff argues that torture and violence against citizens were not an aberration caused by "a few rotten apples," but by "a system, a culture, a way of life that was organized around contempt and violence for other human beings." To what extent do you think his rhetoric and his description of consequences mirror the debate about torture carried out by Americans in the Abu Ghraib prison, and at the Guantanamo Bay detention camp, during the Iraq war?

Archbishop Tutu proclaimed the exemplary success of the commission in healing South Africa's racial wounds and facilitating the emotional unification of the country and a new national identity:

> We have been privileged to help to heal a wounded people ... When we look around us at some of the conflict areas of the world, it becomes increasingly clear that there is not much of a future for them without forgiveness, without reconciliation. God has blessed us richly so that we might be a blessing to others. Quite improbably, we as South Africans have become a beacon of hope to others locked in deadly conflict that peace, that a just resolution, is possible. If it could happen in South Africa, then it can certainly happen anywhere else. Such is the exquisite divine sense of humor. (http://www.info.gov.za/otherdocs/2003/trc/foreword.pdf)

India's Social Revolution: The Mandal Commission. A similar movement against caste discrimination created a social revolution in India that transformed the status of tens of millions of people of the lowest rank, and of many more just somewhat above them.

The Mandal Commission, named for its chairman, B.P. Mandal, was established in 1979 to deal with an economic and social problem that had bedeviled Indian politics for decades: caste discrimination. Many observers have compared caste discrimination to race discrimination, noting that a person's caste is an identity that comes by birth and situates him or her in hierarchical relation to members of other castes. Caste is not racial as it is usually seen in the United States and many other countries. There are hundreds, even thousands of castes throughout India, so caste identification is less clear-cut than racial identity has been in the United States.

Those at the very bottom of the caste hierarchy, formerly called "untouchables" because they were forbidden to come into physical contact with upper caste people, are almost universally recognized as disadvantaged. These former untouchables were given special "reservations" or minimum quotas in public positions. This affirmative action program affected the fields of government jobs, elected offices, and education, and covered 15 percent of the population. Tribals, now more frequently called *adivasis*, or original settlers, usually lived in more remote hilly and mountainous regions, outside the Hindu heartland and usually outside of Hinduism. They formed about seven percent of the population and also received preferential benefits, protected by India's constitution. The next levels up, usually referred to as the Other Backward Classes (OBCs), had also suffered severe discrimination on the basis of caste, although perhaps not quite so extreme as the untouchables or the tribals. In 1980 the Mandal Commission's report argued that OBCs constituted about 52 percent of the nation's population and recommended that 27 percent of the positions in the central administration and in the public sector should be reserved for them. Although the "C" in OBC officially referred to class rather than caste, the Commission argued that caste was the most significant indicator of class. The Commission identified some 3,743 castes as OBCs and recommended them for benefits.

The road to implementation was rocky and often blocked by mass protests and riots by the upper castes. (Americans, accustomed to thinking of class-based public protests coming from below and attacking elites, may be surprised that such protests may also come from above. Backlash protests against racial desegregation in the U.S. in the 1960s, however, were also of this nature.) New parties began to form around the issue of reservations, sometimes led by OBCs themselves, particularly at the state level, and sometimes by upper castes who were committed to concepts of equality, or seeking additional votes, or both.

In 1990, India's prime minister, V.P. Singh, brought the issue to a head nationally by implementing the Mandal Commission's recommendations. This and other of his reformist programs alienated many upper-class and upper-caste people, and Singh was forced from office in 1991 when new elections brought the Congress Party back to power. Nevertheless, a transformation was taking place. In the major north Indian states, from 1984 to 1999 the percentage of upper castes elected to the national parliament dropped by a third, from 47 percent to 31 percent, while the percentage of OBCs doubled, from 11 percent to 22 percent. India's two largest states, Uttar Pradesh and Bihar, were ruled by OBC parties headed by OBC leaders. Singh explained the significance of the shift that was taking place:

> Now that every party is wooing the deprived classes, with every round of elections more and more representatives of the deprived sections will be elected. This will ulti- mately be reflected in the social composition of the local bodies, state governments, and the central government. A silent transfer of power is taking place in social terms. (Jaffrelot, p. 139)

America Elects an African-American President. In 2008, the election of Barack Obama as the first African-American president of the United States was hailed in America and around the world as a triumph of American democracy. The son of a Kenyan father, who left the boy's life when he was very young, and a white woman from Kansas, Obama spent his early years in Indonesia, after his mother remarried to an Indonesian, and then was raised in his teenage years largely by his maternal grand- parents in Hawaii. His biography was international and transracial, and Obama introduced himself to the American electorate as a man whose "story" was quintes- sentially American, and impossible in any other country of the world. He was running not as a candidate primarily of black voters, as some previous African-American can- didates, like Jesse Jackson, had done, but as a representative of the entire population of America. Democratic Party voters, the first to weigh the man and his credentials, chose him in the primary elections over his rival, Hillary Clinton. The primary elec- tion itself was watched with intense interest throughout the world for its historic encounter between the most-serious-ever African-American candidate, and the most-

The Obama family, Chicago, November 5, 2008, the night that Barack Obama was elected President of the United States. *The Times* (of London) wrote: "More than any presidential candidate before him, Barack Obama has fought his campaign on a family ticket. His wife, Michelle, has of course been crucial; but the role of the couple's two girls, Malia, ten, and Sasha, seven, cannot be underestimated."

serious-ever woman candidate. The vote in the end was close, with Clinton, who lost, drawing 18 million votes. One glass ceiling was cracking, but not yet shattered.

In the general election, with an electorate deeply alienated by eight years of government by a widely unpopular president of the opposition Republican Party, two unpopular wars, and a catastrophic collapse of the economy, Obama swept to victory with a margin of nearly eight million votes. Although he carried only 43 percent of the white votes, his margin of 2–1 among Hispanic voters and more than 9–1 among blacks gave him his substantial majority. Many of the white voters who voted Republican were evangelical Christians, probably influenced by party positions on religious/cultural issues more than by race. The total white vote was only about 75 percent of the electorate. America was becoming more multiracial in its demography as well as in its attitudes.

Migration

From the time *Homo sapiens* emigrated out of Africa, migration has been a staple of human life. The establishment of sea routes between the Old World and the New, and between Southeast Asia and Australia reinvigorated that movement, but also triggered a fatal conflict between immigrants and indigenous peoples, not unusual in the history of migration, although extraordinary in the number of indigenous people killed. In addition to long-distance travel, migration from rural farms to the urban factories of the Industrial Revolution, beginning in the nineteenth century, became a hallmark of the modern age.

United States. In the most recent decades, migration continues to affect every region of the earth. The streams of migration bring confrontations between those who are already in place and recent arrivals. The relationships are complicated because both groups need each other, yet they are wary. The most common form of migration is of poorer people in search of work in richer lands. The richer need the poorer for their cheap labor, but they are often put off by the culture of the newcomers, and by their poverty. Americans in the United States, for example, need immigrants from Mexico and other parts of Latin America for their farm and domestic labor at pay scales so low that already settled Americans would not accept them. Nevertheless, they do not want the new migrants to stay after the work is over. They do not want them availing themselves of the benefits of American workers, costly medical care and schooling for their children. So they write laws that make it difficult for foreigners to gain access to the United States and almost impossible to stay. The migrants, desperate for better living conditions, sneak into the country by the millions and find jobs, but they live in fear of being caught and sent back to their home countries. In 2006, the United States government estimated 35 million foreign-born people legally resident in the United States,

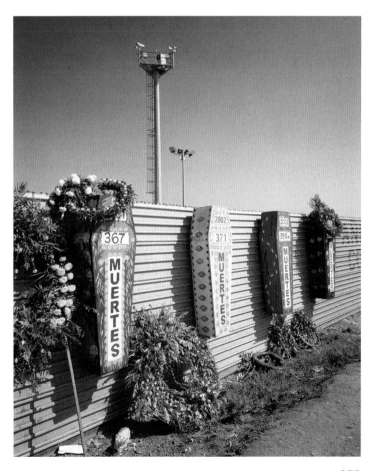

United States–Mexico border fence. As illegal Mexican immigration to the United States increased to an estimated 500,000 per year, demands for barriers across the 2,000 mile long border intensified in the U.S. Fences, walls, and police patrols increased, making the attempt to cross into the U.S. more difficult and more dangerous. Images of coffins along the Mexico–California border memorialize four aspiring migrants who died attempting to enter the country illegally.

12 percent of the total population, and 11.6 million illegally resident. Mexicans comprised slightly more than half of the illegals. America permitted more legal immigrants to enter each year than any other country in the world. Government proposals for illegal immigrants included solutions ranging from according them citizenship to deporting them. In between were proposals to provide some intermediate route to citizenship.

Europe. Europe's dilemmas over migration were newer and more challenging. European countries were not accustomed to large-scale immigration until the economic boom after World War II. Then the combination of war losses, low birth rates, and an expanding economy led them to welcome foreigners for their industrious hands, but not for their culture. European governments did not want to grant them citizenship. In large measure, the new immigrants came from the old colonies.

In the decade 1953–62, Great Britain received 136,000 immigrants from the Commonwealth, made up mostly of former colonies. Of these 66,000 came from the West Indies, 49,000 from India and Pakistan. Young British thugs frequently attacked the new immigrants, especially those from Asia. Some politicians played to racial sentiments. New legislation was passed limiting immigration, and was worded in such a way to discriminate against immigrants of color. Nevertheless, immigrants continued to stream in in ever larger numbers, and by 1990 Great Britain was home to about two million immigrants of color from south Asia and the Caribbean. The 2001 census showed a total of 4.3 million people born overseas, about one million of them from India, Pakistan, and the Caribbean.

France had similar experiences with immigration from its former colonies. At first they were welcome, then restricted. By 1990 there were 615,000 from Algeria, 573,000 from Morocco, 206,000 from Tunisia, and about 100,000 from Senegal and Mali. Most were Muslims. Tensions between the indigenous French and the new immigrants were threefold: class, racial, and religious/cultural. The new immigrants settled in French cities, in some of the worst of urban housing. Fighting became common, with attacks coming from both sides, French against immigrants and immigrants against French. Nevertheless, migrants continued to come. In 2006, the estimated population of foreign-born immigrants in France was 4.9 million.

Germany had not held major colonies, but its economy expanded fastest of all the large European countries, and it had the greatest need for workers. The government therefore agreed to accept immigrants from a wide variety of countries, but only for a set period. Access to citizenship was impossible. By 1973, Germany had accepted almost four million immigrants, by 1996, 7.3 million. As in the other European countries, the immigrants took the lowest-paying jobs and lived in poor housing, usually clustered together in their own neighborhoods. About a third of the immigrants were from Turkey, and their difficulties were greater than most of the other immigrants since they were Asian, Muslim, and had no historic ties to Germany. The Kreuzberg neighborhood of Berlin became known as "Little Istanbul." Only after 1999 did it become legal for someone without a German ancestor to become a citizen, but even then the rules made citizenship difficult to obtain.

Historically, Italy had been a country of emigration, with some 25 million Italians emigrating between 1876 and 1965. After World War II, immigration was largely internal. Italians moved from the impoverished south of the country to the much more prosperous north. But with one of the lowest birth rates in the world, and an economy at last beginning to grow rapidly, Italy offered new opportunities for employment to millions of immigrants in the 1980s. Until the 1990s, these immigrants were largely left undisturbed, even though many entered without legal permission. In the 1990s, new political parties began to attempt to restrict

KEY TERMS

Schengen agreement Set common, restrictive rules limiting immigration and the import of goods to signatory nations.

Fortress Europe The negative designation applied by potential immigrants who were denied entrance to the EU under the terms of the Schengen agreement, implemented after 1990.

immigration. The tolerance of the nation was tested in 1991 when so many Albanians (20,000 in ten days) attempted to enter Italy from across the Adriatic Sea that the Italian government blockaded the ports and deported them as fast as they arrived.

With the tide of popular opinion now running against the immigrants, in 1990 many European nations implemented the **Schengen agreement**, named for the town in Luxembourg where it was promulgated. Schengen addressed the problem created by the freedom of movement inside the EU. Anyone who gained entrance to the EU had complete freedom to travel within any of the member nations. Similarly, imports once inside the Union could be bought and sold anywhere within EU borders. Schengen was designed to insure that all member nations subscribed to equally strict limitations on immigration of people and importation of goods. Immigrants who were refused admission under the more strict Schengen regulations denounced this new policy of "**Fortress Europe**." Italy did not sign right away, feeling that the agreement was too restrictive. In 1998, Italy changed its position. Like the other major countries of Europe, it fortified its borders to the outside so that it could continue to trade more easily with its European neighbors.

A further confrontation occurred in 2007 between Romanian immigrants and the Italian government and public. A Romanian immigrant killed an Italian woman, inflaming public opinion against the immigrants. The problem was complicated. Romania had entered the EU in January 2007, so legal immigration between the two countries was unlimited. Nevertheless, Italy, which had camps of migrant squatters pitched in and around its major cities, now began to enforce restrictions on its immigrants, demanding that they have jobs and legal residences if they wished to stay—even if they came from within the EU. Vigilantes occasionally attacked immigrants and their camps. Meetings between the highest level officials of Italy and Romania helped calm the atmosphere, but migration policy had entered Italian politics. In the national election of 2008 political parties that opposed immigration increased their number of seats in the Parliament.

Immigrants came not only from poor countries to wealthy ones. They also came from extremely poor countries to countries that were somewhat less poor. India, for example, reported tens of millions of illegal immigrants from neighboring Bangladesh and an increasing but much smaller number from Africa. The Bangladeshis, ethnically identical to the Bengalis of India, could slip across the border rather easily, without detection. Many in India accepted them willingly, but others wanted them evicted, especially as they were Muslims in a Hindu majority state.

Anti-immigration election poster, Italy, 2008. "They suffered immigration; now they live on reservations." This election poster of the Northern League (Lega Nord) party of Italy, proclaimed its anti-immigration policy by comparing the situation of contemporary Italians with that of earlier Native American Indians. However far-fetched, and even hysterical, the analogy, no doubt anti-immigrant emotions ran high in Europe. Italy, especially, was just beginning to experience the levels of immigration that countries such as England, France, and Germany had been receiving for decades after World War II.

Refugees

Refugees, even more than migrants, are a social result of political and economic chaos in their home countries. Refugees are immigrants who are fleeing for their safety, and often for their lives. Worldwide the number of refugees fluctuates between 15 and 20

Rwandan refugees at Rusomo, Tanzania, May 1, 1994. Some 250,000 refugees from civil war in Rwanda crossed the border into Tanzania in 1994.

million, about 80 percent of them women and children. In Africa, especially, millions of immigrants poured across borders, partly in search of better economic opportunities, often to escape the threats of oppressive governments. In the 2000s, for example, millions of citizens of Zimbabwe fled the country, seeking refuge from the brutal government of Robert Mugabe. The UN reported, "It is estimated more than two million Zimbabweans are living in South Africa, with another two million in the United Kingdom. As many as 45,000 Zimbabweans live in the United States of America, according to the US-based think-tank, the Association of Zimbabweans Based Abroad" (AZBA). (http://www.irinnews.org/Report.aspx?ReportId=77599)

In 2007 and 2008, so many refugees from Zimbabwe crossed into South Africa that fighting broke out between the immigrants and the local populations, and the government of South Africa blocked new immigration and evicted thousands who had already arrived. In the 1990s, during the wars between Hutus and Tutsis in Rwanda and Congo, two million refugees spilled over the border to Congo. Through the 2000s, millions of refugees from Darfur, in western Sudan, fled to Chad to escape the government-backed militias that attacked them. More than two million refugees fled Iraq during the American-led war beginning in 2003, while another two million were displaced, though they remained within the country. In 1948, some 700,000 refugees fled Palestine. By 2008, their numbers had grown, mostly through natural increase, to three million. In 2004, there were some 17 million refugees worldwide. In 2000 some 550,000 of them were seeking permanent **political asylum**—in fear for their lives because of political positions they had proclaimed.

Rural–Urban Migration. Vast streams of immigrants relocate from rural to urban areas every year. By 2006 the world had become 50 percent urban (3.3 billion people), up from 13 percent in 1900 (220 million) and 29 percent in 1950 (736 million). China's urban population alone grew from 72 million (13 percent) in 1950 to 454 million (35 percent) in 2000. According to UN data, these numbers increased further in just five years, to 530 million (40 percent) in 2005. China's transformation was especially rapid because of a change in government policy. At first, the communist state had forbidden migration from rural to urban areas unless the migrant had already

KEY TERM

political asylum Asylum is normally applied for and granted, or refused, on the basis of individual cases brought by individuals who fear that if they return to their countries they will be persecuted, even murdered, because of their politics. Refugee status is usually a group-based phenomenon and does not imply any specific cause.

Ethnic groups in Africa. The insensitivity to local conditions of many European colonial administrators created territorial boundaries which failed to match the underlying cultural map of Africa and its peoples. The results of this were seen in postindependence internecine conflicts between ethnic groups hemmed into artificial national territories: Congo (Zaire), Nigeria, Uganda, Angola, Zimbabwe, Sudan, and, more recently, Rwanda and Burundi are among those that have reaped this bitter harvest.

secured a job and a residence before moving, tasks that were virtually impossible. When the restrictions were lifted, rural–urban migration shot up. Homeless people seeking employment now became much more numerous and conspicuous in the cities of China, as was true in most third world cities.

Cultural Expression

An important part of the social transformations of globalization, a part that touches billions of people in their daily lives, is the globalization of the arts. Consider singer-songwriter Shakira. She has sold more than 50 million albums worldwide and won two Grammy awards and eight Latin Grammy Awards. She is Colombian. Her mother is of Spanish and Italian ancestry, her father of Lebanese descent. Her fame is global. Consider reggae music, which has come from the Caribbean, with African roots, to win popularity throughout the world, both as music and as protest, especially because of the political songs of the legendary Bob Marley of Jamaica.

fusion In cultural terms, fusion refers to the mixing of different forms into new ones. Often used in terms of food recipes and presentation as well as musical and art forms. The term "hybridity" is used in similar ways, although fusion usually suggests a greater range of imagination in creating the final product.

Consider just a few of the artists who have become musical presences around the world: Zakir Hussein of India, playing tabla, for example; or Nusrat Fateh Ali Khan (1948–97) of Pakistan, chanting the *qawwali* poetry of Sufi mysticism, sometimes fused with western forms, in packed audience halls around the world. Youssou N'Dour, singer and percussionist from Senegal, combines the songs of the griot storytellers of West Africa with Afro-Cuban rhythms, while Toumani Diabaté, of Mali, plays the kora—a 21-string harp/lute central to the classical traditions of West Africa. Diabaté has played "with Taj Mahal, Peter Gabriel, Spain's flamenco-fusion band Ketama, the 52-piece, Japanese/Malian Symmetric Orchestra, and countless jazz musicians who have sought him out in Bamako where he lives." (http://www.afropop.org/explore/artist_info/ID/273/Toumani%20Diabat%C3A9/) **Fusion** has become a cultural norm.

The Festival in the Desert (Festival au Désert), an annual event for world music in Mali, showcases especially the traditional music of North Africa's Tuareg peoples. The Tuareg band, Tinanwen, first came to international attention at the 2001 Festival. Ouagadougou, the capital city of Burkina Faso, has become the showcase for African film. Every two years since 1969 it has hosted the Panafrican Film and TV Festival, the largest on the continent. As many as one million people attend.

Cultural tourism has become a substantial business. Many countries and cities arrange special programming, highlighting their culture—history, music, art, drama—as attractions for tourists. Cultural tourism has become an ever larger component of tourism in general, and travel has been one of the largest and most rapidly growing industries.

Many of the international artists have also participated in relief work for the poor, the hungry, the dispossessed, those suffering from natural disaster, and for the ecological health of the earth. The first of the major benefit concerts by international musicians, the Concert for Bangladesh, in New York City in 1971, raised money for the victims of a cyclone in that newly born country.

The most lucrative of all international benefit concerts was Live Aid, July 13, 1985, dedicated to helping Ethiopia's poor and starving citizens. The concert, organized by

Live Earth concert in Sydney, Australia, 2007. Building on models of huge public concerts by major popular talents for the benefit of particular groups in need, Nobel laureate Al Gore organized twelve "Live Earth" concerts around the world, most of them simultaneous, to call attention to the crisis of global warming.

Bob Geldof and Midge Ure, ran for 16 hours in two parts, the first half at Wembley Stadium in London, the second at JFK Stadium in Philadelphia. Performers in London included Sting, U2, Elton John, and Paul McCartney; in Philadelphia, Madonna, Eric Clapton, Phil Collins, and Led Zeppelin. Parallel concerts took place simultaneously around the world. An estimated 400 million people viewed at least some segments of the multiple concerts on television. The concert ultimately raised £150 million (about US $175 million at current rates of exchange). Live 8, in 2005, was a series of ten concerts, coordinated to take place around the world, dedicated to urging governments to increase aid to poor countries. More than 1,000 musicians performed in the concerts, which were broadcast on 182 television networks and 2,000 radio networks. The first Live Earth concert, organized by Nobel Prize-winner and former U.S. vice president, Al Gore, was dedicated to raising awareness of global warming and took place in multiple locations in 2007: Sydney, Johannesburg, New Jersey, Rio de Janeiro, Antarctica, Tokyo, Kyoto, Shanghai, London, Hamburg, Washington, D.C., and Rome. (A follow-up concert was to have taken place in December, 2008, in Mumbai, India, but was canceled after the city was hit by a wave of terror attacks.)

Many artists individually became almost as famous for their work against poverty and human suffering as for their music. Shakira, for example, performed at the Live 8 benefit concert at the Palace of Versailles, near Paris, and at the German segment of Live Earth in Hamburg, in 2007. Shakira funds the Latin America in Solidarity Action (ALAS) charity and in 2008 she and other Latin artists performed on its behalf in Buenos Aires to 150,000 people and in Mexico City. Perhaps most noteworthy of all has been Bono of the band U2. Bono has participated in numerous benefit concerts, including the 1985 Live Aid concert. In 2002, he joined with others in organizing DATA (Debt, AIDS, Trade, Africa) dedicated to eradicating poverty and HIV/AIDS in Africa. He was also prominent in the worldwide Jubilee 2000 campaign to cancel the debts of some of Africa's poorest countries. In 2005 he joined with others to launch EDUN, dedicated to promoting trade with Africa. *Time* magazine named Bono, along with Bill and Melinda Gates, as "persons of the year" in 2005. In 2008, the UN unveiled a $3 billion plan for eliminating malaria as a mass child killer in Africa. Bono and, again, Bill Gates, joined the many heads of state and UN officials making the announcement.

Sometimes the music itself has been the gift. In 1986, musician Paul Simon went to South Africa to begin recording for his album, *Graceland*. While many criticized Simon for breaking the cultural boycott imposed on apartheid South Africa at the time, he pointed out that he was introducing South African musicians, such as Ladysmith Black Mambazo, and other African artists, such as Ghanaian drummer Okyerema Asante, to wider audiences. Five years after *Graceland*, Simon traveled to Brazil to produce the *Rhythm of the Saints* album, which brought many lesser known Brazilian musicians, and Brazilian music, into a global spotlight. In 1991, Simon's concert in Central Park spotlighted both African and South American musicians.

New recording labels, such as Putumayo and Rough Guides-Music, sprang up, dedicated to producing music of the non-European world (as well as of Europe and the Americas). The TV channel MTV (Music Television) began broadcasting in 1981. Originally it broadcast only music videos, but subsequently its format broadened to include reality shows, movies, and some sitcoms. MTV in the United States generated spinoffs in other countries, in local languages, including MTV channels in the UK, Dubai (targeting markets from Cairo across Saudi Arabia to Bahrain), India, the Philippines, Turkey, Pakistan, Australia, and New Zealand.

Other TV channels, oriented toward news and features, were also reaching out to global audiences. Great Britain's BBC was the first to go international, first as a radio network, later as TV. By 2008 it was reaching about 275 million households in almost every country on earth. The American-based Cable News Network, CNN, began broadcasting in 1980 followed by its related CNNI (International) in 1985. The sister networks now serve most of the nations of the world, reaching about half the number of people as the BBC. Satellite Television for the Asian Region (STAR TV) began broadcasting in 1991 as an Asian TV service, based in Hong Kong, with programming offices in India, Australia, and other South Asian countries. It claims to reach some 300 million viewers in 54 countries. In the Arab world, Al-Jazeera (the [Arabian] Peninsula) became the first TV network headquartered in the Arab world, in Doha, Qatar. It began operations in 1996 with a $150 million grant from the Emir of Qatar, Sheikh Hamad bin Khalifa. It broadcasts in several countries around the world. The channel began building up a reputation for integrity, and for providing a view of the news from within the Arab world, with its broadcasts of the Lebanese civil war, 2000–2001. The network won global attention following the events of 9/11 for its exclusive broadcasts of video statements of Osama bin Laden and other al-Qaeda leaders.

With so many networks, broadcasts could now reach hundreds of millions of people around the world in real time. The most common of these international broadcasts were sporting events, like the World Cup soccer games, and news programming. According to Nielsen Media Research, 4.7 billion viewers worldwide, almost 75 percent of the population of the earth, tuned in to at least some parts of the television coverage of the 2008 Olympic Games in Beijing.

In the years immediately following World War II, when America's military, economic, and cultural power was hegemonic in the world, many nations feared that their cultures would be overwhelmed by music, literature, film, and TV programming originating in the United States. Some began to impose limits on the import, for example, of American films. Subsequently, as other nations became more powerful relative to the United States, anthropological observers of culture contact spoke of **hybridization**, the mixing of cultures to produce new forms. Sometimes this is referred to as cultural fusion. More recently, cultural observers claim to see, also, the carving out of specific niches for individual cultures, in forms that are pristine, or untouched—although in reality cultures change all the time. American (and European) cultural performance remains prominent, but there is less fear now of it overwhelming local cultures.

One index of cultures carving out their own niches appears in the Nobel Prize awards for literature, established in 1901. The first prize to a non-European, non-American writer went to Rabindranath Tagore of India in 1913. The second came only in 1945, to Gabriela Mistral of Chile. Over the next 45 years, only six awardees came from outside the U.S. or Europe, but in the decade of the 1990s there were four (from Mexico, South Africa, the West Indies, and Japan), and since 2000 there have been three, including the first from China and Turkey. Cultures of all regions of the world are not only holding their own, they are winning international recognition and influencing one another as never before.

Nevertheless, many instances of exclusion also appear. For example, China has forced TV networks that want to do business in China to exclude BBC programming. As we noted in Chapter Twenty-three, Iran not only forbade the sale of author Salman Rushdie's writings in the country, as did many Islamic countries, for his alleged blasphemy against Islam in his 1988 novel *The Satanic Verses,* but it also put a bounty on the author's head. Attempts were made on the lives of three of the book's translators; one of them was successful. Huge public demonstrations against publica-

Wole Soyinka at UNESCO, Paris, October 16, 1986. Soyinka is here seen celebrating his Nobel Prize for Literature.

tion of the book led to murders in Islamabad, Pakistan, and in India. Several book-stores and publishers' offices in Great Britain and the United States were bombed, and for years the author lived in hiding, his book almost unavailable in bookstores in Britain and the United States. As Britain protected the author, a British citizen, the Iranian government broke off relations with the government of Great Britain.

Fifteen years later, Azar Nafisi's novel *Reading Lolita in Tehran* (2003) describes the continuing difficulties and dangers of obtaining and reading proscribed literature in Iran. There were limits to the globalization of culture. Many countries around the world censored artistic expression that they found unacceptable or threatening. Cultural exchange, welcomed by some, was resented and feared by others. Censorship did not disappear in the early twenty-first century.

On Technology

We have already written about the technologies of communication and transportation, of computers, the internet, and containerization, and we have discussed genetic engineering and cloning. Here let us look at two additional technologies. One, nanotechnology (technology based on organisms of molecular size and even smaller), is only beginning to come into its own. The other, ecological technology (technology to keep the globe's ecology intact for human life), is already perhaps the most critical for the world today.

Nanotechnology

Nanotechnologies work with substances at the molecular, or even at atomic and sub-atomic, sizes. Nano stands for a substance one billionth of a meter in size. A nanometer is to a meter as the size of a marble is to the size of the planet Earth. Nanosubstances exist in nature, for example, in the enzymes of biological processes that allow the contraction of muscles; in the works of DNA molecules; and in the process of converting minerals and water into living cells. Experiments using and measuring nanosubstances began in the early 1900s, and in 1959 the Nobel laureate physicist Richard Feynman brought the field to greater world attention even outside the scientific community. Feynman noted that when substances are analyzed at atomic size their properties are different from the same substances at the larger scales at which we normally encounter them. For example, opaque substances become transparent (copper); stable materials become combustible (aluminum); solids turn into liquids at room temperature (gold); insulators become conductors (silicon). This last transformation has brought about the use of silicon as a conductor in computers. The term "nanotechnology" was used for the first time in 1974. Substantial research began only in the 1980s.

Making instruments capable of creating and working with such small substances posed problems, but by the 1980s and 1990s, scientists were beginning to create tools for reducing substances to such small dimensions. Some nanotechnology is already in place. Nanomaterials are seeded into materials of larger size, giving them new properties. For example, carbon at the nanoscale is used in some computer hard drives to increase their speed and capacity. Exciting possibilities for further use are under exploration; some seem practicable even now, while others appear more far-fetched. Nanomaterials might be seeded into cancerous cells to track or even destroy them. Carbon in nanoform could be used to create a fiber, or a wire, or a molecular coating. Nanosubstances might be used in desalinating and purifying water at minimal cost, in fuel cells, in controlling pollution, in the bioprocessing of food products. They also promise potential breakthroughs in the production of abundant, cheap, clean energy.

For all of their promise, nanotechnologies are only beginning to provide practical technologies. Producing effective tools to handle materials at such small size is problematic. In addition, substances in such small size may prove dangerous to human and animal life. If they enter the lungs and breathing systems, they may destroy tissues. Because of their tiny size, they may also enter through the skin and, in effect, cut into internal organs. Experience with nanotechnologies is new and limited, as is assessment of their potential harmful effects. They require, and command, further attention.

Ecological Technology

The selection of Al Gore, tireless campaigner for controlling climate change, for the Nobel Peace Prize in 2007 indicated the degree to which the struggle against "global warming" had become one of the world's most important priorities. Two equally remarkable indicators were his Oscar, also in 2007, awarded for his documentary film, *An Inconvenient Truth*, and Waangari Maathai's Nobel Peace Prize in 2004 for her Green Belt movement, in which she has motivated poor women in her country of Kenya to plant some 30 million trees in 30 years.

Gore's Nobel Prize acceptance speech homed in on the global problem of carbon emissions that were threatening to destroy life on earth:

> In the last few months, it has been harder and harder to misinterpret the signs that our world is spinning out of kilter. Major cities in North and South America, Asia and Australia are nearly out of water due to massive droughts and melting glaciers. Desperate farmers are losing their livelihoods. Peoples in the frozen Arctic and on low-lying Pacific islands are planning evacuations of places they have long called home. Unprecedented wildfires have forced a half million people from their homes in one country and caused a national emergency that almost brought down the government in another. Climate refugees have migrated into areas already inhabited by people with different cultures, religions, and traditions, increasing the potential for conflict. Stronger storms in the Pacific and Atlantic have threatened whole cities. Millions have been displaced by massive flooding in South Asia, Mexico, and 18 countries in Africa. As temperature extremes have increased, tens of thousands have lost their lives. We are recklessly burning and clearing our forests and driving more and more species into extinction. The very web of life on which we depend is being ripped and frayed.

Gore called attention to the need for political leadership, which has been sorely lacking, to solve the problem. He identified the need to limit the global emissions of carbon dioxide, CO_2. And he called for market mechanisms to do the job. His positions represent the current state of thinking about the problems and the solutions:

> We must begin by making the common rescue of the global environment the central organizing principle of the world community.
>
> Fifteen years ago, I made that case at the "Earth Summit" in Rio de Janeiro. Ten years ago, I presented it in Kyoto. This week, I will urge the delegates in Bali to adopt a bold mandate for a treaty that establishes a universal global cap on emissions and uses the market in emissions trading to efficiently allocate resources to the most effective opportunities for speedy reductions....
>
> Most important of all, we need to put a price on carbon—with a CO_2 tax that is then rebated back to the people, progressively, according to the laws of each nation, in ways that shift the burden of taxation from employment to pollution. This is by far the most effective and simplest way to accelerate solutions to this crisis.

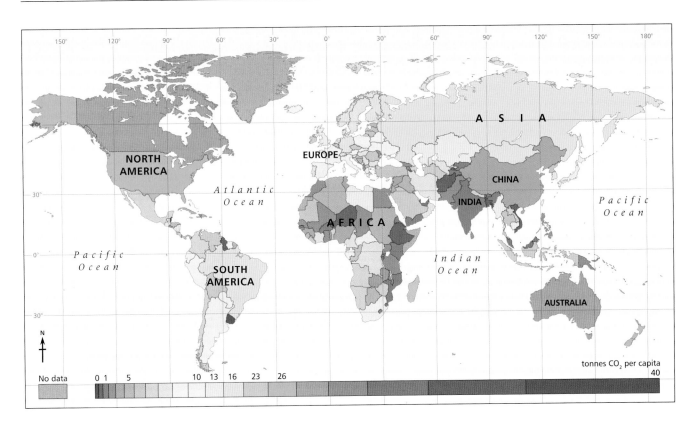

Gore also identified the two largest national culprits creating the CO_2 emissions: the United States, the current leader, and China, coming up fast. In 1980, the United States produced 4,754 million metric tons of CO_2 from fossil fuels; in 2004, the U.S. produced 5,912, an increase of 24 percent. Over the same period, China increased its emissions from 1,454 to 4,707, up 224 percent. Neither nation was willing to take the lead in solving the Earth's climate problems: Quite the contrary.

Advocates of change met resistance, for example from companies that manufactured carbon fuels, and automakers whose products consumed them. Consumers did not want to pay more for carbon fuels. Political leaders were reluctant to take the lead in proposing solutions that had such strong opposition among manufacturers and consumers.

In many parts of the world—Saudi Arabia, Iran, Iraq, Russia, Venezuela—rulers who controlled petrofuels were dictators and could afford to be, since the "petrodollars" left them free to do as they wished. High levels of fossil fuel consumption helped keep them in power. In addition, one attempt to reduce the reliance on petrofuels, especially in the United States and Brazil, by devoting vast acreage of food crops to the production of ethanol, a corn-based fuel, removed that acreage from food production, resulting in increased food costs, a burden falling heaviest on the poor.

In attempting to fight climate change, Gore and his colleagues around the world believed that technological innovation, economic planning, and political action were capable collectively of solving the problems of climate change, and that the process would be commercially rewarding as well. Many companies reaped substantial profits by creating green solutions to energy problems through innovative design, equipment, and application. The production of wind power and solar power began to be economically competitive as pressure on the supply of petrofuels continued to

Greenhouse gas emissions, 2005. As evidence of global warming and climate change became unmistakable, scientists measured more carefully the amount of greenhouse gas emissions, primarily carbon dioxide, CO_2. Here they are computed on a per capita basis, so that countries such as Canada, with a very cold climate and considerable use of coal and gas for heating, register very high, while China registers relatively low. Similar charts giving total emissions by country show China much higher, because of its immense population, and Canada much lower. The United States registers high in both per capita and total emissions.

885

AT A GLANCE: TRADE, SOCIAL REVOLUTION, TECHNOLOGY

DATE	TRADE	SOCIAL REVOLUTION	TECHNOLOGY
1970s		• 1975 First UN Conference on Women	• 1973 Portable cellular phone invented • 1974 "Nanotechnology" term used for first time
1980s		• 1980 Mandal Commission Report on Other Backward Classes (India) • 1981 MTV begins broadcasting • 1985 Schengen agreement; expanded 1997, 1999 • 1985 Live Aid concert • 1987 Palestinian intifada	• 1989 World Wide Web (www) formalized
1990s	• 1994 North American Free Trade Agreement (NAFTA) • 1995 GATT becomes WTO; 153 members in 2008 • 1999 anti-WTO protests	• 1994 One person-one vote democratic elections in South Africa • 1996–98 Truth and Reconciliation Commission in South Africa • 1996 Al Jazeera begins broadcasting	• 1991 First digital cell phone network; first text message
2000s	• 2000 United Nations Millennium Development Goals adopted • 2001 World Social Forum, first meeting • 2002 Euro currency adopted throughout most of EU • 2008 Global economic recession	• 2000 Second Palestinian intifada • 2001 The Netherlands legalizes same-sex marriage • 2004 c. 17 million refugees worldwide • 2008 Barack Obama elected President of the United States	• 2004 Wangari Maathai wins Nobel Peace Prize for Green Belt Movement • 2005 18 million containers make 200 million trips • 2006 2.6 billion cellular phone subscriptions • 2007 Al Gore wins Nobel Peace Prize for ecological advocacy • 2008 1.5 billion people connected to the internet

raise oil prices. Around the world, the public was beginning to accept the need for new initiatives as the evidence piled up of weather changing in peculiar and scary ways, and as arctic glaciers melted faster than ever previously recorded. In some countries, especially in Europe, green political parties began to spring up, dedicated to fighting for ecologically healthy programs. Most solutions for reducing climate change included these key proposals:

- reducing the carbon emissions of automobiles, either by reducing the numbers or usage of cars, or increasing mileage, or changing from fossil fuels to new kinds of fuels;
- increasing the efficiency of electric plants, or converting them to natural gas power;
- reducing the use of energy;
- capturing carbon emissions before they entered the atmosphere;
- increasing reliance on alternative fuels, such as solar, wind, and nuclear;
- preserving the forests and reforesting those that have been cut down; and
- charging more for petrofuels in order to force consumers to cut back on their use and, meanwhile, to recover more of their costs to the environment. This strategy often included plans for putting absolute caps on the national production of carbon emissions, and then buying and selling carbon emissions credits, so that the more efficient could profit from their efficiency in cutting back on emissions, and the less efficient would pay for their inefficiencies, ultimately becoming more efficient.

On Identity: What Difference Does It Make?

The world in 2008 was a very different place from the world of 1988. Just 20 years had made an enormous difference. Consider it in terms of the themes of our text.

In terms of *evolution* and what it means to be a human being, the entire human genome had been mapped. In relationship to the natural world, scientists became able to objectively measure how truly related we are to the entire animal world, especially to the great apes, with whom we share a 97 percent similar DNA. The *urban population* of the world increased by one billion persons between 1990 (2.2 billion) and 2007 (3.3 billion). Fully half of the world's population had become city dwellers. *Empires*, such as the USSR, collapsed. With that collapse, the United States seemed to be the world's lone superpower, but by 2008 it was in deep trouble financially, overstretched militarily, and held in disrepute in many countries around the world. From the time of the Iranian revolution of 1979 especially, *religion* resurfaced as a major factor not only in world culture, but also in world politics. Countries that had kept aloof from world trading systems, like China and India, emerged as major powers in international finance and *trade*. Discrimination in terms of religion, gender, race, caste, nationality, and class was under attack as unworthy of civilized behavior, and was apparently receding as migration forced diverse groups together and schools created educational curricula for a world of diversity. No doubt, some peoples chose to maintain their received traditions and to reject *social change* as firmly as possible. New *technologies* continued their promises and their threats to human life as they always had, but more pervasively.

So much was changing so swiftly that "identity" had become a key issue by the beginning of the twenty-first century. What did it mean to be a male, or a female; black or white; a villager or an urbanite or a suburbanite; a migrant or a local resident; an American, or a Kenyan, or a Brazilian, or a Chinese; a Christian, or a Muslim, or a Buddhist; an economic conservative or a liberal; a cultural traditionalist or a cosmopolitan; technologically savvy or primitive? What does a person stand for and against? What tasks are meaningful and important to undertake, and which seem less important?

Academic researchers ask these questions in formal and disciplined fashion. Historians, for example, trace the ways in which individuals and groups modify their sense of identity over time. But so do everyday people, in more colloquial ways, in conversation with friends and in internal conversation with themselves. It is our hope that this textbook has given its readers some guidelines for thinking about these issues of identity, by demonstrating that they have been with us forever, albeit with different levels of intensity at different times. We hope that readers will go away with the understanding that the study of history is the study of the context of our own lives and identities, individually and collectively. By knowing where we have come from, in the past, we will be better able to understand our choices in determining where we might go in the future.

Asking Questions

- Contemporary history is very difficult to write, because its subject matter keeps changing. The writing of this text was completed in the spring of 2009. What changes have occurred since that time that make elements of this text already seem dated?
- What groups of people seem most likely to be in favor of globalization? What groups against? Have you seen in the past year or two any examples of groups that have changed their position on globalization?

- To what extent is the struggle between Israelis and Palestinians a conflict between religions? To what extent is it a conflict between national groups? To what degree can you separate the two kinds of issues?
- To what degree do women share common issues for struggle regardless of their national identities? To what degree do women in different countries have different issues for struggle? Please give examples.
- In what ways are the struggles of low caste and scheduled caste people in India similar to the struggles that blacks experienced in apartheid South Africa or African-Americans experience in the U.S.? To what extent are they different?
- To what extent are problems of assimilation of migrants similar in all countries? To what extent are they different?
- Considering the many problems of pollution, global warming, and climate change, to what extent can individual initiative help alleviate them? To what extent is national action required? To what extent is international action required?

Suggested Readings

KEY TERMS

globalization see p. 850

outsourcing see p. 853

autarky see p.855

equity see p. 855

protectionism see p. 856

transparency see p. 857

privatization see p. 857

intifada see p. 864

micro-finance or **micro-credit** see p. 868

Schengen agreement see p. 876

"Fortress Europe" see p. 876

political asylum see p. 878

fusion see p. 880

hybridization see p. 882

PRINCIPAL SOURCES

Carter, Jimmy. *We Can Have Peace in the Holy Land: A Plan that Will Work* (New York: Simon and Schuster, 2009). Carter advocates a two-state solution and calls for pressure to be exerted against Israelis and Palestinians to save them from themselves.

Chomsky, Noam. *Middle East Illusions* (Lanham, MD: Rowman and Littlefield, 2004). Chomsky takes to task everyone for failures in Middle East policy. He is especially critical of the United States for its uncritical support of Israel.

Crossley, Pamela Kyle, Lynn Hollen Lees, and John W. Servos. *Global Society: The World since 1900* (Boston, MA: Houghton Mifflin, 2nd ed., 2007). A fine, well-written history of the twentieth century, organized thematically rather than by nations or regions. Special emphasis on technology and useful references to websites for further research.

Edelstein, Jillian. *Truth and Lies: Stories from the Truth and Reconciliation Commission in South Africa* (New York: The New Press, 2001). Portraits and testimony—often quite moving—from individuals who spoke to the commission.

French, Howard. *A Continent for the Taking. The Tragedy and Hope of Africa* (New York: Knopf, 2004). A senior writer for *The New York Times* places the blame for Africa's current difficulties on self-interested political leaders in both Africa and the West, showing that there is plenty of blame to go around.

Human Development Report 2007/08: Fighting Climate Change: Human Solidarity in a Divided World (New York: United Nations Development Programme, 2008). A survey of the nations of the world with an abundance of statistical tables and numerous, brief, specific topical discussions.

Levinson, Marc. *The Box: How the Shipping Container Made the World Smaller and the World Economy Bigger* (Princeton, NJ: Princeton University Press, 2006). The invention and application of containerized technology.

Nussbaum, Martha. *The Clash Within: Democracy, Religious Violence, and India's Future* (Cambridge, MA: Harvard University Press, 2007). Argues that peaceful centrists must work together to defeat violent, radical extremists. The case study is India, but the argument is widely applicable.

Obama, Barack. *Dreams from My Father. A Story of Race and Inheritance* (New York: Three Rivers Press, 2004). Memoirs of America's first multi-racial president. A splendid and insightful autobiography.

Preston, Julia and Samuel Dillon. *Opening Mexico. The Making of a Democracy* (New York: Farrar, Straus and Giroux, 2004). Two *New York Times* reporters narrate the events that marked the contemporary "Opening of Mexico" from about 1968 to 2004. Thoughtful and engaged.

Rosenberg, Rosalind, "The 'Woman Question,'" in Richard W. Bulliet, ed. *The Columbia History of the 20th Century* (New York: Columbia University Press, 1998). Discusses the changing goals of women's movements around the world.

Saadawi, Nawal El. *The Nawal El Saadawi Reader*, p. 4 (New York: Zed Books, 1997). Important spokeswoman for third world feminists. Explains how their issues differ from those in first world counties.

Sassen, Saskia. *The Global City: New York, London, Tokyo* (Princeton, NJ: Princeton University Press, 2001).

Truth and Reconciliation Commission of South Africa Report. http://www.info.gov.za/reports/2003/trc/. The amazing account of the South African government's attempt to heal the breach between black and white, seeking understanding rather than reprisal.

Yale Global. A useful website with information on global poverty and inequality. http://yaleglobal.yale.edu/

Yunus, Muhammad. *Creating a World Without Poverty: Social Business and the Future of Capitalism* (New York: Public Affairs, reprint edition, 2009). An account of his work by the Nobel Prize-winning advocate of micro-finance.

Zakaria, Fareed. *The Post-American World* (New York: W.W. Norton, 2008). Perceptive journalist analyzes current transformations in world economic and political power. America is still very important but China and India are rising fast.

ADDITIONAL SOURCES

Firebaugh, Glenn. *The New Geography of Global Income Inequality* (Cambridge, MA: Harvard University Press, 2003). Sociologist argues that while income inequality is increasing among people within countries, it is decreasing between nations, largely because of China's successful rise.

Foer, Franklin. *How Soccer Explains the World: An (Unlikely) Theory of Globalization* (New York: Harper Perennial, 2005). The subtitle is too grandiose, but a fun introduction to the craze of soccer around the world.

Friedman, Thomas L. *Hot, Flat, and Crowded: Why We Need a Green Revolution and How It Can Renew America* (New York: Farrar, Straus, and Giroux, 2008). *New York Times* columnist urges America to attend to the problems of global warming, and sees economic benefits in new technologies.

Gilbert, Mark and Jonathan T. Reynolds. *Africa in World History: From Prehistory to the Present* (Upper Saddle River, NJ: Prentice Hall, 2nd ed., 2007). A useful survey. Up to date.

Gourevitch, Philip. *We Wish To Inform You That Tomorrow We Will Be Killed With Our Families: Stories from Rwanda* (New York: Farrar, Straus and Giroux, 1998). Brilliant journalistic reporting from the killing fields of Rwanda. Attempts to understand and explain the differences between Tutsis and Hutus.

Hunt, Michael H. *The World Transformed: 1945 to the Present: A Documentary Reader* (Boston, MA: Bedford/St. Martin's, 2004). An outstanding selection of primary documents with global scope and thematic breadth.

Kishwar, Madhu. *Off the Beaten Track: Rethinking Gender Justice for Indian Women* (New Delhi: Oxford University Press, 1999). The editor of one of India's leading feminist journals, *Manushi*, discusses the evolution of her thought in light of the possible and the ideal.

Meade, Teresa. *A Brief History of Brazil* (New York: Checkmark Books, 2nd ed., 2009). Brief, incisive account, with many insights presented in sidebars. Especially interesting on culture, music, and sports. Well-chosen illustrations.

Milanovic, Branko. *Worlds Apart: Measuring International and Global Inequality* (Princeton, NJ: Princeton University Press, 2005). World Bank economist shows methods of evaluating inequality among nations and individuals, and sees little chance of greater equality in the near future.

Shulman, David. *Dark Hope: Working for Peace in Israel and Palestine* (Chicago, IL: University of Chicago Press, 2007). Personal, moving account of actions of individual Israelis to bring humanitarian aid and justice for Palestinian Arabs.

Smick, David. *The World is Curved: Hidden Dangers in the Global Economy* (Portfolio, 2008). Economist and businessman points out the hazards of globalization.

Stiglitz, Joseph and Andrew Charlton. *Fair Trade for All: How Trade Can Promote Development* (New York: Oxford University Press, 2005). Argument for a level playing field among the participants in international trade; until now terms favor the rich and powerful.

Wright, Donald. *The World and a Very Small Place in Africa: A History of Globalization in Niumi, The Gambia* (Armonk, NY: M.E. Sharpe, 2nd ed., 2004). Covers fifteenth century to the present. Fascinating conclusion on globalization and its dangers.

Zinsser, Judith P. "The United Nations Decade for Women: a Quiet Revolution," *The History Teacher*, Vol. 24, No. 1 (Nov., 1990), pp. 19–29. International organizations are helping women organize globally to dream new dreams and to work to achieve otherwise unattainable goals.

For quizzes, flashcards, primary sources, interactive maps, videos, and other activities related to this chapter please go to

www.myhistorylab.com

Glossary

agronomy The systematic concern with field crop production and soil management. The term was first used in 1814.

al-Qaeda "The base." The militant Islamic group of guerrilla warriors mobilized by Osama bin Laden in Afghanistan, first to fight against Russian invaders, and later to attack the United States and its allies. Subsequently, a number of militant Islamic guerrilla groups in different parts of the world adopted the name al-Qaeda, some with ties to bin Laden's group, some without.

Asian tigers The countries in East and Southeast Asia that were doing extremely well economically in the last decades of the twentieth century. The list almost always includes South Korea, Taiwan, Singapore, and Hong Kong, and sometimes Indonesia and Thailand.

asiento The right granted to England by Spain to carry all the slave cargoes from Africa to Spanish America, and the additional right to bring one goods ship each year to Panama.

asymmetrical warfare Warfare between groups armed and equipped very differently, and often using different strategies, usually between lightly armed guerrilla warriors and conventionally equipped armies of powerful states. Terror tactics and disinformation are also considered tactics of asymmetrical warfare. The term came into wide use in the 2000s, but it is also applicable to earlier guerrilla warfare.

autarky An economic system based primarily on internal self-sufficiency with little participation in external trade.

Ayatollah Title of prestigious and powerful Muslim religious leaders in Iran.

balance of power In international relations, a policy that aims to secure peace by preventing any one state or alignment of states from becoming too dominant. Alliances are formed to build up a force equal or superior to that of the potential enemy.

banana republic A country dependent economically on a single cash crop and beholden politically to the company which controls the crop, and to the countries which buy it. Often applied to countries of Central America in their relationships with the United States.

barefoot doctors Paramedical personnel trained in simple, basic levels of medicine and dispatched to work in rural areas of China, where virtually no professionally trained doctors chose to practice.

Bauhaus A movement in architecture arising in Germany between the world wars. It was characterized by an emphasis on streamlined forms, and a rejection of ornamentation. It followed the motto "form follows function." Its work became controversial among political parties. When the Nazis took over Germany they destroyed the Bauhaus school and most of its masters fled the country.

Berlin Conference Convened by Bismarck of Germany in 1884–85 to settle European disputes over territory in Africa peacefully.

big lie, the A propaganda technique, defined by Hitler as a lie so colossal that no one would believe the liar would dare to say it if it weren't true.

blood and iron In nineteenth-century Germany, Prime Minister Bismarck's policy of using warfare against enemies as a means of unifying his new nation. Subsequently the term has been used to designate the policy of any government committed to foreign warfare as a means of internal unification.

bourgeoisie From the French word for town, *bourg*. Originally applied to the inhabitants of walled towns, who occupied a socio-economic position between the rural peasantry and the feudal aristocracy. With the development of industry, it became identified more with employers, as well as with other members of the "middle class," professionals, artisans, and shopkeepers.

bourgeoisie (in Marxism) A collective noun designating the class that owns and directs the means of production. In Marxist thought, the bourgeoisie and the proletariat need each other, but they are also always in conflict over the distribution of wealth.

bourse Another name for stock exchange, especially in Europe.

brain washing The popular term used in the west during Mao's leadership to refer to Chinese methods of group pressure and psychological coercion to extract confessions of political deviance.

Brezhnev Doctrine In 1968 Leonid Brezhnev, head of the USSR government, declared that the USSR would intervene militarily to prevent any of its satellite countries from claiming independence. Issued when Czechoslovakia sought independence.

capitalism An economic system characterized by private or corporate ownership of the means of production and by private control over decisions on prices, production, and distribution of goods in a free, competitive market of supply and demand.

cartel An association of independent producers or businessmen whose aim is to control the supply of a particular commodity or group of commodities in order to regulate or push up prices.

caudillo A military leader who takes political power.

client state A state that is economically, politically, or militarily dependent on another state.

Congress of Vienna The Congress brought together diplomats from the leading countries of Europe to resolve issues raised by the Napoleonic Wars and their aftermath. It redrew national borders, established a balance of power, and enshrined conservative government in Europe for about 30 years.

conquistadores The Spanish soldiers who invaded and conquered the kingdoms of the New World, especially in Mexico and Peru.

containment The postwar policy of the United States, advocated by diplomat George Kennan, to encircle and contain the Soviet Union within limits, through militant confrontation that would stop short of war. Containment advocated a balance of force.

conurbation An enormous, complex city, made up of many parts, each of which may be a small town or city by itself— a megalopolis.

Corn Laws Laws that restricted the import of food into England. These laws favored rural agricultural producers at the expense of urban consumers. Repealed in 1846.

Creole In the sixteenth to eighteenth centuries, a white person born in Spanish America of Spanish parents.

cultivation system, the A system of Dutch rule over Indonesian agriculture that forced peasants to devote 20 percent of their land to cash crops for export. This policy took away the peasant's right to determine his use of his own fields and diminished the production of food.

Cultural Revolution The policy of the Chinese communist government, 1966–76, of basing its economy on rural productivity and quelling the intellectual and cultural life of the cities, subordinating freedom of thought completely in favor of communist ideology.

D-Day Often used in the military as the day on which an important operation is to begin; more generally, signifies any date targeted for special action. Since the Normandy landing, June 6, 1944, the term "D-Day" has most often referred to that historic invasion.

daimyo The feudal lords of Japan, who, by the sixteenth century, controlled almost the entire country.

demographics The study of human populations in quantitative terms, usually considered a sub-field of sociology. Demographers consider such data as birth rates and death rates, fertility and morbidity, and immigration and emigration, among many others.

divide and rule A policy, usually unstated, by which a ruling power would encourage quarrels among its subjects so that they did not unite to challenge the ruling authority, and it could present itself as indispensable to keeping the peace. The rulers claimed that the divisions were inherent among the populations; anti-imperialists claimed that the rulers created them for their own purposes.

divine right of kings A political doctrine influential in the sixteenth and seventeenth centuries which held that the monarch derived his authority from God and was therefore not accountable to earthly authority. James I of England (r. 1603–25) was a foremost exponent.

domesticity An ideal that valued the woman who stayed at home, raising children, keeping the home as comfortable as possible, and making it a safe haven to which her husband could return after his daily work earning a family wage.

domino effect The belief, held by many American policymakers, that if one country in a region became communist, others would follow, one after the other.

dual economy An economy of two largely unconnected tiers: one tier of large-scale, modern, highly mechanized, highly capitalized businesses with large workforces; the other of small-scale workshops with little capital, limited mechanization, and a small workforce, producing traditional goods.

durbar A showy convocation of notables paying obeisance to, and receiving gifts from, the most powerful political leaders; a means of demonstrating and ratifying the relative position of each.

Eastern Ethics; Western Science The watchword of Sakuma Zozan in Japan, urging acceptance of Western science and technology, but rejecting Western culture and ethics in favor of those of Japan. This position was found in many countries colonized by Europeans.

economic liberalism This term has had various meanings at different times. Today it usually refers to a free-market, capitalistic economy, with minimum government intervention. Often referred to as neo-liberalism.

empiricism The theory that all knowledge originates in experience; the practice of relying on direct observation of events and experience for determining reality.

enclosure acts Laws passed in England from 1450–1640, and culminating 1750–1860, which converted public lands held in common into parcels of land to be sold to private owners.

encomienda A concession from the Spanish crown to a colonist, giving the colonist permission to exact tribute from a specified number of Native Americans living in a specific area. Conditions were cruel and the Spanish attempted to convert the Indians to Christianity.

enlightened despotism A benevolent form of absolutism, a system of government in which the ruler has absolute rights over his or her subjects. The term implies that the ruler acts for the good of the people, not in self interest. The ruler/despot was usually a king or emperor. (Compare p. 475 and p. 535.)

equity A condition in which participants in a system believe that the system is fair and unbiased. Equity does not necessarily imply equality, a situation in which all participants have equivalent goods and rights, but it does require that participants share a sense of justice and fairness in the system.

ethnic cleansing A euphemism for genocide. The act of exiling or murdering minority groups from a given territory.

evangelical Christianity Those forms of Protestant Christianity that emphasize the literal truth and authority of the Bible, and salvation through the personal acceptance of Jesus Christ.

extraterritoriality Legal immunities enjoyed by the citizens of a sovereign state or international organization within a host country.

891

family wage A wage, usually earned by a male head-of-household, adequate to support a family. The concept suggested that a woman's place was in the home and that the male husband-father was the family breadwinner.

fascism A political philosophy, movement, or government that exalts the nation over the individual, the antithesis of liberal democracy. It advocates a centralized, autocratic government, often in alliance with major business leaders, led by a disciplined party and headed by a dictatorial, charismatic leader.

finance capital The capital necessary to finance the creation of new industry. The importance of finance capital marked the transition to an age of larger businesses than ever before and gave finance capitalists, who provided the investments, greater power than ever before.

five-year plans State-directed plans, frequently prepared by communist governments, to control the economy and to direct its growth. They contrast with capitalist, laissez-faire, free-market economies, in which the government allows the forces of supply and demand to guide the market.

Fortress Europe The negative designation applied by potential immigrants who were denied entrance to the EU under the terms of the Schengen agreement, implemented after 1990.

free market economy An economic system in which the means of production are largely privately owned and there is little or no government control over the markets.

fusion In cultural terms, fusion refers to the mixing of different forms into new ones. Often used in terms of food recipes and presentation as well as musical and art forms. The term "hybridity" is used in similar ways, although fusion usually suggests a greater range of imagination in creating the final product.

garden city A self-contained planned town combining work, residential, agricultural, and recreational facilities, and surrounded by a rural belt.

gender The social attributes of being male or female, in contrast to the biological attributes of sex. Thus, bearing children is an attribute of the female sex, but caring for children can be done by males or females. If females are expected to care for children, that is an attribute of gender, not sex, since both males and females are capable of doing it.

genocide The act of murdering an entire people. Originally used for the Nazi attempt to exterminate the Jewish people, it has been used since then to indicate the attempt to murder a substantial segment of a designated population.

gentrification The return of wealthier citizens to areas of cities that had become rundown, and their new investment in restoring and revitalizing the areas.

ghetto The part of a city to which a particular group is confined for its living space. Named originally for an area adjacent to an iron foundry (in Italian, *ghetto*) in sixteenth-century Venice where Jews were segregated by government order, the term has been used most often to designate segregated Jewish living areas in European cities. It is also used, more broadly, to indicate any area where specific groups are segregated whether by law, by force, or by choice.

Girondins French revolutionary group formed largely from the middle classes, many of them originally from the Gironde region. Relatively moderate.

globalization The processes by which people, institutions, and nations are brought into unified networks of interaction around the globe. Most commonly the term refers to economic networks and integration, but cultural, political, and technological globalization also occurs.

good wives and wise mothers The stated goal of high-school education for girls in Japan. Women were expected to stay in the home (except, perhaps, for a few years before marriage).

Great Leap Forward The policy of the Chinese communist government in the late 1950s of building China's economy on the basis of small-scale, localized production in rural communities.

Great Trek Between 1834 and 1841 the Dutch settlers in the British Cape Colony left the British-dominated areas to the south to establish their own control in the north. The Dutch felt that the British were too liberal in their treatment of blacks.

green revolution The revolution in agricultural production brought about by the use of new hybrid seeds, with increased use of irrigation, fertilizers, and pesticides.

guild A sworn association of people who gather for some common purpose. In the towns of medieval Europe, guilds of craftsmen or merchants were formed to protect and further their business interests and for mutual aid.

gulag The acronym of Glavnoye, Upravleniye Ispravitelno Trudovykh Lagerey, the "Chief Administration of Corrective Labor Camps," a department of the Soviet secret police founded in 1934 under Stalin. It ran a vast network of forced labor camps throughout the USSR to which millions of citizens accused of "crimes against the state" were sent for punishment.

habeas corpus From the Latin, "you should have the body." A centuries-old principle requiring governments and their agents to publicly present an accused person, held in detention, and state the charges against him or her. It forbids holding a suspect without charges indefinitely.

hacienda A large rural estate in Spanish America, originating with Spanish colonization in the sixteenth century, controlled by one person or family and giving shelter and protection to many dependent workers. The owner was called a *haciendado*.

han In Japan, a territory or feudal estate controlled by a feudal lord, or *daimyo*. *Han* were abolished in 1871.

Hindutva A political–religious slogan calling for the merger of the Hindu religion with the power of the Indian state. It is the rallying cry of several militant Hindu organizations.

humanism Cultural movement initiated in Western Europe in the fourteenth century deriving from the rediscovery and study of Greek and Roman literary texts. Most humanists continued to believe in God, but emphasized the study of humans.

"Hundred Flowers" campaign An invitation by Mao Zedong to the Chinese people in 1956–57 to express their ideas freely and openly. At first viewed as an invitation to democracy; later, after many who spoke out were jailed and punished, it came to be seen as a well-laid trap.

hybridization Originally used in cultural anthropology, and now more widely, to refer to the mixing of cultures to produce new forms. Sometimes referred to as cultural fusion.

indentured labor Labor performed under signed indenture, or contract, which binds the laborer to work for a specific employer, for a specified time, usually years, often in a distant place, in exchange for transportation and maintenance.

indulgences In the Roman Catholic Church, the remission from the punishments of sin, obtainable through good works or special prayers and granted by the Church through the merits of Christ and the saints. In the sixteenth century, the Church began to sell indulgences, precipitating the reforms of Martin Luther.

Industrial Revolution Once defined primarily in terms of new technologies in Britain and Europe, now recognized also as a global phenomenon of unprecedented transformations in social organization and political/military power.

intifada Colloquial Arabic: the act of shaking off; uprising, rebellion.

iron curtain Term introduced by Winston Churchill to describe the division of Europe by the Soviet Union spreading its areas of control in central and Eastern Europe from Western Europe.

iron law of wages The belief that as incomes increased people would choose to have more children. By 1900, this "iron law" reversed: As incomes increased, people chose to have fewer children.

Jacobins A French revolutionary party founded in 1789. It later became the most radical party of the revolution, responsible for implementing the Reign of Terror and the execution of the king (1793).

kulak A prosperous peasant in late tsarist and early Soviet Russia. The leaders of local agricultural communities, kulaks owned sizeable farms and could afford to hire labor.

kulturkampf German, "struggle over culture" or "culture war." The struggle among proponents of different views of culture for recognition and for control over state policies. Such struggles are normal in any society, but in Germany between the world wars they

became intense. They were waged philosophically and physically, and, ultimately, by banishing from the nation unwelcome cultural ideas, and those who held them.

lateen sail A triangular sail affixed to a long yard or crossbar at an angle of about 45 degrees to the mast, with the other free corner secured near the stern. The sail was capable of tacking against the wind on either side. So named when they appeared in the Mediterranean, where they were associated with Latin culture, although their origin was actually far away.

lebensraum In German, "room for living." In 1930s Germany, the claim was that Germany needed to expand and take over the land of its neighbors because its own land was overcrowded. Similar claims on neighbors' lands have been issued by many nations throughout history.

liberation theology A movement within the Catholic Church, especially in Latin America, especially in the 1960s and 1970s, combining some of the social concerns of Marxism with those of the Christian gospel, focusing on serving the needs of poor people, and organizing them for confrontations against governments when necessary.

libertador Literally, "liberator." Term applied to leaders of the independence revolts against Spanish rule in Latin America. Especially applied to Simón Bolívar, but given to others.

made the trains run on time The boast of Mussolini—that he made the trains run on time—became the criticism of his democratic opponents. Both he and they saw the force of the police and military as the means of this accomplishment. For Mussolini it evoked pride; for his critics, despair and even ridicule. For them, the cure— excessive state police power—was greater than the problem: inefficiency. Nowadays usually used to caricature a government eager to achieve efficiency but unconcerned about the effects on individual freedom.

maroon An escaped slave who fled to remote, often hilly areas, and joined with others to create small, free colonies. The process of flight followed by community building is called **maroonage**.

Marshall Plan An American program of economic assistance for rebuilding noncommunist Europe after World War II, proposed by U.S. Secretary of State George Marshall.

mazombo An American-born direct descendant of Portuguese settlers.

McCarthyism A strategy of attacking political opponents by labeling them unpatriotic or even treasonous, named for U.S. Senator Joseph McCarthy, who employed it in his campaign against alleged communists.

medieval The "middle period." Europeans of the Renaissance period, who felt that they were, at last, reconnecting with the glories of ancient Greece and Rome, called the ten centuries in between the end of the Roman empire and the beginning of the Renaissance "the medieval period." They used the term pejoratively. More recent scholars see that very long period as far more complicated and diverse and carve it up by specific geographical regions and into much smaller periods of time.

Meiji restoration The reforms effected in Japan in the name of the emperor Mutsuhito (r. 1867–1912), who was known as the Meiji emperor. During his reign constitutional changes restored the emperor to full power, displacing the militarily powerful shogun, and Japan adopted many Western innovations as it became a modern, industrial, militarized state.

mercantilism An economic policy pursued by many European nations between the sixteenth and eighteenth centuries. It aimed to strengthen an individual nation's economic power at the expense of its rivals by stockpiling reserves of bullion, which involved government regulations of trade.

mestizo A person of mixed race. In Central and South America it usually denotes a person of combined Indian and European descent.

mfecane Literally "time of troubles," the period in southern Africa from about 1816, when Shaka took control of the Zulu kingdom, until about 1841, when the Dutch completed their great trek. The expansion of the Zulus and of the Dutch dislodged local kingdoms and peoples, increasing political instability throughout the region.

micro-finance or **micro-credit** The provision of very small loans, often equivalent to $100 or even less, to very small-scale businessmen and women, people who would not usually have access to conventional commercial bank loans, because the banks do not deal in such small amounts, and because they would not usually recognize the relatively poor borrowers as "bankable." The loans are usually at below market rates, and are usually secured by the common bond among groups of borrowers that they will stand guaranty for one another.

millet **system** The Ottoman Empire's system of rule through religious communities. Legal issues among members of individual *millets*, or religious groups, were administered by the group itself, and taxes were also collected by the *millets* on behalf of the empire. *Millets* kept in close contact with their coreligionists in other countries, sometimes undermining the power of the Ottoman government.

mit'a A system of forced labor in Peru, begun under Inca rule, by which indigenous communities were required to contribute a set number of laborers for public works for a given period. Conditions were virtual slavery.

Montagnards Members of a radical French revolutionary party, closely associated with the Jacobins and supported by the artisans, shopkeepers, and sansculottes. They opposed the more moderate Girondins.

moral economy An economy whose goal is providing basic necessities for all members of a society before allowing any particular members to take profits; in contrast to a free market economy.

mulatto In the Americas, a person of mixed race, usually with parents of European and African origin.

nabob A corruption of the title "Nawab," for an Indian Muslim ruler, nabob referred to a British trader or administrator who grew rich in India.

nation-state A state occupying geographic territory, with its own government, and having a population with a widely shared language, religion, history, and ethnicity. The nation-state defines itself, in part, by its uniqueness and its separation from other nation-states.

nationalism A positive feeling of belonging to a particular nation, often including a desire to serve the nation, based on such elements as birth and ancestry, later choice and naturalization, acceptance of a common future, and/or material and cultural benefits of membership in the nation. In a negative form nationalism may lead to suppression of difference at home, and warfare against others abroad.

neocolonialism The assertion of power by one country over another, usually through economic dominance, but without formal political authority. A common relationship between countries that had previously been in a formal colonial relationship.

New Europes The lands explored, conquered, and settled by Europeans, who brought with them European institutions and ways of life: For example, North and South America, Australia, New Zealand, and South Africa.

NGO Non-governmental organization. Broadly, any organization not controlled by the government, carrying out its own mission. Most commonly refers to voluntary organizations carrying out work of social and community service that the government cannot or does not do.

nonaligned nations Those states, usually newly independent states, that chose not to take sides in the Cold War between the U.S. and the USSR.

other, the Using the term "the other" establishes a relationship between two individuals or groups that define themselves in terms of contrast with one another. Normally the definition implies that one has most of the virtues, and "the other" has most of the vices. Occasionally the word is used in verb form, "othering," meaning the process of defining "the other" in negative terms, and oneself in terms of positive virtues.

outcaste Refers to a person outside the caste system of India, usually also an outcast, rejected by the upper levels of society. Nowadays usually referred to as *dalits*, or oppressed persons.

outsourcing Buying goods and services, including personnel, from sources far away from the place where they are to be used, usually from overseas

locations. A major example is the establishment of overseas call centers in countries where labor is cheap to service customers in places where labor is expensive.

Palestinians Arab residents in the territories of the West Bank of the Jordan River and in the Gaza Strip of land along the Mediterranean coast conquered by Israel in the warfare of 1967. They do not have legal citizenship in Israel, nor in any other recognized state. Another group, Arab residents within the 1948 borders of Israel, are sometimes referred to as Palestinians, but more commonly as Arab Israelis or Israeli Arabs.

paper tiger The mocking comment of the Chinese toward the Americans, who had vast arrays of conventional and nuclear weaponry, but could not cope with simply armed warriors, often guerrilla warriors, fighting for their homelands in Korea, Vietnam, and elsewhere.

partisans Partisan fighters, or partisans, are guerrilla warriors fighting in the resistance against occupying armies. The term is used especially for the resistance against the Germans and Italians in World War II, and against Franco in Spain.

Pax Americana Literally, "American peace," a Latin phrase derived by analogy from *Pax Romana* (the peace enforced within the boundaries of the Roman Empire by Roman rule) to designate the relative tranquility established within the American sphere of influence immediately after World War II.

Pentecostals Christians who stress a direct, personal experience of God, Jesus, and revelation, rather than the authority of scripture or of the church hierarchy.

philosophes A group of eighteenth-century writers and philosophers, mostly French, who emphasized the supremacy of human reason as the key to progress. They advocated freedom of expression and social, economic, and political reform.

pogrom A murderous attack on a group of people—usually based on their ethnicity or religion—that is sanctioned by the government, either officially or unofficially.

political asylum Asylum is normally

applied for and granted, or refused, on the basis of individual cases brought by individuals who fear that if they return to their countries they will be persecuted, even murdered, because of their politics. Refugee status is usually a group-based phenomenon and does not imply any specific cause.

Prague Spring The period in the spring of 1968 when it appeared that Prague, and all of Czechoslovakia, would achieve greater freedom of expression and greater independence of control by the USSR. This hope was crushed by military intervention by the Soviets.

price revolution The massive inflation in Europe from the late 1400s to the early 1600s, caused in large part by the influx of silver and gold from the New World, but also by increased mining of precious metals in Europe, general population increase, and, in particular, increases in urban populations. The inflation tended to help urban entrepreneurs but to harm farmers and land holders.

privatization The act of selling off government-owned enterprises to private business firms.

proletariat A collective noun designating the working class that produces wealth. The singular is "proletarian."

protectionism The policy of protecting domestic production from external competition by limiting or prohibiting imports from other countries.

Protestant Reformation The movement, in sixteenth-century Europe, in which Luther, Calvin, Henry VIII, and others broke away from the Catholic Church.

proxy war A war waged between dependent, client states of larger, more powerful states that do not become directly involved in the fighting.

putting-out system In the putting-out system, employers provide employees with raw materials and the orders for turning them into finished products, which they then buy on completion. The employees carry out the work at home.

realpolitik A German word meaning practical politics, that is, a policy determined by expediency rather than by ethical or ideological considerations.

Red Scare The fear that communists would take over the United States, especially powerful in the years just

after the Communist Revolution in Russia, 1917.

Renaissance From the French word meaning "rebirth," a period of cultural and intellectual creativity in Western Europe between 1300 and 1570. The artists and intellectuals who created the movement saw themselves reconnecting with the traditions of ancient Greece and Rome, thus giving a "rebirth" to European culture. The cultural rebirth was accompanied by an expanding urban economy, another rebirth.

repartimiento A system by which the Spanish crown allowed colonists to employ Indians for forced labor. Conditions were virtual slavery.

Revere the Emperor; Expel the Barbarian In Japan, a much more conservative position than that of Sakuma Zozan (see p. 892), urging rejection of almost everything coming from Western colonization.

samurai The hereditary warrior-aristocrats of Japanese society, known for their codes of honor and loyalty. Only *samurai* were permitted to wear swords in their everyday dress.

sansculottes From the French, "without knee-breeches." Members of the militant, generally poorer classes of Paris, so-called because they wore trousers rather than the knee-breeches of affluent society.

Schengen agreement Set common, restrictive rules limiting immigration and the import of goods to signatory European nations. See also Fortress Europe, p. 892.

scorched earth A strategy of defensive warfare, in which everything that might be of use to an invading army is destroyed by the defending army as it retreats.

scorched-earth retreat A retreat in which everything left behind that might be useful to the enemy is destroyed.

scramble for Africa The rush of European nations to colonize the parts of Africa that were assigned to them in the international negotiations at the Berlin Conference.

serf An agricultural worker or peasant bound to the land and legally dependent on the lord. Serfs had their own homes, plots, and livestock, but they owed the lord labor, dues, and services. These services could be

commuted to rent, but serfs remained chattels of the lord unless they were emancipated, or escaped. Serfdom declined in Western Europe in the late medieval period, but persisted in parts of eastern Europe until the nineteenth century.

shogun The military dictator of Japan, a hereditary title held by three families between 1192 and 1867. Although they were legally subservient to the emperor, their military power gave them effective control of the country.

Sikh Member of a religious community founded in the Punjab region of north India by Guru Nanak in the sixteenth century. Sikhism combines *bhakti*, devotional Hinduism, with Islamic Sufism. In the face of the militant opposition of its neighbours, Sikhs also became a militant armed people.

silk route The set of rough roads, transportation links, across central Asia carrying trade and cultural exchange as far as China, India, and the eastern Mediterranean. The routes flourished only when governments were strong enough to protect them and keep them safe.

social contract A mythical, unwritten agreement among early people in a "state of nature" to establish some form of government. This "contract" generally defines the rights and obligations of the individuals and of the government.

social Darwinism A theory popularized by Herbert Spencer, based on a misreading of Charles Darwin's theory of the survival of the fittest. Darwin argued that those plants and animals best suited to a particular environment survived best in that environment. Spencer took this to mean that whichever creatures were dominant *ought to be* dominant. For example, the rich and powerful deserved to be rich and powerful; conversely, the poor and powerless deserved their low status.

socialist An adherent of the political theory of socialism. Socialists all believed that too much wealth was going into the hands of the owners of property and industry and too little to the workers who actually produced the wealth. The socialists divided sharply among themselves about the precise definition of the problem and the appropriate paths of struggle for change.

soviet (in China) Chinese soviets, governing councils made up of peasants, were modelled in part on Russian examples, but they focused on rural, rather than urban, administration. Founded during the revolutionary movement, they also provided guerrilla warriors for the campaigns.

soviet (in the Soviet Union) A council of workers, the primary unit of government in the Soviet Union at local, regional, and national levels, also adopted by other communist regimes.

Spanish Inquisition A court established with the consent of the Vatican to search out and punish Jews who claimed to have converted to Christianity but were still secretly practicing the Jewish religion, which had been outlawed in Spain in 1492. Subsequently the Inquisition, which was not bound by civil law and which employed torture, also turned against Christians who were not properly observant.

sphere of influence The geopolitical region in which one external power is considered dominant and other powers keep hands off.

state of nature The mythical situation in which people lived without any legal codes or contracts, each free to do exactly as he or she pleased, without the restrictions of law and society, but also without the protections of law and society.

Sufi In Islam, a member of one of the orders practicing mystical forms of worship that first arose in the eighth and ninth centuries C.E.

sunrise industries Industries that are expected to be most profitable in the near future.

sunset industries Industries that are expected to be in decline in the near future.

superpower The term ascribed to both the U.S. and the USSR in recognition of their power, especially their military power, far greater than that of any other country in the world at the time.

supply and **demand** In economics, the relationship between the amount of a commodity that producers are able and willing to sell (supply) and the quantity that consumers can afford and wish to buy (demand).

syncretism Refers to the mixture of different cultural traditions. The term is also used to refer to hybridity in other areas, such as art, music, philosophy, and religion.

theocracy A system of government based on religious beliefs and texts and headed by religious leaders.

third world Today, often refers to economically poor countries, often with ineffective governments, but historically the term referred to a group of newly independent countries that proposed strategies of development different from those of the U.S. and its allies, the first world, and the USSR and its allies, the second world.

totalitarianism A totalitarian state is one that seeks total control of the economy, politics, media, and culture of the state, under a single dictator or party. It does away with individual rights, proclaiming the rights of the state—as defined by its dictator—superior to those of any individual or group.

trade diaspora A dispersion over far-flung territories of a group of people who have a common bond. Usually this is an ancestral bond, such as in the Jewish diaspora and the African diaspora. A trade diaspora refers to the network of international traders who relate to one another through the bonds of their trade.

transhumance A pattern of seasonal migration.

transparency The quality of making public and clear the (financial) transactions of government or of private enterprise. Increasingly, transparency is highly valued as a necessity for successful development.

USSR Union of Soviet Socialist Republics. The name of the country formed from the Union of Russia and some fifteen other nations bound together into a single nation with a single, unifying communist government, 1917–91.

value added An economist's term for the increase in value from the cost of raw materials to the cost of finished products. It is the value added to the raw material by processing, manufacture, and marketing.

vodoun (**voodoo**) A religion of the Caribbean region which blended religious practices brought from Africa with those of Catholicism brought from Europe.

Wahabi Wahabi Islam follows the very conservative teachings of Muhammad ibn Abd-al-Wahhab, an eighteenth-century scholar. It is the dominant form of Islam in Saudi Arabia.

Weimar The constitution of the new German government after World War I was written in the city of Weimar. That government espoused democracy and cultural creativity, but was attacked from communists on the left and Nazis on the right, and was taken over by Nazis in 1933. Since then Weimar has stood for a government democratic and idealistic, but weak and fragile.

welfare state A government that assumes responsibilities for the welfare of its citizens, including such necessities as education, old age pensions, health care, and unemployment benefits. A more capitalist state leaves these responsibilities to private initiative.

White Man's Burden A concept, based on the title of a poem by Rudyard Kipling, that white man was superior to people of color, and that it was their duty to rule over them, serve them, and improve them. The concept was often invoked to justify a colonial system that was, in fact, hugely exploitative, a situation not mentioned in the poem.

white-collar jobs Professional and clerical jobs; office work; clean work. This kind of work became more prevalent as the Industrial Revolution also created these kinds of urban, service jobs.

world system A theory held by some social scientists concerning the political and economic organization of the world in modern times. According to world system theory, a few countries, the "core," dominated most of the others, "the periphery," and exploited them. During the period of imperialism this dominance was both political and economic. Afterward it was mostly economic, taking the form of neocolonialism.

yurt A portable dwelling used by the nomadic people of central Asia, consisting of a tentlike structure of skin, felt, or handwoven textiles arranged over wooden poles, simply furnished with rugs.

Picture and Literary Credits

Picture credits

703 Imperial War Museum, London
704 © Bettmann/Corbis
706 D.O.D. & U.S.A.F.
707 The Granger Collection
709 Camera Press
713 © Richard Kalvar/Magnum Photos
717 © Yevgeny Khaldei/Corbis
719 Reuters
721 Topfoto/Jean Pierre Couderc/Roger-Viollet
724 © Bettmann/Corbis
729 AKG Images
731 N.A.S.A.
733 Rex Features
734 © Burt Glinn/Magnum
736 © Bettmann/U.P.I.
738 ©2009 Josh Gerritsen Photography http://www.joshgerritsen.com
740 Ronald Grant Archive/Zeitgeist Films/Photofest
741 © Bettmann/U.P.I.
743 © Nicolas Tikhomiroff/Magnum Photos
750 South American Pictures
751 Getty Images/Orlando Sierra/AFP
756 Rex Features
760 © Bettmann/Corbis
763 Getty Images/AFP
766 © Bettmann/Corbis
773 Corbis/Hulton-Deutsch Collection
776 © Bettmann/Corbis
778 © Magnum Photos/Cartier-Bresson
779 Topfoto
781 The National Archives
782 © Xinhua/Sovfoto
785 Hulton Getty
788 Popperfoto
791 Topham Picturepoint
793 © Bettmann/Corbis
802 © Stephanie Maze/Corbis
803 (top) © Neal Preston/Corbis
803 (bottom) © Sean Adair/Reuters/Corbis
806 © Paul Lowe/Panos Pictures
809 © Najlah Feanny/Corbis/Saba
812 © Alberto Lowe/Reuters/Corbis
817 Howard Spodek
819 Rex Features/Sipa Press
821 Rex Features
828 © PA Photos/EPA
829 © Associated Press
830 © Kapoor Baldev/Sygma/Corbis
832 © Michel Setboun/Corbis
835 © Corbis/Sygma
839 AFP/Getty Images
842 Andes Press Agency/Carlos Reyes
845 © Wolfgang Hoyt/Esto
848 Peter Turnley/Corbis
851 © Gerry Penny/epa/Corbis
852 © Jonathan Blair/Corbis
861 © PA Photos
862 Rex Features
866 © Goran Tomasevic/Reuters/Corbis
867 Opportunity Organisation/Ron Londen
869 © Bettmann/Reuters
874 AFP/Getty Images
875 Diane Cook and Len Jenshel/Getty Images
878 Popperfoto/Reuters
880 Getty Images
882 © Bettmann/Reuters

Literary credits

For permission to reprint copyright material the publishers gratefully acknowledge the following:

Chapter Twelve
(p. 408): Ibn Battuta, from *Travels in Asia and Africa, 1325–1354*, edited by H.A.R. Gibb (The Hakluyt Society, 1958).
(pp. 415, 418): from *The Travels of Marco Polo*, translated by Ronald Latham (Penguin Classics, 1958), copyright © Ronald Latham, 1958, reprinted by permission of Penguin Books Ltd.

Chapter Sixteen
(p. 556): Pablo Neruda, from *Canto General*, translated by Jack Schmitt (University of California Press, 1991), © 1991 by the Fundación Pablo Neruda and the Regents of the University of California, by permission of University of California Press.

Chapter Nineteen
(pp. 646, 681): Wislawa Szymborska, "The Century's Decline," from *View with a Grain of Sand* (Harcourt Brace, 1995), copyright © 1993 by Wislawa Symborska, English translation by Stanislaw Baranczak and Clare Cavanagh copyright © 1995 by Houghton Mifflin Harcourt Publishing Company, reprinted by permission of the publisher.

Chapter Twenty
(p. 711): Mahatma Gandhi, from *Hind Swaraj* or *Indian Home Rule*, from *The Gandhi Reader*, edited by Homer Jack (Grove Press, 1956).

Chapter Twenty-two
(p. 777): Liu Binyan, from *A Higher Kind of Loyalty* (Pantheon Books, 1990), translation copyright © 1990 by Random House, Inc., used by permission of Pantheon Books, a division of Random House, Inc.
(pp. 784, 786, 787): Mahatma Gandhi, from *Autobiography*, *Hind Swaraj* or *Indian Home Rule*, and *Young India*, June 1, 1921, from *The Gandhi Reader*, edited by Homer Jack (Grove Press, 1956).

Chapter Twenty-four
(pp. 870, 872): Jillian Edelstein, from *Truth and Lies: Stories from the Truth and Reconciliation Commission in South Africa* (The New Press, 2001).

Every effort has been made to obtain permission from all copyright holders, but in some cases this has not proved possible. The publishers therefore wish to thank all authors or copyright holders who are included without acknowledgement. Prentice-Hall Inc./Laurence King Publishing Ltd apologizes for any errors or omissions in the above list and would be grateful to be notified of any corrections that should be incorporated in the next edition

Index